Outcome Uncertain

Cases and Contexts
in Bioethics

D0710814

Outcome Uncertain

Cases and Contexts
in Bioethics

Ronald Munson
University of Missouri–St. Louis

WADSWORTH
CENGAGE Learning

Australia • Brazil • Japan • Korea • Mexico • Singapore • Spain • United Kingdom • United States

WADSWORTH
CENGAGE Learning

Outcome Uncertain: Cases and Contexts in Bioethics
Ronald Munson

Publisher: Holly J. Allen

Philosophy Editor: Steve Wainwright

Assistant Editor: Lee McCraken

Editorial Assistant: Anna Lustig

Marketing Manager: Worth Hawes

Advertising Project Manager: Bryan Vann

Print/Media Buyer: Doreen Suruki

Composition Buyer: Ben Schroeter

Permissions Editor: Bob Kauser

Production Service: The Cooper Company

Text Designer: John Edeen

Copy Editor: Benjamin K. Kolstad

Cover Designer: Preston Thomas

Cover Image: Getty Images

Compositor: Thompson Type

© 2003 Wadsworth, Cengage Learning

ALL RIGHTS RESERVED. No part of this work covered by the copyright herein may be reproduced, transmitted, stored or used in any form or by any means graphic, electronic, or mechanical, including but not limited to photocopying, recording, scanning, digitizing, taping, Web distribution, information networks, or information storage and retrieval systems, except as permitted under Section 107 or 108 of the 1976 United States Copyright Act, without the prior written permission of the publisher.

For product information and technology assistance, contact us at **Cengage Learning Customer & Sales Support, 1-800-354-9706**

For permission to use material from this text or product, submit all requests online at **www.cengage.com/permissions** Further permissions questions can be emailed to **permissionrequest@cengage.com**

Library of Congress Control Number: 2002109035

ISBN-13: 978-0-534-55642-6

ISBN-10: 0-534-55642-6

Wadsworth
10 Davis Drive
Belmont, CA 94002
USA

Cengage Learning is a leading provider of customized learning solutions with office locations around the globe, including Singapore, the United Kingdom, Australia, Mexico, Brazil, and Japan. Locate your local office at **international.cengage.com/region**

Cengage Learning products are represented in Canada by Nelson Education, Ltd.

To learn more about Wadsworth, visit **www.cengage.com/wadsworth**

Purchase any of our products at your local college store or at our preferred online store **www.ichapters.com**

Printed in the United States of America
4 5 6 7 8   13 12 11 10 09
ED210

To Rebecca:
Virisque adquirit eundo.

—Aeneid, IV, 175

Brief Contents

Contents

CHAPTER 6
Reproductive Control   191

CHAPTER *10*
Euthanasia and Physician-Assisted Suicide   326

PART *V*
Foundations of Bioethics: Ethical Theories, Moral Principles, and Medical Decisions   357

Preface

Karen Cramer didn't see the black SUV until it was too late.

The front edge of the bumper struck her at hip level, tossing her into the air like a rag doll. When she fell back, her head struck the concrete curb. Knocked unconscious and bleeding profusely, she was rushed to the Memorial Hospital emergency room by the EMS. Before she arrived, she began to experience difficulty in breathing. Her chest heaved as she gasped for breath.

The trauma team responded like a well-oiled machine. Karen was intubated and attached to a ventilator to take over her breathing. She was given IV blood, electrolytes, and drugs to raise her blood pressure and strengthen her heartbeat. Karen's left hip and left arm were broken, but what worried the trauma team most was the depressed skull fracture. Grayish, red-tinged brain tissue oozed from between pieces of shattered bone.

As soon as Karen's blood gases and blood pressure were stable, the trauma team wheeled her down the hall for an MRI. The scan showed massive damage in the temporal region, the area of the fracture, and bleeding into the brain spaces. The injured brain would start to swell, causing even more damage as the pressure built up within the inelastic vault of the skull.

Karen was rushed to surgery. A neurosurgical team opened her skull, tied off bleeding blood vessels, and removed the debris and damaged tissue. She was given drugs to reduce the pressure, then sent to intensive care.

Later that evening, tests, including an EEG, indicated Karen's brain had no electrical activity. An attempt was made to withdraw her from the ventilator, but after three minutes with no spontaneous breathing, the ventilator was restored. When she was pinched hard, she showed no response to pain. Yet her heartbeat was strong and regular, and her blood showed her organs were getting enough oxygen.

Is Karen dead? Should the ventilator be turned off? Is it all right to remove her heart and kidneys and transplant them into other people? Who should answer these questions? Are there any rules or guidelines? Or are the answers arbitrary?

Bioethics, in my view, begins with cases.

By analyzing and reflecting on them, we identify the important issues, recognize any need for additional information, and seek out relevant principles to help us resolve questions about what we are morally required or permitted to do in the case at hand. We are successful when we're able to frame satisfactory answers to our questions and use them to develop social policies to guide us in dealing with similar cases.

Cases also make us realize how important clear concepts and factual information can be in making moral decisions. In the matter of Karen Cramer, for example, we must have a lucid concept of death to answer the question "Is she dead?" We must also know something about the nature and limits of brain scans and EEGs. In shaping this book, I've tried to capture both the intellectual excitement and the great seriousness that surround the field of bioethics. By emphasizing cases and presenting relevant medical and scientific information, I've attempted to introduce readers to the basic issues and make them active participants in the enterprise of deliberation and problem solving.

I believe that everyone, no matter what their level of knowledge or intellectual sophistication, will find this a useful and engaging book. The problems I present and discuss are ones that face us all as individuals and challenge our society to find solutions.

TOPICS

The topics I've selected are all fundamental ones in bioethics. They reflect the range and variety of the problems we confront and involve the ethical and social issues that have excited the most immediate concern. But more than this, the problems raised are ones so profoundly serious that they lead people to turn hopefully to philosophical consideration in search of satisfactory resolutions.

Part of the intellectual excitement of bioethics is generated by the searing controversies surrounding its issues, and to ignore these conflicts would be misleading. Even worse, it would deny readers the opportunity of dealing directly with proposals and arguments incompatible with their own views. Hence, I've felt an obligation to raise issues that some would prefer to ignore and to discuss ways of resolving them that others reject as wrong or even immoral. I hold, along with most reasonable people, that we must face our problems and consider seriously all proposed solutions. Otherwise, rational inquiry evaporates and power and prejudice take its place.

CHAPTER STRUCTURE

Each chapter of the first four Parts of this book is like a sandwich with multiple layers. Each opens with a Classic Case Presentation, which is followed by the chapter Briefing Session. Next comes a combination of Social Contexts and Case Presentations. The variety and number of these vary by chapter.

In the Case Presentations, I sketch out the most important cases in bioethics in narrative accounts. These are cases that have faced us with crucial issues and shaped our thinking about what we believe is morally legitimate in various areas of clinical practice and medical and biological research.

Some of the people at the focus of the cases are familiar. Nearly everyone has heard of Jesse Gelsinger, Karen Quinlan, Jack Kevorkian, Louise Brown, and

Dax Cowart. Their names have been in headlines and on the evening news many times—some as recently as last week, others almost three decades ago.

I call the opening Case Presentations "classic" because the cases have been at the center of discussion. They raised issues that prompted us to reflect. The image of the young Karen Quinlan slipping into a coma that lasts until her death ten years later, for example, has made us all think hard about when life support ought to be discontinued and whether active euthanasia is ever morally acceptable. Other Classic Cases have forced us to face similar problems. (I should say, however, that some Case Presentations might have been called "classic" with a justification equal to those that were. In this respect, my designation may be considered arbitrary.)

Not all Case Presentations center on individuals. Some focus on defining episodes in the history of clinical research or social practice. These include, for example, the Tuskegee Syphilis Study and the hardly less controversial Willow-brook Hepatitis Experiment. The central concern of such cases is usually with the way groups of individuals were treated by researchers and by society. Or it may be with the way a particular therapy has developed and raised issues.

The most important aspect of all the Case Presentations, in my view, is that they remind us that in dealing with bioethical questions, we are not engaged in some purely intellectual abstract game. Real lives are often at stake.

In the Briefing Session of each chapter, I discuss some of the specific moral problems that occur in actual medical and biological practice, research, and policy making. I also present whatever factual information is needed to understand how such problems arise.

I also suggest in the Briefing Sessions the ways moral theories or principles might be used to resolve some of the problems. Because virtue, care, and feminist ethics don't involve principles, I haven't tried to invoke these theories. My suggestions, in any event, are offered only as starting points in the search for satisfactory answers.

The Social Context sections of each chapter provide information relevant to understanding the current social, political, or biomedical situation in which issues are being debated. They differ from Case Presentations in offering a broader and deeper view of problems like the mammography debate, testing of AIDS drugs in Africa, and the Human Genome Project. If we hope to raise the level of public discussion of an issue and genuinely inform the life of our society, it is essential to consider the relevant scientific and medical facts, as well as the social situation.

The ongoing debate over embryonic stem cells is a good illustration. No one can make a reasoned decision about whether we should allow (or even encourage) embryonic stem cell research without knowing what embryonic stem cells are and without a sense of the therapeutic possibilities they may offer. The debate is not taking place in a vacuum, however. Policies and laws have been proposed and criticized, and anyone wanting to participate in the debate needs some information about the current situation. The Social Context sections offer this information through a "deep-background" briefing to help with the understanding of the issues that are their focus.

FOUNDATIONS OF BIOETHICS

For some readers, the most important feature of this book may be *Part V: Foundations of Bioethics*. In the first section, I sketch the basics of five major ethical theories and indicate how they might be used to answer particular moral questions in medicine and research. In the second section, I present and illustrate several major moral principles. The principles are ones endorsed (or at least expressed in practice) by virtually all ethical theories. Even so, I don't try to demonstrate how the principles follow from or are consistent with particular theories. In the third section, I present the fundamental ideas of three ethical theories usually framed as not involving principles—virtue ethics, care ethics, and feminist ethics.

The main purpose in these sections is to give those without a background in ethics the information they need to frame and evaluate moral arguments about the issues in bioethics. The three parts of the Foundations section are complementary, but they are also self-contained and may be read separately. The aim of each (and of all three together) is to help prepare readers for independent inquiry into bioethics.

INDEPENDENT COMPONENTS

What I've said about the sections of the Foundations part being independent also holds for the components of the chapters—the Case Presentations, Briefing Sessions, and Social Contexts. I have written everything to stand alone. This makes it possible for a reader to turn to any chapter and pick and choose among the materials presented.

Reading the Briefing Session of a chapter may deepen the understanding of the issues involved in (say) paying for health care, but one might choose to read only the Case Presentation discussing the Canadian system. Or one might want to focus only on gene therapy by reading the appropriate Case Presentation and ignore the issues connected with the various other modes of genetic control. The components of the book can be skipped or combined in a variety of ways, depending on one's interest.

This is a useful feature for those using the book as a text. Some instructors, for example, may want to start with *Part V: Foundations of Bioethics* and lay out moral principles or theories, while others may prefer to refer to that part only in the course of discussing some particular topic. Still others may choose to ignore it completely, providing students with whatever information they need in lectures or discussions.

This book, unlike my *Intervention and Reflection: Basic Issues in Medical Ethics,* 6th edition, from which it draws material, includes no readings. Some instructors will prefer focusing on Cases and Contexts and using lectures and class discussions to frame issues and arguments. But those who want to employ assigned readings are free to put together their own set, perhaps by using materials available on the Web or by assembling their own course packets. (The topic-specific bibliographies found on the book's Web site make it simple to assign students outside reading.) This book offers so much flexibility that it is compatible with almost any path an instructor chooses.

TABLE OF CONTENTS

This is a big book and includes a wide variety of topics and materials. To make it easier to navigate, I have included a very detailed table of contents that lists the Case Presentations and Social Contexts and spells out the major subheadings of the Briefing Sessions. The contents pages are designed to reveal all the topics covered in a chapter and prevent readers from getting lost in the thicket of cases and discussions.

NOTES AND REFERENCES

Following the Foundations section at the end of the book, the Notes and References section lists sources for materials used in the Cases, Briefing Sessions, and Social Contexts.

GENERAL RESOURCES IN BIOETHICS

Following the Notes is a brief guide to general resources in bioethics. This includes addresses of some of the more important on-line databases and Web sites. Sites such as the National Library of Medicine, the National Institutes of Health, and the Centers for Disease Control provide access to Medline and Bioethicsline, making it possible to carry out extensive research on almost any bioethical, clinical, or biomedical topic. This section also contains a short list of books that supply addresses of medically related Web sites.

Those interested in diseases like diabetes or breast cancer or therapies such as stem cell rescue or heart transplant can easily acquire a great deal of up-to-the-minute information by consulting relevant Web sites. Everyone knows by now, of course, that Web sites often evaporate like dew in the sun and that the information supplied by some should not be taken on trust.

Also included in this section is a list of prominent bioethics journals, as well as a list of others that publish articles on bioethics frequently. The section also contains a list of printed bibliographies, some quite specialized, that offer another way of getting access to publications relevant to bioethics.

ADDITIONAL RESOURCES

The Additional Resources section can be found on the book's Web site. It is arranged to reflect the chapters in this book. Its bibliographies mirror the topics of the chapters and provide a guide to articles and books. The references are both extensive and recent (although influential older works are also included). Hence, anyone wanting to do additional reading on a topic should have no difficulty locating appropriate works quickly.

ENVOI

I have attempted to supply readers with the kind of information and support they need to understand the issues in bioethics and to move in the direction of coming to reasoned proposals for dealing with them. I hope I have succeeded, and I welcome any comments or suggestions from readers.

I thank the individuals who reviewed the text of this book prior to its publication: Jeremy Koons of the American University of Beirut, Christian Perring of Dowling College, and Richard L. Wilson of Towson University.

Peter Adams, Wadsworth's previous philosophy editor, encouraged me to pursue this project, and his successor, Steve Wainwright, shared Peter's enthusiasm for it. I appreciate the support and encouragement of both. I'm also grateful to Cecile Joyner, Benjamin Kolstad, and Jerry Holloway, whose expertise and industry were crucial to the production of this book.

Miriam Munson's hard work and keen judgment not only made this project better, they made it possible. I also thank Miriam, as well as Rebecca Munson, for encouragement and understanding. Writer's families always pay a price and deserve a share of whatever credit may be available.

I have not always listened to those who have taken the trouble to warn and advise me, and this is reason enough for me to claim the errors here as my own.

Ronald Munson

Ronald Munson

University of Missouri–St. Louis, 2002
munson@umsl.edu

Outcome Uncertain

Cases and Contexts
in Bioethics

CHAPTER 1

Research Ethics and Informed Consent

Jesse Gelsinger: The First Gene-Therapy Death

When Jesse Gelsinger was three months short of his third birthday, he was watching cartoons on TV when he fell asleep. Except it was a sleep from which his parents were unable to arouse him. Panicked, they rushed him to a local hospital.

When Jesse was examined, he responded to stimuli but didn't awaken. The physicians classified him as being in a level-one coma. Laboratory tests showed he had a high level of ammonia in his blood, but it was only after several days and additional blood assays that Jesse's physicians arrived at a diagnosis of ornithine transcarbamylase deficiency—OTC.

OTC is a rare genetic disorder in which the enzyme ornithine transcarbamylase, one of the five involved in the urea cycle, is either missing or in short supply. The enzymes in the cycle break down the ammonia that is a by-product of protein metabolism.

A deficiency of OTC means the body cannot get rid of the ammonia, and it gradually accumulates in the blood. When the ammonia reaches a crucial level, it causes coma, brain damage, and eventually death. The disease results from a mutation on the X chromosome; thus females are carriers of the gene, which they pass on to their sons. The disorder occurs in one of every forty thousand births. Infants with the mutation usually become comatose and die within seventy-two hours of birth. Half die within a month of birth, and half of those who remain die before age five.

Although OTC is a genetic disease, no one else in Jesse's immediate family or ancestry had ever been diagnosed with the disease. His disease was probably the result of a spontaneous mutation. He was a genetic mosaic, which meant his body contained a mixture of normal and mutated cells. For this reason, Jesse had a comparatively mild form of OTC. His body produced enough of the enzyme that he could remain in stable health, if he stuck to a low-protein diet and took his medications. These included substances, like sodium benzoate, that chemically bind to ammonia and make it easier for the body to excrete it.

At age ten, after an episode of consuming too much protein, Jesse once again fell into a coma and was hospitalized. But five days later, he was back home with no apparent neurological damage. During his teens, Jesse's condition was monitored by semiannual visits to a metabolic clinic in his hometown of Tucson, Arizona.

In 1998 Jesse, now seventeen, and his father, Paul Gelsinger, heard from Dr. Randy Heidenreich, a doctor at the clinic, about a clinical trial at the University of Pennsylvania. Researchers at the Institute for Human Gene Therapy, Heidenreich told the Gelsingers, were trying to use gene therapy to supply the gene for OTC. Their success would not be a cure for the disease, but it would be a treatment that might be able to bring babies out of comas and prevent their having brain damage.

The Gelsingers were interested, but Jesse was still a year short of being old enough to participate. In April 1999, during another visit to the clinic, they again talked to Dr. Heidenreich about the trial, and Paul mentioned that the family would be taking a trip to New Jersey in June. They would be able to make a side trip to Philadelphia and talk to the investigators.

Dr. Heidenreich contacted an investigator at the Institute and mentioned the Gelsingers' interest in the research, and Paul received a letter from him in April. Jesse would be interviewed and tested at the university hospital on June 22 to determine whether he met the criteria for becoming a research participant.

A bioethicist at the university, Arthur Caplan, had advised the researchers that it would be morally wrong to use infants born with OTC as participants in the gene-therapy trial. Because they could not be expected to live, Caplan reasoned, their parents would be desperate to find a way to save their child's life. Hence, driven by desperation, their consent would not be free. The appropriate participants would be women who were carriers of the gene or men in stable health with only a mild form of the disease. Jesse would celebrate his eighteenth birthday the day the family flew to the East Coast, and his age would then make him eligible to become a participant.

On June 22, 1999, Jesse and Paul Gelsinger met with Dr. Steven Raper for forty-five minutes to review the consent forms and discuss the procedure for which Jesse might volunteer, if he qualified. Dr. Raper, a surgeon, would be the one performing the gene-therapy procedure.

According to Paul Gelsinger's recollections, Raper explained that Jesse would be sedated and two catheters inserted: one in the artery leading to his liver, the second in the vein leaving it. A weakened strain of adenovirus (the virus causing colds), genetically modified to include the OTC gene, would be injected into the hepatic artery. Blood would then be taken from the vein to monitor whether the viral particles were being taken up by the liver cells.

To reduce the risk of a blood clot's breaking loose from the infusion site, Jesse would have to remain in bed for eight hours after the procedure. Most likely, he would soon develop flu-like symptoms lasting for a few days. He might develop hepatitis, an inflammation of the liver. The consent form mentioned that if hepatitis progressed, Jesse might need a liver transplant. The consent form also mentioned that death was a possible outcome.

Paul Gelsinger saw this as such a remote possibility that he was more concerned about the needle biopsy of the liver to be performed a week after the procedure. The risk of death from the biopsy was given as 1 in 10,000. Paul urged Jesse to read the consent document carefully and to make sure he understood it. Paul thought the odds looked very good.

Dr. Raper explained that Jesse couldn't expect to derive any personal medical benefit from participating in the clinical trial. Even if the genes became incorporated into his cells and produced OTC, the effect would only be transitory. His immune system would attack the viral particles and destroy them within a month to six weeks.

Jesse, at the end of the information session, agreed to undergo tests to determine how well the OTC he produced got rid of ammonia in his blood—a measure of OTC efficiency. Samples of his blood were taken; then he drank a small amount of radioactively tagged ammonia. Later, samples of his blood and urine were taken to see how much of the ingested ammonia had been eliminated. The results showed his body's efficiency was only 6 percent of a normal performance.

A month later, the Gelsingers received a letter from Dr. Mark Bratshaw, the pediatrician at the Institute who proposed the clinical trial. Bratshaw confirmed the 6 percent efficiency figure from additional test results and expressed his wish to have Jesse take part in the study. A week later, Bratshaw called Jesse and talked to him. Jesse had already expressed to his father a wish to participate, but he told Bratshaw to talk to his father.

Bratshaw told Paul about the results of their animal studies. The treatment had worked well in mice, preventing the death of those given a lethal injection of ammonia. Also, the most recent patient treated had shown a 50 percent increase in her ability to excrete ammonia. Paul Gelsinger later recalled saying, "Wow! This really works. So, with Jesse at 6 percent efficiency, you may be able to show exactly how well this works."

Bratshaw said their real hope was to find a treatment for newborns lacking any OTC efficiency and with little chance of survival. Also, another twenty-five liver disorders could potentially be treated with the same gene-therapy technique. The promise, then, was that hundreds of thousands, if not millions, of lives might be saved. Bratshaw and Paul never talked about the dangers to Jesse of becoming a subject in the clinical trial.

Paul discussed participation with Jesse. They both agreed that it was the right thing to do. Jesse would be helping babies stay alive and, perhaps in the long run, he might even be helping himself.

APPROVAL

The clinical trial was supported by a National Institutes of Health grant awarded to Dr. James Wilson, the head of the Institute, and Mark Bratshaw. Their protocol had been reviewed by the federal Recombinant-DNA Advisory Committee (RAC) and the FDA. The animal studies Bratshaw had mentioned to Paul included twenty studies on mice to show the efficacy of the proposed technique. Wilson and his group had also conducted studies on monkeys and baboons to demonstrate the safety of the procedure.

Three of the treated monkeys had died of severe liver inflammation and a blood-clotting disorder when they had been given a stronger strain of adenovirus at a dose twenty times that proposed in the human trial. Both of the scientists assigned by the RAC to review the proposal thought the trial was too dangerous to include stable, asymptomatic volunteers. But Wilson and Bratshaw, using Caplan's argument, convinced the panel that using subjects capable of giving consent was morally preferable to using OTC newborns.

The initial protocol called for the modified viruses to be injected into the right lobe of the liver. The thinking was that if the treatment caused damage, the right lobe could be removed and the left lobe spared. But the RAC objected to injecting the viruses into the liver and the investigators agreed to change the protocol. The decision was later reversed by the FDA, on the grounds that wherever the viruses were injected, they would end up in the liver. The RAC was in the process of being reorganized and, in effect, taken out of the approval loop for proposals; it never received notice of the change. The investigators continued to operate under the modified protocol.

PROTOCOL

The study was a Phase 1 Clinical Trial. According to its protocol, eighteen patients were to receive an infusion of the genetically modified adenovirus. The aim of the study was to determine "the maximum tolerated dose." The investigators wanted to determine the point at which the transferred gene would be producing OTC in the maximum amount compatible with side effects that could be tolerated.

The eighteen patients were divided into six groups of three. Each successive group was to receive a slightly higher dose than the preceding one. The idea behind this common procedure is to protect the safety of the study participants. By increasing doses slightly, the hope is to spot the potential for serious side effects in time to avoid causing harm to the participants.

PREPARATION

On Thursday, September 9, Jesse Gelsinger, carrying one suitcase of clothes and another of videos, caught a plane for Philadelphia. He checked into the hospital alone. His father, a self-employed handyman, stayed in Tucson to work. Paul planned to arrive on the 18th to be present for what he considered the most dangerous part of the trial—the liver biopsy.

"You're my hero," Paul told Jesse. He looked him in the eye, then gave him a big hug.

The level of ammonia in Jesse's blood was tested on Friday and Sunday. Sunday night he called his father, worried. His ammonia level was high, and his doctors had put him on IV medication to lower it. Paul reassured his son, reminding him that the doctors at the Institute knew more about OTC than anybody else in the world.

TRAGEDY

On the morning of Monday, September 13, Gelsinger became the eighteenth patient treated. He was transported from his room to the hospital's interventional radiology suite, where a catheter was snaked through an artery in his groin to the hepatic artery. A second catheter was placed in the vein exiting the liver.

Dr. Raper then slowly injected thirty milliliters of the genetically altered virus into Jesse's hepatic artery. This was the highest dose given to any participant. Patient 17, however, had received the same size dose from a different lot of the virus and had done well. The procedure was completed around noon, and Jesse was returned to his room.

That evening Gelsinger, as expected, began to develop flu-like symptoms. He was feeling ill and feverish when he talked to his father and his stepmother, Mickie, that evening. "I love you, Dad," Jesse told his father. They all said what turned out to be their last goodbyes.

During the night, Jesse's fever soared to 104.5 degrees. A nurse called Raper at home, and, when he arrived at the hospital around 6:15 that morning, the whites of Jesse's eyes had a yellowish tinge. This was a sign of jaundice, not something the doctors had encountered with the other trial participants. Laboratory findings revealed that Jesse's bilirubin, the product of red blood cell destruction, was four times the normal level.

Raper called Dr. Bratshaw, who was in Washington, to tell him their patient had taken a serious turn. Bratshaw said he would catch the train and arrive in Philadelphia in two hours. Raper also called Paul Gelsinger to explain the situation.

The jaundice was worrying to Jesse's physicians. Either his liver was not functioning adequately or his blood was not clotting properly and his red blood cells were breaking down faster than his liver could process them. Such a breakdown was life threatening for someone with OTC, because the destroyed cells released protein the body would have to metabolize. Jesse was showing the same problem as the monkeys that had been given the stronger strain of the virus.

Tuesday afternoon Paul received a call from Dr. Bratshaw. Jesse's blood-ammonia level had soared to 250 micromoles per deciliter, with 35 being a normal measure. He had slipped into a coma and was on dialysis to try to clear the ammonia from his blood. Paul said he would catch a plane and be at the hospital the next morning.

By the time Paul arrived at eight o'clock on Wednesday and met Bratshaw and Raper, Jesse had additional problems. Dialysis had brought his ammonia level down to 70 from its peak of 393, but he was definitely having a blood-clotting problem. Also, although placed on a ventilator, he continued to breathe for himself, causing hyperventilation. This increased the pH of his blood, which increased the level of ammonia circulating to his brain. Paul gave his permission for the doctors to give Jesse medications that would paralyze his breathing muscles and allow the machine to take over completely.

By Wednesday afternoon, Jesse's breathing was under control. His blood pH had fallen back to normal, and the clotting disorder was improving. Bratshaw returned to Washington. Paul began to relax, and at 5:30 he went out to dinner with his brother and his wife. But he returned to the hospital to find Jesse had been moved to a different intensive care ward, and as he watched the monitors, he saw the oxygen content of Jesse's blood was dropping. A nurse asked him to wait outside.

At 10:30 that evening, a doctor told Paul that Jesse's lungs were failing. Even by putting him on pure oxygen, they were unable to get an adequate amount of oxygen into his blood. The doctors had also talked with a liver transplant team and learned that Jesse was not a good candidate for a transplant.

Raper, very worried, discussed Jesse's problems with Bratshaw and Wilson, and the three of them decided to put Jesse on extracorporeal membrane oxygenation— ECMO. The machine would remove carbon dioxide from Jesse's blood and supply it with the needed oxygen. The procedure was far from standard, however. Only half of the 1000 people placed on ECMO had lived, but Paul was informed that Jesse had only a 10 percent chance of surviving without ECMO.

"If we could just buy his lungs a day or two," Raper later told a reporter, "maybe he would go ahead and heal up."

Jesse was not hooked up to the ECMO unit until five o'clock Thursday morning. Bratshaw attempted to return from Washington, but he was trapped in an Amtrak train outside Baltimore. Hurricane Floyd was headed toward the East Coast; Jesse's stepmother arrived from Tucson just before the airport closed.

The ECMO appeared to be working. But Paul was told that Jesse's lungs were so severely damaged that, if he survived, it would take a long time for him to recover.

When Paul finally saw his son at mid-morning, Jesse was still comatose and bloated beyond recognition. Only the tattoo on his right calf and a scar on his elbow assured Paul that the person in the bed was Jesse.

That evening, unable to sleep, Paul walked the half-mile from his hotel to the hospital to check on Jesse. His son was no better, and Paul noticed that the urine-collecting bag attached to Jesse's bed contained blood. He realized that this meant Jesse's kidneys were shutting down. "He was sliding into multiple-organ-system failure," Raper later recalled.

The next morning, Friday, September 17, Raper and Bratshaw met with Paul and Mickie to give them the bad news that Paul had already predicted. Jesse had suffered irreversible brain damage, and the doctors wanted Paul's permission to turn off the ventilator. At Paul's request, he and Mickie were left alone for a few minutes. He then told the doctors he wanted to bring in his family and have a brief service for Jesse.

Paul and Mickie, seven of Paul's fifteen siblings and their spouses, and about ten staff members crowded into Jesse's room. Paul leaned over Jesse, then turned and told the crowd, "Jesse was a hero." The chaplain said a prayer; then Paul gave a signal. Someone flipped one switch to turn off the ventilator, and flipped a second to turn off the ECMO unit.

Dr. Raper watched the heart monitor. When the line went flat, he put his stethoscope against Jesse's chest. At 2:30 P.M. Raper officially pronounced him dead. "Goodbye, Jesse," he said. "We'll figure this out."

GATHERING STORM

Dr. James Wilson, the head of the Institute, immediately reported Jesse's death to the FDA. Paul Gelsinger, sad as he was, didn't blame Jesse's physicians for what had happened. Indeed, he supported them in the face of an initial round of criticism. "These guys didn't do anything wrong," he told reporters.

Then journalists began to bring to light information that raised questions about whether Jesse and his father had been adequately informed about the risks of the trial that claimed Jesse's life. Also, it raised questions about a conflict of interest that might have led researchers to minimize the risks. The FDA initiated an investigation, and the University of Pennsylvania conducted an internal inquiry.

Paul Gelsinger decided to attend the December 1999 RAC that discussed his son's death. He learned for the first time at that meeting, according to his account, that gene therapy had never been shown to work in humans. He had been misled, not necessarily deliberately, by the researcher's accounts of success in animals. As Paul listened to criticisms of the clinical trial, his faith in the researchers waned and was replaced by anger and a feeling of betrayal.

Other information fed his anger. When a month earlier he had asked James Wilson, "What is your financial position in this?" Wilson's reply, as Paul recalled, was that he was an unpaid consultant to the biotech company Genovo that was partially funding the Institute. Then later Paul learned that both Wilson and the University of Pennsylvania were major stockholders in Genovo and that Wilson had sold his 30 percent share of the company for $13.5 million.

Wilson and the university, as Paul saw it, had good reason to recruit volunteers for the clinical trial and produce positive results. Thus, they might not have been as careful in warning the Gelsingers about the risks of the study as they should have been. Also, the bioethicist approving the trial was someone who held an appointment in the department headed by Wilson. This, in effect, made Wilson his superior and thus automatically raised a question about the independence of his judgment.

A year and a day after Jesse's death, the Gelsinger family filed a wrongful-death lawsuit against the people conducting the clinical trial and the University of Pennsylvania. The university settled the suit out of court. The terms of the settlement were not disclosed.

FDA FINDINGS

An investigation by the FDA resulted in a report to Wilson and the University of Pennsylvania pointing to two flaws in the way the clinical trial was conducted. First, the investigators failed to follow their protocol and failed to report liver toxicity in four patients treated prior to Gelsinger. Second, the investigators failed to acknowledge the death of two rhesus monkeys injected with a high level of a similar vector.

Wilson's response was that he had sent the FDA the liver–toxicity information prior to the final approval of the protocol, although his report had been late. Further, the two monkeys that died were part of another study that used a different, stronger virus. In effect, then, Wilson was claiming that he and his colleagues had done nothing wrong and the FDA criticisms were unjustified.

Critics point out, apart from the question of how legitimate the criticisms were, that the FDA itself does not have enough power to oversee clinical trials properly. Most important, it is prohibited by law from distributing some so-called "adverse-event" reports. Difficulties encountered by patients in the fifty or so gene-therapy trials are often not made public, or even shared with investigators conducting similar trials, because drug-company sponsors regard information about adverse events as proprietary. This, critics say, puts participants in the position of having to take risks that they know nothing about. The law seems to favor protecting the investments of the pharmaceutical industry more than the protection of human subjects.

OUTCOME

What caused the death of Jesse Gelsinger? Even after the autopsy, the answer isn't clear. The most suggestive finding was that Jesse had abnormal cells in his bone marrow. This may have been a pre-existing condition, and it may account for why his immune system reacted in such an unpredicted way to the viral injection. He apparently died from an immunological response.

The FDA, after Jesse's death, shut down all gene-therapy operations temporarily for review. The University of Pennsylvania, after its internal review, restricted the role of the Institute for Human Gene Therapy to conducting basic biological research. Unable to carry out clinical trials, the Institute was de facto put out of business. A year or so later, it ceased to exist.

Because of Jesse's death, the Office for the Protection of Human Research Subjects committed itself to a major effort to educate researchers in the requirements for protecting participants in clinical trials and to stress the importance of Institutional Review Boards in seeing to the safety of participants. Even so, adverse-event reporting is still prohibited by law, when it can be deemed to constitute proprietary information. Critics continue to see this as incompatible with the idea behind informed consent.

Briefing Session

In 1947, an international tribunal meeting in Nuremberg convicted fifteen German physicians of "war crimes and crimes against humanity." The physicians were charged with taking part in "medical experiments without the subjects' consent." But the language of the charge fails to indicate the cruel and barbaric nature of the experiments. Here are just some of them:

✦ At the Ravensbrueck concentration camp, experiments were conducted to test the therapeutic powers of the drug sulfanilamide. Cuts were deliberately made on the bodies of people; then the wounds were infected with bacteria. The infection was worsened by forcing wood shavings and ground glass into the cuts. Then sulfanilamide and other drugs were tested for their effectiveness in combatting the infection.

✦ At the Dachau concentration camp, healthy inmates were injected with extracts from the mucous glands of mosquitos to produce malaria. Various drugs were then used to determine their relative effectiveness.

✦ At Buchenwald, numerous healthy people were deliberately infected with the spotted-fever virus merely for the purpose of keeping the virus alive. Over 90 percent of those infected died as a result.

✦ Also at Buchenwald, various kinds of poisons were secretly administered to a number of inmates to test their efficacy. Either the inmates died or they were killed at once so that autopsies could be performed. Some experimental subjects were shot with poisoned bullets.

✦ At Dachau, to help the German Air Force, investigations were made into the limits of human endurance and existence at high altitudes. People were placed in sealed chambers, then subjected to very high and very low atmospheric pressures. As the indictment puts it, "Many victims died as a result of these experiments and others suffered grave injury, torture, and ill-treatment."

Seven of the physicians convicted were hanged, and the other eight received long prison terms. From the trial there emerged the Nuremberg Code, a statement of the principles that should be followed in conducting medical research with human subjects.

Despite the moral horrors that were revealed at Nuremberg, few people doubt the need for medical research involving human subjects. The extent to which contemporary medicine has become effective in the treatment of disease and illness is due almost entirely to the fact that it has become scientific medicine. This means that contemporary medicine must conduct inquiries in which data are gathered to test hypotheses and general theories related to disease processes and their treatment. Investigations involving nonhuman organisms are essential, but the ultimate tests of the effectiveness of medical treatments and their side effects must involve human beings as research subjects. Human physiology and psychology are sufficiently different to make animal studies alone inadequate.

The German physicians tried at Nuremberg were charged with conducting experiments without the consent of their subjects. The notion that consent must be given before a person becomes a research subject is still considered the basic requirement that must be met for an experiment to be morally legitimate. Moreover, it is not merely consent—saying yes—but informed consent that is demanded. The basic idea is simply that a person decides to participate in research after he or she has been provided with background information relevant to making the decision.

This same notion of informed consent is also considered a requirement that must be satisfied before a person can legitimately be subjected to medical treatment. Thus, people are asked to agree to submit themselves to such ordinary medical procedures as blood transfusion or to more extraordinary ones such as surgical operations or radiation therapy.

The underlying idea of informed consent in both research and treatment is that people have a right to control what is done to their bodies. The notion of informed consent is thus a recognition of an individual's autonomy—of the right to make decisions governing one's own life. This right is recognized both in practice and in the laws of our society. (Quite often, malpractice suits turn on the issue of whether a patient's informed consent was valid.)

In the abstract, informed consent seems a clear and straightforward notion. After all, we all have an intuitive grasp of what it is to make a decision after we have been supplied with information. Yet in practice informed consent has proved to be a slippery and troublesome concept. We will identify here only a few of the moral and practical difficulties that make the concept controversial and hard to apply.

Our focus will be on informed consent in the context of research involving human subjects. But most of the issues that arise here also arise in connection with giving and securing informed consent for the application of medical therapies. (They also arise in special forms in abortion and euthanasia.) In effect, then, we will be considering the entire topic.

Before discussing informed consent, it will be useful to have an idea of what takes place in a typical clinical trial. Perhaps the most common type of research involves testing new drugs, so let's begin by considering a sketch of what this involves.

DRUG TESTING

Traditions of medical research and regulations of the U.S. Food and Drug Administration more or less guarantee that the development of new drugs follows a set procedure. The procedure consists of two major parts: preclinical and clinical testing. When it is thought likely that a chemical substance might be useful, animal experiments are conducted to determine how toxic it is. These tests are also used to estimate the drug's therapeutic index (the ratio of a dose producing toxic effects to a dose producing desired effects). The effects of the substance on particular organs and tissues, as well as on the whole animal, are studied. Efforts are made to determine the drug's potential side effects and hazards. (Does it produce liver or kidney damage? Is it carcinogenic? Does it cause heart arrythmias?)

Clinical testing of the substance occurs in three phases. In phase one, healthy human volunteers are used to determine whether the drug produces any toxic effects. If the outcome of giving them the drug is acceptable, in phase two the drug is administered to a limited number of patients who might be expected to benefit from it. If the drug produces desirable results, and has no serious side effects, then phase three studies are initiated.

The drug is administered to a larger number of patients by a larger number of clinical investigators. Such multicenter trials usually take place at teaching hospitals or in large public institutions. Usually they are sponsored by the drug's manufacturer. Successful results achieved in this phase ordinarily lead to the licensing of the drug for general use.

In the clinical part of testing, careful procedures are followed to attempt to exclude bias in the results. Investigators want their tests to be successful and patients want to get well, and either or both of these factors may influence test results. Investigators may perceive a patient as "improved" just because they want or expect him to be. What is more, medications may produce a "placebo effect." That is, when patients are given inactive substances (placebos), they nevertheless may show improvement.

To rule out these kinds of influences, a common procedure followed in drug testing is the "double-blind" (or "double-masked") test design. In the classic version of this design, a certain number of patients are given the drug being tested, and the remainder of the test group are given placebos. Neither the investigators nor the patients are allowed to know who is receiving the drug and who is not—both are kept "blind." Sometimes a test group is divided so that part receives placebos all of the time, part only some of the time, and part receives genuine medication all of the time.

Often placebos are no more than just sugar pills. Yet, frequently, substances are prepared to produce side effects like those of the drug being tested. If, for example, the drug causes drowsiness, a placebo will be used that produces drowsiness. In this way, investigators will not be able to learn which patients are being given placebos on the basis of irrelevant observations.

In recent decades, placebo trials have been replaced, for the most part, with trials in which an established drug used to treat a condition is compared to a new drug. The old drug represents the "standard of care," and the question is whether the new drug is more effective.

The double-blind test design is employed in many kinds of clinical investigations, not just in drug testing. Thus, the testing of new vaccines and even surgeries often follows the same form. A major variation is the "single-blind" design, in which those who must evaluate the results of some treatment are kept in ignorance of which patients have received it.

THE "INFORMED" PART
OF INFORMED CONSENT

Consent, at first sight, is no more than agreement. A person consents when he or she says "yes" when asked to become a research subject. But legitimate or valid consent cannot be merely saying yes. If people are to be treated as autonomous agents, they must have the opportunity to decide whether they wish to become participants in research.

Deciding, whatever else it may be, is a process in which we reason about an issue at hand. We consider such matters as the risks of our participation, its possible advantages to ourselves and others, the risks and advantages of other alternatives that are offered to us, and our own values. In short, valid consent requires that we deliberate before we decide.

But genuine deliberation requires both information and understanding. These two requirements are the source of difficulties and controversies. After all, medical research and treatment are highly technical enterprises. They are based on complicated scientific theories that are expressed in a special vocabulary and involve unfamiliar concepts.

For this reason, some physicians and investigators have argued that it is virtually useless to provide patients with relevant scientific information about research and treatment. Patients without the proper scientific background, they argue, simply don't know what to make of the information. Not only do patients find it puzzling, but they find it frightening. Thus, some have suggested, informed consent is at worst a pointless charade and at best a polite fiction. The patient's interest is best served by allowing a physician to make the decision.

This obviously paternalistic point of view (see Chapter 2) implies, in effect, that all patients are incompetent to decide their best interest and that physicians must assume the responsibility of acting for them.

An obvious objection to this view is its assumption that, because patients lack a medical background, they cannot be given information in a form they can understand that is at least adequate to allow them to decide how they are to be treated. Thus, proponents of this view confuse difficulty of communication with impossibility of communication. While it is true that it is often hard to explain technical medical matters to a layperson, this hardly makes it legitimate to conclude that people should turn over their right to determine what is done to them to physicians. Rather, it imposes on physicians and researchers the obligation to find a way to explain medical matters to their patients.

The information provided to patients must be usable. That is, patients must understand enough about the proposed research and treatment to deliberate and reach a decision. From the standpoint of the researcher, the problem here is to determine when the patient has an adequate understanding to make informed consent valid. Patients, being people, do not like to appear stupid and say they don't understand an explanation. Also, they may believe they understand an explanation when, as a matter of fact, they don't.

Until recently, little effort was made to deal with the problem of determining when a patient understands the information provided and is competent to assess it. In the last few years, researchers have investigated situations in which individuals have been asked to consent to become research subjects. Drawing upon these data, some writers have attempted to formulate criteria for assessing competency for giving informed consent. The problem is not one that even now admits of an ideal solution, but, with additional empirical investigation and philosophical analysis, the situation may improve even more.

THE "CONSENT" PART OF INFORMED CONSENT

We have talked so far as though the issue of gaining the legitimate agreement of someone to be a research subject or patient involved only providing information to an ordinary person in ordinary circumstances and then allowing the person to decide. But the matter is more complicated than this, because often either the person or the circumstances possess special features. These features can call into question the very possibility of valid consent.

It's generally agreed that, in order to be valid, consent must be voluntary. The person must of his or her "own free will" agree to become a research subject. This means that the person must be capable of acting voluntarily. That is, the person must be competent.

This is an obvious and sensible requirement accepted by all. But the difficulty lies in specifying just what it means to be competent. One answer is that a person is competent if he or she is capable of acting rationally. Because we have some idea of what it is to act rationally, this is a movement in the direction of an answer.

The problem with it, however, is that people sometimes decide to act for the sake of moral (or religious) principles in ways that may not seem reasonable. For example, someone may volunteer to be a subject in a potentially hazardous experiment because she believes the experiment holds out the promise of helping countless others. In terms of self-interest alone, such an action would not be reasonable.

VULNERABLE POPULATIONS

Even in the best of circumstances, it is not always easy to determine who is competent to consent and who is not. Yet researchers and ethicists must also face the issue of how children, the mentally retarded, prisoners, and those suffering from psychiatric illnesses are to be considered with respect to consent. Should no one in any of these vulnerable populations be considered capable of giving consent? If so, then is it ever legitimate to secure the consent from some third party—from a parent or guardian—in some cases?

One possibility is simply to rule out all research that involves such people as subjects. But this has the undesirable consequence of severely hampering efforts to gain the knowledge that might be of use either to the people themselves or to others with similar medical problems. Later we will consider some of the special problems that arise with children and other vulnerable groups as research subjects.

The circumstances in which research is done can also call into question the voluntariness of consent. This is particularly so with prisons, nursing homes, and mental hospitals. These are all what the sociologist Erving Goffman called "total institutions," for within them all aspects of a person's life are connected with the social structure. People have a definite place in the structure and particular social roles. Moreover, there are social forces at work that both pressure and encourage an inmate to do what is expected of him or her.

We will discuss below some of the special problems that arise in research with prisoners. Here we need only point out that gaining voluntary consent from inmates in institutions may not be possible, even in principle. If it is possible, it's necessary to specify the kinds of safeguards that must be followed to free them from the pressures resulting from the very fact that they are inmates. Those who suffer from psychiatric illnesses may be considered just as capable intellectually of giving consent, but here too safeguards to protect them from the pressures of the institution need to be specified.

In recent years, researchers have expanded the testing of new drugs and drug regimens into developing countries. The citizens of these countries are typically less well educated and less scientifically sophisticated than their counterparts in industrialized nations. They may also be more likely to trust that what they are asked to do by some medical authority will be in their best interest. Hence, securing informed consent from them that is valid presents particular difficulties.

It's important to keep in mind that ordinary patients in hospitals may also be subject to pressures that call into question the voluntariness of the consent that they give. Patients are psychologically predisposed to act in ways that please physicians. Not only do physicians possess a social role that makes them figures of authority, but an ill person feels very dependent on those who may possess the power to make her well. Thus, she will be inclined to go along with any suggestion or recommendation made by a physician.

The ordinary patient, like the inmate in an institution, needs protection from the social and psychological pressures that are exerted by circumstances. Otherwise, the voluntariness of consent will be compromised, and the patient cannot act as a free and autonomous agent.

MEDICAL RESEARCH
AND MEDICAL THERAPY

Medical therapy aims at relieving the suffering of people and restoring them to health. It attempts to cure diseases, correct disorders, and bring about normal bodily functioning. Its focus is on the individual patient, and his or her welfare is its primary concern.

Medical research, by contrast, is a scientific enterprise. Its aim is to acquire a better understanding of the biochemical and physiological processes involved in human functioning. It is concerned with the effectiveness of therapies in ending disease processes and restoring functioning. But this concern is not for the patient as an individual. Rather it's directed toward establishing theories. The hope, of course, is that this theoretical understanding can be used as a basis for treating individuals. But helping a particular patient get well is not a goal of medical research.

The related but distinct aims of medical research and medical therapy are a source of conflict in human experimentation. It's not unusual for a physician to be acting both as a researcher and as a therapist. This means that although she must be concerned with the welfare of her patient, her aims must also include acquiring data that are important to her research project. It is possible, then, that she may quite unconsciously encourage her patients to volunteer to be research subjects, provide them with inadequate information on which to base their decisions, or minimize the risks they are likely to be subject to.

The patient, for his part, may be reluctant to question his physician to acquire more information or to help him understand his role and risks in research. Also, as mentioned above, the patient may feel pressured into volunteering for research, just because he wants to do what his physician expects of him.

Medical research is a large-scale operation in this country and affects a great many people. It has been estimated that 400,000–800,000 people a year are patients in research programs investigating the effectiveness of drugs and other therapies. Since 1980, the number of clinical studies has increased more than 30 percent, from about 3500 to 5000. Informed consent is more than an abstract moral issue.

The aims of therapy and the aims of research may also cause moral difficulties for the physician that go beyond the question of consent. This is particularly so in certain kinds of research. Let's look at some of the ethical issues more specifically.

PLACEBOS AND RESEARCH

As we saw earlier in the description of a typical drug experiment, placebos are often considered essential to determine the true effectiveness of the drug being tested. In practice, this means that during all or some of the time they are being "treated," patients who are also subjects in a research program will not be receiving genuine medication. They are not, then, receiving the best available treatment for their specific condition.

This is one of the risks that a patient needs to know about before consenting to become a research subject. After all, most people become patients in order to be cured, if possible, of their ailments, not to further science or anything of the kind. The physician-as-therapist will continue to provide medical care to a patient, for under double-blind conditions the physician does not know who is being given placebos and who is not. But the physician-as-researcher will know that a certain number of people will be receiving medication that cannot be expected to help their condition. Thus, the aims of the physician who is also a researcher come into conflict.

This conflict is particularly severe in cases in which it is reasonable to believe (on the basis of animal experimentation, in vitro research, and so on) that an effective disease preventative exists, yet, to satisfy scientific rigor, tests of its effectiveness involve the giving of placebos.

This was the case with the development of a polio vaccine by Thomas Weller, John F. Enders, and Frederick C. Robbins in 1960. The initial phase of the clinical testing involved injecting 30,000 children with a substance known to be useless in the prevention of polio—a placebo injection. It was realized, statistically, that some of those children would get the disease and die from it.

Since Weller, Enders, and Robbins believed they had an effective vaccine, they can hardly be regarded as acting in the best interest of these children. As physicians they were not acting to protect the interest and well-being of the children. They did, of course, succeed in proving the safety and effectiveness of the polio vaccine. The moral question is whether they were justified in failing to provide 30,000 children with a vaccine they believed to be effective, even though it had not been tested on a wide scale with humans. That is, did they correctly resolve the conflict between their roles as researchers and their role as physicians?

Placebos also present physician-researchers with another conflict. As we noticed in the earlier discussion, placebos are not always just "sugar pills." They often contain active ingredients that produce in patients effects that resemble those caused by the medication being tested—nervousness, vomiting, loss of appetite, and so on. This means that a patient receiving a placebo is sometimes not only failing to receive any medication for his illness, but also receiving a medication that may do him some harm. Thus, the physician committed to care for the patient and to relieve his suffering is at odds with the researcher who may be harming the patient. Do the aims of scientific research and its potential benefits to others justify treating patients in this fashion? Here is another moral question that the physician must face in particular and we must face in general.

We should not leave the topic of the use of placebos without the reminder of what was mentioned earlier—that it is possible to make use of an experimental design in research that does not require giving placebos to a control group. An investigator can compare the results of two treatment forms: a standard treatment whose effectiveness is known and a new treatment with a possible but not proven effectiveness. This is not as scientifically satisfactory as the other approach because the researcher must do without a control group that has received no genuine treatment. But it does provide a way out of the dilemma of both providing medical care and conducting research.

This way of proceeding has associated with it another moral issue. If a clinical trial of a drug is scheduled to last for a long period of time (perhaps years) but accumulating statistical results indicate the drug is more effective in the treatment or prevention of a disease than the established one it is being compared with, should the trial be stopped so that all the patients in the study can gain the benefits of the test drug? Or does the informed consent of the participants warrant continuing the trial until the therapeutic value of the test drug is fully established?

The view generally accepted now is that if the evidence strongly indicates that a treatment being tested is more effective than the standard one, researchers have an obligation to discontinue the trial and offer the new treatment to those who were not receiving it.

THERAPEUTIC AND NONTHERAPEUTIC RESEARCH

We have mentioned the conflict that faces the physician who is also an investigator. But the patient who has to decide whether or not to consent to become a research subject is faced with a similar conflict.

Some research holds out the possibility of a direct and immediate advantage to those patients who agree to become subjects. For example, a new drug may, on the basis of limited trials, promise to be more effective in treating an illness than those drugs in standard use.

Or a new surgical procedure may turn out to give better results than one that would ordinarily be used. By agreeing to participate in research involving such a drug or procedure, a patient may then have a chance of gaining something more beneficial than he or she would gain otherwise.

Yet the majority of medical research projects do not offer any direct therapeutic advantages to patients who consent to be subjects. The research may eventually benefit many patients, but seldom does it bring more than usual therapeutic benefits to research participants. Ordinarily, the most that participants can expect to gain are the advantages of having the attention of physicians who are experts on their illness and receiving close observation and supervision from researchers.

These are matters that ought to be presented to the patient as information relevant to the decision the patient must make. The patient must then decide whether he or she is willing to become a participant, even if there are no special therapeutic advantages to be gained. It is in making this decision that one's moral beliefs can play a role. Some people volunteer to become research subjects without hope of reward because they believe that their action may eventually be of help to others.

Let us now examine some problems of medical research when special groups are its focus. We will also consider some of the related issues of fetal research.

RESEARCH INVOLVING CHILDREN

One of the most controversial areas of all medical research has been that involving children as subjects. The Willowbrook project discussed in the Case Presentation that follows is just one among many investigations that have drawn severe criticism and, quite often, court action.

Why Study Children at All?

The obvious question is: Why should children ever be made research subjects? Children clearly lack the physical, psychological, and intellectual maturity of adults. It does not seem that they are as capable as adults of giving informed consent because they can hardly be expected to grasp the nature of research and the possible risks to themselves.

Furthermore, because children have not yet developed their capacities, it seems wrong to subject them to risks that might alter, for the worse, the course of their lives. They are in a position of relative dependency, relying upon adults to provide the conditions for their existence and development. It seems almost a betrayal of trust to allow children to be subjected to treatment that is of potential harm to them.

Such considerations help explain why we typically regard research involving children with deep suspicion. It is easy to imagine children being exploited and their lives blighted by callous researchers. Some writers have been sufficiently concerned by the possibility of dangers and abuses that they have advocated an end to all research with children as subjects.

But there is another side to the coin. Biologically, children are not just small adults. Their bodies are developing, growing systems. Not only are there anatomical differences; there are also differences in metabolism and biochemistry. For example, some drugs are absorbed and metabolized more quickly in children than in adults, whereas other drugs continue to be active for a longer time. Often some drugs produce different effects when administered to children.

Also, precisely because the bodies of children are still developing, their nutritional needs are different. Findings based on adult subjects cannot simply be extrapolated to children, any more than results based on animal studies can be extrapolated to human beings.

Further, children are prone to certain kinds of diseases (measles or mumps, for example) that are either less common in adults or occur in different forms. It is important to know the kinds of therapies that are most successful in the treatment of children afflicted with them.

Children also have problems that are not seen in adults, because children with them do not survive unless the problems are treated effectively. Various heart anomalies, for example, must be corrected to keep children alive. Thus, the development of new surgical techniques must necessarily involve children.

Finally, even familiar surgical procedures cannot be employed in a straightforward way with children. Their developing organ systems are sufficiently different that special pediatric techniques must often be devised.

For many medical purposes, children must be thought of almost as if they were wholly different organisms. Their special biological features set them apart and mark them as subjects requiring special study. To gain the kind of knowledge and understanding required for effective medical treatment of children, it is often impossible to limit research solely to adults.

Excluding Children

Failing to conduct research on children raises its own set of ethical issues. If children are excluded from investigations, then the development of pediatric medicine will be severely hindered. In general, this would mean that children would receive medical therapies that are less effective than might be possible. Also, since it is known that children differ significantly from adults in drug reactions, it seems wrong to subject children to the risks of drugs and drug dosages that have been tested only on adults.

Research involving children can also be necessary to avoid causing long-term harm to numerous people. The use of pure oxygen in the environments of prematurely born babies in the early 1940s resulted in hundreds of cases of blindness and impaired vision. It was not until a controlled study was done that retinal damage was traced to the effects of the oxygen. Had the research not been allowed, the chances are very good that the practice would have continued and thousands more infants would have been blinded.

Ethical Issues

Yet, even if we agree that not all research involving children should be forbidden, we still have to face up to the issues that such research generates. Without attempting to be complete, we can mention the following three issues as among the more prominent.

WHO IS A CHILD?   Who is to be considered a child? For infants and children in elementary school, this question is not a difficult one. But what about people in their teens? Then the line becomes hard to draw. Indeed, perhaps it is not possible to draw a line at all without being arbitrary.

The concern behind the question is with the acquisition of autonomy, of self-direction and responsibility. It is obvious on the basis of ordinary experience that people develop at different rates, and some people at sixteen are more capable of taking charge of their own lives than others are at twenty. Some teenagers are more capable of understanding the nature and hazards of a research project than are many people who are much older.

This suggests that many people who are legally children may be quite capable of giving their informed consent. Of course, many others probably are not, so that decisions about capability would have to rest on an assessment of the individual. Where medical procedures that have a purely therapeutic aim are concerned, an individual who is capable of deciding whether it is in his or her best interest should probably be the one to decide. The issue may be somewhat different when the aim is not therapy. In such cases, a better policy might be to set a lower limit on the age at which consent can be given, and those below that limit should not be permitted to consent to participate in research. The problem is, of course, what should that limit be?

PARENTAL CONSENT.   Can anyone else consent on behalf of a child? Parents or guardians have a duty to act for the sake of the welfare of a child under their care. In effect, they have a duty to substitute their judgment for that of the child. We generally agree to this because most often we consider the judgment of an adult more mature and informed than a child's. And because the responsibility for care rests with the adult, we customarily recognize that the adult has a right to decide. It is almost as though the adult's autonomy is being shared with the child—almost as though the child were an extension of the adult.

Society and its courts have recognized limits on the power of adults to decide for children. When it seems that the adult is acting in an irresponsible or unreasonable manner, then society steps in to act as a protector of the child's right to be cared for. Thus, courts have ordered that lifesaving procedures or blood transfusions be performed on children even when their parents or guardians have decided against it. The criterion used in such judgments is "the best interest of the child."

What sort of limits should govern a parent's or guardian's decision to allow a child to become a research subject? Is it reasonable to believe that, if a parent would allow herself to be the subject of research, then it is also right for her to consent to her child's becoming a subject? Or should something more be required before consent for a child's participation can be considered legitimate?

THERAPEUTIC BENEFITS. Should children be allowed to be subjects of research that does not offer them a chance of direct therapeutic benefits? Perhaps the "something more" that parents or guardians ought to require before consenting on behalf of a child is the genuine possibility that the research will bring the child direct benefits. This would be in accordance with a parent's duty to seek the welfare of the child. It is also a way of recognizing that the parent's autonomy is not identical with that of the child: one may have the right to take a risk oneself without having the right to impose the risk on someone else.

This seems like a reasonable limitation, and it has been advocated by some writers. Yet there are difficulties with the position. Some research virtually free from risk (coordination tests, for example) might be stopped because of its lack of a "direct therapeutic value."

More important, however, much research promising immense long-term benefits would have to be halted. Research frequently involves the withholding of accepted therapies without any guarantee that what is used in their place will be as effective. Sometimes the withholding of accepted treatment is beneficial. Thus, as it turned out, in the research on the incidence of blindness in premature infants in the 1940s, premature infants who were not kept in a pure oxygen environment were better off than those who received ordinary treatment.

But no one could know this in advance, and such research as this is, at best, ambiguous as to the promise of direct therapy. Sheer ignorance imposes restrictions. Yet if the experiment had not been done, the standard treatment would have continued with its ordinary course of (statistically) disastrous results. Here, at least, there was the possibility of better results from the experimental treatment.

But in research that involves the substitution of placebos for medications or vaccines known to be effective, it is known in advance that some children will not receive medical care considered to be the best. A child who is a subject in such research is then put in a situation in which he or she is subjected to a definite hazard. The limitation on consent that we are considering would rule out such research. But the consequence of doing this would be to restrict the development of new and potentially more effective medications and treatment techniques. That is, future generations of children would be deprived of at least some possible medical advances.

These, then, are some of the issues that we have to face in arriving at a view of the role of children in research. Perhaps the greatest threat to children, however, has to do with social organization. Children, like prisoners, are often grouped together in institutions (schools, orphanages, detention centers, and so on) and are attractive targets for clinical investigators because they inhabit a limited and relatively controlled environment, can be made to follow orders, and do not ask too many questions that have to be answered. It is a misimpression to see researchers in such situations as "victimizing" children, but at the same time careful controls are needed to see that research involving children is legitimate and carried out in a morally satisfactory way.

Guidelines
In response to some of these difficulties, the Department of Health and Human Services has issued guidelines specifically designed to protect children as research subjects. First, for children to become participants, permission must be obtained from parents or guardians, and children must give their "assent." Second, an Institutional Review Board is assigned the responsibility of considering the "ages, maturity, and psychological states" of the children and determining whether they are capable of assenting. (A failure to object cannot be construed as assent.)

Third, children who are wards of the state or of an institution can become participants only if the research relates to their status as wards or takes place in circumstances in which the majority of subjects are not wards. Each child must also be supplied with an "advocate" to represent her or his interest.

RESEARCH INVOLVING PRISONERS

Prisoners are in some respects social outcasts. They have been found guilty of breaking the laws of society and, as a consequence, are removed from it. Stigmatized and isolated, prisoners in the relatively recent past were sometimes thought of as less than human. It seemed only reasonable that such depraved and corrupt creatures should be used as the subjects of experiments that might bring benefits to the members of the society that they wronged. Indeed, it seemed not only reasonable, but fitting.

Accordingly, in the early part of this century, tropical medicine expert Richard P. Strong obtained permission from the Governor of the Philippines to inoculate a number of condemned criminals with plague bacillus. The prisoners were not asked for their consent, but they were rewarded by being provided with cigarettes and cigars.

Episodes of this sort were relatively common during the late nineteenth and early twentieth centuries. But as theories about the nature of crime and criminals changed, it became standard practice to use only volunteers and to secure the consent of the prisoners themselves.

In the 1940s, for example, the University of Chicago infected over 400 prisoners with malaria in an attempt to discover new drugs to treat and prevent the disease. A committee set up by the Governor of Illinois recommended that potential volunteers be informed of the risks, be permitted to refuse without fear of such reprisals as withdrawal of privileges, and be protected from unnecessary suffering. The committee suggested also that volunteering to be a subject in a medical experiment is a form of good conduct that should be taken into account in deciding whether a prisoner should be paroled or have his sentence reduced.

Consent and Coercion

But the committee also called attention to a problem of great moral significance. They pointed out that, if a prisoner's motive for volunteering is the wish to contribute to human welfare, then a reduction in his sentence would be a reward. But if his motive is to obtain a reduction in sentence, then the possibility of obtaining one is really a form of duress. In this case, the prisoner cannot be regarded as making a free decision. The issue of duress or "undue influence," as it is called in law, is central to the question of deciding whether, and under what conditions, valid informed consent can be obtained for research involving prisoners. Some ethicists have argued that, to avoid undue influence, prisoners should never be promised any substantial advantages for volunteering to be research subjects. If they volunteer, they should do so for primarily moral or humane reasons.

Others have claimed that becoming research subjects offers prisoners personal advantages that they should not be denied. For example, participation in a research project frees them from the boredom of prison life, gives them an opportunity to increase their feelings of self-worth, and allows them to exercise their autonomy as moral agents. It has been argued, in fact, that prisoners have a right to participate in research if the opportunity is offered to them and they wish to do so. To forbid the use of prisoners as research subjects is thus to deny to them, without adequate grounds, a right that all human beings possess. As a denial of their basic autonomy, of their right to take risks and control their own bodies, not allowing them to be subjects might constitute a form of cruel and unusual punishment.

By contrast, it can also be argued that prisoners do not deserve to be allowed to exercise such autonomy. Because they have been sentenced for crimes, they should be deprived of the right to volunteer to be research subjects: that right belongs to free citizens. Being deprived of the right to act autonomously is part of their punishment. This is basically the position taken by the House of Delegates of the American Medical Association. The Delegates passed a resolution in 1952 expressing disapproval of the use as research subjects of people convicted of "murder, rape, arson, kidnapping, treason, and other heinous crimes."

A more worrisome consideration is the question of whether prisoners can be sufficiently free of undue influence or duress to make their consent legitimate. As we mentioned earlier, prisons are total institutions, and the institutional framework itself puts pressures on people to do what is desired or expected of them.

There need not be, then, promises of rewards (such as reduced sentences) or overt threats (such as withdrawal of ordinary privileges) for coercion to be present. That people may volunteer to relieve boredom is itself an indication that they may be acting under duress. That "good conduct" is a factor in deciding whether to grant parole may function as another source of pressure.

The problem presented by prisoners is fundamentally the same as that presented by inmates in other institutions, such as nursing homes and mental hospitals. In these cases, once it has been determined that potential subjects are mentally competent to give consent, then it must also be decided whether the institutional arrangements allow the consent to be "free and voluntary."

RESEARCH INVOLVING THE POOR

In the eighteenth century, Princess Caroline of England requested the use of six "charity children" as subjects in the smallpox vaccination experiments she was directing. Then, and well into the twentieth century, charity cases, like prisoners, were regarded by some medical researchers as prime research subjects.

A horrible example of medical research involving the poor is the Tuskegee Syphilis Study that was conducted under the auspices of the U.S. Department of Public Health (USPH). From 1932 to 1970, a number of black males suffering from the later stages of syphilis were examined at regular intervals to determine the course their disease was taking. The men in the study were poor and uneducated and believed that they were receiving proper medical care from the state and local public health clinics.

As a matter of fact, they were given either no treatment or inadequate treatment, and at least forty of them died as a result of factors connected with their disease. Their consent was never obtained, and the nature of the study, its risks, and the alternatives open to them were never explained.

It was known when the study began that those with untreated syphilis have a higher death rate than those whose condition is treated, and although the study was started before the advent of penicillin (which is highly effective against syphilis), other drugs were available but were not used in ways to produce the best results. When penicillin became generally available, it still was not used.

The Tuskegee Study clearly violated the Nuremberg Code, but it was not stopped even after the War Crimes trials. It was reviewed in 1969 by a USPH ad hoc committee, and it was decided that the study should be phased out in 1970. The reasons for ending the experiment were not moral ones. Rather, it was believed nothing much of scientific value was to be gained by continuing the work. In 1973, a United States Public Health Department Ad Hoc Advisory Panel, which had been established as a result of public and congressional pressure to review the Tuskegee Study, presented its final report. It condemned the study both on moral grounds and because of its lack of worth and rigor. (See the *Classic Case Presentation: Bad Blood, Bad Faith* in Chapter 4 for more details.)

No one today argues that disadvantaged people ought to be made subjects of research simply as a result of their social or economic status. The "back wards" in hospitals whose poor patients once served as a source of research subjects have mostly disappeared as a result of such programs as Medicare and Medicaid. Each person is now entitled to his or her own physician and is not under the general care of the state or of a private charity.

Yet many research projects continue to be based in large public or municipal hospitals. And such hospitals have a higher percentage of disadvantaged people as patients than do private institutions. For this reason, such people are still more likely to become research subjects than are the educated and wealthy. If society continues to accept this state of affairs, special precautions must be taken to see to it that those who volunteer to become research subjects are genuinely informed and free in their decisions.

RESEARCH INVOLVING THE TERMINALLY ILL

People who have been diagnosed with a terminal illness characteristically experience overwhelming feelings of despair. Within a few days or weeks, some are able to acknowledge and accept the situation, but others are driven to desperation by the imminent prospect of their death.

When they learn that conventional therapies offer little hope of prolonging their lives, they vow to fight their disease by other means. They look for hope in a situation that seems hopeless, and with the encouragement of family and friends, they seek new therapies.

Some turn to quack medicine or suspect remedies, but others seek out clinical trials of new drugs for their diseases. They seek acceptance into trials from the hospitals and medical centers where they are being conducted.

Critics of the policy of accepting terminally ill patients into clinical trials base their objections on the vulnerability of patients. Most often, critics charge, such patients are not sufficiently aware of what they are getting into, nor are they aware of how little personal payoff they may reasonably expect to receive from an experimental therapy.

To be enrolled in a drug trial, patients must satisfy the study's research protocol. They must meet diagnostic criteria for having a particular disease or their disease must be at a certain stage in its natural history. Or perhaps the patients must not have received certain treatments, such as radiation, or must not have been taking a particular drug for several weeks. Perhaps the patients must not have signs of liver damage or kidney disease. Some of the criteria may require that patients be tested. The testing may involve only drawing blood for analysis, but it may also require submitting to painful and potentially harmful surgical procedures to biopsy tissue.

A patient who qualifies for admission to a study may still have a difficult time ahead. If the study is at an institution that is hundreds, even thousands, of miles away, the patient must either move nearer or travel to the institution regularly. In either case, much expense and inconvenience may be involved.

Critics also charge that patients may have unreasonable expectations about the effectiveness of experimental therapies. Patients may believe, for example, that a drug has at least some record of success, but in fact the therapeutic benefits of the drug may be uncertain at best. Indeed, in the initial stage of drug testing with human subjects, Phase I trials, the aim is not to determine the therapeutic effectiveness of the drug, but to determine such matters as its toxicity, rate of metabolism, or most effective mode of administration.

The chance that a drug under investigation will actually prolong the life of a patient in the final stages of a terminal illness is small. One study reviewed the results of forty-two preliminary reports on drugs used to treat colon cancer and thirty-three on drugs used to treat nonsmall-cell lung cancer, but only one drug was found to have therapeutic effects.

Furthermore, critics charge, patients may not realize the extent to which an experimental drug may turn out to cause unpleasant, painful, or harmful side effects. Patients may suffer nausea, vomiting, chills, fevers, neurological damage, or lowered immunological functioning.

Such effects may not even be known to the investigators, and so they cannot inform patients about them at the time consent is sought. The last weeks or months of terminally ill patients may thus be spent more painfully than if they had simply waited for death, and in fact, patients may even shorten their lives by becoming subjects in a study.

As a sort of final disappointment, critics point out, the study that a dying patient was counting on to give her a last chance at lengthening her life might drop her as a subject. The aim of a clinical trial of a new drug, for example, is to discover such medically important characteristics of the drug as its side effects, what constitutes an effective dosage, and whether the drug has therapeutic benefits. Patients in the study are sources of data, and if a patient who is receiving no therapeutic benefit from a drug turns out to be of no value to the study, she may be dropped from it. Dying patients may be hit particularly hard by such a rejection.

In the view of critics, the desperation of terminally ill patients makes them too vulnerable to be able to give meaningful consent to participate in experimental trials. Even if they are fairly informed that a drug trial will offer them only a remote possibility of prolonging their lives, they are under such pressure from their illness that, in a sense, they are not free to consent. Patients and their families may be so frightened and emotionally distraught that they hear only what they want to hear about an experimental therapy. They may be unable to grasp that the therapy probably will not benefit them and may even harm them.

Opponents of enrolling terminally ill patients in clinical investigations charge that the patients are often treated as though they are only a research resource, a pool from which subjects can be selected for whatever testing needs to be done. That people are dying does not mean that it is justifiable to exploit them, and the only way to avoid this is to exclude them as eligible candidates for research subjects.

While no one advocates the exploitation of terminally ill people, most observers believe it is morally legitimate to include them in clinical trials. The patients themselves may have something to gain. The very act of trying a new drug might make some patients feel better, even if it is only a placebo effect. Also, patients and their families can feel that they are genuinely doing everything possible to improve the patient's health. Moreover, the drug might be of some therapeutic benefit to the patient, even if the chance of its prolonging the patient's life is remote.

Furthermore, defenders of the policy hold, allowing dying patients to participate in research is to recognize their status as autonomous persons, and to exclude them as candidates for research subjects is to deny them that status.

Finally, defenders claim, in connection with their status as moral agents, dying patients deserve to be given a chance to do something for others. In fact, when dying patients are recruited or seek to enroll in a study, instead of stressing the possible therapeutic benefit they might secure, the experimenter should emphasize the contribution that patients' participation might make to helping others in the future.

To put this last point in perspective, consider the responses of twenty-seven cancer patients enrolled in a Phase I clinical trial who were interviewed by Mark Siegler and his colleagues at the University of Chicago. Eighty-five percent of the patients said they had agreed to participate because they hoped for therapeutic benefits, 11 percent enrolled at the suggestion of their physicians, and 4 percent did so at the urging of their families. No one reported enrolling out of a desire to help others.

RESEARCH INVOLVING FETUSES

In 1975 legal charges were brought against several physicians in Boston. They had injected antibiotics into living fetuses that were scheduled to be aborted. The aim of the research was to determine by autopsy, after the death of the fetuses, how much of the drug got into the fetal tissues.

Such information is considered to be of prime importance because it increases our knowledge of how to provide medical treatment for a fetus still developing in its mother's womb. It also helps to determine ways in which drugs taken by a pregnant woman may affect a fetus and so points the way toward improved prenatal care.

Other kinds of research involving the fetus also promise to provide important knowledge. Effective vaccines for preventing viral diseases, techniques for treating children with defective immune-system reactions, and hormonal measurements that indicate the status of the developing fetus are just some of the potential advances that are partially dependent on fetal research.

But a number of moral questions arise in connection with such research. Even assuming that a pregnant woman consents to allow the fetus she is carrying to be injected with drugs prior to abortion, is such research ethical? Does the fact that the fetus is going to be aborted alter in any way the moral situation? For example, prior to abortion should the fetus be treated with the same respect and concern for its well-being as a fetus that is not scheduled for abortion?

After the fetus is aborted, if it is viable—if it can live separated from the mother—then we seem to be under an obligation to protect its life. But what if a prenatal experiment threatens its viability? The expectation in abortion is that the fetus will not be viable, but this is not in fact always the case. Does this mean that it is wrong to do anything before abortion to threaten the life of the fetus or reduce its chance for life, even though we do not expect it to live?

These are difficult questions to answer without first settling the question of whether the fetus is to be considered a person. (See the discussion of this issue in the *Briefing Session* in Chapter 9.) If the fetus is a person, then it is entitled to the same moral considerations that we extend to other persons. If we decide to take its life, if abortion is considered to be at least sometimes legitimate, then we must be prepared to offer justification. Similarly, if we are to perform experiments on a fetus, even one expected to die, then we must also be prepared to offer justification. Whether the importance of the research is adequate justification is a matter that currently remains to be settled.

If the fetus is not a person, then the question of fetal experimentation becomes less important morally. Since, however, the fetus may be regarded as a potential person, we may still believe it is necessary to treat it with consideration and respect. The burden of justification may be somewhat less weighty, but it may still be there.

Let us assume that the fetus is aborted and is apparently not viable. Typically, before such a fetus dies, its heart beats and its lungs function. Is it morally permissible to conduct research on the fetus before its death? The knowledge that can be gained, particularly of lung functions, can be used to help save the lives of premature infants, and the fetus is virtually certain of dying, whether or not it is made a subject of research.

After the death of a fetus that is either deliberately or spontaneously aborted, are there any moral restraints on what is done with the remains? It is possible to culture fetal tissues and use them for research purposes.

These tissues might, in fact, be commercially grown and distributed by biological supply companies in the way that a variety of animal tissues are now dealt with. Exactly when a fetus can be considered to be dead so that its tissues and organs are available for experimentation, even assuming that one approves of their use in this manner, is itself an unsettled question.

Scientists have long been concerned about federal guidelines and state laws regulating fetal research. Most investigators feel that they are forced to operate under such rigid restrictions that research is slowed and, in some instances, even prohibited. Everyone agrees, however, that fetal research involves important moral and social issues. (See Chapter 9 for more detail.)

Fetal research has to be considered a part of human research. Not only are some fetuses born alive even when deliberately aborted, but all possess certain human characteristics and potentialities. But who should give approval to what is done with the fetus? Who should be responsible for consent?

To some it seems peculiar to say that a woman who has decided to have an abortion is also the one who should consent to research involving the aborted fetus. It can be argued that in deciding to have an abortion she has renounced all interest and responsibility with respect to the fetus. Yet, if the fetus does live, we would consider her, at least in part, legally and morally responsible for seeing to its continued well-being.

But if the woman (or the parents) is the one who must give consent for fetal experimentation, are there limits to what she can consent to on behalf of the fetus?

With this question we are back where we began. It is obvious that fetal research raises both moral and social issues. We need to decide, then, what is right as a matter of personal conduct and what is right as a matter of social policy. At the moment, issues in each of these areas remain highly controversial.

RESEARCH INVOLVING ANIMALS

The seventeenth-century philosopher René Descartes doubted whether animals experience pain. They may act as if they are in pain, but perhaps they are only complicated pieces of clockwork designed to act that way. Humans feel pain, but then, unlike animals, humans have a "soul" that gives them the capacity to reason, be self-conscious, and experience emotions. The bodies of humans are pieces of machinery, but the mental states that occur within the bodies are not.

If the view of animals represented by Descartes and others in the mechanistic tradition he initiated is correct, we need have no moral concern about the use of animals in research. Animals of whatever species have the status of any other piece of delicate and often expensive lab equipment. They may be used in any way for any purpose.

Here are some of the ways in which animals are or have been used in biomedical research:

♦ A standard test for determining the toxicity of drugs or chemicals is the "lethal dose-50" (LD-50) test. This is the amount of a substance that, when administered to a group of experimental animals, will kill 50 percent of them.

♦ The Draize test, once widely used in the cosmetics industry, involves dripping a chemical substance into the lidless eyes of rabbits to determine its potential to cause eye damage.

♦ The effects of cigarette smoking were investigated by a series of experiments using beagles with tubes inserted into holes cut into their tracheas so that, when breathing, they were forced to inhale cigarette smoke. The dogs were then "sacrificed" and autopsied to look for significant changes in cells and tissues.

♦ Surgical procedures are both developed and acquired by using animals as experimental subjects. Surgical residents spend much time in "dog labs" learning to perform standard surgical procedures on live dogs. Limbs may be deliberately broken and organs damaged or destroyed to test the usefulness of surgical repair techniques.

♦ A traditional medical-school demonstration consisted in exsanguinating (bleeding to death) a dog to illustrate the circulation of the blood. High school and college biology courses sometimes require that students destroy the brains of frogs with long needles (pithing) and then dissect the frogs to learn about physiological processes.

♦ Chimpanzees and other primates have served as experimental subjects for the study of the induction and treatment of infectious diseases. Perfectly healthy chimps and monkeys have been inoculated with viruses resembling the AIDS virus; then the course of the resulting diseases is studied.

A list of the ways in which animals are used would include virtually all basic biomedical research. The discovery of an "animal model" of a disease typically signals a significant advancement in research. It means that the disease can be studied in ways it cannot be in humans. The assumption is that animals can be subjected to experimental conditions and treatments that humans cannot be subjected to without violating basic moral principles.

Is the assumption that we have no moral obligation toward animals warranted? Certainly the crude "animal machine" view of Descartes has been rejected, and no one is prepared to argue that no nonhuman animal can experience pain.

Exactly which animals have the capacity for suffering is a matter of dispute. Mammals undoubtedly do, and vertebrates in general seem to experience pain, but what about insects, worms, lobsters, and clams? Is the identification of endorphins, naturally occurring substances associated with pain relief in humans, adequate grounds for saying that an organism that produces endorphins must experience pain?

Once it is acknowledged that at least some animals can suffer, most philosophers agree that we have some moral responsibility with respect to them. At the least, some (like W. D. Ross) say that, since we have a prima facie duty not to cause unnecessary suffering, we should not inflict needless pain on animals.

This does not necessarily mean that biomedical research should discontinue the use of animals. Strictly construed, it means only that the animals should be treated in a humane way. For example, surgical techniques should be practiced only on dogs that have been anesthetized. Understood in this way, the principle raises no objection to humanely conducted animal research, even if its purpose is relatively trivial.

Philosophers like Kant and most of those in the natural law tradition would deny that we have any duties to animals at all. The only proper objects of duty are rational agents; unless we are prepared to argue that animals are rational, we have to refuse them the status of moral persons. We might treat animals humanely because we are magnanimous, but they are not in a position to lay claims against us. Animals have no rights.

Some contemporary philosophers (Tom Regan, in particular) have argued that, although animals are not rational agents, they have preferences. This gives them an autonomy that makes them "moral patients." Like humans, animals possess the right to respectful treatment, and this entails that they not be treated only as a means to some other end. They are ends in themselves, and this intrinsic worth makes it wrong to use them as subjects in research, even when alternatives to animal research are not available.

Contrary to Regan, a number of philosophers have taken a utilitarian approach to the issue of animal experimentation. Some (like Peter Singer) have argued that, although animals cannot be said to have rights, they have interests. If we recognize that the interests of humans are deserving of equal consideration, then so too are the interests of nonhuman animals. Hence, we can recognize that animals have inherent worth without assigning them rights, but this does not mean that we must treat them exactly as we treat humans.

Most people, whether utilitarians or not, argue that at least some forms of animal experimentation can be justified by the benefits produced. After all, they point out, the understanding of biological processes we have acquired since the time of Aristotle has been heavily dependent on animal experimentation. This understanding has given us insights into the causes and processes of diseases, and, most important, it has put us in a position to invent and test new therapies and modes of prevention.

Without animal experimentation, the identification of the role played by insulin, the development of the polio vaccine, and the perfection of hundreds of major surgical techniques surely would not have been possible. The list could be extended to include virtually every accomplishment of medicine and surgery. Countless millions of human lives have been saved by using the knowledge and understanding gained from animal studies.

Animals, too, have benefited from the theoretical and practical knowledge of research. An understanding of nutritional needs has led to healthier domestic animals, and an understanding of environmental needs has produced a movement to protect and preserve many kinds of wild animals. At the conceptual and scientific levels, veterinary medicine is not really distinct from human medicine. The same sorts of surgical procedures, medicines, and vaccines that benefit the human population also benefit many other species.

However, even from a broadly utilitarian perspective, accepting the general principle that the results justify the practice does not mean that every experiment with animals is warranted. Some experiments might be trivial, unnecessary, or poorly designed. Others might hold no promise of yielding the kind or amount of knowledge sufficient to justify causing the animal subjects to suffer pain and death.

Furthermore, the utilitarian approach supports (as does a rights view like Regan's) looking for an alternative to animal experimentation. If good results can be obtained, for example, by conducting experiments with cell cultures (in vitro), rather than with whole organisms (in vivo), then in vitro experiments are to be preferred. However, if alternatives to animal testing are not available and if the benefits secured promise to outweigh the cost, animal testing may be morally legitimate.

The utilitarian justification faces what some writers see as a major difficulty. It is one posed by the fact that animals like chimpanzees and even dogs and pigs can be shown to possess mental abilities superior to those of humans suffering from severe brain damage and retardation. If experiments on mammals are justifiable by appealing to the benefits, then why aren't experiments on humans with serious mental impairments equally justified? Indeed, shouldn't we experiment on a human in a chronic vegetative state, rather than on a healthy and alert dog?

The use made of animals in biomedical research is a significant issue, but it is no more than one aspect of the general philosophical question about the status of animals. Do animals have rights? If so, what grounds can be offered for them? Do animals have a right to coexist with humans? Do animals have a right to be free? Is it wrong to eat animals or use products made from their remains? These questions and many others like them are now being given the most careful scrutiny they have received since the last century. How they are answered will do much to shape the character both of medical research and of our society.

WOMEN AND MEDICAL RESEARCH

Critics have charged that medical research has traditionally failed to include women as experimental subjects, even when women might also stand to benefit from the results. Most strikingly, a study showing the effectiveness of small doses of aspirin in reducing the risk of heart attack included 2201 subjects—all male. The relevance of the study to women is in doubt, for, although more men than women die of heart disease, after women reach menopause the difference in mortality rates between genders becomes much smaller.

Until recently, studies of the therapeutic effectiveness of drugs characteristically included only males. Although the effects of many drugs are the same for women as for men, this is not always true. Hormonal differences may alter drug reactions, so conclusions based on the reactions of men may be misleading when applied to women.

In the view of critics, the traditionally male-dominated research establishment has been responsible for perpetuating an unacceptable state of affairs. To change the situation so that both women and men are included in studies adds to their costs. By introducing gender as a variable, a study must include more subjects in order to get the degree of statistical reliability that could be achieved with fewer subjects of the same gender. However, such studies have the additional value of yielding results known to be applicable to women.

That this issue is a matter of social fairness is obvious, but its connection with informed consent is less direct. As we mentioned in connection with prisoners, not allowing someone to consent may be viewed as treating that person as having less worth than someone who is allowed to consent. From this perspective, then, women have traditionally been denied the opportunity to be full persons in the moral sense. They have not been able to exercise their autonomy in ways permitted to men. Of course, they have also not been permitted to gain benefits that might be associated with the research projects from which they have been excluded. (For more details on women and medical research, see Chapter 4, *Race, Gender, and Medicine.*)

SUMMARY

There are other areas of medical experimentation that present special forms of moral problems. We have not discussed, for example, research involving military personnel or college and university students. Moreover, we mentioned only a few of the special difficulties presented by the mentally retarded, psychiatric patients, and old people confined to institutions.

We have, however, raised such a multiplicity of questions about consent and human research that it is perhaps worthwhile to attempt to restate some of the basic issues in a general form.

Basic Issues
Three issues are particularly noteworthy:

1. Who is competent to consent? (Are children? Are mental patients? If a person is not competent, who—if anyone—should have the power to consent for him or her?) Given that animals have no power to consent, is research involving them legitimate?

2. When is consent voluntary? (Is any institutionalized person in a position to offer free consent? How can even hospitalized patients be made free of pressures to consent?)

3. When are information and understanding adequate for genuine decision making? (Can complicated medical information ever be adequately explained to laypeople? Should we attempt to devise tests for understanding?)

Standards

Although we have concentrated on the matter of consent in research, there are other morally relevant matters connected with research that we have not discussed. These often relate to research standards. Among them are the following:

1. Is the research of sufficient scientific and medical worth to justify the human risk involved? Research that involves trivial aims or that is unnecessary (when, for example, it merely serves to confirm what is already well established) cannot be used to justify causing any threat to human well-being.

2. Can the knowledge sought be obtained without human clinical research? Can it be obtained without animal experimentation?

3. Have animal (and other) studies been done to minimize as far as is possible the risk to human subjects? A great deal can be learned about the effects of drugs, for example, by using "animal models," and the knowledge gained can be used to minimize the hazards in human trials. (Ethical issues involving animals in research may also be called into question.)

4. Does the design of the research meet accepted scientific standards? Sloppy research that is scientifically worthless means that people have been subjected to risks for no legitimate purpose and that animals have been harmed or sacrificed needlessly.

5. Do the investigators have the proper medical or scientific background to conduct the research effectively?

6. Is the research designed to minimize the risks and suffering of the participants? As we noted earlier, it is sometimes possible to test new drugs without using placebos. Thus, people in need of medication are not forced to be without treatment for their condition.

7. Have the aims and the design of the research and the qualifications of the investigators been reviewed by a group or committee competent to judge them? Such "peer review" is intended to assure that only research that is worthwhile and that meets accepted scientific standards is conducted. And although such review groups can fail to do their job properly, as they apparently did in the Tuskegee Syphilis Study, they are still necessary instruments of control.

Most writers on experimentation would agree that these are among the questions that must be answered satisfactorily before research involving human subjects is morally acceptable. Obviously, however, a patient who is asked to give his or her consent is in no position to judge whether the research project meets the standards implied by these questions. For this reason, it is important that there be social policies and practices governing research. Everyone should be confident that a research project is, in general, a legitimate one before having to decide whether to volunteer to become a participant.

Special problems are involved in seeing to it that these questions are properly answered. It is enough for our purposes, however, merely to notice that the character of the research and the manner in which it is to be performed are factors that are relevant to determining the moral legitimacy of experimentation involving human subjects.

ETHICAL THEORIES: MEDICAL RESEARCH AND INFORMED CONSENT

We have raised too many issues in too many areas of experimentation to discuss how each of several ethical theories might apply to them all. We must limit ourselves to considering a few suggestions about the general issues of human experimentation and informed consent.

UTILITARIANISM

Utilitarianism's principle of utility tells us, in effect, to choose those actions that will produce the greatest amount of benefit. Utilitarianism must approve human research in general, since there are cases in which the sacrifices of a few bring great benefits to many. We might, for example, design our social policies to make it worthwhile for people to volunteer for experiments with the view that, if people are paid to take risks and are compensated for their suffering or for any damage done to them during the course of a research project, then the society as a whole might benefit.

The principle of utility also tells us to design experiments to minimize suffering and the chance of harm. Also, it forbids us to do research of an unnecessary or trivial kind—research that is not worth its cost in either human or economic resources.

As to the matter of informed consent, utilitarianism does not seem to require it. If more social good is to be gained by making people research subjects without securing their agreement, then this is morally legitimate. It is not, of course, necessarily the best procedure to follow. A system of rewards to induce volunteers might be more likely to lead to an increase in general happiness. Furthermore, the principle of utility suggests that the best research subjects would be "less valuable" members of the society, such as the mentally retarded, the habitual criminal, or the dying. This, again, is not a necessary consequence of utilitarianism, although it is a possible one. If the recognition of rights and dignity would produce a better society in general, then a utilitarian would also say that they must be taken into account in experimentation with human beings.

For utilitarianism, that individual is competent to give consent who can balance benefits and risks and decide what course of action is best for him or her. Thus, if informed consent is taken to be a requirement supported by the principle of utility, those who are mentally ill or retarded or senile have to be excluded from the class of potential experimental subjects. Furthermore, investigators must provide enough relevant information to allow competent people to make a meaningful decision about what is likely to serve their own interests the most.

KANT

For Kant, an individual capable of giving consent is one who is rational and autonomous. Kant's principles would thus also rule out as research subjects people who are not able to understand experimental procedures, aims, risks, and benefits. People may volunteer for clinical trials if they expect them to be of therapeutic benefit to themselves, or they may act out of duty and volunteer, thus discharging their imperfect obligation to advance knowledge or to improve human life.

Yet, for Kant, there are limits to the risks that one should take. We have a duty to preserve our lives, so no one should agree to become a subject in an experiment in which the likelihood of death is great. Additionally, no one should subject himself to research in which there is considerable risk that his capacity for rational thought and autonomy will be destroyed. Indeed, Kant's principles appear to require us to regard as morally illegitimate those experiments that seriously threaten the lives or rationality of their subjects. Not only should we not subject ourselves to them, but we should not subject others to them.

Kant's principles also rule out as potential research participants those who are not in a position to act voluntarily, that is, those who cannot exercise their autonomy. This makes it important to determine, from a Kantian point of view, whether children and institutionalized people (including prisoners) can be regarded as free agents capable of moral choice. Also, as in the case of abortion, the status of the fetus must be determined. If the fetus is not a person, then fetal experimentation presents no particular moral problems. But if the fetus is a person, then we must accord it a moral status and act for its sake and not for the sake of knowledge or for others.

Kant's view of people as autonomous rational beings requires that informed consent be obtained for both medical treatment and research. We cannot be forced to accept treatment for "our own good," nor can we be turned into research subjects for "the good of others." We must always be treated as ends and never as means only. To be treated in this way requires that others never deliberately deceive us, no matter how good their intentions. In short, we have a right to be told what we are getting into so that we can decide whether we want to go through with it or not.

ROSS

Ross's theory imposes on researchers prima facie duties to patients that are similar to Kant's requirements. The nature of people as autonomous moral agents requires that their informed consent be obtained. Researchers ought not to deceive their subjects, and protocols should be designed in ways in which suffering and the risk of injury or death are minimized.

These are all prima facie duties, of course, and it is possible to imagine situations in which other duties might take precedence over them. In general, however, Ross, like Kant, tells us that human research cannot be based on what is useful; it must be based on what is right. Ross's principles, like Kant's, do not tell us, however, how we are to deal with such special problems as research involving children or prisoners.

NATURAL LAW

The principle of double effect and the principle of totality, which are based on the natural law theory of morality, have specific applications to experimentation. (See *Part V: Foundations of Bioethics*). Because we hold our bodies in trust, we are responsible for assessing the degree of risk to which we might be put if we agree to become research subjects. Thus, others have an obligation to supply us with the information that we need in order to make our decision. If we decide to give our consent, it must be given freely and not be the consequence of deception or coercion.

If available evidence shows that a sick person may gain benefits from participating in a research project, then the research is justified. But if the evidence shows that the benefits may be slight or if the chance of serious injury or death is relatively great, then the research is not justified.

In general, the likelihood of a person's benefiting from becoming a participant must exceed the danger of the person's suffering greater losses. The four requirements that govern the application of the principle of double effect determine what is and what is not an allowable experiment. (See *Part V: Foundations of Bioethics* for a discussion of these requirements.)

People can volunteer for experiments from which they expect no direct benefits. The good they seek in doing so is not their own good but the good of others. But there are limits to what they can subject themselves to. A dying patient, for example, cannot be made the subject of a useless or trivial experiment. The probable value of the knowledge to be gained must balance the risk and suffering the patient is subjected to, and there must be no likelihood that the experiment will seriously injure or kill the patient.

These same restrictions also apply to experiments involving healthy people. The principle of totality forbids a healthy person to submit to an experiment that involves the probability of serious injury, impaired health, mutilation, or death.

The status of the fetus is clear in the Roman Catholic version of the natural law theory: the fetus is a person. As such, the fetus is entitled to the same dignity and respect we accord to other persons. Experiments that involve doing it injury or lessening its chances of life are morally prohibited. But not all fetal research is ruled out. That which may be of therapeutic benefit or which does not directly threaten the fetus's well-being is allowable. Furthermore, research involving fetal tissue or remains is permissible, if it is done for a serious and valuable purpose.

RAWLS

From Rawls's point of view, the difficulty with utilitarianism with respect to human experimentation is that the principle of utility would permit the exploitation of some groups (the dying, prisoners, the retarded) for the sake of others. By contrast, Rawls's principles of justice would forbid all research that involves violating a liberty to which a person is entitled by virtue of being a member of society.

As a result, all experiments that make use of coercion or deception are ruled out. And since a person has a right to decide what risks she is willing to subject herself to, voluntary informed consent is required of all subjects. Society might, as in utilitarianism, decide to reward those who volunteer to become research subjects. As long as this is a possibility open to all, it is not objectionable.

It would never be right, according to Rawls, to take advantage of those in the society who are least well off to benefit those who are better off. Inequalities must be arranged so that they bring benefits (ideally) to everyone or, at least, to those who are most disadvantaged. Research involving direct therapeutic benefits is clearly acceptable (assuming informed consent), but research that takes advantage of the sick, the poor, the retarded, or the institutionalized and does not benefit them is unacceptable. The status of the fetus—whether or not it is a person in the moral sense—is an issue that has to be resolved before we know how to apply Rawls's principles to fetal research.

We have been able to provide only the briefest sketch of some of the ways in which our moral theories might apply to the issues in human experimentation. The remarks are not meant to be anything more than suggestive. A satisfactory moral theory of human experimentation requires working out the application of principles to problems in detail, as well as resolving such issues as the status of children and fetuses and the capability of institutionalized people to act freely.

In the Case Presentations and Social Contexts that follow, the issues we have discussed can be recognized as pressing problems requiring decisions about particular situations and general policies.

CASE PRESENTATION

Baby Fae

On October 14, 1984, a baby was born in a community hospital in southern California with a malformation known as hypoplastic left-heart syndrome. In such a condition, the mitral valve or aorta on the left side of the heart is underdeveloped, and essentially only the right side of the heart functions properly. Some 300 to 2000 infants a year are born with this defect, and most die from it within a few weeks.

The infant, who became known to the public as Baby Fae, was taken to the Loma Linda University Hospital Center. There, on October 26, a surgical team headed by Dr. Leonard Bailey performed a heart transplant; Baby Fae became the first human infant to receive a baboon heart. She died twenty days later.

Baby Fae was not the first human to receive a so-called xenograft, or cross-species transplant. In early 1964, a sixty-eight-year-old deaf man, Boyd Rush, was transplanted with a chimpanzee heart at the University of Mississippi Medical Center. The heart failed after only an hour, and the patient died. Before Baby Fae, three other cross-species transplants had also ended in a quick death.

MORAL QUESTIONS

In the case of Baby Fae, questions about the moral correctness and scientific legitimacy of the transplant were raised immediately. Hospital officials revealed that no effort had been made to find a human donor before implanting the baboon heart, and this led some critics to wonder if research interests were not being given priority over the welfare of the patient. Others questioned whether the parents were adequately informed about alternative corrective surgery, the Norwood procedure, available from surgeons in Boston and Philadelphia.

Other observers wondered whether the nature of the surgery and its limited value had been properly explained to the parents. Also, some critics raised objections to sacrificing a healthy young animal as part of an experiment not likely to bring any lasting benefit to Baby Fae.

Scientific critics charged that not enough is known about crossing the species barrier to warrant the use of transplant organs at this time. The previous record of failures, with no major advances in understanding, did not make the prospect of another such transplant reasonable. Furthermore, critics said, chimpanzees and gorillas are genetically more similar to humans than baboons, so the choice of a baboon heart was not a wise one. The only advantage of baboons is that they are easier to breed in captivity. Also, other critics claimed Dr. Bailey was merely engaged in "wishful thinking" in believing that Baby Fae's immune system would not produce a severe rejection response because of its immaturity.

POSTMORTEM

An autopsy on Baby Fae showed that her death was caused by the incompatibility of her blood with that of the baboon heart. Baby Fae's blood was type O, the baboon's type AB. This resulted in the formation of blood clots and the destruction of kidney function. The heart showed mild signs of rejection.

In an address before a medical conference after Baby Fae's death, Dr. Bailey commented on some of the criticisms. He is reported to have said that it was "an oversight on our part not to search for a human donor from the start." Dr. Bailey also told the conference that he and his team believed that the difference in blood types between Baby Fae and the baboon would be less important than other factors and that the immunosuppressive drugs used to prevent rejection would also solve the problem of blood incompatibility. "We came to regret those assumptions," Dr. Bailey said. The failure to match blood types was "a tactical error that came back to haunt us."

On other occasions Dr. Bailey reiterated his view that, because infant donors are extremely scarce, animal-to-human transplants offer a realistic hope for the future. Before the Baby Fae operation, Dr. Bailey had transplanted organs in more than 150 animals. None of his results were in published papers, however, and he performed all his work on local grants. He indicated that he would use the information obtained from Baby Fae to conduct additional animal experiments before attempting another such transplant.

NIH REPORT

In March of 1985 the National Institutes of Health released a report of a committee that made a site visit to Loma Linda to review the Baby Fae matter. The committee found that the informed-consent process was generally satisfactory, in that "the parents were given an appropriate and thorough explanation of the alternatives available, the risks and benefits of the procedure and the experimental nature of the transplant." Moreover, consent was obtained in an "atmosphere which allowed the parents an opportunity to carefully consider, without coercion or undue influence, whether to give permission for the transplant."

The committee also pointed out certain flaws in the consent document. First, it "did not include the possibility of searching for a human heart or performing a human heart transplant." Second, the expected benefits of the procedure "appeared to be overstated," because the consent document "stated that 'long-term survival' is an expected possibility with no further explanation." Finally, the document did not explain "whether compensation and medical treatment were available if injury occurred."

The committee did not question the legitimacy of the cross-species transplant. Moreover, it made no mention of the Norwood procedure, except to say that it had been explained to the mother at the community hospital at the birth of the infant. (The consent document described the procedure as a generally unsuccessful "temporizing operation.")

Although the committee was generally critical of Loma Linda's Institutional Review Board in "evaluating the entire informed-consent process," it reached the conclusion that "the parents of Baby Fae understood the alternatives available as well as the risks and reasonably expected benefits of the transplant."

Officials at Loma Linda University Medical Center promised that before performing another such transplant they would first seek a human infant heart donor.

SOCIAL CONTEXT
Clinical Trials, HIV, and Pregnancy: A Third World Tuskegee?

In 1995 the National Institutes of Health and the Centers for Disease Control and Prevention initiated clinical trials with the aim of finding a cheap and effective way of preventing HIV-positive pregnant women in developing countries from transmitting the virus to their newborn babies. The studies involved 12,211 women in five African countries, Thailand, and the Dominican Republic.

REGIMEN 076

The results of clinical trials conducted in the United States and reported in 1994 showed that if pregnant women testing positive for HIV followed a treatment regimen using the drug zidovudine (ZDV, previously called AZT), the risk of the virus being transmitted to their children was reduced by almost two-thirds. The chance of untreated HIV-positive women passing on the virus is about 25 percent, but when the women are treated with ZDV, the transmission drops to around 8 percent. By employing a ZDV treatment regimen, the United States has reduced the number of HIV-positive babies to about 500 per year.

The treatment requires women to take ZDV during the last twelve weeks of their pregnancy, then receive an intravenous dose of it during delivery. The newborns are then given the drug for the first six weeks of their lives. Because the federal study establishing the effectiveness of this treatment was assigned the number 076, the treatment is referred to as the 076 regimen.

A THOUSAND HIV-POSITIVE BABIES A DAY

The CDC estimates that in the world as a whole about one thousand HIV-positive babies are born every day. Most of them are born in countries too poor to pay for the treatment needed to lower this number substantially. The 076 regimen costs about $1000, putting it out of the reach of all but the richest individuals or nations.

Aside from the expense of the drug, other factors stand in the way of using the 076 regimen in underdeveloped countries. Most of them lack the hospitals and equipment needed to administer ZDV intravenously during delivery. Also, most mothers in third-world countries breast feed their babies, and while generally the practice is beneficial to the infant, the HIV virus can be transmitted through breast milk. Yet feeding infants prepared formula not only goes against custom, it costs more than most women—and their countries—can afford.

Against this backdrop, representatives of the World Health Organization, the United Nations, the National Institutes of Health and the Centers for Disease Control and Prevention met in Geneva in 1994 to design clinical trials to determine whether any short-term regimen using oral doses of ZDV could be effective in reducing the maternal-fetal transmission (vertical transmission) of the HIV virus. A short-term course of oral medication would be both cheaper and easier to administer and thus would make treatments possible in poor countries with limited medical resources.

HOW SHOULD EFFECTIVENESS BE JUDGED?

But what comparison group should be used to judge the effectiveness of the experimental regimens? One possibility would be to compare them to 076. This was rejected by the planners, however, because administering 076 to those who might benefit from it in the countries involved was not a realistic prospect. The test regimens needed to be compared to something that was realistic.

Another possibility was to use as a comparison the standard of medical care in the countries where the trials would be conducted. The care received by HIV-positive pregnant women could be measured against the outcome of the clinical trials. But the difficulty with this approach was that the standard of care in the countries where the trials would be conducted didn't exist. Essentially, HIV-positive pregnant women received no care at all. Thus, the Geneva group decided that results of the clinical trials involving different doses of zidovudine could best be judged by comparing them with the results obtained by administering a substance known to possess no therapeutic value—that is, with a placebo.

Tests involving placebos in the United States have become rare when a potentially lethal or disabling disease is involved. The principle is generally accepted that people deserve to receive treatments that represent the standard of medical care for their problem. Experimental treatments must show promise of being superior in at least some respects to the standard of care or there is no justification for employing them. Thus, the results of a test of an experimental treatment are compared with the results of the standard treatment.

The Geneva group, however, took the standard of care for preventing vertical HIV transmission to be that for the countries in which the test would be conducted, not the standard of care in North America or Western Europe. Because women in those countries would receive no treatment, the planners reasoned that women receiving placebos would be no worse off than otherwise. Indeed, because even those in the placebo group would be provided with free general health care, they would gain benefits they wouldn't ordinarily receive.

USE OF PLACEBOS CHALLENGED

The decision to give placebos to about half the women in the ZDV study was controversial from the beginning. Marc Lallemant, an NIH–sponsored investigator working in Thailand, refused to administer them to his patients. (Some Thai women, treated by CDC investigators, did receive placebos.) CDC researchers in Ivory Coast wrote to the agency's headquarters to report that their African collaborators didn't feel comfortable giving patients placebos. Critics estimated that because of the deliberate withholding of a known and effective treatment, more than a thousand babies would become HIV-positive who might have escaped infection.

"We have turned our backs on these mothers and their babies," said a representative of Public Citizen, a rights organization. The group also wrote to then-Secretary of Health and Human Services, Donna Shalala, and demanded that the clinical trial be redesigned to eliminate placebos. Instead, the group argued, a short course of ZDV should be compared with the 076 regimen, despite the higher cost this would entail. Because ZDV is known to be effective against HIV and in reducing vertical transmission of the virus, all women in the trial would at least be receiving doses of a drug appropriate as a treatment for their disease.

The head of the CDC's AIDS program, Helene Gayle, defended the clinical trial as it was designed. "This was done with a lot of discussion from the international community, following international codes of ethics," she said. "Part of doing ethical trials is that you are answering questions that are relevant for those countries."

Physicians and officials in some of the countries objected to ethical questions being raised about the trials. Viewing the objections as a form of condescension, they saw them as suggesting Africans were unable to decide what was in their best interest. "One has the impression that foreigners think that once white people arrive here they can impose what they want and we just accept it in ignorance," said Dr. Toussaint Sibailly of Ivory Coast. "If that was once the case, those days are long past."

"We already know what the alternative is to what we are doing," said Dr. Rene Ekpini in Abidjan. "The alternative is giving everyone here the placebo treatment, because that is what pregnant women with the disease are getting here—nothing."

This view was supported by AIDS researchers Joseph Saba and Arthur Ammann. They suggested that yielding to critics and giving every pregnant woman some level of treatment with an effective drug would require extending the studies several more years. But with over 1000 children a day becoming HIV infected, they suggested such a delay was unacceptable. "Americans should not impose their standard of care on developing countries," they claimed.

ANOTHER TUSKEGEE?

In contrast to the defenders of the trial, Marcia Angell, the Executive Editor of the *New England Journal of Medicine*, denounced the study in an editorial in the journal, comparing it to the Tuskegee syphilis experiments. "Some of the same arguments that were made in favor of the Tuskegee study are emerging in a new form in the [ZDV] studies in the third world," she said. (See in Chapter 4 the *Classic Case Presentation: Bad Blood, Bad Faith*.)

Investigators in the Tuskegee syphilis study never told the participants they were experimental subjects who might receive no relevant treatment for their disease. Indeed, participants with syphilis were never given a specific diagnosis of their disease. In this respect, at least, the ZDV clinical trials can be distinguished from the Tuskegee study. The design of the trials required that participants be informed of their diagnosis and consent to treatment. Investigators were also required to inform potential participants that they might be receiving a placebo, rather than an effective drug.

Even given the requirement of informed consent, some observers have questioned whether ordinary people in underdeveloped countries were capable of giving legitimate consent to becoming participants. Most of the people in the countries in which the trials took place are generally uneducated and technically unsophisticated. It is not clear whether they could be considered capable of understanding the medical and scientific information provided to them. But if they were not, their consent could not be considered genuine.

IS INFORMED CONSENT GENUINE?

When some patients agreed to become participants in the clinical trials, they appeared to have had little or no grasp of what they were consenting to and what the potential risks might be. After interviewing study participants in Abidjan, Ivory Coast, reporter Howard W. French concluded that "despite repeated explanations by project case workers, the understanding of these mostly poor and scantily educated subjects does not match the complexity of the ethical and scientific issues involved."

One educated women, a thirty-one-year-old mother with a law degree, who spoke with French said she hadn't received an explanation making it clear to her that ZDV was already known to be effective in controlling the transmission of HIV from mother to infant. How would she feel if she learned she had been in the placebo group? "I would say it was an injustice for sure," she told French.

This attitude was in contrast with that of another woman in the study. "People are trying to help us," she said. "And if a bunch of people have to die first, I am ready to risk my life too, so that other women and their babies survive. If I got the placebo, that will hurt for sure. But there is no evil involved."

AN END TO PLACEBOS

On February 18, 1998, the Centers for Disease Control and Prevention announced that placebos would no longer be used in the clinical trials. The use was not discontinued for moral reasons, but because data showed that the use of about $80 worth of ZDV administered in the last four weeks of pregnancy could reduce transmission of the HIV virus by about 50 percent.

The decision was based on a study of 393 women in Thailand, some of whom received placebos. "We are very pleased," Philip Nieburg said. "The controversy was unfortunate, but we feel the placebo-controlled trial that we did was very necessary."

Sidney Wolfe, Director the Public Citizen's Health Research Group, claimed the trial was unnecessary, because data supporting the outcome were already known from the trials of the 076 regimen. "This is inexcusable, sloppy research," he charged. "They have wasted a large number of lives and a huge amount of money."

EQUIVOCAL RESULTS

More recent findings make it unclear how effective a drug regimen can be in reducing maternal-fetal transmission of the HIV virus. A study conducted by the United Nations involved giving AZT and 3TC (lamivudine) to the mother for four weeks before expected delivery and during labor, then giving both mother and infant the drugs for an additional week.

The study showed that after eighteen months, the rate at which the infants acquired the virus through breast-feeding cancelled the preventive effects of the drug regimen. If this is the case, preventing the transmission of the virus at birth is probably not worth the investment of cost and effort.

Yet a second study by the National Institute of Allergy and Infectious Disease offers more hope. Researchers gave a single dose of the drug nevirapine to women during labor, then a dose to the newborn. After six to eight weeks, infants and mothers receiving the treatment were 42 percent less likely to be infected with HIV than those treated with AZT. This figure held for eighteen months, but mothers continued to infect their infants through breast-feeding.

In Africa breast-feeding may last for two years or longer. Hence, whether drugs are effective or not in preventing the transmission of HIV at birth, ways must be found to make breast-feeding safer.

Was it worth a widespread clinical trial using a placebo control to acquire data relevant to formulating public health and political policies about controlling the transmission of AIDS to infants in Africa? The question is still being debated.

The Cold-War Radiation Experiments

Amelia Jackson was a cook at Pogue's department store in Cincinnati, in 1966, when she was diagnosed with colon cancer. In October, she was treated with 100 rads of full-body radiation—the equivalent of 7500 chest X rays. Until the treatment, Ms. Jackson was strong and still working, but after the treatment, she bled and vomited for days and was never again able to care for herself.

Ms. Jackson was treated as part of a program operated by the University of Cincinnati and supported in part by funds from the Pentagon. She was one of several cancer patients in a research program in which people were subjected to radiation in massive doses to determine its biological effects.

The aim of the study, according to researchers, was to develop more effective cancer treatments. However, the military was interested in determining how much radiation military personnel could be subjected to before becoming disoriented and unable to function effectively.

A PATCHWORK OF RADIATION EXPERIMENTS

The Cincinnati project was only one of a patchwork of human experiments involving radiation that were carried out with funding from a variety of military and civilian agencies of the U.S. government over a period of at least thirty years. The experiments took place at government laboratories and university hospitals and research centers. Some experiments involved exposing patients to high-energy beams of radiation, while others involved injecting them with such dangerous radioactive substances as plutonium.

The experiments started toward the end of World War II. They were prompted by both scientific curiosity and the practical and military need to know more about the damaging effects of radiation on people. The advent of the Cold War between the United States and the Soviet Union and the real possibility that the political conflict would lead to nuclear war gave a sense of urgency to the research. Little was known about the harmful effects of radiation, and researchers believed their experiments would not only contribute to understanding, but would provide the basis for more effective medical therapies.

In the late 1940s, Vanderbilt University exposed about 800 pregnant women to radiation to determine its effects on fetal development. A follow-up study of the children born to the women showed a higher-than-average rate of cancer.

At the Oak Ridge National Laboratory in Tennessee, patients with leukemia and other forms of cancer were exposed to extremely high levels of radiation from isotopes of cesium and cobalt. Almost two hundred patients, including a six-year-old boy, were subjected to such treatment, until the experiment was ended in 1974 by the Atomic Energy Commission, on the grounds of lack of patient benefit.

From 1963 to 1971, experiments were conducted at Oregon State Prison in which the testicles of sixty-seven inmates were exposed to X rays to determine the effects of radiation on sperm production. Prisoners signed consent statements that mentioned some of the risks of the radiation. However, the possibility that the radiation might cause cancer was not mentioned. A similar experiment was conducted on sixty-four inmates at Washington State Prison.

At Columbia University and Montefiore Hospital in New York, during the late 1950s, twelve terminally ill cancer patients were injected with concentrations of radioactive calcium and strontium-85 to measure the rate at which the substances are absorbed by various types of tissues.

At a state residential school in Fernald, Massachusetts, from 1946 to 1956, nineteen mentally retarded teenaged boys were fed radioactive iron and calcium in their breakfast oatmeal. The aim of the research was to provide information about nutrition and metabolism. In the consent form mailed to parents of the boys, no mention was made of radiation.

THE EXPERIMENTS BECOME PUBLIC

The radiation experiments became public only in 1993 when reporters for the *Albuquerque Tribune* tracked down five of the eighteen patients who had been subjects in an experiment conducted from 1945 to 1957, in which patients were injected with plutonium. The work was done at the University of Rochester, Oak Ridge Laboratory, the University of Chicago, and the University of California, San Francisco Hospital. Apparently, some of the patients did not receive information about their treatment and were injected with radioactive materials without first giving consent.

Relying on the Freedom of Information Act, Eileen Welsome, a reporter for the newspaper, attempted to get documents from the Department of Energy concerning the radiation research, including ones containing the names of subjects. However, she was able to secure little information, and Tara O'Toole, the assistant secretary of energy for environment, safety, and health at the time, expressed reservations about releasing documents containing the names of research subjects. "Does the public's right to know include releasing names?" O'Toole asked. "It is not clear to me that it is part of the ethical obligation of the Government."

DID PARTICIPANTS GIVE THEIR INFORMED CONSENT?

Secretary of Energy Hazel R. O'Leary soon committed her department to a full investigation of the radiation experiments. A major focus of the inquiry was on whether patients were fully informed about the risks of the treatments they received and whether they gave meaningful consent to them.

In a number of cases, the government discovered, the experimental subjects were not informed of the risks they faced and did not consent to participate in the research. Patients were sometimes misled about the character of the treatments and in some cases even the signatures on consent forms were forged. Ms. Jackson's granddaughter claims that although her grandmother was illiterate, she could sign her name, and the signature on the form used by the University of Cincinnati was not hers. The same claim is made by other relatives of subjects in the study.

In one known instance, a researcher found the radiation experiments to be morally suspect and warned his colleagues against pursuing them. C. E. Newton at the Hanford nuclear weapons plant wrote in an internal memorandum about the work done with prisoners at Washington State Prison: "The experiments do not appear to have been in compliance with the criminal codes of the state of Washington, and there is some question as to whether they were conducted in compliance with Federal laws."

Similarly, in a 1950 memorandum, Joseph G. Hamilton, a radiation biologist, warned his supervisors that the experiments "might have a little of the Buchenwald touch." Hamilton warned that the Atomic Energy Commission would be "subject to considerable criticism."

Some observers claim that work carried out twenty or thirty years ago cannot be judged by the same ethical standards as we would use today. Robert Loeb, speaking for Strong Memorial Hospital, where some of the studies were carried out, put the point this way: "In the 1940s, what was typical in research involving human subjects was for physicians to tell the patients that they would be involved in a study and not always give full details. That is not the standard today. Many of these studies would be impossible to conduct today."

By contrast, Dr. David S. Egilman, who has investigated instances of research with human subjects conducted by the military and the Atomic Energy Commission, claims there is adequate evidence to conclude the researchers and their supporting agencies knew they were conducting immoral experiments. "They called the work, in effect, Nazi-like," he says. "The argument we hear is that these experiments were ethical at the time they were done. It's simply not true."

The initial question about the use of human subjects in radiation experiments conducted under the auspices of what is now the Department of Energy was expanded to include those conducted by several federal agencies. It seems as if at least 1000 people were exposed to varying levels of radiation in a variety of experiments conducted over a number of years at various locations. Some observers believe the actual figures are much higher.

The President's Advisory Committee on Human Radiation Experiments reviewed records from the Energy Department, Defense Department, Central Intelligence Agency, NASA, and federal health agencies to attempt to locate research projects involving radiation and identify the people who were their experimental subjects. After eighteen months of investigation, the committee reported in 1995 that many of the government-sponsored experiments had been illegal and that their survivors ought to be compensated.

COMPENSATION

In November 1996 the federal government agreed to pay $4.8 million as compensation for injecting twelve people with plutonium or uranium. At the time of the settlement, only one of the twelve was still alive, and the $400,000 award was paid to the families of the other participants. In 1998 the Quaker Oats Company and M.I.T. agreed to pay $1.85 million to the more than one hundred men who, as boys, had been fed the radioactive oatmeal at the Fernald School and other study sites.

A large number of claims from other experiments involving radiation and consent were filed against the Federal government, universities, and hospitals. Advocates for those whose rights may have been violated charge the government with failing to make an effort to find the names of the people who were participants in the various radiation experiments. This would be a difficult and time-consuming process, because often names and addresses were not made a part of the experimental records.

The National Archives has placed all the hundreds of thousands of pages of records acquired by the Presidential Commission in files available to the public, and instead of the government notifying people that they may have a legal claim for compensation, individuals must come forward on their own initiative.

NEW REGULATIONS

In 1997 President Clinton endorsed a stringent set of policies governing all human research receiving federal support. Under the new rules, explicit informed consent is required, the sponsor of the experiment must be identified to the subject, the subject must be told whether the experiment is classified, and permanent records of the experiment and the subjects must be kept. Further, an external review must be conducted before the experiment can proceed. The hope was that the new rules would put an end to secret experiments in which human subjects are subjected to radioactive, chemical, or other dangerous substances without their knowledge or consent.

With respect to the radiation experiments, Representative David Mann of Ohio summed up the views of most citizens: "I believe we have no choice but to conclude that the radiation experiments were simply wrong and that the Government owes a huge apology to the victims, their families, and the nation."

CASE PRESENTATION
The Willowbrook Hepatitis Experiments

The Willowbrook State School in Staten Island, New York, is an institution devoted to housing and caring for mentally retarded children. In 1956 a research group led by Saul Krugman and Joan P. Giles of the New York University School of Medicine initiated a long-range study of viral hepatitis at Willowbrook. The children confined there were made experimental subjects of the study.

Hepatitis, a disease affecting the liver, is now known to be caused by one of two (possibly more) viruses. Although the viruses are distinct, the results they produce are the same. The liver becomes inflamed and increases in size as the invading viruses replicate themselves. Also, part of the tissue of the liver may be destroyed and the liver's normal functions impaired. Often the flow of bile through the ducts is blocked, and bilirubin (the major pigment in bile) is forced into the blood and urine. This produces the symptom of yellowish or jaundiced skin.

The disease is generally relatively mild, although permanent liver damage can be produced. The symptoms are ordinarily flu-like—mild fever, tiredness, inability to keep food down. The viruses causing the disease are transmitted orally through contact with the feces and bodily secretions of infected people.

Krugman and Giles were interested in determining the natural history of viral hepatitis—the mode of infection and the course of the disease over time. They also wanted to test the effectiveness of gamma globulin as an agent for inoculating against hepatitis. (Gamma globulin is a protein complex extracted from the blood serum that contains antigens, substances that trigger the production of specific antibodies to counter infectious agents.)

ENDEMIC HEPATITIS

Krugman and Giles considered Willowbrook to be a good choice for investigation because viral hepatitis occurred more or less constantly in the institution. In the jargon of medicine, the disease was endemic. That this was so was recognized in 1949, and it continued to be so as the number of children in the school increased to over 5000 in 1960. Krugman and Giles claimed that "under the chronic circumstances of multiple and repeated exposure . . . most newly admitted children became infected within the first six to twelve months of residence in the institution."

Over a fourteen-year period, Krugman and Giles collected over 25,000 serum specimens from more than 700 patients. Samples were taken before exposure, during the incubation period of the virus, and for periods after the infection. In an effort to get the kind of precise data they considered most useful, Krugman and Giles decided to deliberately infect some of the incoming children with the strain of the hepatitis virus prevalent at Willowbrook.

JUSTIFYING DELIBERATE INFECTION

They justified their decision in the following way: It was inevitable that susceptible children would become infected in the institution. Hepatitis was especially mild in the three- to ten-year age group at Willowbrook. These studies would be carried out in a special unit with optimum isolation facilities to protect the children from other infectious diseases such as shigellosis (dysentery caused by a bacillus), and parasitic and respiratory infections which are prevalent in the institution.

Most important, Krugman and Giles claimed that being an experimental subject was in the best medical interest of the child, for not only would the child receive special care, but infection with the milder form of hepatitis would provide protection against the more virulent and damaging forms. As they say: "It should be emphasized that the artificial induction of hepatitis implies a 'therapeutic' effect because of the immunity which is conferred."

CONSENT

Krugman and Giles obtained what they considered to be adequate consent from the parents of the children used as subjects. Where they were unable to obtain consent, they did not include the child in the experiment. In the earlier phases of the study, parents were provided with relevant information either by letter or orally, and written consent was secured from them. In the later phases, a group procedure was used:

> First, a psychiatric social worker discusses the project with the parents during a preliminary interview. Those who are interested are invited to attend a group session at the institution to discuss the project in greater detail. These sessions are conducted by the staff responsible for the program, including the physician, supervising nurses, staff attendants, and psychiatric social workers. . . . Parents in groups of six to eight are given a tour of the facilities. The purposes, potential benefits, and potential hazards of the program are discussed with them, and they are encouraged to ask questions. Thus, all parents can hear the response to questions posed by the more articulate members of the group. After leaving this briefing session parents have an opportunity to talk with their private physicians who may call the unit for more information. Approximately two weeks after each visit, the psychiatric social worker contacts the parents for their decision. If the decision is in the affirmative, the consent is signed but parents are informed that signed consent may be withdrawn any time before the beginning of the program. It has been clear that the group method has enabled us to obtain more thorough informed consent. Children who are wards of the state or children without parents have never been included in our studies.

Krugman and Giles point out that their studies were reviewed and approved by the New York State Department of Mental Hygiene, the New York State Department of Mental Health, the Armed Forces Epidemiological Board, and the human-experimentation committees of the New York University School of Medicine and the Willowbrook School. They also stress that, although they were under no obligation to do so, they chose to meet the World Medical Association's Draft Code on Human Experimentation.

ETHICAL CONCERNS

The value of the research conducted by Krugman and Giles has been recognized as significant in furthering a scientific understanding of viral hepatitis and methods for treating it. Yet serious moral doubts have been raised about the nature and conduct of the experiments. In particular, many have questioned the use of retarded children as experimental subjects, some claiming children should never be experimental subjects in investigations that are not directly therapeutic. Others have raised questions about the ways in which consent was obtained from the parents of the children, suggesting that parents were implicitly blackmailed into giving their consent

CASE PRESENTATION
Echoes of Willowbrook or Tuskegee? Experimenting with Children

In April 1998 the National Bioethics Advisory Committee was asked to investigate three experiments conducted from 1993 to 1996 at the New York State Psychiatric Institute.

The subjects of the experiment were almost 100 boys ranging in age from six to eleven. All were from New York City, and many were Black or Hispanic. The boys were chosen as subjects because their older brothers had been legally charged with some form of delinquency.

Researchers identified the potential subjects by combing through court records and by interviewing the mothers of the boys charged with crimes. The ones chosen for the experiment were considered by the researchers to be boys who had experienced "adverse rearing practices." The mothers of the boys selected were asked to take their children to the Psychiatric Institute to take part in the experiment. Mothers bringing in their boys were given a $125 cash payment.

The research subjects were given a small intravenously administered dose of the drug fenfluramine, and their blood was then assayed for a change in the level of neurotransmitters. The aim of the experiment was to test the hypothesis that violent behavior can be predicted by the use of neurochemical markers. The boys were given only a single dose of the drug.

In two of the three studies conducted at the Psychiatric Institute, the sixty-six boys who served as subjects were between seven and eleven and had been diagnosed as having Attention Deficit Hyperactivity Disorder. They were taken off their medication for a period of time before the fenfluramine was administered.

Fenfluramine has now been withdrawn from medical practice by the Federal Drug Administration. In combination with another drug ("fen-phen"), it was used to treat obesity, until it was discovered that in some people it caused damage to the heart valves. Experts on the use of the fenfluramine consider it unlikely that the boys in the experiments suffered any harm from the drug. They were given only a single small dose, whereas those with heart damage used the drug in larger doses over a period of months.

Even so, critics of the experiments charge that the boys were exposed to a substantial risk in experiments in which they had no chance of receiving any benefit. The experiments were for the sake of science, not for their own sake. Further, the drug is not free of such side effects as nausea, headache, dizziness, anxiety, and irritability. The children, then, suffered to some extent without gaining any advantage.

While the critics have not mentioned the role played by the boys' mothers, we might ask whether they can be said to have acted in the best interest of their children. Some of the women may have been induced by the $125 payment to ignore their child's interest. Thus the payment itself raises the question of whether the consent of the mothers to their children's participation was legitimate. If their income was low, the prospect of receiving money may have tainted the quality of their consent.

"What value does the President's apology for Tuskegee have when there are no safeguards to prevent such abuses now?" asked Vera Sharay, director of Citizens for Responsible Care in Psychiatry and Research. "These racist and morally offensive studies put minority children at the risk of harm in order to prove they are generally predisposed to violence in the future," she charged. "It demonstrates that psychiatric research is out of control."

A spokesperson for Mount Sinai Hospital, which participated in the studies, refused to reveal how many of the subjects were black or Hispanic. He commented only that the subjects chosen reflected "the ethnically diverse population of the catchment area."

Dr. John Oldham, director of the New York Psychiatric Institute, said during an interview that such studies are crucial to acquiring an understanding of the biological basis of behavior. "Is there a correlation between certain biological markers and conduct disorders or antisocial behaviors?" he asked. "This study was an effort to look at this with a relatively simple method using fenfluramine."

At the instigation of Disability Advocates, the experiments are also being investigated by the Department of Health and Human Services' Office of Protection from Research Risks.

CASE PRESENTATION

The Use of Morally Tainted Sources: The Pernkopf Anatomy

In November 1996 Howard A. Israel and William E. Seidelman wrote a letter to *JAMA*, the Journal of the American Medical Association, asking that the University of Vienna attempt to determine the source of the cadavers used as subjects of the illustrations in the multi-volume book known as the *Pernkopf Anatomy*. Rumors surrounding the book's author and artists had long suggested that some of the cadavers employed in the dissections might have been victims of the Nazis.

Eduard Pernkopf, the book's author, was a member of the Nazi party, and, although never charged with war crimes, he spent three years in an Allied prison camp. He returned afterward to his academic position at the University of Vienna and worked on his atlas of anatomy until he died in 1955. The four main artists illustrating the anatomy were also Nazi party members, and one of them sometimes incorporated into his signature a swastika and the lightning bolts of the SS. These have been airbrushed out in contemporary printings of the book.

Pernkopf began his work in 1933, well before the beginning of the war, but he died in 1955, and the book was completed by others and published in 1960. While the American edition has dropped Pernkopf's text, it uses the original illustrations, which some anatomists consider to be masterpieces of medical paintings. The atlas is admired for its accuracy and is widely used by anatomists and others in medical schools.

After investigating the charge that cadavers from concentration camps or the bodies of Nazi opponents from the district prison were used as subjects, the anatomist David P. Williams concluded that either was possible but couldn't be proved one way or the other. Because of this doubt about the source of the cadavers, uncertainty about the moral legitimacy of using the atlas continues to be debated.

Anatomist E. W. April expressed the opinion of one faction. The atlas is "a phenomenal book," he told reporter Nicholas Wade, "very complete and thorough and authoritative, and you can't detract from that regardless of the fact that [Pernkopf] might not have been a good person or belonged to the wrong party."

The opposite view is expressed by Howard Israel, the coauthor of the letter to *JAMA*. "I have looked at a lot of anatomy textbooks, and these [volumes] are terrific in terms of the quality of pictures," he told Wade. "But that doesn't mean it's right to use them."

What if the source of the cadavers was known? What if they turned out to be the bodies of victims of the Holocaust? Would it be wrong to use an anatomy text based on the dissection of the victims? This is one aspect of the general question of whether it is morally acceptable to use scientific data or any other sort of information that has been obtained in an immoral way. In the view of some, we have a moral duty to avoid tainted data, because to use it is in an indirect way to benefit from the wrongdoing that produced it. Others, however, believe that using the data is a way of rescuing something worthwhile from something that was wrong. As such, it is a way of honoring those who suffered a terrible injustice by making sure their sacrifice is not wasted.

CHAPTER 2

Physicians, Patients, and Others:
Autonomy, Truth Telling, and Confidentiality

Donald (Dax) Cowart Rejects Treatment—and Is Ignored

The man stretched out on the steel platform of the sling with his knees drawn up is thin to the point of emaciation. His face and numerous patches of bare, raw flesh are slathered with layers of thick white salve. A pad covers one eye, and the eyelid of the other is sewn shut. Bandages wrapped around his legs and torso give him the look of a mummy in a low-budget horror movie.

In obvious pain, he writhes on the platform. With rock music playing in the background, white-uniformed attendants in gauze masks raise the sling and lower him into a steel tank of clear liquid.

The real horror began for Donald Cowart in July of 1973. The previous May he had left active duty in the Air Force after three years of service, including a tour of duty in Vietnam, to take a slot in the Air Force Reserve. He returned to his family home in east Texas to wait for an opening as a commercial airline pilot. He was twenty-five years old, a college graduate, unmarried, and in excellent health and top physical condition. A high school athlete who had played football and basketball and run track, he had stayed athletic. He played golf, surfed when he could, and rodeoed. As a pilot for a large airline, he'd be busy, but not too busy to continue the active life he was used to. But in 1973 the airlines weren't looking for new pilots, and while Don waited for them to start hiring again, he decided to join his father as a real estate broker. The two had always been close, so working together was a pleasure for both of them.

And then everything changed forever.

One hot Wednesday afternoon in July, Don and his father drove out to the country to take a look at a piece of land Don thought might be a good buy. They parked the car in a shady, cool spot at a low place in the road beside a bridge. They took a walking tour of the land, but when they returned to the car, it wouldn't start.

Mr. Cowart got out, raised the hood, and tinkered with the carburetor. Don, in the driver's seat, turned the key repeatedly, grinding the engine around so much he got afraid he would run down the battery. Then, after three or four minutes of trying, a blue flame suddenly shot from the carburetor, and a tremendous explosion rocked the car, throwing Don sideways onto the passenger seat. A huge ball of live fire enveloped the car.

Don managed to get the door open, then, still surrounded by fire, he ran three steps toward the woods, the only place that wasn't on fire. But seeing that the undergrowth was so thick that he was likely to get trapped in it and burn to death, he turned away and ran straight down the road. He hurtled through three thick walls of fire, and when he cleared the last one, he threw himself to the ground and rolled to smother the flames.

Getting to his feet, he ran again, shouting for help. He noticed his vision was blurred, as if he were looking at everything from under water, and he realized his eyes had been seared by the fire. *This can't be happening,* he thought as he ran. But the pain assured him that it was. He heard a voice shouting, "I'm coming!" and only then did he stop running and lie down beside the road.

He thought at the time that the car's gas tank had exploded, and only after he had been in a hospital for several days did he learn that the blast and fire were caused by a leak in a propane gas transmission line. Seeping from the line, the gas had collected in the hollow by the bridge, saturating the air to such an extent that the car wouldn't start because the engine couldn't get enough oxygen. The spark from the starter had ignited the gas.

When the farmer who had heard Don's shouts arrived, he said, "Oh, my God." Then Don knew for the first time that he was burned more badly than he had thought. After the farmer came back from looking for Mr. Cowart, Don asked him to get him a gun. "Why?" the man asked.

"Can't you see I'm a dead man," Don told him. "I'm going to die anyway."

"I can't do that," the farmer said gently.

When the first ambulance arrived, Don sent it to pick up his father. When the second came, he didn't want to go to the hospital. "All I wanted to do was die and to die as quickly as possible," he recalled nine years later. Despite his protest, the attendants put him in the ambulance. He asked them to pick him up by his belt, because his burns were so excruciating he couldn't bear to be touched.

Don and his father were taken to a small nearby hospital, but because of the extent of their injuries, they were soon transported to the burn unit of Parkland Hospital in Dallas, 140 miles away. "I'm sorry, Donny boy," his father told him as they were placed in the ambulance. Mr. Cowart died on the way to Parkland. Don continued to insist that he be allowed to die.

Charles Baxter, Don's attending physician, estimated that Don had extremely deep burns over about 65 percent of his body. His face, upper arms, torso, and legs had suffered severe third-degree burns, and both ears were virtually destroyed. His eyes were so damaged that his left eye had to be surgically removed, and he eventually lost the vision in his right eye. His fingers were burned off down to the second joint, making it impossible for him to pick up anything. The pain was tremendous, and even though he was given substantial doses of narcotics, it remained unbearable for more than a year.

Don's mother had heard about an accidental explosion on the radio, but she learned her husband and son were involved only when the police called her out of an evening church service to tell her. After rushing to Dallas to be with Don, she was approached by his physicians to sign consent forms for surgery and treatment.

Knowing nothing about burn therapies, she took the advice offered to her by the physicians. She knew of Don's protest against being treated, but she expected his wish to be allowed to die to pass as soon as he began to recover.

Rex Houston, the family's attorney and close friend, filed a lawsuit with the owners of the propane transmission line for damages resulting from the explosion. He was concerned with going to trial as soon as possible. Don was unmarried and had nobody depending on him, so if he died before the case was heard, the lawsuit would be likely to produce little money. But with Don as a living plaintiff and a young man who had lost the use of both hands and both eyes, the suit had the potential to be of tremendous value. "I had to have a living plaintiff," Houston said years later. Dr. Baxter later said he had discussed the legal and moral aspects of Don's treatment with Mr. Houston.

Don continued to want to die. He asked a nurse with whom he had developed a rapport to give him a drug that would kill him or at least to help him do something to take his own life. As sympathetic as she was, she was forced to refuse his request. Don also asked a family friend to get a gun for him, but then, even while he was asking, he observed that getting him a gun would be pointless, because he had no fingers to pull the trigger.

Dr. Baxter's initial response to Don's request to die was dismissive: "Oh, you don't want to do that," he would say. For a while, though, Don convinced Dr. Baxter he was serious and not simply reacting out of the immediate pain and shock. But eventually Dr. Baxter decided Don talked about wanting to die only to manipulate the people around him and gain control over his environment. Don later rejected this interpretation.

Mrs. Cowart considered her son's medical condition too serious to allow him to make decisions about accepting or rejecting treatment. "Everything was discussed with her in detail," Dr. Baxter recalled. "She was most cooperative and most helpful. We approached the problem of his desire to die very openly." Also, Dr. Baxter remembered, "Even the possibility that it could be allowed was discussed with her. She was never in favor of it, because basically she thought he did not have this desire."

When his burns had healed enough that he was out of danger, Don was moved to the Texas Institute of Rehabilitation in Houston. He agreed to give the program a try, but after about three weeks, he began to refuse treatment again. He had learned that rehabilitation would take years of pain and suffering. The doctors at the Institute honored his request that he not be treated, and in a few days, the burns on his legs became infected again, and the grafted skin peeled away. He came near death.

Dr. Robert Meier, a rehabilitation specialist responsible for Don's care, called a meeting with Don's mother and attorney. They decided that because Don's burns had become infected again due to his refusal to have his dressings changed, he should be hospitalized in an acute care center again.

Don was transferred to the University of Texas Medical Branch at Galveston in April of 1974. Once there, he again refused treatment. Psychiatrist Robert B. White was called in by the surgeons in charge of Don's case, because they thought Don's refusal might be the result of clinical depression or some form of mental illness. If he were found incompetent, a legal guardian could be appointed to give permission for the additional surgery he needed. After examining Don and with the concurrence of a second psychiatrist, Dr. White concluded that Don was fully competent and not suffering from any kind of mental illness. He was, moreover, intelligent, self-aware, and highly articulate.

To control the many infected areas on his body, Don had to be submerged daily in a tank of highly chlorinated water to destroy the microorganisms breeding on the surface of his wounds. The experience was excruciatingly painful, and despite Don's protests and refusals, the "tankings" were carried out anyway. He refused to give his permission for surgery on his hands, which had become more clawlike due to scarring and contracture. Eventually, he consented, with his surgeon's assurance that he would give Don enough drugs to control the pain.

Don wanted to leave the hospital so he could go home and die. But he couldn't leave without help, and neither his physicians nor his mother would agree to help. His mother wanted him taken care of, and moving him home to die of massive infection was more than she could accept. Don accused her of being responsible for prolonging his hopeless condition.

Surgeon Duane Larson was puzzled by Don's ongoing insistence that he wanted to die. Don wasn't on the verge of death and would surely recover some degree of normalcy. He would find new ways to enjoy life. "In essence he was asking people to participate in his death," Dr. Larson recalled.

One alternative Dr. Larson mentioned to Don was for him to be treated until he was well enough to leave the hospital, then he could kill himself, if he still wanted to. Another alternative was to get Don to see that new things could be done to lessen his pain and make him more comfortable. But Dr. Larson also thought Don might be brought to see that some of his outbursts were merely angry "little boy feelings" anyone would experience after going through such a terrible ordeal.

The tankings were by far the worst treatments. "It was like pouring alcohol on an open wound," Don remembered. Being lifted out of the tank was even worse, because the room was freezing, and every nerve in the damaged parts of his body produced agony. "All I could do was scream at the top of my lungs until I would finally pass out with exhaustion. The tankings took place seven days a week—week after week after week."

"Don't ask us to let you die," Dr. Meier had told Don at the rehabilitation center, "because in a sense what that means is we're killing you. If you want to die, then let me fix your hands, operate on them and open them up so at least you can do something with them, and if you want to commit suicide then, you can. But don't ask us to stand here and literally kill you."

"The argument that not treating a patient is the same as killing borders on the ridiculous," Don said years later. "If letting the patient die is characterized as playing God, then treating the patient to save his life has to be as well. In the final analysis, I was nothing but a hostage to the current state of medical technology." Just a few years earlier, he would have died, but the management of burns had advanced sufficiently to keep him alive. He was, he said, "forced to receive treatment," because he was "too weak to resist and unable to walk out on my own." Ironically, as Don later saw the situation, what was happening to him was taking place when the country was emphasizing the importance of individual liberties and freedom of choice by the individual.

Don was treated for ten months. He lost all ten fingers, was blind and terribly scarred and disfigured. He had to have help with everything and was unable to take care of even his most basic bodily needs. His pain was still constant, and he couldn't walk.

Discharged from the hospital, he took up residence in his mother's house. At first he was relieved to be out of the hospital, but in a few weeks he fell into a deep depression. Frustration built up as he experienced his loss of independence, grew bored, and worried about what he was going to do with the rest of his life. Marriage seemed at best a remote possibility.

Because of his disfigurement, he thought about never going out in public, but eventually he began to go to stores and restaurants, protected by his blindness from the stares and reactions of others. Money from the court settlement gave him the financial independence to do what he wanted and was able to do.

Starting law school, he lived with a married couple and learned to do some things for himself. But in the spring of that year, beset by a sleep disturbance and upset by the breakdown of a personal relationship, he tried to kill himself with an overdose of sleeping pills and tranquilizers. He was found in time for him to be taken to the hospital and have his stomach pumped. Despite what Dr. Larson and others had told him while his burns were being treated, he wasn't going to be allowed to kill himself. Don was rehospitalized for depression and insomnia for about a month and eventually returned to law school.

After graduating, Don—who was called Dax—set up a practice in Corpus Christi. He married Karen, someone he had known in high school, in 1983.

His mother is sure she made the right decision in signing the consent forms for treatment, particularly now that her son's life is filled with the satisfactions of marriage and a job he likes. She wishes she had asked the doctors to give him more pain medication, though. They hadn't told her it was possible.

Dax doesn't blame his mother for her decisions. He blames his doctors for putting her in the position of having to make them. *He* should have been the one asked. "The individual freedom of a competent adult should never be restricted," he says, "except when it conflicts with the freedom of some other individual." For him the individual should be able to decide what minimum quality of life is acceptable to him or her. This is not a decision that should be made by physicians or anyone else on behalf of another person.

Now that Donald Cowart is living a satisfactory life, is he glad his physicians and his mother continued his treatment against his wishes? "I'm enjoying life now, and I'm glad to be alive," Cowart says. "But I still think it was wrong to force me to undergo what I had to, to be alive."

Nor would the assurance of pulling through be enough to make him change his mind. "If the same thing were to occur tomorrow, knowing I could reach this same point, I still would not want to undergo the pain and agony that I had to undergo to be alive now. I should want that choice to lie entirely with myself and not others."

Briefing Session

Consider the following cases:

1. A state decides to require that all behavioral therapists (that is, all who make use of psychological conditioning techniques to alter behavior patterns) be either licensed psychologists or psychiatrists.

2. A member of the Jehovah's Witnesses religion, which is opposed to the transfusion of blood and blood products, refuses to consent to a needed appendectomy. But when his appendix ruptures and he lapses into unconsciousness, the surgical resident operates and saves his life.

3. A physician decides not to tell the parents of an infant who died shortly after birth that the cause of death was an unpredictable birth defect, because he does not wish to influence their desire to have a child.

4. A janitor employed in an elementary school consults a psychiatrist retained by the school board and tells her that he has on two occasions molested young children; the psychiatrist decides that it is her duty to inform the school board.

5. A six-year-old develops a high fever accompanied by violent vomiting and convulsions while at school. The child is rushed to a nearby hospital. The attending physician makes a diagnosis of meningitis and telephones the parents for permission to initiate treatment. Both parents are Christian Scientists, and they insist that no medical treatment be given to her. The physician initiates treatment anyway, and the parents later sue the physician and the hospital.

6. A thirty-year-old woman who is twenty-four weeks pregnant is involved in an automobile accident that leaves her with a spinal cord injury. Her physician tells her that she would have had a greater chance of recovery had she not been pregnant. She then requests an abortion. The hospital disagrees with her decision and gets a court order forbidding the abortion.

There is perhaps no single moral issue that is present in all these cases. Rather, there is a complex of related issues. Each case involves acting on the behalf of someone else—another individual, the public at large, or a special group. And each action comes into conflict with the autonomy, wishes, or expectations of some person or persons. Even though the issues are related, it is most fruitful to discuss them under separate headings. We will begin with a brief account of autonomy, then turn to a discussion of paternalism and imposed restrictions on autonomy.

AUTONOMY

We are said to act autonomously when our actions are the outcome of our deliberations and choices. To be autonomous is to be self-determining. Hence, autonomy is violated when we are coerced to act by actual force or by explicit and implicit threats or when we act under misapprehension or under the influence of factors that impair our judgment.

We associate autonomy with the status we ascribe to rational agents as persons in the moral sense. Moral theories are committed to the idea that persons are by their nature uniquely qualified to decide what is in their own best interest. This is because they are ends in themselves, not means to some other end. As such, persons have inherent worth, rather than instrumental worth. Others have a duty to recognize this worth and to avoid treating persons as though they were only instruments to be employed to achieve a goal chosen by someone else. To treat someone as if she lacks autonomy is thus to treat her as less than a person.

All the cases above may be viewed as involving violations of the autonomy of the individuals concerned. Consider: (1) laws requiring a license to provide therapy restrict the actions of individuals who do not qualify for a license; (2) the Jehovah's Witness is given blood he does not want; (3) information crucial to decision making is withheld from the parents of the child with the genetic disease, so their future decision cannot be a properly informed one; (4) by breaking confidentiality, the psychiatrist is usurping the prerogative of the janitor to keep secret information that may harm him; (5) by treating the girl with meningitis, the physician is violating the generally recognized right of parents to make decisions concerning their child's welfare; (6) by refusing the woman's request for an abortion, the hospital and the court are forcing her to remain pregnant against her will.

The high value we place on autonomy is based on the realization that without it we can make very little of our lives. In its absence, we become the creatures of others, and our lives assume the forms they choose for us. Without being able to act in ways to shape our own destiny by pursuing our aims and making our own decisions, we are not realizing the potential we have as rational agents. Autonomy permits us the opportunity to make ourselves; even if we are dissatisfied with the result, we have the satisfaction of knowing that the mistakes were our own. We at least acted as rational agents.

One of the traditional problems of social organization is to structure society in such a way that the autonomy of individuals will be preserved and promoted. However, autonomy is not an absolute or unconditional value, but just one among others. For example, few would wish to live in a society in which you could do what you wanted only if you had enough physical power to get your way. Because one person's exercise of autonomy is likely to come into conflict with another's, we are willing to accept some restrictions to preserve as much of our own freedom as possible. We value our own safety, the opportunity to carry out our plans in peace, the lives of other rational beings, and perhaps even their welfare.

Because autonomy is so basic to us, we usually view it as not requiring any justification. However, this predisposition in favor of autonomy means that to violate someone's autonomy, to set aside that person's wishes and render impotent her power of action, requires that we offer a strong justification. Various principles have been proposed to justify conditions under which we are warranted in restricting autonomy.

The most relevant principle in discussing the relationships among physicians, patients, and society is that of paternalism. The connection of paternalism with the physician-patient relationship and with truth telling and confidentiality in the medical and social context will be discussed in the following section. (For a fuller account of autonomy, as well as the principles invoked to justify restricting its exercise, see the *Foundations of Bioethics* in Part V of this book. The harm principle is of particular relevance to the topics presented here.)

PATERNALISM

Exactly what paternalism is, is itself a matter of dispute. Roughly speaking, we can say that paternalism consists in acting in a way that is believed to protect or advance the interest of a person, even if acting in this way goes against the person's own immediate desires, or limits the person's freedom of choice. Oversimplifying, paternalism is the view that "Father knows best." (The word "parentalism" is now sometimes preferred to "paternalism," because of the latter's gender association. See the *Foundations* section for the distinction between the weak and strong versions of the principle of paternalism.) Thus, the first three cases presented above are instances of paternalistic behavior.

It is useful to distinguish what we can call "state paternalism" from "personal paternalism." State paternalism, as the name suggests, is the control exerted by a legislature, agency, or other governmental body over particular kinds of practices or procedures. Such control is typically exercised through laws, licensing requirements, technical specifications, and operational guidelines and regulations. (The first case above is an example of state paternalism.)

By contrast, personal paternalism consists in an individual's deciding, on the basis of his own principles or values, that he knows what is best for another person. The individual then acts in a way that deprives the other person of genuine and effective choice. (Cases two and three are examples of this.) Paternalism is personal when it is not a matter of public or semipublic policy but is a result of private, moral decision making.

The line between public and private paternalism is often blurred. For example, suppose a physician on the staff of a hospital believes a pregnant patient should have surgery to improve the chances for the normal development of the fetus. The physician presents his view to the hospital's attorney, and, agreeing with him, the attorney goes to court to request a court order for the surgery. The judge is persuaded and issues the order. Although the order is based on arguments that certain laws are applicable in the case, the order itself is neither a personal decision nor a matter of public policy. The order reflects the judgment of a physician who has succeeded in getting others to agree.

Despite the sometimes blurred distinction between state and personal paternalism, the distinction is useful. Most important, it permits us to separate issues associated with decisions about public policies affecting classes of individuals (for example, people needing medication) from issues associated with decisions by particular people affecting specific individuals (for example, a Dr. Latvia explaining treatment options to a Mr. Zonda).

STATE PATERNALISM IN MEDICAL AND HEALTH CARE

At first sight, state paternalism seems wholly unobjectionable in the medical context. We are all certain to feel more confident in consulting a physician when we know that she or he has had to meet the standards for education, competence, and character set by a state licensing board and medical society. We feel relatively sure that we aren't putting ourselves in the hands of an incompetent quack.

Indeed, that we can feel such assurance can be regarded as one of the marks of the social advancement of medicine. As late as the early twentieth century in the United States, the standards for physicians were low, and licensing laws were either nonexistent or poorly enforced. It was possible to qualify as a physician with as little as four months' formal schooling and a two-year apprenticeship.

Rigorous standards and strictly enforced laws have undoubtedly done much to improve medical care in this country. At the very least, they have made it less dangerous to consult a physician. At the same time, however, they have also placed close restrictions on individual freedom of choice. In the nineteenth century, a person could choose among a wide variety of medical viewpoints. That is no longer so today.

We now recognize that some medical viewpoints are simply wrong and, if implemented, may endanger a patient. At the least, people treated by those who espouse such views run the risk of not getting the best kind of medical care available. Unlike people in the nineteenth century, we are confident that we know (within limits) what kinds of medical therapies are effective and what kinds are useless or harmful. The scientific character of contemporary medicine gives us this assurance.

Secure in these beliefs, our society generally endorses paternalism by the state in the regulation of medical practice. We believe it is important to protect sick people from quacks and charlatans, from those who raise false hopes and take advantage of human suffering. We generally accept, then, that the range of choice of health therapy ought to be limited to what we consider to be legitimate and scientific.

This point of view is not one that everyone is pleased to endorse. In particular, those seeking treatment for cancer have sometimes wanted to try drugs rumored to be effective but not approved by the Food and Drug Administration. Such drugs cannot be legally prescribed in the United States, and those wishing to gain access to them must travel to foreign clinics, often at considerable discomfort and expense. Some have claimed that FDA regulations make it impossible for them to choose the therapy they wish and that this is an unwarranted restriction of their rights. It should be enough, they claim, for the government to issue a warning if it thinks one is called for. But after that, people should be free to act as they choose.

The debate about unapproved therapies raises a more general question: To what extent is it legitimate for a government to restrict the actions and choices of its citizens for their own good? It is perhaps not possible to give a wholly satisfactory general answer to this question. People don't object that they are not permitted to drink polluted water from the city water supply or that they are not able to buy candy bars contaminated with insect parts. Yet some do object if they have to drink water that contains fluorides or if they cannot buy candy bars that contain saccharine. But all such limitations result from governmental attempts to protect the health of citizens. Seeing to the well-being of its citizens certainly must be recognized as one of the legitimate aims of a government. And this aim may easily include seeing to their physical health. State paternalism with respect to health seems, in general, to be justifiable. Yet the laws and regulations through which the paternal concern is expressed are certain to come into conflict with the exercise of individual liberties. Perhaps the only way in which such conflicts can be resolved is on an issue-by-issue basis. Later, we will discuss some of the limitations that moral theories place on state paternalism.

State paternalism in medical and health-care matters may be more pervasive than it seems at first sight. Laws regulating medical practice, the licensing of physicians and medical personnel, regulations governing the licensing and testing of drugs, and guidelines that must be followed in scientific research are some of the more obvious expressions of paternalism. Less obvious is the fact that government research funds can be expended only in prescribed ways and that only certain approved forms of medical care and therapy will be paid for under government-sponsored health programs. For example, it was a political and social triumph for chiropractors and Christian Science readers when some of their services were included under Medicare coverage. Thus, government money, as well as laws and regulations, can be used in paternalistic ways.

PERSONAL PATERNALISM IN MEDICAL AND HEALTH CARE

That patients occupy a dependent role with respect to their physicians seems to be true historically, sociologically, and psychologically. The patient is sick, the physician is well. The patient is in need of the knowledge and skills of the physician, but the physician does not need those of the patient. The patient seeks out the physician to ask for help, but the physician does not seek out the patient. The patient is a single individual, while the physician represents the institution of medicine with its hospitals, nurses, technicians, consultants, and so on. In his dependence on the physician, the patient willingly surrenders some of his autonomy. Explicitly or implicitly, he agrees to allow the physician to make certain decisions for him that he would ordinarily make for himself.

The physician tells him what to eat and drink and what to avoid, what medicine he should take and when to take it, how much exercise he should get and what kind it should be. The patient consents to run at least part of his life by "doctor's orders" in the hope that he will regain his health or at least improve his condition.

The physician acquires a great amount of power in this relationship. But she also acquires a great responsibility. It has been recognized at least since the time of Hippocrates that the physician has an obligation to act in the best interest of the patient. The patient is willing to transfer part of his autonomy because he is confident that the physician will act in this way. If this analysis of the present form of the physician-patient relationship is roughly correct, two questions are appropriate.

First, should the relationship be one in which the patient is so dependent on the paternalism of the physician? Perhaps it would be better if patients did not think of themselves as transferring any of their autonomy to physicians. Physicians might better be thought of as people offering advice, rather than as ones issuing orders. Thus, patients, free to accept or reject advice, would retain fully their power to govern their own lives. If this is a desirable goal, it is clear that the present nature of the physician-patient relationship needs to be drastically altered.

The problem with this point of view is that the patient is ordinarily not in a position to judge the advice that is offered. The reason for consulting a physician in the first place is to gain the advantage of her knowledge and judgment. Moreover, courses of medical therapy are often complicated ones involving many interdependent steps. A patient could not expect the best treatment if he insisted on accepting some of the steps and rejecting others. As a practical matter, a patient who expects good medical care must rather much put himself in the hands of his physician.

For this reason, the second question is perhaps based on a more realistic assessment of the nature of medical care: How much autonomy must be given up by the patient? The power of the physician over the patient cannot be absolute. The patient cannot become the slave or creature of the physician—this is not what a patient consents to when he agrees to place himself under the care of a physician. What, then, are the limits of the paternalism that can be legitimately exercised by the physician?

INFORMED CONSENT
AND MEDICAL TREATMENT

Traditionally, many physicians believed they could do almost anything to a patient so long as it was in the patient's best interest. Indeed, many thought they could act even against the patient's wishes, because they considered themselves to know the patient's interest better than the patient himself and thought that eventually the patient would thank them for taking charge and making hard decisions about treatment. (See the Dax Cowart Classic Case Presentation which begins this chapter for what has become the standard example of this way of thinking.)

While some physicians may still wish to press treatments on patients for the patients' own good, patients need not choose to do as they are advised. Some people refuse to take needed medications, change their diets, quit smoking, exercise more, or undergo surgical procedures that promise to improve the quality of their lives, if not lengthen them. Valuing autonomy, we now realize, requires recognizing that people do not always do what is good for them in a medical way, and accepting this outcome as a consequence of the exercise of autonomy.

People may even choose to reject treatment necessary to save their lives. Over the past two decades, the courts have recognized repeatedly and explicitly that the right to refuse or discontinue medical treatment has a basis in the Constitution and in common law. To receive medical treatment, people must first give their consent, and if they wish to reject it, even after it has been started, they are legally and morally entitled to do so.

FREE AND INFORMED CONSENT

Both ethicists and the courts have understood *consent* (in the context of agreeing to treatment) to mean that several specific conditions must be fulfilled. For consent to be morally and legally meaningful, individuals must be: (1) competent to understand what they are told about their condition and capable of exercising judgment; (2) provided with relevant information about their illness and the proposed treatment for it in an understandable form; (3) free to make a decision about their treatment without coercion. (For a fuller discussion of consent in the context of becoming an experimental subject, see the *Briefing Session* in the previous chapter.)

Most public and legal attention to the topic of refusing to consent to therapy has focused on cases in which terminally ill patients wished to have ventilators disconnected or in which the guardians of patients in chronic vegetative states wanted their nutrition and hydration to be discontinued. The issues have concerned the rights of patients themselves, and in this respect the questions were more or less straightforward.

The matter of refusing treatment becomes more complicated when the interest of someone other than or in addition to the patient is involved. Two sorts of cases, in particular, present difficulties: cases in which parents' beliefs cause them to deny their children necessary medical attention and cases in which a pregnant woman's behavior results in damage to her fetus.

PARENTS AND CHILDREN

First is the situation in which parents, acting on the basis of their beliefs, refuse to authorize needed medical treatment for their child. The duty of the physician is to provide the child the best medical care possible. The duty of the parent is to protect and promote the welfare of the child. Ordinarily, in the medical context, these two duties are convergent with respect to the line of action they lead to. The parents ask the physician to "do what is best" for their child, and the physician discusses the options and risks with the parents and secures their consent on behalf of the child. (See the discussion of informed consent in the previous chapter for details.)

However, this convergence of duties leading to agreement about action is dependent on physicians and parents sharing some fundamental beliefs about the nature of disease and the efficacy of medical therapy in controlling it. When these beliefs are not shared, then the outcome is a divergence of opinion about what should be done in the best interest of the child. The actions favored by the physician will be incompatible with the actions favored by the parents.

As in the Case Presentation about Robyn Twitchell at the end of this chapter and example 5 on page 58, some parents are adherents of religions like Christian Science that teach that disease has no reality but is a manifestation of incorrect or disordered thinking. People with such beliefs think that the appropriate response to illness is to seek spiritual healing, rather than to employ medical modalities.

What about the children of those with such beliefs? Their parents can legitimately claim that by refusing to seek or accept medical treatment for their children they are doing what they consider best. It is a recognized principle that parents should decide the best interest of their children, except in very special circumstances. We don't think, for example, that a psychotic or clinically depressed parent should be allowed to decide about a child's welfare. Should Christian Scientists and others with similar beliefs be put in the category of incompetent parents and forced to act against their beliefs and seek medical care for their children?

A strong case can be made for answering yes. If mentally competent adults wish to avoid or reject medical treatment for themselves, the principle of autonomy supports a public policy permitting this. However, when the interest of someone who lacks the abilities to deliberate and decide for himself is concerned, it is reasonable to favor a policy that will protect that person from harm. This is particularly so when matters as basic as the person's health and safety are at stake.

Hence, to warrant restricting the generally recognized right of parents to see to the welfare of their children, we can appeal to the harm principle. We might say that, if a parent's action or failure to take action tends to result in harm to a child, then we are justified in restricting his or her freedom to make decisions on behalf of the child. We could then look to someone else—a court or an appointed guardian—to represent the child's best interest.

In general, we consider a legitimate function of the state to be the protection of its citizens. When parents fail to take reasonable steps to secure the welfare of their children, then doing so becomes a matter of interest to the state.

PREGNANCY AND AUTONOMY

The second kind of case is one that involves an actual or potential conflict between the actions of a pregnant woman and the interest of the fetus she is carrying. (This kind of case is illustrated in example 6 on page 58 and discussed in the *Social Context: Pregnancy and Responsibility* below.)

An obvious way of dealing with an alleged conflict between what a pregnant woman wants or does and the interest of her fetus is to deny that conflict is possible. If one holds that the fetus, at every developmental stage, is a part of the woman's body and that she is free to do with her body as she pleases, then there can be no conflict. The woman is simply deciding for herself, and it would be an unjustifiable violation of her autonomy to regulate her actions in ways that the actions of men or nonpregnant women are not regulated.

However, a number of difficulties are associated with this position. The most significant one is that as a fetus continues to develop, it becomes increasingly implausible to hold that it is no different from any other "part" of a woman's body. The problem of when the fetus is a person in the moral sense is one that plagues the abortion dispute (see Chapter 9), and it is no less relevant to this issue.

Furthermore, even if one is not prepared to say that the fetus can claim any serious consideration to life, particularly at the very early stages of pregnancy, it seems prima facie wrong to act as if the fetus (barring miscarriage or abortion) is not going to develop into a child.

Suppose a woman knows that she is pregnant and knows that continuing to drink alcohol even moderately is likely to cause the child who will be born to suffer from birth defects. Most people would consider it wrong for her to disre-gard the consequences of her actions. Once she has decided against (or failed to secure) an abortion, then it seems she must accept the responsibility that goes with carrying a child to term. On even a moderate view, this would imply avoid-ing behavior she knows will be likely to cause birth defects.

However, another aspect of the question of whether a pregnant woman has any responsibility to protect the welfare of the fetus is to what extent, if any, we are justified in regulating the woman's actions. Should a pregnant woman retain her autonomy intact? Or is it legitimate for us to require her, by virtue of being pregnant, to follow a set of rules or laws not applicable to other people?

Once again, the status of the fetus as a person makes such a question hard to answer. Should we regard cases of "fetal neglect" or "fetal abuse" as no different from cases of child neglect or abuse? If the answer is yes, then the pregnant woman does not differ from the parent of a minor child. In the same way the state might order a Christian Science parent to seek medical help for a sick child, we might consider ourselves justified in insisting that a pregnant woman get prenatal care and avoid drugs and alcohol. Just as parents are subject to laws and rules that other people are not, so then are pregnant women.

Assuming this answer is accepted, then the question becomes one of how far we should go in prescribing behavior for a pregnant woman. Should we require a basic minimum, or should we establish an obtainable ideal? Even the basic questions surrounding the issue of pregnancy and responsibility remain unan-swered by our society. We have yet to develop a social policy to reduce the inci-dence of fetal alcohol syndrome and drug-damaged babies while also protecting the autonomy of pregnant women.

TRUTH TELLING IN MEDICINE

The question of the limits of paternalism arises most forcefully when physicians deceive patients. When, if ever, is it justifiable for a physician to deceive her or his patient?

The paternalistic answer is that deception by the physician is justified when it is in the best interest of the patient. Suppose, for example, that a transplant sur-geon detects signs of tissue rejection in a patient who has just received a donor kidney. The surgeon is virtually certain that within a week the kidney will have to be surgically removed and the patient transferred to dialysis equipment again. Although in no immediate clinical danger, the patient is suffering from postoper-ative depression. It is altogether possible that, if the patient is told at this time that the transplant appears to be a failure, his depression will become more se-vere. This, in turn, might lead to a worsening of the patient's physical condition, perhaps even to a life-threatening extent.

Eventually the patient will have to be told of the need for another operation. But by the time that need arises, his psychological condition may have improved. Is the surgeon justified in avoiding giving a direct and honest answer to the patient when he asks about his condition? In the surgeon's assessment of the situation, the answer is likely to do the patient harm. His duty as a physician, then, seems to require that he deceive the patient, either by lying to him (an act of commission) or by allowing him to believe (an act of omission) that his condition is satisfactory and the transplant was successful.

Yet doesn't the patient have a right to know the truth from his physician? After all, it is his life that is being threatened. Should he not be told how things stand with him so that he will be in a position to make decisions that affect his own future? Is the surgeon not exceeding the bounds of the powers granted to him by the patient? The patient surely had no intention of completely turning over his autonomy to the surgeon.

The issue is one of "truth telling." Does the physician always owe it to the patient to tell the truth? Some writers make a distinction between lying to the patient and merely being nonresponsive or evasive. But is this really a morally relevant distinction? In either case, the truth is being kept from the patient. Both are instances of medical paternalism.

PLACEBOS

The use of placebos (from the Latin *placebo,* meaning "I shall please") in medical therapy is another issue that raises questions about the legitimate limits of paternalism in medicine. The "placebo effect" is a well-documented psychological phenomenon: even patients who are seriously ill will sometimes show improvement when they are given any kind of medication (a sugar pill, for example) or treatment. This can happen even when the medication or treatment is irrelevant to their condition.

The placebo effect can be exploited by physicians for the (apparent) good of their patients. Many patients cannot accept a physician's well-considered judgments. When they come to a physician with a complaint and are told that there is nothing organically wrong with them, that no treatment or medication is called for, they continue to ail. They may then lose confidence in their physician or be less inclined to seek medical advice for more serious complaints.

One way to avoid these consequences is for the physician to prescribe a placebo for the patient. Since the patient (we can assume) suffers from no organic disease condition, he is not in need of any genuine medication. And because of the placebo effect, he may actually find himself relieved of the symptoms that caused him to seek medical help. Moreover, the patient feels satisfied that he has been treated, and his confidence in his physician and in medicine in general remains intact.

Since the placebo effect is not likely to be produced if the patient knows he is being given an ineffective medication, the physician cannot be candid about the "treatment" prescribed. She must either be silent, say something indefinite like "I think this might help your condition," or lie. Since the placebo effect is more likely to be achieved if the medication is touted as being amazingly effective against complaints like those of the patient, there is a reason for the physician to lie outright. Because the patient may stand to gain a considerable amount of good from placebo therapy, the physician may think of herself as acting in the best interest of her patient.

Despite its apparent advantages, placebo therapy may be open to two ethical criticisms. First, we can ask whether giving placebos is really in the best interest of a patient. It encourages many patients in their belief that drugs can solve their problems. Patients with vague and general complaints may need some kind of psychological counseling, and giving them placebos merely discourages them from coming to grips with their genuine problems. Also, not all placebos are harmless (see the discussion in the *Briefing Session* to Chapter 1). Some contain active chemicals that produce side effects (something likely to enhance the placebo effect) so the physician who prescribes placebos may be subjecting her patient to some degree of risk.

Second, by deceiving her patient, the physician is depriving him of the chance to make genuine decisions about his own life. Because the person is not genuinely sick, it does not seem legitimate to regard him as having deputized his physician to act in his behalf or as having transferred any of his power or autonomy to the physician. In Kant's terms, the physician is not acknowledging the patient's status as an autonomous rational agent. She is not according him the dignity that he possesses simply by virtue of being human. (A utilitarian who wished to claim that telling the truth to patients is a policy that will produce the best overall benefits could offer essentially the same criticism.)

Some of the traditional ethical problems about using placebos as a form of treatment rests, in part, on the assumption that placebos can be an effective form of therapy. At least one recent study analyzing investigations employing placebos as part of the experimental design casts doubt on the so-called placebo effect. Yet, even assuming the result is correct, we still must deal with the issue of whether it is ever morally legitimate to mislead a patient by giving her an inactive substance in the guise of an effective medication.

DIGNITY AND CONSENT

Deception is not the only issue raised by the general question of the legitimacy of medical paternalism. Another of some importance is difficult to state precisely, but it has to do with the attitude and behavior of physicians toward their patients. Patients often feel that physicians deal with them in a way that is literally paternalistic—that physicians treat them like children.

The physician, like the magician or shaman, is often seen as a figure of power and mystery, one who controls the forces of nature and, by doing so, relieves suffering and restores health. Some physicians like this role and act in accordance with it. They resent having their authority questioned and fail to treat their patients with dignity and respect.

For example, many physicians call their patients by their first names, while expecting patients to refer to them as "Dr. X." In our society, women in particular have been most critical of such condescending attitudes displayed by physicians.

More serious is the fact that many physicians do not make a genuine effort to educate patients about the state of their health, the significance of laboratory findings, or the reasons why medication or other therapy is being prescribed. Patients are not only expected to follow orders, but they are expected to do so without questioning them. Patients are, in effect, denied an opportunity to refuse treatment and consent is taken for granted.

The amount of time that it takes to help a patient understand his medical condition and the reason for the prescribed therapy is, particularly in this era of managed care, one reason why physicians do not attempt to provide such information. A busy physician in an office practice might see thirty or forty patients a day, and it is difficult to give each of them the necessary amount of attention. Also, patients without a medical background obviously can find it hard to understand medical explanations—particularly in the ways in which they are often given.

The result, for whatever reasons, is a situation in which physicians make decisions about patients without allowing patients to know the basis for them. Explanations are not given, physicians sometimes say, because patients "wouldn't understand" or "might draw the wrong conclusions about their illness" or "might worry needlessly." Patients are thus not only not provided information, they are discouraged from asking questions or revealing their doubts.

The moral questions here concern the responsibility of the physician. Is it ultimately useful for patients that physicians should play the role of a distant and mysterious figure of power? Do patients have a right to ask that physicians treat them with the same dignity as physicians treat one another? Should a physician attempt to educate her patients about their illnesses? Or is a physician's only real responsibility to provide patients with needed medical treatment?

Furthermore, is it always obvious that the physician knows what will count as the all-around best treatment for a patient? Patients, being human, have values of their own, and they may well not rank their best chance for effective medical treatment above all else. A woman with breast cancer, for example, may wish to avoid having a breast surgically removed (mastectomy) and so prefer another mode of treatment, even though her physician may consider it less effective. Can her physician legitimately withhold from her knowledge of alternative modes of treatment and so allow her no choice? Can he make the decision about treatment himself on the grounds that it is a purely medical matter, one about which the patient has no expert knowledge?

If patients have a right to decide about their treatment, physicians have an obligation to provide them with an account of their options and with the information they need to make a reasonable choice. Thus, treating patients with dignity requires recognizing their status as autonomous agents and securing their free and informed consent.

CONFIDENTIALITY (PRIVACY)

"Whatever I see or hear, professionally or privately, which ought not be divulged, I will keep secret and tell no one," runs one of the pledges in the Hippocratic Oath.

The tradition of medical practice in the West has taken this injunction very seriously. That it has done so is not entirely due to the high moral character of physicians, for the pledge to secrecy also serves an important practical function.

Physicians need to have information of an intimate and highly personal sort to make diagnoses and prescribe therapies. If physicians were known to reveal such personal information, then patients would be reluctant to cooperate, and the practice of medicine would be adversely affected.

Furthermore, because psychological factors play a role in medical therapy, the chances of success in medical treatment are improved when patients can place trust and confidence in their physicians. This aspect of the physician-patient relationship actually forms a part of medical therapy. This is particularly so for the "talking cures" characteristic of some forms of psychiatry and psychotherapy.

BREACHING CONFIDENTIALITY

A number of states recognize the need for "privileged communication" between physician and patient and have laws to protect physicians from being compelled to testify about their patients in court. Yet physicians are also members of a society, and the society must attempt to protect the general interest. This sometimes places the physician in the middle of a conflict between the interest of the individual and the interest of society.

For example, physicians are often required by law to act in ways that force them to reveal certain information about their patients. The clearest instance of this is the legal obligation to report to health departments the names of those patients who are carriers of such communicable diseases as syphilis and tuberculosis. This permits health authorities to warn those with whom the carriers have come into contact and to guard against the spread of the diseases. Thus, the interest of society is given precedence over physician-patient confidentiality.

Confidentiality may also be breached in cases when the interest of the patient is at stake. Thus, a woman seeking medical attention for trauma resulting from abuse by a husband or boyfriend may have no choice about whether the police are notified. State laws may give the physician no choice about whether to report a suspected case of assault.

Similarly, physicians usually have no discretion about whether to report cases of suspected child abuse. While the parents of the child may deny responsibility for the child's injuries, if the physician suspects the parents of abuse, she must make a report notifying police of her suspicions.

Few people question society's right to demand that physicians violate a patient's confidence when protecting the health of great numbers of people is at stake. More open to question are laws that require physicians to report gunshot wounds or other injuries that might be connected with criminal actions. (In some states, before abortion became legal, physicians were required to report cases of attempted abortion.) Furthermore, physicians as citizens have a legal duty to report any information they may have about crime unless they are protected by a privileged-communication law.

Thus, the physician can be placed in a position of conflict. If he acts to protect the patient's confidences, then he runs the risk of acting illegally. If he acts in accordance with the law, then he must violate the confidence of his patients. What needs to be decided from a moral point of view is to what extent the laws that place a physician in such a situation are justified.

The physician who is not in private practice but is employed by a government agency or a business organization also encounters similar conflicts. Her obligations run in two directions: to her patients and to her employer.

Should a physician who works for a government agency, for example, tell her superiors that an employee has confided in her that he is a drug addict? If she does not, the employee may be subject to blackmail or bribery. If she does, then she must violate the patient's confidence.

Or what if a psychiatrist retained by a company decides one of its employees is so psychologically disturbed that she cannot function effectively in her job? Should the psychiatrist inform the employer, even if it means going against the wishes of the patient? (Consider also the fourth case cited at the beginning of the *Briefing Session* on page 58.)

DUTY TO WARN?

Even more serious problems arise in psychiatry. Suppose that a patient expresses to his psychiatrist feelings of great anger against someone and even announces that he intends to go out and kill that person. What should the psychiatrist do? Should he report the threat to the police? Does he have an obligation to warn the person being threatened?

This is the fundamental issue dealt with by the California Supreme Court in the *Tarasoff* case. The court ruled that therapists at the student health service of the University of California, Berkeley were negligent in their duty to warn Tatiana Tarasoff that Prosenjit Poddar, one of their patients, had threatened her life. The therapists reported the threat orally to the police, but they did not warn Tarasoff. Two months later, after her return from a trip to Brazil, she was murdered by Poddar.

Poddar was tried and convicted of second-degree murder. The conviction was overturned on appeal, on the grounds that the jury had not been properly instructed. The state decided against a second trial, and Poddar was released on condition that he return to India.

The parents of Tatiana Tarasoff sued the university for damages and eventually won a favorable judgment in the California Supreme Court. The court ruled that not only were the therapists justified in breaking the confidentiality of a patient, they had a duty to warn her that her life was in danger. Since this ruling, many psychiatrists and other therapists have argued that the court went too far in its demands.

MANAGED CARE

A worrying trend, with the rise of managed care, is the availability of intimate information about patients that the patients provided to their physicians on the assumption that it would remain confidential. For patients to have their medical bills paid, their physicians may have to reveal to the insurer information concerning such matters as a patient's sexual history and practices, drug use, and troubling psychological problems. Most observers now believe that the assumption that what one tells one's physician will remain private no longer holds. The result is that patients are becoming less willing to tell their physicians anything that might cause them harm if it were known to their spouse, employer, or insurance company.

The basic question about confidentiality concerns the extent to which we are willing to go to protect it. It is doubtful that anyone would want to assert that confidentiality should be absolutely guaranteed. But, if not, then under what conditions is it better to violate it than to preserve it?

ETHICAL THEORIES: AUTONOMY, TRUTH TELLING, CONFIDENTIALITY

What we have called state paternalism and personal paternalism are compatible with utilitarian ethical theory. But whether they are justifiable is a matter of controversy. According to the principle of utility, if governmental laws, policies, practices, or regulations serve the general interest, then they are justified. It can be argued that they are justified even if they restrict the individual's freedom of choice or action, because for utilitarianism autonomy has no absolute value. Personal paternalism is justified in a similar way. If a physician believes that she can protect her patient from unnecessary suffering or relieve his pain by keeping him in ignorance, by lying to him, by giving him placebos, or by otherwise deceiving him, these actions are morally legitimate.

However, John Stuart Mill did not take this view of paternalism. Mill argued that freedom of choice (autonomy) is of such importance that it can be justifiably restricted only when it can be shown that unregulated choice would cause harm to other people. Mill claimed that compelling people to act in certain ways "for their own good" is never legitimate. This position, Mill argued, is one that is justified by the principle of utility. Ordinarily, then, people have the freedom to decide what is going to be done to them, so free and informed consent is a prerequisite for medical treatment. Clearly, utilitarianism does not offer a straightforward answer to the question of the legitimacy of paternalism.

What we have said about paternalism applies also to confidentiality. Generally speaking, if violating confidentiality seems necessary to produce a state of affairs in which happiness is increased, then the violation is justified. This might be the case when, for example, someone's life is in danger or someone is being tried for a serious crime and the testimony of a physician is needed to help establish her innocence. Yet it also might be argued from the point of view of rule utilitarianism that confidentiality is such a basic ingredient in the physician-patient relationship that, in the long run, more good will be produced if confidentiality is never violated.

The Kantian view of paternalism, truth telling, and confidentiality is more clear-cut. Every person is a rational and autonomous agent. As such he or she is entitled to make decisions that affect his or her own life. This means that a person is entitled to receive information relevant to making such decisions and is entitled to the truth, no matter how painful it might be. Thus, for treatment to be justified, the informed consent of the individual is required.

The use of placebos or any other kind of deception in medicine is morally illegitimate in a Kantian view, because this would involve denying a person the respect and dignity to which he or she is entitled. The categorical imperative also rules out lying, for the maxim involved in such an action produces a contradiction. (There are special difficulties in applying the categorical imperative that are discussed in the *Foundations of Bioethics*. When these are taken into account, Kant's view is perhaps not quite so straightforward and definite as it first appears.)

It can be argued that Kant's principles also establish that confidentiality should be regarded as absolute. When a person becomes a patient, she does so with the expectation that what she tells her physician will be kept confidential. Thus, in the physician-patient relationship there is an implicit promise. The physician implicitly promises that he will not reveal any information about his patient, either what he has been told or what he has learned for himself. If this analysis is correct, then the physician is under an obligation to preserve confidentiality, because keeping promises is an absolute duty. Here, as in the case of lying, there are difficulties connected with the way a maxim is stated. (See *Foundations of Bioethics* for a discussion.)

Ross's principles recognize that everyone has a moral right to be treated as an autonomous agent who is entitled to make decisions affecting his own life. Thus, free and informed consent to medical treatment is required. Also, everyone is entitled to know the truth and to be educated in helpful ways. Similarly, if confidentiality is a form of promise keeping, everyone is entitled to expect that it will be maintained. Thus, paternalism, lying, and violation of confidence are prima facie morally objectionable.

But of course it is possible to imagine circumstances in which they would be justified. The right course of action that a physician must follow is one that can be determined only on the basis of the physician's knowledge of the patient, the patient's problem, and the general situation. Thus, Ross's principles rule out paternalism, deception, and violations of confidence as general policies, but they do not make them morally illegitimate in an absolute way.

Rawls's theory of social and political morality is compatible with state paternalism of a restricted kind. No laws, practices, or policies can legitimately violate the rights of individuals. At the same time, however, a society, viewing arrangements from the original position, might decide to institute a set of practices that would promote what they agreed to be their interests. If, for example, health is agreed to be an interest, then they might be willing to grant to the state the power to regulate a large range of matters connected with the promotion of health. Establishing standards for physicians would be an example of such regulation.

But they might also go so far as to give the state power to decide (on the advice of experts) what medical treatments are legitimate, what drugs are safe and effective to use, what substances should be controlled or prohibited, and so on. So long as the principles of justice are not violated and so long as the society can be regarded as imposing these regulations on itself for the promotion of its own good, then such paternalistic practices are unobjectionable.

With respect to personal paternalism, consent, deception, and confidentiality, Rawls's general theory offers no specific answers. But since Rawls endorses Ross's account of prima facie duties (while rejecting Ross's intuitionism), it seems reasonable to believe that Rawls's view on these matters would be the same as Ross's.

The natural law doctrine of Roman Catholicism suggests that paternalism in both its forms is legitimate. When the state is organized to bring about such "natural goods" as health, then laws and practices that promote those goods are morally right. Individuals do have a worth in themselves and should be free to direct and organize their own lives. Thus, they generally should be informed and should make their own medical decisions. Yet at the same time, individuals may be ignorant of sufficient relevant information, lack the intellectual capacities to determine what is really in their best interest, or be moved by momentary passions and circumstances. For these reasons, the state may act so that people are protected from their own shortcomings, and yet their genuine desires, their "natural ends," are satisfied.

Thus, natural law doctrine concludes that because each individual has an inherent worth, she is entitled to be told the truth in medical situations (and others) and not deceived. But it reasons too that because a physician has superior knowledge, he may often perceive the interest of the patient better than the patient herself. Accordingly, natural law doctrine indicates that, although the physician should avoid lying, he is still under an obligation to act for the best interest of his patient. This may mean allowing the patient to believe something that is not so (as in placebo therapy) or withholding information from the patient. In order for this to be morally legitimate, however, the physician's motive must always be that of advancing the welfare of the patient.

In the matter of confidentiality, the natural law doctrine recognizes that the relationship between physician and patient is one of trust, and a physician has a duty not to betray the confidences of her patients. But the relationship is not sacrosanct and the duty is not absolute. When the physician finds herself in a situation in which a greater wrong will be done if she does not reveal a confidence entrusted to her by a patient, then she has a duty to reveal the confidence. If, for example, the physician possesses knowledge that would save someone from death or unmerited suffering, then it is her duty to make this knowledge available, even if by doing so she violates a patient's trust.

We have only sketched an outline of the possible ways in which ethical theories might deal with the issues involved in paternalism, consent to treatment, truth telling, and confidentiality. Some of the views presented are open to challenge, and none has been worked out in a completely useful way. That is one of the tasks that remains to be performed.

Autonomy, paternalism, truth telling, and confidentiality are bound together in a complicated web of moral issues. We have not identified all the strands of the web, nor have we traced out their connections with one another. We have, however, mentioned enough difficulties to reveal the seriousness of the issues.

As the following cases and contexts illustrate, some of the issues are social ones and require that we decide about the moral legitimacy of certain kinds of laws, practices, and policies. Others are matters of personal morality, ones that concern our obligations to society and to other people. Our ethical theories, we can hope, will provide us with the means of arriving at workable and justifiable resolutions of the issues. But before this point is reached, much intellectual effort and ingenuity will have to be invested.

CASE PRESENTATION
Medical ID Cards and Privacy

When Tod Whitman, a Denver police officer, saw Carol Kanfield collapse on the sidewalk outside a coffee shop, he rushed over to her and checked to see whether she required CPR. Seeing that she didn't, he called the EMS and gave the operator the medical I.D. number from the card he found in her purse.

By the time the ambulance arrived, the EMTs and Denver General knew she was a twenty-four-year-old insulin dependent diabetic who was allergic both to penicillin and to animal-derived insulin. The information had been retrieved by using Carol's medical I.D. number from the National Medical Database and displayed on the EMS and hospital computers. The technicians were able to stabilize Carol and bring her out of her coma by using insulin produced by genetically altered bacteria. Without the information from the database, it would have taken much longer to diagnose Carol's problem, and even then, had she been given bovine insulin, an allergic reaction might have killed her. The case of Carol Kanfield is imaginary, but in the near future, cases like it may become common. In 1996, Congress mandated that every American be assigned a "unique health identifier" or medical identification number, which can be used to create a national computer database containing the lifetime medical records of every citizen. This was passed as a part of the Health Insurance Portability Act, which is supposed to allow people to keep their insurance when they change jobs.

Such a database would benefit everyone considerably. Individuals would have their medical records available for inspection by any physician or hospital whenever they need treatment. This might be of crucial importance in an emergency, but even for a scheduled examination it would be helpful. Patients would no longer have to make an effort to get their records sent to a new physician, and physicians would no longer have to examine patients without having the details of their known medical history. Patients with a complex of disorders or a rare disease might also benefit, if their physicians were able to find out how other patients with the same problem responded to specific treatments.

Insurance companies would benefit, because patients could no longer hide the parts of their medical history that might make them a bad risk or show a preexisting condition. Also, billing would be streamlined. This would reduce the administrative cost of medical care and thus lower the overall cost of care. Scientists would benefit, because they would be able to analyze genetic factors in disease and look for geographical or seasonal patterns. They would also be able to compare the effectiveness of various treatments for the same disease.

Critics of assigning a medical I.D. number to each person and establishing a medical-records databank point to several serious potential abuses. Connected databases of health records, financial and credit histories, and criminal records would make it possible for government agencies and knowledgeable individuals to pry into almost every aspect of a person's life.

Those gaining access to the records could make decisions about such matters as employment, admission to college, approving home loans or life or health insurance policies without the applicant knowing what information is being used. Someone who is HIV-positive, for example, might be turned down for a sales job, because the employer doesn't want to risk hiring a person with an infectious disease. Laws protecting against discrimination would be weakened.

People are already reluctant to tell their physicians intimate details of their lives, even though some of the information may be important to diagnosing their problem or providing them with the right treatment. If they knew that everything they revealed could end up in a database accessible to a large number of people, they would probably reveal even less about themselves than now. This would undercut the quality of medical care.

While at least thirty-five states have passed laws to protect patient privacy and insurance companies are legally required to develop procedures to protect the privacy of their policy holders, no uniform and generally accepted standards currently protect the information in databases or regulate access to it. In part this is because no national consensus on patient privacy appears to exist. Critics of a medical I.D. system fear that, given the nature of political compromises, any federal privacy standards Congress passes to regulate it will be weaker than most current state standards.

Do people care about their medical privacy? A 1993 Lou Harris poll showed that only 18 percent of those surveyed thought it was all right for medical records to be used in research without a person's consent. Some 60 percent thought it was unacceptable for pharmacists to supply medical data about their customers to marketing companies, and 96 percent wanted legal penalties for the unauthorized disclosure of medical information.

Privacy is clearly valued, but equally clearly, having people's medical records easily available in a national database can benefit them, even to the extent of saving their lives. Further, the database can benefit society by lowering health-care costs and by allowing us to discover more about the causes of disease and the most effective ways to treat them. Perhaps the basic question is whether we can gain the benefits of a national medical identification system without having to surrender the benefits of privacy.

SOCIAL CONTEXT

Autonomy and Pregnancy

Pamela Rae Monson was a twenty-seven-year-old mother of two living in San Diego, California. When she became pregnant again, toward the end of her term, she began to experience vaginal bleeding. The cause was diagnosed as placenta previa, and her physician advised her to stay off her feet as much as possible and to get immediate medical treatment if she began to bleed again. She was also told not to engage in sexual intercourse and not to use amphetamines.

Monson disregarded virtually all of these instructions. On November 23 she began to bleed, but instead of seeking medical treatment, she stayed home, took illegally obtained amphetamines, and had sex with her husband. Later that day, she began to have contractions, and several hours after they began, she finally went to a hospital. She gave birth that evening to a boy with massive brain damage. He lived for six weeks.

The San Diego police wanted Monson prosecuted for homicide, but the district attorney charged her with a misdemeanor under a child-support statute. Under the California law, a parent must provide "medical attendance" to a child who requires it. However, the judge threw out the case, on the grounds that an appeals court had already ruled that a conceived but unborn child is not to be considered a person within the intended scope of the child-abuse law.

OTHER CASES

The 1985 Monson case was the first of its kind, and despite its legal outcome, it had considerable national influence. In particular, the case suggested to prosecutors in various states that they might use the law to punish pregnant women for acting in ways that cause harm to the fetuses they are carrying.

After Monson, at least 200 women in at least thirty states were charged with threatening the safety of their unborn children by engaging in behavior that put them at risk. Most often, the behavior involved the pregnant woman's use of alcohol or illegal drugs. For example:

+ In Laramie, Wyoming, in February 1990, Diane Pfannensteil, twenty-nine years old, was charged with felony child abuse because she drank alcohol while pregnant. A blood test had earlier determined that Pfannensteil was legally intoxicated, and a judge had ordered her to remain alcohol free to protect the fetus. The charge against her was dismissed by a judge who ruled that, according to the law, "the child already has to have suffered," and it might be years before it could be determined whether Pfannensteil's child was damaged.

+ In May 1990, a New York State appeals court ruled that the presence of cocaine in the blood of a newborn infant and admission of drug use by the mother were grounds enough to hold a child-neglect hearing to consider what action should be taken in the best interest of the child.

+ On August 7, 1992, twenty-four-day-old Hanna Gillispie of Corona, California, was found dead in the apartment of her mother, Alicia. The coroner determined that the child had died from ingesting methamphetamine obtained from her mother's milk. Her mother was said to be an habitual user of illegal drugs. In October, Ms. Gillispie pleaded guilty to three counts of child endangerment and was sentenced to six years in prison. Her other two children, ages two and five, were placed in foster homes. The public defender explained the guilty plea by saying that it avoided the possibility of Ms. Gillispie's being charged with second-degree murder.

WHY PROSECUTE?

Civil liberties groups have been highly critical of the prosecutorial approach toward pregnant women taken by some cities and states. Even prosecutors admit that the cases they bring are on novel legal grounds, but they claim that something must be done to protect developing fetuses and newborns. "We're really not interested in arresting women and sending them to jail," the solicitor of Charleston said. "We're just interested in getting them to stop using drugs before they do something horrible to their babies."

This also seems to be the motivation of physicians who cooperate in the prosecution of pregnant women who use drugs. However, the actions physicians take in the interest of protecting the developing child may conflict with their traditional commitment to preserving the confidentiality of their patients.

Is it morally permissible for a physician to inform the police that a pregnant patient tested positive for illegal drugs? Should there be laws requiring physicians to make such reports? The preservation of confidentiality is not a value that overrides all others. For example, we justify requiring physicians to report communicable diseases and gunshot wounds on the grounds that the social good this produces (controlling diseases and crime) outweighs infringing on an individual's privacy.

The obvious drawback to such a reporting requirement is that drug-using pregnant women might not seek medical care to avoid the risk of being prosecuted for a crime. Hence, a law intended to benefit the developing child might work in the opposite way in some cases. Indeed, if physicians made it a practice of reporting pregnant women for drug use even though not required to do so, these women might be expected to avoid getting prenatal care.

CASES REVERSED

The great majority of the legal cases of "pregnancy abuse" were appealed and lower court decisions reversed. Indeed, court decisions tended to recognize that pregnant women are not guilty of child abuse, even though their actions might result in harm to the developing fetus:

◆ The Connecticut Supreme Court ruled in 1992 that a pregnant woman who injected cocaine into a vein as she was about to go into labor was not guilty of abusing her child, even though when the child was born he was traumatized, pale, and suffering from oxygen deprivation. The court decided that state laws give no legal rights to the unborn and that, until the child was born, the mother could not be considered to have engaged in abusive "parental conduct" toward a "child."

◆ In July 1992, the Florida Supreme Court overturned the 1989 conviction of Jennifer Johnson for "delivering" drugs to her children through the umbilical cord during the first few moments after their birth. Johnson was tested after the births of two of her children in 1987 and 1989 and found positive for cocaine each time.

In the nineteen cases prosecuted in Florida, Johnson was the only defendant convicted. The court reasoned that she could have avoided delivering the drugs only by severing the umbilical cord, which might have killed her children. Further, the court held, the legislature's concept of "delivering" drugs was not intended to cover such cases. In fact, an attempt to pass legislation punishing pregnant women for actions endangering their fetuses had failed.

SOUTH CAROLINA—CHARGE UPHELD BY STATE SUPREME COURT

Matters played out in a different way in South Carolina. On June 6, 1995, Talitha Renee Garrick called paramedics complaining of abdominal pains and cramps. She admitted to having smoked crack cocaine an hour or two earlier. Physicians at the hospital to which she was taken found that her placenta had detached and her fetus had suffocated. On autopsy metabolic products of cocaine were detected, indicating that the fetus had been alive. In 1996 Garrick was charged with murder by child abuse and faced a maximum of five years in prison.

In 1997, on appeal, the state Supreme Court allowed her to plead guilty to involuntary manslaughter and handed down a sentence of three years probation and two hundred hours of community service, to take the form of speaking to expectant mothers about the dangers of drugs. South Carolina was the only appellate court to uphold charges against a woman for actions resulting in the death of her fetus.

RACIAL BIAS

At least one study shows a racial bias in the prosecution of pregnant women addicted to illegal drugs. In Florida, all drug use during pregnancy must be reported to health departments and pregnant women using illegal drugs prosecuted. A study of urine collected during a one-month period in public health clinics and obstetricians' offices showed a 15 percent incidence of drug use by both blacks and whites. Blacks were ten times more likely to be prosecuted than whites, however, and poor women more likely than middle-class women.

Although the incidence of illegal drug use is about the same for black and white women, the frequency of cocaine use is much higher among black women. White women use marijuana more frequently, and although it is associated with fetal harm, the harm is much less than that caused by cocaine.

DRUG DAMAGE

Everyone agrees the problem of infants damaged or put at risk by drug use is enormous. By some estimates, as many as 375,000 newborns each year may be affected by drug abuse by pregnant women. Alcohol is estimated to cause harm in 2 or 3 of every 1000 fetuses.

Cocaine or crack cocaine used by women during pregnancy poses severe risks to newborns. Because the drug triggers spasms in the fetus's blood vessels, oxygen and nutrients can be severely restricted for long periods. Prenatal strokes and seizures may occur, and malformations of the kidneys, genitals, intestines, and spinal cord may develop. "Crack babies" are twice as likely to be premature and 50 percent more likely to need intensive care. Although intensive therapy may reverse effects of the drug to a greater extent than was once thought, "crack babies" still suffer from a high incidence of irreversible brain damage.

Pregnant women who consume alcohol put their developing fetuses at risk for the same kind of damage. Fetal alcohol syndrome includes growth retardation before and after birth, facial malformations, such abnormal organ development as heart and urinary tract defects and underdeveloped genitals, and various degrees of brain damage. Alcohol use is believed to be one of the leading causes of retardation. Furthermore, the damage done by alcohol seems permanent, so that even excellent postnatal nutrition and compassionate care cannot alter the growth retardation or the brain damage.

Some studies suggest that even three or four drinks a week can cause fetal damage. Further, more women are consuming alcohol during pregnancy than ever before. An April, 1997 Centers for Disease Control survey found that 3.5 percent of 1313 pregnant women surveyed admitted to having seven or more drinks a week or to binging on five or more drinks at least once during the previous month. This was an increase from 1 percent of 1053 pregnant women surveyed in 1991.

The sample indicates 140,000 women admitted to frequent drinking in 1995, compared to 32,000 in 1991. The study also showed 16.3 percent of pregnant women in 1995 had at least one drink in the preceding month, compared with 12.4 percent in 1991.

FETAL INTEREST?

Cases against pregnant women were usually based on the notion that the fetus has legally recognizable interests apart from the woman, while acknowledging that the pregnant woman has a legally recognizable right to seek an abortion. The basic idea is that if a woman decides not to have an abortion, then she acquires a duty to protect the fetus.

This position faces a number of problems. First, the legal basis is at best murky. Most courts do not consider a fetus a child, so child-abuse laws do not apply in any obvious way. Similarly, the notion of "delivering" drugs by maternal-fetal circulation is an apparently significant departure from the notion of "delivering" that lies behind antidrug legislation.

Second, what counts as "fetal abuse" is unclear and elastic. Should a pregnant woman who has two drinks be seen as endangering the fetus? Since there is no safe level of alcohol consumption, the answer might be yes. But what about making sure she eats a diet proper to nourishing the developing fetus? Should the woman be charged with a crime if she fails to provide whatever the medical profession believes to be proper prenatal care? Should she be prosecuted even though she cannot afford to provide the right care?

Third, what about the interests of the pregnant woman herself? Does becoming pregnant and not having an abortion commit her to subordinating her own welfare to that of the fetus? Does she have an obligation to avoid using drugs and alcohol, even though no one else—woman or man—may have such an obligation? Does she have an obligation to avoid engaging in any activities likely to cause a miscarriage?

In general, does the pregnant woman have a duty to live in such a way that whenever there is a conflict of interest between what she wishes to do and what others consider the best interest of the fetus, the conflict must be resolved in favor of the fetus?

The prospect of a continuing number of children damaged by preventable causes is appalling. No one believes that the legal punishment of pregnant women is a satisfactory solution. It is more an act of frustration and desperation. But what solution is satisfactory?

UNITED STATES SUPREME COURT DECISION

In a six-to-three decision in March 2001, the United States Supreme Court overturned a Court of Appeals Decision in a South Carolina case. A public hospital in Charleston had an arrangement with the police department that led to the arrest of pregnant women whose urine tested positive for cocaine. Under the program, the women were offered the chance to enter a treatment program or go to trial on drug charges. The aim was to protect the unborn child from the effects of cocaine use.

Before Charleston altered then eliminated its program, thirty women were arrested after drug screening. Nearly all charges were dropped after the women agreed to participate in a drug rehabilitation program. Crystal Ferguson was one of the women tested by the hospital.

The Supreme Court ruled in *Ferguson v. Charleston* that it is unconstitutional to order pregnant women tested for drugs without a warrant on the grounds of the "special needs" of getting the women into a treatment program. A "special needs" exception to the Fourth Amendment guarantee against unlawful searches and seizures has been recognized by the court to hold in circumstances in which drug testing was needed to protect health and safety (e.g., testing railroad workers), but the Court rejected the notion that the Charleston program satisfied this criterion.

"While the ultimate goal of the [Charleston] program may well have been to get the women into substance abuse treatment and off drugs," Justice John Paul Stevens wrote in the majority opinion, the immediate objective of the searches [i.e., drug test] was to generate evidence *for law enforcement purposes* in order to reach that goal." Because law enforcement "always serves some broader social purpose or objective," a reference to such a purpose does not justify a constitutional exception.

The "stark and unique" fact of the Charleston case, Justice Stevens said, is that the relationship between the hospital and the police was such that it was designed to collect evidence against patients to be turned over to the police for potential use in a criminal prosecution.

The Supreme Court decision effectively blocks programs that involve the involuntary screening of pregnant women for drug use. Thus, unless women agree to be tested or ask for help with drug rehabilitation, states have little power to intervene for the purpose of protecting the developing fetus.

Whether the state should have such power continues to be a matter of debate. Further, the questions we raised earlier about whether and to what extent a pregnant woman has responsibility for the developing child remain unanswered.

CASE PRESENTATION

The Death of Robyn Twitchell and Christian Science

Two-year-old Robyn Twitchell ate very little for dinner on April 3. Then, shortly after eating, he began to cry. The crying was soon replaced by vomiting and screaming.

Robyn lived in Boston, the city where the Christian Science religion was founded, and both his parents, David and Ginger Twitchell, were devout Christian Scientists. The tenets of the religion hold that disease has no physical being or reality but, rather, is the absence of being. Because God is complete being, disease is an indication of the absence of God, of being away from God. Healing must be mental and spiritual, for it consists in bringing someone back to God, of breaking down the fears, misperceptions, and disordered thinking that stand in the way of having the proper relationship with God. When someone is ill, the person may need help getting to the root cause of the estrangement from God. The role of a Christian Science practitioner is to employ teaching, discussion, and prayer to assist someone suffering from an illness to discover its spiritual source.

Acting on the basis of their beliefs, the Twitchells called in Nancy Calkins, a Christian Science practitioner, to help Robyn. She prayed for Robyn and sang hymns, and, although she visited him three times during the next five days, he showed no signs of getting better. A Christian Scientist nurse was brought in to help feed and bathe Robyn, and on her chart she described him as "listless at times, rejecting all food, and moaning in pain" and "vomiting." On April 8, 1986, Robyn began to have spasms, and his eyes rolled up into his head. He finally lost consciousness, and that evening he died.

Robyn was found to have died of a bowel obstruction that could have been treated by medicine and surgery. Medical experts were sure that he wouldn't have died had his parents sought medical attention for him.

MANSLAUGHTER CHARGES

David and Ginger Twitchell were charged with involuntary manslaughter. In a trial lasting two months, the prosecution and defense both claimed rights had been violated. The Twitchells' attorneys appealed, in particular, to the First Amendment guarantee of the free exercise of religion and claimed that the state was attempting to deny it to them.

Prosecutors responded by pointing out that courts have repeatedly held that not all religious practices are protected. Laws against polygamy and laws requiring vaccinations or blood transfusions for minors, for example, have all been held to be constitutional.

The prosecutors also claimed that Robyn's rights had been violated by his parents' failure to seek care for him as required by law. They also cited the 1923 Supreme Court ruling in *Prince v. Massachusetts* that held that "Parents may be free to become martyrs of themselves, but it does not follow they are free to make martyrs of their children."

GUILTY

The jury found the Twitchells guilty of the charge, and the judge sentenced them to ten years' probation. John Kiernan, the prosecutor, had not recommended a jail sentence. "The intent of our recommendation was to protect the other Twitchell children." Judge Sandra Hamlin instructed the Twitchells that they must seek medical care for their three children, if they showed signs of needing it, and they must take the children to a physician for regular checkups.

"This has been a prosecution against our faith," David Twitchell said. Although, speaking of Robyn, at one point he also said most sadly, "If medicine could have saved him, I wish I had turned to it."

The prosecutor called the decision "a victory for children." However, Stephen Lyons, one of the defense attorneys, said it was wrong to "substitute the imperfect and flawed judgment of medicine for the judgment of a parent." A spokesman for the Christian Science church said it was not possible to combine spiritual and medical healing as the ruling required. "They're trying to prosecute out of existence this method of treatment," he said.

During the last several years a number of children have died because religious beliefs kept their parents from getting them necessary medical care. Christian Science parents have been convicted of involuntary manslaughter, felony child abuse, or child endangerment in California, Arizona, and Florida.

The Twitchell case was one of several initially successful prosecutions. The case directly challenged the First Church of Christ Scientist (the proper name of the church) in the city where it was founded and has its headquarters, and the church recognized the challenge and helped in providing leading attorneys to defend the case. "The message has been sent," John Kiernan said after the Twitchells were sentenced. "Every parent of whatever religious belief or persuasion is obligated to include medical care in taking care of his child."

APPEAL

The Twitchells' attorneys immediately announced they would appeal the decision on the grounds that the ruling rested on the judge's misinterpretation of a Massachusetts child-neglect law, which explicitly exempts those who believe in spiritual healing. Because of this, legal authorities considered it possible the Twitchell decision would be overturned on appeal.

A spiritual-healing exemption is found in similar laws in forty-four states. Such exclusions make it difficult to successfully prosecute Christian Scientists or others on the grounds of child neglect. The American Academy of Pediatrics is one of several groups that have campaigned to eliminate the exceptions from child-protection laws, but so far only South Dakota has actually changed its laws.

Despite legal exemptions, parents belonging to religious groups like the Church of the First Born, Faith Assembly, and True Followers of Christ have been convicted and imprisoned for failing to provide their children with medical care. However, so far no Christian Scientist has gone to jail. When a Christian Scientist has been convicted, the sentence has been suspended or has involved probation or community service and the promise to seek medical care for their children in the future.

Critics claim Christian Scientists have been treated more leniently than members of more fundamentalist groups, because a high proportion of church members are middle to upper-middle class and occupy influential positions in business, government, and the law. They also suggest that the legal exceptions for spiritual healing in child-protection laws are there because of the influence of the Christian Science church and its members.

Some legal observers initially believed that the Twitchell case would spur wider and more intense efforts to eliminate the spiritual-healing exception, and groups representing the rights of children consider such a change to be long overdue.

However, the Twitchell conviction was overturned on appeal in 1993, and it did not turn out to have the impact on the law many hoped it would. Except in exceptional cases, the religious beliefs of parents continue to take precedence over the medical welfare of their children.

CHAPTER *3*

HIV–AIDS

CLASSIC CASE PRESENTATION

The Way It Was: Tod Thompson, Dallas, 1993–1994

Tod Thompson opened his sock drawer and took out a round, white-enameled snuff box. A green dragon breathing a jagged tongue of fire was painted on the lid. Alan Lauder had given him the box almost five years earlier as a memento of their trip to Cancun.

Tod had never bought cocaine, but when somebody gave him a little he kept it in the dragon box. Those days now seemed as obscure and fragmentary as scenes from a movie watched in childhood. After Alan got sick, Tod never felt happy enough to risk doing drugs of any kind.

After Alan died, he even stopped drinking. He had actually stopped a few months before that. Alan had been too sick even to eat, and Tod had no wish to drink alone. Now he drank only water and fruit juice, not even wine.

Tod opened the hinged lid of the snuff box and looked at the blunt purple and gray capsules of Seconal inside. He dumped them into the palm of his hand and counted them, pushing each to one side with a fingertip.

Eight. Six was supposed to be enough, but with eight he felt much better. How ghastly it would be to wake up in a hospital feeling very sick and knowing you had failed. If you were going to do it, you should be sure you could pull it off. And he was sure he was going to do it. He had watched Alan, and nothing would make him want to go through that.

Tod put the snuff box under his socks in the back corner and closed the drawer. He looked up at the mirror hanging above the dresser, and the reflection still shocked him. He couldn't believe how he had changed.

He still looked young, but in the way photographs of children in concentration camps made them look simultaneously young and old. His gray eyes were abnormally large as they stared out of deep sockets, and his cheeks were drawn into dark hollows beneath sharp cheekbones. His blond hair was fine and wispy, barely hiding the pale skin of his scalp. His body was shrunken, and his thin shoulders hunched inward like the folded wings of a bat.

He pulled back his shirt collar, exposing an edge of one of the bluish patches that ran across his chest and back and covered his arms and legs—Kaposi's sarcoma. The patches had been late in coming. Maybe the ZDV had slowed down the process. The drug had appeared too late to do much for Alan.

Alan had introduced him to a world he never suspected existed. A world of glittering parties, long weekends on yachts, trips to Mexico, San Francisco, and New

York. Above all, abundant and virtually unrestrained sex. Tod found himself the object of much attention, and he liked it.

Hardly two months after Alan died, Tod got sick. First the night sweats started. He would wake up at three or four in the morning so drenched with sweat he would be freezing and burning up simultaneously. Then the mild but persistent fever had started, and diarrhea had come along with it.

He had put off seeing his doctor for almost a month. He hadn't taken the blood test, because he was sure he would test positive, and then he wouldn't be able to deny that something so horrible was going to happen to him. When the symptoms finally started, it was almost a relief in a twisted way. Now he knew the worst and didn't have to fear it anymore.

He finally went to his doctor—to Alan's doctor—when he developed shingles on his legs. The rash was too painful to ignore. By then he had already lost a lot of weight. The diarrhea and the fever seemed to keep him tired. That and the lack of sleep. He was exhausted, but he felt too anxious to sleep. He would wake in the early morning hours while it was still dark and lie in bed and wonder what was going to happen to him.

He always asked for the early shift at the bookstore where he worked. Because he couldn't sleep, it was a relief to get up and have a place to go to. Also, few customers came in during the morning hours. Keeping up a normal front was very hard. He started the day by stocking the shelves, and usually he did as much as necessary before getting too exhausted. He was working only half-days now, but even so he was tired all the time.

When he first got the diagnosis, he resolved to fight the disease and not give in. He wanted to try everything that people told him to try. He spent six weeks eating a macrobiotic diet, but it seemed to make his diarrhea worse. He tried smuggled doses of Compound Q, but he could tell no difference in what was happening to him. Eventually he simply took ZDV.

It was the only drug he took for half a year. Then, when the first bruiselike Kaposi patch appeared on his leg, his doctor put him on alpha-interferon. When he developed a cough and a fever and was found to have pneumonocystis pneumonia, he was given pentamidine spray. And now he was also trying one drug after another to try to control the diarrhea that had become chronic.

He knew he was lucky to be an employee of the bookstore. He was covered by the Blue Cross group policy, and so far it had paid for everything except 20 percent of his medical bills and medicines. He had tried to get a supplemental policy before Alan died, but he couldn't find a company willing to accept him without a blood test. So far he had been able to pay his part of the bills, but it wouldn't be long before he became so weak he would have to quit his job.

He couldn't ask his parents to help him. They knew the kind of life he had been living, and they didn't approve of it. But that's not why he couldn't turn to them. It was because they themselves had nothing, and he would become another burden for them. Besides, to be honest, he was afraid of their reaction to him. He couldn't stand the idea that they would treat him like a leper, not wanting to touch him or come near him. In sparing them, he was also sparing himself.

When he could no longer work, he knew what would happen, because he had seen it happen to other people. First they moved to a cheaper apartment, if they could find someone willing to rent to them. Then they sold their car. After that, they began to sell whatever furniture, stereo, or video equipment they had. Finally, they were forced to turn to Medicaid and the state welfare agencies for everything—medical care, medicine, rent money, telephone, and even the food they didn't want to eat. Most people grew poorer faster than they grew sicker, and that guaranteed their dying in complete poverty.

He heard the sharp ding of the kitchen timer. His frozen pasta dinner was ready. He'd have to get it out of the oven before it burned. He picked up his cane from the bed and started to walk away. Then he turned around and pulled open the drawer. He picked up the snuff box and shook it. The capsules inside rattled reassuringly.

He put the box back inside and closed the drawer.

On a warm April day in 1994, Tod was sitting in a chair by the window when a call came from Dr. Katz at Southwest Medical Center. For the first time since he had been diagnosed with HIV, his viral load had dropped. One of the experimental drugs he had been taking along with the ZDV was a protease inhibitor, and Dr. Katz proposed adding another drug to the ones he was taking.

"You've responded so well, I think you can look forward to seeing some of your symptoms regressing," Dr. Katz said. "I can't promise you'll be cured, but I believe you can count on seeing your life return to something like normal." He paused. "I'd say you're one of the lucky ones."

Tod felt a tightness in his throat that made it impossible to speak, and tears stung the corners of his eyes. He'd keep the snuff box, but it was time to throw away the contents.

Briefing Session

Only a few years ago, the disease known as Acquired Immunodeficiency Syndrome, or AIDS, was routinely described as the worst plague to strike the world since the Black Death devastated Europe and much of Asia in the fourteenth century. Now that treatment with a combination of new drugs can keep HIV infection from progressing to full-blown AIDS and can extend the life of those with the disease, some of the fear and dread associated with AIDS have lessened.

Yet the majority of the pressing moral and social issues associated with the disease have not gone away. We are still faced with questions about such matters as deciding what proportion of medical research funding should be allocated for AIDS, restricting individual freedom to protect society, balancing the need to protect confidentiality against the need to inform, and allocating the new and effective AIDS drugs. Further, while the burden of AIDS has lessened for the United States and other industrialized countries, it has increased for the rest of the world. The infectious and fatal character of AIDS continues to give its issues an immediacy and urgency with few parallels in the history of medicine.

COMBINATION THERAPY: AIDS ON THE RUN

Like a snarling werewolf in a horror movie, AIDS has devastated the lives of hundreds of thousands of people unlucky enough to encounter the virus. The disease doomed friends and family, destroyed sons and daughters, fathers and mothers, and condemned children to short, unhappy lives.

Causing heartbreak and sorrow, the virus has also generated unreasoning fear and sweaty terror. *Am I infected?* people asked themselves. *I have a fever— could it be AIDS?* The disease abolished all hope, because becoming infected with HIV (the human immunodeficiency virus) was the equivalent of receiving a death sentence.

The virus is still a threat, the AIDS monster still stalks the streets, but in 1994-1995 for the first time in the sixteen years since the disease made its appearance, the number of cases of AIDS started to go down. In 1997, for the first time since 1990, AIDS was no longer among the top ten causes of death in the United Sates. The trend has continued. New drugs and combinations of drugs have been so effective that AIDS has become a chronic disease most people can treat and live with, instead of an invariably fatal one.

Cocktails of the new protease inhibitors plus one or more other antivirals— *combination drug therapy* or HAART (highly active antiviral therapy)—have worked treatment wonders. The new drugs may make it possible for someone to be infected with HIV and stay alive without symptoms for decades, living long enough to die of something besides AIDS. Those infected with HIV can now contemplate a future that includes them. Instead of studying about death and dying, they can think about living.

A silver bullet to slay the werewolf hasn't been found, but the new combination drug therapy at least provides protection. It thus offers hope where once there was only despair.

DECLINE IN DEATH RATE

The effects of combination drug therapy are most obvious in the decline in the number of deaths due to AIDS that resulted when HAART was first introduced. In a study sponsored by the Centers for Disease Control and Prevention and involving 1255 patients at nine medical centers, researchers found the AIDS death rate declined an astounding 75 percent from January, 1994 to June, 1997.

The sharpest decline began in early 1996 when people who were HIV positive began to take drug combinations that included a protease inhibitor. Between the first and second quarter of the year, AIDS-related deaths dropped almost 50 percent, and by the end of the next six months, it fell another 50 percent.

In the first quarter of 1994, the AIDS death rate was 35.2 per 100 person-years; in the first quarter of 1995, it was 31.2. The rate began to drop when physicians started using the antiviral drugs ZDV (also called AZT) and 3TC in combination and began aggressively treating the adventitious infections that the compromised immune systems of AIDS patients couldn't fight off.

Then in 1996 protease-inhibiting drugs came into widespread use, and the death rates plunged. In the first quarter of the year they dropped from 29.4 (per 100 person-years) to 15.4, and by the end of the first quarter of 1997, they had dropped again to 8.8. The results of the CDC study showed that HIV infections could be treated successfully and that the great majority of premature deaths caused by AIDS could be prevented.

INFECTION RATES

The rate at which people are becoming infected with HIV has remained relatively constant, but the rate at which people develop AIDS has dropped significantly. The CDC reported that from 1994 to mid-1997 the number of people newly diagnosed with an HIV infection was a relatively steady 20,000 a year. From 1995 to 1996, infection declined 3 percent among men (10,762 new cases), but it increased by the same percentage among women (4253 new cases). Among African Americans, HIV infection fell about 3 percent (8300 new cases), but among Whites fell only 2 percent (4966 new cases). Infection increased 10 percent among Hispanic Americans (1070 new cases).

Young people ages 13 to 24 continue to be the main source of new infections. From January 1994 to June 1997, 7200 people in this age group tested positive for the virus. In 1997 (the latest figures), 25 percent of new infections were in people under 25.

In 1999 black youths (47 percent) and young women (23 percent) constituted major parts of the increase. At least 15 percent of the infections were the result of heterosexual conduct. Male homosexual contact was involved in 34 percent of the new cases, and intravenous drug use was involved in 22 percent. Despite the relatively constant rate of HIV infection, combination drug therapy has sharply lowered the number of deaths from AIDS.

PROTEASE INHIBITORS AND COMBINATION DRUG THERAPY

About 200,000 people in the United States are now taking a protease-inhibiting drug. The number almost doubled from 1996 to 1997, and by now almost everyone who has been diagnosed as HIV positive either is being treated or has been treated by one of the drugs. The protease inhibitor is usually administered in combination with one or more other antiretrovirals.

The first drug to treat HIV infection, Zidovudine (AZT or ZDV), was introduced in 1986. A failed cancer drug, ZDV turned out to be highly effective against reverse transcriptase, an enzyme essential in the early phases of HIV replication. Researchers quickly developed a number of other drugs to interrupt reverse transcriptase. The family is called nucleoside analogs and includes widely used drugs like ddC and 3TC.

Because of HIV's rapid mutation rate, new strains soon emerged that could survive attacks by the available nucleoside analogs. Researchers eventually developed a second class of drugs known as non-nucleoside reverse-transcriptase inhibitors.

While drugs in this class also work on the earlier part of the HIV replication cycle, they employ a different mechanism to inhibit reverse transcriptase. Thus, they can be successful in treating HIV, even after ZDV-type drugs have failed.

Protease inhibitors belong to a third family of drugs that prevent HIV from making copies of itself. They work by blocking a necessary enzyme—protease. Protease cuts a long protein chain into fragments that ordinarily form the functioning virus. Thus, protease inhibitors forestall the increase of viral particles, and so protect uninfected cells from infection.

Protease inhibitors work at a later stage of HIV replication than nucleoside analogs and non-nucleoside reverse-transcriptase inhibitors. Thus, it is possible to combine the three types of drugs in ways that attack replication at different stages of the cyle. Viral particles not prevented from replicating by drugs of the first two types may be stopped by protease inhibitors. This is the basic idea of HAART.

None of the drugs do anything to treat cells that are already infected. But if the viral particles can be kept from multiplying, this will prevent the infection of additional cells. The infected cells will then eventually die off, and the symptoms caused by the virus will retreat.

LIMITS OF THE THERAPY

As effective as protease inhibitors in combination with other drugs have shown themselves to be in preventing the development of AIDS in people infected with HIV, HAART has definite limitations. It is by no means a cure for AIDS, and it is not effective nor tolerable for everyone who is HIV-positive.

BEST WITH NEW INFECTIONS

Some evidence indicates that protease inhibitors work best in recently infected people whose immune systems have not yet been severely damaged by the AIDS virus. Those who have been infected for ten or fifteen years and have devastated immune systems may not get any long-term benefits from adding a protease in-hibiting drug to the antiviral drugs.

Thus, what offers a new hope for some HIV-positive people may be only an-other source of frustration and sorrow for those who have become long-term survivors. They still haven't hung on long enough for the long-anticipated "cure" for AIDS.

DRUG RESISTANCE

The mechanisms of HIV infection are still not adequately understood, and the pre-cise manner in which the virus becomes drug resistant is unknown. But protease-inhibiting drugs, like the standard antiviral drugs, can lose their effectiveness due to drug resistance.

From a therapeutic standpoint, the strategy is to change drugs as soon as pa-tients stop responding to the ones they are taking. Even so, it is possible for someone to stop responding to all available drugs. Almost thirty protease in-hibitors are now available, and pharmaceutical companies are working rapidly to produce new ones. Drugs from the three types are used in as many as 250 combinations. For some HIV-infected people, there is a race between the virus' development of drug resistance and the companies' development of new drugs, and their lives are at stake.

There is a race, too, for those who are newly infected and don't respond to the standard therapies, because they are infected by a mutant strain. A 2001 study showed that drug-resistant strains of HIV have increased to 14 percent among newly diagnosed HIV cases. This is up from 5.8 percent during the years 1999–2000, which was significantly higher than .04 percent for the period 1995–1998.

VIRUS REMAINS

Viral load, rather than a count of T-cells or CD4 cells, is now considered to be the best prediction of the outcome of someone who is HIV positive. A follow-up study of infected people who gave blood samples in 1984–1985 showed that at the end of a decade only 17 of 45 men with a viral load averaging less than 5300 RNA strands (per cubic milliliter of blood) had died of AIDS. Out of 45 with a viral load average of above 37,000 RNA strands, 34 had died. In short, the lower the viral load, the more likely an infected person is to survive.

While combination drug therapy can reduce the viral load so low that the presence of HIV particles cannot be detected by a blood test, the drugs never completely eliminate the virus from the body. Despite initial hopes, several studies have shown that copies of the virus remain hidden in the memory T-cells of the immune system.

The memory cells may remain in a resting phase for years (perhaps decades), waiting to make copies of themselves or the viruses infecting them. It is this mechanism that makes vaccinations against polio and measles possible—the immune system remembers the viruses and can produce antibodies against them whenever it needs to. Combination drug therapy works only against actively reproducing viral particles. Thus, it is ineffective against the HIV particles hidden in the memory cells. Ironically, the same adaptation that protects us against some infectious diseases also preserves the agents that cause others.

The discovery of HIV in the memory cells explains why HIV-infected people eventually develop a new viral load after no particles could be detected in their blood. The discovery also means that those who are HIV positive must continue to take their drugs, even when they no longer have a detectable viral load and their CD-4 (or T-cell) count is in the normal range.

On the positive side, however, knowing that copies of the virus are stored in the memory T-cells gives researchers a new target. If a drug or combination of drugs could be found to eliminate the sequestered copies of the virus, as well as the viral particles in the blood, this would constitute a cure for HIV infection.

COSTS

A typical combination-therapy cocktail for HIV infections includes the drugs ZDV, 3TC, and a protease inhibitor like Crixivan. The cost of treating someone with this combination, not counting other drugs, is $10,000–$15,000 a year. In addition, monitoring the effectiveness of the treatment costs another $5000 to $6000 for laboratory work and physician's office visits. Thus, when the expense of other drugs is added, it costs about $25,000–$30,000 a year to treat someone who is HIV positive.

Only about 20 percent of the roughly 1 million people who are HIV positive have insurance adequate to cover most of the expense of HIV treatment. All fifty states have established joint state and federal AIDS Drug Assistance programs (ADAPS), but a patchwork of regulations that differ from state to state make it difficult for many in need of treatment to find the money to pay for it.

While the $20,000 a year treatment costs are high, the costs for treating full-blown AIDS can be $100,000 a year or more. As usual in medicine, just in terms of dollars, preventing a problem from becoming worse costs less than neglecting it, then dealing with the consequences.

SIDE EFFECTS

The immediate side effects of the combination therapy can be worse than the earlier effects of AIDS itself. Uncontrollable diarrhea, severe stomach cramps, nausea, dizziness, disorientation, skin sensitivity, and a feverish feeling are among the more common reactions to the drugs. Some people find the side effects so devastating that they can't take the drugs, even though they are potentially life saving. "I early reached the point where death was the preferable alternative," one person with AIDS told a reporter.

The drugs may also cause life-threatening harm. In some susceptible people, they may damage the liver. Those affected develop jaundice as their liver becomes unable to function effectively in breaking down red blood cells. Continuing to take the drugs may lead to liver failure and death.

By mechanisms that are not understood, the drugs may also affect fat metabolism and blood sugar levels. Some taking the drugs experience a potentially dangerous rise in the level of blood cholesterol and even grow a fatty hump between their shoulder blades. A recent study has revealed a rare bone disorder called avascular necrosis, in which bone dies because its blood supply is cut off, in 4 percent of the HIV patients studied. It is unclear whether this is a result of protease inhibitors or other drugs taken by HIV patients.

Some in whom the drugs produce an increase in the level of sugar in their blood may develop diabetes, indicating some sort of failure in the metabolic process. If they are not taken off the drugs or treated for diabetes, they may suffer damage to their eyes, kidneys, and other organ systems caused by diabetes.

The side effects of combination drug therapy are not ones that need to be tolerated for only a short time while the individual recovers from the infection. Because the drugs do not eliminate all HIV particles from the body, those who are infected must continue to take the drugs for the rest of their lives. If the reactions are too severe or too toxic this may prove to be impossible.

A question not yet answered is what the long-term effects of combination drug therapy for HIV will be. While the risks are unknown at present, most people who are HIV positive are willing to bet that combination drug therapy will save their lives. They have a better chance of surviving it than they do surviving AIDS.

DIFFICULT REGIMEN

When combination therapy was first initiated, some of the drugs had to be taken five or six times a day, some with food, and others on an empty stomach. Some had to be taken every six hours and kept refrigerated, requirements making it difficult to travel very far from home or even stay overnight in most hotels. Responding to these problems, drug companies have made following the necessary regimens easier. They have developed tablets that include a combination of three drugs and have reduced both the number of tablets and the number of times they must be taken. More sophisticated treatment regimens have also been developed. A patient with few complications and a low viral load typically has to take fewer drugs than someone at an advanced stage of HIV infection.

Even with such advances, an HIV-infected patient typically must still follow a demanding drug regimen. While the number of tablets involved in the triple therapy may be fewer, most patients must also take drugs to prevent side effects from the anti-retrovirals or to treat secondary infections resulting from a damaged immune system.

Missing a dose of some of the drugs can have serious consequences for some patients. It presents a window of opportunity to mutant strains of the virus, allowing them to replicate and spread to new cells. As a result, the drugs in that particular combination may cease being effective against the new drug-resistant strains. Physicians must then try new combinations of drugs and hope they are effective for the patient. Patients who continue to miss doses for different combinations of drugs may find themselves in the unhappy position of being infected with a strain of the virus that is resistant to all drugs currently available. Further, such patients pose a threat, for if they should spread the drug-resistant strain, a rekindling of the AIDS epidemic is possible.

The ideal drug against HIV is one that is taken orally and is easily tolerated, has no serious side effects, does not interact dangerously with other drugs, is effective against the AIDS virus in all tissues and cell types, and is inexpensive. No drug promising even most of these characteristics is expected to be available soon. Until then, adherence to the regimen of combination therapy offers the most hope of keeping the virus under control in the individual and the nation.

FALSE SECURITY

About 1 million Americans are infected with HIV, and some 350,000 of them have gone on to develop AIDS. Each year, about 14,000 more become infected with the virus. The rate of HIV infection has remained more or less constant, even though the death rate from AIDS has dropped.

Many public-health researchers think the failure of the infection rate to decline is due, in part, to a false sense of security produced by combination therapy.

Supporting this is a 1999 study of 416 gay men that found that the more optimistic they were about new drug treatments, the more likely they were to practice unsafe sex.

Too many people appear to believe that HIV infection is no longer worth worrying about—that someone infected need take only a few pills to bring it under control. But, of course, the infection remains life-threatening, and its treatment, even when it succeeds in bringing the infection under control, is difficult, fraught with severe side effects, and expensive.

The FDA took a step toward promoting a more realistic view of HIV infection in 2001. In a letter to drug companies, the FDA insisted that advertising eliminate images that are "not generally representative" of patients with HIV. Particularly, the ads should not show "robust individuals engaged in strenuous physical activities" like mountain climbing.

Such ads do not provide an accurate picture of people living with AIDS. While their aim may be to encourage people with AIDS to have a positive attitude, an unintended consequence may be that they encourage the false belief that the disease is no more debilitating than a bout with the flu. This may then translate into rationalizations for avoiding practices known to reduce the risk of HIV infection.

ORIGIN OF THE AIDS VIRUS

In 1999 Beatrice Hahn of the University of Alabama at Birmingham announced that she and her collaborators had established a close connection between a simian virus and HIV-I, the virus that causes AIDS. The simian virus, known as SIV.cpz (simian immunodeficiency virus.chimpanzee) has such a close resemblance to HIV-I that differences can easily be accounted for by changes that have taken place as the virus has crossed to the human species.

Hahn and her coworkers recovered the simian virus from the frozen remains of a chimpanzee named Marilyn that had been brought to the United States from Africa in 1959. Marilyn was used as a breeder for research animals, and in 1985 she was the only member of the breeding colony to test positive for the virus. She died that same year, although an autopsy showed no evidence she had an immunodeficiency disease.

Hahn's group found that the virus recovered from Marilyn and two other viruses from another two infected chimpanzees could be arranged in a phylogenetic tree that demonstrated the closeness of their relationship. A fourth virus from another chimp was very different, and it was this virus that had led some researchers to doubt the connection between chimpanzee viruses and HIV-I. Additional tests by Hahn's group showed that all known strains of HIV-I are closely related to strains of SIV.cpz. These strains infect only a subspecies of chimpanzees known as *Pan troglodytes troglodytes*.

The natural habitat of *troglodytes* includes the areas of central and western Africa where HIV-I was first identified. Hahn and her collaborators speculate that the simian virus was transmitted to humans by means of an exposure to chimpanzee blood as a result of the slaughtering of chimpanzees for meat. The opening of roads into what were once isolated tribal areas then promoted the spread of the virus to human population centers.

The oldest documented case of infection with the AIDS virus is that of a Bantu man from what is now Kinshasa in the Democratic Republic of Congo. Molecular analysis of the 1959 blood sample and comparisons with other examples of the virus suggest AIDS probably occurred in people in the late 1940s or early 1950s. It may have been accidentally spread in local populations by the use of needles in smallpox and polio vaccination programs.

As a result of easier access to transportation, from Africa the disease spread to the Caribbean, was acquired by American homosexuals in Haiti, then began to spread in the United States, probably from New York, then to San Francisco. Recent evidence indicates that the disease appeared several times as early as the late 1950s and 1960s in Britain, the United States, and elsewhere but failed to establish itself within the local population. That did not happen until the 1980s. (The retrospective diagnosis of a British sailor who died, perhaps of AIDS, in 1959 has not been confirmed.)

Discovering the origin of the AIDS virus will make it possible to study the virus in new ways. Chimpanzees, despite infection with SIV.cpz, apparently do not develop AIDS or AIDS-like diseases. An understanding of the mechanisms preventing this from happening might allow the development of an AIDS vaccine or new and more effective drugs to treat the disease.

SPREAD OF THE DISEASE

The World Health Organization reported in 1997 that an improved method of gathering statistics showed that earlier estimates of the spread of HIV should be doubled, and figures released in 2000–2002 reveal a world burdened by infection. The most recent estimates indicate that 36.1 million adults and children in the world are infected with HIV. The infections are split almost evenly between males and females.

Cases in Western Europe number 600,000, with 30,000 new cases every year. Eastern Europe and central Asia report more than 375,000–475,000. The number has increased to fifteen times the number three years previously (1999). Ukraine alone in 2002 had an estimated 300,000–400,000 cases, making it the first country in Europe with 1 percent of the adult population infected.

South and Southeast Asia now have more than 6.4 million cases; Latin America has 1.3 million and the Caribbean half a million. North American cases now number some 920,000, with 45,000 new cases per year. The Middle East and North Africa have 400,000 cases, with an estimated 80,000 new cases within the last year. Australia and New Zealand have dropped to around 15,000 infections, with only 500 new cases a year.

Two-thirds of the people now thought to be infected with HIV live in the countries of sub-Saharan Africa. The most accurate figure now available puts the figure at an astounding 25.3 million. South Africa, with 4.5 million cases, has the highest number of any single country. (Countries with the highest number of infected people also include Ivory Coast, Kenya, Tanzania, Uganda, and Zimbabwe.) In 2000, however, for the first time the number of new infections in the region stabilized.

CHILDREN

The U.N. estimates that 600,000 children under age 15 become infected with HIV each year. In addition, 1200 children a day die of AIDS. About 10 percent of all new infections are in children under the age of 15. More than half are in people 15 to 24.

DEATHS

As many as 21.8 million people have died of AIDS since the beginning of the epidemic in the late 1970s. By U.N. estimates, 9.7 million of the deaths have been among people in Sub-Saharan Africa. South Asia and Southeast Asia account for 740,000 deaths, Latin America 470,000, Western Europe 190,000, and Caribbean countries 110,000. Deaths in North America are estimated to have been 420,000. Deaths in China, with an estimated 500,000–700,000 cases, are expected to increase at a rapid rate over the next few years, both because of the size of the population and the slow response of the government in providing needed treatments.

THE FUTURE

The spread of the disease is a worldwide phenomenon. As the numbers show, the African continent has been hit particularly hard as AIDS has spread from the cities to the countryside. African nations face a bad situation that is likely to worsen, but other countries are also experiencing an increase in infection.

Infection rates in India have tripled since 1992 and risen tenfold in Thailand. Within ten to fifteen years, as many as 37 million people could be infected in India. In China the number of people infected is increasing at a rate of almost 30 percent a year. Sexually transmitted diseases are on the rise there, and HIV infection may follow. Health officials fear that the virus will break out in an unprepared population before steps can be taken to combat its spread. New outbreaks have already occurred in Eastern Europe, Russia, Vietnam, and Cambodia.

U.N. experts believe China, India, and Thailand are likely to follow the pattern set by Africa. Poverty and cultural attitudes will allow outbreaks of HIV to spread in the population until the incidence rate becomes massive.

The North American and Western European countries have been able to use new drugs to prevent HIV infection from developing into AIDS. Yet even wealthy and technologically advanced countries have been able to do very little to reduce the rate of HIV transmission. The underdeveloped countries in Africa and Asia are unable to afford the huge cost of treating HIV with combination drug therapy. The only way they can have a hope of controlling the epidemic is through preventive measures, but those measures often come into conflict with such cultural practices as a refusal to use condoms. Also, cultural disapproval of homosexuality and IV drug use makes it difficult for public health officials to speak openly about prevention strategies. In the view of some observers, only a vaccine will make it possible to bring AIDS under control in impoverished nations.

What everyone in public health accepts is that AIDS–HIV is a worldwide catastrophe. The developed nations, out of self-interest, if not out of altruism, will eventually have to invest billions to bring the pandemic under control. But as the Social Contexts and Cases in this chapter illustrate, the ethical issues in our own country have not disappeared either.

CASE PRESENTATION
Will Teresa Blair Take Her Medicine?

Teresa Blair (as we will call her) is twenty years old, and for two years she had been infected with HIV—the human immunodeficiency virus.

Dr. Martha McIntosh, Teresa's physician at the Gilman Street Clinic, has explained Teresa's disease to her and warned her that without treatment she will develop the life-threatening symptoms of AIDS. It is unclear to Dr. McIntosh whether Teresa grasps the seriousness of her condition. Teresa appears to understand the explanation, but she doesn't seem able to keep in mind the need to take her medicine and have her regularly scheduled checkups.

But Teresa doesn't seem able to keep much of anything in mind. "I'm the kind of person who likes to stay on the go and have fun," she says. "I do what I want when I want. I don't sit around and study about what's happening to me or what I'm going to be doing next week. Or even tomorrow, really."

Teresa doesn't have a regular job. She lives with various aunts and cousins, moving frequently, and she picks up work as a cleaner or busperson when she needs some cash. She dropped off the welfare roll, rather than show up five days a week for the required eleven to two shift of picking up trash in the city parks. "It was demeaning," she said. "Besides, it interfered with my social life." Because she has no income or insurance, her medical expenses are paid for under Medicaid.

NO PROTEASE INHIBITOR

Although Dr. McIntosh has prescribed ZDV (AZT) to treat Teresa's HIV infection, after a lot of thought she decided not to prescribe a protease inhibitor. The most effective treatment for Teresa would be a combination therapy of a protease inhibitor and one or more antiviral agents, but Dr. McIntosh doesn't think Teresa's life is sufficiently organized for her to adhere to such a demanding drug regimen. This judgment is based on what she knows about Teresa. Teresa has missed six of her last ten appointments and takes the ZDV only when she happens to think about it.

Like many physicians who treat a large number of HIV-positive patients, Dr. McIntosh is reluctant to prescribe a protease inhibitor for patients who are likely to be careless about taking it. Physicians who withhold the combination therapy say they do so out of a concern for the patient and for the public.

To bring an HIV infection under control requires that a patient adhere religiously to the doses, times and restrictions of the prescribed drugs. Even when only three drugs are involved—a protease inhibitor and two antivirals—the drug taking regimen can be bewilderingly complex. Some drugs must be taken three times a day, some twice, others once. Some must be taken without food or water, others after eating. When other drugs to prevent or treat the infections commonly found in people with a compromised immune system are added, the number of pills, tablets, and capsules taken daily may increase to fifty or sixty or even more.

An HIV-positive person who starts with a combination drug therapy but misses scheduled doses gives the virus a chance to mutate and rebound. The patient may then stop responding to the drugs, and some other combination will have to be tried. Eventually, if the patient continues to be careless about taking the drugs as prescribed, the virus might stop responding to all available drugs.

What worries some physicians and scientists even more is that some of the new mutated strains of HIV might spread from the individual to the population. If that happened, the recently acquired ability to beat back, if not eliminate, the virus could be lost. Once again, HIV would sweep through vulnerable groups, unchecked by any of the drugs in our arsenal.

A DUTY TO WITHHOLD?

Some physicians believe they have a duty to withhold combination therapy from patients who are a poor risk for adherence. This view is highly controversial, however, and some critics of the practice hold that all who might benefit from combination therapy are entitled to at least a chance to show whether they can take the drugs as prescribed. In their view, excluding people who are homeless, drug addicts, or live chaotic lives without a trial run of the medication most effective for their problem is unfair.

A number of social workers and physicians claim that their experience shows that no matter how unplanned their lives, some HIV-infected people find the resources to keep to the demanding regimen of combination therapy. This is particularly so when they realize that their lives are at stake and that the therapy is effective. Also, when those who have not been feeling well for a long time experience the difference the drugs can make, they become more motivated to follow the schedule.

The other side of this, however, is that some HIV-positive people, like Teresa, don't feel sick. Indeed, the combination therapy, with its diarrhea, stomach cramps and worse, may well make them feel much worse than they ordinarily do. When this is coupled with a free-spirited, disorganized approach to life, the chance someone will take the drugs as prescribed becomes slim.

Teresa has people she can stay with, but not everyone is even that fortunate. Being homeless presents immense difficulties for anyone who must take drugs according to a schedule. Some people don't even have a watch. Moreover, some of the drugs must be refrigerated, an impossibility for a homeless person.

In the view of some, prescribing combination therapy for people who have no means of complying with it is, at best, foolish. At worst, it's against the best interest of the individual and potentially dangerous to anyone who might become infected with the human immunodeficiency virus.

Dr. McIntosh hasn't written off Teresa. If Teresa takes her ZDV, the virus will be kept in check for an indeterminate time, and perhaps before it stops working, Teresa's life will become less chaotic. Maybe she will get a steady job, enroll in a training program, or at least settle down enough to focus on her future. Or perhaps as the virus continues to damage her immune system, she will start developing more symptoms and lose the feeling that she's not sick.

If the time comes when Teresa takes seriously the need to treat her disease, Dr. McIntosh is prepared to prescribe combination therapy for her. The main danger for Teresa, though, is that the time will never come. Or it will come too late for combination therapy to be effective.

SOCIAL CONTEXT
What About a Vaccine?

When the AIDS virus was identified, people hoped that a vaccine for it would be developed immediately. AIDS would then become a member of the family of diseases like smallpox and rabies that can be effectively prevented by vaccination. Unfortunately, HIV has turned out to be a virus that mutates rapidly and exists in many variant forms. Some researchers have expressed skepticism about the possibility of developing a vaccine that will provide protection against all forms of the disease.

Even so, researchers have invested considerable effort in the last decade, and more than sixty trials involving thirty candidate vaccines are currently underway. Various vaccines have been shown to protect chimpanzees from HIV infection, but the same vaccines have not been effective for humans. Some vaccines have turned out to increase the number of circulating antibodies against the HIV virus, producing so-called humoral immunity. Humoral immunity is often enough to protect against an infectious agent, but this does not seem to be the case with the HIV virus. Even in the presence of antibodies, it continues to infect cells.

Thus many experts think it is necessary to find a vaccine that will also activate the body's system of cellular immunity. Cells infected with HIV display a characteristic protein marker on their surface. Thus, if researchers can find a way of provoking the body to produce killer T-cells that can recognize this marker, they will destroy the infected cells.

The search for an effective vaccine has so far proved elusive, but even partial success would have its rewards. The usual measure of effectiveness of a vaccine is that it produces immunity in 90 percent of the cases in which it is administered. Yet with 15,000 people (worldwide) becoming infected every day, even a vaccine that produces immunity only 50 percent of the time would save millions of lives. Indeed, according to some calculations, a vaccine available now that is 60 percent effective would prevent twice as many infections as one that is 90 percent effective but will not be available until five years from now.

The cost of treating AIDS and its rapid spread in poor countries in Africa, in particular, make finding a vaccine to prevent or reduce HIV infection a matter of global concern.

SOCIAL CONTEXT

AIDS in Africa: What Should Be Done?

Only a few times has the world been faced with a pandemic, the ravaging of an infectious disease on a global scale. It happened most notably with the spread of the Black Death (the bubonic plague) in the fourteenth century. During the long period of its initial outbreak, it killed from 20 to 30 percent of the world's population. Only the remotest regions of the planet were safe from it.

HIV/AIDS is now a global phenomenon. While the developed countries of the West have reduced its ravages, the disease is out of control in many of the countries of sub-Saharan Africa. Those with a high incidence of infection include South Africa, Ivory Coast, Tanzania, Zimbabwe, and Kenya.

Home to only one-tenth of the world's population, the region accounted for 72 percent of new HIV infections in 2000. Seventy percent of all people infected with HIV (including those with AIDS) live in the region, and 80 percent of HIV deaths occur there.

The number infected with HIV is more than 25 million, and the figure is going up by about 4 million a year. The United Nations estimates that in the most affected countries more than one-third of the children now 15 years old are destined to die of AIDS. By 2010 the life expectancy is calculated to be thirty for those living in sub-Saharan Africa. Already 13 million children have been orphaned by AIDS, most of them in that region.

A BROADER PROBLEM

In the United States and other developed countries, infection with HIV is a straight-forward medical problem with a limited scope. Those infected are started on a drug regimen, then examined and tested regularly. They are given instructions about safe sex and referred to social programs for help with diet and living problems. Also, a variety of public health programs (TV and radio ads, school talks, counseling sessions for parents, etc.) spread the word about preventive measures and the options open to those who believe they may be HIV infected.

The situation is radically different in undeveloped countries. People may lack a general trust in medicine and may not even share the general scientific worldview needed for understanding diseases and their treatment. They may be unable to read and have no access to testing; they may not believe they could be infected, and, if they are, they cannot afford to buy the drugs most effective in treating HIV/AIDS.

People cannot, in general, do what is best for their health, for they lack the education and the resources. HIV infection is just one among many other disease conditions they may not understand or see themselves as able to do much about.

Dealing with HIV in third-world countries is not simply a matter of addressing a medical problem. It involves educational, social, and economic factors in an essential way. Some factors, particularly the economic one, are so serious that some observers doubt the problems of HIV in Africa can be solved at all. The most the world might be able to do is to slow the spread of infection and work to develop a vaccine to prevent it.

The U.N. estimates that by 2005 it will take $2 billion a year to reduce the spread of HIV to the level achieved by countries like Uganda and Senegal. This will involve putting into place modest programs like distributing condoms, counseling prostitutes, educating students about risks, treating sexually-transmitted diseases (which increase the likelihood of HIV infections), and testing for HIV. Even this would be only for people with access to a medical system able to treat diseases like tuberculosis that accompany HIV infection and to administer drugs to prevent maternal-infant transmission of HIV.

The money for drugs will go for relatively cheap antibiotics to treat people with compromised immune systems. Some will buy anti-retroviral drugs, but these will go only to a fraction of those infected with HIV. The reason for this is not so much the costs (see page 102), but that their administration must be carefully monitored. Undeveloped countries lack the physicians, nurses, clinics, and hospitals to make this possible on a wide scale.

By 2005 the U.N. plans to see about 40 percent of Africans dying of AIDS receiving some form of care and 10 percent of those who are HIV positive receiving treatment with anti-retroviral drugs. The U.N. calculations assume that the cost of the anti-retrovirals will be $1400 a year per patient, compared to about ten times that amount for an American patient.

No one believes it is possible for Africans (or Asians) to receive the sort of care given in the developed world. To provide it would cost hundreds of billions of dollars, because an entire health-care infrastructure would have to be built to provide what by Western standards would be adequate treatment.

DRUGS

The Pharmaceutical Manufactures Association of South Africa, representing some thirty-nine major international drug companies, filed a suit against the South African government in 1999. The suit alleged that a law that would allow the country to import brand-name drugs from wherever they could be most cheaply obtained would violate the patent rights of the drug companies. The government, for its part, argued that the country was facing a crisis of HIV infection that it could not afford to buy medicines for and that it was unfair for the companies to sell the same drug in South Africa that could be bought from another country for only a fraction of the price.

The lawsuit was only another skirmish in a battle between the international drug companies and those working to make cheap drugs available to those needing them. Human rights groups had been pressuring the companies for several years to lower the prices of their patent drugs for all poor countries. The companies initially resisted, arguing that doing so would both weaken their patent claims and make them lose money on the drugs they had spent millions developing. Then in a sudden shift led by

Merck, the companies offered to negotiate deep discounts for African countries. The cost of treating someone with AIDS for a year with combination therapy (see the Briefing Session in this chapter) would then drop from $10,000 to $350.

But critics quickly pointed out that cutting the price of combination therapy would not be enough to assure adequate treatment. The tendency of HIV-infected people to develop adventitious infections, because of their impaired immune systems, means that treating them requires antibiotics, antifungals, and a range of other medications. The companies would have to offer discounts on all the drugs necessary, if those needing treatment were to benefit.

Deciding they were losing the public relations battle and tarnishing their reputations, in April 2001, the pharmaceutical companies dropped the lawsuit. South Africa was thus free to import drugs from wherever they could buy them most cheaply. This included brand-name drugs manufactured by the pharmaceutical companies. Still unresolved, even now, is whether the drugs can come from manufacturers of generic versions of those drugs in countries like India that were not signatories of the international patent agreements.

Whatever the source of drugs and however cheap they are, they would still be expensive for countries like South Africa. When the costs of distributing and administering the drugs in complicated treatment regimens and testing and monitoring patients is taken into account, the price of the drugs is seen as only one component of an expensive process. Where could the money come from? South Africa rejected in 2000 an offer from the United States for loans to buy patented drugs, on the grounds that it and similar countries were already burdened by too much debt.

MONEY

In an unprecedented meeting in June 2001, the United Nations General Assembly met to discuss the problem of HIV/AIDS in the developing world. The meeting was contentious, but in the end the delegates approved a "Declaration of Commitment" that calls on governments to show leadership in dealing with the AIDS epidemic. "Prevention must be the mainstay of our response," the document declares. The Assembly then laid out a timetable for bringing the disease under control, which includes helping countries develop their own national strategies.

The cost of the program the Declaration set at $7–$10 billion, with countries with an increasing number of cases of HIV/AIDS being given priority in spending. The Declaration urges developed countries to strive to meet the target of contributing about 10 percent of their GNP to the program. The resolution also calls on lender nations to cancel the debts owed by poor countries, on the understanding that the countries will take measurable steps to eradicate poverty and improve the health care for people with HIV/AIDS and other infections.

The U.N. Declaration underscored the position taken by Secretary-General Kofi Annan at an AIDS conference in Nigeria in April 2001. Annan announced the establishment of a Global Fund to Fight AIDS that would begin operation in 2002.

The Fund, Annan said, would need from $7 to $10 billion a year to deal with HIV/AIDS alone. (This is seven to ten times the $1 billion spent in 2000 in developing countries.) He recommended that the money go to prevent the spread of the disease by reducing mother–infant transmission, educating people about risks, and buying drugs to treat the disease.

The money is supposed to go initially to the African countries most devastated by AIDS, and leaders from 43 African states have committed themselves to increase spending on health in their countries and on HIV/AIDS in particular.

The World Bank, International Monetary Fund, and Group of Seven (the world's most industrialized nations) endorsed the idea of a global fund. Initially it was to be operated by the United Nations, but dissatisfaction with the management of other U.N. programs raised questions about whether the money contributed to the fund would be properly used. The fund was established with independent management.

The money for the fund has been slow in coming. The U.S. contributed $200 million in 2001 and committed itself to $480 million in 2002. Critics called the amounts paltry and urged the U.S., the country that produces 26 percent of the world's wealth, to make a stronger effort. The country should be offering at least $1 billion a year. This, critics point out, would be only 10 percent of the amount needed to slow the progress of the epidemic.

HIV IN COMPETITION

The focus on treating HIV/AIDS, despite its humanitarian appeal, worries some experts on public health. Their major fear is that scarce funds will not be put to the most effective use for saving lives.

Each year some 54 million people die of various causes worldwide. Most (31 percent) of them die of heart disease, but 25 percent die from an infectious disease. Ninety percent of these deaths are caused by six diseases: measles, malaria, tuberculosis, diarrhoeal diseases, acute respiratory infections, and AIDS.

People in developed countries often respond sympathetically when they think about people with AIDS, because they may know of someone who died of the disease. While the other diseases are not unknown in the developed world, relatively few people die of them. This is not the case in the undeveloped world, where the combined deaths from the other five infectious diseases greatly outnumber deaths from AIDS.

Talk of responding to AIDS in Africa by spending large amounts of money makes some public health officials worry that this may divert resources from other diseases and problems that, if not more pressing than HIV/AIDS, are more likely to be solvable.

If resources are shifted away from (for example) childhood vaccination programs, a great number of preventable deaths will occur. Providing retrovirals to treat an HIV-positive African may cost $1100–$1400, but childhood immunizations for diseases like measles, mumps, diphtheria, whooping cough, and polio cost no more than a few cents per child. Immunization programs save as many as 3 million lives a year in Africa alone. Also, millions of lives could be saved (and many millions more significantly improved) in remote areas if people were guaranteed a supply of safe drinking water.

The basic way of dealing with epidemics before HIV was to focus on preventing the spread of the disease. We do not, even now, have a cure for polio, influenza, or smallpox. We have developed therapies for supporting patients to help their bodies cope with the disease, but historically, we have invested most resources in preventing the diseases. (The eradication of smallpox is a major triumph of public health.)

Only with the arrival of AIDS and the rise of AIDS activism did the biomedical establishment began to focus on finding a cure for the disease. While one has yet to emerge, treatments for the disease have grown more effective over the decades. Yet they are so expensive and require such a large and sophisticated system of medical care, some public health experts question whether the treatment model is the best way to approach dealing with AIDS in Africa.

The most realistic approach may be the classical one of focusing on reducing the spread of the infection. The U.N. resolution recognizes that prevention is the "mainstay" of dealing with the disease. Public education must be a key ingredient in any effective prevention plan, but the real hope for the future lies in the development of a vaccine to prevent infection. Even a vaccine falling short of the 90 percent protection typically required would be a major step forward. If a vaccine were effective only 50 percent of the time, in Africa alone it could cut the number of new cases of infection from about 4 million to 2 million.

Emphasizing the prevention strategy means recognizing that millions of people in Africa and other undeveloped regions will die without receiving medical treatment that developed nations consider standard. No strategy has to be all-or-none, however, and strong financial support from the developed nations can do much to relieve the suffering of millions of people with HIV/AIDS, even if not enough money is available to prolong their lives.

What is most pressing is that decisive steps be taken immediately to prevent the spread of HIV and end the most devastating epidemic to sweep across the world in 600 years.

CHAPTER 4

Race, Gender, and Medicine

CLASSIC CASE PRESENTATION

Bad Blood, Bad Faith: The Tuskegee Syphilis Study

The way the United States Public Health Service conducted the Tuskegee Study of Untreated Syphilis in the Negro Male probably did more than any other single event to promote suspicion and distrust of physicians, treatment, and the entire medical establishment in the African-American community.

Ironically, the Tuskegee Study was the outgrowth of a program of deliberate efforts to improve the health of poor African Americans in the rural South. It is a story of good intentions paving the road to hell.

Medicine at the beginning of the twentieth century was in the process of becoming scientific, and thanks to the work of bacteriologists like Pasteur, Koch, and Ehrlich in the preceding century, it was able to diagnose and treat a wide range of infectious diseases. Perhaps more important, it had acquired a good understanding the ways in which such diseases spread, and public health medicine had been founded to put the new knowledge into practice. The prevention of disease on a grand scale became a major goal of public health, and because preventing disease often meant treating those capable of spreading it, joint public programs of treatment and prevention became common.

Since its occurrence in Europe in the fifteenth century, syphilis had been viewed much the way AIDS was when it made its first appearance in the United States during the early 1980s. Syphilis was spread primarily by sexual contact, and so could be passed on to sexual partners. Women could infect their children, and the children could be born dead or blind and diseased. Its association with sex, particularly illicit sex, turned it into a shameful disease for many and made its diagnosis and treatment difficult. In the Victorian age mental hospitals housed many people suffering from the "insanity" marking the final stage of the disease, and this underscored the idea that syphilis was a disease affecting only people with loose moral conduct.

The causative agent of syphilis, a small corkscrew shaped bacterium, was isolated in 1905, and a year later August Wassermann introduced a diagnostic blood test for the disease. In 1911 Paul Ehrlich (who coined the phrase "magic bullet") tested over six hundred chemical compounds before identifying one, salvarsan (number 606), that seemed effective in the treatment of syphilis. The hope of public health officials in developed countries was that, armed with the Wassermann test and salvarsan, they could soon eradicate syphilis.

MACON COUNTY, ALABAMA

Salversan did not turn out to be the miracle drug public health officials had hoped for, but even so researchers soon discovered that injections of arsenic derivatives over a period of about eighteen months would halt the disease and render it noninfectious. This kept alive the dream of eliminating syphilis, and it was in pursuit of that dream that in 1930 in Macon County, Alabama, the United States Public Health Service, building on experience recently acquired in Mississippi, initiated a program to diagnose and treat 10,000 African Americans for syphilis.

Sampling showed that 35 percent of the black population was infected with syphilis, however, and the Public Health Service soon realized it had underestimated the costs of eradicating the disease in even one county. By 1931, in the midst of the Depression, the money for the program ran out, with only some 1400 people receiving even partial treatment. Additional money from the Federal government or the Julius Rosenwald Fund, a Chicago charitable foundation that had supported the project, could not be expected.

Taliaferro Clark of the Public Health Service (PHS) was determined to salvage something from the Macon Project. He decided that if there was no money for the extensive treatments, the Service could at little cost do a six-month study of the natural history of untreated syphilis. Did the disease behave the same in Blacks as in Whites or did genetic differences make Blacks more susceptible? Or were Blacks, once infected, more resistant than Whites to the effects of the disease?

The PHS accepted Clark's proposal and, in doing so, tacitly endorsed a research program that involved deceiving a group of people about the nature of their illness and deliberately withholding potentially effective treatments from them, while giving them the impression that they were being appropriately treated. That the people were all rural, impoverished, and poorly-educated Black males makes it hard to avoid the conclusion that the PHS regarded the subjects as hardly more than experimental animals.

Representatives of the PHS approached the Tuskegee Institute with its research proposal, and in 1932 Tuskegee agreed to participate in the observational study. The institute would be paid for its participation, and its interns and nurses would have the opportunity to work for the government, a major incentive during the worst of the depression in the rural South.

With the help of Tuskegee and black churches and community leaders, men were recruited for the study. They were promised free medical examinations, blood tests, and medicines. In rural Alabama, where few people, black or white, could afford to consult a physician even when sick, such an offer by an agency of the Federal government seemed a golden opportunity.

NO DIAGNOSIS, NO TREATMENT

What the subjects weren't told was that they wouldn't be given a more specific diagnosis than "bad blood" and would be treated only with placebos. The Public Health doctors sometimes claimed that "bad blood" was the term used by rural Blacks to mean syphilis. But the term was really a catch-all category that could include anything from iron deficiency and sickle cell disease to leukemia and syphilis. It was used to explain why people felt sluggish, tired easily, or had a low energy level.

In its primary stage syphilis causes a genital, anal, or mouth ulcer. Known as a chancre, this is a pus-filled sore teeming with bacterial spirochetes that heals within a month or two. Six to twelve weeks after infection, the disease enters its secondary stage. It is marked by skin rashes that may last for months, swollen lymph nodes, headaches, bone pain, fever, loss of appetite, and fatigue. Sores that are highly infectious may develop on the skin. The secondary stage lasts for about a year, then the disease becomes latent. During this inactive stage, which may last for many years or even a lifetime, the person seems wholly normal.

About 30 percent of the time, however, people with untreated syphilis progress to the tertiary stage. One marked effect is the destruction of the tissues making up the bones, palate, nasal septum, tongue, skin, or almost any organ in the body. The infection of the heart may lead to the destruction of the valves or the aorta, causing aneurysms that can rupture and cause immediate death. The infection of the brain can lead to general paralysis and to progressive brain damage, which produces the "insanity" noted in the nineteenth century.

Study participants diagnosed with "bad blood" were given, at different times, vials of liquids, round pills, and capsules. But the drugs were nothing more than placebos, vitamins at best, and contained no ingredient active against syphilis. A sham diagnosis was matched by a sham treatment.

Unfortunately, despite the medical counterfeiting, the disease was real enough to maim and kill. At the end of the six-month study period, the data showed that untreated syphilis in Blacks was just as deadly as in Whites. This was seen as an important and exciting finding, because it contradicted the widely-held opinion that Blacks tolerated syphilis better and were less harmed by it.

STUDY EXTENDED

Raymond A. Vonderlehr, a Public Health Service officer, obtained permission to extend the study to collect more data. An African-American nurse, Eunice Rivers, was added to the staff. She was assigned to recruit men to the study who were free of the disease and so could serve as a control group. The study came to involve six hundred black men—399 diagnosed with syphilis and 201 free of the disease.

Nurse Rivers also had the job of keeping up with the study participants and making sure they showed up for their annual examinations and tests administered by the PHS physicians. She was given a government car, and it was a sign of pride in the black community of Macon County to be driven by Miss Rivers to the school where the exams were conducted. Because the study offered participants $50 for burial expenses if they agreed to an autopsy at their death, they spoke of themselves as belonging to Nurse Rivers' Burial Society.

Reports from the Tuskegee Study were published in peer-reviewed medical journals like the *Journal of the American Medical Association,* and from time to time Public Health Service officers presented the study results to Congress. No one raised any questions about the ethics of the study or asked whether the men participating in it had been informed that they had syphilis and weren't being treated for it.

In 1938 the passage of the National Venereal Disease Control Act required the PHS to provide treatment for people suffering from syphilis or other venereal diseases, even if they couldn't afford to pay for it. Yet participants in the study were considered experimental subjects and not subject to the requirements of the law. Participants who sought treatment from venereal disease clinics were turned away.

At the outbreak of the Second World War, local draft boards were persuaded to exempt at least fifty participants from military service so their symptoms wouldn't be diagnosed and treated by military physicians. When penicillin, which is highly effective against the syphilis spirochete, became available in the mid-1940s, the PHS withheld it from the study participants. Even as participants became blind or insane, the study went on without any treatments being offered.

In 1947 Nazi physicians and scientists who had taken part in vicious, senseless, and often deadly human experiments were tried for war crimes at Nuremberg. One of the outcomes of the trial was the formulation of the Nuremberg Code to govern the participation of subjects in experimentation. (See the *Briefing Session* in Chapter 1.) The key element of the Code is the requirement that subjects give their free and informed consent before becoming participants. Although this requirement was consistently violated by the Tuskegee Study, even after the Nuremberg Code was enunciated, officials at the PHS failed to grasp its relevance to the research they were conducting.

BEGINNING OF THE END

In 1964 Irwin J. Schatz, a Detroit physician responding to an article, wrote to PHS researcher Anne Q. Yobs that he was "utterly astounded by the fact that physicians allow patients with a potentially fatal disease to remain untreated when effective therapy is available," but Schatz received no reply. Two years later Peter Buxtun, a social worker hired by the PHS as a venereal disease investigator, heard rumors about the Tuskegee Study, and after reading the research publications based on it, sent a letter to the director of the Division of Venereal Disease, William J. Brown, to express his serious moral concerns about the experiment.

Buxtun received no response, but eventually, he was invited to a meeting at the headquarters of the Centers for Disease Control, and there he was verbally attacked by John Cutler, a health officer knowledgeable about the study. "He was infuriated," Buxtun said. He "thought of me as some sort of lunatic who needed immediate chastisement." Cutler explained to Buxtun the importance the experiment would have in helping physicians treat black patients with syphilis.

Buxtun left the PHS voluntarily to go to law school, but he didn't forget about Tuskegee. In 1968 he wrote another letter to Brown. Pulling few punches, he pointed out that the racial makeup of the study supported "the thinking of Negro militants that Negroes have long been used for 'medical experiments' and 'teaching cases' in the emergency wards of county hospitals." He said they could hardly be regarded as volunteers and observed that whatever justification could have been offered for the experiment in 1932 was no longer relevant. He expressed the hope that the subjects in the study would be given appropriate treatments.

This time Buxtun's letter produced action—but not much. In 1969 the Centers for Disease Control convened a panel to review the Tuskegee Study. With only one dissenting member, it concluded that the study should go on, because it had gone on so long already that treating the subjects with penicillin might cause them more harm than leaving them untreated would. (More than half of the patients treated for syphilis with penicillin suffer a severe reaction in response to the sudden killing of so many spirochetes.) In short, treatment might cause the participants more harm than doing nothing would.

Early in July, 1972 Peter Buxtun turned over the materials he had accumulated on the Tuskegee Study to Associated Press reporter Jean Heller, and on July 25, after interviewing officials in the PHS, Heller broke the story nationally.

Public anger was swift in coming. The experiment was denounced by the Assistant Secretary of Health, Education, and Welfare, who launched an investigation into why study participants never received treatment for their disease. Congressional hearings were conducted, government research agencies reviewed their recruiting practices, and human subject committees were established to oversee all research involving people.

Most important, the Tuskegee Study came to an immediate halt. It lasted for forty years, and twenty-eight of its participants had died by the time it ended. Since 1972, the Federal government has paid out $10 million in out-of-court settlements to the subjects, their families, or heirs. Eight of the participants were still alive in 1998, but their number is dwindling.

On May 16, 1997 President Bill Clinton formally apologized to the survivors of the Tuskegee Study. "What is done cannot be undone, but we can end the silence," he said in a White House ceremony. "We can stop turning our heads away. We can look at you in the eye and finally say on behalf of the American people: 'What the United States did was shameful, and I am sorry.'"

Briefing Session

Ethical and social issues connected with the health of minorities, particularly African Americans, and women have received little attention until recent decades.

Traditional Western medicine centered the great majority of its efforts on understanding and treating the disorders of the white male. The white male was implicitly taken as the standard patient and research subject. Perhaps this is not surprising, considering that the white male was also the standard physician and researcher.

Society has changed. It has become more diverse, and people of color and women in increasing numbers have become scientists and health-care professionals. Even so, the past has left both thumbprints and bruises on the present. Social inequalities, including those connected with inequalities of income, are still with us, as are entrenched differences in the ways women and people belonging to ethnic minorities are dealt with, despite changed public policies. Clashes of cultures continue to occur, particularly as an increasing number of immigrants from a variety of non-European countries become residents and citizens.

All these factors have consequences for the health of individuals belonging to groups that to various degrees have been marginalized or neglected. As a result, decisions we make about health care policy and the treatment of individuals must take into consideration both economic and cultural differences and the ways women and minorities have been dealt with in the past.

African Americans can lay a strong claim to special attention in any discussion of social issues connected with health care. To a considerable extent, the black population continues to suffer from the effects of social prejudice, including an endemic distrust of physicians and hospitals rooted in historical and personal experience. Further, not only do African Americans constitute the largest minority in the United States, they have the highest death rate of any group, minority or not. Thus, we need to be particularly concerned about the impact of social practices and policies on the black community.

African Americans are not the only minorities with health problems, of course. American Indians have a higher level of diabetes, and Hispanic Americans suffer more from fatal and disabling strokes. Puerto Rican–American children are more prone to asthma, and tuberculosis among Asian Americans is some fifteen times higher than among Whites and twice as high as among Blacks. Each ethnic group has its own health problems, and while in some instances the problems can be connected with prejudice, negative attitudes, or flawed social policies, in other cases they may be the result of language difficulties or differences in cultural beliefs and patterns.

AFRICAN AMERICANS AND HEALTH CARE

The cost of hospitalization and treatment, the cost of insurance, and the rise of HMOs and other managed care schemes lead some observers to worry that the United States is moving in the direction of a two-tier health-care system—one for the rich and the other for everybody else. Yet in the view of many critics, the U.S. already has a two-tier system, only the marker for separation isn't money alone. It's also race.

The gap between the health of African Americans and that of the general population is evident in the overall mortality, infant mortality, and most major chronic and fatal diseases. While heart attacks, strokes, and cancer have declined overall, Blacks are still more likely to suffer them sooner than Whites.

The situation is tellingly reflected in a comment by Donald Berwick, a member of the President's Commission on Health Care Quality. "Tell me someone's race," says Dr. Berwick. "Tell me their income. And tell me whether they smoke. The answers to those three questions will tell me more about their longevity and health status than any other questions I could possibly ask. There's no genetic blood test that would have anything like that for predictive value."

The numbers comparing black Americans with the entire population support the view that when it comes to health, race matters very much:

A Statistical Snapshot

	General Population*	African Americans*
Years of healthy life	63.8	55.6
Infant mortality	7.6	15.1
Maternal mortality	7.1	22.1
Tuberculosis deaths	8.7	23.9
Cancer deaths	130	172
Heart disease deaths	108	147
Stroke deaths	26.7	46
Diabetes-related deaths	40	76

*Per 100,000. Figures are for 1995.

Source: U.S. Department of Health and Human Services, *Health United States 1996–1997* (Washington, D.C.: Government Printing Office)

PROGRAMS HAVEN'T ELIMINATED THE DIFFERENCE

Medicare and Medicaid, along with a variety of new social programs introduced in the 1990s, were expected to close the yawning gap between the health of Blacks and Whites, but the results have been mixed.

Research by the National Institute for Aging shows that black people enjoy eight fewer years of relatively good health than do white people or Hispanic Americans. The Institute also found that while only one-fifth of Whites from 51 to 61 described their health as fair to poor, one third of Blacks applied the description to themselves.

Far from having diminished, the incidence of asthma, obesity, maternal mortality, and fetal alcohol syndrome in the black population has actually increased. Further, cases of all types of cancer have dropped or stayed the same for men and women of all races—except for black men. Since the early 1960s, deaths from cancer among black males have increased some 62 percent, compared with 19 percent for all American males. The incidence of prostate cancer is 30 percent higher for black men. This means they have the highest rate of cancer of any group in the nation.

In addition, while 81 percent of white men survive for at least five years after diagnosis, the figure for black men is 66 percent. (This is partly explained by the later diagnosis of the disease in Blacks; because the cancer is at a later stage, its treatment is less successful.)

From 1980 to 1994 (the most recent comprehensive figures), the number of cases of diabetes increased 33 percent among Blacks—three times the increase among Whites. Infectious disease like tuberculosis have increased among Blacks in a similar proportion.

African Americans are more likely than Whites to die of heart disease. Yet a study published in 2001 showed that black people who have a heart attack are less likely than Whites to undergo diagnostic cardiac catheterization, regardless of the race of their physicians. A review of the hospital records from various regions of the country of 40,000 Medicare patients (35,675 Whites, 4039 Blacks) who had experienced a heart attack showed that doctors referred white patients for catheterization 40 percent more often than Blacks, no matter what the physician's race.

*Deaths from Heart Disease in Men**

African American	841
White	666
American Indian/Alaska Native	465
Hispanic	432
Asian/Pacific Islander	372

*Per 100,000; 1991–1995

Source: Centers for Disease Control

This may happen because Whites have access to better medical care, or black patients may be more reluctant to agree to the procedure than white patients. Another possibility is that doctors may be more aggressive in treating white patients. Whatever the explanation, the findings support the general view that Blacks receive less care and less sophisticated care than Whites.

For most American women, advances in the diagnosis and treatment of breast cancer have been, to some extent, a success story. Between 1990 and 1995 the death rate from breast cancer fell 10 percent, going from 23.1 per 100,000 women to 21. But the success story didn't extend to black women. The death rate for them didn't increase, but it did remain steady at 27.5 per 100,000 women. Black women are also more than twice as likely as white women to die of breast cancer, primarily because their disease more often reaches an advanced stage before it is diagnosed and treatment is initiated.

In a 1994 study involving 1100 women (roughly half black and half white) who had just received a diagnosis of breast cancer, researchers found black women were 2.2 times more likely to die than white women. Forty percent of the higher death rate was attributed to the cancer's being more advanced when it was detected. One of the authors of the study, J.W. Eley, was satisfied with the way medicine treats breast cancer in black women, but not with the lateness of the diagnosis: "So we have to concentrate on access to mammography and physical breast exams and educating women to understanding the risk of breast cancer."

Late diagnosis wasn't the only factor involved in the higher rate of breast cancer deaths among black women, according to the researchers. In their view, 15 percent of the death rate was the result of the cancer's being more aggressive in black women. "That's not to say the difference is due to genetics," said Eley. Differences in diet or unknown environmental factors might account for the more aggressive tumors.

A hopeful sign is that since 1992 black women have been having mammograms at the same rate as white women. By 2000 the decline in breast cancer deaths among Blacks should begin to approach that of Whites.

WHY THE GAP?

The failure of social programs to close the health gap is a matter of considerable puzzlement to public health experts. Blacks have generally improved their status in American society over the last few decades. They have increased the level of their education, found better jobs, raised their incomes, and moved into better housing. While prejudice and discrimination have not ended, many black people have become highly successful, and even more have entered the mainstream of American life.

Despite such major changes, the health of African Americans has not improved. The gap between them and the rest of society has remained the same or even widened during the decades when so much else was getting better.

Evidence suggests African Americans as a population have a genetic predisposition to develop diseases like sickle-cell anemia and perhaps prostate cancer; they may also have a predisposition to obesity and to the hazards that accompany it, such as high blood pressure. Yet even if all such predispositions were known to have a genetic basis (and most are still matters of scientific controversy or speculation), they would still not account for the large discrepancies between Blacks and others for diseases like cancer (all forms) and for the significant differences in life spans or in the number of well years of life. Others factors have to be involved.

Blacks generally receive less health care than Whites, and often it is received later in an illness when it is not as likely to be effective. Also, sometimes the care delivered is not as good as that delivered to Whites. Some evidence indicates that when white patients and black, both with insurance, are hospitalized for a heart attack, white patients receive more advanced care more often than black patients.

A greater proportion of African Americans are poor and so are more likely to lack insurance or means to pay for medical care. This may keep more Blacks out of doctor's offices or hospitals. Yet it can't be the whole explanation of the gap between the health of Blacks and the rest of the population. Hispanic Americans are also poor and are even less likely to have health insurance. Yet data from the Centers for Disease Control indicate that they stay healthy longer than all other groups.

Also, even when Blacks have adequate insurance, they don't always make use of it. A study carried out by Roshan Bastani, an expert on cancer and minorities, found that when white women were diagnosed with a breast abnormality, almost 99 percent of them returned to their physicians for follow-up treatment. However, when the same diagnosis was made in a group of minority women, who were predominantly Black or Hispanic, only 75 percent returned for additional care. "Part of this has to do with attitude," according to Bastani. "Like, 'It may go away' or 'I don't have sick leave, so if I go in for this, I'm going to lose a day's pay.'"

Prejudice may also play a role in determining not only the quality of health care provided, but in directly affecting health. A 1996 study of hypertension found that hypertension may be connected with the way black people respond to racial discrimination. When working class Blacks experienced two or more cases of discrimination (such as in looking for a job), they had higher normal blood pressure than working class Whites or black professionals. Black professionals, by contrast, who were aware of experiencing cases of racial discrimination and challenged them, were at a lower risk of developing higher blood pressure. However, as the investigators acknowledged, the study, while suggestive, did not give a full account of why Blacks are more likely to be hypertensive than other groups.

THE TUSKEGEE EFFECT

The medical establishment—physicians, nurses, therapists, clinics, and hospitals—is viewed with suspicion and distrust by millions of poor people in the United States. Distrust is especially high among black people, but it extends to white, Hispanic, and Indian people as well.

While public programs like Medicaid and Medicare now offer mostly equal care to all people, this was not the case in the past. Those unable to pay physicians avoided consulting them until their illness or that of a family member was so serious that desperation forced them to act. If they were hospitalized, it was most likely in a charity ward. They were dependent on the benevolence of their physicians and, given the paternalistic attitude prevalent in medicine until recent years, constrained to do what they were told without asking for information or explanations. Further, the doctrine of informed consent had not yet achieved general acceptance in a form offering much protection to a patient's autonomy and well-being. Hence, the poor often received second-rate medical care and, without being told anything in useful detail, could become the subjects of medical or surgical experimentation.

The emblem of the way in which the trust of black patients was taken advantage of and betrayed by the biomedical establishment is the Tuskegee Study. (See the *Classic Case Presentation: Bad Blood, Bad Faith*.) But while Tuskegee illustrates the most flagrant abuse of medical authority, it was preceded by a more general pattern of abuse.

The distrust of physicians and hospitals was present before Tuskegee, which only confirmed and reinforced the fears and doubts of people in the black community. But all poor people knew you couldn't trust doctors and hospitals to look out for your interest. Thus, while we may talk of a "Tuskegee effect" to suggest why Blacks are suspicious of medicine, the phrase isn't historically accurate. (Vanessa Gamble has documented the distrust as preceding Tuskegee by decades.)

Also, even now those who have never heard of the Tuskegee study are distrustful. The distrust has been passed along to them as part of the lore of what's involved in coping with being poor. Probably at least years and perhaps decades must pass before the medical establishment can overcome the faults of its own past and earn the trust of all people, whatever their income or race.

AIDS

HIV/AIDS is a major health problem among African Americans. In 1995 the death rate per 100,000 of population for black males from AIDS was about 172; for black females it was 64.5. (The comparable figures for whites were 47 and 6.)

Black males tested HIV positive at a rate of 186 per 100,000 and black females at a rate of 62.

Protease-inhibiting drugs are effective in reducing levels of virus in people who are HIV positive, and when the drugs are used in combination with others, life-threatening or debilitating infections can often be brought under control. Yet the distrust of the medical establishment by African Americans hampers the efforts of the medical community to deliver the appropriate care to many who are HIV-positive or have developed AIDS.

People delay seeking care until they are suffering from consequences of the disease that are harder to bring under control, and some begin treatment only to drop out because they don't trust those involved in their care to be acting in their best interest. Some are afraid they are being used as subjects in life-threatening experiments which they are told nothing about.

With respect to HIV, the distrust of the medical establishment extends further and deeper than doubt about receiving good care. A significant number of people in the black community believe that AIDS is a genocidal plot against them. A study by the University of North Carolina at Chapel Hill discovered that about 33 percent of 1054 churchgoers in five cities believed that HIV/AIDS was created by Whites as a form of genocide, and another 30 percent said they weren't sure. Other studies have produced similar results.

A variant of the story is that although a cure for AIDS exists, it is not being used, because the disease affects many more black people than white. As soon as enough Blacks die off, "the doctors" will start using the cure.

CLINICAL TRIALS

African Americans participate in clinical trials of new drugs at a rate significantly below their number in the population. Some fear they are being used as "guinea pigs" by physicians who will "poison" them with experimental drugs. The result is unfortunate both for individuals and for the group. Without a representative number of black participants, it is impossible to acquire the data needed to determine whether Blacks respond to drugs and drug regimens in the same way as the population in general. Not until ten years after the introduction of ACE inhibitor beta blockers and converting enzyme inhibitors were researchers able to compile enough data to realize that these groups of drugs are less effective in the treatment of hypertension among Blacks than in Whites.

By not participating in clinical trials, African Americans can also miss the chance to benefit from experimental drugs. Until recently, promising drugs like taxol for breast cancer and antiretroviral drugs for HIV infection could be obtained by patients only through programs of experimental investigation. While receiving experimental drugs can be a mixed blessing for patients, everyone should at least have the opportunity to decide whether to participate in a drug trial on the basis of relevant considerations. For many African Americans, distrust does not permit them to get so far as to make an informed choice about participation.

African Americans are underrepresented in drug trials for reasons other than their own suspicion. A 1996 survey of some five hundred physicians in central

Tennessee found that black urban physicians were more likely to refer black and white AIDS patients to clinical trials than were white or rural physicians. In interviews, the nonreferring physicians explained that they didn't think the drug testing system was set up to deal with AIDS patients who were African American, women, or IV-drug abusers.

Factors such as the costs of transportation and the difficulty of scheduling office visits also play a role in keeping African Americans from enrolling in clinical trials. Further, one study has shown that black women, in particular, tend to consider clinical trials unethical. They feel that researchers don't care about them and that by participating in research they would deprive themselves of the best treatment available.

The traditional underrepresentation of black people in clinical trials is likely to change eventually under the influence of a new federal policy. Since 1993 the National Institutes of Health has required that all NIH-supported biomedical research include minorities and women, unless there are clear and compelling reasons to justify their exclusion.

Implementing the mandate, however, is likely to require special recruitment efforts. Patients need to be educated about clinical trials and their importance, more African American health care personnel need to be involved, and attempts need to be made to involve community groups. Most of all a strong and continuing effort must be made to earn and deserve the trust of the black community.

CHILDREN'S HEALTH

Surveys show that twice as many African-American children as white children under the age of fifteen are in fair or poor health. To a considerable extent, this is the result of poverty. In 1995 the poverty rate for black children was 42 percent, while the rate for white children was 11 percent. Lack of money can translate into poor diet, unsafe housing, and inadequate health care.

Even a small sampling of relevant statistics shows the impact of poverty:

+ In 1994 almost 90 percent of children in families with an income over $35,000 were in good or excellent health, while this was true for only about 60 percent of those in families with an income below $10,000.

+ A study of women who plan and prepare their family's main meal found that African American women were less likely than white women to know the relationship between diet and health.

+ The death rate for black males between 15 and 19 almost doubled between 1985 and 1994, primarily due to death by firearms. The number of such deaths almost tripled from 46.5 per 100,000 to 152.7.

+ In 1995 only 66 percent of children living in poverty received the standard course of immunization, while 77 percent of those living above the poverty line were immunized.

✦ In 1994 children in low-income households were 16 times more likely to report they didn't have enough to eat "sometimes" or "often."

Disproportionate numbers of African-American babies are born with low birth weight (under 5.5 pounds). These infants are more likely to die or suffer from such severe long-term disabilities as brain damage and blindness.

For many years, the mortality rates have been twice as high for African Americans as for Whites, and in 1995 the rate for Blacks was 2.4 times that of whites. The infant mortality gap between Blacks and Whites can be explained in part by such factors as a greater frequency of drug use among black women and a lower level of nutrition, but even when these factors are taken into account, a gap still remains. Why it does has become something of a medical mystery.

The health of African-American children is likely to be improved by a 1997 federal program. Under the program, $20 billion will be available to states over a period of five years for health care for children in families not eligible for Medicaid. Each state must develop eligibility requirements and provide matching funds. States are also required to pay for such health services as immunizations, X rays, laboratory tests, outpatient care, and hospital stays.

ORGAN TRANSPLANTS

African Americans are at a higher risk for hypertension and kidney disease than the general population, and this increases the chances that they will eventually suffer from kidney failure and need a transplant. Blacks make up 12 percent of the population, but they constitute 30 percent of end-stage kidney disease patients needing dialysis. They also constitute 30 percent of those on the waiting list for a kidney transplant.

About 20 percent of African Americans needing a kidney transplant are likely to do better with a kidney donated by someone of their own race. Kidneys are matched with patients not only by blood type, but by protein antigens, and the closer the match, the more likely the transplanted kidney will "take." Kidney donation by Blacks is significantly lower than donation by Whites, but from a rate of 8 per million in 1980, it rose to 20 per million in 1996.

Why don't African Americans donate organs as often as others? Some people don't donate for personal religious reasons (no organized religion in the United States objects to organ donation), but many are simply inadequately informed about how donated organs are distributed and don't trust the fairness of the system.

"There's a belief that only rich Whites, especially those who are famous, become organ recipients," said Jackie Lynch, a recruiter of minorities for the Regional Organ Bank of Illinois. "They don't see a black role, other than as those who are dying and donating the organs." (Ironically, because of their relatively low rate of donation, it is Blacks who receive a disproportionate number of organs.) Lynch said that black families sometimes ask his non-black colleagues to leave the room so they can ask him about the fairness of the organ distribution system. The rise in organ donation among African Americans suggests it will continue to increase to at least the level of other ethnic groups. For this to happen, however, more public education about donation and the fairness of the system is needed. Black people will have to come to trust that the organs they donate will be used to save or extend the lives of people who may belong to any ethnic or racial group.

CLOSING THE GAP

Discrimination, genetics, cultural patterns, education, and personal history are among the numerous factors that play a role in producing the relatively poor health of African Americans in the United States. But there are signs that improvements are taking place. In 1993 the overall death rate for Blacks was 785 per 100,000; for Whites it was 465. In 1995 (the latest available figures), the rate for Blacks had dropped to 571. This is still considerably higher than the 365 rate for Whites, but the size of the decline is greater.

Also, the Centers for Disease Control, in a 2002 survey of seventeen "health indicators," reported that death rates from lung, breast, colorectal, and prostate cancer fell for all groups during the 1990s. The decline was not as much for Blacks as for the general population, but the trend was in the right direction.

New federal and state programs to assist children living in poverty and provide prenatal care for expectant mothers should eventually be reflected in improved health statistics. New federal requirements that African Americans be included in clinical trials have been accompanied by discussions in the research community of ways to recruit Blacks by providing them with information and transportation expenses and making it easier for them to become part of a study. Organ donations by African Americans have increased over the years, and as more black people come to have confidence in the integrity and fairness of the distribution system, donations should continue to rise.

Perhaps the most important change likely to lead to improvements in the health of African Americans is the development of trust in the black community for the medical establishment. The Tuskegee effect is likely to linger for years, and to overcome it the medical establishment must make a special effort to earn and deserve the trust of black patients. Treating patients with respect, taking seriously their reservations about diagnostic tests or proposed treatments, and taking the time to educate them about their medical condition and the therapy for it are important in securing the trust of any group of patients. If African Americans are more distrustful, it's because they have more reason to be.

AMERICAN INDIANS AND
ALASKA NATIVES AND HEALTH CARE

With respect to health care, the native peoples of the United States have a relationship with the Federal government shared by no other minority group. As a result of the historical evolution of a hodgepodge of treaties and laws, the U.S. is obligated to build hospitals and provide physicians and medical supplies to see to the health needs of the native people. Finding ways to discharge this obligation eventually led to the creation of the Indian Health Service.

INDIAN HEALTH SERVICE

Almost 2 million Indians and Alaska natives live in the United States, and the Indian Health Service (IHS) serves about 1.5 million of them. It operates 76 clinics and 42 hospitals and contracts with a number of tribes to administer their own heath care in 64 clinics and 8 hospitals located on Indian reservations and in 172 village clinics in Alaska. The IHS also runs a small urban Indian Health Program with clinics and referral centers that is intended to provide health resources to those who live off reservations.

The IHS budget is around $2 billion, and while this may seem like a lot of money, given the size of the population that must be served, the per capita expenditure is less than half the average for other U.S. citizens. For each Native American, the spending on health care is $1500, while for someone in the general population it is $3100.

Severe budget constraints have put the IHS in the business of rationing care, and not even all necessary health services can be provided to their patient population. Only about 15 of the 500 IHS health facilities can supply patients with the basic health benefits outlined in the American Health Security Act.

Also, the distribution of resources is skewed and inequitable, with some geographical regions or locations within regions allocated resources to provide a wider range of care than others. The discrepancies are often the result of such factors as historical commitments, population density, and relative isolation. Indians who live in areas without hospitals or clinics within a reasonable distance are often de facto denied the care supplied to others.

Health is generally connected to a large extent with income, and the income of Indians on reservations is substantially below that of the U.S. average. Median household income in the U.S. is $30,000, while that of Indians is below $20,000. About half the population of Indians and Alaskan Natives live on reservations, and 46 percent of them are unemployed. Of those who have jobs, only 28 percent earn as much as $7000 a year. Most Indians who receive health care are almost completely dependent on its being provided by the Indian Health Service. Because the IHS lacks the budget to provide a level of heath care comparable to that provided to private citizens or military veterans, Indians and Alaskan Natives have no guarantee of receiving what for others is the basic minimum of care.

CAUSES OF DEATH

Many of the causes of death among Indians, as among other populations, are related to life style. Although heart disease and cancer are among the leading killers of Indians, the rates are lower for Indians than for the general population. But alcoholism and alcohol abuse are associated with five of the top ten causes of death. This includes accidents and violence connected with excessive drinking.

Leading Causes of Death

	Males*	Females*	U.S.*
Heart disease	143.1	97.8	166.3
Cancer	74.9	73.1	132.7
Accident	133	43.9	35
Diabetes	19.6	26.7	10.7
Stroke	24.7	24	29.7
Liver disease	25.5	21.1	9

*Per 100,000 population.
Source: U.S. Indian Health Service, 1993

The two leading causes of death for those 15–44 are accidents and liver disease. Research shows that Indian women die from liver disease at three times the rate of black women and six times the rate for white women. Women account for half of all deaths of Indians from cirrhosis. The rate of alcohol-related mortality for Indians in the age group 35–44 is five times the overall U.S. rate, and for those 45–54, it is eight times the U.S. rate.

While it has been suggested for decades that Indians are genetically predisposed to become alcoholics, the best evidence at present indicates that historical, cultural, and social factors, not genes, are responsible for the high incidence of alcoholism in Indian populations.

Diabetes, like liver disease, is connected with alcohol consumption, and diabetes is a major health problem in Indian communities. Three times as many Indian men and women die from diabetic complications as do in the general U.S. population. Type II or "adult onset" diabetes is responsible for the high rate of amputations among Indian women. Critics claim that IHS policies restrict the foot care diabetics need for the treatment of ulcers and tissue breakdown and that, as a result, a disproportionate number of diabetics lose legs that could be saved with proper medical care. Sadly, 70 percent of the amputees will have a second leg amputated within five years of the first.

Diabetes among Indians may be connected with both predisposing genetic factors and diet. Some evidence suggests that when Indians eat their traditional foods and avoid the high carbohydrate–high fat diet that has become typical in the U.S., obesity goes down and the incidence of diabetes declines.

Although the rate for cancer is lower than for the U.S. population as a whole, in Indians it is diagnosed later on the average. This means that the death rate for the disease is greater. Certainly screening and prevention services are woefully inadequate. Some of the clinics have historically treated mammography not as a screening technique, but as a diagnostic test to be used only when a women is discovered to have a lump in her breast. The severe budget limitation of the IHS has seriously restricted the use of procedures that are not immediately life-saving.

SUMMARY

The American Indian and Native Alaskan people are caught in a situation in which they have little control over their health care. Although the government is responsible for seeing to their welfare, the government has done a poor job. Facilities and funding are both inadequate.

The need for increasing the level and quality of care is pressing, and only a strong and continuing political and financial commitment can eventually raise the health of the Indian population even to the level of that of the general population. Evidence also suggests that prevention and treatment programs that build on Indian cultures and make use of traditional ways are more likely to succeed than ones imported from the majority culture.

ASIAN AND PACIFIC ISLANDERS AND HEALTH CARE

The hospital staff was worried about Mrs. Tai Li. After giving birth to a healthy baby boy, the thirty-two-year-old woman wouldn't accept the cold water that was offered to her. Her refusal continued for the next five days, with the nurses trying to give her juice and even soft drinks. She was on the verge of becoming seriously dehydrated, and her physicians were on the verge of giving her fluid intravenously, so a translator was called in to explain the situation to her.

As soon as the translator arrived, the situation became clear. Mrs. Li was refusing to drink, because all the beverages that had been offered to her were cold. In Chinese culture, it is thought to bring bad luck to the child for the mother to consume anything cold immediately after childbirth. She willingly accepted the cups of tea that were then offered to her.

By the year 2010 the Asian American–Pacific Islander (AAPI) population will have increased by more than 100 percent, making it the fastest growing minority group. In 1980 the number of people of Asian origin in the United States was roughly 3.5 million. By the time of the 1990 census, it had more than doubled to 7.2 million, and it has continued to increase. About 62 percent of Asian Americans are foreign born, and more than 75 percent speak a language other than English at home.

Present day Asian Americans and Pacific Islanders are not a homogenous group. Rather, the category is made up of as many as forty-eight distinct ethnic populations. Those of Chinese, Japanese, Filipino, Vietnamese, or Hawaiian ancestry, for example, all qualify as members of the group, but all have different cultural backgrounds. They differ in beliefs, diets, lifestyles, and general attitude toward life, and all these factors may play a role in determining their health or the way that they seek health care. Capturing much of importance that is true of the group in a generalization is virtually impossible.

HEALTH PROFILE

Partly because the Asian-American population has increased so rapidly, it has not been studied by epidemiologists and medical sociologists as much as other minority groups. Even so, it is possible to make out some of the significant features of its health profile by looking at death rates for major diseases. (At the moment, state agencies reporting health data usually do not distinguish among the various groups.)

Asian-American females die of cancer at a rate of about 68 per 100,000 and males at a rate of almost 100; comparable figures for Whites are 107 and 156. Lung cancer kills Asian-American females at a rate of 12 per 100,000 and males at 27.4. Breast cancer for Asian-American women is comparatively low at a rate of 10 per 100,000, compared to the population figure of 21.

Death by stroke, at a rate of 22 per 100,000 for Asian-American women, is about the same as that for white women, but the rate of 30 per 100,000 for Asian-American men is substantially higher than the 26 for white men. The rate of death by heart disease for Asian-American women is 57 per 100,000 and much lower than the 97 per 100,000 rate for white females. Yet it is not as dramatically lower as the Asian-American male rate of 107 per 100,000 compared to the white male rate of 186. Hypertension is less common among Asian Americans, but it is also less successfully controlled.

Deaths from chronic obstructive lung disease among Asian Americans, at 5 per 100,000 for women and 13 for men, is about in the middle of the population spread. The death rate from AIDS is low at .06 per 100,000 for Asian-American females and 6 for males. Indeed, these are the lowest rates of any minority group and substantially lower than the 3.8 per 100,000 for white females and 33 for white males.

Hepatitis B is endemic in the Asian-American community. The infection occurs in the U.S. population at a rate of only 0.2 percent, but for those claiming origin from China, Korea, Philippines, Southeast Asia, or the Pacific Islands, the rate of infection ranges from 5–15 percent.

About 11 percent of those infected are pregnant women, and 54 percent of all infants that carry hepatitis B in the U.S. are born to these women. Most of the women are foreign born and have received late or no prenatal care and have not been tested for the virus. The good news, though, is that from 1987 to 1995, the number of cases among AAPI children declined, even though it remains two to three times higher than for other children.

The tuberculosis incidence for AAPIs is about five times higher than the rate for the general population. What is more, the rate is increasing for them, while it is decreasing for others. During 1988 to 1995, it went from 36 to 46 per 100,000.

The population of Asian-American women is not receiving proper screening for cancer. While only 5 percent of white women report they have never had a Pap smear to test for cervical cancer, 45 percent of Chinese-American women and 51 percent of Vietnamese-American women say they have never had one.

The situation is comparable for mammograms. Thirty percent of white women say they have never had the test, but the figure rises to 48 percent for Vietnamese-American women, 55 percent for Hawaiians, 68 percent for Chinese Americans, and 71 percent for those in other Asian-American groups.

On the positive side, life expectancy for Asian American and Pacific Islanders is more than 80 years, about five years higher than that of the general population. Japanese have the highest life expectancy at 82.1 years, while native Hawaiians have the shortest at 68.3 years.

Asian Americans are second only to Hispanic Americans in numbers of people who are uninsured. Some 30 percent of those under age 65 have no health insurance, compared to 16 percent of those under 65 in the general population.

SUMMARY

As much as or more than those belonging to any minority population, the majority of Asian American–Pacific Islanders face formidable barriers to acquiring appropriate medical care. The rate of poverty and unemployment is high, making it difficult for them to obtain private insurance or purchase health care. But perhaps more important, because so many are foreign born and have come to the U.S. relatively recently, they speak little or no English. Even those who might qualify for Medicaid or Medicare programs may be unable to take advantage of them. Either they don't know about the programs or, if they do, they aren't able to cope with the demands of the social and medical systems to gain access.

Moreover, as a non-Western population with many new immigrants, AAPIs are more likely to come into conflict with the medical establishment. Their entrenched cultural beliefs and practices include ones about the causes of diseases and the proper way to prevent or deal with them. Effective treatments by Western medicine may be delayed or replaced by less effective or even harmful folk treatments. The need for medical care may not be recognized or may be delayed, and the importance of taking prescribed drugs, adhering to a treatment regimen, or taking advantage of life-saving surgery may not be appreciated or even accepted.

HISPANIC AMERICANS/LATINOS AND HEALTH CARE

Like the "Asian American" category, the "Hispanic American" or "Latino" category is made up of people from more than twenty countries. It includes those who identify themselves as having their origins in Mexico, Puerto Rico, Cuba, Central or South America, Spain, and some locations in the Caribbean. While all the subgroups may share a Spanish or Latino heritage, they differ significantly from one another. Data on Hispanics are usually not collected in terms of such refined categories; most data are about Mexican Americans.

In 1994 26.4 million Hispanic Americans were living in the United States. They constitute roughly 10 percent of the total population. In terms of origin, 64 percent were Mexican, 11 percent Puerto Rican, 13 percent from Central or South American or the Caribbean, while 5 percent were classified as "Other Hispanics." By the year 2010, demographers estimate that Hispanics will become the largest minority group in the U.S. and constitute 13 percent of the population.

Hispanic individuals are the youngest of any minority group. The median age is 26.7 years, compared to 34.4 for others. At $23,000, their income remains significantly below the general population figure of $38,000. Unemployment is high at about 10–12 percent, and more than 25 percent of Hispanic families live below the poverty level. Partly this is because Hispanics are less likely than others to have two workers in a two-parent family. More than half of Hispanic women (52 percent) are in the labor force, but for non-Hispanics the figure is close to 58 percent. Also, about 16 percent of Hispanic mothers are under the age of twenty, compared to 10 percent of white mothers and 23 percent of black mothers.

HEALTH PROFILE

The Hispanic population is perhaps the healthiest of minority groups. While AIDS in particular kills a disproportionate number of Hispanic males, compared with the population as a whole, Hispanics are doing well.

Leading Causes of Death *

	Males	Females	Population
AIDS	94.5	23	26
Lung disease	12.5	6.9	21.1
Lung cancer	25.1	8.3	40.2
Breast cancer	—	12.6	21.3
Cancer (other)	97.8	66.1	131.3
Stroke	23	17.1	26.6
Heart disease	121.9	68.1	138.3
All causes	515	274.4	503.9

*Per 100,000; figures are for 1995.

Source: U.S. Department of Health and Human Services, *Health United States 1996–1997* (Washington, D.C.: Government Printing Office)

Heart disease and cancer are the top two causes of deaths in Hispanic men and women. But for Hispanic men, the next two causes are accidental injury and AIDS, while for women the causes are stroke and diabetes, with accidental injury coming in a distant fifth.

Several recent changes reveal that in some respects the health of Hispanic Americans has taken a turn for the worse compared with the rest of the population. A survey published in 2002 showed that the incidence of syphilis was three times that of whites, and that tuberculosis was six times as high. Most striking, an earlier study showed that the homicide rate among Hispanic males 15–34 increased to 52.2 per 100,000 in 1994 from the 1987 baseline of 41.3. Yet the 2002 survey showed that homicide was six times as high for Hispanics as for whites.

Diabetes is another reason for concern. While the prevalence of the disease in the U.S. population increased from 28 to 30 cases per 1000 in less than a decade, for Mexican Americans the increase went from 54 to 66. Also, the number of pregnancies among Hispanic females 15–19 has increased from 143 per 1000 to 180. However, the number of pregnant Hispanic women receiving care in the first trimester of pregnancy increased to 70 percent in 1995.

Some other changes have also been positive. The most recent data show that 50 percent of Hispanic-American women who are 50 or older have received a breast examination and a mammogram. Data gathered in 2002 showed that the death rate from breast cancer in Hispanic women had declined by 13 percent. (It fell 18 percent for Whites, but only 4 percent for Blacks.) Further, the proportion of Hispanic American women receiving a Pap test has increased from about 75 percent ten years ago to over 91 percent today.

These increases in the number of women screened for disease may be connected with the fact that the proportion of Hispanic Americans over eighteen who now have a primary health care provider has increased to 71 percent. While lower than the total population figure of 84 percent, it is a significant improvement over the 1991 figure of 63 percent.

WOMEN AND HEALTH CARE

Researcher Charles H. Hennekens showed in a 1982 study, the Physician's Health Survey, that small, regular doses of aspirin could reduce the likelihood of a first heart attack by as much as 30 percent. This was an important finding from the standpoint of preventive medicine, and it served as the basis for physicians to recommend that those at risk of heart disease take aspirin in low doses prophylactically.

But did the study's finding also apply to women?

Critics immediately pointed out that the 22,071 subjects in Hennekens' study were all men. What grounds were there to be sure that the same measure that prevented a heart attack in men would also prevent one in women? Why weren't women included in the study? Cardiovascular disease kills about as many women as men.

Hennekens replied to his critics that the study participants had all been physicians, and at the time the study was initiated, only about 10 percent of physicians in the country were women. The population was simply not large enough to supply him with subjects. Also, twice as many women as men would have been needed in the study to get the same statistically significant result, because while one in five men has a heart attack by age sixty, only one in seventeen women does.

"We didn't want to neglect women," Hennekens said later, "but we couldn't study them in that population."

Whatever the merits of Hennekens's explanation, the gender-exclusive character of the study led many advocates for women to look at other scientific studies. When they did, many decided women weren't being adequately represented as subjects in medical research. Important studies, such as the Multiple Risk Factor Intervention Trial (MR FIT) involved 15,000 men and no women. Drug trials were just as exclusive. The great majority of tests to determine the safety and effectiveness of new drugs included no women. They were routinely excluded on the basis of concerns about the effects of the drugs on actual or future pregnancies. Pregnant women were excluded because new drugs of unknown effects might harm the fetus and cause birth impairments.

Also, because some women might be pregnant without knowing it or become pregnant while taking the experimental drug, most researchers considered it safer and easier simply to exclude women of childbearing age. Some drugs, they said, might also affect a woman's potential for becoming pregnant. Further, researchers argued, the variation in hormone levels associated with menstruation made it difficult to separate the effects of a drug from the effects of biochemical changes.

A result of this systematic exclusion of women, as advocates pointed out, is that most drugs and treatment regimens have been developed (until recently) using data from studies conducted exclusively with men as subjects. For the most part, it has simply been taken for granted that the best drugs and most effective treatments for men are also the best and most effective for women. Yet without studies that include women or ones that focus on the way women respond to treatment, there is no way of knowing to what extent a particular drug (or a certain dose of a drug) or treatment may benefit women. Man cannot be the measure of all things medical.

INCLUDE WOMEN, STUDY WOMEN

Beginning in the late 1980s, advocates for women, armed with facts about the exclusionary practices of scientific research, began pressing researchers, first of all, to include more women in their studies. It was unacceptable to exclude women from all studies on the slim grounds that a woman's capacity to become pregnant might sometimes lead to harm. Most often, pregnancy was at best a speculative consideration, and women deserved to have confidence that conclusions about their medical treatments were based on data acquired from studies including women. What could be more relevant to predicting the response of women to a drug than a study of the drug that included women as subjects?

Second, advocates demanded that more attention be paid to the variations in responses between men and women. They pointed out that even when women were included in a study, investigators typically failed to make an effort to determine how the gender of the research subjects affected the study's results.

For example, although asthma deaths increase in women during the time before menstruation occurs, researchers have not attempted to determine whether the hormonal changes taking place during menstruation affect the bronchi or interact with asthma medications. Differences in men and women that are connected with differences in responses are often ignored and simply buried in statistical measurements that count men and women as the same.

Third, advocates for women also claimed that health problems specific to women have received relatively little attention from researchers. Perhaps because researchers are predominantly male, they have traditionally focused on problems or diseases affecting mostly men. Thus, data are scarce on the effects of hormone replacement therapy on heart disease, of a low-fat diet on breast cancer, or of alcohol consumption on ovarian cancer.

Fourth, advocates demanded that women receive medical care equal to that of men. One study found that women with kidney disease sufficiently severe to require dialysis were 30 percent less likely to receive a kidney transplant than were men. A second study found there was a 25 percent difference. Moreover, men in every age category were more likely to receive a transplant than were women in the same category.

Similar disparities were found in diagnostic testing. All smokers, regardless of gender, have the same risk of lung cancer, yet a study found that men were twice as likely as women to be tested for the disease. Also, a 1987 study found that men with symptoms of heart disease were much more likely to receive a diagnostic cardiac catheterization than women.

Interpreting diagnostic results showed the same sort of bias as did the tests themselves. When abnormal results were found in thallium scans of the heart, women were more than twice as likely to have their symptoms attributed to psychiatric or noncardiac causes than were men.

ADDITIONAL SUPPORT

In 1985 the Task Force on Women's Health Issues of the United States Public Health Service concluded that because of the lack of research data on women, it was difficult to assess women's health needs. This conclusion was taken by advocates to endorse the view that gender bias had deprived us of the information needed to recognize and deal with the health needs of women. Women, it appeared clear, were being shortchanged.

The American Medical Association's Council on Ethical and Judicial Affairs 1990 Report "Gender Disparities in Clinical Decision-Making" offered additional support to the contention that women were not being treated fairly by the American health care system. The Council reviewed forty-eight studies published in a variety of medical journals between 1970 and 1990. The basic question was whether gender improperly affected the amount and kind of medical care patients received. (The findings on diagnostic testing and kidney transplants have already been mentioned.)

The Council's conclusion was that there were definitely "non-biological or nonclinical factors which affect clinical decision making." Although the Council did not have the data to identify the exact nature of the nonclinical factors, it pointed to their existence as a cause for concern.

The Council recommended that "physicians examine their practices and attitudes for the influence of social or cultural biases which could be inadvertently affecting the delivery of medical care" and eliminate them. Furthermore, "more research in women's health issues and women's health problems should be pursued." The Council ended by encouraging the promotion of more female physicians to positions of leadership in teaching, research, and the practice of medicine.

POSITIVE CHANGES

Partly in response to political pressure from the women's movement but also as a result of the recognition that women had a good case and hadn't been dealt with fairly in medical research and practice, several significant changes were made in the treatment of women by the biomedical research establishment.

In 1990 the National Institutes of Health established the Office of Research on Women's Health. It was given the responsibility of determining what research of benefit to women needed to be done and of making sure women were included in future federally-funded research projects intended to benefit both genders. It is currently sponsoring research into heart disease and cancer among women.

Researcher Charles Hennekens, who had conducted the study showing the benefit of aspirin therapy in preventing heart attacks in men, proposed a study to establish the effects of aspirin in preventing heart attacks in women. Scientists who reviewed the proposal for the federal granting agency to which it was submitted, the National Heart, Lung, and Blood Institute, rejected the proposal twice. They held that the preliminary data did not support a case for repeating

Hennekens' original study with women. The proposal was rejected a third time on a 5-to-4 vote on technical grounds, although the reviewing panel said that determining the benefits and risks of aspirin therapy in a healthy population of women was of "the highest priority."

The director of the Institute, Claude J. Lenfant, decided to set aside the recommendation of the grant reviewing panel and approve the $10 million needed to fund the study. In addition to intense Congressional interest in the project, he cited the potential health significance of the study. He mentioned several differences between men and women with respect to heart disease:

+ Women develop heart disease about ten years later than men and tend to be twenty years older than men when they have a first heart attack.

+ Women learn they have heart disease when they experience the chest pain of angina, men when they have a heart attack.

+ A first heart attack is more often fatal in women, and the death rate during the following year is greater.

+ Women have more painless heart attacks.

+ Women suffer more complications from clot-dissolving drugs used to treat heart attacks.

Hennekens' study was designed to include 45,000 women nurses. The sample size was designed to be large enough to assess whether the findings apply to Whites, Blacks, Hispanics, and other minorities.

The funding for programs affecting women's health has significantly increased in the 1990s. This is particularly true for breast cancer, a disease of particular concern to women. In 1990 the federal funding for breast cancer research was $90 billion, and in 1997 it rose to a phenomenal $600 billion. The increase in research funding for studying health issues affecting women has been accompanied by an increase in the number of professional journals devoted to women's health. At least eight new titles have appeared since 1990.

The increase in research findings concerning women is also reflected in the increase in the number of publications. From 1986–1991, Medline, the database for medical research, listed 159 articles with the key words "women's health." For the period 1992–1996, the number had increased to 1426. More recent numbers suggest a continuing upward trend.

BACKLASH OR BALANCE?

In the view of some critics, the success of advocates for women in shifting the focus of research and funding onto women's health issues has produced a bias against men's health, with a disproportionate amount of resources being spent on women.

First, the claim that diseases affecting women have been studied less than those affecting men has been used by advocates as a basis for demanding that women's diseases receive more attention. The factual basis for this claim has been denied by some, however. Curtis L. Meinert, an epidemiologist at Johns Hopkins University, asserts that when research published in the period 1980–1993 is surveyed, the number of projects focusing only on men is virtually matched by ones focusing only on women.

Second, critics charge, the politics of health care have been manipulated to favor women, even when the scientific evidence does not support the demands made by advocates. The principal example of this was a policy change concerning the use of mammography in breast-cancer screening. Because of pressure from Congress, particularly from the women members, the National Cancer Institute reversed its original position. A panel of experts convened by the NCI considered the question of whether women in their forties with no family history of breast cancer should have regular mammograms. The panel found that the evidence did not establish that mammograms saved lives in women in their forties and recommended that the test not be made a part of every woman's medical exam. Although the NCI initially endorsed the recommendation, the director reversed this position in response to public and political pressure. Bills were then immediately introduced in Congress to require that insurers pay for the procedure for women under fifty.

(Critics point out that the director of the Heart Institute acted similarly in setting aside the recommendations of the grant reviewing panel and funding Hennekens' study of the effect of aspirin on heart attacks in women.)

Congress has also devoted considerable attention to whether insurers should be required to pay for longer hospital stays for women recovering from mastectomies. Yet Congress has completely ignored the same question about prostate surgery, although prostate cancer kills almost as many people every year as breast cancer.

Third, research money is spent on women disproportionately. In 1996, 16 percent of National Institutes of Health funds were directed to the study of diseases exclusive to women, while only 5.7 percent went to studies of diseases exclusive to men. The majority of funds, 78.3 percent went to diseases affecting both genders. Past funding was similar. In 1987, the figures were 13.5 percent for women's diseases, 6.5 percent for men's, and 80 percent for both. Furthermore, the National Cancer Institute spends more on cancers affecting women (breast and ovarian) than on prostate cancer.

Defenders of this pattern of research spending claim that, even though it appears to favor women, the appearance is deceiving. The spending is disproportionate because our ignorance is disproportionate. We simply lack an understanding of the diseases affecting women. A larger amount of research money goes for research on women because that is where our scientific understanding is most incomplete.

So far as breast cancer is concerned, it should be given special consideration— more consideration than prostate cancer. Breast cancer kills women at an earlier age than prostate cancer. Thus, the money spent on preventing it or treating it buys more years of life than does money spent on prostate cancer.

Nevertheless, some critics reject the whole idea that American medicine has not served women well. If anything, they charge, women receive better health care than men. "There's no question that women seek out medical attention more," says A. G. Kadar. "Whether they are less healthy is another issue . . . especially since there are diseases that keep you from feeling your best but don't shorten your life expectancy." Kadar suggests that a better measure is life expectancy. Given that women live about 7.5 years longer than men, this may be taken as showing that women are healthier than men.

While no one can doubt the influence of politics on health-care research and policy, the historical record supports the claim of advocates that women have received scant attention as research subjects. It may be true that women's response to drugs and treatments do not, for the most part, differ significantly from those of men. But the point some critics miss is that we have little scientific evidence for embracing this view. Past practices have kept us so ignorant of how women may respond that we have scant grounds for generalization.

Things may not be significantly changing either. A 2000 report from the General Accounting Office suggests that the 1993 law requiring that women be included in federally supported clinical trials in numbers sufficient to determine whether men and women respond differently to drugs, surgical procedures, and treatments is being followed only in the letter.

While scientists generally include women in the study group, they don't always analyze the data to look for differences in gender-specific responses to treatments. Also, sometimes the number of women included is not large enough for a reliable statistical analysis of the data to indicate whether a therapy leads to different outcomes for women and men.

Debates over research related to women's health are likely to continue. Eventually, as more is learned about how diseases affect women and how women respond to treatment, funding may reach something like parity. What is more important is that the health needs of women have now been explicitly recognized, because this makes it unlikely that women will ever be completely left out of scientific studies. Women, as well as men, will then be in a position to benefit from new knowledge and understanding.

CONCLUSION

In a society committed to fairness, no one questions in principle that we must be sure that disadvantaged groups receive a just allocation of the society's health care resources. A number of significant steps have been taken to see to it that research into issues affecting women's health is given the same emphasis as that affecting the health of men. Eventually, the institutional structures that have been put into place, such as the Office of Research on Women's Health, are likely to bring about and sustain gender equity in medical research. Attitudes toward women as patients may be slower to change.

The society has been more effective in correcting the imbalance of resources with respect to gender than it has with respect to minority status. Evidence suggests that the health of African Americans and American Indians and Native Alaskans, in particular, is considerably more at risk than that of the general population. The gap between both minority groups and others is so wide that special and continuing efforts need to be made to close it.

A larger budget for the Indian Health Service would solve part of the problem of providing the basic care not currently supplied, and perhaps a way could be devised to extend the care to Indians living in isolated areas.

But Indians are in need of more preventive care. Disease screening, such as mammograms and PSA testing, needs to be made available to a larger proportion of the population. Further, problems like unemployment and alcoholism that are connected with high death rates need a social and political solution. Public health programs can educate people about the importance of good health habits and make a strong contribution to disease prevention, but it cannot give people jobs.

Many of the factors responsible for the gap between the health of African Americans and that of the general population are unknown. Yet many of them are known and can be modified in a positive direction by political, social, and individual effort. Programs designed to promote preventive screening among blacks have shown themselves to be effective. Programs to encourage blacks to participate in clinical trials, to consult physicians when a health concern arises (instead of waiting until it becomes unbearable), and to become organ donors could make use of the same principles. All such programs need to take into account the distrust of the medical establishment in the black community (the Tuskegee effect), as well as restrictions imposed by income and transportation and child-care needs.

Part of the public health message to Indians and Blacks also needs to stress the importance of personal responsibility in health. Louis Sullivan, President George Bush's Secretary of Health and Human Services, stresses that "the top ten causes of premature death in our nation are significantly influenced by personal behavior and life-style choices." He advises African Americans to give up smoking, reduce drinking, and lose weight. Taking such steps, he claims, could eliminate 45 percent of deaths from heart disease, 23 percent of deaths from cancer, and more than 50 percent of the disabling consequences of diabetes.

The death rates for cancer for African Americans was once lower than for Whites, but as more Blacks took up smoking, the rates surpassed that of Whites. Heart disease rose along with cancer. But it might be due in part to the traditional African-American diet that is high in both salt and fat. Also, almost half of black women are seriously overweight, as are almost a third of black men. This is a risk factor for heart disease but also for diabetes and hypertension. Because African Americans are particularly prone to these diseases, a change in personal behavior might lead to significant changes in health statistics.

If we want to improve the health of minority groups in our society, a crucial step is to bridge the gap between the dominant culture and minority cultures. This is particularly true for Hispanics, who may have to cope with a language difficulty, and with Asian Americans, who may have to cope both with a language difficulty and a radically different cultural understanding of disease and its treatment.

Interpreters for non-English speakers are crucial for providing even adequate health care for many minority individuals. Increasing the number of minorities in the health care profession is another obvious way to help bring minorities into the health care system. So, too, is opening clinics in urban areas where immigrant populations are concentrated. All these steps have been taken by some major medical centers and several health maintenance organizations.

From the national perspective, perhaps the most important project was Healthy People 2000: National Health Promotion and Disease Prevention. The effort was a collaboration between private organizations, public agencies, and health professionals led by the U.S. Public Health Service. The project attempted to reduce preventable death and disability, enhance the quality of life, and reduce disparities in health status among Americans.

Listing 300 objectives to be achieved, the project enjoined all participants to work in a professional and personal capacity to achieve whatever targets (increasing immunizations among the Hmong, reducing amputations among the Plains Indians, encouraging African Americans to quit smoking) were most appropriate for their situation.

Project 2000 was successful in moving in the direction of achieving its goals. Yet for the majority of minority people, a Project 2025 or maybe even a Project 2050 will be needed before the disparities in health care can be expected to disappear.

CASE PRESENTATION
Lee Lor: Caught in a Culture Conflict

The Hmong are a Southeast Asian mountain people who were American allies during the Vietnam war. At the end of the war, to protect them from reprisals, whole families of Hmong were airlifted to the United States. Most of the Hmong settled in California, and more than 35,000 now live in or near Fresno.

The Hmong (pronounced *mung*) brought their culture with them and have not abandoned it in favor of the general western or American culture in which they now live. This is unproblematic so far as matters like dress, food preferences, and modes of worship are concerned. But some Hmong practices have brought them into conflict with the law. Over the years, the Fresno police have been required to deal with complaints about the Hmong slaughtering pigs and other animals in their apartments. The police have also raided the patches of ground where the Hmong were growing opium poppies and mounted an education campaign to discourage Hmong men from pursuing their traditional practice of abducting teenage girls to marry.

Hmong beliefs about illness, its causes, and its treatment have led to even more conflicts with sometimes tragic results. Adhering to their traditional beliefs, the Hmong don't accept the view of the world put forward by Western science. They are animists who view the everyday world as a place shared with spirits, and the interactions between spirits and humans help to shape the course of human life. Spirits can be angered or seek revenge for insults or wrongs, and often the vengeful actions of the spirits are manifested as diseases. Propitiating the spirits may involve praying, performing healing rituals, burning incense, and carrying out animal sacrifices.

The cultures of the Hmong and of the West come into sharp conflict where the treatment of sick children is concerned. Hmong parents of a child with club feet avoided getting the child treated, because they thought the child's feet were deformed to atone for the wrongdoing of an ancestor. To try to correct the problem might result in another family member's becoming sick.

Other Hmong parents have refused surgery, because they believe it maims the body and makes it impossible for the child to be reincarnated. But one case of conflict between Hmong cultural beliefs and the Western notion of the legal and moral responsibility to provide children with appropriate medical care was the focus of considerable attention.

LEE LOR

Lee Lor, a fifteen-year-old girl, was admitted to Valley Children's Hospital in late September of 1994 with a complaint of severe stomach pains. Her physicians diagnosed acute appendicitis and operated immediately. During the surgery, however, they discovered that Lee Lor had a cancerous tumor growing in her abdomen. In removing the tumor, the surgeon took out an ovary and part of one of her fallopian tubes. Her family later claimed they were not told about the cancer or the surgery for it until three days later. A hospital spokesman said the Lees were told, but he suggested they may have not have understood because of problems with the translation.

Failing to get permission from Lee's family to initiate chemotherapy, the hospital notified the Fresno County Department of Social Services of the situation. The agency obtained a court order requiring Lee to submit to chemotherapy. The police, facing a barrage of stones hurled by a group of Hmong, removed Lee from her home strapped to a stretcher. Her father was so upset that a police officer had to wrestle a knife out of his hand to keep him from killing himself. A guard was posted outside Lee's room in the hospital.

To protest Lee's forced treatment, several hundred Hmong marched through the city twice. At a town meeting, they accused the county and the hospital of racism.

Lee was given chemotherapy for a week, then allowed to return home. On the day of her discharge, a court hearing was initiated to determine whether she should be placed in a foster home until the completion of her course of chemotherapy. Her physicians estimated that with treatment she had an 80 percent chance of survival, but without it her chances dropped to 10 percent.

Lee made her own decision about treatment by running away from home on October 28. Her parents saw her as she slept on a couch with her eight siblings, but the next morning she was gone. She left with little or no money but with a supply of herbal medicines. Her parents notified the police, but they also called in the family shaman. She reported that she had a vision of Lee out in the open and well.

Some two months later, Lee returned home. She had spent the time wandering around the state and was apparently no worse for the wear. While she was gone, the Department of Social Services had dropped its efforts to get a court order to continue Lee's chemotherapy. In one sense, Lee and her parents and the Hmong community had won their battle against Western medicine.

LINGERING QUESTIONS

While the parents of Lee Lor were devoted to their daughter, they could not free themselves of their culturally acquired beliefs and adopt in their place the scientific ones of Western medicine.

They did what they believed best for their child. Yet the fact remains that the beliefs of Western medicine are more effective in dealing with cancer than are ones based on the Hmong's animistic view of the world. Granted this is so, does a respect for the beliefs of others require us to refrain from interfering when a sick child is given a treatment we consider ineffective?

Or, by contrast, does out knowledge of what is more likely to be effective require us to intervene to make sure the child receives the treatment most likely to benefit her—even if this means acting against the wishes of her parents?

These questions are not prompted just by "alien" cultures like that of the Hmong. It's necessary only to think of Jehovah's Witnesses or Christian Scientists (see the *Case Presentation: The Death of Robyn Twitchell* in Chapter 2) to realize that where the best treatment for a child's illness is at issue, the beliefs of parents can come into conflict with the beliefs of scientific medicine.

Our society is strongly committed to individual autonomy and to recognizing the responsibility of parents in caring for their children. Hence, we are ambivalent about abnegating parental responsibility. When the beliefs of an entire culture are concerned, we become even more ambivalent, not wishing to be guilty of cultural arrogance.

But the question that must be addressed above all is—What is in the best interest of the child? Allowing a competent adult to refuse medical care or choose a treatment with little or no chance of success is quite different from allowing an adult to make a similar choice for a child. Children are not in a position to have any say in the matter and must look to society to see that their interest is protected.

SOCIAL CONTEXT
The Mammography Debate

Susan Arcadan, as we will call her, was forty-one years old and enjoying life to the fullest.

She had a nice apartment, a wide circle of friends, and best of all, she had recently been promoted to head a new products group at the online computer company where she worked.

Not bad for a college history major who had known next to nothing about computers when she was hired as a sales representative six years earlier. Now she was riding herd over bright, talented, amusing people and loving it.

Susan took care of her health, too. She ate lots of fruits and vegetables, avoided fats, biked or jogged every day, and when the weather permitted, worked in the garden she had carved out of the wasteland behind her building. She had regular physical exams, and when she turned thirty-nine, she started getting mammograms, even though no one in her family had ever been diagnosed with breast cancer. She was the sort of person who took pride in being cautious.

Despite her exercise and careful diet, a couple of weeks after her promotion, Susan began to gain weight. At first she thought it was only because she was over forty and cut back on her calories, but when she noticed a dimpling in the skin of her left breast, she decided she should see her doctor. Her methods of weight control weren't working.

After only the briefest exam, Dr. Long found a lump in her left breast. "You need a biopsy immediately," he told Susan. "I'll arrange for you to see a surgeon." The dimpling in the skin, she learned, was a sign of breast cancer past its earliest stage.

Susan was numb with shock. She had gotten her yearly mammogram eight months earlier, and it had shown nothing abnormal. She had done everything, and it had turned out to be useless.

STATISTICAL PICTURES

Susan was one of the roughly 200,000 women in the United States diagnosed with breast cancer every year. In about 140,000 of these women, the cancer has not spread beyond the breast, but in 60,000 of them the cancer is not a new diagnosis but a recurrence of the disease. Eventually, around 65,000 women in the group of 200,000 will die of the disease, and by this estimate, during the last ten years, breast cancer killed more than half a million women.

Studies show that women fear breast cancer more than any other disease. Fearing the disease is quite reasonable, because it is one of the major causes of death in women. It is far from being the leading cause, however, and many women believe they are at greater risk for the disease than they are. An unfortunate aspect of this is that they may fail to take steps that might prevent some of the diseases more likely to kill them.

Heart disease, which causes death in women at a rate of 100.4 per 100,000, is a far greater threat to their lives. The same is true of lung cancer, which has a death rate of 27.5, and stroke, with a death rate of 24.8. By contrast with these diseases, breast cancer has a death rate of 21 per 100,000—high but about one-fifth that of heart disease.

While little is known about how to prevent breast cancer, much is known about reducing the risk for heart disease, lung cancer, and stroke. This is why women's health experts worry that too restricted a focus on breast cancer may fail to promote the overall health of women.

A woman's lifetime risk of dying of breast cancer is one in nine, while her risk of dying of heart disease is one in two. Her risk of dying of diabetes is one in three and of stroke one in five.

But even the one in nine figure, high as it is, needs to be kept in perspective. What the figure taken alone does not show is that the risk of breast cancer increases with age. Relatively few women die of the disease in their twenties, thirties, or even early- to mid-forties, but when they reach their fifties, the incidence begins to rise. It then soars for women in their sixties and beyond. The lifetime risk is one in nine, but the longer a woman lives, the greater her risk becomes. The following chart illustrates this.

Breast Cancer Deaths by Age*

25–34	2.7
35–44	15
45–54	41.4
55–64	69.8
65–74	103.3
75–84	142
85–	203.7

*Per 100,000; figures are for 1995.

Source: U.S. Department of Health and Human Services, *Health United States 1996–1997* (Washington, D.C.: Government Printing Office)

At thirty-eight Susan Arcadan was statistically unlikely to develop breast cancer. With good health habits and no family history of the disease, she was only one of the unlucky so-called sporadic cases that have no explanation. (For a discussion of known breast cancer genes, see Chapter 5.) Susan was also unlucky in another way. Although she had gotten a mammogram eight months before she was diagnosed with breast cancer, the X-ray image had appeared to be completely normal.

MAMMOGRAMS

In 1987 the National Cancer Institute recommended that women start having breast-cancer screening mammograms at age forty and get one every year or two. The American Cancer Society endorsed the recommendation and continued an intensive advertising campaign stressing the importance of early detection in cancer treatment, and the message that "Mammograms Save Lives" was widely disseminated.

No one questioned the diagnostic usefulness of mammograms, and the number of cases of cancer detected in women over fifty made their importance in examining this group unquestionable. However, even while the general value of mammograms was being promoted, a long-simmering scientific debate over the value of using them for women in their forties continued over the next six years.

Then, in 1993, the National Cancer Institute changed its original recommendation and announced that "experts do not agree on the value of routine screening mammography for women ages 40 to 49." The American Cancer Society and a dozen or more cancer advocacy groups continued to adhere to the original guidelines.

Hoping to resolve the long dispute, in 1997 the Director of the National Cancer Institute, Richard Klausner, convened a panel of thirteen medical experts and public representatives and asked them to address a number of specific questions. They were to consider, for example, "Do mammograms prevent women in their forties from dying of breast cancer?" and "What are the disadvantages of mammograms for women in their forties?" Klausner hoped the panel would function as a consensus conference and establish guidelines for the use of mammograms that could be adopted by both clinicians and public groups.

The panel, headed by Leon Gordis, an epidemiologist from Johns Hopkins, met for six weeks, considered hundreds of scientific papers, and listened to presentations from thirty-five authorities on breast cancer. The scientific findings presented to the committee were not always clear-cut and didn't support an obvious conclusion.

Studies done in Sweden and Scotland indicated women in their forties getting mammograms were less likely to die of breast cancer, but another study conducted in Canada found no such effect. All researchers agreed that even if there was a positive effect, it was so slight that huge numbers of women would have to be screened to save even a few.

Suzanne W. Fletcher pointed out that if the most optimistic estimate of the value of mammograms was correct, for every 1000 women having a yearly mammogram, in a ten-year period only one or two would be saved from death by breast cancer. Ordinarily, eight women could be expected to die of the disease in that time, so mammograms would not save the lives of six or seven of them.

Lazlo Tabar, a principal investigator in the Swedish study, claimed mammograms had "a tremendous potential" to reduce breast cancer deaths in women in their forties by as much as 16 percent, but Ingvar Andersson, also a Swedish researcher, disagreed. According to his figures, a yearly screening of 10,000 women for 10 years would save 15 women from dying of breast cancer. However, the test would produce 1250 false positives—results indicating women have tumors when they don't. Further testing would be required in each case. Biopsies would be performed 56 times, and they would lead to 10 cases of surgery for noncancerous lumps. Further, at least one woman every ten years would die of cancer caused by radiation exposure from mammograms.

A 1998 study showed that a woman who has a yearly mammogram for ten years has a 50 percent chance of having at least one false positive. She has a 19 percent chance of undergoing an unnecessary biopsy. For the 32 million American women between ages 40 and 79, this could mean 16 million false positives in 10 years and over 5 million biopsies. The worry, anxiety, and general difficulties are incalculable.

RECOMMENDATION

On January 23, 1997, the panel made public the results of its deliberations. "At the present time," it said in a public statement, "the available data do not warrant a single recommendation for mammography for all women in their 40s. Each woman should decide for herself whether to undergo mammography."

At best, the panel concluded, mammography might prolong, but not necessarily save, the lives of 10 women of every 10,000 getting a yearly mammogram. While mammograms can reduce the breast-cancer death rate for women fifty and above by as much as 30 percent, the panel found no evidence for any such reduction for women in their forties. Some studies found no effect in the death rate at all, and some found only a slight effect.

As a statistician on the panel put the point, 98.5 percent of women in their forties who have yearly mammograms get no benefit at all. The other 1.5 percent have their lives extended 200 days, but how the days are distributed—all to one person or some to all ten—cannot be known.

Also, mammograms would involve much worry, additional testing, and surgery with its hazards and potential complications. During the ten-year period from forty to fifty, with the women getting yearly mammograms, 30 percent of the supposed abnormalities detected will be false positives. All these women will have to have additional tests, and some will need surgery to be sure cancer is not present. Forty percent of the tumors detected in women in their forties turn out to be intraductal carcinoma in situ, which may or may not turn into invasive lethal tumors. Forty percent of the women with tumors of this type have mastectomies, while the others have lumpectomies, sometimes with radiation and sometimes without. Many women must suffer worry, expense, pain, surgical mutilation and the risks of surgery and radiation to benefit only a few.

Further, for every 10,000 women getting an annual mammogram, 3 or so might develop breast cancer as a result of the exposure to radiation. Also, because mammograms miss about 25 percent of invasive tumors in women in their forties, having mammograms might give women a false sense of security. The breast tissue in women fifty or older is less dense, and tumors are missed only about 10 percent of the time.

RESPONSES

The Director of the National Cancer Institute said he was shocked by the panel's recommendation. He himself was persuaded of the importance of the Swedish study indicating the value of mammograms in reducing deaths in women in their forties and thought the panel hadn't given it the weight it deserved.

The American Cancer Society said it was "disappointed" in the report. Some radiologists were outraged. "I do feel this is tantamount to a death sentence for women in their forties," one said. Another said the panel's report was "fraudulent" and should not be released to the public. The former Director of the National Institutes of Health, Bernardine Healy, said she was shocked by the panel's conclusion. "I am very disturbed that a group of so-called experts challenged the notion of early detection," she said. "What they are saying is that ignorance is bliss."

Women who had recovered after a diagnosis of breast cancer were among the sharpest critics of the report. In an op-ed piece in the *New York Times* titled "Luckily, I Had a Mammogram," Kathlyn Conway told how, thanks to a mammogram, she had been diagnosed with breast cancer at the age of forty-three. What is more, while waiting to get a second opinion on a biopsy, she talked to several women in the waiting room, and none was over fifty. "Yes, my evidence is anecdotal," she wrote. "But it is evidence I can't ignore." Conway and others pointed out that the insurance industry would use the panel's report to deny coverage for mammograms for women under fifty.

Politicians were quick to respond to the panel's report. Leon Gordis, the head of the panel was called to testify before Congress on the panel's report. The Senate voted 98 to 0 in favor of a nonbinding resolution endorsing the value of mammograms for women in their forties.

Some thought the panel's conclusions about the value of mammograms was reasonable but were dissatisfied with its recommendation. It was supposed to be an expert panel, but it said to women, you've got to decide for yourself. But how could women be expected to decide for themselves, if a group of experts couldn't decide?

While most of the responses to the panel's report were ones of angry disbelief, some praised the panel for its courage and candor. Some breast cancer activists pointed out that the idea of early detection of breast cancer had been oversold and most people were unaware of how often mammograms failed to reveal the presence of a tumor in women in their forties.

Also, despite the repeated message, early detection doesn't always save lives. Some cancers aren't deadly even if they aren't found, while others are still deadly even if they are. This was not a message the public wanted to hear about breast cancer. Instead, they wanted to hear the old, simplistic message that a mammogram would lead to early detection, which would save your life.

Others suggested that many radiologists, hospitals, breast centers, and equipment manufacturers had too much of a professional and financial stake in promoting mammograms to be happy with the panel's report. Mammography has become a big business and a profit center for institutions providing the service, so those with something to lose by reducing the number of mammograms might be expected to object.

A REVERSAL

In April 1997, Klausner called a press conference and announced that the NCI was retracting the panel's recommendation. Instead, the NCI recommended that women between 40 and 49 should have a mammogram every one to two years. Women with a family history of breast cancer would talk to their doctors and perhaps have the procedure sooner and more often.

President Bill Clinton immediately praised the new NCI policy and announced that future federal health care programs would pay for mammograms. He encouraged private insurers to follow the federal example.

Critics charged that the NCI was giving in to public opinion and heavy lobbying by members of Congress and women's advocacy groups. What should have been settled by scientific evidence was being resolved on political grounds. NCI officials claimed they had never planned for the panel's recommendation to be the final word on mammograms. "More evidence from clinical trials led us, about a year ago, to begin a process of reevaluating our recommendations," Klausner said.

Without a doubt, the change in the NCI position reflected the opinion of most women. Of those surveyed in a *New York Times*/CBS poll, 44 percent said they thought mammograms should start at age 40, and 40 percent thought they should begin even earlier.

DEBATE CONTINUES

In October 2001, *Lancet*, a leading British medical journal, published an article in which the authors claimed that a review of past studies showed that mammography had only a marginal benefit in saving lives. Moreover, the studies contained statistical flaws so significant as to make it doubtful it had any value at all in preventing breast-cancer deaths.

A couple of months later, in January 2002, a group of experts called the P.D.Q. Screening and Editorial Board, which is responsible for reviewing the information for the National Cancer Society database, expressed similar doubt. The P.D.Q. said that its review of seven large studies of mammography revealed that they had such serious statistical flaws as to cast doubt on the reliability of their conclusions.

While the debate continues, such health organizations as the American Cancer Society recommend that women continue to have regular mammograms for breast-cancer screening.

TREATMENT

Susan Arcadan was among the 25 percent of women in their forties whose breast cancer went undetected by mammography. After a biopsy, her disease was staged.

The clinical staging of breast cancer is the best predictor of the patient's chances of recovery. The stage of the cancer is determined by three variables: tumor size, number of lymph nodes involved, and whether the cancer has metastasized (spread) to other parts of the body. Using a classification scheme worked out by the American Joint Committee on Cancer, a patient's breast cancer is assigned a stage ranging from Stage I (carcinoma in situ) to Stage IV (an invasive tumor that has spread beyond the lymph nodes to distant sites).

Cells that are well differentiated are likely to grow slowly, while cells that are un-differentiated are more abnormal and faster growing. The presence of estrogen or progesterone receptors on the cancer cells are also indicators of how malignant a tumor is. The more receptors on the cells, the less malignant the tumor.

Susan Arcadan's cancer was classified as a Type III that was negative for estro-gen receptors. It had spread to seven lymph nodes but couldn't be detected at other sites. The cancer was aggressive, and Susan had a mastectomy, with the removal of affected lymph nodes. The surgery was followed by a course of chemotherapy, then radiation treatments.

A year after her breast cancer was diagnosed, Susan showed no sign of the dis-ease. She was in remission. Perhaps the cancer was gone forever, perhaps not. The question of whether to have mammograms during her forties was moot for her.

SOCIAL CONTEXT
The Prostate Cancer Epidemic

The prostate is a walnut-sized gland unique to men.

It contributes secretions that go to make up the seminal fluid discharged in ejac-ulation. It surrounds the upper part of the urethra and is located directly under the bladder and in front of the rectum.

The prostate reaches its normal size around age twenty, but it starts to grow again in most men around fifty. Called benign prostatic hyperplasia, the condition may require surgery, if the prostate begins to compress the urethra and makes uri-nation difficult or even impossible. While prostate cancer can also make the prostate increase in size, benign prostatic hyperplasia doesn't lead to cancer.

PROSTATE CANCER

The American Cancer Society estimates that about 182,000 men will be diagnosed with prostate cancer in the United States this year. This exceeds the 142,000 new cases of breast cancer, and excluding skin cancer, prostate cancer accounts for al-most a quarter of all cancer.

The number of deaths predicted from prostate cancer for the year is roughly 37,000; the number predicted for breast cancer is 44,000. The lifetime odds for a man being diagnosed with prostate cancer is 1 in 6, compared to the 1 in 8 risk of breast cancer in women. If it can be said there is an epidemic of breast cancer, then there is also an epidemic of prostate cancer.

Like breast cancer, the risk of prostate cancer increases with age. It most often develops in men in their sixties and seventies. As life expectancy has increased and men have escaped death from accidents, heart disease, and strokes, more are likely to develop prostate cancer and die from it. About 20 percent of American men will develop prostate cancer in their fifties, and the risk rises with age. Although deaths from breast and prostate cancer are similar, women with breast cancer tend to die at an earlier age. Thus, more years of life are lost to breast cancer than to prostate cancer.

The increase in diagnosed cases of prostate cancer is also due to a better diagnostic test. The traditional test was limited to a digital rectal examination (DRE), in which the physician uses a finger inserted into the rectum to palpate the prostate. If it felt abnormal, the next step was to have a biopsy.

The PSA (for prostate specific antigen) test was pioneered in the late 1980s and has now become a standard test for men of fifty or older. The test measures the blood level of a protein produced by prostate cells. Measured in nanograms of PSA per milliliter of blood, measurements usually rise gradually with age, because after fifty, the number of cells in the prostate increase. A sharp increase in the PSA measurement can indicate the presence of cancer, because it involves the rapid increase of cells.

The normal range for PSA is from 0 to 4 (some researchers put the upper limit at 3 or even 2.5), and a measurement of 4 or above is a cause for further diagnostic inquiry. This now involves an examination of the prostate by ultrasound and, most likely, a needle biopsy of all quadrants of the prostate.

A PSA level below 4 is an indicator that prostate cancer is not likely to be present, but it doesn't rule it out. The probability of cancer increases as the measurement rises to between 2 and 22. When the PSA is within the 4–10 range, the chance of prostate cancer is about 25 percent. When the measurement is over 10, cancer is very likely.

The PSA tests became relatively common in the late 1980s, and a study of Medicare recipients by the National Cancer Institute found that by 1994 half of American men over 65 had had at least one. The incidence of prostate cancer per 100,000 men was 190.4 in 1990, but it dropped to 139.1 in 1997. This may not reflect a genuine decrease, but only more precise diagnoses.

Since 1991, the death rate from prostate cancer has dropped 16 percent among white men. In black men, who have a higher incidence of prostate cancer, the death rate has dropped 11 percent since 1993.

No one can be sure to what extent this decrease can be attributed to early detection. A clinical trial was initiated in 1973 to follow 75,000 men with the aim of determining whether early diagnosis prolongs lives, but the trial will not be finished for years. Even those who were initially skeptics have come to regard the PSA test as a valuable tool, but whether their confidence can be given a scientific basis can only be determined when more data are available.

TREATMENTS

Treatments for prostate cancer are all hard on the patient, offer no certainty of success, and have results that can substantially affect the patient's quality of life.

PROSTATECTOMY   The prostate is surgically removed through an incision in the abdomen or behind the scrotum. This is major surgery, with a hospital stay of several days and a recovery time of months. If the cancer has not spread beyond the prostate, the surgery can be curative.

Because sphincter muscles may be cut or damaged, about 8 percent of patients are incontinent, and 20 to 50 percent will have only partial bladder control. Until recently impotence was virtually inevitable, but the development of a nerve-sparing surgical technique has reduced its incidence.

RADIATION THERAPY   Treatment can be performed on an outpatient basis, eliminating the need for a hospital stay and for coping with the trauma of surgery. But while radiation can shrink the tumor, it does not always kill all the cancer cells. After ten years, 75 to 80 percent of those treated show signs of recurrence. Impotence occurs in as many as half the patients.

RADIOACTIVE SEEDS   Instead of using an external source of radiation, dozens of tiny pellets of radioactive palladium or iodine are implanted in the prostate. The damage to healthy tissue produced by a beam of radiation going into the body is reduced, but incontinence is common for several weeks and is permanent in about 5 percent of those treated. Men under seventy have a 15 percent ratio of impotence, with a higher rate for older men. Short-term studies suggest the method has a lower rate of tumor recurrence, but the cure rate is not established.

CRYOTHERAPY   The destruction of prostate tissue by liquid nitrogen circulating through a transurethral probe may be most useful after a tumor returns. The tissue destruction usually includes nerves, producing impotence in 60 percent of the men treated, but incontinence is usually not a problem. An important limitation of the procedure is that cancer cells may escape destruction and grow again and spread.

HORMONE THERAPY   Testosterone stimulates the growth of prostate cancer cells, so treatment with another hormone that shuts it down may stop the cells from multiplying and even shrink the tumor. The treatment produces a loss of sex drive and is limited in its effects. Within a year or two, the cancer cells will start to multiply again.

Whatever treatment is chosen, about 35 percent of the men diagnosed with prostate cancer eventually will have a recurrence of cancer. At this point, options are limited and their outcomes not encouraging.

A DILEMMA

The availability of the PSA test, coupled with the lack of a benign and effective way of treating prostate cancer, often presents a dilemma to men and their physicians. The average prostate cancer takes a decade to produce symptoms. Someone advanced in years may choose "watchful waiting," instead of treatment. He will have regular PSA tests, DREs, and occasional biopsies to monitor the cancer. If it shows signs of becoming more aggressive, treatment can be instituted. The aim is for an elderly man to die *with* the cancer, not *from* it.

But what about men who might reasonably be expected to live for more than ten years? Should they choose watchful waiting? The answer is controversial. "Men with prostate cancer should have two goals," according to researcher William Catalona. "One should be to live longer if they can, and the second should be to avoid dying of prostate cancer. A quick heart attack is far preferable." Catalona advocates widespread PSA testing and aggressive intervention.

Unfortunately, PSA readings are insufficient to distinguish between aggressive and slow-growing tumors. A high reading may incline men, with the encouragement of their physicians, to choose treatments that are not needed and are themselves harmful. Thus, widespread PSA testing may lead to an increase in the number of cases treated unnecessarily.

"How many people is it okay to treat without benefit, and even with harm, in order to save one life?" asks urologist Gerald Chodak. Chodak presents his patients with relevant information about the PSA test, then allows them to make the decision as to whether to have it. He tells his patients, "If you want to see if you have cancer, then take the test. If you want to minimize your risk of undue harm, then don't take the test."

Part of the doubt about how men diagnosed with prostate cancer should be treated may be resolved eventually by the results of the Prostate Cancer Intervention Versus Observation Trial. PIVOT will monitor 2000 prostate cancer patients for fifteen years to determine if prostatectomies save enough lives to make surgery preferable to watchful waiting.

The causes of prostate cancer are unknown. Evidence suggests that diet plays a role. The disease is relatively rare in Japan, but incidence among second- and third-generation Japanese Americans is much higher. The incidence in Japan has also increased as many have switched to a more Western diet.

African Americans have a 37 percent higher risk of getting prostate cancer than Whites and are two to three times more likely to die of the disease. Why this is so is not known. Genetic factors may be at work, but perhaps not.

Unanswered questions about prostate cancer are more numerous than answered ones: Is there a gene or genes that predispose men to prostate cancer? How can the disease be prevented? How can its incidence be reduced? Does early detection save lives? What is the best of the available treatments? What treatment might be better than the ones we have? "Our knowledge of prostate cancer is woefully limited," says the head of the American Cancer Society.

FUNDING

If it were possible to find a cellular marker to distinguish between aggressive and slow-growing prostate tumors when they are detected early, this would help resolve the question of who should be treated and who kept under surveillance. But that knowledge is currently lacking. While a gene may have been identified for prostate cancer that runs in some families, none is known that predisposes men in general to the disease.

Only recently has prostate cancer received much attention from researchers. Prostate-cancer activists point out that the lack of research attention is almost certainly due to a lack of funding. In their view, prostate cancer has been unjustly ignored, considering the number of people it kills.

The number of deaths from prostate cancer each year is comparable to the number of deaths from AIDS and breast cancer, yet the funding for prostate cancer is much lower than for either of the other two diseases. The Federal government spends about $1.3 billion a year on AIDS research and about $313 million on breast cancer research. Yet it spends only $59 million on prostate cancer research.

Until quite recently, men didn't talk openly about prostate cancer. Having the disease was almost shameful, and most men suffered and died in silence. They didn't speak out and demand more research, and there was no prostate cancer lobby or political action group. As a result of silence, activists say, research into prostate cancer is only now moving ahead.

Like other kinds of research, it would move faster if only more research money were available. The drugs, chemotherapies, vaccines, and viruses designed to destroy cancer cells that might be effective against prostate cancer could be tested and developed with greater speed. As with breast cancer, people are dying for the lack of better treatments.

CHAPTER 5

Genetic Control

CLASSIC CASE PRESENTATION
Huntington's Disease: Genetic Testing and Ethical Dilemmas

Huntington's disease (HD) is a particularly cruel and frightening genetic disorder. It has no effective treatment and is invariably fatal. Furthermore, each child of an affected parent has a 50 percent chance of developing the disease.

The disease typically makes its appearance between the ages of thirty-five and forty-five in men and women who have shown no previous symptoms. The signs of its onset may be quite subtle—a certain clumsiness in performing small tasks, a slight slurring of speech, a few facial twitches. But the disease is progressive. Over time the small signs develop into massive physical and mental changes. Walking becomes jerky and unsteady, the face contorts into wild grimaces, the hands repeatedly clench and relax, and the whole body writhes with involuntary muscle spasms. The victim eventually loses the power of speech, becomes disoriented, and gives way to irrational emotional outbursts. Before mental deterioration becomes too advanced, HD victims often kill themselves out of sheer hopelessness and despair. Death may occur naturally from fifteen to twenty years after the beginning of the symptoms. Usually, it results from massive infection and malnutrition—as the disease progresses, the victim loses the ability to swallow normally.

In the United States, at any given time, some 30,000 people are diagnosed as having the disease, and as many as 150,000 more may have the gene responsible for it. The incidence of the disease is only 1 in 10,000, but for the child of someone with the disease, the chances of having it are 1 in 2.

GENE IDENTIFIED

The gene causing the disease was identified in 1993 after ten years of intensive research carried out in six laboratories in the United States, England, and Wales. Following the leads provided by genetic markers for the disease, the gene was finally located near the tip of chromosome 4. When researchers sequenced the nucleotides making up the gene, they discovered that the mutation was a trinucleotide repeat. In healthy individuals, the nucleotides CAG are repeated eleven to thirty-four times, whereas in individuals with HD, the repetitions typically range from thirty-seven to eighty-six. Some evidence suggests that higher numbers of repetitions are associated with earlier onset.

When the HD gene was identified, it was expected this would have almost immediate consequences for the development of an effective treatment. This has not turned out to be the case because the mechanism of the gene's action is not yet understood. Furthermore, the gene was expected to be found functioning only in the brain, but in fact radioactive tagging has shown that the gene operates in virtually every tissue of the body, including the colon, liver, pancreas, and testes. The protein the gene codes for is believed to be toxic to neuronal development, but the protein itself has not yet been isolated. (In 1998 it was discovered that the disease involves the formation of a protein plaque in brain cells that destroys them, but this hasn't yet led to a therapy.)

Before the HD gene was identified or a marker for it discovered, the disease was known to be transmitted from generation to generation in the sort of hereditary pattern indicating it is caused by a single gene. However, because the disease makes its appearance relatively late in life, an unsuspecting victim may already have passed on the gene to a child before showing any sign of the disease. In the absence of a genetic test to detect the gene, the individual could not know whether he or she was a carrier.

In 1983 a major step toward the development of such a test was announced by James F. Gusella and his group at Massachusetts General Hospital. The team did not locate the gene itself, but discovered a "genetic marker" indicating its presence. They began by studying the DNA taken from members of a large American family with a history of Huntington's disease, then employed recombinant-DNA techniques to attempt to locate DNA segments that might be associated with the HD gene.

The techniques involved using proteins known as restriction enzymes. A particular enzyme, when mixed with a single strand of DNA, cuts the strand at specific locations known as recognition sites. After the DNA strand has been cut up by restriction enzymes, short sections of radioactive, single-stranded DNA are added to serve as probes. The probes bind to particular segments of the DNA. Because the probes are radioactive, the segments to which they are attached can be identified on photographic film. The various fragments of DNA produced by the restriction enzymes and identified by probes form a pattern that is typical of individuals. Thus, if the pattern of someone who does not have the disease is compared with the pattern of a family member who does, the fragments that include the faulty gene can be identified, even when the gene itself is unknown. The pattern serves as a marker for the presence of the gene.

Gusella's group faced the problem of finding a marker consistently inherited by those with Huntington's disease but not by those free of the disease. This meant identifying perhaps as many as 800 markers and determining whether one could serve as the marker for the HD gene. Incredibly, the team identified a good candidate on its twelfth try. It was a marker found in all members of the family they were studying. Those with the disease had the same form of the marker, while those free of the disease had some other form.

Gusella and other researchers were supported in their work by the Hereditary Disease Foundation. The organization was founded by Milton Wexler after his wife was diagnosed with Huntington's. Wexler hoped a treatment for the disease could be found that might benefit his daughters, Nancy and Alice, who stood a 50 percent chance of developing the disease. Nancy Wexler soon became an active participant in research activities aimed at discovering a genetic marker.

In collaboration with the Hereditary Disease Foundation, plans were made to test Gusella's candidate marker in a large population. It was known that a large family with a high incidence of HD lived along the shores of Lake Maracaibo in Venezuela. Nancy Wexler led a team to this remote location to collect family history and to obtain blood and skin samples for analysis. The lake-dwelling family included some 100 people with the disease and 1100 children with the risk of developing it. Analysis of the samples showed that those with the disease also carried the same form of the marker as their American counterparts. Gusella estimated that the odds were 100 million to 1 that the marker was linked to the HD gene. Subsequent work by Susan Naylor indicated the marker was on chromosome 4. When the gene itself was identified in 1993, this turned out to be correct.

GENETIC TEST AVAILABLE

Once the location of the gene for Huntington's disease was known, a genetic test for its presence was quickly developed. The availability of the test, however, raises a number of serious ethical and social issues. The basic question people with a family history that puts them at risk for the disease must ask is whether they should have the test.

A study conducted in Wales revealed that more than half of those whose parents or relatives were victims of Huntington's disease would not want to have a test that would tell them whether they had the HD gene, even if such a test were available. Considering that the disease cannot be effectively treated and is invariably fatal, this is not a surprise finding.

Nancy Wexler confided to a reporter that she and her sister had assumed that once a test for determining whether they were carrying the HD gene was available, they would take it. However, when they met with their father to work out the details for a test based on a genetic marker, he suddenly said, "What are we doing here? Are we sure we want to do this?" The sisters, Nancy recalled, "had a visceral understanding that either one of us could get bad news and that it would certainly destroy my father."

But do those who are at risk have obligations to others? Because a test is available, is it fair to a potential marriage partner to marry without finding out whether one is a carrier of the HD gene and informing the potential partner of the result? Perhaps he or she may be willing to take the chance that the offspring of an HD parent will not have the disease. Even so, because of the tremendous burden the disease places on the other spouse, the possibility of being tested for the presence of the gene deserves serious consideration.

The decision about whether to have children can also be affected by the knowledge that one partner is a carrier of the HD gene so that there is a 50 percent chance that any child will also develop the disease. Should a potential carrier of the gene impose on the other partner the risk of having a child who will inherit the gene? Should such a risk be imposed on a potential child? The genetic test can determine whether an individual carries the gene. If he or she does, then the couple has knowledge of the relevant facts that will put them in a position to make a decision about having a child.

PRENATAL TEST

The test now in use can also be employed in conjunction with amniocentesis to determine whether a developing fetus carries the HD gene. Possessing such information may add a particular difficulty to making an abortion decision for some. A child born with the HD gene will inevitably develop the disease but may not do so for three, four, or even five or more decades. Is the fact that the child will eventually succumb to the disease reason enough to make an abortion morally obligatory? On the other hand, should the parents even have the fetus tested, if they are not prepared to have it aborted in the event of a positive test for the HD gene?

One disadvantage of the direct testing of the fetus for the presence of the HD gene is that if the fetus is found to have the gene, then the parent with the family history of the disease will know that she or he has the gene also. To avoid this consequence, a so-called nondisclosing prenatal test can be performed. The test employs a gene-probe method to determine how a segment of fetal chromosome 4 compares with segments from grandparents. If the segment resembles that of a healthy grandparent, the child is not likely to have the gene. If it matches that of the grandparent with the disease, there is a 50 percent chance that the child possesses the gene.

This is the same as the risk for a mother or father with one parent who developed the disease. Hence, the potential parent has learned nothing new about his or her own chances of having the gene, and it is this that makes the test nondisclosing. However, if the potential parents do not plan to abort the fetus should they learn that it has a 50 percent chance of possessing the HD gene, there is no reason to perform the test.

SOCIAL RISKS

The advent of a standard, inexpensive test for the HD gene raises various other moral and social issues. For example, insurance companies may refuse to provide life or health insurance to those from families with Huntington's disease, unless they prove that they are not carriers of the gene. Employers may refuse to provide health benefits to family members unless they are tested and found to lack the gene. Adoption agencies have requested that infants available for adoption be tested to assure potential adopting families that the children are not at risk for HD. As Nancy Wexler put the point, "In our culture, people assume that knowledge is always good. . . . But our experience with Huntington's has shown that some things may be better left unknown."

Informing someone that he or she carries the gene also has problems associated with it. Such news can be devastating, both to the person and to the person's family. About 10 to 12 percent of HD victims kill themselves, and 30 percent of those at risk say that this is what they will do if they learn they have the disease. Thus, the mere act of conveying the information that someone will later develop the signs of a fatal disease can itself constitute a threat to life. Nancy Wexler has refused to disclose publicly whether she has been tested for the HD gene. "I don't want to influence anyone's decision," she says.

In the best of worlds, an effective means of preventing the onset of Huntington's disease or treating it effectively would be available. Then the moral and social issues associated with a genetic test for it would disappear without having to be resolved. Regrettably, that world still lies in the future.

Briefing Session

The two great triumphs of nineteenth-century biology were Darwin's formulation of the theory of organic evolution and Mendel's statement of the laws of transmission genetics. One of the twentieth century's outstanding accomplishments was the development of an understanding of the molecular structures and processes involved in genetic inheritance. All three great achievements give rise to moral and social issues of considerable complexity. The theories are abstract, but the problems they generate are concrete and immediate.

Major problems are associated with our increased knowledge of inheritance and genetic change. One class of problems concerns the use we make of the knowledge we possess in dealing with individuals. We know a great deal about the ways genetic diseases are transmitted and the sorts of errors that can occur in human development. We have the means to make reliable predictions about the chances of the occurrence of a disease in a particular case, and we have the medical technology to detect some disorders before birth.

To what extent should we employ this knowledge? One possibility is that we might use it to detect, treat, or prevent genetic disorders. Thus, we might require that everyone submit to screening and counseling before having children. We might require that children be tested either prenatally or immediately after birth. We might recommend or require selective abortions. We might require or recommend for some couples in vitro fertilization, then the selection of embryos free of a disease-producing gene for implantation. Using some combination of these methods, we might be able to bring many genetic diseases under control (although we could never eliminate them) in the way we have brought contagious diseases under control.

Requiring screening and testing suggests another possibility, one that involves taking a broader view of human genetics. Eliminating genetic disease might simply become part of a much more ambitious plan for deliberately improving the entire species. Shall we attempt to control human evolution by formulating policies and practices designed to alter the genetic composition of the human population? Shall we make use of "gene surgery" and recombinant-DNA technology to shape physical and mental attributes of our species? That is, shall we practice some form of eugenics?

Another class of problems has to do with the wider social and environmental consequences of genetic research and technology. Research in molecular genetics concerned with recombinant DNA has already revealed to us ways in which the machinery of cells can be altered in beneficial ways. We are able to make bacteria synthesize such important biological products as human insulin, and we are able to alter bacteria to serve as vaccines against diseases. In effect, recombinant-DNA technology produces life forms that have never existed before. Should biotech industries be allowed to patent such forms in the way new inventions are patented? Or do even altered organisms belong to us all?

Also, what are we to say about the deliberate release of genetically modified organisms into the environment? Is the threat that such organisms pose greater than the benefits they are likely to produce? We have already witnessed the great damage that can be done by pesticides and chemical pollution. Is there any way we can avoid the potential damage that might be caused by genetically engineered organisms?

In the following three sections, we shall focus attention on the issues raised by the actual and potential use of genetic information. Our topics are these: genetic intervention (screening, counseling, and prenatal diagnosis), eugenics, and genetic research (therapy, technology, and biohazards).

GENETIC INTERVENTION: SCREENING, COUNSELING, AND DIAGNOSIS

Our genes play a major role in making us what we are. Biological programs of genetic information work amazingly well to produce normal, healthy individuals. But sometimes things go wrong, and when they do, the results can be tragic.

Almost 5000 human diseases have been identified as involving genetic factors. Some of the diseases are quite rare, whereas others are relatively common. Some are invariably fatal, whereas others are comparatively minor. Some respond well to treatment, whereas others do not.

The use of genetic information in predicting and diagnosing diseases has significantly increased during the last few decades. New scientific information, new medical techniques, and new social programs have all contributed to this increase.

Three approaches in particular have been adopted by the medical community as means of acquiring and employing genetic information related to diseases: genetic screening, genetic counseling, and prenatal genetic diagnosis. Each approach has been the source of significant ethical and social issues, but before examining the approaches and the problems associated with them, we need to consider the idea of a genetic disease.

GENETIC DISEASE

The concept of a "genetic" disease is far from being clear. Roughly speaking, a genetic disease is one in which genes or the ways in which they are expressed are causally responsible for particular biochemical, cellular, or physiological defects. Rather than rely upon such a general definition, it's more useful for understanding genetic diagnosis to consider some of the ways genes may play a role in producing diseases.

Gene Defects
The program of information coded into DNA (the genetic material) may in some way be abnormal because of the occurrence of a mutation at some time or other.

(That is, a particular gene may have been lost or damaged, or a new gene added.) Consequently, when the DNA code is "read" and its instructions followed, the child that develops will have impairments.

For example, a number of diseases, like phenylketonuria (PKU), are the result of "inborn errors of metabolism." (For an explanation of PKU, see *Genetic Screening* later in the Briefing Session.) The diseases are produced by the lack of a particular enzyme necessary for ordinary metabolic functioning. The genetic coding required for the production of the enzyme is simply not present—the gene for the enzyme is missing.

A missing or defective gene may be due to a new mutation, but more often the condition has been inherited. It has been transmitted to the offspring through the genetic material contributed by the parents. Because defective genes can be passed on in this way, the diseases they produce are themselves described as heritable. (Thus, PKU is a genetically transmissible disease.) The diseases follow regular patterns through generations, and tracing out those patterns has been one of the great accomplishments of modern biology and medicine.

Developmental Defects

The biological development of a human being from a fertilized egg to a newborn child is an immensely complicated process. It involves an interplay between both genetic and environmental factors, and the possibility of errors occurring is quite real.

Mistakes that result as part of the developmental process are ordinarily called "congenital." Such defects are not in the original coding (genes) but result either from genetic damage or from the reading of the code. When either happens, the manufacture and assembly of materials required for normal fetal development are affected.

Radiation, drugs, chemicals, and nutritional deficiencies can all cause changes in an otherwise normal process. Also, biological disease agents, such as certain viruses, may intervene in development. They may alter the machinery of the cells, interfere with the formation of tissues, and defeat the carefully programmed processes that lead to a normal child.

Finally, factors internal to fetal development may also alter the process and lead to defects. The most common form of Down syndrome, for example, is caused by a failure of chromosomes to separate normally. The outcome is a child who has failed to develop properly and displays physical anomalies and some degree of mental retardation.

Defects occurring during the developmental process are not themselves the results of inheritance. Consequently, they cannot be passed on to the next generation.

Genetic Carriers

Some diseases are produced only when an individual inherits two copies of a gene (two alleles) for the disease from the parents. Parents who possess only one copy of the gene generally show none of the disease's symptoms. However, sometimes a parent may have symptoms of the same kind as are associated with the disease, although much less severe.

In the metabolic disease PKU, for example, individuals who have inherited only one allele (that is, who are heterozygous, rather than homozygous) may show a greater-than-normal level of phenylalanine in their blood. Such people are somewhat deficient in the enzyme required to metabolize this substance, but the level of the substance may not be high enough to cause them any damage. Even so, they are carriers of a gene that, when passed on with another copy of the same gene from the other parent, can cause the disease PKU in their offspring. (As we will see later, this is also true for carriers of sickle-cell trait.) The individual who receives both alleles for PKU obviously has the disease, but what about the parents? The point at which a condition becomes a disease is often uncertain.

Genetic Predisposition

It's been suggested that every disease involves a genetic component in some way or other. Even when people are exposed to the same new virus their bodies react differently; some may destroy the virus, while others may become infected. Genetic variations may play a role in these differences. For example, while AIDS researchers noted in the 1980s that some who had been HIV positive for years hadn't developed AIDS, it wasn't until a mutation in the gene called CCR5 was identified that a potential explanation was found. The mutation is present in 10 to 15 percent of Whites and appears to be absent in Blacks and Asians.

In some cases genes play a larger role in producing disease than in others. We have good evidence that hypertension, heart disease, various forms of cancer, and differential responses to environmental agents (such as sunlight, molds, or chemical pollutants) run in families, and the genetic makeup of particular individuals may predispose them to specific diseases.

For example, women who carry the BRCA1 gene are more likely to develop breast cancer at an early age than others in the population. Of course not every woman who carries the gene develops breast cancer. What distinguishes the two groups? Their diet? Possessing other genes? No one knows, and what's true for familial breast cancer is also known to hold for dozens of other diseases.

Even granted the role of genes in producing diseases, it's important to keep in mind that predispositions are not themselves diseases. At best they can be regarded only as causal conditions that, in conjunction with other conditions (likely to be unknown), can produce disease.

The action of genes in disease processes are even more complicated than described here. Nevertheless, our general categories are adequate to allow us to talk about the use made of information in genetic diagnosis.

GENETIC SCREENING

In 1962 Dr. Robert Guthrie of the State University of New York developed an automated procedure for testing the blood of newborn children for the disease PKU. Although a diagnostic test for PKU had been available since 1934, it was time consuming and labor intensive. The Guthrie test made it practical to diagnose a large number of infants at a relatively low price.

PKU is a serious metabolic disorder. Infants affected are deficient in the enzyme phenylalanine hydroxylase. Because the enzyme is necessary to convert the amino acid phenylalanine into tyrosine as part of the normal metabolic process, a deficiency of the enzyme leads to a high concentration of phenylalanine in the infant's blood. The almost invariable result is severe mental retardation.

If the high level of phenylalanine in an infant's blood is detected very early, the infant can be put on a diet low in that amino acid. Keeping children on the diet until they are around the age of six significantly reduces the severity of the retardation that is otherwise inescapable.

The availability of the Guthrie test and the prospects of saving newborn children from irreparable damage encouraged state legislatures to pass mandatory screening laws. Massachusetts passed the first such law in 1963, and by 1967 similar legislation had been adopted by forty-one states.

The term *genetic screening* is sometimes used to refer to any activity having to do with locating or advising people with genetically connected diseases. We will restrict the term's application here and use it to refer only to public health programs that survey or test target populations with the aim of detecting individuals at risk of disease for genetic reasons.

The Massachusetts PKU law pointed the way for the development of public screening programs. PKU was the first disease tested for, but before long others were added to the list. A number of public health programs now screen particular populations for such conditions as sickle-cell anemia, sickle-cell trait, metabolic disorders, hypothyroidism, and chromosome anomalies. Technological developments make it possible to use a single drop of blood to test for some forty disease conditions in one analysis. New York state developed plans in 2002 to test newborns for all forty.

Although genetic screening is relatively new as a social program, the concept is historically connected with public health measures for the detection and prevention of communicable diseases like tuberculosis and syphilis. (HIV has been added to the list by states and the federal Centers for Disease Control.) If an individual with such a disease is identified, he can receive treatment, but most important, he can be prevented from spreading the disease to other members of the population.

Similarly, it is possible to think of diseases with a genetic basis as resembling contagious diseases. Individuals are affected, and they can pass on the disease. With genetic diseases the potential spread is not horizontal through the population, however, but vertical through the generations.

In terms of this model, public health measures similar to the ones that continue to be effective in the control of contagious diseases might be used to help bring genetic diseases under control. When screening locates an individual with a genetic disorder, then steps can be taken to ensure she receives appropriate therapy. Furthermore, when carriers of genes that produce diseases are identified, they can be warned about their chances of having children that are genetically impaired. Thus, a limited amount of control over the spread of genetic disease can be exercised, and the suffering of at least some individuals can be reduced or eliminated. Public

---

Screening Newborns

PKU Metabolic disorder causing seizures and retardation; 1 in 12,000 newborns.
MCAD Enzyme needed to convert fat to energy is missing; causes seizures, respiratory failure, cardiac arrest, and death; 1 in 15,000 newborns.
Congenital hypothyroidism Deficiency of thyroid hormone retards growth and brain development; 1 in 4000 newborns.
Congenital adrenal hyperplasia Defects in the synthesis of the adrenal hormones; can alter sexual development and in severe cases of metabolic disturbance result in death; 1 in 5000 newborns.
Biotinidase deficiency Results in failure to synthesize biotin (a B vitamin), causing seizures, uncontrolled movements, deafness, and mental retardation; 1 in 70,000 births.
Maple-syrup urine disease (branched-chain ketoaciduria) In-born metabolic error causing mental retardation and death; 1 in 250,000 births.
Galactosemia Missing enzyme needed to convert galactose sugar into glucose, causing mental retardation, blindness, and death; 1 in 50,000 births.
Homocystinuria Missing enzyme needed to produce chemical necessary for normal brain development, causing mental retardation, blindness, bone abnormalities, and stroke; 1 in 275,000 births.
Sickle-cell disease Disorder of the red blood cells, causing damage to vital organs resulting in heart attack and stroke, pain, ulceration, and infection; 1 in 400 births among blacks (including African Americans), 1 in 1000–30,000 among Hispanics.

Source: March of Dimes Foundation to Prevent Birth Defects, 2002.

---

health experts estimate about 3000 babies a year are identified as having diseases in which early intervention can save their lives or prevent serious disabilities.

The justification of laws mandating screening programs can be sought in the power and responsibility of government to see to the welfare of its citizens. Here again, the public health measures employed to control contagion might be looked to as a model. We do not permit the parents of a child to decide on their own whether the child should be vaccinated against smallpox. We believe that society, operating through its government, has a duty to protect the child. Similarly, some argue that society owes it to the child with PKU to see to it that the condition is discovered as quickly as possible so treatment can be instituted.

Critics of screening programs haven't been convinced that the contagious-disease model is appropriate in dealing with genetic diseases. Because the way in which genetic diseases are spread is so different, only a very small part of the population can be said to suffer any risk at all. By contrast, an epidemic of smallpox may threaten millions of people. Furthermore, some genetic screening programs don't have follow-up or counseling services attached to them, so often nothing is done that benefits the participants. By being told they are the carriers of a genetic disease, people may be more harmed than helped by the programs.

In general, whether the benefits of screening programs are sufficient to outweigh the liabilities remains a serious question. In particular, are screening programs so worthwhile that they justify the denial of individual choice entailed by required participation? What if parents don't want to know whether their child has the genes responsible for a particular disease? Is it legitimate for a state, in the interest of protecting the child, to require parents to find this out, whether or not they want to know?

These issues and others related to them are easier to appreciate when considered in the context of particular kinds of screening programs. We'll discuss briefly two programs that have been both important and controversial.

PKU Screening

Screening for PKU was not only the first mass testing program to be mandated by state laws, it's generally agreed it has also been the most successful program.

PKU is a relatively rare disease. It accounts for only about 0.8 percent of mentally retarded people who are institutionalized, and among the infants screened during a year in a state like Massachusetts, only three or four cases of PKU may be discovered. (The incidence is 5.4 per 100,000 infants.) Given this relatively low incidence of the disease, critics have argued that the abrogation of the freedom of choice required by a mandatory program doesn't make the results worthwhile.

This is particularly true, they suggest, because of the difficulties with the testing procedure itself. The level of phenylalanine in the blood may fluctuate so that not all infants with a higher-than-normal level at the time of the test actually have PKU. If they are put on the restricted diet, then they may suffer consequences from the diet that are harmful to their health. Thus, in attempting to protect the health of some infants, a mandatory program may unintentionally injure the health of other infants.

Tests more refined than the Guthrie one are possible. However, their use increases considerably the cost of the screening program, even if they are employed only when the Guthrie test is positive for PKU. From the statistical standpoint of public health, then, the financial cost of preventing a few cases of PKU may be much greater than allowing the cases to remain undetected and untreated.

Furthermore, there are additional hidden social costs. Female infants successfully treated for PKU may grow into adults and have children of their own. Their children run a very high risk of being born with brain damage. The reason for this is not genetic but developmental. The uterine environment of PKU mothers is one high in phenylalanine, and in high concentrations it causes damage to the infant. Thus, one generation may be saved from mental retardation by screening only to cause mental retardation in the next.

Sickle-Cell

Sickle-cell disease is a group of genetic disorders involving the hemoglobin in red blood cells. Because of faulty hemoglobin, the cells assume a characteristic sickle shape and do not transport oxygen as well as normal red cells. They are also fragile and break apart more frequently. The result is anemia and, often, the blocking of blood vessels by fragments of ruptured cells. The pain can be excruciating, and infections in tissues that have broken down because of oxygen deprivation can be life threatening. Stroke and heart disease often cause death in the early thirties.

The disease occurs only in those who have inherited both alleles for the disease from their parents. (That is, the gene for the disease is recessive, and those who are homozygous for the gene are the ones who develop the disease.) Those with only one allele for the disease (that is, are heterozygous) are said to have sickle-cell trait. Sickle-cell disease may develop at infancy, or it may manifest itself later in life in painful and debilitating symptoms. Those with sickle-cell trait rarely show any of the more serious clinical symptoms.

In the United States, the disease is most common among African Americans, but it is also found among those of Mediterranean, Caribbean, and Central and South American ancestry. The trait is carried by about 7 to 9 percent of African Americans (about 3 million people), and the disease occurs in about 0.3 percent of the population. Many people with the disease are not severely affected and can live relatively normal lives. However, the disease may also be fatal, and at present there is no cure for it. It can be diagnosed prenatally, however.

In 1970 a relatively inexpensive and accurate test for sickle-cell hemoglobin was developed, making it possible to identify the carriers of sickle-cell trait. This technological development combined with political pressures generated by rising consciousness among African Americans led to the passage of various state laws mandating sickle-cell screening. During 1971 and 1972, twelve states enacted sickle-cell legislation.

The results were socially disastrous. Some laws required African Americans who applied for a marriage license to undergo screening. Because the only way to reduce the incidence of the disease was for two carriers to avoid having children (now embryos may be screened before implantation), many African Americans charged that the mandatory screening laws were a manifestation of a plan for genocide.

Medical reports that carriers of sickle-cell trait sometimes suffer from the pain and disability of sickling crises served as a new basis of discrimination. Some employers and insurance companies began to require tests of African American employees, and as a result some job possibilities were closed off to people with sickle-cell trait.

In 1972, Congress passed the National Sickle-Cell Anemia Control Act. In order to qualify for federal grants under the act, states were required to make sickle-cell screening voluntary, provide genetic counseling, and take steps to protect the confidentiality of participants. The most significant impact of the act was to force states to modify their laws to bring them into conformity with the act's requirements. In response, thirty-four states with sickle-cell screening laws now require universal screening.

The National Genetic Diseases Act, passed in 1976 and funded annually since then, provides testing and counseling for the diagnosis and treatment of a number of genetic diseases. The act further strengthens the commitment to voluntary participation and to guarantees of confidentiality.

The lesson learned from the public controversy over the first sickle-cell screening programs is that genetic information can be used in ways that are harmful to the interests of individuals. Furthermore, the information can be used as a basis for systematic discrimination.

In April 1993, an expert panel assembled by the Agency for Health Care and Policy (a part of the Public Health Service) recommended that all newborns, regardless of race, be screened for sickle-cell. In making its recommendations, the panel stressed that sickle-cell is not uniquely a disease of African Americans or blacks and that the general belief that it is can result in failing to see to it that people of non-African origin receive appropriate treatment.

Furthermore, the panel claimed, targeted screening of high-risk groups is not adequate to identify all infants with sickle-cell disease because it is not always possible to know an individual's racial heritage. Targeted screening, according to one study, may miss as many as 20 percent of cases.

What the panel did not point out was that one advantage of universal screening is that it permits individuals needing treatment to be identified without stigmatizing them just by requiring screening. However, whether having the disease or the trait becomes a social stigma is not a matter that can be resolved by an expert panel. It's something that must be dealt with by law, social policy, and public education.

GENETIC COUNSELING

Much is known about the ways in which a number of genetic diseases are inherited. Those like PKU, sickle-cell, and Tay–Sachs follow the laws of Mendelian genetics. Accordingly, given the appropriate information, it is often possible to determine how likely it is that a particular couple will have a child with a certain disease.

Suppose, for example, an African-American couple is concerned about the possibility of having a child with sickle-cell disease. They will be tested to discover whether either or both of them are carriers of sickle-cell trait.

Sickle-cell disease occurs only when two recessive alleles are both present—one inherited from the mother, one from the father. If only one of the parents is a carrier of the trait (is heterozygous), no child will have the disease. If both parents are carriers of the trait, the chances are one out of four that their child will have the disease. (This is determined simply by considering which combinations of the two genes belonging to each parent will produce a combination that is a homozygous recessive. The combination of Ss and Ss will produce ss in only 25 percent of the possible cases.)

Such information can be used to explain to potential parents the risks they might run in having children. But, as the case of sickle-cell disease illustrates, it is often very difficult for individuals to know what to do with such information.

Is a 25 percent risk of having a child with sickle-cell disease sufficiently high that a couple ought to decide to have no children at all? If the couple is opposed to abortion, the question becomes especially crucial. Answering it is made more difficult by the fact that sickle-cell disease varies greatly in severity. A child with the disease may be virtually normal, or doomed to a short life filled with suffering. No one can say in advance of its birth which possibility is more likely.

If a couple isn't opposed to abortion, is a 25 percent risk high enough to warrant a prenatal test? Or perhaps they should avoid the question of abortion by relying on artificial insemination so the embryos could be screened before one is implanted. This would be expensive and probably not covered by insurance.

It is generally agreed that the question of whether or not to have a child when a serious risk is involved is a decision that must be made by the couple. The counselor may provide information about the risk, and—just as important—the counselor may provide information about medical therapies that are available for a child born with a hereditary disease.

In diseases in which prenatal diagnosis is possible, the option of abortion may be open to potential parents. Here, too, the object of counseling is to see to it that the couple is educated in ways relevant to their needs.

PRENATAL GENETIC DIAGNOSIS

A variety of new technological developments now make it possible to secure a great amount of information about the developing fetus while it is still in the uterus. Ultrasound, radiography, and fiber optics allow examination of soft-tissue and skeletal development. Anatomical abnormalities can be detected early enough to permit an abortion to be safely performed, if that is the decision of the woman carrying the fetus.

Amniocentesis and CVS

Yet the most common methods of prenatal diagnosis are amniocentesis and chorionic villus sampling (CVS), which involve direct cell studies. In amniocentesis, the amnion (the membrane surrounding the fetus) is punctured with a needle and some of the amniotic fluid is removed for study. The procedure cannot be usefully and safely performed until fourteen to sixteen weeks into the pregnancy. Until that time, there is an inadequate amount of fluid. The risk to the woman and to the fetus from the procedure is relatively small, usually less than 1 percent. (The risk that the procedure will result in a miscarriage is about 1 in 200.) A recent study shows that if amniocentesis is performed eleven to twelve weeks after conception, there is an increase in foot deformity from 0.1 percent to 1.3 percent in the child.

Chorionic villus sampling involves retrieving hairlike villi cells from the developing placenta. The advantage of the test is that it can be employed six to ten weeks after conception. Although the procedure is as safe as amniocentesis, a 1994 study by the Centers for Disease Control found that infants whose mothers had undergone CVS from 1988 to 1992 had a 0.03 percent risk of missing or undeveloped fingers or toes. The normal risk is 0.05 percent. A later study questioned this finding and found reason to believe that the risk of fetal damage is greater than normal.

Amniocentesis came into wide use only in the early 1960s. At first, it was mostly restricted to testing fetuses in cases in which there was a risk of Rh incompatibility. When the mother lacks a group of blood proteins called the Rh (or Rhesus) factor, and the fetus has it, the immune system of the mother may produce antibodies against the fetus. The result for the fetus may be anemia, brain damage, and even death.

It was soon realized that additional information about the fetus could be gained from further analysis of the amniotic fluid and the fetal cells in it. The fluid can be chemically assayed, and the cells can be grown in cultures for study. An examination of the DNA can show whether there are any known abnormalities that are likely to cause serious physical or mental defects. Some metabolic disorders (such as Tay–Sachs disease) can be detected by chemical analysis of the amniotic fluid. However, some of the more common ones, such as PKU and Huntington's or muscular dystrophy, require an analysis of the genetic material. Because only males have a Y chromosome, it's impossible to examine fetal cells without also discovering the gender of the fetus.

Amniocentesis and CVS do have some hazards attached to them. Accordingly, it is not at all regarded as a routine procedure to be performed in every pregnancy. There must be some indication that the fetus is at risk from a genetic or developmental disorder. One indication is the age of the mother. Down syndrome is much more likely to occur in fetuses conceived in women over the age of thirty-five. Because the syndrome is produced by a chromosome abnormality, an examination of the chromosomes in the cells of the fetus can reveal the defect.

A relatively new test for Down syndrome employs a blood sample taken from the pregnant woman. The sample is examined for the presence of three fetal proteins. About sixteen to eighteen weeks after gestation, fetuses with the syndrome are known to produce abnormally small quantities of estriol and alpha fetoprotein and abnormally large amounts of chorionic gonadotropin. The levels of the proteins, plus such factors as the woman's age, can be used to determine the statistical probability of a child with the syndrome.

Genetic screening can also provide an indication of a need to perform amniocentesis. For example, Tay–Sachs disease is a metabolic disorder that occurs ten times as often among Jews originating in central and eastern Europe (the Ashkenazi) as in the general population. (The disease is invariably fatal and follows a sad course. An apparently normal child progressively develops blindness and brain damage, then dies at an early age.) Carriers of the Tay–Sachs gene can be identified by a blood test, and couples who are both carriers of the trait run a 25 percent risk of having a child with the disease. In such a case, there would be a good reason to perform amniocentesis.

When Is a Test Justified?

Our ability to test for the presence of certain genes gives rise to some cases some people find particularly troubling. Suppose, for example, a woman with a family history of breast and ovarian cancer wants to know whether the fetus she is carrying has the BRCA1 gene. If the gene is present, she wants to have an abortion, then get pregnant again.

Chances are good that no clinic or testing center would agree to test the fetus for the BRCA1 gene. After all, its presence only increases the probability that a woman will develop breast and ovarian cancer. Unlike, say, the gene for Huntington's disease, the BRCA1 gene doesn't inevitably produce the disease. Hence, a testing center is likely to reject the woman's request, on the grounds that it's unwilling to support anyone's attempt to get a "perfect baby."

Yet the woman, not the center, is the one who has responsibility for her child. Hence, if she wants to have a child that, so far as can be determined by the tests available, is free from the threat of disease, shouldn't she be allowed to seek that aim? What's wrong about trying to have a baby lacking the gene predisposing her to two forms of cancer?

Another controversy has developed as pregnant women younger than thirty-five with no particular risk factors in their background have increasingly sought prenatal screening. The women argue that even though their risk of having a child with a detectable genetic abnormality is small, the financial and emotional consequences of raising an impaired child are so serious that they should be allowed to take advantage of the technology available to minimize even the slight risk.

Opponents of this view point out that the risk of a miscarriage from a diagnostic procedure is around 1 in 200 while the risk of a woman below the age of forty having an impaired child is about 1 in 192. Hence, the chance of losing a normal child to miscarriage is almost as great as the chance of having an impaired child. Further, amniocentesis costs from $1000 to $2500 to perform, and the money spent on such unnecessary screening procedures contributes to the general rise in health-care costs.

Such replies aren't convincing to those advocating wider access to prenatal testing. Some see the issue as one of the right of a woman to make choices affecting her body and her life. For some, the distress caused by a miscarriage is much less than that they would experience by having to raise an impaired child, but in any case, women should be the ones to decide what risks and burdens they are willing to bear. Such decisions should not be made unilaterally by physicians, hospitals, and health-policy planners.

Advocates of access to prenatal testing argue that, as far as increasing the cost of health care is concerned, when the costs of raising an impaired child are considered, the money spent on testing is insignificant. It costs about $100,000 to support a Down syndrome child during just the first year of life, and expenditures in the millions may be required to meet the needs of a severely impaired person over a lifetime. In addition, the potential emotional burden of the parents and other family members must be taken into account, even though they can't be assigned a dollar cost.

Some women want the added feeling of control prenatal screening can provide. The test can give them information that will put them in a position to make a decision about abortion, depending on the test results, or will provide them the peace of mind that comes from knowing their pregnancy is proceeding with only a small likelihood that the developing child will suffer a serious impairment. The general attitude is that the technology to secure relevant information exists, and it should be available to anyone who wants to make use of it. It certainly shouldn't be under the complete control of physicians.

Selective Abortion

In most cases in which prenatal diagnosis indicates that the fetus suffers from a genetic disorder or developmental defect, the only means of avoiding the birth of an impaired child is abortion. Because those who go through the tests required to determine the condition of the fetus are concerned with having a child, abortion performed under such circumstances is called *selective*. That is, the woman decides to have an abortion to avoid producing a child with birth impairments, not just to avoid having a child.

Those who oppose abortion in principle (see Chapter 9) also oppose selective abortion. In the view of some, the fact that a child will be born impaired is in no way a justification for terminating the life of the fetus.

Those prepared to endorse abortion at all typically approve of selective abortion as an acceptable way of avoiding suffering. In their view, it's better that the potential person—the fetus—not become an actual person, full of pain, disease, and disability.

The painful decision between having an abortion or giving birth to an impaired child may be avoided by employing ova, sperm, or embryo screening. This means, however, using the techniques developed in assisted reproduction (see Chapter 6), and the costs in time, frustration, and money can be considerable.

In the last few years, another way to avoid abortion has opened up as the techniques of fetal surgery have been employed to correct at least some abnormal physical conditions. Repairs to the heart, the insertion of shunts to drain off excess brain fluids, and the placement of tubes to inflate collapsed lungs are some of the intrauterine surgical procedures now being performed. Some surgeons believe it may be possible to expose the fetus within the uterus, perform surgery, then close up the amnion again. This would make possible more extensive surgery for a greater variety of conditions.

The present hope is that as new surgical techniques for the treatment of fetuses are perfected and extended, the need to rely on abortion to avoid the birth of impaired children will significantly decline. Of course, surgery cannot, even in principle, provide a remedy for a large number of hereditary disorders. It can do nothing for a child with Tay-Sachs, sickle cell, cystic fibrosis, muscular dystrophy, or PKU.

Helplessness in this regard is balanced by the hope that in future years pharmaceutical and biochemical therapies will be available to employ in cases involving missing enzymes; or perhaps gene therapy will make it possible to insert the proper gene for manufacturing a needed biochemical into the DNA of the cells of a fetus.

Embryo Selection
Potential parents who learn they are carriers of genes responsible for lethal or life-threatening diseases may decide to use the techniques of assisted reproduction to avoid having a child affected with the disease. Their embryos, produced by in vitro fertilization, can be genetically screened, then only those free of the disease-causing genes transferred to the woman's uterus. (See Chapter 6 for a fuller discussion.)

Embryo screening allows couples to avoid the risk their genetic heritage poses for their offspring. Those carrying the Tay–Sachs gene or the gene responsible for cystic fibrosis, for example, can be sure they don't have children with these diseases. It also makes selective abortion unnecessary. (However, some consider destroying embryos, for whatever reason, the moral equivalent of abortion.)

The painful present reality is that for most children born with genetic diseases or defects little can be done. Embryo selection and selective abortion are the primary means of avoiding the birth of a child known to be genetically impaired, and only abortion offers the possibility of avoiding the birth of a child discovered to be developmentally impaired.

ETHICAL DIFFICULTIES WITH GENETIC INTERVENTION

Genetic screening, counseling, prenatal diagnosis, and embryo selection present bright possibilities for those who believe in the importance of exercising control through rational planning and decision making. They see the prospect of avoiding the birth of children with crippling impairments as one of the triumphs of contemporary medicine.

Furthermore, the additional prospect of wholly eliminating some genetic diseases by counseling and reproductive control holds the promise of an even better future. For example, if people who are carriers of diseases caused by a dominant gene (such as Huntington's) produced no children with the disease, the disease would soon disappear entirely. The gene causing the disease would simply not be passed on to the next generation.

A vision of a world without the misery caused by genetic defects is a motivating factor among those who are strong advocates of programs of genetic intervention. (See the section on eugenics later in this Briefing Session.) The vision must have its appeal to all who are moved by compassion in the face of suffering. Yet whether or not one shares this vision and is prepared to use it as a basis for social action, serious ethical questions about genetic intervention must be faced.

We've already mentioned some of the issues in connection with particular programs and procedures. We can now add some more general questions to that list. The moral and social issues connected with genetic intervention are woven into a complicated fabric of personal and social considerations, and we can merely sketch the main outline of the pattern.

1. *Is there a right to have children who are likely to be impaired?* Suppose a woman is informed, after an alphafetoprotein (AFP) test and amniocentesis, that the child she's carrying will be born with a neural tube defect. Does she have the right to refuse an abortion and have the child anyway?

Those opposed to all abortion on the grounds of natural law would favor the woman's having the child. By contrast, a utilitarian might argue that the decision would be wrong. The amount of suffering the potential child might be expected to undergo outweighs any parental loss. For different reasons, a Kantian might endorse this same point of view. Even if we assume the fetus is a person, a Kantian might argue that we are obliged to prevent its suffering.

Suppose we decide a woman does have a right to have a child that is almost certain to be impaired. If so, then is society obligated to bear the expense of caring for the child? On the natural law view, the answer is almost certainly yes.

The child, impaired or not, is a human person and, as such, is entitled to the support and protection of society. If we agree that the impaired child is a person, he or she is also a disadvantaged person. Thus, an argument based on Rawls's principles of justice would support the view that the child is entitled to social support.

2. *Is society justified in requiring that people submit to genetic screening, counseling, or prenatal diagnosis?* Children born with genetic diseases and defects require the expenditure of large amounts of public funds. Mandatory diagnosis need not be coupled with mandatory abortion or abstention from bearing children. (A related question is whether society ought to make available genetic testing to all who wish it, regardless of their ability to pay.)

On utilitarian grounds, it might be argued that society has a legitimate interest in seeing to it that, no matter what people ultimately decide, they should at least have the information about the likelihood that they will produce an impaired child.

If this view is adopted, then a number of specific medically related questions become relevant. For example, who should be screened? It's impractical and unnecessary to screen everyone. Why should we screen schoolchildren or prisoners, those who are sterile, or those past the age of childbearing?

This is closely connected with a second question: What should people be screened for? Should everyone be screened for Tay–Sachs disease, even though it's the Jewish population that is most at risk? Should everyone be screened for the cystic-fibrosis gene, even though the disease occurs primarily among Whites?

Those who accept the contagious-disease model of genetic screening frequently defend it on the utilitarian grounds that screening promotes the general social welfare. However, one might argue that screening can also be justified on deontological grounds. It could be claimed that we owe it to developing fetuses, regarded as persons, to see to it they receive the opportunity for the most effective treatment. For example, it might be said that we have an obligation to provide a PKU child with the immediate therapy required to save him or her from severe mental retardation. The restriction of the autonomy of individuals by requiring screening might be regarded as justified by this obligation. If screening is voluntary, the welfare of the child is made to depend on ignorance and accidental opportunity.

3. *Do physicians have an obligation to inform their patients who are prospective parents about the kinds of genetic tests that are available?* A study of one population of women screened for Tay–Sachs disease showed that none had sought testing on the recommendation of her physician.

If the autonomy of the individual is to be preserved, then it seems clear it is the duty of a physician to inform patients about genetic testing. A physician who disapproves of abortion might be reluctant to inform patients about tests that might encourage them to seek an abortion or embryo screening. Nevertheless, to the extent that abortion is a moral decision, it is a decision properly made by the individual, not by someone acting paternalistically in her behalf.

The duty of a physician to inform patients about the possibility of genetic tests seems quite straightforward. Yet the issue becomes more complicated in light of the next question about truth telling.

4. *Do patients have a right to be informed of all of the results of a genetic test?* Ethical theories based on respect for the autonomy of the individual (such as Kant's and Ross's) suggest that patients are entitled to know what has been learned from the tests.

But what if the test reveals that the fetus carries the gene for a minor genetically transmissible disease or for increased susceptibility to a serious disease? Should the physician risk the patient's deciding to have an abortion merely because she is committed to the ideal of a "perfect" baby? Or is such a decision one for the physician to make?

Furthermore, what about the matter of sex determination? Screening tests can also reveal the gender of the fetus. Are prospective parents entitled to know this information? When an abortion is elective, it's possible for the woman to decide to avoid giving birth to a child of a particular gender. (The same possibility is presented by embryo selection.)

It might be argued on both utilitarian and deontological grounds that the sex of the fetus is information that isn't relevant to the health of the fetus. Accordingly, the physician is under no obligation to reveal the gender. Indeed, the physician may be under an obligation not to reveal the gender to avoid the possibility of its destruction for a trivial reason. But, again, is this really a decision for the physician?

5. *Should public funds be used to pay for genetic tests when an individual is unable to pay?* This is a question that holders of various ethical theories may not be prepared to answer in a simple yes-or-no fashion. Those who oppose abortion on natural law grounds might advocate providing funds only for genetic testing and counseling. That is, they might favor providing prospective parents with information they might use to decide whether to refrain from having children. Yet opponents of abortion might be against spending public money on tests that might encourage the use of abortion to prevent the birth of an impaired child.

The views of Rawls and of utilitarianism might support the use of public funds for genetic testing as part of a more general program of providing for health-care needs. Whether genetic testing programs are funded and what the level of funding might be would then depend on judgments about their expected value in comparison with other health-care programs.

A present ethical and social difficulty is caused by the fact that federal funds may be employed to pay for genetic screening and testing, yet federal money cannot legally be used to pay for abortions. Consequently, it's possible for a woman to discover she is carrying a fetus with a serious genetic disease, wish to have an abortion, yet lack the means to pay for it.

Issues about the confidentiality of test results, informed consent, the use of genetic testing to gather epidemiological information, and a variety of other matters might be mentioned here in connection with genetic intervention. Those that have been discussed are sufficient to indicate that the difficulties presented by genetic intervention are at least as numerous as the benefits it promises.

EUGENICS

Like other organisms, we are the products of millions of years of evolutionary development. This process has taken place through the operation of natural selection on randomly produced genetic mutations. Individual organisms are successful in an evolutionary sense when they contribute a number of genes to the gene pool of their species proportionately greater than the number contributed by others.

Most often, this means that the evolutionarily successful individuals are those with the largest number of offspring. These are the individuals favored by natural selection. That is, they possess the genes for certain properties that are favored by existing environmental factors. (This favoring of properties is natural selection.) The genes of "favored" individuals will thus occur with greater frequency than the genes of others in the next generation. If the same environmental factors continue to operate, these genes will spread through the entire population.

Thanks to Darwin and the biologists who have come after him, we now have a sound understanding of the evolutionary process and the mechanisms by which it operates. This understanding puts us in a position to intervene in evolution. We no longer have to consider ourselves subject to the blind working of natural selection, and if we wish, we can modify the course of human evolution. As the evolutionary biologist Theodosius Dobzhansky expressed the point: "Evolution need no longer be a destiny imposed from without; it may conceivably be controlled by man, in accordance with his wisdom and values."

Those who advocate eugenics accept exactly this point of view. They favor social policies and practices that, over time, offer the possibility of increasing the number of genes in the human population responsible for producing or improving intelligence, beauty, musical ability, and other traits we value.

The aim of increasing the number of favorable genes in the human population is called *positive eugenics*. By contrast, *negative eugenics* aims at decreasing the number of undesirable or harmful genes. Those who advocate negative eugenics are most interested in eliminating or reducing from the population genes responsible for various kinds of genetic diseases.

Both positive and negative eugenics require instituting some sort of control over human reproduction. Several kinds of policies and procedures have been advocated, and we will discuss a few of the possibilities.

NEGATIVE AND POSITIVE EUGENICS

The discussion of genetic screening, counseling, prenatal genetic diagnosis, and embryo selection makes it unnecessary to repeat here information about the powers we possess for predicting and diagnosing genetic diseases. It is enough to recall that, given information about the genetic makeup and background of potential parents, a large number of genetic diseases can be predicted with a certain degree of probability as likely to occur in a child of such parents. Or the presence of the genes can be determined by genetic analysis of the chromosomes. This is true of such diseases as PKU, sickle cell, hemophilia, Huntington's disease, Tay–Sachs, and muscular dystrophy.

When genetic information isn't adequate for a reliable prediction or direct determination, information about the developing fetus can often be obtained by employing one of several procedures of prenatal diagnosis. Even when information is adequate for a reliable prediction, whether the fetus has a certain disease can be determined by prenatal testing. Thus, in addition to the genetic disorders named above, prenatal tests can be performed for such developmental defects as neural tube anomalies and Down syndrome. Also, other tests can be performed on ova, sperm, or embryos.

A proponent of negative eugenics might advocate that a screening process for all or some currently detectable genetic diseases or dispositions (or developmental impairments) be required by law. When the probability of the occurrence of a disease is high (whatever figure that might be taken to be), then the potential parents might be encouraged to have no children. Indeed, the law might require that such a couple either abstain from having children or rely on embryo selection and prescribe a penalty for going against the decision of the screening board.

If those carrying the genes for some genetic diseases could be prevented from having children, over time the incidence of the diseases would decrease. In cases when the disease is the result of a dominant gene (as it is in Huntington's disease), the disease would eventually disappear. (It would appear again with new mutations, however.)

When the disease is of the sort that can be detected only after a child is conceived, if the results of a prenatal diagnosis show the developing fetus has a heritable disease, an abortion might be encouraged. Or a couple identified as at risk might be encouraged to seek artificial insemination and embryo testing and transfer.

Short of a law requiring abortion, a variety of social policies might be adopted to make abortion or embryo selection an attractive option. (For example, the cost of an abortion might be paid for by government funds or women choosing abortion might be financially rewarded. Or the costs of embryo selection might be paid for under a federal program.) The aborting of a fetus found to have a transmissible genetic disease would not only prevent the birth of an impaired infant, it would also eliminate a potential carrier of the genes responsible for the disease.

Similarly, the sterilization of people identified as having genes responsible for certain kinds of physical or mental impairments would prevent them from passing on these defective genes. In this way, the number of such genes in the population would be proportionately reduced.

Currently, no state or federal laws make it a crime for couples who are genetically a bad risk to have children. Yet a tendency toward more genetic regulation may be developing. Screening newborns for certain genetic diseases that respond well to early treatment is an established practice. Also, genetic testing programs are frequently offered in communities to encourage people to seek information about particular diseases.

At present, genetic testing (for adults) and counseling are voluntary. They aim at providing information and then leave reproductive decisions up to the individuals concerned. Most often, they are directed toward the immediate goal of decreasing the number of children suffering from birth defects and genetic diseases. Yet genetic testing and counseling might also be viewed as a part of negative eugenics. To the extent they discourage the birth of children carrying deleterious genes, they also discourage the spread of those genes in the human population.

Obviously, genetic testing and genetic counseling programs might also be used to promote positive eugenics. Individuals possessing genes for traits society values might be encouraged to have large numbers of children. In this way, genes for those traits would increase in relative frequency in the population.

No programs of positive eugenics currently operate in the United States. It is easy to imagine, however, how a variety of social and economic incentives (such as government bonuses) might be introduced as part of a plan to promote the spread of certain genes by rewarding favored groups of people for having children.

USE OF DESIRABLE GERM CELLS

Developments in reproductive technology have opened up possibilities once considered so remote as to be the stuff of science fiction. Artificial insemination by the use of frozen sperm is already commonplace. So too is the use of donor eggs and embryos. While some of the embryos may be donated by couples who don't need or want them, some are produced in infertility clinics by combining sperm from commercial sperm banks with donor ova. The developing embryos can be divided into several genetically identical embryos, and before long it may be possible to clone a human being from a single body cell.

Those wishing to have a child now have the option of selecting donor eggs or sperm from individuals with traits considered desirable. Alternatively, they may select a frozen embryo on the basis of descriptions of the gamete contributors. They may also turn to physicians who may offer them embryos they've created from sperm and eggs obtained from what they judge to be outstanding traits.

We have available to us right now the means to practice both negative and positive eugenics at the level of both the individual and the society. If we wished, we could encourage groups of individuals to avoid having their own biological children and, instead, make use of the "superior" sperm, ova, and embryos currently offered at sperm banks and infertility centers. In this way, we could increase the number of genes for desirable traits in the population. (See Chapter 6.)

ETHICAL DIFFICULTIES WITH EUGENICS

Critics have been quick to point out that the proposals mentioned suffer from serious drawbacks. First, negative eugenics isn't likely to make much of a change in the species as a whole. Most hereditary diseases are genetically recessive and so occur only when both parents possess the same defective gene. Even though a particular couple might be counseled (or required) not to have children, the gene will still be widespread in the population among people we would consider wholly normal. For a similar reason, sterilization and even embryo selection would have few long-range effects.

Also, the uncomfortable fact is that geneticists have estimated that, on the average, everyone carries recessive genes for five genetic defects or diseases. Genetic counseling and the use of the techniques of assisted reproduction may help individuals, but negative eugenics doesn't promise much for the population as a whole.

Positive eugenics can promise little more. It's difficult to imagine we would all agree on what traits we'd like to see increased in the human species. But even if we could, it's not clear we'd be able to increase them in any simple way.

For one thing, we have little understanding of the genetic basis of traits such as "intelligence," "honesty," "musical ability," "beauty" and so on. It's clear, however, there isn't just a single gene for them, and the chances are they are the result of a complicated interplay between genetic endowment and social and environmental factors. Consequently, the task of increasing their frequency is quite different from that of, say, increasing the frequency of short-horned cattle. Furthermore, desirable traits may be accompanied by less desirable ones, and we may not be able to increase the first without also increasing the second.

Quite apart from biological objections, eugenics also raises questions of a moral kind. Have we indeed become the "business manager of evolution," as Julian Huxley once claimed? If so, do we have a responsibility to future generations to improve the human race? Would this responsibility justify requiring genetic screening and testing? Would it justify establishing a program of positive eugenics? Affirmative answers to these questions may generate conflicts with notions of individual dignity and self-determination.

Of the ethical theories we have discussed, it seems likely that only utilitarianism might be construed as favoring a program of positive eugenics. The possibility of increasing the frequency of desirable traits in the human species might, in terms of the principle of utility, justify placing restrictions on reproduction. Yet the goal of an improved society or human race might be regarded as too distant and uncertain to warrant the imposition of restrictions that would increase current human unhappiness.

As far as negative eugenics is concerned, the principle of utility could be appealed to in order to justify social policies that would discourage or prohibit parents who are carriers of the genes for serious diseases from having children. The aim here need not be the remote one of improving the human population but the more immediate one of preventing the increase in sorrows and pain that would be caused by an impaired child.

Natural law doctrines of Roman Catholicism forbid abortion, sterilization, and embryo selection. Thus, these means of practicing negative eugenics are ruled out. Also, the natural law view that reproduction is a natural function of sexual intercourse seems, at least prima facie, to rule out negative eugenics as a deliberate policy altogether. It could be argued, however, that voluntary abstinence from sexual intercourse or some other acceptable form of birth control would be a legitimate means of practicing negative eugenics.

Ross's prima facie duty of causing no harm might be invoked to justify negative eugenics. If there is good reason to believe a child is going to suffer from a genetic disease, we may have a duty to prevent the child from being born. Similarly, Rawls's theory might permit a policy that would require the practice of some form of negative eugenics for the benefit of its immediate effects of preventing suffering and sparing all the cost of supporting those with genetic diseases.

It is difficult to determine what sort of answer to the question of negative eugenics might be offered in terms of Kant's ethical principles. Laws regulating conception or forced abortion or sterilization might be considered to violate the dignity and autonomy of individuals. Yet moral agents as rational decision makers require information on which to base their decisions. Thus, programs of genetic screening and counseling might be considered to be legitimate.

GENETIC RESEARCH, THERAPY, AND TECHNOLOGY

By replacing natural selection with artificial selection that is directly under our control, we can, over time, alter the genetic composition of populations of organisms. This has been done for thousands of years by animal and plant breeders, and our improved understanding of genetics allows us to do it today with more effectiveness and certainty of results. Yet such alterations require long periods of time. Molecular genetics holds out the possibility of immediate changes. Bacteria continue to be the major organisms of research, but genetic technology is already being applied to plants and animals. The same technology is now on the verge of being applied to humans.

RECOMBINANT DNA

The information required for genetic inheritance is coded in the two intertwined strands of DNA (deoxyribonucleic acid) found in plant and animal cells—the double helix. The strands are made up of four kinds of chemical units called nucleotides, and the genetic message is determined by the particular sequence of nucleotides. Three nucleotides in sequence form a triplet codon. Each codon directs the synthesis of a particular amino acid and determines the place it will occupy in making up a protein molecule. Since virtually all properties of organisms (enzymes, organs, eye color, and so on) depend on proteins, the processes directed by DNA are fundamental.

Alterations in the nucleotide sequence in DNA occur naturally as mutations—random changes introduced as "copying errors" when DNA replicates (reproduces) itself. These alterations result in changes in the properties of organisms, because the properties are under the control of DNA. Much research in current molecular genetics is directed toward bringing about desired changes by deliberately manipulating the nucleotide sequences in DNA. The major steps toward this goal have involved the development of techniques for recombining DNA from different sources.

The recombinant process begins by taking proteins known as restriction enzymes from bacteria and mixing them with DNA that has been removed from cells. These enzymes cut open the DNA strands at particular nucleotide locations. DNA nucleotide sequences from another source can then be added, and certain of these will attach to the cut ends. Thus, DNA from distinct sources can be recombined to form a single molecule.

This recombinant DNA can then be made to enter a host cell. The organism most widely employed is the one-celled bacterium *E. coli* that inhabits the human intestine by the billions. In addition to the DNA in the nucleus, *E. coli* also has small circular strands of DNA known as *plasmids*. The plasmid DNA can be recombined with DNA from an outside source and returned to the cell. When the plasmid replicates, it will make copies of both the original nucleotides and the added segments. Thus, a strain of bacteria can be produced that will make limitless numbers of copies of the foreign DNA.

The obvious question is, what benefits might recombinant DNA technology produce? From the standpoint of theory, it might lead to a better understanding of the molecular processes involved in such diseases as cancer, diabetes, and hemophilia. Or it might provide more effective treatment for metabolic diseases like PKU and Tay–Sachs.

From the practical standpoint, recombinant-DNA technology has already led to the development of new breeds of plants able to utilize nitrogen from the air and requiring little or no fertilizer. Specially engineered bacteria might be used to clean up the environment by breaking down currently nonbiodegradable compounds like DDT. Other bacteria might convert petroleum into other useful chemical compounds, including plastics.

The most immediate benefits of recombinant DNA technology is the use of bacteria modified into chemical factories that produce biological materials of medical importance. A glance at a few of the many recent research developments gives an appreciation of the powerful potential of genetic technology:

+ Hypopituitary dwarfism is a condition caused by a deficiency in growth hormone. The hormone itself consists of molecules too large and structurally complex to synthesize in the laboratory, but as early as 1979 researchers employed recombinant-DNA technology to induce bacteria to produce the hormone. It's now available in quantities large enough to be used as a therapy.

+ Modified bacteria now produce human insulin in quantities large enough to meet the need of diabetics, some of whom are allergic to swine or bovine insulin.

+ Genetically engineered bacteria have been used to produce a vaccine against hepatitis B and against a strain of genital herpes. The clotting factor employed in the treatment of hemophilia has been similarly produced.

+ Genetically engineered flu vaccines grown in moth cells may replace some of those currently grown in fertilized chicken eggs, reducing production time from six to nine months to two to three.

+ In 1985 the Cetus Corporation was awarded the first patent for an altered form of the protein interleukin-2. Il-2 activates the immune system and is used in the treatment of some cancers. It occurs naturally but in very small amounts; thus, it wasn't possible to use it therapeutically until it was produced in quantity by genetically altered bacteria.

+ Researchers have inserted human genes into plants and induced the plants to produce large quantities of medically significant proteins. Antibodies, serum albumin, enkephalins, hormones, and growth factors are among those currently produced.

✦ Substances occurring in the human body in minute amounts that can be important as drugs when widely available are now being produced in large quantities by genetic engineering. For example, tissue plasminogen activator (TPA), which is produced in blood vessels, dissolves blood clots and is a useful drug in the treatment of heart attacks. Also, blood factor-VIII, a clotting agent, may improve the lives and health of hemophiliacs by reducing their chances of viral infection from donated blood.

✦ Researchers in 1997 genetically engineered mice to serve as an animal model for sickle-cell disease by inserting into the mice human genes for the defective hemoglobin that causes the disease. Having animal models may speed up the testing of new drugs and suggest approaches for an effective treatment.

✦ Researchers have inserted into mouse embryos human DNA equivalent to an entire chromosome and discovered the DNA is passed on to the next mouse generation. Such research promises to lead to an understanding of the ways in which genes work normally and in disease processes. Further, animals containing segments of human DNA might be induced to produce medically useful products. (See *Social Context: Hello, Dolly,* in Chapter 6)

GENE THERAPY

The rapid advancement in genetic knowledge during the last few years has led to the use of recombinant-DNA techniques in experimental medical therapies. Therapy in which a missing or nonfunctioning gene is inserted into a patient's cells is already being employed. So is the use of altered cells to induce the formation of new blood vessels to treat unhealing leg ulcers and, perhaps soon, coronary artery blockages. (See the *Case Presentation: Gene Therapy* in this chapter for more details.)

The ability to alter the basic machinery of life to correct its malfunctioning is surely the most powerful form of therapy imaginable. The immediate prospects for gene therapy involve the relatively modest, but very dramatic, task of splicing into the DNA of body cells a gene that controls the production of a specific substance. Diseases such as PKU that are caused by the absence of an enzyme might then be corrected by inducing the patient's cells to manufacture that enzyme. Some genetic diseases involve dozens or even hundreds of genes, and often the mechanism by which the genes produce the disease is not understood. Consequently, it's likely to be a long while before most genetic diseases can be treated by gene therapy. Even so, the effective treatment of single-gene disorders is a most promising possibility.

Few special moral or social issues are raised by the use of gene therapy as long as the cells modified are somatic (body) cells. The issues change significantly with the prospect of modifying human germ-line (sex) cells. Somatic-cell changes cannot be inherited, but germ-line cell changes can be. This possibility holds out the benign prospect of eliminating forever a number of genetic diseases. However, we need not wait for germ-line therapy to accomplish this. Embryo testing and selection before implantation, a technology already in common use, would be a simpler way to achieve the same goal.

While germ-line therapy may have no medical use, it points toward a frightening prospect. It offers us a way of "engineering" human beings by tinkering with the sex cells to produce people who meet our predetermined specification. Because we'll discuss this possibility below, it's only relevant to note here that the technology required to alter human sex cells doesn't exist at present.

BIOHAZARDS

The issues connected with gene therapy, testing, and screening may be overshadowed in significance by questions concerning dangers inherent in the development of genetic technology and the release of its products into the environment.

The question of whether recombinant-DNA research ought to be halted is no longer a serious social issue. However, this hasn't always been so. In 1974 a group of scientists active in such research issued a report recommending that scientists be asked to suspend work voluntarily on recombinant experiments involving tumor viruses, increased drug resistance in harmful bacteria, and increased toxicity in bacteria. The discussion that ensued resulted in the formulation of guidelines by the National Institutes of Health to regulate research.

The major concern initially was that recombinant techniques might be employed to produce essentially new organisms that would threaten human health. Suppose that the nucleotide sequence for manufacturing a lethal toxin were combined with the DNA of *E. coli*. This usually harmless inhabitant of the intestine might be transformed into a deadly organism that would threaten the existence of the entire human population. (In recent years we've seen how deadly naturally occurring mutant forms of *E. coli* can be when they appear in the food supply.)

Or to take another scenario, perhaps a nucleotide sequence that transforms normal cells into cancerous ones might trigger an epidemic of cancer. Without a thorough knowledge of the molecular mechanisms involved, little could be done to halt the outbreak. Indeed it isn't even clear what would happen if one of the engineered insulin-producing strain of bacteria escaped from the lab and spread through the human population.

These and similar dangers prompted some critics to call for an end to all genetic-engineering research. However, almost two decades of recombinant-DNA research have passed without the occurrence of any biological catastrophes. Most observers regard this as sufficient proof of the essential safety of the research. Yet, in the view of others, the fact that no catastrophes have yet occurred must not be allowed to give us a false sense of security. Almost no one advocates that the research be abandoned, but several molecular geneticists have argued that the very fact that we still do not know enough to estimate the risks involved with a high degree of certainty is a good reason for continuing to control it severely.

Quite apart from the possible hazards associated with genetic engineering, many people continue to be uneasy about the direction of research. A number of biotechnological possibilities are on the horizon, some of which might have far-reaching consequences. As we discussed earlier, gene surgery offers more possibilities than just medical therapy. If undesirable DNA segments can be sliced out of the genetic code and replaced with others, this would permit the "engineering" of human beings to an extent and degree of precision never before imagined.

The eugenic dream of producing people to match an ideal model would be a reality. What would happen then to such traditional and moral values as autonomy, diversity, and the inherent worth of the individual?

The same techniques employed to manufacture the ideal person might also be used to design others to fit special needs. It's not difficult to imagine using genetic surgery to engineer a subhuman race to serve as a slave class for the society. The scenarios of cautionary science fiction might be acted out in our own future.

Further, the technique of asexual reproduction known as cloning might be employed to produce individuals that are exact genetic copies of someone whose DNA has been engineered to suit our needs or ideals. While human cloning is not yet a practical reality, a giant step toward it was taken in 1997 when Ian Wilmut and his colleagues at the Roslin Institute in Scotland cloned a sheep. (See *Social Context: Hello, Dolly* in Chapter 6.)

We might use reproductive technology in combination with genetic engineering to have several children that are copies of ourselves. If the embryos were stored, some of these might be born years apart.

Consider one last possibility. Virtually new organisms might be produced by splicing together DNA from two or more sources. Thus, the world might be faced with creatures of an unknown and unpredictable nature that are not the product of the natural processes of evolution.

It's little wonder molecular biologists have become concerned about the nature and direction of their research. As Robert Sinsheimer says, "Biologists have become, without wanting it, custodians of great and terrible power." Such power in the hands of a tyrannical government could be used with irresistible effectiveness to control its subjects. Societies might create a race of semihuman slaves or armies of genetically engineered soldiers. The possibilities are both fantastic and unlimited.

ETHICAL DIFFICULTIES WITH GENETIC RESEARCH, THERAPY, AND TECHNOLOGY

The risks involved in gene therapy are not unique ones. In most respects, they exactly parallel those involved in any new medical treatment. Accordingly, it seems reasonable to believe that the same standards of safety and the same consideration for the welfare of the patient that are relevant to the use of other forms of therapy should be regarded as relevant to gene therapy.

The principles of Kant and Ross suggest that the autonomy of the individual must be respected and preserved. The individual ought not to be viewed as an experimental case for testing a procedure that may later prove helpful. If the person is adequately informed, competent to consent, and no alternative therapy is likely to be effective, it would be morally legitimate for the patient to be given the opportunity to benefit from the therapy. However, if the hazards are great or completely unknown, it's doubtful whether the patient would be justified in risking his or her life.

By contrast, on utilitarian principles, if the outcome of gene therapy can be reasonably expected to produce more benefit than harm, its use might be considered justifiable. If we assume a person is likely to die anyway, that in itself might be enough to warrant the use of the therapy. In addition, since each case treated is likely to contribute to increased understanding and to benefit others, this tends to support the use of gene therapy, even in cases in which it is of doubtful help to the individual. (See the Case Presentation for a fuller discussion.)

Genetic research and its associated technology present issues much greater in scope than those raised by gene therapy. They are issues that require us to decide what sort of society we want to live in.

Very few responsible people currently believe we should call a halt to research in molecular genetics and forgo the increase in power and understanding it has already brought. However, the possibilities of genetic engineering include ones that are frightening and threatening, ones that could wholly alter our society and destroy some of our most cherished values. These are the possibilities that require us to make decisions about whether or to what extent we want to see them realized.

The natural law view of ethics would not, in general, support any policy of restricting scientific inquiry in the area of molecular genetics. For on this view there is a natural inclination (and hence a natural duty) to seek knowledge. Yet certain types of experiments and gene engineering would be ruled out. Those that aim at altering human beings or creating new species from mixed DNA are most likely to be considered to violate the natural order. On the Roman Catholic view, such a violation of nature would run counter to God's plan and purpose and so be immoral.

The principle of utility might be invoked to justify limiting, directing, or even ending research in molecular genetics. If research or its results are more likely to bring about more harm than benefit, regulation would be called for. Yet if the promise of relieving misery or increasing well-being is great, then some risk that we might also acquire dangerous knowledge in the process might be acceptable.

On the utilitarian view, knowledge may be recognized as a good, but it's only one good among others. Possessing the knowledge to alter human beings in accordance with a eugenic ideal or to create new species means we have to make a decision about whether doing so would result in an overall benefit. That judgment will then be reflected in our social policies and practices.

Such an analysis also seems to be consistent with Rawls's principles. There is not, for Rawls, an absolute right to seek knowledge, nor is there any obligation to employ knowledge that is available. Restriction might well be imposed on scientific research and on the technological possibilities it presents if the good of society seems to demand it.

SOCIAL CONTEXT
The Holy Grail of Biology: The Human Genome Project

The Holy Grail in medieval Christian legend is the lost cup used by Christ at the Last Supper. Because the Grail delivers salvation to whoever possesses it, finding the Grail was the aim in many tales of valorous quests. While deciphering the human genome cannot promise eternal life, it offers the benefits of genetic knowledge, including the possibility of exercising control over our genes and the ways they affect us. This is promise enough to give the Human Gene Project the status of a secular Holy Grail.

GENOME

On June 26, 2000, Francis Collins, Director of the National Genome Research Institute, and J. Craig Venter, president of Celera Genetics, announced that, thanks to the joint work of the two groups, the human genome had been sequenced.

This means that the estimated 3.2 billion base pairs making up human DNA have been identified and sequenced—that is, the precise order of the base pairs has been established. Human DNA is now thought to contain about 30,000 genes. Earlier estimates had put this figure around 100,000, so the lower number came as a considerable surprise. Using the comparison by writer Nicholas Wade, if the complete DNA sequence was published in the *New York Times,* it would cover 75,490 pages.

This complete set of genes contained in the forty-six chromosomes is known as the *genome.* Metaphorically, it is the total set of coded instructions for assembling a human being that is stored in the nucleus of each cell. About 75 percent of the genome is thought to be (as geneticists say) junk, consisting of repetitive DNA sequences accumulated during evolution and contributing nothing to human development or functioning. Yet biologists are also quick to say that we don't yet know enough to declare the junk DNA absolutely useless. It may contain sequences that in the future we will realize are crucially important.

BACKGROUND

In 1985, biologist Robert Sinsheimer began promoting the idea that the entire human genome should be mapped and its genes sequenced. Because the genome was recognized as involving some three billion base pairs, the genome project would be on a scale unprecedented in the biological sciences. It would compare with the efforts of physicists to develop the atomic bomb during World War II and with the manned space project in the 1960s.

The size of the genome project made many scientists skeptical about supporting it. Some believed it would drain money away from smaller projects of immediate value in favor of one with only distant and uncertain promise. Also, some feared the genome project would turn out to be too much like the space project, emphasizing the solution to engineering problems more than the advancement of basic science.

Attitudes changed in 1988 when the National Research Council endorsed the genome project and outlined a gradual approach of coordinated research that would protect the interest of the basic sciences. When James Watson (who, along with Francis Crick, worked out the structure of DNA in 1953) agreed to be director of the project, most critics dropped their opposition, and many became enthusiastic participants. Watson headed the project with great success until he resigned in 1993, when the position was taken over by Francis S. Collins.

Mapping and sequencing the human genome was expected to take fifteen to twenty years and cost between $3 and $5 billion. In 1989, Congress approved $31 million to initiate the program, but the project eventually came to cost about $200 million per year, and most biological and medical scientists view the money as well and wisely spent. The project was divided among nine different centers at both national laboratories and universities, and hundreds of scientists participated in the research and contributed to the final product.

The project was expected to be completed by 2005, but in response to a challenge by a commercial enterprise to the federal project and eventual cooperation between the two, the project was completed five years ahead of schedule.

Biologist J. Craig Venter, head of the Celera Corporation, claimed he would begin sequencing in 1999 and finish in 2001. Venter's group took a different approach than the federal project. Celera sequenced millions of DNA fragments, then used a computer program to piece them together on the basis of their overlaps. Unlike the HEP approach, Celera did not break DNA into fragments, then create a map of each piece's location.

The payoff of the genome project is considered by most biological and medical researchers to be of inestimable worth. The information has already provided us with a better understanding of the patterns and processes of human evolution and clarified our degree of genetic relatedness with other organisms.

Most important, the detailed genetic information is giving us a much improved understanding of the relationships between certain genes and particular diseases. This information may eventually permit us to develop gene therapy to such a degree that genetic diseases can be wholly eliminated or their results effectively controlled.

The genome project achieved its goal sooner than even its most avid supporters ever thought possible. In 1993, Daniel Cohen, assembling data from some 129 researchers, published a complete map of human chromosomes. The map was sketchy, but it was four times more detailed than the first chromosomal-linkage map published in 1987. The map made it ten times quicker to locate a particular gene than by using earlier linkage maps. After the Cohen map a number of other maps, based on increasingly more complete data, were published.

Another milestone was reached in 1997 when the team led by David Schlessinger of the Washington University Medical School completed a high-resolution map of the X chromosome. The 160 million base pairs of the chromosome were mapped with markers around every 75,000 pairs. Because a number of sex-linked diseases, such as hemophilia, result from a defective gene on the X chromosome, the map made it easier to locate the genes responsible for them. (Females have two copies of the X chromosome. Males have only one; so if it carries a defective gene, they lack a backup gene to prevent the consequences.)

IDENTIFIED GENES

The rapidity with which the genes responsible for a large number of human diseases have been identified has been astounding. A sampling from a list of about a thousand gives some idea of how successful researchers have been in locating actual genes or gene markers for diseases:

Colon cancer For the familial form of colon cancer, a marker was found on the upper end of chromosome 2 for a "repair" gene that corrects minor errors in cellular DNA. In its mutant form, the gene seems to function by triggering hundreds of thousands of mutations in other genes. One in 200 people has the gene; 65 percent of the carriers are liable to develop cancer. The familial form accounts for about 15 percent of all colon tumors. (A blood test is expected to be available soon.)

Amyotrophic lateral sclerosis The familial form of ALS (Lou Gehrig's Disease) results from a mutation of a gene on chromosome 21 that codes for the enzyme superoxide dismutase, which plays a role in eliminating free radicals. If they aren't controlled, it's believed they may damage motor neurons, which will then lead to muscle degeneration. The familial form of the disease accounts for only about 10 percent of cases, but those with a family history of the disease can now be screened for the defective gene.

Type II (adult onset) diabetes A still unidentified gene on chromosome 7 codes for glucokinase, an enzyme that stimulates the pancreas to produce insulin. At least twenty-three mutated forms of the gene may cause the disease by encoding for a faulty enzyme that apparently fails to trigger insulin production. A screening test for the mutated genes is available.

Alzheimer's disease The gene ApoE on chromosome 19 codes for a protein that transports cholesterol. People who have both alleles for the form of the protein known as E4 have eight times the risk of developing Alzheimer's; those with one allele have two to three times the risk. The gene could account for as many as half of those with the disease, although the causal role of E4 in producing it is not yet known.

X-linked SCID Severe combined immunodeficiency diseases (SCID) is caused by a defective gene passed from mothers to sons on the X chromosome. The normal gene codes for part of the receptor of interleukin-2, which serves in the cytokine messenger system that keeps the T-cells of the immune system functioning. Newborns with the mutated gene have few or no T-cells, and even a mild infection is life threatening. The disease occurs in only 1 in every 100,000 births.

(The cells used in the study were from "David," who died in Houston after he was removed from the sterile environment where he had spent almost twelve years of his life and given a bone marrow transplant. Because of the publicity surrounding him, SCIDS is known popularly as "the Bubble Boy disease.")

This list could be multiplied to include spinocerebellar ataxia (a degenerative disease linked to a gene on chromosome 6), Huntington's disease (see the Classic Case Presentation: Huntington's Disease that opens this chapter), Lorenzo's disease (adrenoleukodystrophy, or ALD, which involves the degeneration of the myelin sheath around nerves), Canavan disease (a rare and fatal brain disorder affecting mostly Ashkenazi Jews and similar to ALD), achondroplastic dwarfism, (the gene FGR3 causes about one-third of the cases of dwarfism), and cystic fibrosis (in which mucus accumulates in the lungs and pancreas; the gene, discovered on chromosome 7, is known to exist in hundreds of mutant forms).

More and more genes associated with particular disorders are likely to be identified in the near future. The map of the genome is a powerful tool for understanding the role of genes that in the past could only be guessed at or located only by determined research and good luck.

THE PROTEINS PROJECT

The Human Genome Project's achievement of mapping, identifying, and sequencing all the genes in the human body is a major milestone on the way to our acquiring something like a complete understanding of our genetic makeup. Being able to locate a gene and knowing it consists of a certain segment of DNA is a crucial step toward understanding the complex roles of genes, but a knowledge of where genes appear on the map of the genome is incomplete in a crucial way. It has to be accompanied by an understanding of what proteins are determined by the genes and what role those proteins play.

Genes do most of their work through the production of proteins. The proteins interact with other proteins to regulate human development, cell division, physiological functioning, immunological responses, tissue repair, and so on.

An enzyme or hormone that is missing or deficient, for example, is responsible for diseases like Tay–Sachs and diabetes. Indeed, perhaps all diseases can be viewed as involving genetically-based responses. We already know of genes that predispose people to heart disease and breast cancer, and many researchers think it is reasonable to believe there are scores (if not hundreds) of predisposing genes for many other diseases, ranging from schizophrenia to glaucoma.

In the future, we can expect researchers to unravel some of the connections between proteins and diseases. When this happens, we can also hope to see new approaches to diagnosing and treating diseases that have often been mysterious and lacking an effective therapy. Instead of a broad diagnostic category like "breast cancer," for example, the disease may be subdivided into many more specific categories, and each may have its own prognosis and its own therapy.

Indeed, pharmaceutical companies may be able to design drugs that are specific for individuals and their particular genetic makeup. By tailoring an individual treatment to an individual version of a disease, not only could such designer drugs be more effective, they could lack some of the worst side effects of drugs aimed at a general population of patients. Thus, if Sonia Henty is treated for breast cancer, she will receive drugs designed to treat her genetically-characterized disease, and if the drugs hit their target more specifically, she may not suffer the literally sickening effects of wide-spectrum chemotherapy.

When we understand the interplay among genes, development, and environmental factors, we will be well on the way to grasping the causes of diseases. Understanding these causes, will put us on the road to finding effective measures to prevent them, treat them, or even cure them.

That is the promise of the secular Holy Grail.

SOCIAL CONTEXT
Genetic Testing and Screening

The discovery of dozens of new disease-predisposing genes has been followed by the development of new screening tests. Given the increasing sophistication of biotechnology, tests that are now complex and expensive are likely to become simple and cheap quite soon. By using cells from a blood sample in an automated process involving biochip arrays of genetic probes, it should be possible to screen simultaneously for the presence of literally hundreds of genes. Already researchers test for the presence of many genes simultaneously and instantaneously by using a modified form of DNA and mass spectrometry.

While researchers are well on the way to identifying an entire catalogue of genes and their associated diseases, the concept of a genetic disease is not as clear-cut as it may seem. Rarely is it the case that if a person carries a certain gene, she will invariably develop a certain disease. While single-gene disorders like sickle cell and Huntington's diseases have been the focus of research, they account for only about 2 percent of genetic disorders. Most diseases result from a multiplicity of conditions such as the particular form of a gene (many genes have scores and even hundreds of mutated versions), the presence or absence of other genes, and the presence or absence of specific environmental factors. Being predisposed to develop a disease raises a number of questions about the value and dangers of genetic screening.

A Sample of DNA Tests Currently Available

Disease	*Description*
Huntington's disease	Progressive neurological disorder, onset in 40s or 50s
Polycystic kidney disease	Multiple kidney cysts leading to loss of kidney function
Cystic fibrosis	Mucus clogs lungs and pancreas; death in 30s is common
Sickle cell disease	Hemoglobin defect; anemia, strokes, and heart damage
Alpha-1-Antitrypsin deficiency	Can cause hepatitis, cirrhosis, and emphysema
Familial adenomatous polyposis	Colon polyps by age 35, often leading to cancer
Muscular dystrophy	Progressive muscle deterioration
Hemophilia	Blood fails to clot properly
Tay–Sachs disease	Lipid metabolism disorder causing death in first one to four years of life
Retinoblastoma	Cancerous tumor of the eye; most common in childhood
Phenylketonuria	Enzyme deficiency producing mental retardation
Retinitis pigmentosa	Progressive retinal degeneration leading to blindness
Familial breast cancer	5 to 10 percent of breast cancers
Familial hypercholesterolemia	High levels of cholesterol leading to early heart disease
Spinocerebellar ataxia	Neurological disorder producing lack of muscle control

INDIVIDUALS AND SCREENING

The ambivalence we all feel about genetic testing is shown by the results of a recent survey. When five hundred people were asked if they would like to take a genetic test that would tell them what diseases they would suffer from later in life, 50 percent said they would want to take it, and 49 percent said they wouldn't. We are torn between seeing the value of knowing and the comfort of not knowing.

Information about a genetic predisposition to a particular disease can be beneficial to individuals. It can alert them to the need to seek medical surveillance so they can receive appropriate therapy for the disease, should it develop, at the earliest time. Further, it can make them aware of the need to avoid environmental factors that may trigger the disease. For example, those with the gene for xeroderma pigmentosum are extremely sensitive to ultraviolet radiation, and exposure to it is likely to lead to a form of melanoma that is usually incurable. However, if those with the gene avoid prolonged exposure to sunlight, they have a good chance of avoiding developing melanoma.

By contrast, in the case of some single-gene diseases like Huntington's, knowing one is a carrier of the gene opens up no ways of altering the outcome of the disease. No way of preventing the disease is known, and early intervention makes no difference in the course of the illness. While some might want to know whether they are carriers of the gene in order to make informed decisions about such personal matters as marriage, childbearing, and life style, others might prefer to live their lives without knowing. (See the Classic Case Presentation: *Huntington's Disease* in this chapter.)

Equally difficult issues are associated with screening for the genes known to be associated with familial breast cancer. Mutations in the gene BRCA1, located on chromosome 17, were identified in 1994 as being responsible for the susceptibility to breast cancer and ovarian cancer in a group of families with multiple incidence of the diseases. A "frame-shift mutation" apparently causes the translation of codons to start in the wrong place, producing a nonsense protein. A second gene, BRCA2, located on chromosome 13, that also causes susceptibility to breast cancer was discovered in 1995. More than 200 mutations have been identified on the BRCA genes, but one study suggests it is a mutation in BRCA1 most likely to cause cancer in younger women.

Women who carry on the mutated genes are estimated to have an 85 percent chance of developing breast cancer and a 60 percent chance of developing ovarian cancer by age 65. Whether these figures can be generalized to any carrier of the gene is in some dispute, because they are based on samples from families with a history of breast cancer. Critics suggest a more realistic figure for breast cancer for a woman with the BRCA mutation is 56 percent.

The two mutated genes may explain the majority of hereditary breast cancers. (BRCA1 appears responsible for about 50 percent and BRCA2 for 30 to 40 percent.) Yet to the surprise of researchers, no evidence suggests the BRCA1 or BRCA2 gene plays a role in the 90 to 95 percent of "sporadic" breast cancers—ones not known to be due to inherited susceptibility. (The possibility that mutations in other genes are responsible is under investigation.)

But susceptibility to breast cancer means only that a woman is more likely than average to develop the disease. The extent to which she might control the outcome by altering such factors as diet, alcohol consumption, and exercise aren't known. Some evidence suggests the chance of developing cancer might be reduced by a prophylactic double mastectomy. Even so, cancer can still occur in the remaining tissue, and ovarian cancer might remain as likely. While the grounds for recommending that women be screened for the breast cancer genes are shaky, some women may still want to be tested. They might find a psychological value in knowing, and this might have practical consequences, even though not preventive or therapeutic ones.

EMPLOYMENT

Whether or not individuals find value in knowing their own genetic predispositions to develop diseases, some observers worry that our newly acquired understanding of parts of the human genome may result in opening the way for new forms of discrimination—ones based on genetic predisposition.

This worry is reflected in the responses to the survey mentioned earlier. While individuals may be ambivalent about knowing their own genetic predispositions, they are virtually unanimous in wanting such information kept from employers. In response to the question "Do you think it should be legal for employers to use genetic tests in deciding whom to hire?" only 9 percent of the 500 people surveyed said yes; an overwhelming 87 percent said no.

While individuals may be sure about what they don't want employers to know, employers may believe they have good reasons to know anything likely to affect the health and performance of employees. Because employers have financial responsibilities and legal liabilities with respect to their employees, they may believe they are entitled to all relevant health information.

The way in which genetic screening for disease predisposition becomes entangled with thorny issues of public policy is illustrated by a telling example occurring early in the history of genetic screening. People prone to develop an acute form of anemia after exposure to naphthalene should avoid jobs in which the chemical is employed. In principle, susceptible workers could be assigned to jobs allowing them to avoid being exposed to the chemicals particularly harmful to them.

With such an aim in view, in 1982 some 59 percent of large companies surveyed indicated they either had a genetic screening program or intended to institute one. Their motivation was partly based on economic self-interest; the costs of damage suits and insurance premiums could be lowered by keeping susceptible workers out of danger.

By 1986, however, the majority of plans to screen workers had been abandoned by corporations that had initially favored them. This was mostly in response to criticisms from civil rights groups, women's organizations, and labor unions. The critics pointed out that the results of genetic screening could be used to discriminate against the hiring of entire classes of workers. Because African Americans are more susceptible to environmentally induced anemia, they would be effectively shut out of jobs in which the risk to them was greater than to other workers.

Similarly, because fetuses are likely to be affected by a number of chemicals used in manufacturing, pregnant women would not be hired for a wide variety of jobs. Indeed, the possibility that a woman might be or become pregnant without knowing it might result in the exclusion of women as a group.

As this case illustrates, the possibility of genetic screening in connection with employment presents us with a number of dilemmas of a moral and social kind. We wish to promote equal opportunity for workers, yet we also wish to protect their health and safety. If those genetically predisposed to certain diseases are allowed to compete for jobs that place them at risk, then we are not seeing to their health and safety. Yet if we see to their health, we are not allowing them equal opportunity. Similarly, we wish to promote individual freedom in the society, but at what point do we decide that an individual is taking an unacceptable risk? If we allow someone to risk her health, are we willing to bear the social cost associated with her falling ill?

A worker found to be susceptible to a common manufacturing chemical would be at a clear disadvantage in attempting to get a job and might claim that an employer who required him to take a screening test as a condition of employment was violating his right to privacy. Yet should employers be allowed no protection from the added costs of damage suits and higher insurance premiums caused by a higher rate of illness among susceptible workers?

The Equal Employment Opportunities Commission construes the Americans with Disabilities Act as making it unlawful to use the results of genetic testing to refuse employment. EEO's opinion has not yet been supported by any court rulings, however, and until that happens both employees nor employers must make decisions without a definite policy to guide them.

INSURANCE

Quite apart from the issues of employment, individuals who are screened for whatever reason and found to be at risk for some genetic diseases may find they can get only very expensive health insurance, if they can get it at all. Insurance companies, for their part, may attempt to make genetic screening for probabilities of certain known disorders a condition of insurability. Are individuals entitled to keep such information about themselves private? Are insurers entitled to know what risk they are taking before insuring an applicant?

While some states have passed laws forbidding insurers to require genetic testing or to use the results of genetic tests as a reason for denying applicants for health insurance, federal laws currently offer little or no protection against genetic discrimination. Recent efforts to pass such legislation have met with strong opposition from the insurance industry.

SOCIAL ISSUES

In addition to issues connected with employment and insurance, genetic screening opens up the possibility of identifying a class of people that may become regarded as socially undesirable. Being predisposed to a genetic disease may become a stigma in a society that prizes health. Genetic carriers of disease-causing genes

might be shunned as marriage partners or find it difficult to make their way into positions of social power and influence. Regarded as genetic pariahs, they might come
to be outcasts in their own society, stigmatized by their biological inheritance.

These are merely some of the difficulties raised by the new possibilities of screening for the genetic predisposition to diseases. The promise of being able to prevent
the occurrence of some disease in many individuals is genuine, but we have yet to
make an adequate effort to resolve the social and moral issues that fulfilling the
promise presents. Until we deal with them satisfactorily, a powerful technology may
remain underutilized.

SCREENING AND CHILDREN

Researchers attempting to identify a gene predisposing women to breast cancer
conducted their work among families with a high incidence of the disease. During
the course of their work, they learned which females in the family had to be carriers
of the BRCA1 gene and so had an 85 percent chance of developing the disease. The
question they faced was, should they inform the women that they or their children
were at such risk?

Some researchers decided they would not volunteer any information and would
provide it only to women eighteen or older who asked for it. They refused to divulge
any information about children, even when pressed to do so by their parents, because
being predisposed to breast cancer is not a condition for which there is a treatment.
Also, the researchers reasoned, if a child knew she was predisposed to breast cancer,
she might be inclined to think of herself as sick and her breasts as likely to kill her.

Some critics of screening have argued that children should not be included in
screening tests, except when there is some direct benefit for them. The acquisition
of knowledge is not in itself a justification for screening children, the critics hold,
nor is the usefulness of the knowledge in the treatment of others. Screening tests
and the results they yield have the potential to damage or destroy a child's self
esteem, causing emotional harm, or altering the way in which the family views the
child. In some instances, upon learning that a child is likely to develop a disease,
some families have distanced themselves from the child, even to the point of placing the child in a foster home. When the child herself receives no benefit, the threat
of such an outcome makes the test unjustifiable.

At least one survey shows, however, that parents often believe children should be
aware of their risks for developing a particular disease. Some 61 percent of parents
visiting prenatal testing clinics said they should be permitted to have their children
tested for Alzheimer's, and 47 percent said that parents should inform the children of
the results.

However, another survey of families with members already diagnosed with genetic diseases shows a different result. Survey participants seemed to feel strongly
that parents should have their children tested for a disease only when it is a treat-
able or preventable one. When the disease is neither, as is the case with
Alzheimer's, the screening should not be done.

The issue may be complicated in some cases by the recent discovery that a disease that is mild or even asymptomatic in a parent may be much worse in an

offspring. This was discovered to be the case with myotonic muscular dystrophy, the most common form of the disease. A segment of DNA on chromosome 19 appears to repeat itself with increasing frequency over generations. Hence, someone who does not have any clinical sign of the disease may pass on the gene to a child, who will develop a devastating form of the disease. It might be argued that if a parent knows that a child is at high risk for developing a life-threatening disease, the parent has a duty to inform the child, although perhaps only after the child has reached a certain level of maturity.

The questions of whether children should be tested and who should decide when and how much they should know are issues that are likely to become more pressing as the number of tests for disease-causing genes increases.

CASE PRESENTATION

Gene Therapy

On September 14, 1990, at the National Institutes of Health in Bethesda, Maryland, a four-year-old girl became the first patient under an approved protocol to be treated by gene therapy. The child, whose parents initially asked that her identity not be made public, lacked the gene for producing adenosine deaminase (ADA), an enzyme required to keep immune cells alive and functioning.

Her life expectancy was low because without ADA she would almost certainly develop cancers and opportunistic infections that cannot be effectively controlled by conventional treatments. The aim of the therapy was to provide her with cells that would boost her immune system by increasing the production of essential antibodies. During the following months, she received four injections of altered cells.

The treatment, under the direction of W. French Anderson, R. Michael Blaese, and Kenneth Culver, involved taking blood from the patient, isolating the T-cells and then growing a massive number of them. These cells were infected with a weakened retrovirus into which a copy of the human gene for ADA had been spliced. The cells were then injected into the patient in a blood transfusion.

The idea behind the therapy was for the ADA gene to migrate to the cellular DNA, switch on, and begin producing ADA. If the cells produced enough of the enzyme, the child's immune system would not be destroyed. Because most T-cells live for only weeks or months, the process had to be repeated at regular intervals. The girl's parents, from a Cleveland suburb, later revealed their daughter's identity. She is Ashanthi Desilva, and over a decade later, she is alive and doing well. Soon after her treatment, on January 30, 1991, nine-year-old Cynthia Cutshall, became the second person to receive gene therapy.

Laboratory tests showed both children's immune systems were functioning effectively. But the need to replace short-lived T-cells meant Ashanthi and Cynthia had to continue to receive regular injections of altered cells. However, Anderson and his collaborators had always hoped to find a way around this need, and the break came when an NIH group developed a procedure for isolating stem cells from the bone marrow. If enough stem cells could be obtained and genetically altered, when injected back into the patient, the cells might produce enough T-cells for an adequately functioning immune system.

In May 1993, Cynthia's stem cells were harvested, exposed to the retrovirus containing the normal ADA gene, and reinjected. She tolerated the procedure with no apparent ill effects, and later that year essentially the same procedure was repeated with Ashanthi. While the immune systems of both continue to function within the normal range, the evidential value of the experiment is difficult to assess, because both subjects have also been treated with a standard drug regimen. At the moment, the therapy can't be said to have produced a cure for ADA, but advocates of the therapy believe that eventually it will.

This belief is strengthened by announcements of the results of clinical trials conducted in Paris in 2000 and in Great Britain in 2002. Researchers report that they have successfully used gene therapy to treat the genetic disorder known as SCID (severe combined immunodeficiency disease). If the reports hold up to scientific scrutiny, for the first time gene therapy can be said to have cured a genetic disease.

WIDE PROMISE

The promise gene therapy holds for those who suffer from a variety of genetic disorders is enormous. Experimental clinical protocols for the treatment of a wide range of relatively common diseases such as cystic fibrosis, hemophilia, phenylketonuria, sickle-cell anemia, hypercholesterolemia, AIDS, cardiovascular disease, cancer, lupus erythematous, and blood-clotting disorders either have already been initiated or are under consideration. Below are a few examples.

Parkinson's Disease Parkinson's disease, which affects about 400,000 people in the United States, is a progressive disorder in which cells in the part of the brain called the *substantia nigra* die off, resulting in a lack of the neurotransmitter dopamine. This leads to symptoms such as hand tremors, a stooped posture, and a shuffling walk. As more cells die, the symptoms become progressively worse.

A new treatment aims to slow cell loss by using a modified cold virus to transport copies of the gene for glial cell–derived neurotrophic factors or GDNF into the cells of the substantia nigra. Studies show GDNF can block cell degeneration, and experiments with rats indicate that those treated with GDNF suffered less brain cell death than untreated ones. The therapy will next be tested with primates, and if it is effective, it will then be ready for application to humans.

Sickle Cell Disease Sickle cell disease, affecting about 1 in 400 African Americans, is produced by a gene that affects the folding of the two chains making up the hemoglobin molecule. In a developing treatment, molecular fragments called *chimeraplasts* will be induced to enter red blood cell–producing stem cells in the bone marrow.

If a stem cell takes up the fragment and incorporates it into the nucleus, the cell's own repair system should eliminate the code for the defective hemoglobin chain and substitute that provided by the chimeraplast. If enough stem cells are altered and function, the amount of red blood cells produced should eliminate the tissue damage and strokes that often cause early death in those with the disease.

Malignant melanoma In one proposed cancer treatment, researchers will make trillions of copies of the gene that codes for the antigen HLA-B7, then inject them directly into the tumors of those with melanoma. The DNA is expected to enter the cells of the tumor, insert itself in the cellular DNA, then trigger the production of HLA-B7. The antigen will then extrude from the cell, causing the cell to be attacked by killer T-cells. Animal experiments suggest the immune system will attack not only tumor cells with the antigen markers, but those around it.

Leukemia A genetic abnormality known as the Philadelphia chromosome triggers cancerous changes in stem cells in the bone marrow. The resulting disease is chronic myelogenous leukemia, which affects about 7000 people a year and is responsible for 20 to 25 percent of all cases of leukemia. The best standard treatment is to inject patients with stem cells from a bone marrow donor. Sometimes, however, a compatible donor can't be located; also, the therapy has a lower level of success in people over fifty-five.

A new gene-based therapy is used to alter the patient's own stem cells by adding an antisense sequence to the cellular DNA. The sequence is designed to block the formation of the protein leading to cancerous growth, thus making the cancer cells behave like normal cells. The sequence will also have attached to it a gene making the altered cells more resistant to the chemotherapeutic drug methotrexate. When a patient receives chemotherapy, the cancerous cells will be killed, while the altered ones will survive and reproduce. The altered stem cells should then produce normal red blood cells. The main difficulty, at present, is to get the stem cells to incorporate the new genes.

Hypercholesterolemia Hypercholesterolemia is a disease in which the excess production of cholesterol often leads to heart attacks and early death. The gene therapy being developed to treat it involves removing part of a patient's liver, then culturing the cells and inserting into them a gene that produces the low-density lipoprotein receptor. The receptor plays an important role in removing cholesterol from the blood. The treated cells are then injected into the patient's liver, where they attach themselves to the liver's capillaries and start producing the protein of the receptor. Six months after the experimental study was started, the results were so satisfactory that federal approval was given to include more patients in the study.

Collateral blood vessel growth Every year thirty to forty thousand people in the U.S. develop almost complete blockage in the arteries of their legs. Shut off from a blood supply, the tissues in the leg develop ulcers that don't heal, and, eventually, when gangrene sets in, the leg must be amputated to save the person's life. Twenty percent of the patients died in the hospital, and forty percent died within the next year. No drugs are available to increase the blood flow to the legs.

A new treatment uses the gene that codes for vascular endothelial growth factor, or vegF, a protein that stimulates the growth of collateral blood vessels. When billions of vegF genes are injected into leg muscle, about 5 percent of them are incorporated into muscle cells, causing them to start producing the vegF protein. Because the vessel cells beyond the blockage are deprived of blood, their membranes become altered so as to be more receptive to the vegF molecule. When it attaches to the surface of cells, the cells begin to produce tiny new blood vessels that grow around the blockage. While only a few people have been treated with vegF gene therapy, it has shown itself to be effective. Plans are now underway to test the effectiveness of the therapy in heart disease. If vegF can establish collateral circulation in the heart, the need for coronary artery bypass surgery may be reduced or even eliminated. Those too frail or sick to undergo a bypass or even angioplasty might eventually be helped by the new technique.

Cystic fibrosis In April 1993, a twenty-three-year-old man became the first patient to receive human gene therapy for the treatment of cystic fibrosis. An altered form of the adenovirus was used to transport into his lungs the gene that codes for cystic fibrosis transmembrane conductance regulator. The regulator controls the flow of chloride through body cells. Cystic fibrosis patients lack the regulator gene, and as a result, they suffer severe salt imbalances that cause abnormal mucus excretions in the lungs and pancreas.

The first test of the therapy was evaluated in 1996. While the evidence did not demonstrate that it was effective, most investigators think ultimately it will be. Part of the difficulty is to find a way of getting the gene into the cells of the lungs. If the problems can be solved, gene therapy will offer the 30,000 Americans who suffer from cystic fibrosis a cure for the disease.

AIDS Several experiments are underway utilizing gene therapy to treat AIDS. In one of them, a few CD4 cells, the principle target of the HIV virus, will be taken from an AIDS patient, and a molecule called a "hairpin ribozyme" spliced into their DNA. The ribozyme slices up RNA, and because HIV depends on RNA for replication, cells with altered DNA should prevent the virus from reproducing. If enough altered CD4 cells were present in an HIV-positive individual, the level of infection might be lowered.

Paralleling the development of gene therapy are other treatment strategies based on the technology of recombinant DNA. One of the most promising is the use of drugs to alter the function of genes not behaving normally. The drugs in effect "turn on" a malfunctioning gene so it plays the role it is supposed to. Some promising results in the treatment of thalassemia and sickle-cell anemia have been reported.

Another technique involves transplanting cells into the brain, and it has been used experimentally in the treatment of Parkinson's disease. Researchers in Sweden have reported success in transplanting cells from fetal tissue into the substantia nigra of the brain. Other work also supports the idea that transplant therapy for diseases such as Parkinson's and Alzheimer's will be effective in the not-too-distant future.

GERM-LINE THERAPY

The gene therapy in humans currently under development is somatic-cell therapy, where modifications take place in the body cells of patients, not in the sex cells. This means that even if the therapy can eliminate the disease produced in an individual who has inherited a defective gene, the therapy will do nothing to alter the probability that a child of that person will inherit the same defective gene. To change this circumstance, germ-line cells would have to be altered. That is, the defective gene in an ovum or sperm cell would have to be replaced.

If this were possible, then certain genetic diseases could be eliminated from families. Germ-line therapy would make it unnecessary to perform somatic-cell therapy for each generation of affected individuals. As appealing as this prospect is, at present germ-line therapy has many more technical difficulties associated with it than does somatic-cell therapy. Uniformly encouraging results have not so far been produced in animal research, and even somatic-cell therapy in humans remains a distant prospect.

Moreover, some question the value of germ-line therapy. If the aim is to eliminate heritable diseases from a family, the most direct and effective way to achieve this is to screen embryos and avoid implanting those that carry the flawed gene. This process is currently available at infertility clinics and doesn't involve the risks and uncertainties of tinkering with the DNA of germ cells.

Most of the moral issues discussed in connection with gene therapy have centered around germ-line therapy. It holds out the prospect of genetically engineering sex cells to produce offspring with virtually any set of characteristics desired. This possibility has led many critics to warn that "genetic surgery" may be leading us into a sort of "Brave New World" in which we practice eugenics and manufacture our children to order. (See the Briefing Session in this chapter for a fuller discussion.) However, any dangers posed by germ-line therapy are far from immediate.

While somatic-cell therapy continues to be experimental, some of its forms are likely to become standard therapies within the next two to five years. Other forms will for some time remain experimental, and as such they will raise the same sorts of moral questions typical of any experimental procedure—questions of informed consent, benefit, and risk.

CHAPTER 6

Reproductive Control

CLASSIC CASE PRESENTATION
The Stem-Cell Debate

Research groups headed by James Thomson of the University of Wisconsin, Madison and John Gearhart of Johns Hopkins University announced in November 1998 that they had succeeded in isolating and culturing human embryonic stem cells. Embryonic stem cells are undifferentiated cells produced after a fertilized egg has divided several times and developed into a blastocyst.

EMBRYONIC STEM CELLS VS. ADULT STEM CELLS

The *blastocyst,* a hollow ball of cells, contains a little lump called the inner-cell mass consisting of fifteen to twenty embryonic stem cells. As development proceeds, embryonic stem cells differentiate and become specialized. They turn into so-called *adult* stem cells. These are cells that go on to produce the approximately 120 different cell types that form tissues and organs such as the blood, brain, bone, and liver. Adult stem cells have been found in the bone marrow and the brain, but biologists believe that adult stem cells are associated with every organ.

Before embryonic stem cells begin to differentiate, they have the potential to become any of the specialized cells. Afterwards, their fate is determined, and they cannot go back to their previous state. When heart cells divide, for example, they produce only heart cells. (Success in cloning mammals demonstrates, however, that the genetic material in a body cell can be made to return to its default position. Each cell retains the genetic information needed to develop into a complete individual—including all the cell types.)

SOURCE OF STEM CELLS

Thomson retrieved embryonic stem cells from surplus embryos produced for fertility treatments. (He obtained consent from the egg and sperm donors.) Gearhart used a different method. A group of cells known as embryonic germ cells form the sperm and ova that transmit genetic information to the next generation, and these cells are protected from the process that turns stem cells into specialized components of tissues and organs. Gearhart retrieved embryonic germ cells from aborted fetuses and cultured them to produce stem cells. Stem cells obtained in this way are apparently no different from the ones obtained directly from blastocysts.

NEW TREATMENT POSSIBILITIES

The identification of embryonic stem cells and the ability to culture them are important steps in opening up an amazing new range of possibilities for treating many chronic, debilitating, and life-threatening diseases. Cultures of embryonic stem cells appear to be what biologists call *immortal* cell lines. That is, the cells can replicate for an indefinite number of generations without dying or accumulating genetic errors. This capacity reduces the need to acquire new stem cells with great frequency. Cell lines can be established to supply the needs of researchers and physicians. If scientists learn how to control the system of chemical messengers and receptors that regulate the development of "blank" embryonic stem cells into specialized brain, heart, liver, or pancreas cells, it may be possible to repair those organs by injections of stem cells.

This may make it possible, for example, to treat Parkinson's disease by injecting stem cells into the substantia nigra in the brain to boost the production of the neurotransmitter dopamine. (The lack of dopamine produces the symptoms of the disease.) Or diabetes might be brought under control by inducing the pancreas to incorporate insulin-producing islet cells developed from stem cells.

Because embryonic stem cells have the capacity to become cells of any type, it looks as if they could be used to produce whatever sort of cells are needed to treat a particular disease. Damaged spinal nerves that keep people from walking or even moving their bodies might be repaired, and faulty retinas that cause blindness might be replaced with functional ones.

An even more dramatic prospect is that embryonic stem cells might be used to grow body tissues and even whole organs for transplantation. People could be provided with bone or skin grafts, liver segments, lung lobes, or even new kidneys or hearts. The problems caused by the intractable shortage of transplant organs would simply disappear. (See Chapter 7.)

Growing transplant organs is, at best, a distant dream. By one estimate, about 14,000 genes may be involved in the immensely complicated signal-receptor system governing embryonic development in higher mammals. A better understanding of the system is necessary to orchestrate the development of embryonic stem cells to produce replacement organs. The goal is in sight, however, and that has never been true before.

TREATMENTS WITH ADULT STEM CELLS

The therapeutic promises of embryonic stem cells are, to an extent, paralleled by the promises of adult stem cells. How adult stem cells can be used in treatments is currently being investigated vigorously. Evidence from animal studies suggests, for example, that heart muscle damaged by a heart attack can be treated effectively by an injection of adult stem cells. These cells produce normal heart cells, forming new tissue to replace damaged tissue. Amazingly, the stem cells employed come from the bone marrow, where they ordinarily produce blood cells. No adult stem cells have been found in the heart. Apparently, the bone-marrow cells respond to the biochemical environment of the heart, and it reprograms them to produce heart cells.

Swedish scientists in January 1999 identified *neural stem cells.* These are brain cells that have differentiated to become cavity-lining cells, yet when they divide, their progeny can differentiate into either *glial* (structural) cells or neurons. When the brain is injured, the cavity-lining cells begin reproducing, and the neural stem cells produce glial cells that form scars. If a way could be found to induce the neural stem cells to produce more neurons at the injury site, more brain function might be preserved.

REJECTION POTENTIALLY SOLVED

Embryonic and adult stem cells, like the tissues and organs derived from them, cannot escape the problem of immunological rejection that results from the triggering of an individual's immune response. All cells have protein markers on their surfaces that the immune system recognizes as self or not-self. Hence, an injection of neural stem cells donated by Romano into Walters will result in Walters' immune system attacking the cells as foreign.

The problem of the rejection of tissue and organ transplants is now dealt with by using powerful immunosuppressive drugs. Good antigen (proteins on the cell surface) matching, which reduces the severity of the immune response, might be achieved by maintaining a bank of stem cells. With a wide range of (say) embryonic stem-cell lines to choose from, transplant physicians could select the cells most compatible with the individual.

A second solution is to find a way to suppress or disguise markers on the surfaces of stem cells so they don't provoke the immune response. But researchers concerned with preventing the rejection of transplant organs have been trying without success to accomplish this for a long time.

The third and most elegant solution is to make use of embryonic stem cells acquired from an embryo created by using the techniques of cloning. This involves removing the nucleus from a donor egg, then replacing it with the DNA taken from a cell of an individual. The egg will contain only the DNA of the donor. Thus, when the egg develops into an embryo and the stem cells are removed, they will be genetically identical with those of the individual contributing the DNA. (This is called *therapeutic cloning,* in contrast with *reproductive cloning.* For more details on cloning, see the *Social Context: Cloning* later in this chapter.)

REGENERATIVE MEDICINE

Stem cells have the potential to serve as the foundation for treatments that will allow us to repair or replace most, if not all, of our ailing organs. They hold the promise of a secular miracle. They could provide a way to still the tremors of Parkinson's disease, knit together a severed spinal cord, supply the cells needed to produce the enzyme required to metabolize sugar, replace the cells in a malfunctioning retina, and heal a damaged heart. Stem cells could become treatments for diseases like Alzheimer's and Huntington's for which there are no effective therapies. And the list goes on and on.

Stem cells may offer us the chance to redeem from disease and injury the lives of countless numbers of people. In this respect, they may usher in a new era of medicine. Regenerative medicine, therapies that produce new tissues and perhaps whole organs, holds out the promise of cures in dozens of cases where no effective treatments now exist.

ETHICAL ISSUES

The retrieval of embryonic stem cells from human fetuses or embryos raises ethical problems for those who oppose abortion or believe that a fetus or embryo has a special moral status. From this perspective, a fertilized egg (an embryo) has the potential to develop into a human being, and (in a strong version) this makes it entitled to be treated as a person in the moral sense. Because it is wrong to kill an innocent person, it is thus wrong to destroy a human embryo. (See the discussion in Chapter 9.)

Taking embryonic stem cells from an aborted fetus is also seen as morally wrong by the same critics. Because abortion is viewed as a wrongful act, it is considered morally wrong to benefit from it. Also, as with the use of fetal tissue generally, by giving stem cells an instrumental value (in using them to treat a disease, for example), we are tacitly encouraging abortion and endorsing its practice. We are also showing a lack of respect for the fetus, given the special status bestowed on it by its potential to develop into a human being, by treating it as a product or commodity we are free to use to suit our needs.

Those who do not assign a special status to a fetus or embryo typically do not oppose the use of embryonic stem cells. Rather, their concerns resemble ones associated with cloning and genetic manipulation in general. They oppose reproductive cloning, for example, because they think it cheapens human life. To consider another example, genes could be added to embryonic stem cells to produce individuals with some special trait that could be inherited. Potentially, then, the whole human species might be altered by altering stem cells.

Some critics maintain that to choose such a course of action would be dangerous, because of its unforeseen biological and social consequences. Others hold that it would be wrong, because tampering with the human genome would violate our notion of what it is to be human.

ALTERNATIVES TO EMBRYONIC STEM CELLS

1. Most critics object to the way embryonic stem cells are acquired, not to the use of the cells. Thus, those who consider the destruction of an embryo to obtain stem cells immoral, may (but not always) consider it legitimate to obtain stem cells from spontaneously aborted fetuses. But those ascribing a different moral status to the human embryo, claim this way of getting stem cells is expensive and difficult. Also, because a fetus is spontaneously aborted, the stem cells may be abnormal in some way.

2. Some critics think research should be restricted to adult stem cells. If they can be used to develop effective treatments, we would not need embryonic stem cells. Hence, there would be no need to destroy human embryos. Most researchers are not satisfied with the prospect of restricting research to adult stem cells. They point out that we don't yet know enough about embryonic stem cells to know whether their

therapeutic potential could be equaled by using adult stem cells. Only research with embryonic and adult stem cells will answer this question.

3. Some who oppose acquiring stem cells from embryos or aborted fetuses would find stem cells produced by a process of parthenogenesis morally acceptable. That is, if an unfertilized human egg could be induced by biochemical means to divide and produce stem cells, the stem cells recovered could be legitimately used. Because the unfertilized egg would lack the genetic information needed for development, even if implanted into a uterus, it would not be a human embryo and thus would have no special moral status.

REGULATIONS AND STEM CELL RESEARCH

A 1995 law prohibits the use of federal funds to support research in which a human embryo is destroyed, and nine states ban all research involving fetal tissue. The research by Thomson and Gearhart leading to the recovery and culturing of stem cells was not supported by federal grants but by the Geron Corporation, a small biotechnology company. When Gearhart and Thomson announced their success, the question of the moral legitimacy of obtaining and using embryonic stem cells quickly became the topic of a national debate.

The National Conference of Catholic Bishops and other social-conservative groups and politicians opposed spending any federal money on stem-cell research. This included many of the traditional opponents of abortion. They argued, fundamentally, that human embryos have the status of persons, so that retrieving their stem cells, thus killing them, would be morally wrong.

In contrast, many disease-advocacy groups, seeing the possibility of cures by means of stem cells, advocated making stem-cell research eligible for federal funding. Without such funding, they argued, the chances that effective treatments would be found for many diseases would be significantly reduced. Private funding would be inadequate. Also, the United States would fall behind in medical innovation as other countries moved into the research gap that a lack of federal support would produce. Those pressing for going ahead with research included many politicians who ordinarily aligned themselves with the social conservatives.

Many people, politicians included, found it hard to object to removing stem cells from embryos that had been created at reproductive clinics, then not used. Ordinarily, such embryos are discarded. If so, then why not retrieve the stem cells and use them to develop treatments for diseases?

Social conservatives, Roman Catholics in particular, did not find this argument persuasive. So far as they were concerned, it was morally wrong to create and destroy embryos for the purpose of assisted reproduction. Hence, destroying them to acquire stem cells would also be wrong. (Even if the stem cells were used to treat disease, it would be wrong. The morally poisoned tree bears only poisoned fruit.)

President George Bush faced this politically vexed situation in 2001, and in August of that year he announced a policy to guide future federal funding of research involving human embryonic stem cells. The decision he made was to allow research on the (alleged) sixty-four human embryonic stem cell lines already established, but not permit federal funds to be used to acquire new stem cells through the destruction of new embryos. "This allows us to explore the promise and potential of stem cell research without crossing a fundamental moral line, by providing taxpayer funding that would sanction or encourage further destruction of human embryos that have at least the potential for life," he said in announcing his decision. He also established a President's Council on Bioethics to consider the consequences of stem cell research.

The new policy met with a mixed response. It was denounced by the National Conference of Catholic Bishops as "morally unacceptable," while many researchers and patient advocates viewed the policy as placing an unwarranted restriction on research. Scientists were particularly concerned about limiting research to already established cell lines. No one could say in advance, they pointed out, exactly how many genetically different kinds of stem cells would be adequate for treating diseases.

Yet many observers also welcomed the decision as being less restrictive than they had feared. Many had been afraid the President would respond to the pressure from social conservatives by presenting a policy that would forbid using stem cells, no matter when or how obtained, in federally funded projects.

Perhaps the most unfortunate effect of the policy, in the view of most patient advocates and researchers is that it forecloses the possibility of therapeutic cloning. Because embryos cannot be destroyed, the process described above of acquiring embryonic stem cells genetically identical with one's own cells cannot be employed.

Advocates of cloning for therapeutic purposes stress that they are not advocating reproductive cloning—that is, producing an embryo that is transferred to someone's uterus and allowed to develop into a child. Critics of cloning generally oppose it for any reason.

Embryonic stem-cell research, including therapeutic cloning, is likely to remain a flashpoint of controversy for the immediate future. While its promises are too powerful to ignore, its opponents consider the destruction of human embryos to acquire stem cells the moral equivalent of murder. Finding an acceptable political compromise will be a long-term challenge.

Briefing Session

"Oh, brave new world that has such people in it!" exclaims Miranda in Shakespeare's *The Tempest*.

This is the line from which Aldous Huxley took the title for his dystopian novel *Brave New World*. A dystopia is the opposite of a utopia, and the future society depicted by Huxley is one we're invited to view with shock and disapproval.

In Huxley's dystopia, "pregnancy" is a dirty word, sex is purely recreational, and children are produced according to explicit genetic standards in the artificial wombs of state "hatcheries." Furthermore, one's genetic endowment determines the social position and obligations one has within the society, and everyone is conditioned to believe the role she finds herself in is the best one to have.

In significant ways, that future society is now. The new and still-developing technologies of human reproduction have reached a stage in which the innovations imagined by Huxley in 1932 to make such a society possible are well within the limits of feasibility.

We have no state hatcheries and no artificial uteruses. But we do have sperm banks, donor ova, artificial insemination, frozen embryos, and surrogate pregnancies. We have it within our power to remove an ovum from a woman's body, fertilize it, then place it in her uterus so it may develop into a child. We can remove one or more of the cells of a growing embryo and allow them to develop into separate embryos. Because we have the power to clone mammals, producing a genetically identical twin, we most likely also have the power to clone humans.

The new technology of human-assisted reproduction is so powerful it differs only in degree from that of Huxley's dystopian world. What we have yet to do is to employ the technology as part of a deliberate social policy to restructure our world along the lines imagined by Huxley.

Yet the potentiality is there. Perhaps more than anything else, it is the bleak vision of such a mechanistic and dehumanized future that has motivated much of the criticism of current reproductive technology. The "brave new world" of Huxley is one in which traditional values associated with reproduction and family life, values based on individual autonomy, have been replaced by values of a purely social kind. In such a society, it is the good of the society or the species, not the good of individuals, that is the touchstone of justification.

The possible loss of personal values is a legitimate and serious concern. The technologies of human reproduction are sometimes viewed as machines that may be employed to pave the road leading to a world of bleakness and loss. Yet it is important to remember that these same technologies also promise to enhance the lives of those presently living and prevent potential suffering and despair.

Thousands of women (as well as a lesser number of men) unable to have children may find it possible to do so through the use of reproductive technology. It offers a means of conception when biological dysfunction makes the normal means unlikely or impossible. Women past the age of ovulation or who have lost their ovaries to surgery and men with a low sperm count are among those who have an opportunity where not long ago none existed.

These are all potentialities that have become actualities. But in the view of some, current methods merely mark a beginning, and the possibilities inherent in reproductive technology still remain relatively unrealized. It may be possible before long, for example, to avoid sexual reproduction and use in vitro fertilization and surrogate pregnancy to reproduce clones of an individual. The technology is so powerful that, if we wish, we can employ it to change the basic fabric and pattern of our society.

Should we do that? Or will the use of the technology promote the development of a dystopia? One way of thinking about these general questions is to turn once more to Huxley.

In 1962 Huxley published a utopian novel entitled *Island.* Like the society in *Brave New World,* Huxley's ideal society also relies on the principles of science, but they are used to promote autonomy and personal development. For over a hundred years, the society on the island of Pala has shaped itself in accordance with the principles of reason and science. Living is communal, sexual repression is nonexistent, children are cared for by both biological parents and other adults,

drugs are used to enhance perceptual awareness, and social obligations are assigned on the basis of personal interest and ability.

Reproductive technology is one of the means the society uses to achieve its
ends. It practices contraception, eugenics, and artificial insemination. Negative
eugenics to eliminate genetic diseases is considered only rational. But more than
this, by the use of DF and AI (Deep Freeze and Artificial Insemination), sperm
from donors with superior genetic endowments is available for the use of couples who wish to improve their chances of having a child with special talents or
higher-than-usual intelligence.

Huxley's ideal society is not above criticism, even from those sympathetic toward the values he endorses. Yet *Brave New World* is such a powerful cautionary
tale of what might happen if science were pressed into the service of repressive
political goals that it makes it difficult to imagine other possible futures in which
some of the same technology plays a more benign role. *Island* is an attempt to
present such an alternative future, so in thinking about the possibilities inherent
in reproductive technology, fairness demands that we also consider Palinese society and not restrict our attention to the world of soma and state hatcheries.

IVF, GIFT, ZIFT, AND OTHER TECHNIQUES

The birth of Louise Brown in 1978 (see the Case Presentation) was a major media
event. Photographs, television coverage, interviews, and news stories presented
the world with minute details of the lives of the people involved and close accounts of the procedures leading to Louise's conception.

Despite the unprecedented character of the event, few people seemed surprised
by it. The idea of a "test-tube baby" was one already familiar from fiction and
folklore. Medieval alchemists were thought capable of generating life in their re-
torts, and hundreds of science fiction stories depicted a future in which the creation of life in the laboratory was an ordinary occurrence. Thus, in some ways,
the birth of Louise Brown was seen as merely a matter of science and medicine
catching up with imagination. Indeed, they didn't quite catch up, for the "test
tube" contained sperm and an egg, not just a mixture of chemicals.

While it's doubtful the public appreciated the magnitude of the achievement
that resulted in the birth of Louise Brown, it was one of considerable significance. The first embryo transfer was performed in rabbits in 1890, but it wasn't
until the role of hormones in reproduction, the nutritional requirements of developing cells, and the reproductive process itself were better understood that it became possible to consider seriously the idea of fertilizing an egg outside the
mother's body and then returning it for ordinary development. By 2002 considerably more than 100,000 babies worldwide had been born through the use of in
vitro fertilization or some other form of assisted reproduction.

IVF

In vitro is a Latin phrase that means "in glass," and in embryology, it is used in
contrast with *in utero,* or "in the uterus." Ordinary human fertilization takes

place in utero (strictly speaking, in the fallopian tubes) when a sperm cell unites with an ovum. In vitro fertilization, then, is fertilization that is artificially performed outside the woman's body—in a test tube, so to speak.

The ovum that produced Louise Brown was fertilized in vitro. But the remainder of the process involved *embryo transfer*. After the ovum from her mother's body was fertilized and had become an embryo, it was transferred—returned for in utero development.

Robert Edwards and Patrick Steptoe, who were responsible for developing and performing the techniques that led to the birth of Louise Brown, followed a process that, allowing for technical improvements, is basically the same as the one still employed.

The patient is given a reproductive hormone to cause ova to ripen. Several mature eggs are extracted from the ovarian follicles and placed in a nutrient solution to which sperm is then added. With luck, sperm cells penetrate several ova, fertilizing them. The fertilized eggs are transferred to another nutrient solution where they undergo cell division. The embryo (also called a zygote or, by some, pre-embryo) is then transferred to the woman, who has been given injections of hormones to prepare her uterus to receive it.

Numerous modifications and extensions of Steptoe and Edwards's techniques have been introduced since 1978. It's now common to employ a nonsurgical procedure for securing ova. After hormones stimulate the ovarian follicles, ultrasound is used to locate the follicles, and a hollow needle is inserted through the vaginal wall and into a follicle. Fluid is withdrawn and egg cells identified under the microscope. They are then fertilized with the sperm, cultured, and the resulting embryos implanted.

Also, it's now not unusual to implant two, three, or even as many as ten fertilized ova at a time. (Implanting more than four is coming to be viewed as not good medical practice.) This makes it more likely that at least one will attach to the uterine wall and so eliminates the need for a woman to have eggs removed another time. Yet the practice also has the disadvantage of increasing the chances of multiple births. (See the Septuplets Case Presentation and Multiple Births in following pages.)

GIFT, ZIFT, IVC, ULER, PZD, ICSI, DNA TRANSFER, AND CD

Gamete intrafallopian transfer or GIFT uses some of the same manipulative techniques as IVF. It involves inserting both ova and sperm into the fallopian tubes through a small abdominal incision so if fertilization takes place, it does so inside the woman's body. Some regard the procedure as being more "natural" than in vitro fertilization.

Zygote intrafallopian transfer or ZIFT involves culturing eggs and sperm outside the body, then placing the zygotes into a woman's fallopian tubes. If the transfer is done at a particular developmental stage, it is called *pronuclear stage tubal transfer* or PROST. Both are variants of *tubal embryo transfer* or TET and reflect the view that the fallopian tubes provide the most protective environment for embryo development.

Intravaginal culture or IVC is another attempt at naturalness. Ova are placed in a tube to which sperm cells are added, and the tube is then inserted into the vagina and kept next to the cervix by a diaphragm. Normal sexual intercourse can take place with the tube in place. Two days later, the tube is removed, the contents decanted, and any fertilized ova transferred into the uterus.

Uterine Lavage Embryo Retrieval or ULER is a method for assisting pregnancy in a woman with a functioning uterus but who is either incapable of ovulation or for some reason (e.g., she knows she is the carrier of a lethal gene) doesn't wish to use her own ova. An ovulating woman is inseminated with donor sperm, then after around five days, the fertilized egg is washed out of the uterus (this is the lavage) before it becomes implanted in the uterine wall. Once retrieved, the embryo is implanted in the woman being assisted. Because fertilization takes place in vivo, instead of in vitro, a potential difficulty is that the embryo may not be washed out before it becomes embedded in the uterine wall. If this happens, the woman must then decide whether to have an abortion.

Partial zona dissection or PZD involves using microtechniques to drill holes in the *zona*, or protective membrane surrounding an ovum, to facilitate the passage of sperm into the interior. This increases the chances of fertilization by reducing the egg's resistance to penetration, which is particularly useful when the sperm involved may be constitutionally weak.

Intracytoplasmic sperm injection or ICSI is a technique that can help 50 to 60 percent of infertile men become fathers. Sperm are examined microscopically and one that seems best shaped and most active is injected directly into the egg cell.

DNA Transfer involves replacing the nucleus of an older egg with one taken from a younger donor egg. The aim is to take advantage of the cellular mechanisms of the younger egg, while keeping the maternal genetic material.

Cytoplasmic Donation or CD involves removing the cytoplasm from a younger donor egg and injecting it into an older egg. Some data indicate this will increase the developmental success of the recipient egg.

New techniques to assist reproduction are being developed at a rapid rate. That so many are available means that if one technique doesn't work, a woman may try another. Yet having so many possibilities makes it difficult for some women who wish to become pregnant to give up the attempt, even after repeated failure.

NEED, SUCCESS RATES, AND COSTS OF ASSISTED REPRODUCTION

In 1995 the U.S. population included 60.2 million women of reproductive age. Some 6.1 million of them, almost 10 percent, were infertile. By some estimates, at least 4 million men are infertile, and one in nine married couples have difficulty conceiving a child. In 1995 alone about 600,000 infertile women sought assistance at the over 300 clinics specializing in treating infertility.

The Centers for Disease Control reported in 1997 the result of its study (the most recent) of the effectiveness of assisted reproductive technology. Attempts to produce pregnancy involve one-month cycles, and during 1995 infertility clinics intervened in 59,142 cycles. The interventions resulted in 11,315 live births (some of them multiple), for a success rate of 19.6 percent. The success rate of individual clinics ranged from 7 to 35 percent.

About 24 percent of the women treated got pregnant, and 78 percent of the pregnancies resulted in live births. (These figures exclude the use of donor eggs or frozen embryos.) Single births occurred in 49.8 percent of the cases, twins in 23.8 percent, and triplets or more in 4.5 percent. Adverse outcomes, such as miscarriage, stillbirth, or ectopic pregnancy, occurred in 21.9 percent of the pregnancies.

According to these figures, the chance of a woman's becoming pregnant with the help of reproductive technology is roughly the same (by some estimates) as that of a normal, healthy couple attempting conception during the woman's regular monthly cycle. But of course not all the pregnancies result in births, and almost three-quarters of the women treated in infertility programs never become pregnant.

The financial cost of an attempt to become pregnant can be staggering. Each fertilization cycle costs from $10,000 to $11,000, and most women who get pregnant go through three or four cycles before pregnancy occurs. Only a dozen states require insurers to cover infertility treatments, and many people go deeply into debt to pay for them. By some estimates the money spent on fertility-related medical services exceeds $2 billion a year.

Cost is not the only drawback to assisted reproduction. Both the consequences of the methods and the methods themselves are associated with a variety of moral and social difficulties.

MULTIPLE BIRTHS

One of the hazards of assisted reproduction is that the fertility drugs given to women to speed up the production of ova can increase the chances that the women will become pregnant with multiple fetuses. Also, if in vitro fertilization is employed, the practice of transferring several embryos into a woman's fallopian tubes to improve the probability that at least one will implant in the uterus may result in the implanting of several embryos.

Unless selective abortion (called *fetal reduction*) is performed, a pregnancy with multiple fetuses puts the pregnancy at risk for miscarriage. A woman carrying quadruplets has a 25 percent chance of a miscarriage in the first trimester; a woman carrying quintuplets has a 50 percent chance.

Also, even if a miscarriage doesn't occur, a multiple pregnancy puts the infants at risk. Normal pregnancies last about forty weeks, but multiple pregnancies rarely go full term. Triplets are born at around 33.5 weeks and quadruplets after 31 weeks. Because of their prematurity, babies born as multiples often suffer from such problems as blindness, stroke, brain damage, and impaired motor skills.

The number of women taking fertility drugs has almost tripled in the last decade, rising from about 1 million to 2.7 million, and the number of multiple births has *quadrupled* in the last twenty-five years. In 1995, 4973 children were born in groups of three or more. Triplets were most common, but already three sets of sextuplets have been born, and no doubt more are on the way.

Should women who become pregnant with multiple fetuses be permitted to decide to try to carry them all to term? Should infertility specialists be restricted in the use they make of fertility drugs? The costs of carrying multiples includes a social cost along with the personal costs of the parents. Should our society insist on selective reduction? (See the *Case Presentation: Septuplets* in this chapter for more details.)

FREEZING EMBRYOS

An important development in the technology of assisted reproduction is the perfection of techniques for freezing embryos. Evidence to date indicates embryos can be stored in a frozen condition and then unfrozen and implanted without any damage to the chromosomes. One advantage of the procedure is that it eliminates the need for a woman to undergo the lengthy and uncomfortable process required to secure additional ova. If a woman fails to become pregnant at a first attempt, an embryo saved from the initial fertilization can be employed in another effort.

The technique also makes it possible to delay an embryo transplant until the potential mother has reached the most favorable time in her menstrual cycle. Furthermore, because embryos survive storage better than ova, when a woman who wants to preserve her option to have a child undergoes chemotherapy, she may have her ova fertilized and the embryos preserved.

Each year around 25,000 embryos are frozen at fertility clinics. Not all the embryos are implanted, and this raises what many consider to be the serious question of what should be done with them. What if a couple storing their embryos get divorced? What if both die? (See the Case Presentation: Embryos in Court.) What if the woman changes her mind about wanting to be pregnant? What if no surrogate is found?

Because more embryos are usually stored than are used to produce a pregnancy, what should be done with the leftovers? Fertility clinics typically offer the options of having excess embryos destroyed, used for research, or offered to an infertile couple. Sometimes, though, couples cannot be traced, and centers are unwilling to give away an embryo without their permission. When embryos are unclaimed in this way or the bills for storage are left unpaid, frozen embryos are usually destroyed simply by being allowed to thaw. (A frozen embryo is only a tiny speck, because development is at the four- to eight-cell stage.)

A British law requires the destruction of unclaimed embryos after five years. The law took effect in August of 1996, and in the face of some protest about 3300 frozen embryos were destroyed. The courts had refused to set aside the law, and the Prime Minister ignored appeals that he intervene. Protesters held a vigil outside Westminster Cathedral, and the Vatican newspaper denounced the destruction as a "prenatal massacre."

Another layer of complexity has been added by the practice at some fertility centers of creating embryos from donated eggs and sperm from commercial sperm banks. The rationale is that donor eggs are scarce, and when more are available than are needed in a particular case, they shouldn't be wasted. Having on hand a collection of embryos that don't belong to any person or couple allows the centers to offer what fertility specialists call *embryo adoption*. This means a woman or couple can choose ("adopt") an embryo for transfer on the basis of a description of the social and educational background and physical characteristics of the gamete donors. A couple can thus try for a resemblance between them and their potential child.

Some critics are troubled by the move from the creation of embryos to help particular people to the production of embryos on the speculation that someone who wants one may appear at the clinic. The practice is open to the charge that reproductive technology is a step nearer to treating human embryos as commercial products to be offered to discriminating consumers. At present there are no national regulations or guidelines for dealing with frozen embryos. Fertility centers set their own policies, and as might be expected, the rules followed by various centers are far from uniform.

The current controversy over embryonic stem cells has focused attention on unused embryos. Those who oppose the use of embryonic stem cells usually do so on the ground that acquiring them typically means destroying human embryos, which they consider to have the moral status of a person. By contrast, those favoring the use of embryonic stem cells argue that it is legitimate to retrieve them from unwanted embryos. Otherwise the embryos will discarded, and the potential to use the stem cells to help cure diseases will be lost.

GESTATIONAL SURROGATES AND DONOR OVA

This is perhaps the most dramatic possibility opened up by in vitro fertilization. A woman whose uterus has been removed, making her incapable of normal pregnancy, can contribute an ovum that, after being fertilized in vitro, is implanted in the uterus of a second woman whose uterus has been prepared to receive it. The "host" or gestational surrogate then carries the baby to term.

In a similar procedure, when a woman is incapable of producing ova, as the result either of disease, injury, or normal aging, a donor ovum may be fertilized in vitro then implanted in her uterus, and she then carries the child to term. Thus, postmenopausal women or many women once considered hopelessly barren may now become pregnant and give birth to a baby, even though they are genetically unrelated to the child.

Gestational surrogacy is a relatively new practice, and it opens up a number of possibilities that may have significant social consequences. That women past the natural age of childbearing can now become mothers is a stunning possibility that has already given rise to ethical and policy questions. (For a discussion, see Social Context: Postmenopausal Motherhood.) Second, women using the services of a gestational surrogate do so at present because they are unable to bear children themselves. However, it is only a short step from being unable to bear children to being *unwilling* to bear children.

Thus, it is easy to imagine that some women might choose to free themselves from the rigors of pregnancy by hiring a gestational surrogate. The employer would be the source of the ovum, which would then be fertilized in vitro and implanted as an embryo in the uterus of the surrogate. Women who could afford to do so could have their own genetic children without ever having to be pregnant.

Although a few have advocated using "genetically superior" women as a source of ova and "less superior" women as gestational surrogates, it is unlikely such a program will ever be endorsed by society. (See the *Briefing Session* in Chapter 5 for the difficulties in determining genetic "superiority.") Nevertheless, such practices are entirely possible, and it's likely they will continue to excite discussion.

The possibilities inherent in the use of gestational surrogacy, donor ova and IVF mentioned so far are all currently employed or easily implemented. By contrast, the development of "baby factories" or "hatcheries" similar to those described in *Brave New World* is technologically unlikely, judged by current science and medicine. Machines would have to serve the function now served by the uterus, and designing such machines would require knowing enough about the needs of the developing fetus to reproduce that function. At present, it's not possible even to state all the problems that would have to be solved.

CRITICISMS OF ASSISTED REPRODUCTION PRACTICES

While admitting the present and potential values of reproductive technology in assisting women who want to have children, many critics think it has been oversold. Despite their hopes, the majority of women who must rely on it don't become pregnant. Also, women aren't always properly informed about their chances. A particular clinic may have a success rate of 25 percent, but for a woman in her early forties, the rate may be only a 1 to 2 percent chance per month of trying. (Only about 25 percent of those who seek assistance overcome their infertility.)

Critics also point out that the expense of trying to become pregnant can be quite high. Each attempt costs about $10,000 or more, and several attempts are usually required for success. Further, the procedures involve anxiety and discomfort. While the risk of injury and infection isn't great, it is real. In addition, the safety of the fertility drugs used to trigger ovulation and to prepare the uterus for implantation has been questioned. Also, there is a possibility the high hormone levels in the blood the drugs produce may increase a woman's risk of breast cancer.

An increase in the use of "donated" eggs raises serious issues about donors. All are young women, many are college students, and most are motivated to contribute their eggs for money. A typical fee is around $2000, and some women contribute two or more times. Sperm donors (see further on) usually receive only about $50, but egg donors must spend more time, experience discomfort, and run risks to their own health. They must agree to be injected with drugs to stimulate their ovaries (which may produce nausea and fatigue) and have frequent blood tests and ultrasound scans to determine when the ova are ready. They must then be anesthetized and the eggs retrieved from their follicles.

Donated ova are a scarce commodity, and some fertility clinics and programs make an effort to recruit donors so ova will be available for their clients. Some critics regard the situation as one in which young women in need lack the protection of the law and risk being exploited by those in a financial position to offer them money. As matters stand, only the moral principles of those who recruit donors regulate the practice.

BENEFITS OF IVF AND OTHER FORMS OF ASSISTED REPRODUCTION

Assisted reproduction is complicated, expensive, and requires a great investment of skill, knowledge, and resources. An obvious question is, What is to be gained by it? That is, what benefits might justify the use of the technically difficult and expensive medical procedures involved?

The most direct and perhaps the most persuasive answer is that assisted reproduction makes it possible for many people to have children who wouldn't otherwise be able to do so. For those people, this is a decisive consideration. Research shows that more than 10 percent of married couples in the United States are infertile—that is, they have attempted to conceive a child for a year or longer without success. As noted earlier, infertility affects 6.1 million women and an estimated 4 million men. In 1995 alone more than 1 million people sought professional help in conceiving a child.

Assisted reproduction isn't a solution to all problems of fertility, but it's the only solution possible in a large number of cases. Figures show that as many as 45 percent of all cases of female infertility are caused by abnormal or obstructed fallopian tubes. Although normal ova are produced, they cannot move down the tubes to be fertilized. In some cases, tissue blocking the tubes may be removed, or the tubes reconstructed. In other cases, however, the tubes may be impossible to repair or may be entirely absent. (Only 40 to 50 percent of infertile women can be helped through surgery.) This means that the only way in which these women can expect to have a child of their own is by means of some sort of assisted reproduction. This is also true when the woman has no uterus or is postmenopausal and must rely on a donated ovum. Thus, technology offers a realistic possibility of becoming parents to many people who once had no hope of having a child.

Critics of assisted reproduction often claim there is no *right* to have a child and suggest that those unable to conceive should simply accept the fact and perhaps adopt a child. Proponents don't justify assisted reproduction in terms of rights, however. They refer primarily to the strong desire some people have to become parents, and some point out that assisted reproduction, as it is most often employed, is nothing more than a means of facilitating a natural function that can't be carried out because of some sort of biological failure.

ETHICAL AND SOCIAL DIFFICULTIES

Several aspects of the technology of assisted reproduction and the way it is being employed are regarded by some people as troublesome. Briefly, we will consider a few sources of unease not mentioned earlier.

1. *Destroyed embryos.* Ova removed for fertilization may not all be used. Although they may be mixed with sperm and several become fertilized, only a few embryos are selected for implantation. The others may be simply discarded. Unclaimed and unused frozen embryos may be treated the same way. For those who believe that human life begins at conception, the destruction of embryos may be viewed as tantamount to abortion. Thus, the destruction may be regarded as destroying innocent human life.

Others, who are not prepared to ascribe personhood to an embryo, may still be troubled by its pointless destruction. They may believe its potential to develop into a human being at least requires that it be treated with concern and respect. Those who subscribe to such views might argue that the only legitimate form of assisted reproduction is one in which the effort is made to fertilize only a single ovum. A failure in fertilization would then be similar to the failure that occurs naturally, and what would be eliminated would be the necessity of destroying fertilized eggs that cannot be implanted.

2. *Danger to the fetus.* Some critics worry that the use of reproductive technology like IVF, GIFT, or frozen embryos may pose risks to the fetus and to the person it may become. But experience has taken the teeth out of this objection. The rate of birth impairments in children born using established forms of reproductive technology is about 3 percent, virtually the same as that of ordinary births.

So far there is no evidence that children conceived by means of assisted reproduction differ in any way from other children. Where a new technology like cloning is concerned, however, this objection may still have bite. So far the necessary animal experiments haven't been done to establish a cloning procedure as reliable and safe.

3. *Eugenics.* The use of reproductive technology may encourage the development of eugenic ideas about improving the species. Rather than having children of their own, would-be parents might be motivated to seek out ova (and sperm) from people who possess physical and intellectual characteristics that are particularly admired. Thus, even without an organized plan of social eugenics (see Chapter 4), individuals might be tempted to follow their own eugenic notions. This includes the tendency to try to have "the perfect baby," and this cheapens human life by promoting the view that human babies are commodities produced to order.

4. *Sex selection.* Similarly, would-be parents might be inclined to exercise the potential for control over the sex of their offspring. Only males contain both an

X and a Y chromosome, and their presence is detectable in the cells of the developing embryo. Determination of the sex of the embryo would allow the potential parents to decide whether they wish to have a male or female child. Consequently, a potential human being (the developing fetus) might be destroyed for what is basically a trivial reason.

5. *Weakening of family.* Reproductive technology may promote a social climate in which having children becomes severed from the family. The procedures emphasize the mechanics of conception and so minimize the significance of the shared love and commitments of the parents of a child conceived by intercourse.

Similarly, the technology dilutes the notion of parenthood by making possible peculiar relationships. For example, as many as five people may become involved in having a child, for a couple can use donor sperm and donor eggs and rely on the services of a surrogate for pregnancy. Because there is no clear sense in which the child belongs to any of them, parenthood is radically severed from conception.

Obviously, these difficulties are not ones likely to be considered equally serious by everyone. Those who do not believe life begins at conception will hardly be troubled by the discarding of unimplanted embryos. Research and experience will likely reduce the risks of new and still unused technologies like cloning. Sex choice is possible now by the use of amniocentesis, so it's not a problem unique to reproductive technology, and the same is true of the implementation of eugenic ideas.

Finally, whether assisted reproduction actually leads to a weakening of the values associated with the family is partly an empirical question that only additional experience will show. Even if childbearing does become severed from current family structure, it still must be shown this is in itself something of which we ought to disapprove. It's not impossible that alternative social structures for childbearing and childrearing might be superior to ones currently dominant in Western culture.

CLONING AND TWINNING

Cloning involves producing individuals that are exact genetic copies of the donor from whom the DNA was obtained. Some animal cells have been cloned for more than five decades, but it wasn't until 1997 that the first mammal was cloned. Nothing in principle seems to stand in the way of cloning a human, but if human cloning became a practical reality, it would present serious moral and social issues. (See the Social Context: Hello, Dolly.)

Many of the issues raised in a speculative way by cloning are raised in a more immediate way by the procedure known as *twinning.* In 1993 Jerry Hall and Robert Stillman took 17 two- to eight-cell human embryos, separated the *blastomeres* (the individual cells) and coated them with artificial *zona pellucida* (the protective coat surrounding egg cells), then placed them in various nutrient solutions. The outcome was the production of forty-eight new embryos from the original ones.

The cells continued to divide, but development stopped after six days, partly because the embryos were abnormal—the original ones were chosen just because they were defective. The work was purely experimental, and it was never intended that the embryos would be implanted.

The immediate advantage of the techniques developed by Hall and Stillman (as well as many others) is to increase the supply of implantable embryos for couples with fertility problems. If a couple's embryos, produced by in vitro fertilization, can be used to produce several embryos, these can be used in repeated implantation attempts. Thus, the woman does not have to undergo repetitions of the unpleasant, expensive, and somewhat risky procedures involved in triggering ovulation, then retrieving ova for in vitro fertilization. Regarded from this point of view, for some couples, the techniques may make having a child easier, cheaper, and less time-consuming.

The process used by Hall and Stillman was, strictly speaking, not actually cloning, which requires taking a somatic cell from a developed organism, extracting the DNA, then growing an embryo from it. Even so, the process of twinning they employed showed it would take very little more technically to use the techniques of assisted reproduction and produce a number of genetically identical humans.

Such techniques, when combined with the freezing of embryos, open up a number of social possibilities as surprising and controversial as those cloning would make possible:

1. The production of several identical embryos would make a market in embryos possible. If a child had already been born and could be shown to have desirable qualities, the couple who had produced the embryos might sell them at high prices. It would then be possible for someone to have a child genetically identical to the one with the desirable qualities.

2. Parents could have a family in which all their children are genetic copies of one another. The oldest and the youngest would have the same genetic endowment. If several gestational mothers were employed, it would be possible to produce a dozen or more genetically identical children of the same age.

3. A couple might have a child, while also freezing an embryo twin as a spare. If the child should die, then the genetic twin could be grown from the embryo. The twin would be as much like the lost child as genetics makes possible.

4. If embryo twins were frozen and stored, they could be implanted in a gestational mother years apart. Thus, one twin might be sixty years old, while the other is only six.

5. Twins of an individual might be stored so that if the person needed something like a bone marrow or kidney transplant, the twin could be implanted in a gestational surrogate and allowed to develop. The tissue match from the twin would be perfect, and the problem of rejection would not arise.

The issues raised by twinning differ little from those raised by cloning, and twinning is already a practical reality. Some of the uses are so benign as to be hardly debatable, while others may result in such a cheapening or commercialization of human life as to be undesirable options.

ARTIFICIAL INSEMINATION

In 1909, an unusual letter appeared in the professional journal *Medical World*. A. D. Hard, the author of the letter, claimed that when he was a student at Jefferson Medical College in Philadelphia, a wealthy businessman and his wife consulted a physician on the faculty about their inability to conceive a child. A detailed examination showed the man was incapable of producing sperm. The case was presented for discussion in a class of which Hard was a member. According to Hard, the class suggested semen should be taken from the "best-looking member of the class" and used to inseminate the wife.

The letter claimed this was done while the woman was anesthetized and that neither the husband nor the wife was told about the process. The patient became pregnant and gave birth to a son. The husband was then told how the pregnancy was produced, and, although he was pleased with the result, he asked that his wife not be informed.

The event described by Hard took place in 1884, and Hard was probably "the best-looking member of the class."

The Philadelphia case is usually acknowledged to be the first recorded instance of the artificial insemination of donor sperm in a human patient. However, the process itself has a much longer history. Arab horsemen in the fourteenth century apparently inseminated mares with semen-soaked sponges, and in the eighteenth century the Italian physiologist Spallansani documented experiments in which he fertilized dogs, reptiles, and frogs.

THE PROCEDURE

Artificial insemination has become one of the basic techniques of assisted reproduction. It's initiated when the woman's body temperature indicates that ovulation is to take place in one or two days, then is repeated once or twice more until her body temperature shows that ovulation is completed. Typically, three inseminations are performed during a monthly cycle.

The procedure is simple. The patient is usually placed in a position so that her hips are raised. A semen specimen, collected earlier through masturbation or taken from a sperm bank, is placed in a syringe attached to a catheter. The catheter is inserted into the cervical canal and the semen slowly injected into the uterus. The patient then stays in her position for fifteen or twenty minutes to increase the chances that the sperm will fertilize an ovum.

The overall success rate of artificial insemination is about 85 to 90 percent. Success on the first attempt is quite rare, and the highest rate occurs in the third month. In unusual cases, efforts may be made every month for as long as six months or a year. Such efforts are continued, however, only when a detailed examination shows that the woman is not suffering from some unrecognized problem preventing her from becoming pregnant.

When sperm taken from donors is used, the rate of congenital abnormalities is a little lower than that for the general population. There is no evidence that manipulating the sperm causes any harm. Some physicians prefer to employ fresh, rather than frozen, sperm to minimize the amount of environmental change the sperm is subjected to. Other physicians, however, claim that frozen sperm is to be preferred, for it provides an opportunity for screening out defective sperm or chromosome abnormalities.

REASONS FOR SEEKING ARTIFICIAL INSEMINATION

Artificial insemination may be sought for a variety of reasons. When a couple is involved, the reasons are almost always associated with factors that make it impossible for the couple to conceive a child in the usual sexual way. About 10 percent of all married couples are infertile, and 40 percent of those cases are due to factors involving the male.

In some instances, the male may be unable to produce any sperm at all (a condition called asospermia), or the number of sperm he produces may be too low to make impregnation of the female likely (a condition called oligospermia). In other cases, while adequate numbers of sperm cells may be produced, they may not function normally. They may not be sufficiently motile to make their way past the vaginal canal and through the opening to the uterus. Hence, their chances of reaching and penetrating an ovum are slight. Finally, the male may suffer from a neurological condition that makes ejaculation impossible or from a disease (such as diabetes) that renders him impotent.

If the female cannot ovulate, or if her fallopian tubes are blocked so that ova cannot descend, artificial insemination can accomplish nothing. (See the earlier section on in vitro fertilization.) Yet there are factors affecting the female that artificial insemination can be helpful in overcoming. For example, if the female has a vaginal environment that is biochemically inhospitable to sperm, the artificial insemination may be successful. Because the sperm need not pass through the vagina, they have a better chance of surviving. Also, if the female has a small cervix (the opening to the uterus) or if her uterus is in an abnormal position, then artificial insemination may be used to deliver the sperm to an advantageous position for fertilization, a position they otherwise might not reach.

A couple might also seek artificial insemination for genetic reasons. Both may be carriers of a recessive gene for a genetic disorder (Tay–Sachs disease, for example) or the male may be the carrier of a dominant gene for a genetic disorder (Huntington's disease, for example). In either case, the couple may not want to run the statistical risk of their child's being born with a genetic disease, yet may also not be willing to accept prenatal testing and abortion. To avoid the possibility they fear, they may choose to make use of artificial insemination with sperm secured from a donor.

The traditional recipient of artificial insemination is a married woman who, in consultation with her husband, has decided to have a child. Some physiological or physical difficulty in conceiving leads them to turn to artificial insemination. But the traditional recipient is no longer the only recipient.

Those seeking to have the procedure performed now include single women who wish to have a child but do not wish to have it fathered in the usual fashion. The number of such inseminations may increase in the future if the notion of being a single parent continues to be met with acceptance or approval within our society. The increase may be quite rapid if the attitudes of physicians, in particular, change. At present, single women who wish to become mothers are likely to be discouraged, and some physicians and infertility centers won't accept them as candidates for artificial insemination.

TYPES OF ARTIFICIAL INSEMINATION

Artificial insemination can be divided into types in accordance with the source of the sperm employed. Artificial insemination (homologous) or AIH uses sperm obtained from the male partner. Artificial insemination (heterologous) or AID uses sperm from a sperm donor. The use of semen obtained from a donor is the most frequent of AI procedures and gives rise to most of the social and legal issues surrounding the practice.

Artificial insemination (confused) or CAI employs a mixture of sperm from the male partner and sperm obtained from a donor. CAI has no particular biological advantage, but it offers a couple a degree of psychological support. Because they cannot be sure that it was not sperm from the male partner that resulted in conception, they may be more inclined to accept the child as the product of their union. The role of the third-party sperm donor is thus psychologically minimized.

SPERM DONORS

Sperm donors are typically selected from medical or college student volunteers. Commercial sperm banks may recruit widely, but generally an effort is made to employ as donors people in excellent health with a high level of intellectual ability. Their family histories are reviewed to reduce the possibility of transmitting a genetic disorder, and their blood type is checked to determine its compatibility with that of the AID recipient. Such general physical features of the donor as body type, hair and eye color, and complexion are matched in a rough way with those of the potential parents. To be a donor, an individual must also be known to be fertile. This means he must already be a biological parent or that he must fall within the normal range in several semen analyses.

Donors are typically paid for their services. What is more, their identity is kept secret from the recipient and her husband. A coding system is ordinarily used both to preserve the anonymity of the donor and to ensure that the same donor is used in all inseminations.

Sperm contributed by a donor might be employed in an insemination within one to three hours after the semen is obtained. As mentioned earlier, some physicians prefer to use freshly obtained sperm in the procedure. But sperm may also be maintained in a frozen condition and, after being restored to the proper temperature, used in the same way as fresh sperm. Sperm banks are no more than freezers containing racks of coded plastic tubes holding donated sperm.

The semen stored in sperm banks is not necessarily that of anonymous donors. For a variety of reasons, individuals may wish to have their sperm preserved and pay a fee to a sperm-bank operator for this service. For example, a man planning a vasectomy or one expecting to become sterile because of a progressive disease may store his sperm in the event that he may later want to father a child.

ISSUES IN ARTIFICIAL INSEMINATION

Artificial insemination presents a variety of moral, legal, and social issues that have not been addressed in a thorough fashion. Legal scholars have explored some of the consequences that AI has for traditional legal doctrines of paternity, legitimacy, and inheritance. They have also made recommendations for formulating new laws (or reformulating old ones) to take into account the reality of the practice of AI.

Others who have written about AI have focused mostly on its potential for altering the relationship between husbands and wives and for producing undesirable social changes. Many of the objections to assisted reproduction in general have also been offered to AI. For example, it's been argued that AI will take the love out of sexual procreation and make it a purely mechanical process, that AI will promote eugenics and so denigrate the worth of babies that fall short of some ideal, and that AI is just another step down the road toward the society of *Brave New World*.

Some of the issues that need close attention from philosophers concern individual rights and responsibilities. For example, does a man who has served as a sperm donor have any special moral responsibilities? He certainly must have some responsibilities. For example, it would be wrong for him to lie about any genetic diseases in his family history. But does he have any responsibilities to the child that is produced by AI employing his sperm? If donating sperm is no different from donating blood, then perhaps he does not. But is such a comparison apt?

Can a child born as a result of AI legitimately demand to know the name of his biological father? We need not assume mere curiosity might motivate such a request. Someone could need to know his family background in order to determine how likely it is that a potential child might have a genetic disorder. Perhaps the current practice of maintaining the anonymity of sperm donors is not one that can stand critical scrutiny.

Should a woman be allowed to order sperm donated by someone who approximates her concept of an ideal person? Should she be able to request a donor from a certain ethnic group, with particular eye and hair color, certain minimum or maximum height, physical attractiveness, with evidence of intelligence, and so on? At present, the physician who performs the procedure also makes the choice of the donor. But why should the physician be granted the right to make the selection? One might argue that allowing the physician to exercise such a power violates the autonomy of the AI recipient.

A number of other ethical questions are easily raised about AI: Does any woman (married or single, of any age) have the right to demand AI? Should a physician make AID available to a married woman even if her husband is opposed?

Other questions concerning the proper procedures to follow in the practice of AI are also of considerable significance. For example, how thoroughly must sperm donors be screened for genetic defects? What standards of quality must sperm as a biological material be required to satisfy? What physical, educational, or general social traits (if any) should individual donors possess? Should records be maintained and shared through an established network to prevent the marriage or mating of individuals born from AID with the same biological father?

At present, these questions have been answered only by individual physicians or clinics, if at all. There are no general medical or legal policies governing the practice of AI. Even if present practices are adequate, most people would agree there is a need to develop uniform policies to regulate AI.

Obviously, we have touched upon only a few of the ethical and social issues that the practice of artificial insemination generates. Indeed, at the moment, it is not wholly clear even what the more significant issues may be.

OVA DONORS

The use of donor ova presents virtually the same set of issues as those raised by artificial insemination. In addition, as mentioned earlier, unlike AI, egg donation raises questions about the exploitation of donors. They are typically young women who agree to donate ova because they want to earn the several thousand dollars fertility clinics are willing to pay.

To earn the money, they must put themselves through an uncomfortable process involving treatment with powerful drugs and the retrieval of the eggs by a small surgical incision or a needle puncture. The risk to their health is small but real. Critics point out that women willing to submit themselves to the process must be young and are likely to be naive and vulnerable. A need for money will thus make them ripe for exploitation. Paying money to someone for performing a service does not in itself constitute exploitation, however, and critics could make a stronger case if they were able to show how women are harmed by the practice.

SURROGATE PREGNANCY

A *gestational surrogate* (see the discussion above) is a "host mother," a woman who is implanted with an embryo produced from the ovum of another woman. *Surrogate mothers* are women who agree to become pregnant by means of artificial insemination. The surrogate mother carries the baby to term, then turns the baby over for adoption to the couple or individual with whom she made the agreement.

Surrogate mothers are typically sought by couples who wish to have a child with whom at least the man has a genetic link and who have been unsuccessful in conceiving one themselves. Also, a woman unable to conceive but wanting a child may also arrange for the services of a surrogate mother by using donor sperm.

Various legal complications surround surrogate pregnancy, and at least eighteen states have passed laws regulating surrogacy arrangements. Some laws, like those in Michigan and New Jersey, make it illegal for couples to adopt a child born to a surrogate mother. The aim is to discourage surrogacy.

When surrogacy arrangements are allowed, a major problem is to find a way to pay women who agree to be surrogates. Adoption laws forbid the selling of children or even the payment of money to one of the biological parents in connection with adoption. The child must be freely surrendered. Because a child born to a surrogate mother is, in the absence of laws to the contrary, legally her child, the child must be adopted by the couple securing her services. How then can the surrogate mother be paid?

Some women have simply volunteered to be surrogate mothers so the issue of payment would not arise. In general, however, the difficulty has been resolved by paying the mother to compensate her for her inconvenience and the loss of her time. Technically, then, she is not being paid for conceiving and bearing a child, nor is she being paid for the child who is handed over for adoption. Hence, laws against selling a child are not violated, and the surrogate is paid from $10,000 to $25,0000.

A second problem is finding a way to permit surrogacy, while avoiding turning it into a commercial operation resembling the breeding of horses or show dogs. Surrogacy is often arranged by an attorney acting as a broker on behalf of a couple who want a child. The attorney finds the surrogate and draws up a contract between her and the couple. (The contract can include such items as a prorated fee if the surrogate miscarries or a requirement that the surrogate have an abortion if prenatal tests reveal a fetal abnormality.) The surrogate must agree to relinquish her maternal rights and not stand in the way of adoption by the contracting couple. For arranging the surrogacy, as well as for drawing up the contract, the broker receives a fee of $15,000 to $25,000.

Despite the claim that a surrogate is being paid for her time and inconvenience, some critics charge that surrogacy arrangements are no more than "baby selling." To avoid this appearance, New York State passed a law with the aim of removing the profit motive from surrogacy arrangements and making them completely noncommercial. The state kept it legal for a woman to become a surrogate but made it illegal to pay a broker to handle the arrangements. Further, the state made it illegal to pay a surrogate for anything more than her medical expenses. A contract agreeing to pay a fee to a broker or to a woman acting as a surrogate would have no legal standing in court.

Some of the same reasons offered to justify assisted reproduction can also be offered for surrogate pregnancy. Fundamentally, couples who wish to have a child of their own but are unable to do so because of some uncorrectable medical difficulty experienced by the woman view surrogate pregnancy as the only hope remaining to them. Some rule out adoption because of the relative shortage of available infants, and some simply want a genetic connection between them and the child. Many people are quite desperate to have a child of their own.

Some critics have charged that surrogate pregnancy is no more than a specialized form of prostitution. A woman, in effect, rents out her body for a period of time and is paid for doing so. Such a criticism rests on the assumption that prostitution is morally wrong, and this is a claim at least some would deny is correct. Furthermore, the criticism fails to take into account the differences in aims. Some surrogate mothers have volunteered their services with no expectation of monetary reward, and some women have agreed to be surrogate mothers at the request of their sister, friend, daughter, or son. Even those who are paid mention that part of their motivation is to help those couples who so desperately want a child. Far from condemning surrogate mothers as acting immorally, it is possible to view at least some as acting in a morally heroic way by contributing to the good of others through their actions.

Perhaps the most serious objection to surrogate mothers is that they are likely to be recruited from the ranks of those most in need of money. Women of upper- and middle-income groups are not likely to serve as surrogate mothers. Women with low-paying jobs or no jobs at all are obviously the prime candidates for recruiters. It might be charged, then, that women who become surrogate mothers are being exploited by those who have money enough to pay for their services.

Merely paying someone in need of money to do something does not constitute exploitation, however. To make such a charge stick, it would be necessary to show that women who become surrogate mothers are under a great deal of social and economic pressure and have no other realistic options. Furthermore, it could be argued that, within limits, individuals have a right to do with their bodies as they choose. If a woman freely decides to earn money by serving as a surrogate mother, then we have no more reason to object to her decision than we would have to object to a man's decision to earn money by working as a laborer.

As the population ages and women with careers postpone having children, the employment of surrogate mothers is likely to increase. The practice is now well established, but the ethical and social issues are far from being resolved to the general satisfaction of our society.

ETHICAL THEORIES AND REPRODUCTIVE CONTROL

One of the themes of Mary Shelley's famous novel *Frankenstein* is that it is both wrong and dangerous to tamper with the natural forces of life. It is wrong because it disturbs the natural order of things, and it is dangerous because it unleashes forces beyond human control. The "monster" that is animated by Dr. Victor Frankenstein stands as a warning and reproach to all who seek to impose their will on the world through the powers of scientific technology.

The fundamental ethical question about the technology of human reproductive control is whether it ought to be employed at all. Is it simply wrong for us to use our knowledge of human biology to exercise power over the processes of human reproduction?

The natural law view, as represented by currently accepted doctrines of the Roman Catholic Church, suggests that all the techniques for controlling human reproduction that we have discussed here are fundamentally wrong.

Children may ordinarily be expected as a result of sexual union within marriage. However, if no measures are wrongfully taken to frustrate the possibility of their birth (contraception, for example), then a married couple has no obligation to attempt to conceive children by means such as artificial insemination or in vitro fertilization. Certainly, they have no reason to resort to anything as extreme as cloning or using donor embryos.

Indeed, many of the technological processes are themselves inherently objectionable. Artificial insemination, for example, requires male masturbation, which is prima facie wrong, since it is an act that can be considered to be unnatural, given the natural end of sex. AI, even when semen from the husband is used, tends to destroy the values inherent in the married state. It makes conception a mechanical act.

In vitro fertilization is open to the same objections. In addition, the process itself involves the destruction of fertilized ova. On the view that human conception takes place at the moment of fertilization, this means that the discarding of unimplanted embryos amounts to the destruction of human life.

On the utilitarian view, no reproductive technology is in itself objectionable. The question that has to be answered is whether the use of any particular procedure, in general or in a certain case, is likely to lead to more good than not. In general, it is reasonable to believe that a utilitarian would be likely to approve of all the procedures we've discussed here.

A rule utilitarian, however, might oppose any or all of the procedures. If there is strong evidence to support the view that the use of reproductive technology will lead to a society in which the welfare of its members will not be served, then a rule utilitarian would be on firm ground in arguing that reproductive technology ought to be abandoned.

According to Ross's ethical theory, we have prima facie duties of beneficence. That is, we have an obligation to assist others in bettering their lives. This suggests that the use of reproductive technology may be justified as a means to promote the well-being of others. For example, if a couple desires to have a child but is unable to conceive one, then either in vitro fertilization procedures or artificial insemination might be employed to help them satisfy their shared desire. Twinning might be used to increase the number of embryos, and even cloning seems prima facie unobjectionable.

Kantian principles don't seem to supply grounds for objecting to assisted reproduction or reproductive technology in general as inherently wrong. However, the maxim involved in each action must always be one that satisfies the categorical imperative. Consequently, some instances of in vitro fertilization, artificial insemination, twinning, and cloning would no doubt be morally wrong.

The technology of reproduction is a reality of ordinary life. So far it has made our society into neither a dystopia nor a utopia. It's just one set of tools among the many that science and medicine have forged.

Yet the tools are powerful ones, and we should beware of allowing familiarity to produce indifference. The moral and social issues raised by reproductive technology are just as real as the technology. So far we have not treated some of them with the seriousness they deserve.

SOCIAL CONTEXT
Hello, Dolly: The Advent of Cloning

On February 3, 1997, Ian Wilmut of the Roslin Institute in Edinburgh, Scotland, made public the information that he and his research group had successfully produced a clone of an adult sheep. The younger genetic twin, the clone they named Dolly, had been born about seven months earlier and appeared to be healthy and normal in every respect.

The procedure Wilmut followed had a cookbook simplicity but was scientifically highly sophisticated. He took cells from the mammary tissue of a Finn Dorset ewe and got them to stop going through the ordinary process of cell division by culturing them in a medium with a low level of nutrients. Retrieving egg cells from a Scottish Blackface ewe, he removed their nuclei (hence the DNA), then mixed them with the mammary cells. By passing a weak current of electricity through the mixture, Wilmut got some of the egg cells and mammary cells to fuse together. He then used a second pulse of electricity to activate the machinery responsible for cell division.

Six days later, some of the fused cells had divided, becoming embryos in the way a fertilized egg develops into an embryo. Using the technology of embryo transfer, Wilmut succeeded in implanting one of the embryos in the uterus of a third sheep, another Blackface ewe. At the end of her pregnancy, the ewe gave birth to a lamb that was the genetic twin of the Finn Dorset sheep that supplied the mammary cells.

Wilmut and his group made 277 tries at fusing the body cells with the enucleated cells, but they managed to produce only 29 embryos that lasted longer than six days, the usual time in vitro fertilization specialists allow for a fertilized egg to develop into an embryo before transferring it into the uterus. Of the embryos Wilmut implanted, Dolly was the sole success.

The great majority of biologists were amazed at Wilmut's achievement. While they acknowledged that the DNA in the nucleus of a body cell contains a complete set of genes and so, in principle, could be used to produce another genetically identical individual, they didn't believe our understanding of cells was detailed enough actually to do it. The view accepted by most researchers was that once a cell finds its place in the body, it switches off all the genes it contains, except those it needs to do its job and to reproduce itself. But to become an embryo, the genes must be switched on again. When the embryo is implanted in a uterus, they must be able to orchestrate the stunningly complicated process of development, changing the embryo into an offspring.

Wilmut demonstrated that what the majority of scientists considered only a distant possibility could be achieved in a relatively straightforward fashion. Placing the mammary cells in a culture low in nutrients seemed to return them to the state when their genetic potential is still open, and the pulse of electricity seemed to trigger them into dividing and developing. Wilmut showed it wasn't necessary to understand the underlying biology of the process to control it. Under the right conditions, the DNA would reprogram itself to initiate and direct development.

ESTABLISHED AS REAL

Wilmut's achievement was initially greeted with skepticism by some in the research community. Cloning was demonstrated as a phenomenon beyond doubt, however, in July 1998. Ryuzo Yanagimachi and his team at the University of Hawaii reported that they had produced more than fifty mouse clones. Some of the mice, moreover, were clones of clones.

Yanagimachi's technique was a variation of Wilmut's. Using the genetic material from a mouse cumulus cell in the resting phase, he injected it into an enucleated mouse egg, then used chemicals to get the cell to divide. The cell was then implanted into a surrogate mother and allowed to develop into a mouse. In one experiment, tan mice were used as genetic donors, black mice as egg donors, and white mice as gestational surrogates. The clones were all tan.

After Yanagimachi's demonstration, doubt about the reality of cloning evaporated. Scientists have now succeeded in cloning cows, goats, pigs, and cats. The first cat was cloned in 2002 only because researchers at Texas A&M failed (as others had) to clone a dog. Called cc, for "carbon copy" or "copycat," the kitten was the only successful result of attempts using eighty-seven cloned embryos transferred to gestational surrogates.

DRAWBACKS

Despite cc's name, she really isn't an exact copy of her biological mother, a two-year-old calico cat named Rainbow. Although the two are genetically identical, the color and pattern of cc's coat is different. Coat color results from the separation and distribution of pigmented cells. This takes place during development and is not completely determined by genes.

While cc is apparently healthy and normal, some cloned animals have not been so fortunate. A number die soon after birth, while others suffer from a variety of birth anomalies. Developmental delays, defective hearts, underdeveloped lungs, neurological deficits, and faulty immune systems are the more common flaws. Some cloned mice appear normal, then as they grow, they become extremely fat. Developing calves become oversized and die prematurely.

Scientists don't know exactly what happens to cause these adverse results. Apparently, however, cloning promotes the occurrence of random changes. During normal reproduction, both egg and sperm mature before they combine, but in cloning, eggs are harvested and the DNA in cells combined with them must all be reprogrammed during a period of minutes or hours. During the process, researchers think, genes are altered and random errors occur. These cause unpredictable problems that can crop up at any time during development or after birth.

That cloning works at all is surprising to some researchers, given what needs to happen to make it possible. Still, even under the best laboratory conditions and in skilled hands,only about 3 percent of attempts at cloning mammals are successful. Only about one attempt in a hundred results in a viable calf.

When Dolly was born, some scientists speculated that it was likely she would age prematurely. The cell from which the nuclear DNA was removed had already undergone a number of cell divisions and, given that cells divide only about fifty times before they die, perhaps the clock for Dolly had already been ticking before she was born. Experience with cloned animals, however, has so far not shown that they age prematurely.

PRACTICAL USES

1. Cloning is expected to be the foundation of what is now called *pharming*—the use of animals to produce drugs. The Roslin Institute is an agricultural research

center, and a third of Wilmut's funding came from PLP Therapeutics, a biotechnology firm. Wilmut's aim, as well as PLP's, is to produce a flock of sheep genetically
engineered to give milk containing such medically valuable and expensive substances as blood-clotting factor, insulin, and human growth hormone. If a single
sheep able to secrete one of these substances in her milk could be created, cells
from her could be cloned into a herd. Cloning would make it possible to produce
whatever number of animal drug factories are needed, insuring us a supply of useful substances at lower prices.

2. The interest in cloning cattle is to produce a line that has properties that are valued for commercial reasons. A cow that produces substantially more milk than usual,
for example, could be cloned to produce a herd of dairy cows. The milk yield from
such a herd would significantly reduce the cost of milk production and boost profits.

3. The research that produced cc, the cloned cat, was supported by Genetics
Saving and Clone, a biotech company that aims to profit from cloning valued pets.
The company is already storing, for a fee, DNA samples from pets, with the expectation that cloning technology will soon be adequate to producing a genetic replica
of a beloved pet. Dogs were the first target, but when cloning them turned out to be
intractable, the company turned to cats.
Critics object to the whole idea of the enterprise, pointing out that in the U.S.
alone millions of dogs and cats are destroyed each year as an unwanted surplus.
Thus, it is pointlessly cruel to create even more. Those who believe they will get an
identical version of their cat or dog are simply mistaken. Cc's coat color was different from her mother's, and very likely her behavior and personality will also be different. Developmental factors, including environmental ones, are likely to result in
a very different animal.

4. In 2002 Immerge Biotherapeutics and PPL Therapeutics independently announced that they had succeeded in cloning pigs from which the gene encoding the
sugar GAL had been "knocked out." The GAL molecule on the surface of cells triggers hyperacute rejection in humans. (The molecule is not expressed in primates.)
Thus, the hope is that the production of pigs lacking this molecule will make it more
likely that pig organs can be used as transplants in humans.

5. Advanced Cell Technologies announced in 2002 that it had cloned cow eggs
and, when the embryos had developed into fetuses, had removed kidney cells and
transferred them to a spongelike matrix. The cells developed into what researchers
described as a small kidney. When the kidney was implanted into the cow contributing the DNA, it produced a small amount of urine. While no one sees this as
an acceptable procedure for use with human cells, it demonstrates the possibility of
growing transplant organs without relying on stem cells. (For the controversy over
stem cells, see the Classic Case Presentation: The Stem-Cell Debate at the beginning of this chapter.)

6. The possibility of using human embryonic stem cells to treat diseases, repair
organs, and even grow whole organs makes cloning outstandingly important.

Embryonic stem cells are obtained from embryos. If someone with (say) diabetes needed stem cells for treatment, to overcome the problem of tissue rejection, her DNA could be used to replace the nucleus in a donor egg. When the egg formed a blastocyst, the stem cells could be removed. They would be a perfect genetic match with her own tissue. This is an example of *therapeutic cloning*. That is, the cloning is for the purpose of getting materials for treatment, not for the purpose of reproduction. Because embryos must be destroyed to secure the stem cells, those who consider human embryos to have the status of persons regard even therapeutic cloning as a serious moral wrong.

WHAT ABOUT HUMANS?

Most of the public discussion has focused on human *reproductive cloning*. People have been quick to realize that if a sheep and other mammals have been cloned, there seems to be no technical reason a human can't be also.

Assuming the procedure were perfected, here are a few of the possibilities it opens up:

1. When one of a couple carries a gene responsible for a devastating illness like Tay–Sachs disease, the couple could decide to have a child using only the genetic material from the non-carrier.
2. Women who have entered menopause as a result of chemotherapy, had their ovaries removed for therapeutic reasons, or are postmenopausal could still have a genetically connected child by employing the DNA from their somatic cells. The child would be a genetically identical twin, as well as an offspring.
3. Similarly, men who are sterile for any reason or who no longer are capable of producing undamaged sperm (as a result of cancer surgery or radiation treatments, for example) may still father a child.
4. The parents of a dying child could decide to have another child who will be a genetically identical replacement.
5. A woman could decide to use the DNA of a dying (or just dead) partner to have a child who would be the partner's genetic twin. A man could achieve the same end by finding a woman who would agree to be a gestational surrogate.
6. A "family" could be made up of several offspring who are genetically identical with the mother or the father. The father would also be a twin brother and the mother a twin sister, although separated by years.

These possibilities, which many regard as potential benefits, are shadowed by other possibilities which some see as offering serious objections to human cloning.

1. Those who are rich and egocentric might decide to clone themselves for no reason except to perpetuate their unique combination of genes.
2. Dictators or powerful political leaders could replace themselves with a clone, thus promoting an indefinite continuation of their influence.

3. The cellular DNA from popular figures such as athletes and movie stars might become marketed as commodities. Or because cloning would make "popular" DNA valuable, it might be stolen and used to produce children without the consent of an unwitting and unwilling donor.

Some fears about cloning seem to reflect the mistaken belief that the clone of an individual will grow up to be exactly the same as the individual—a sort of photocopy. But of course genetic identity doesn't result in exact similarity. We already know that identical twins, even when brought up in the same family, may turn out to be quite distinct in personality, interests, and motivations.

A child who develops in a different uterine environment, then grows up in a world filled with different people, practices, events, and experiences, is quite unlikely to be exactly like the person cloned. Even individuals can become "different people" with experience and education.

The most serious objection to human reproductive cloning at the moment is that it would lead to so many tragic outcomes. With a success rate with mice hovering around a mere 3 percent, the number of failed pregnancies is not likely to be better. Also, the chance of children being born with either lethal or seriously debilitating impairments is unacceptably high. We know from cloned mammals that unpredictable genetic and developmental errors occur.

No serious researcher thinks it would be anything but premature and morally indefensible to attempt to clone a human at the moment. Even if it is not wrong in principle, it would be wrong to produce children who would most likely be severely impaired, assuming they didn't die shortly after birth.

But what of the future? In what circumstances, if any, would the cloning of humans be legitimate? Are we willing to take the risks involved in its development? Are we prepared to accept the alterations in our society that successful human cloning would produce?

POLITICS

Research involving cloning human embryos has been controversial from the start. On February 4, 1997, the day after Ian Wilmut announced the cloning of Dolly, President Clinton asked the National Bioethics Advisory Committee to report to him in ninety days "with recommendations on possible federal actions" to prevent the "abuse" of cloning. Meanwhile, on March 4, the President issued an Executive Order banning the use of federal funds to support research leading to the cloning of humans. On June 9, the committee made its report to the President, and he immediately called for legislation banning cloning "for the purpose of creating a child."

Human cloning for the purpose of reproduction continues to be denounced, even in principle, by many, and researchers in the area have repeatedly asserted they have no plans to carry out experiments like the ones that have produced other mammals. The fundamental practical interest in cloning is with therapeutic cloning—the creation of human embryos to acquire stem cells to treat diseases and injuries.

The potential of stem cells to cure diseases is so significant that it has split social conservatives. Many who once joined to oppose abortion are now divided on the question of whether an early human embryo before it is implanted in a uterus should be regarded as equivalent to a fetus. (See the Classic Case Presentation on stem cells earlier in this chapter.) Those who think not are often willing to support therapeutic cloning, although they condemn reproductive cloning.

In August 2001 President George Bush announced he was prepared to allow human embryonic stem-cell research supported by federal funds to continue on stem cells that had already been recovered from embryos. Federal money could not be used, however, to create new embryos. Thus, the decision left no room for even therapeutic cloning.

The President also announced that he would appoint a President's council "to monitor stem cell research, to recommend appropriate guidelines and regulations and to consider all of the medical and ethical ramifications of biomedical innovation."

CASE PRESENTATION

Louise Brown: The First "Test-Tube Baby"

Under other circumstances, the birth announcement would have been perfectly ordinary, the sort appearing in newspapers every day: *Born to John and Lesley Brown: a baby girl, Louise, 5 lbs. 12 ozs., 11:47 P.M., July 25, 1978, Oldham (England) General Hospital.*

But the birth of Louise Brown was far from being an ordinary event, and the announcement of its occurrence made headlines throughout the world. For the first time in history, a child was born who was conceived outside the mother's body under controlled laboratory conditions. Louise Brown was the world's first "test-tube baby."

For John and Lesley Brown, the birth of Louise was a truly marvelous event. "She's so small, so beautiful, so perfect," her mother told a reporter. Her father said, "It was like a dream. I couldn't believe it."

The joy of the Browns was understandable. From the time of their marriage in 1969, they had both very much wanted to have a child, then they discovered that Lesley Brown was unable to conceive because of blocked Fallopian tubes—the ova would not descend so fertilization could not occur. In 1970, she had surgery to correct the condition, but the procedure was unsuccessful.

The Browns decided they would adopt a child, because they couldn't have one of their own. After two years on a waiting list, they gave up that plan. But the idea of having their own child was rekindled when a nurse familiar with the work of embryologist Robert Edwards and gynecologist Patrick Steptoe referred the Browns to them.

For the previous twelve years, Steptoe and Edwards had been working on the medical and biochemical techniques required for embryo transfer. Steptoe developed techniques for removing a ripened ovum from a woman's ovaries, then reimplanting it in the uterus after it has been fertilized. Edwards improved the chemical solutions needed to keep ova functioning and healthy outside the body and perfected a method of external fertilization with sperm.

Using their techniques, Steptoe and Edwards had successfully produced a pregnancy in one of their patients in 1975, but it had resulted in a miscarriage. They continued to refine their procedures and were confident their techniques could produce a normal pregnancy that would result in a healthy baby.

They considered Lesley Brown a superb candidate for an embryo transfer. She was in excellent general health, at thirty-one she was within the usual age range for pregnancy, and she was highly fertile. In 1976, Steptoe did an exploratory operation and found her Fallopian tubes were not functional and could not be surgically repaired. He removed them so he would have unimpeded access to the ovaries.

In November 1977, Mrs. Brown was given injections of a hormone to increase the maturation rate of her egg cells. Then, in a small private hospital in Oldham, Dr. Steptoe performed a minor surgical procedure. Using a laparoscope to guide him— a tube with a built-in eyepiece and light source that is inserted through a tiny slit in the abdomen—he extracted an ovum with a suction needle from a ripened follicle.

The ovum was then placed in a small glass vessel containing biochemical nutrients and sperm secured from John Brown. Once the egg was fertilized, it was transferred to another nutrient solution. More than fifty hours later, the ovum had reached the eight-cell stage of division. Guided by their previous experience and research, Steptoe and Edwards had decided that it was at this stage an ovum should be returned to the womb. Although in normal human development the ovum has divided to produce sixty-four or more cells before it completes its descent down the Fallopian tube and becomes attached to the uterine wall, they had learned that attachment is possible at an earlier stage. The stupendous difficulties in creating and maintaining the proper biochemical environment for a multiplying cell made it reasonable to reduce the time outside the body as much as possible.

Lesley Brown had been given another series of hormone injections to prepare her uterus. Two and a half days after the ovum was removed, the fertilized egg—an embryo—was reimplanted. Using a laparoscope and a hollow plastic tube (a *cannula*), Dr. Steptoe introduced the small sphere of cells into Mrs. Brown's uterus. It successfully attached itself to the uterine wall.

Lesley Brown's pregnancy proceeded normally. But, because of the special nature of her case, seven weeks before the baby was due she entered the Oldham Hospital maternity ward so she could be continuously monitored. About a week before the birth was expected, the baby was delivered by Cesarean section. Mrs. Brown had developed toxemia, a condition associated with high blood pressure that can lead to stillbirth.

The baby was normal, and all concerned were jubilant. "The last time I saw the baby it was just eight cells in a test tube," Dr. Edwards said. "It was beautiful then, and it's still beautiful now." After the delivery, Dr. Steptoe said, "She came out crying her head off, a beautiful normal baby."

John Brown almost missed the great event, because no one on the hospital staff had bothered to tell him his wife was scheduled for the operation. Only when he had been gone from the hospital for about two hours and called to talk to his wife did he find out what was about to happen.

He rushed back and waited anxiously until a nurse came out and said, "You're the father of a wonderful little girl." As he later told a reporter, "Almost before I knew it, there I was holding our daughter in my arms."

Like many ordinary fathers, he ran down the halls of the hospital telling people he passed, "It's a girl! I've got a baby daughter."

To calm down, he went outside and stood in the rain. It was there a reporter from a London newspaper captured Mr. Brown's view of the event. "The man who deserves all the praise is Dr. Steptoe," he said. "What a man to be able to do such a wonderful thing."

On July 25, 1998 Louise Brown turned twenty. While working part-time in a fast-food restaurant, she was studying to become a school nurse. Despite dire predictions of opponents of in vitro fertilization, Louise didn't turn out to be either grossly abnormal or psychologically scarred. The main feature distinguishing her from most twenty-somethings turns out to be her trust fund composed of earnings from a book by her parents and various television projects over the years.

"I want to have my own children, whatever it takes," she told a reporter from London's *Daily Mail*. "I would use the in vitro method if I couldn't have a baby."

CASE PRESENTATION:

Septuplets: The Perils of Multiple Pregnancies

Shortly before noon on November 19, 1997, in the small town of Cheerlessly, Iowa, a twenty-nine-year-old woman named Bobbi McCaughey gave birth by cesarean section to seven babies.

Mrs. McCaughey (pronounced McCoy) had set a world record for the number of live babies born in a single pregnancy. The family was immediately bathed in the glare of worldwide media attention, and for a while they became emblems of the American family—hard-working, religious, and committed to the welfare of their children. Bobbi McCaughey was admired for her courage and fortitude for coping so well with a difficult thirty-one week pregnancy.

To help prevent a miscarriage, she had been confined to bed in the nineteenth week, and for the last months, she had been hospitalized. While all the babies had a lower than normal birth rate, ranging from 2.5 to 3.4 pounds, with the help of the more than forty obstetricians, neonatologists, pediatricians, and other specialists who attended the birth, the babies all survived. Some suffered difficulties, but eventually even they were pulled to safety by aggressive medical management.

FERTILITY DRUGS AND MULTIPLE BIRTHS

Because the McCaugheys had experienced difficulty conceiving their first child, Mikayla, when they were ready to have another, they sought help from an infertility clinic. Bobbi McCaughey was treated with Pergonal to increase her chances of becoming pregnant, which she soon did.

Pergonal is one of several fertility drugs associated with multiple pregnancies. The drugs increase the likelihood of pregnancy by causing more than one egg to be released per menstrual cycle, but this also increases the likelihood that more than one egg will be fertilized.

Early in Mrs. McCaughey's pregnancy, her physician informed the couple she was carrying seven fetuses and recommended some of them be terminated. The elimination procedure, called *selective reduction,* involves deliberately destroying and removing fetuses and is performed to increase the chances that the remaining fetuses will develop into healthy babies. The McCaugheys rejected the recommendation on the ground that their religious beliefs made abortion unacceptable. "God gave us those babies," Mrs. McCaughey told a reporter. "He wants us to raise them."

While Mrs. McCaughey's pregnancy set a record, it is only one of an increasing number of multiple pregnancies. During the period 1988 to 1997, the number of women taking fertility drugs almost tripled, rising from about 1 million to 2.7 million. Not coincidentally, the number of multiple births has *quadrupled* over the last thirty years. In 1995 (the latest year with complete figures), 4973 children were born in groups of three or more. Triplets were most common, but already three sets of sextuplets have been born, and no doubt more are on the way.

DANGERS

A multiple pregnancy increases the risk of a miscarriage. Mark Evans, a fertility expert at Wayne State Hospital, estimates that a woman pregnant with quadruplets has a 25 percent chance of a miscarriage in the first trimester; a woman pregnant with quintuplets has a 50 percent chance. Cases of pregnancies with a larger number of fetuses are too few to permit significant generalizations.

The risk of losing all fetuses to a miscarriage was sadly illustrated by the case of Mary Atwood in England. Pregnant with eight fetuses, she arranged to sell her story to a tabloid, with the amount she would be paid dependent on the number of surviving babies. All eight were lost in a miscarriage.

Even when a miscarriage doesn't occur, multiple pregnancies rarely reach the end of a full forty-week term. Triplets are born after an average of 33.5 weeks and quadruplets after 31 weeks. The result is that babies born as multiples often suffer from one or more of the many problems of prematurity: retinal damage causing blindness, bleeding into the brain producing permanent brain damage, retardation, learning disabilities, impaired motor skills, chronic lung problems, or cerebral palsy.

IRRESPONSIBLE?

The McCaugheys were lucky with their seven babies, but they and their fertility specialists aren't without critics. Some believe the specialists should have stopped the fertility drugs sooner and perhaps prevented the release of so many eggs. Others think the specialists should have required the McCaugheys to agree to a selective reduction of multiple fetuses before starting Mrs. McCaughey's treatment. Also, when it became apparent how many fetuses were present, they should have pressed the McCaugheys harder to eliminate some of them.

Critics also see the McCaugheys as having acted irresponsibly. If they weren't prepared to accept selective reduction, they shouldn't have sought help from an infertility clinic. Also, because they were lucky enough to have a good outcome, their example may suggest multiple pregnancies are now safe and reliable and thus others may be encouraged to believe they can safely have multiple babies.

COSTS

Further, the cost of medical care for Mrs. McCaughey and her children has been estimated at around $1.5 million. This is money the McCaugheys can't afford to pay, and it must be picked up in some way by the health-care system and the society. With so much medical need unmet, society cannot afford to indulge the wishes of others like the McCaugheys.

Infertility specialists discourage multiple pregnancies. Their aim is to assist a woman in having one or at most two healthy babies. A multiple pregnancy carried to term is viewed not so much as a mark of success as a sign of failure. But because infertility clinics are almost completely self-regulated, the penalty for the failure is borne by the woman, her babies, the family, and society, but not by the clinic treating her. If the number of multiple births continues to rise, however, infertility clinics will be under increasing pressure either to reduce the number or to become subject to government regulation. While multiple births can sometimes be occasions for joy, they are too often times of trouble and tragedy.

SOCIAL CONTEXT
Postmenopausal Motherhood

In late 1996 sixty-three-year-old Arceli Keh gave birth to a healthy baby girl. This made her the oldest woman ever to become a first-time mother.

This highly unusual event was not an accident of nature, but the result of deliberate planning and technological manipulation. Even so, Dr. Richard Paulson, the physician at the University of Southern California infertility clinic who treated Keh, hadn't known her true age. She had lied to her previous doctors, and the age on her chart was recorded as fifty.

Fifty was already five years over the clinic's limit for in vitro fertilization, but Keh was in excellent health and did well on tests for strength and endurance. Paulson approved her for IVF, and by the time he discovered her true age, she was pregnant with an embryo formed by a donor egg fertilized with sperm provided by her sixty-year-old husband Isagani Keh.

The Kehs, who had immigrated from the Philippines, lived in Highland, California, about sixty miles east of Los Angeles. Although they had been married sixteen years, they had been unsuccessful in conceiving a child.

"I wasn't trying to make history," Arceli told a reporter for the London newspaper *The Express.* "We are working people," she said. "I only retired to have my baby." Isagani was still working as a carpenter to help pay the more than $60,000 they spent on the procedures resulting in the birth of their daughter, whom they named Cynthia.

Keh was the oldest postmenopausal woman to bear a child, but she wasn't the first. On Christmas Day, 1993, a fifty-nine-year-old British woman, identified only as Jennifer F., gave birth to twins. Jennifer F. was married and highly successful in business, but even though she was a millionaire, there came a time when she realized she regretted not having a child. By then she had undergone menopause, making it impossible for her to conceive.

Refusing to surrender her dream, Jennifer F. visited a National Health Service fertility clinic in London and asked for help. She wanted to be made pregnant with an embryo produced from her husband's sperm and a donor egg. Physicians at the clinic declined to perform the procedure, telling her she was too old to cope with the physical and emotional stress required to be a mother.

Determined to do everything possible to have a child, Jennifer F. then went to the clinic operated by Severino Antinori in Rome. Antinori agreed to accept her as a patient and performed the in vitro fertilization and embryo transfer procedure. Antinori claims he has assisted more than fifty women over the age of fifty to become pregnant.

Although both Arceli Keh and Jennifer F. attracted much media attention, other postmenopausal women had earlier become pregnant and borne children. In 1993 Geraldine Wesoloski, fifty-three, gave birth to a baby who was both her child and her grandchild. She was the gestational surrogate for her son, Mark, and his wife Susan. As a result of an accident, Susan had undergone a hysterectomy, but she and Mark were able to provide the embryo that was then transferred to Wesoloski.

A year earlier, Mary Shearing, also fifty-three, gave birth to twin girls. She was made pregnant with embryos produced by donated eggs and sperm from her thirty-two-year-old husband. Even though Mary Shearing was no longer ovulating, she and her husband had decided to have a child of their own.

Since 1987 it has been technologically possible for a postmenopausal woman to become pregnant with donor eggs, but relatively few pregnancies have occurred. Partly this may be the result of the policies of infertility clinics. Most clinics in the United States will not accept as patients women past their early- or mid-forties on the ground that such pregnancies have a low success rate. Given the scarcity of donor eggs, some specialists argue, they ought to be reserved for younger women, who are more likely to have successful pregnancies.

Critics favoring barring access by postmenopausal women to fertility procedures generally raise three additional objections. First, older women may have their health damaged by undergoing the rigors of pregnancy, and they appear more prone to complications. Indeed, Keh developed gestational diabetes and high blood pressure, although both were successfully treated.

Second, it is best for a child to have physically and mentally active parents. Older parents may be unable to keep up with the demands of growing children, and the children will thus be cheated by not having parents who do things with them. Third, older parents are more likely to die, leaving behind young children still in need of guidance and financial support.

Defenders of granting access to fertility services to older women argue it is pure gender bias to deny them the possibility of having a child. Men often father children well into their old age and are often admired for doing so. Charlie Chaplin was seventy-three when he had his last child, and Senator Strom Thurmond had four children during his sixties and seventies. The actor Tony Randall became a father for the first time when he was seventy-seven. By contrast, a woman no longer ovulating, even with a younger husband, has no way to have a child without relying on assisted reproduction.

Also, just because a woman is relatively young does not mean she will be a better mother. On the contrary, it seems likely an older woman with more psychological and financial security will be a better parent than many young women. Besides, younger women do not have to prove they will be good mothers before they are allowed to have children, so why should older women? Finally, while it is true that pregnancy poses more health risks for older women, careful medical monitoring can significantly reduce the chances that either the mother or the developing child will be harmed. Babies born to older women using eggs obtained from younger women do just as well as babies born to younger women.

The number of women past menopause wishing to become pregnant is never expected to become great. Even so, the conflict between those who argue that older women are entitled to access to assisted reproduction and those who argue access should be denied to them is likely to continue over the next few years. Eventually, after a number of children have been born to older mothers, factual questions about safety and how the children fare may be resolved, and this may make it easier to resolve the ethical and policy questions.

CASE PRESENTATION
Embryos in Court—The Davis and Nahmani Cases

The subject of the dispute between Mary Sue Davis and her estranged husband, Junior Davis, was seven embryos lying frozen in liquid nitrogen in the Fertility Center of East Tennessee. Junior Davis did not want Mary Sue Davis to use the embryos to bear their child after their divorce. Mary Sue Davis wished to be free to do just that. In her view, the embryos were already living children, while for Junior Davis they were not alive in any significant way. For him, the only issue was the legal one of settling a joint property dispute, and he had no wish to be forced into fatherhood against his wishes. That was why he sued his estranged wife to gain recognition of what he considered his right to exercise a veto power over the use of the embryos.

The Davises had met when both were in the army and stationed in Germany. They married in 1979 and, after their military discharge, moved to Maryville, Tennessee. Mrs. Davis got a job as a service representative for a boat dealer, and Mr. Davis found work as a refrigeration technician. They tried to start a family, but luck was not with them. Mrs. Davis suffered five ectopic pregnancies. The last resulted in the rupturing and scarring of one fallopian tube and the tying off of the other for medical reasons.

Convinced that normal conception was impossible, in October of 1988 the couple entered an in vitro fertilization program in Knoxville. Originally nine ova were retrieved and fertilized with Mr. Davis's sperm. An attempt was made to implant two of the embryos, but it was unsuccessful. The plan was to try again at a more propitious time in Mrs. Davis's reproductive cycle, and the remaining seven embryos were frozen. Unfortunately, for reasons the Davises have not made public, their marriage began to break down, and on February 24, 1989, Junior Davis filed for divorce. Mr. Davis also filed suit to exercise joint control over the frozen embryos. During the trial, Mary Sue Davis took the position that the embryos were the product of her years of suffering through surgery, tests, and injections and represented her best chance to have a child. "I consider [the embryos] life," Mrs. Davis said. "To me it would be killing them if you destroyed them." In her view, the case involved the issues of custody of children and a woman's right to decide whether to bring a pregnancy to term. Her lawyer argued the frozen embryos should be regarded as "preborn children."

In contrast with Mary Sue Davis's position, Junior Davis testified he would feel "raped of my reproductive rights" if his wife were allowed to use the embryos to produce a child. He also opposed their donation for use by someone else. He insisted he did not wish to be a father and he had the right to make that decision. His attorney argued the embryos were "mere tissue" and should be kept frozen indefinitely.

Testimony by fertility experts put Mary Sue Davis's chances of bearing a child with the implanted embryos at about 10 percent. Testimony also supported the view the embryos would probably cease to be viable after two years.

COURT RULING

Circuit Judge W. Dale Young rendered his decision on September 21, 1989. He ruled that "the temporary custody of the seven human embryos is vested in Mrs. Davis for the purpose of implantation." Furthermore, "Human embryos are not property. Human life begins at conception. Mr. and Mrs. Davis have produced human beings, in vitro, to be known as their child or children."

The judge's decision was explicitly based on the notion the embryos already have the status of children. According to the decision, "It is in the manifest interest of the child or children for their mother, Mrs. Davis, to be permitted the opportunity to bring them to term through implantation." Furthermore, Judge Young held, "To allow the seven human embryos to remain so preserved for a period exceeding two years is tantamount to the destruction of these human beings." Judge Young declared that, if Mrs. Davis had a baby after implantation of the embryos, he would then decide the issues of child custody, support, and visitation rights.

Mr. Davis announced he would appeal the ruling, and Mary Sue Davis said she would make no attempt to implant the ova until the appeal was heard. Soon afterward she married again, and in May 1990, without explaining her reasons, she said she didn't want to use the embryos. However, she wanted to be free to donate them to some childless couple who might be able to benefit from them. Junior Davis said he was totally against this. In September 1990 the Appeals Court granted joint custody of the embryos to Junior Davis and Mary Sue Davis Stowe.

STATE SUPREME COURT

In 1992, the Tennessee Supreme Court decided that the embryos "are not, strictly speaking, either 'persons' or 'property,' but occupy an interim category that entitles them to special respect because of their potential for human life." On this basis, the court refused to assign the embryos an independent legal status, holding that the only rights involved were those of the donors of the eggs and the sperm. Those rights revolve around the concept of "procreational autonomy," which is composed of the right to procreate and the right to avoid procreation. Hence, Junior Davis could not be forced to procreate against his wishes.

Mary Sue Davis Stowe, the court decided, had ways of having a child other than being implanted with the embryos, including adoption. As a result, her wishes could not automatically outweigh the interest of her ex-husband in not having a child. Junior Davis had argued that, as an orphan himself, he could not stand the idea the embryos might be donated and implanted. If a child were born, he would be forced to remain ignorant of the fate of his own offspring. Citing this consideration, the court decided his ex-wife could not donate the embryos. "Donation, if a child came of it, would rob him twice, in that his procreational autonomy would be defeated and his relationship with his offspring would be prohibited."

Junior Davis was described by his lawyer as grateful for the court's decision. Mary Sue Davis Stowe said through her lawyer that the decision would mean "seven unique potential children" would be denied the opportunity to live and grow.

NAHMANI CASE

In 1997, in an almost exact reprise of the Davis case, Israel's Supreme Court reached the completely opposite decision. "A woman's right to be a parent prevails over the husband's right not to be a parent," Judge Dalia Dorner wrote in the majority opinion.

The ruling ended a four-year legal battle between Ruti and Danny Nahmani over 11 frozen embryos. The embryos were the result of the in vitro fertilization of ova taken from Ruti with sperm contributed by Danny. Mrs. Nahmani had lost her uterus as a result of cancer surgery, and before they separated, the couple had planned on having a child by employing a surrogate. After the separation, Mr. Nahmani began living with another woman and demanded that the embryos be destroyed. While the court battle raged, Mr. Nahmani fathered two children and initiated divorce proceedings.

In the United States, no federal law governs the disposition of frozen embryos. The precedent, however, is that until both parties agree to their implantation, they remain in storage. Having observed the Davis case and others like it, storage facilities now require that couples sign an agreement covering various foreseeable contingencies.

SOCIAL CONTEXT
Father Shopping: Sperm by Mail

Several commercial sperm banks now offer potential mothers the opportunity to browse through a catalogue of sperm donors and choose the one they prefer. One has a web site providing detailed information about a donor's medical history, appearance, and interests, while another, with the permission of its donors, includes photographs and donor profiles online.

A California web site employs a search function to allow shoppers to specify donor characteristics ranging from blood type and race to level of education, hair color, and appearance. The computer then searches its data banks for particular donors that meet the specifications.

Some sperm banks also offer ways of allowing donors to reveal aspects of their personality. While preserving their anonymity, the banks give them the option of writing a personal essay or letter about themselves that can be read by a prospective recipient and, later, by a child conceived by the use of the sperm. Donors are sometimes even asked to indicate their willingness to meet their biological child in the future, if the child requests it.

The frozen sperm from the favored recipient chosen by the potential recipient can be ordered and shipped by mail, but the ordering must be done by a physician. Both the physician and the patient must sign a consent form.

CASE PRESENTATION

Baby M and Mary Beth Whitehead: Surrogate Pregnancy in Court

On March 30, 1986, Elizabeth Stern, a professor of pediatrics, and her husband William accepted from Mary Beth Whitehead a baby who had been born four days earlier. The child's biological mother was Whitehead, but she had been engaged by the Sterns as a surrogate mother. Even so, it was not until almost exactly a year later that the Sterns were able to claim legal custody of the child.

The Sterns, working through the Infertility Center of New York, had first met with Whitehead and her husband Richard in January of 1985. Whitehead, who already had a son and a daughter, had indicated her willingness to become a surrogate mother by signing up at the Infertility Center. "What brought her there was empathy with childless couples who were infertile," her attorney later stated. Her own sister had been unable to conceive.

According to court testimony, the Sterns considered Mrs. Whitehead a "perfect person" to bear a child for them. Mr. Stern said it was "compelling" for him to have children, for he had no relatives "anywhere in the world." He and his wife planned to have children, but they put off attempts to conceive until his wife completed her medical residency in 1981. In 1979, however, she was diagnosed as having an eye condition indicating she probably had multiple sclerosis. When she learned the symptoms of the disease might be worsened by pregnancy and that she might become temporarily or even permanently paralyzed, the Sterns "decided the risk wasn't worth it." It was this decision that led them to the Infertility Center and to Mary Beth Whitehead.

The Sterns agreed to pay Whitehead $10,000 to be artificially inseminated with Mr. Stern's sperm and to bear a child. Whitehead would then turn the child over to the Sterns, and Elizabeth Stern would be allowed to adopt the child legally. The agreement was drawn up by a lawyer specializing in surrogacy. Mr. Stern later testified that Whitehead seemed perfectly pleased with the agreement and expressed no interest in keeping the baby she was to bear. "She said she would not come to our doorstep," he said. "All she wanted from us was a photograph each year and a little letter on what transpired that year."

BIRTH AND STRIFE

The baby was born on March 27, 1986. According to Elizabeth Stern, the first indication Whitehead might not keep the agreement was her statement to the Sterns in the hospital two days after the baby's birth. "She said she didn't know if 'I can go through with it,'" Dr. Stern testified. Although Whitehead did turn the baby over to the Sterns on March 30, she called a few hours later. "She said she didn't know if she could live any more," Elizabeth Stern said. She called again the next morning and asked to see the baby, and she and her sister arrived at the Sterns' house before noon.

According to Elizabeth Stern, Whitehead told her she "woke up screaming in the middle of the night" because the baby was gone, her husband was threatening to leave her, and she had "considered taking a bottle of Valium." Stern quoted Whitehead as saying, "I just want her for a week, and I'll be out of your lives forever." The Sterns allowed Mrs. Whitehead to take the baby home with her.

Whitehead then refused to return the baby and took the infant with her to her parents' home in Florida. The Sterns obtained a court order, and on July 31 the child was seized from Whitehead. The Sterns were granted temporary custody. Then Mr. Stern, as the father of the child, and Mrs. Whitehead, as the mother, each sought permanent custody from the Superior Court of the State of New Jersey.

TRIAL

The seven-week trial attracted national attention, for the legal issues were without precedent. Whitehead was the first to challenge the legal legitimacy of a surrogate agreement in a U.S. court. She argued the agreement was "against public policy" and violated New Jersey prohibitions against selling babies. In contrast, Mr. Stern was the first to seek a legal decision to uphold the "specific performance" of the terms of a surrogate contract. In particular, he argued Whitehead should be ordered to uphold her agreement and to surrender her parental rights and permit his wife to become the baby's legal mother. In addition to the contractual issues, the judge had to deal with the "best interest" of the child as required by New Jersey child-custody law. In addition to being a vague concept, the "best interest" standard had never been applied in a surrogacy case.

On March 31, 1987, Judge Harvey R. Sorkow announced his decision. He upheld the legality of the surrogate-mother agreement between the Sterns and Whitehead and dismissed all arguments that the contract violated public policy or prohibitions against selling babies.

Immediately after he read his decision, Judge Sorkow summoned Elizabeth Stern into his chambers and allowed her to sign documents permitting her to adopt the baby she and her husband called Melissa. The court decision effectively stripped Mary Beth Whitehead of all parental rights concerning this same baby, the one she called Sara.

APPEAL

The Baby M story did not stop with Judge Sorkow's decision. Whitehead's attorney appealed the ruling to the New Jersey Supreme Court, and on February 3, 1988, the seven members of the court, in a unanimous decision, reversed Judge Sorkow's ruling on the surrogacy agreement.

The court held that the agreement violated the state's adoption laws, because it involved a payment for a child. "This is the sale of a child, or at the very least, the sale of a mother's right to her child," Chief Justice Wilentz wrote. The agreement "takes the child from the mother regardless of her wishes and her maternal fitness . . . ; and it accomplishes all of its goals through the use of money."

The court ruled that surrogacy agreements might be acceptable if they involved no payment and if a surrogate mother voluntarily surrendered her parental rights. In the present case, though, the court regarded paying for surrogacy as "illegal, perhaps criminal, and potentially degrading to women."

The court let stand the award of custody to the Sterns, because "their household and their personalities promise a much more likely foundation for Melissa to grow and thrive." Mary Beth Whitehead, having divorced her husband three months earlier, was romantically involved with a man named Dean Gould and was pregnant at the time of the court decision.

Despite awarding custody to the Sterns, the court set aside the adoption agreement signed by Elizabeth Stern. Whitehead remained a legal parent of Baby M, and the court ordered a lower court hearing to consider visitation rights for the mother.

The immediate future of the child known to the court and to the public as Baby M was settled. Neither the Sterns nor Mary Beth Whitehead had won exactly what they had sought, but neither had they lost all.

CASE PRESENTATION:
The Calvert *Case: A Gestational Surrogate Changes Her Mind*

Disease forced Crispina Calvert of Orange County, California to have a hysterectomy, but only her uterus was removed by surgery, not her ovaries. She and her husband, Mark, wanted a child of their own, but without a uterus Crispina would not be able to bear it. For a fee of $10,000 they arranged with Anna Johnson to act as a surrogate.

Unlike the more common form of surrogate pregnancy, Johnson would have no genetic investment in the child. The ovum that would be fertilized would not be hers. Mary Beth Whitehead, the surrogate in the controversial Baby M case, had received artificial insemination. Thus, she made as much genetic contribution to the child as did the biological father.

Johnson, however, would be the gestational surrogate. In an in vitro fertilization process, ova were extracted from Crispina Calvert and mixed with sperm from Mark. An embryo was implanted in Anna Johnson's uterus, and a fetus began to develop.

Johnson's pregnancy proceeded in a normal course, but in her seventh month she announced she had changed her mind about giving up the child. She filed suit against the Calverts to seek custody of the unborn child. "Just because you donate a sperm and an egg doesn't make you a parent," said Johnson's attorney. "Anna is not a machine, an incubator."

"That child is biologically Chris and Mark's," said the Calverts' lawyer. "That contract is valid."

Critics of genetic surrogate pregnancy are equally critical of gestational surrogate pregnancy. Both methods, some claim, exploit women, particularly poor women. Further, in gestational pregnancy the surrogate is the one who must run the risks and suffer the discomforts and dangers of pregnancy. She has a certain biological claim to be the mother, because it was her body that produced the child according to the genetic information supplied by the implanted embryo.

Defenders of surrogate pregnancy respond to the first criticism by denying surrogates are exploited. They enter freely into a contract to serve as a surrogate for pay, just as anyone might agree to perform any other service for pay. Pregnancy has hazards and leaves its marks on the body, but so do many other paid occupations. As far as gestational surrogacy is concerned, defenders say, since the surrogate makes no genetic contribution to the child, in no reasonable way can she be regarded as the child's parent.

The Ethics Committee of the American Fertility Society has endorsed a policy opposing surrogate pregnancy "for non-medical reasons." The apparent aim of the policy is to permit the use of gestational surrogate pregnancy in cases like that of Mrs. Calvert, while condemning it when its motivation is mere convenience or an unwillingness to be pregnant. When a woman is fertile but, because of diabetes, uncontrollable hypertension, or some other life-threatening disorder, is unable to bear the burden of pregnancy, then gestational surrogacy would be a legitimate medical option.

BIRTH AND RESOLUTION

The child carried by Anna Johnson, a boy, was born on September 19, and for a while, under a court order, Johnson and the Calverts shared visitation rights. Then, in October, 1990, a California Superior Court denied Johnson the parental right she had sought. Justice R. N. Parslow awarded complete custody of the child to the Calverts and terminated Johnson's visitation rights.

"I decline to split the child emotionally between two mothers," the judge said. He said Johnson had nurtured and fed the fetus in the way a foster parent might take care of a child, but she was still a "genetic stranger" to the boy and could not claim parenthood because of surrogacy.

Justice Parslow found the contract between the Calverts and Johnson to be valid, and he expressed doubt about Johnson's contention that she had "bonded" with the fetus she was carrying. "There is substantial evidence in the record that Anna Johnson never bonded with the child till she filed her lawsuit, if then," he said. While the trial was in progress, Johnson had been accused of planning to sue the Calverts from the beginning to attempt to make the case famous so she could make money from book and movie rights.

"I see no problem with someone getting paid for her pain and suffering," Parslow said. "There is nothing wrong with getting paid for nine months of what I understand is a lot of misery and a lot of bad days. They are not selling a baby; they are selling pain and suffering."

The Calverts were overjoyed by the decision.

CHAPTER 7

Scarce Medical Resources

CLASSIC CASE PRESENTATION
Selection Committee for Dialysis

In 1966 Brattle, Texas, proper had a population of about 10,000 people. In Brattle County there were 20,000 more people who lived on isolated farms deep within the pine forests, or in crossroads towns with a filling station, a feed store, one or two white frame churches, and maybe twenty or twenty-five houses. Brattle was the market town and county seat, the place all the farmers, their wives, and children went to on Saturday afternoon.

It was also the medical center because it had the only hospitals in the county. One of them, Conklin Clinic, was hardly more than a group of doctors' offices. But Crane Memorial Hospital was quite a different sort of place. Occupying a relatively new three-story brick building in downtown Brattle, the hospital offered new equipment, a well-trained staff, and high-quality medical care.

This was mostly due to the efforts of Dr. J. B. Crane, Jr. The hospital was dedicated to the memory of his father, a man who had practiced medicine in Brattle County for almost fifty years. Before Crane became a memorial hospital, it was Crane Clinic. But J. B. Crane, Jr., after returning from Johns Hopkins Medical School, was determined to expand the clinic and transform it into a modern hospital. The need was there, and private investors were easy to find. Only a year after his father's death, Dr. Crane was able to offer Brattle County a genuine hospital.

It was only natural that, when the County Commissioner decided that Brattle County should have a dialysis machine, he would turn to Dr. Crane's hospital. The machine was bought with county funds, but Crane Memorial Hospital would operate it under a contract agreement. The hospital was guaranteed against loss by the county, but the hospital was also not permitted to make a profit on dialysis. Furthermore, although access to the machine was not restricted to county residents, residents were to be given priority.

Dr. Crane was not pleased with this stipulation. "I don't like to have medical decisions influenced by political considerations," he told the Commissioner. "If a guy comes in and needs dialysis, I don't want to tell him that he can't have it because somebody else who doesn't need it as much is on the machine and that person is a county resident."

"I don't know what to tell you," the Commissioner said. "It was county tax money that paid for the machine, and the County Council decided that the people who supplied the money ought to get top priority."

"What about the kind of case that I mentioned?" Dr. Crane asked.

237

"What about somebody who could wait for dialysis who is a resident as opposed to somebody who needs it immediately who's not a resident?"

"We'll just leave that sort of case to your discretion," the Commissioner said. "People around here have confidence in you and your doctors. If you say they can wait, then they can wait. I know you won't let them down. Of course, if somebody died while some outsider was on the machine . . . well, that would be embarrassing for all of us, I guess."

Dr. Crane was pleased to have the dialysis machine in his hospital. Not only was it the only one in Brattle County, but none of the neighboring counties had even one. Only the big hospitals in places like Dallas, Houston, and San Antonio had the machines. It put Crane Memorial up in the top rank.

Dr. Crane was totally unprepared for the problem when it came. He hadn't known there were so many people with chronic renal disease in Brattle County. But when news spread that there was a kidney machine available at Crane Memorial Hospital, twenty-three people applied for the dialysis program. Some were Dr. Crane's own patients or patients of his associates on the hospital staff. But a number of them were referred to the hospital by other physicians in Brattle and surrounding towns. Two of them were from neighboring Lopez County.

Working at a maximum, the machine could accommodate fourteen patients. But the staff decided that maximum operation would be likely to lead to dangerous equipment malfunctions and breakdowns. They settled on ten as the number of patients that should be admitted to the program.

Dr. Crane and his staff interviewed each of the program's applicants, reviewed their medical history, and got a thorough medical workup on each. They persuaded two of the patients to continue to commute to Houston, where they were already in dialysis. In four cases, renal disease had already progressed to the point that the staff decided that the patients could not benefit sufficiently from the program to make them good medical risks. In one other case, a patient suffering intestinal cancer and in generally poor health was rejected as a candidate. Two people were not in genuine need of dialysis but could be best treated by a program of medication.

That left fourteen candidates for the ten positions. Thirteen were from Brattle County and one from Lopez County.

"This is not a medical problem," Dr. Crane told the Commissioner. "And I'm not going to take the responsibility of deciding which people to condemn to death and which to give an extra chance at life."

"What do you want me to do?" the Commissioner asked. "I wouldn't object if you made the decision. I mean, you wouldn't have to tell everybody about it. You could just decide."

"That's something I won't do," Dr. Crane said. "All of this has to be open and aboveboard. It's got to be fair. If I decide, then everybody will think I am favoring my own patients or just taking the people who can pay the most money."

"I see what you mean. If I appoint a selection committee, will you serve on it?"

"I will. As long as my vote is the same as everybody else's."

"That's what I'll do, then," the Commissioner said.

The Brattle County Renal Dialysis Selection Committee was appointed and operating within the week. In addition to Dr. Crane, it was made up of three people chosen by the Commissioner. Amy Langford, a Brattle housewife in her mid-fifties whose husband owned the largest automobile and truck agency in Brattle County, was one member. The Reverend David Johnson was another member. He was the only African American on the committee and the pastor of the largest predominantly African American church in Brattle. The last member was Jacob Sims, owner of a hardware store in the nearby town of Silsbee. He was the only member of the committee not from the town of Brattle.

"Now I'm inclined to favor this fellow," said Mr. Sims at the Selection Committee's first meeting. "He's twenty-four years old, he's married, and he has a child two years old."

"You're talking about James Nelson?" Mrs. Langford asked. "I had some trouble with him. I've heard that he used to drink a lot before he got sick, and from the looks of his record he's had a hard time keeping a job."

"That's hard to say," said Reverend Johnson. "He works as a pulp-wood hauler, and people who do that change jobs a lot. You just have to go where the work is."

"That's right," said Mr. Sims. "One thing, though. I can't find any indication of his church membership. He says he's a Methodist, but I don't see where he's told us what his church is."

"I don't either," said Mrs. Langford." And he's not a member of the Masons or the Lions Club or any other sort of civic group. I wouldn't say he's made much of a contribution to this community."

"That's right," said Reverend Johnson. "But let's don't forget that he's got a wife and baby depending on him. That child is going to need a father."

"I think he is a good psychological candidate," said Dr. Crane. "That is, I think if he starts the program he'll stick to it. I've talked with his wife, and I know she'll encourage him."

"We should notice that he's a high school dropout," Mrs. Langford said. "I don't think we can ever expect him to make much of a contribution to this town or to the county."

"Do you want to vote on this case?" asked Mr. Sims, the chairman of the committee.

"Let's talk about all of them, then go back and vote," Reverend Johnson suggested.

Everyone around the table nodded in agreement. The files were arranged by date of application, and Mr. Sims picked up the next one from the stack in front of him.

"Alva Algers," he said. "He's a fifty-three-year-old lawyer with three grown children. His wife is still alive, and he's still married to her. He's Secretary of the Layman's Board of the Brattle Episcopal Church, a member of the Rotary Club and the Elks. He used to be a scoutmaster."

"From the practical point of view," said Dr. Crane, "he would be a good candidate. He's intelligent and educated and understands what's involved in dialysis."

"I think he's definitely the sort of person we want to help," said Mrs. Langford. "He's the kind of person that makes this a better town. I'm definitely in favor of him."

"I am too," said Reverend Johnson. "Even if he does go to the wrong church."

"I'm not so sure," said Mr. Sims. "I don't think fifty-three is old—I'd better not, because I'm fifty-two myself. Still, his children are grown; he's led a good life. I'm not sure I wouldn't give the edge to some younger fellow."

"How can you say that?" Mrs. Langford said. "He's got a lot of good years left. He's a person of good character who might still do a lot for other people. He's not like that Nelson, who's not going to do any good for anybody except himself."

"I guess I'm not convinced that lawyers and members of the Rotary Club do a lot more good for the community than drivers of pulp-wood trucks," Mr. Sims said.

"Perhaps we ought to go on to the next candidate," Reverend Johnson said.

"We have Mrs. Holly Holton, a forty-three-year-old housewife from Mineral Springs," Mr. Sims said.

"That's in Lopez County, isn't it?" Mrs. Langford asked. "I think we can just reject her right off. She didn't pay the taxes that bought the machine, and our county doesn't have any responsibility for her."

"That's right," said Reverend Johnson.

Mr. Sims agreed, and Dr. Crane raised no objection.

"Now," said Mr. Sims, "here's Alton Conway. I believe he's our only African American candidate."

"I know him well," said Reverend Johnson. "He owns a dry-cleaning business, and people in the black community think very highly of him."

"I'm in favor of him," Mrs. Langford said. "He's married and seems quite settled and respectable."

"I wouldn't want us to take him just because he's black," Reverend Johnson said. "But I think he's got a lot in his favor."

"Well," said Mr. Sims, "unless Dr. Crane wants to add anything, let's go on to Nora Bainridge. She's a thirty-year-old divorced woman whose eight-year-old boy lives with his father over in Louisiana. She's a waitress at the Pep Cafe."

"She is a very vital woman," said Dr. Crane. "She's had a lot of trouble in her life, but I think she's a real fighter."

"I don't believe she's much of a churchgoer," said Reverend Johnson. "At least she doesn't give us a pastor's name."

"That's right," said Mrs. Langford. "And I just wonder what kind of morals a woman like her has. I mean, being divorced and working as a waitress and all."

"I don't believe we're trying to award sainthood here," said Mr. Sims.

"But surely moral character is relevant," said Mrs. Langford.

"I don't know anything against her moral character," said Mr. Sims. "Do you?"

"I'm only guessing," said Mrs. Langford. "But I wouldn't say that a woman of her background and apparent character is somebody we ought to give top priority to."

"I don't want to be the one to cast the first stone," said Reverend Johnson. "But I wouldn't put her at the top of our list either."

"I think we had better be careful not to discriminate against people who are poor and uneducated," said Dr. Crane.

"I agree," said Mrs. Langford. "But surely we have to take account of a person's worth."

"Can you tell us how we can measure a person's worth?" asked Mr. Sims.

"I believe I can," Mrs. Langford said. "Does the person have a steady job? Is he or she somebody we would be proud to know? Is he a churchgoer? Does he or she do things for other people? We can see what kind of education the person has had, and consider whether he is somebody we would like to have around."

"I guess that's some of it, all right," said Mr. Sims. "But I don't like to rely on things like education, money, and public service. A lot of people just haven't had a decent chance in this world. Maybe they were born poor or have had a lot of bad luck. I'm beginning to think that we ought to make our choices just by drawing lots."

"I can't approve of that," said Reverend Johnson. "That seems like a form of gambling to me. We ought to choose the good over the wicked, reward those who have led a virtuous life."

"I agree," Mrs. Langford said. "Choosing by drawing straws or something like that would mean we are just too cowardly to make decisions. We would be shirking our responsibility. Clearly, some people are more deserving than others, and we ought to have the courage to say so."

"All right," said Mr. Sims. "I guess we'd better get on with it, then. Simon Gootz is a forty-eight-year-old baker. He's got a wife and four children. Owns his own bakery—probably all of us have been there. He's Jewish."

"I'm not sure he's the sort of person who can stick to the required diet and go through the dialysis program," Dr. Crane said.

"I'll bet his wife and children would be a good incentive," said Mrs. Langford.

"There's not a Jewish church in town," said Reverend Johnson. "So of course we can't expect him to be a regular churchgoer."

"He's an immigrant," said Mr. Sims. "I don't believe he has any education to speak of, but he did start that bakery and build it up from nothing. That says a lot about his character."

"We can agree he's a good candidate," said Mrs. Langford.

"Let's just take one more before we break for dinner," Mr. Sims said. "Rebecca Scarborough. She's a sixty-three-year-old widow. Her children are all grown and living somewhere else."

"She's my patient," Dr. Crane said. "She's a tough and resourceful old woman. I believe she can follow orders and stand up to the rigors of the program, and her health in general is good."

Reverend Johnson said, "I just wonder if we shouldn't put a lady like her pretty far down on our list. She's lived a long life already, and she hasn't got anybody depending on her."

"I'm against that," Mrs. Langford said. "Everybody knows Mrs. Scarborough. Her family has been in this town for ages. She's one of our most substantial citizens. People would be scandalized if we didn't select her."

"Of course, I'm not from Brattle," said Mr. Sims. "And maybe that's an advantage here, because I don't see that she's got much in her favor except being from an old family."

"I think that's worth something," said Mrs. Langford.

"I'm not sure it's enough, though," said Reverend Johnson.

After dinner at the Crane Memorial Hospital cafeteria, the Selection Committee met again to discuss the seven remaining candidates. It was past ten o'clock before their final decisions were made. James Nelson, the pulp-wood truck driver, Holly Holton, the housewife from Mineral Springs, and Nora Bainridge, the waitress, were all rejected as candidates. Mrs. Scarborough was rejected also. The lawyer, Alva Algers, the dry cleaner, Alton Conway, and the baker, Simon Gootz, were selected to participate in the dialysis program. Others selected were a retired secondary school teacher, an assembly-line worker at the Rigid Box Company, a Brattle County Sheriff's Department patrolman, and a twenty-seven-year-old woman file clerk in the office of the Texas Western Insurance Company.

Dr. Crane was glad that the choices were made so the program could begin operation. But he was not pleased with the selection method and resolved to talk to his own staff and with the County Commissioner about devising some other kind of selection procedure.

Without giving any reasons, Mr. Sims sent a letter to the County Commissioner resigning from the Renal Dialysis Selection Committee. Mrs. Langford and Reverend Johnson also sent letters to the Commissioner. They thanked him for appointing them to the committee and indicated their willingness to continue to serve.

Briefing Session

Few of us have as much as we desire of the world's goods. Usually, this is because we don't have enough money to pay for everything we want. We have to make choices. If we wish to spend a month in Paris, we can't afford a new car. Even when an abundance of goods is available, we can't buy everything we want. Sometimes, even when we have the money, we can't buy some item because the supply is inadequate or nonexistent. A computer manufacturer, for example, might not be turning out a new laptop fast enough to meet the demand. Or, to take a different sort of case, we can't buy fresh figs in Minnesota in January, because they simply aren't available.

In some circumstances, we can't acquire an item because its supply is limited and our society has decided that it falls into the category of things that require more than money to acquire. The item may be rationed on the basis of priorities. During wartime, for example, the military is supplied with all the food it needs, and food for civilians is rationed. Thus, even those able to pay for a pound of butter may not be permitted to buy it.

Medical goods and services include medications, care by physicians, visits to the emergency room, stays in hospitals, surgical operations, MRIs, diagnostic laboratory tests, in vitro fertilization, bone-marrow transplants, blood transfusions, genetic screening . . . and so on. Not everyone who wants these goods and services or even everyone who needs them can get them. To acquire them in our society, except in special circumstances, you must have the means of paying for them. This means having cash or adequate insurance coverage or being covered by a government entitlement program. You can't get so much as a CT-scan, unless you can demonstrate your ability to pay. (Emergency services to get you medically stable must be provided by hospitals receiving federal money.)

In the case of some medical goods and services, however, the need and ability to pay are not enough. That was the way it was with dialysis machines at the beginning. That's the way it sometimes is when there is a shortage of a crucial drug. That's the way it always is when we have to decide who gets the next donor liver, heart, or kidney that becomes available.

These are decisions about distributing scarce resources. Most of this chapter will focus on the distribution of transplant organs. Aside from the distribution of health care itself, which is addressed in the next chapter, parceling out donated organs to people likely to die unless they receive them is the most pressing medical distribution problem in our society. The issues that arise in distributing transplant organs are not in principle different from those that arise in connection with any scarce commodity.

Transplant organs are of particular concern, however. Not only because they can save and extend lives and so ought not be wasted, but because we have no way of eliminating the shortage. We can't simply crank up production, the way we can with drugs and diagnostic equipment. Nor is there an equivalent of building more hospitals or training more physicians and nurses.

TRANSPLANTS, KIDNEYS, AND MACHINES

The story of Robin Cook's novel *Coma* takes place in a large Boston hospital at the present time. What sets the novel apart from dozens of others with similar settings and characters is the fact that the plot hinges on the operations of a large-scale black market in transplant organs. For enormous fees, the criminals running the operation will supply corneas, kidneys, or hearts to those who can pay.

Cook claims that the inspiration for his novel came from an advertisement in a California newspaper. The anonymous ad offered to sell for $5000 any organ that a reader wanted to buy. In this respect, Cook's novel seems rooted firmly in the world we know today and not merely a leap into the speculative realms of science fiction.

Organ transplants have attracted a considerable amount of attention in the last few years. Not only are transplants dramatic, often offering last-minute salvation from an almost certain death, but the very possibility of organ transplants is bright with promise. We can easily imagine a future in which any injured or diseased organ can be replaced almost as easily as the parts on a car. The present state of biomedical technology makes this more than a distant dream, although not a current reality. Kidneys, hearts, lungs, livers, intestines, and pancreases are now transplanted as a matter of routine, and perhaps before long the list will be extended to include ovaries, testes, spleen, gall bladder, esophagus, and stomach. The basic problem with organ transplants is the phenomenon of tissue rejection by the immune system.

CONTROLLING REJECTION

Alien proteins trigger the body's defense mechanisms. In pioneering work with kidneys, the proteins in the transplanted tissues were matched as carefully as possible with those of the recipient; then powerful immunosuppressive drugs were used in an effort to allow the host body to accommodate itself to the foreign tissue. These drugs left the body open to infections that it could normally cope with without much difficulty.

Use of the drug cyclosporine dramatically improved the success of organ transplants when it was first used almost three decades ago. Cyclosporine selectively inhibits only part of the immune system and leaves enough of it functional to fight off most of the infections that were once fatal to large numbers of transplant recipients. Also, although tissue matching is important, particularly for kidneys, matches do not have to be as close as before and may be dispensed with altogether.

Now 90 to 96 percent of transplanted kidneys function after one year; in the 1970s only about 50 percent did. Since 1970, the one-year survival rate for children with liver transplants has increased from 38 percent to more than 75 percent, and there is good reason to believe that if children survive for as long as one year, they have a genuine chance to live a normal life. About 82 percent of heart transplant recipients now live for at least one year, a major increase from the 20 percent of the 1970s. Lung and heart–lung transplants have a success rate of about 54 percent.

Some new drugs promise to be even more effective than cyclosporine in controlling acute rejection. One of the drugs, FK-506, was approved by the FDA in 1994, and some data suggest that up to 8 percent more adult liver-transplant patients and 15 percent more pediatric patients survive with the drug than with cyclosporine. Although the drug was approved only for liver transplants, some studies of patients receiving it for transplanted kidneys, bone marrow, and intestines indicate it may also be more effective than cyclosporine in those cases.

ALLOCATION AND SCARCITY

Because of the relatively high rate of success in organ transplants, the need for organs (kidneys in particular) is always greater than the supply. (The black-market operation in Cook's novel is not wholly unrealistic.) In such a situation, where scarcity and need conflict, it is frequently necessary to decide who among the candidates for a transplant will receive an available organ.

Relatively objective considerations such as the "goodness" of tissue matching, the size of the organ, and the general medical condition of the candidates may rule out some individuals. But it does happen that choices have to be made. Who should make such choices? Should they be made by a physician, following her own intuitions? Should they be made by a committee or board? If so, who should be on the committee? Should a patient have an advocate to speak for his interest—someone to "make a case" for his receiving the transplant organ? Should the decision be made in accordance with a set of explicit criteria? If so, what criteria are appropriate? Are matters such as age, race, gender, and place of residence irrelevant? Should the character and accomplishments of the candidates be given any weight? Should people be judged by their estimated "worth to the community"? Should the fact that someone is a parent be given any weight?

What if one is a smoker, an alcoholic, or obese? Are these to be considered "medical" or "behavioral" risk factors that may legitimately be employed to eliminate someone as a candidate for a transplant? Or, on the other hand, are these to be treated as aspects of people's chosen "lifestyle" that cannot be used as a basis for denying them an organ needed to save their lives?

These are just some of the questions relevant to the general issue of deciding how to allocate medical goods in situations in which the available supply is surpassed by a present need. Transplant organs are an example of one type of goods. (See *Social Context: Acquiring and Allocating Transplant Organs* in this chapter.) Even so, most of the ethical issues raised by the distribution of organs also arises when we have to consider how we're going to parcel out such goods and services as hospital beds, physician consultations, nursing care, physical therapy, medications, diagnostic MRIs, chemotherapy, coronary angiography, or any of the hundreds of other resources used in delivering medical care. All resources, economists remind us, are limited, and so we must always face the problem of how to distribute them. It was a shortage of machines, rather than organ transplantation, that first called public attention to the issue of medical resource allocation.

SEATTLE AND KIDNEY MACHINES

This occurred most dramatically in the early 1960s when the Artificial Kidney Center in Seattle, Washington, initiated an effective large-scale treatment program for people with renal diseases. Normal kidneys filter waste products from the blood that have accumulated as a result of ordinary cellular metabolism—salt, urea, creatinine, potassium, uric acid, and other substances. These waste products are sent from the kidneys to the bladder, where they are then secreted as urine. Kidney failure, which can result from one of a number of diseases, allows waste products to build up in the blood. This can cause high blood pressure and even heart failure, tissue edema (swelling), and muscular seizure. If unremedied, the condition results in death.

When renal failure occurs, hemodialysis is a way of cleansing the blood of waste products by passing it through a cellophane-like tube immersed in a chemical bath. The impurities in the blood pass through the membrane and into the chemical bath by osmosis, and the purified blood is then returned to the patient's body.

At the beginning of the Seattle program, there were many more candidates for dialysis than units ("kidney machines") to accommodate them. As a response to this situation, the Kidney Center set up a committee to select patients who would receive treatment. (See the *Classic Case Presentation* in this chapter for an account of how such a committee might work.) In effect, the committee was offering to some a better chance for life than they would have without access to dialysis equipment.

As other centers and hospitals established renal units, they faced the same painful decisions that Seattle did. Almost always there were many more patients needing hemodialysis than there was equipment available to treat them. It was partly in response to this situation that Section 299-1 of Public Law 92-603 was passed by Congress in 1972. Those with end-stage renal disease who require hemodialysis or kidney transplants are now guaranteed treatment under Medicare.

DIALYSIS COSTS AND DECISIONS

More than 300,000 patients are now receiving dialysis paid for by Medicare. Present costs are over $10 billion per year, and the patient load is increasing by about 50,000 per year. Dialysis saves lives, but the cost is high.

Although the average cost of each treatment session has dropped from $150 in 1973 to $115 in 1997, many more groups of patients now have dialysis than were treated earlier. In particular, the treatment population now includes many more elderly and diabetic people than was envisioned when the dialysis program was established.

Quite apart from the cost, which is about four times higher than originally expected, dialysis continues to present moral difficulties. Resources are still finite, so, while virtually everyone needing dialysis can be accomodated, physicians face the problem of deciding whether everyone should be referred. If a physician believes a patient isn't likely to gain benefits from dialysis sufficient to justify the expense or isn't likely to show up for appointments, should she recommend the patient for dialysis anyway? Not to do so may mean death for the patient in the near future, yet the social cost (measured in terms of the expense of equipment and its operation, hospital facilities, and the time of physicians, nurses, and technicians) may be immense—$100,000 or more per year for a single person.

Nor does dialysis solve all problems for patients with terminal kidney diseases. Although time spent on the machine varies, some patients spend five hours, three days per week, attached to the machine. Medical and psychological problems are typical even when the process works at its most efficient. Prolonged dialysis can produce neurological disorders, severe headaches, gastrointestinal bleeding, and bone diseases. Psychological and physical stress is always present, and particularly before dialysis treatments, severe depression is common. One study showed that 5 percent of dialysis patients take their own lives, and "passive suicide," resulting from dropping out of treatment programs, is the third most common cause of death among older dialysis patients. (The overall death rate for those on dialysis is about 25 percent per year. The worst outlook is for diabetics starting dialysis at age 55 or older. After one year, only 18 percent are still alive.) For these reasons, strong motivation, psychological stability, age, and a generally sound physical condition are factors considered important in deciding whether to admit a person to dialysis.

The characteristics required to make someone a "successful" dialysis patient are to some extent "middle-class virtues." A patient must not only be motivated to save his life, but he must also understand the need for the dialysis, be capable of adhering to a strict diet, show up for scheduled dialysis sessions, and so on. As a consequence, where decisions about whether to admit a patient to dialysis are based on estimates of the likelihood of the patient's doing what is required, members of the white middle class appear to have a definite edge over others. Selection criteria that are apparently objective may actually involve hidden class or racial bias.

Various ways of dealing with both the costs and the personal problems presented by dialysis are currently under discussion. In the view of some, increasing the number of kidney transplants would do the most to improve the lives of patients and to reduce the cost of the kidney program. (This would have the result of increasing even more the demand for transplant organs. See the *Social Context: Acquiring and Allocating Transplant Organs* later in this chapter for a discussion of proposals for doing this.) Others have pressed for training more patients to perform home dialysis, which is substantially cheaper than dialysis performed in clinics or hospitals. However, those who are elderly, live alone, or lack adequate facilities are not likely to be able to use and maintain the complicated equipment involved. Other things being equal, should such people be given priority for transplants?

MICROALLOCATION VERSUS MACROALLOCATION

Some critics have questioned the legitimacy of the dialysis program and pointed to it as an example of social injustice. While thousands of people have benefited from the program, why should kidney disease be treated differently from other diseases? Why should the treatment of kidney disease alone be federally funded? Why shouldn't society also pay for the treatment of those afflicted with cancer or neurological disorders? Perhaps only the development of a new national health-care policy will render this criticism irrelevant.

The problems of transplants and dialysis involve decisions that affect individuals in a direct and immediate way. For example, a person either is or is not accepted into a dialysis program. As we will see in the next chapter, there are a number of broader social issues connected with providing and distributing medical resources. But our concern here is with decisions involving the welfare of particular people in specific situations in which demand exceeds supply. The basic question becomes, Who shall get it and who shall go without?

Any commodity or service that can be in short supply relative to the need for it raises the issue of fair and justifiable distribution. Decisions that control the supply itself—that determine, for example, what proportion of the federal budget will be spent on medical care—are generally referred to as macroallocation decisions. These are the large-scale decisions that do not involve individuals in a direct way. Similarly, deciding what proportion of the money allocated to health care should be spent on dialysis is a macroallocation decision.

By contrast, microallocation decisions directly impinge on individuals. Thus, when one donor heart is available and six people in need of a transplant make a claim on it, the decision as to who gets the heart is a microallocation decision. In Chapter 8, in discussing paying for health care, we will focus more on macroallocation, but here we will be concerned mostly with microallocation. (The distinction between macroallocation and microallocation is often less clear than the explanation here suggests. After all, decision making occurs at many levels in the distribution of resources, and the terms "macro" and "micro" are relative ones.)

The examples we have considered have been restricted to transplant organs and dialysis machines, but, as mentioned earlier, the question of fair distribution can be raised just as appropriately about other medical goods and services. This includes cardiac resuscitation teams, microsurgical teams, space in burn units or intensive-care wards, hospital beds, drugs and vaccines, medical-evacuation helicopters, operating rooms, physicians' time, and all other medical commodities that are in limited supply with respect to the demand for them. (See the *Case Presentation: The Drug Lottery* later in this chapter.)

Earlier, in connection with transplants, we considered some of the more specific questions that have to be asked about distribution. The questions generally fall into two categories: Who shall decide? What criteria or standards should be employed in making the allocation decision? These are questions that must be answered whenever there is scarcity relative to needs and wants.

ETHICAL THEORIES AND THE ALLOCATION OF MEDICAL RESOURCES

Discussions of the distribution of limited medical resources frequently compare such a situation to the plight of a group of people adrift in a lifeboat. If some are sacrificed, the others will have a much better chance of surviving. But who should be sacrificed?

One answer to this question is that no one should be. Simply by virtue of being human, each person in the lifeboat has an equal worth. Any action that involved sacrificing someone for the good of the others in the boat would not be morally defensible. This suggests that the only right course of action would be simply to do nothing.

This point of view may be regarded as compatible with Kant's ethical principles. Because each individual may be considered to have inherent value, considerations such as talent, intelligence, age, social worth, and so on are morally irrelevant. Accordingly, there seem to be no grounds for distinguishing those who are to be sacrificed from those who may be saved. In the medical context, this would mean that when there are not enough goods and services to go around, then no one should receive them.

This is not a result dictated by Kant's principles, however. One might also argue that the fact that every person is equal to every other in dignity and worth does not require the sacrifice of all. A random procedure—such as drawing straws—might be used to determine who is to have an increased chance of survival. In such a case, each person is being treated as having equal value, and the person who loses might be regarded as exercising autonomy by sacrificing him- or herself.

The maxim underlying the sacrifice would, apparently, be one that would meet the test of the categorical imperative. Any rational person might be expected to sacrifice himself in such a situation and under the conditions in which the decision was made. In the case of medical resources, a random procedure would seem to be a morally legitimate procedure.

Both the natural law view and Ross's would seem to support a similar line of argument. Although we all have a duty, on these views, to preserve our lives, this does not mean that we do not sometimes have to risk them. Just such a risk might be involved in agreeing to abide by the outcome of a random procedure to decide who will be sacrificed and who saved.

Utilitarianism does not dictate a specific answer to the question of who, if anyone, should be saved. It does differ radically in one respect, however, from those moral views that ascribe an intrinsic value to each human life. The principle of utility suggests that we ought to take into account the consequences of sacrificing some people rather than others. Who, for example, is more likely to make a contribution to the general welfare of the society, an accountant or a nurse? This approach opens the way to considering the "social worth" of people and makes morally relevant such characteristics as education, occupation, age, record of accomplishment, and so on.

To take this approach would require working out a set of criteria to assign value to various properties of people. Those to be sacrificed would be those whose point total put them at the low end of the ranking. Here, then, a typical "calculus of utilities" would be relied on to solve the decision problem. The decision problem about the allocation of medical resources would follow exactly the same pattern.

This approach is not one required by the principle of utility, however. Some might argue that a policy formulated along those lines would have so many harmful social consequences that some other solution would be preferable. Thus, a utilitarian might argue that a better policy would be one based on some random process. In connection with medical goods and services, a "first-come, first-served" approach might be superior. (This is a possible option for rule utilitarianism. It could be argued that an act utilitarian would be forced to adopt the first approach.)

Rawls's principles of justice seem clearly to rule out distributing medical resources on the criterion of "social worth." Where special benefits are to be obtained, those benefits must be of value to all and open to all. It is compatible with Rawls's view, of course, that there should be no special medical resources. But if there are, and they must be distributed under conditions of scarcity, then some genuinely fair procedure, such as random selection, must be the procedure used.

No ethical theory that we have considered gives a straightforward answer to the question of who shall make the selection. Where a procedure is random or first-come, first-served, the decision-making process requires only establishing the right kind of social arrangements to implement the policy. Only when social worth must be judged and considered as a relevant factor in decision making does the procedure assume importance. (This is assuming that medical decisions about appropriateness—decisions that establish a class of candidates for the limited resources—have already been made.)

A utilitarian answer as to who shall make the allocation decision might be that the decision should be made by those who are in a good position to judge the likelihood of an individual's contributing to the welfare of the society as a whole. Since physicians are not uniquely qualified to make such judgments, leaving decisions to an individual physician or a committee of physicians would not be the best approach. A better one would perhaps be to rely on a committee composed of a variety of people representative of the society.

Many more questions of a moral kind connected with the allocation of scarce resources arise than have been mentioned here. We have not, for example, considered whether an individual should be allowed to make a case for receiving resources. Nor have we examined any of the problems with employing specific criteria for selection (such as requiring that a person be a resident of a certain community or state; the *Classic Case Presentation* in this chapter illustrates such a selection process). We have, however, touched upon enough basic issues to make it easy to see how other appropriate questions might be asked.

SOCIAL CONTEXT
Acquiring and Allocating Transplant Organs

Organ transplantation is perhaps the most dramatic example of how contemporary medical technology can extend or improve the lives of tens of thousands of people. Developments in surgical techniques, improvements in organ preservation, and the advent of new immunosuppressive drugs have made organ transplantation into a standard surgical therapy.

Yet behind the wonder and drama of transplant surgery lies the troubling fact that the need for transplant organs seriously and chronically outstrips the supply. Thus, against a background of a chronic shortage, physicians, surgeons, and committees must make judgments that will offer an opportunity for some, while destroying the last vestige of hope for others.

While transplanting kidneys began as early as the 1950s, the list of organs now transplanted with a significant degree of success has been expanded over the last twenty years to include corneas, bone marrow, bone and skin grafts, livers, lungs, pancreases, intestines, and hearts. All involve special problems, but we will limit discussion to solid organs—those like the heart and liver that are complete functional units.

Worldwide, more than 150,000 kidney transplants have been performed, and about 93 percent of the organs are still functioning one year later. (Some recipients are still alive after more than thirty years.) Thomas Starzl and his team successfully transplanted the first liver in 1967, and the rate of survival rate after three years is about 75 percent. Also in 1967, Christian Barnard transplanted a human heart, and now around 75 percent of the procedures are considered successful. Lung transplants, though still a relatively new procedure, have a 55 percent three-year survival rate. New techniques of management and the development of drugs to suppress part of the immune response have done much to increase the success rate of transplants, but additional improvements will probably require improvements in the ability to control tissue rejection. (See the Briefing Session for more details.)

Costs

A major social and moral difficulty of transplant surgery is that it is extremely expensive. For example, a kidney transplant may cost about $40,000, a heart transplant about $150,000, and a liver transplant in the range of $200,000 to $300,000. The immunosuppressive drugs needed to prevent the rejection of a transplanted organ cost from $10,000 to $20,000 a year, and they must be taken for the remainder of the patient's life. Despite the high costs of transplantation, it may offer cost savings over dialysis and medical treatments. Further, combined costs constitute less than 1 percent of all health care costs.

Questions have been raised in recent years about what restrictions, if any, should be placed on access to transplants. Should society deny them to everyone, pay for all who need them but cannot afford them, or pay for only some who cannot pay? (For a discussion of some of these issues, see Chapter 8.) Medicare, Medicaid, and most, but not all, insurance companies pay for organ transplants and at least part of the continuing drug and treatment costs. The End-Stage Renal Disease Program covers kidney transplants for everyone, yet people needing any other sort of transplant who don't qualify for public programs and lack appropriate insurance must find some way of raising the money. Otherwise, hospitals are not likely to provide them with an organ. Every transplant candidate, in Starzl's phrase, must pass a wallet biopsy to qualify.

Availability

The second major problem, after cost, is the availability of donor organs. The increase in the number of transplant operations performed during the last twenty-five years has produced a chronic scarcity of organs. While in 1996 more than 20,000 people received transplants at the nation's 278 transplant centers, more than 3000 more died waiting for organs. On the last day of 1996 (the last year for which figures are available), 50,407 were on the transplant waiting list, and during the year there was a total of 33,000 new registrations. For every organ transplanted, two more people enter the waiting list, and those on the waiting list currently die at a rate of ten a day.

Those in need of a kidney or pancreas can rely on dialysis and insulin injections to treat their diseases, but those in need of a liver, heart, or lung have limited alternative treatments available. Artificial livers remain experimental, and left ventricular-assist devices can help only some heart patients. For those waiting for livers, lungs, or hearts, the lack of a suitable transplant organ spells almost certain death. Given the currently limited supply of organs, we face two key questions: How can the supply be increased? How are those who will actually receive organs to be selected from the pool of candidates?

Increasing Supply

An obvious answer to the first question is that the supply of organs can be increased by increasing donations. Exactly how many organs that could be used for transplant aren't retrieved from those declared dead is unclear. According to one estimate, between 6900 and 10,700 potential donors are available, but because of such factors as the next of kin's not being asked to donate or refusing to donate or because of the circumstances of death or condition of the organs, only about 37 to 57 percent of potential donors become actual donors.

REQUIRED REQUEST AND REQUIRED RESPONSE LAWS

The federal Uniform Anatomical Gift Act of 1984 served as a model for state laws, and virtually all states have enacted laws to promote the increase of organ donation. Some have "required response" laws requiring people to declare when renewing their driver's license whether they wish to become organ donors, and most make it easy for people to decide to become donors by printing organ donation cards on the backs of driver's licenses. State laws based on the act spell out a person's right to donate all or part of his body and to designate a person or institution as a recipient. Starting in 1997, a new federal law mandates that organ donor cards be included with tax refund checks.

Even with the support of such laws, physicians and hospital administrators have been reluctant to intrude on a family's grief by asking that a deceased patient's organs be donated for use as transplants. Even if a patient has signed an organ donation card, the permission of the immediate family is required, in most cases, before the organs can be removed. In 1991, a federal appeals court ruled in favor of an Ohio woman who argued that the coroner who had removed her husband's corneas during an autopsy and donated them to the Cincinnati Eye Bank had violated her property rights. Her property interest in her husband's body was found to be protected under the due process clause of the Fourteenth Amendment.

In an attempt to overcome the reluctance of physicians to request organ donations, a 1986 federal law requires that hospitals receiving Medicare or Medicaid payments (97 percent of the nation's hospitals) identify patients who could become organ donors at death. The law also requires that hospitals discuss organ donations with the families of such patients and inform them of their legal power to authorize donations. Although this "required request" law has been in effect for about ten years, because of difficulties in administering it, including overcoming the reluctance of physicians to approach worried or bereaved families, the law has led to only a modest (about 10 percent) increase in the supply of transplant organs.

Non–Heart Beating Donors

An approach devised recently at the University of Pittsburgh involves acting on the requests of patients (or their representatives) to remove their organs when their hearts stop beating, even though they may not yet be brain-dead. (See Chapter 10 for a discussion of criteria for determining death.) Hence, someone on a respirator wanting to be weaned off the machine may ask that her organs be used for transplant, should the withdrawal result in her death. The respirator is removed in an operating room, and at least three minutes after the patient's heart has stopped beating, the transplant organs are removed. In practice, most donor candidates are not like the one described. They have suffered severe brain damage but are not brain-dead, and permission has been obtained from their families.

Critics of the practice have raised questions about using the cessation of heartbeat as a proper criterion for death. (Perhaps the patient could be resuscitated. Is three minutes long enough to wait?) Some have also wondered if the practice doesn't put pressure on mentally competent, but seriously ill, patients to give up the struggle for their lives by volunteering to become organ donors. Similarly, critics have charged, by providing a rationalization, the practice may make it too easy for the parents or other representatives of comatose patients on life support to decide to withdraw support and end the person's life.

Organ Protection Before Obtaining Consent

Another innovative but controversial approach employed by some medical centers involves injecting organ-protective drugs and preservatives into patients who die in an emergency room or en route. The organs are not removed from the body (although some surgical steps may be taken), but by making sure the organs have a good blood supply and so are protected from damage, physicians gain additional time to seek permission from the families. Otherwise, the organs would deteriorate and be useless for transplantation.

Critics of this practice claim that hospitals do not always wait to determine that a patient is dead before injecting drugs with the aim of preserving the organs. Thus, physicians can cause harm to still-living patients. Others claim the practice borders on desecration and denies dignity to individuals whose dead bodies are subjected to an invasive procedure without their prior consent. Further, critics say, we have no generally accepted ideas about what it is legitimate to do to a newly dead body to provide benefit to others.

Defenders of the practice say it gives families time to recover from the shock of learning about the death of a loved one and allows them to make a more considered decision. In this respect, the practice is more humane than asking a family for permission to take an organ from a loved one right at the time they learn of the loved one's death. Also, taking steps to preserve the organs of a dead body enables us to use them to save the lives of others.

Using organs from non–heart beating cadavers and preserving the organs of the newly dead before securing consent to use them are both practices that aim to provide a way to fill the gap between the number of transplant organs obtainable from brain-dead individuals and the number needed by those awaiting transplant. While 10,000 to 12,000 people are declared brain-dead every year, 60,000 are in need of transplants.

Selling Organs

Another possibility for increasing the organ supply is to permit organs to be offered for sale on the open market. Before death, an individual might arrange payment for the posthumous use of one or more of his organs. Or after his death, his survivors might sell his organs to those needing them. In a variation of this proposal, donors or their families might receive tax credits, or a donor might be legally guaranteed that if a family member or friend required a transplant organ, that person would be given priority in the distribution. Under either plan, there would be a strong incentive to make organs available for transplant.

The public reaction to any plan for marketing organs has been strongly negative. People generally regard the prospect of individuals in need of transplants bidding against one another in an "organ auction" as ghoulish and morally repugnant, and this attitude extends to all forms of the market approach. (A government-regulated market with fixed prices is likely to be preferable to a genuine open market.) In 1984, the National Organ Transplantation Act made the sale of organs for transplant illegal in the United States. At least twenty other countries, including Canada, Britain, and most of Europe, have similar laws.

A third possibility would be to allow living individuals to sell their nonvital organs to those in need of transplants. Taking hearts and livers from living people would be illegal as it would involve homicide by the surgeon who removed them. However, kidneys occur in pairs, and we already permit individuals to donate one of their kidneys—indeed, we celebrate those who do. It is only a short step from the heroic act of giving away a kidney to the commercial act of selling one.

Kidney donors must undergo surgery that involves incurring a 12-inch incision, the removal of a rib, and three to six weeks of recuperation. Donors face odds of 1 in 20,000 of dying from surgical complications, but the risk of dying as a result of having only one kidney is extremely small. People with one kidney are slightly more likely to develop high blood pressure than those with two.

Allowing the sale of an organ would be in keeping with the generally acknowledged principle that people ought to be free to do as they wish with their own bodies. We already permit the sale of blood, plasma, bone marrow, ova, and sperm. The decisive disadvantage to allowing such transactions as a matter of social policy, however, is that it would be the poor who would be most likely to suffer from it.

It is all too easy to imagine a mother wishing to improve the lives and opportunities of her children deciding to sell a kidney to help make that possible. That the economically advantaged should thrive by literally exploiting the bodies of the poor seems morally repulsive to most people. (The 1984 Organ Transplant Act was in direct response to the operations of the International Kidney Exchange, which was established in Virginia for the purpose of selling kidneys from living donors. The donors were predominantly indigent.) It is no answer to object that someone should be permitted to do as he wishes with his body to provide for the welfare of his family. If selling a kidney and putting his own life and health at risk is the only option open to someone with that aim, this in itself constitutes a prima facie case for major social reform.

"Everyone Makes a Fee, Except for the Donor"

Despite strong public sentiment against selling organs, a telephone poll conducted by the United Network for Organ Sharing and the National Kidney Foundation showed that 48 percent of the people interviewed favored some form of "donor compensation." Under the Transplant Act, there can be none.

The law does permit payments associated with removing, preserving, transporting, and storing human organs. As a result, a large industry has developed around organ transplants. Sixty-nine procurement organizations, operating in federally defined geographical regions, collect organs from donors and transport them to the 278 hundred hospitals with transplant facilities.

A procurement agency may be paid about $25,000 for its services. This includes ambulance trips to pick up and deliver the organ, fees to the hospital for the use of the operating room where the organ is removed, costs of tissue matching and blood testing, and overhead expenses for the agency and its personnel.

In addition, costs involved in a transplant may include fees paid to local surgeons to prepare the patient for organ removal and fees paid to a surgical team coming into town to remove the organ. Such fees typically amount to several thousand dollars.

Hospitals pay for the organs they receive, but they pass on their costs and more. Hospitals charge, as a rough average, $16,000 to $18,000 for a kidney or a heart and $20,000 to $22,000 dollars for a liver. According to one study, hospitals may mark up the cost of an organ by as much as 200 percent to cover costs that patients are unable to pay or that exceed the amount the government will reimburse. A donor of several organs can produce considerable income for the transplanting hospital.

Some critics of current transplant practices have pointed out that everyone makes a fee from donated organs except for the donor. Yet matters show little sign of changing. A representative of the National Kidney Foundation proposed to a congressional committee that the law be changed to allow a relatively small amount of money (perhaps $2000) to be given to the families of organ donors as a contribution to burial expenses. The recommendation was not acted on, and similar proposals are no more likely to meet with success.

Given current transplant practices, it is understandable why donor families can sometimes become bitter. When Judy Sutton's daughter Susan killed herself, Mrs. Sutton donated Susan's heart and liver and so helped save the lives of two people. Mrs. Sutton then had to borrow the money to pay for Susan's funeral. "Susan gave life even in death," Mrs. Sutton told a reporter. "It's wrong that doctors make so much money off donors. Very wrong."

Presumed Consent

A possibility widely discussed as a means of increasing the number of transplant organs is the adoption of a policy of "presumed consent." That is, a state or federal law would allow hospitals to take it for granted that a recently deceased person has tacitly consented to having any needed organs removed, unless the person had indicated otherwise or unless the family objects. The burden of securing consent would be removed from physicians and hospitals, but the burden of denying consent would be imposed on individuals or their families. To withdraw consent would require a positive action.

A policy of presumed consent has been adopted by several European countries. Critics of the policy point out that this has not, in general, done much to reduce the shortage of transplant organs in those countries. Although legally empowered to remove organs without a family's permission, physicians continue to be reluctant to do so. It is doubtful that a policy of presumed consent would be any more successful in this country. Also, if families are to be given the opportunity to deny consent, they must be notified of the death of the patient, and in many cases this would involve not only complicated practical arrangements, but also considerable loss of time. Thus, it is doubtful that presumed consent would do a great deal to increase the number of usable transplant organs.

Altruistic Donation

In the view of many observers, the present system of organ procurement by voluntary donation for altruistic reasons is the best system. It appeals to the best in people, rather than to greed and self-interest, it avoids exploiting the poor, and it's efficient. Families who donate organs can gain some satisfaction from knowing that the death of a loved one brought some benefit to others.

Living Donors

Some centers have relaxed or eliminated rules requiring that a living donor belong to the same family as the recipient. This allows those who wish to act in a generous and commendable fashion to directly benefit a friend, a coworker, or (in principle) a complete stranger. In 1995 over 3000 people received a kidney from a living donor. The majority of kidneys were donated by siblings (46 percent) or came from parents (22 percent), but they were also donated by spouses, children, and other relatives.

Kidneys are no longer the only organs transplanted from living donors. A healthy liver rapidly regenerates, and liver segments have been transplanted with great success. More recently, lung segments have been added to the list. Kidneys from living donors have a better success rate than ones from cadavers, but it is too early to tell whether this holds for liver and lung segments. Also, the history of using living kidney donors shows that the risk to donors is slight, with death as a result of the surgery occurring in about 3 in 10,000 cases. Experience with liver and lung segment donors isn't sufficiently extensive to be statistically meaningful, but the early data suggest they too pose little risk to the donor.

While the use of living donors can help reduce the chronic scarcity of some organs, the practice is not without critics. Thomas Starzl, the developer of liver transplants, refuses to use living donors, because too often the person in a family who "volunteers" to be a donor does so only because of the pressures of family dynamics. In effect, Starzl charges, consent cannot be voluntary. Those favoring the practice argue that Starzl's criticism is not a reason to reject the use of living donors so much as it is a reason to design a system of securing consent that will protect vulnerable individuals.

The chronic shortage of transplant organs can probably not be relieved by any one of the proposals mentioned here. Some combination of them might come close to solving the problem. Most likely, however, we must wait for a technological solution. If genetic engineering made it possible to breed pigs with organs invisible to the human immune system, the shortage of transplant organs would be ended. Not all moral problems would be solved, however, for some already question the breeding and use of animals solely to serve human wants and needs.

ORGAN ALLOCATION

Whatever the future may promise, the fact remains that at present there is a limited supply of transplant organs, and the demand far exceeds the supply. Thus, the key question today is, How are organs to be distributed when they become available? Currently, no national policies or procedures supply a complete answer to this question. Usually, with some exceptions, such decisions are made in accordance with policies adopted by particular regional or hospital-based transplant programs.

Typically, a transplant center employs a screening committee made up of surgeons, physicians, nurses, social workers, and a psychologist to determine whether a candidate for a transplant should be admitted to the waiting list. Medical need— whether the candidate might benefit from the transplant—is the first consideration, but it is far from the only one. A committee's decisions may also be based on the patient's general medical condition, age, and ability to pay for the operation, as well as whether he has the social support needed to assist him during recovery, shows evidence of being able to adhere to a lifetime regimen of antirejection drugs, and he belongs to the constituency that the center is committed to serving. Factors like race and gender are considered irrelevant, but in practice the individual's "social worth" (education, occupation, accomplishments) may also be taken into account.

Some large transplant centers employ a scoring system that involves assigning values to a list of what the center considers relevant factors. Those with the highest score are accepted as candidates and given a priority ranking. If their medical condition worsens, they may later be moved up in the ranking. At most centers this process is done in a more informal fashion.

Guidelines for Distribution

Once a patient is admitted to a center's waiting list, the allocation rules of the federally funded United Network for Organ Sharing (UNOS) also apply. UNOS policies stipulate the ways in which organs are distributed. Until recently, when an organ became available within one of the nine UNOS regions of the country, the institutions in the region had first claim on it, without respect to the needs of patients in other regions. In practice few organs ever left the region in which they were donated. In a recent move, UNOS now stipulates that an organ must go to a patient with the greatest need, no matter what the region, assuming the organ can be transported in good condition to the patient.

The policy is likely to have the effect of creating something like a national waiting list. Proponents say it will get more organs to the patients who need them most, while critics charge it will mean the greatest number of organs will go to the largest transplant centers, because the largest number of patients in acute need are there. Consequently, a number of centers will have to close. Some observers view this positively, for not all of the 278 centers do enough transplants to gain the experience needed to offer patients the best outcomes possible.

Some of the factors considered by transplant centers in admitting a patient to the waiting list have been criticized by many as morally irrelevant to deciding who is to receive a transplant organ. A patient's social worth and ability to pay are rejected by most critics, but opinion is divided over how much weight should be given to factors such as alcoholism, drug abuse, and poor health habits. Because of the shortage of organs, people needing transplants as a result of "lifestyle diseases" caused in part by obesity, smoking, or alcohol abuse would be automatically excluded as transplant candidates by some. By contrast, others would ask only that such people demonstrate a willingness to change their behavior. At present, transplant centers have much leeway in deciding which candidates they will accept.

A good example of an effort to formulate acceptable guidelines for making decisions about allocating organs is the Massachusetts Task Force on Organ Transplantation. The group issued a unanimous report that included the following recommendations:

1. Transplant surgery should be provided "to those who can benefit most from it in terms of probability of living for a significant period of time with a reasonable prospect for rehabilitation."

2. Decisions should not be based on "social worth" criteria.

3. Age may be considered as a factor in the selection process, but only to the extent that age is relevant to life expectancy and prospects for rehabilitation. Age must not be the only factor considered.

4. If not enough organs are available for all those who might benefit from them, final selections should be made by some random process (for example a lottery or first-come, first-served basis).

5. Transplants should be provided to residents of New England on the basis of need, regardless of their ability to pay, as long as this does not adversely affect health-care services with a higher priority. Those who are not residents of New England should be accepted as transplant candidates only after they have demonstrated their ability to pay for the procedure.

Organ transplantation continues to face two crucial problems: the chronic shortage of organs and the inability of some people needing a transplant to pay for one. The shortage problem might eventually be solved by developments in biotechnology, but the financial problem could be solved immediately by a change in social policy.

CASE PRESENTATION
Sandra Jensen Gets a Transplant

Sandra Jensen was born with a deformed heart, but it wasn't until she was thirty-five that it began to make her so sick that she needed a heart–lung transplant to extend her life. She was young and otherwise healthy, but transplant centers at both Stanford University and the University of California, San Diego rejected her as a candidate.

Sandra Jensen also had Down syndrome, and the transplanters doubted she had sufficient intelligence to care for herself after the surgery. She would have to follow the complicated routine of taking doses of dozens of medications daily that is the lot of every transplant recipient. If she failed to adhere to the postoperative requirements, she would die, and the organs that might have saved the life of one or two other people would be wasted.

William Bronston, a state rehabilitation administrator and a friend of Jensen, became her advocate. He pointed out that she had demonstrated a high level of intellectual functioning. She was a high school graduate who worked with people with Down syndrome, and she had lived on her own for several years. She spoke for the disabled in California and attended the Washington signing by George H. Bush of the Americans with Disabilities Act in 1990.

Thanks to strong lobbying by Bronston and the threat of adverse publicity, Stanford reversed its decision. On January 23, 1996, in a five-hour operation, Ms. Jensen became the first seriously mentally retarded person in the United States to receive a major organ transplant.

More than a year later, on May 4, 1997, after her health began deteriorating, Ms. Jensen entered Sutter General Hospital in San Francisco. She had been admitted to the hospital several times before because of her reaction to the immunosuppressive drug. But this time was the last, and she died there on May 25, 1997. "Every day was always precious and lived well by her," her friend William Bronston said.

Prompted by Ms. Jensen's struggle to be accepted for a transplant, the California Assembly passed a bill to prohibit transplant centers from discriminating against impaired people needing a transplant.

CASE PRESENTATION
The Ayalas' Solution: Having a Child to Save a Life

Anissa Ayala was fifteen years old in 1988 when she was diagnosed with chronic myelogenous leukemia. She received radiation and chemotherapy treatments to destroy diseased bone marrow and blood cells, but the usual outcome of such treatments is that the bone marrow is left unable to produce an adequate number of normal blood cells.

Anissa's parents, Mary and Andy Ayala, were informed that without a bone marrow transplant of stem cells her survival chances were virtually zero, while with a transplant she would have a 70 to 80 percent chance.

Tests showed that neither the Ayalas nor their nineteen-year-old son, Airon, had bone marrow sufficiently compatible for them to be donors for Anissa. They turned to a public registry to assist them and during the next two years searched for a donor. The odds of a match between two nonrelated people is only 1 in 20,000, and as time passed and no one was found, the Ayalas began to feel increasingly desperate. Anissa's health had stabilized, yet that condition couldn't be counted on to last forever.

The Ayalas decided that the only way they could do more to help save their daughter's life was to try to have another child. Anissa's physician tried to discourage them, pointing out that the odds were only one in four that the child would have the right tissue type to be a stem-cell donor. Furthermore, the possibility that they could conceive another child was doubtful. Andy Ayala was forty-five years old and had had a vasectomy performed sixteen years earlier. Mary Ayala was forty-two, well past the period of highest fertility. Nevertheless, the Ayalas decided to go ahead with their plan, and as the first step Andy Ayala had surgery to repair the vasectomy.

Against all the odds, Mary Ayala became pregnant. When it became known that the Ayalas planned to have a child because their daughter needed compatible bone marrow, they became the subjects of intense media attention and received much harsh criticism. Some said that they were treating the baby they expected to have as a means only and not as a person of unique worth. One commentator described their actions as "outrageous." Others said they were taking a step down the path that would lead to conceiving children merely to be sources for tissues and organs.

A few opposed this outpouring of criticism by noting that people decide to have children for many and complex reasons and sometimes for no reason at all. No one observed that a reason for having a child need not determine how one regards the child. Also, those who condemned the Ayalas often emphasized the "child-as-an-organ-bank" notion but never mentioned the relative safety of a bone marrow transplant.

The Ayalas were hurt by the criticisms. Mary Ayala said she had wanted a third child for a number of years but had been unable to get her husband to agree. Andy Ayala admitted that he wouldn't have wanted another child if Anissa hadn't become ill, but he said he also had in mind the comfort a child would bring to the family if Anissa should die. The whole family said they would want and love the child, whether or not its bone marrow was a good match for Anissa's.

In February 1990 the Ayalas found they had beat the odds once more. Tests of the developing fetus showed that the stem cells were nearly identical with Anissa's. During an interview after the results were known, Anissa Ayala said "A lot of people think 'How can you do this? How can you be having this baby for your daughter?' But she's my baby sister and we're going to love her for who she is, not for what she can give me."

Then, on April 6, in a suburban Los Angeles hospital, more than a week before the predicted date, Mary Ayala gave birth to a healthy six-pound baby girl. The Ayalas named her Marissa Eve. Anissa's physician, pediatric oncologist Patricia Konrad, collected and froze blood from the baby's umbilical cord. Umbilical blood contains a high concentration of stem cells, and she wanted the blood available should Anissa need it before Marissa was old enough to be a donor.

When Marissa Eve was fourteen months old and had reached an adequate weight, she was given general anesthesia and marrow was extracted from her hipbone. After preparation, the donated marrow was injected into one of Anissa's veins. The procedure was successful, and the stem cells migrated to Anissa's marrow and began to multiply. Anissa's own bone marrow began to produce normal blood cells.

In 1993 Anissa married Bryan Espinosa, and Marissa Eve was the flower girl at the wedding. Radiation treatments destroyed Anissa's chances of having a child of her own, but she claims that the bond between her and Marissa Eve is especially close. "Marissa is more than a sister to me," Anissa told reporter Anni Griffiths Belt. "She's almost like my child too."

"I was struck by the extraordinary bond between the sisters," Belt said. "The fact is, neither one would be alive today without the other."

SOCIAL CONTEXT
Fetal-Cell Implants

Parkinson's disease often begins with tremors and a mild stiffening of the limbs that is followed, usually over a period of years, by a gradual but progressive loss of muscle control. Although remaining intellectually lucid, people with the disease are often unable to walk, use the toilet, wash, or even eat without assistance.

Their behavior also has a peculiar and disturbing off/on aspect. Someone may be walking or talking when, without the least warning, he freezes during the action. Some find this feature of the disease so disconcerting that they become recluses, fearful of freezing in midmotion in public or in a dangerous place. Over 1.5 million people, most of them over sixty, are estimated to suffer from the disease. In 1996 what might be the gene responsible for the disease was traced to chromosome 4, but the gene itself has not been identified.

The disease is causally connected with the dying off of cells in a darkly pigmented part of the brain called the *substantia nigra*. These cells produce dopamine, a neurotransmitter essential in conveying impulses to brain cells that control muscle movements. A major therapeutic advance in the treatment of Parkinsonism occurred with the introduction of the drug L-dopa. L-dopa is a biochemical precursor of dopamine, and when the body converts the drug to dopamine, people often make an amazing recovery from the effects of the disease. Unfortunately, within a few years L-dopa ceases to be effective, and the old problems of rigidity, "freezing," and general loss of muscle control return.

In 1987, Ignacio Madrazo reported in Mexico that he had successfully transplanted cells from the adrenal cortex of two Parkinson patients into the caudate nucleus area of their brains. The adrenal gland is known to produce dopamine, and Madrazo described his patients as making substantial functional recoveries that he expected to continue over the long term. (Five years previously, Swedish researchers performed a similar operation but reported that their patients made only slight and transitory improvements.) Madrazo's results were never reported in a scientific journal, and although scientists made efforts to repeat the work, no one was successful. Thus, early hopes for adrenal-cell transplants as an effective treatment for Parkinsonism were disappointed.

Then in February 1990, matters began to look hopeful again. Olle Lindvall of University Hospital in Lund, Sweden, reported in *Science* that he and his research team had implanted fetal brain cells into the brain of a forty-nine-year-old man with severe Parkinson's disease. The cells were injected into the left putamen, an area known to be the site of numerous dopamine pathways.

The man's symptoms were significantly relieved. Previously, even with medication, he had spent more than half his time in a frozen "off" position, but within three months after the implant, he had only one or two brief "off" periods each day. (The man's course was followed from eleven months before the surgery, and it was still being followed at the time of publication five months afterward.) Most important, brain-imaging methods indicated that the fetal cells were continuing to function and to produce dopamine.

Lindvall's team had been working on the problem since 1979, and the team's reputation, experimental procedures, and data convinced most of the biomedical community that their results were reliable. Other researchers indicated that they had experiments underway that were likely to confirm Lindvall's results.

The Swedish procedure involved taking neural tissue from four fetuses eight to nine weeks old. Fetal brain tissue offers the possibility of a better biological match than cells even from an individual's own adrenal gland. Further, neural fetal tissue seems to be unlikely to provoke an autoimmune response and cause graft-host rejection. Treating Parkinsonism with fetal-cell implants is an exciting therapeutic possibility that may benefit hundreds of thousands of sufferers. Furthermore, the treatment points the way toward the development of other therapies involving fetal tissues.

Fetal liver cells may be used to generate new bone marrow to treat those suffering from leukemia, sickle-cell anemia, thalassemia, aplastic anemia, or radiation sickness. (Robert Gale employed fetal liver cells to treat some victims of the Chernobyl disaster, although without success.) Alzheimer's disease and Huntington's disease may yield to treatments involving fetal neural cells. Fetal heart tissue may be used to replace damaged heart muscle, and the bodies of the more than 2 million insulin-dependent (Type-I) diabetics may someday be able to produce their own insulin, if implants of islet cells from fetal pancreatic tissue should be successful.

In 1997 scientists at the Veterans Affairs Medical Center in Gainesville, Florida initiated a clinical trial involving treating ten patients with spinal cord injuries with injections of cells from fetal spinal cord tissue. The hope is that the fetal cells will reproduce and fill in the gaps in the spinal cavity where nerves have been destroyed. Adult neural tissue does not regenerate, but fetal neural tissue still has the capacity to grow. Animal studies, as well as experiments performed in Russia and Sweden hold out the hope that the new neural tissue will make it possible for some patients to regain some control over their bodies. Tissue from five to eight fetuses will be required to treat each patient. About 10,000 people are paralyzed by spinal cord injuries each year, and no therapy has yet been shown to reverse paralysis.

The potential therapeutic marvels promised by fetal cells hold out the only hope for literally millions of people suffering from a wide range of diseases. However, fetal-cell implants and their use in research and therapy have also produced serious moral and social issues we have yet to resolve.

The most vexed issue is that of induced abortion as the source of fetal tissue. Opponents of elective abortion argue that research and therapy using fetal tissue both condone and encourage abortion. According to a National Right to Life Committee representative, the medical use of fetal tissue will "offer an additional rationalization to those who defend the killings."

Also, both opponents and advocates of elective abortion express concern over the possibility that some women might deliberately conceive a child, then have an abortion for the sole purpose of obtaining the fetal tissue. The tissue could then either be used to help some member of the woman's family or sold as a commodity. Although a 1988 amendment to the National Organ Transplant Act prohibits the sale of fetal organs and tissue, the success of fetal-cell therapy could lead to a repeal. Some have suggested that fetal tissue, like blood, bone marrow, ova, and sperm, can be considered a renewable resource. The potential for a fetal-tissue market exists, and some have speculated that the current law may only encourage the establishment of an off-shore source of supply. People will seek out illegal sources of supplies of fetal tissue in much the same way they seek illegal sources of drugs they believe are crucial to their survival.

Some critics see the possibility that women might be exploited. The idea that women might be put under pressure by social expectations or by their friends, husbands, or families to have an abortion to provide fetal tissue needed to treat an ailing relative is not farfetched. Further, if there were a market in fetal tissue, women might be under pressure to produce a fetus to secure money needed to support themselves or their families. (It should be kept in mind, though, that even in the absence of pressure, a woman might choose to sell or donate fetal tissue for a variety of reasons.)

While the Catholic Church condemns induced abortion, it condones the use of fetal tissue, at least that obtained from spontaneous abortions, within certain limits. The "fetal organ donor" must be treated with the same respect as any other organ donor, and it is necessary to be certain the donor is dead. This requirement presents a difficulty, however, for the standards for fetal brain death are far from clear.

About 1.25 million abortions are performed each year, and most fetal tissue used in research is obtained from those performed during the first four months of pregnancy. Although the matter is in dispute, some researchers regard tissue from eight- to nine-week-old fetuses as preferable, while some claim older tissue is better. In either case, social and economic pressure on a woman to delay an abortion may start to build and the best interest of the woman may be compromised by the need for mature fetal tissue. Instead of using a drug like RU-486 to inhibit the implantation of a fertilized ovum or instead of having an early abortion, a woman might carry the fetus until a time dictated by needs other than her own health.

The possibility of using only spontaneously aborted fetuses is dimmed by the fact that up to 60 percent show chromosomal abnormalities or other defects that might affect the tissue recipient. But one way of addressing the abortion objection to the use of fetal tissue is to employ cells from a single fetus, grow them in cultures, then harvest them as needed. This would eliminate the need for a large number of mature fetuses and make the research and treatment more independent of abortion.

Another possibility is to use the techniques of molecular biology to clone cells taken from an individual patient. If the cells can be made to multiply in sufficient quantity, the patient can be treated with his own cells. The problem of an immune reaction would be eliminated, and cell therapy would be severed from abortion.

Because fetal cells are now available and not dependent on technological development, people suffering from Parkinson's disease, spinal-cord injuries, and other disorders that might be helped by fetal-cell implants are understandably not eager to see research in this area delayed. For a great number, the development of a future technology that will disconnect cell therapy and abortion will come too late to help.

In 1987, the Department of Health and Human Services suspended the support of research projects using fetal tissue obtained through induced abortions. After two reviews of the issues, a special panel of the National Institutes of Health decided in 1988 that the use of fetal tissue for research and treatment can be morally legitimate. The panel separated the question of elective abortion from that of the use of fetal tissue and took no position on the moral status of abortion. The panel also recommended that women not be permitted to donate fetal tissue for the treatment of their friends or family.

In April 1989, NIH, following most of the recommendations of its panel, issued guidelines for the use of fetal tissue in research and experimental therapy. The ban on the use of such tissue initiated during the Reagan administration was continued by the Bush administration, however, and federal funds could not be used for human fetal-tissue implants. In addition, at least seven states passed laws forbidding the use of fetal tissue obtained from induced abortions. Many researchers objected to these restrictions. Some claimed that the restrictions were immoral because they seriously impeded the development of effective treatments for devastating diseases. Others used funds from private foundations to continue their research.

Despite objections from the research community, the ban on federal financing of studies using cells from aborted fetuses remained in effect until it was lifted by President Clinton in one of his first official acts. In January 1994, the National Institute of Neurological Disorders announced grants of $4.5 million to three institutions to study the effects of fetal-cell implants in Parkinson's patients.

One of the grants was awarded to researchers at the University of Colorado, in Denver. During the ban, the researchers, operating on private financing, injected fetal brain cells into sixteen patients with Parkinson's disease. The outcome was that about one-third of the patients improved significantly, one-third improved some, and one-third showed no measurable improvement.

Patients with diseases that might be relieved by fetal-cell therapy, as well as their families, are eager to see it developed as rapidly as possible. Some are angered by what they see as an unjustified delay in federal research funding. Others are angered by what they see as an endorsement of abortion.

CASE PRESENTATION

Drug Lottery: The Betaseron Shortage

Multiple sclerosis (MS) is a neurological disorder affecting almost 300,000 Americans. Its symptoms include fatigue, dizziness, slurred speech, vision loss, numbness, tingling sensations, and muscle spasticity that affects coordination and makes walking difficult. The disease strikes adults from twenty to forty years old. It is progressive and, in extreme cases, can lead to paralysis.

About one third of those with the disease have a form known as relapsing–remitting multiple sclerosis. They can live free of symptoms for months, then have an attack during which their symptoms return, and they may be confined to a wheelchair for weeks. Typically, the symptoms are worse than they were during the last episode, and as the attacks continue to occur, people become progressively more disabled.

The hopes of some sufferers were raised in 1993 when the FDA announced its approval of a new drug that had been shown in clinical trials to reduce the frequency of attacks by about 30 percent in early stages of the relapsing–remitting form. What's more, magnetic resonance imaging indicated that brain changes associated with the symptoms were fewer than those seen in untreated patients. The drug was a genetically engineered form of interferon known as interferon beta IB with the trade name Betaseron. An injectable drug, it promised to help an estimated 100,000 to 175,000 people with multiple sclerosis. It was the first drug that promised to slow the course of the disease, rather than merely treat its symptoms.

By the fall of 1993, immediately after FDA approval, MS patients throughout the country were pressuring their physicians to prescribe the drug for them. Most physicians were happy to do so, but the problem was there wasn't enough Betaseron to meet the needs of the patients who might benefit from it. Berlex Laboratories, its developer, had been caught by surprise by FDA's fast-track approval process and so were not in a position to manufacture large quantities of the drug rapidly. Further, because Betaseron can be manufactured only in a fermentation process using genetically engineered E. coli bacteria, its production could not be speeded up to meet demand.

Berlex's response to the situation was to establish a lottery, the first of its kind, as a means of determining who would receive the drug. The lottery was open only to those with relapsing–remitting multiple sclerosis who were certified by their doctors to be in the earlier stages of the disease and able to walk at least 100 yards unassisted. Some 67,000 people applied for the drug by the September 15 deadline, and another 7000 applied after the deadline.

As people applied, they were assigned randomly to positions on a waiting list by a computer program. Enough doses of the drug were available to help 17,000 people immediately. Those receiving higher numbers would have to wait for additional supplies to be manufactured.

Berlex was especially concerned that those treated with Betaseron receive an uninterrupted course of the drug. "A lot of patients on and off therapy is no good for anybody," Jeffrey Latts, a Berlex vice president said. "We felt it was better for some patients to get continuous therapy rather than intermittent therapy."

Before announcing the lottery, Berlex officials talked with patient groups, drug distribution experts, and physicians. Patients tended to favor a lottery, but physicians were generally not happy with the idea of giving up control over choosing which patients might benefit from the drug.

"We felt it was important to keep this process completely clean," Latts said about the lottery. "I personally can guarantee that no one got moved up, no matter how influential. We said, 'No, Governor, we can't,' and 'I'm sorry, Senator, it's not possible.' We heard rumors that someone was offering to pay for a lower number, but we have records of what number went to what patient where."

Despite Berlex's commitment to fairness, some patients did receive Betaseron without going through the lottery. Some 3500 doses of the drug were sent to 100 medical centers, and the centers decided how to distribute them. "I feel guilty I was chosen and other people weren't," said a fifty-seven-year-old lawyer who was one of those who got the drug without entering the lottery. "But not guilty enough not to take it. When you've had MS for many years, you just look for some ray of hope."

Some patients not meeting the lottery guidelines pressured their physicians into certifying them as in the early stages of the disease, permitting them to qualify for the lottery. An even larger number objected to being excluded from the lottery, claiming that they had as much right as anyone to get whatever benefit they could from Betaseron. Most physicians, however, rejected this point of view. They considered it wrong to give the drug to patients for whom it had not been proved effective, when there was an inadequate supply of the drug for patients for whom its effectiveness had been demonstrated.

Along with the lottery, Berlex Laboratories introduced a second program with the aim of assuring access to Betaseron by those who might benefit from it. The cost of the drug was $989 a month, putting it out of the financial reach of many people. To address this problem Berlex provided the drug free to those who were uninsured and earned less than $20,000 a year. For those uninsured and earning up to $50,000, it employed a sliding scale of charges. Medicaid and most private insurance companies paid for the drug, but Medicare did not. To encourage patients to adhere to the best treatment schedule, Berlex committed itself to providing free drugs to all patients for the eleventh and twelfth months.

By 1994 the shortage of Betaseron was over. While some physicians and patients were unhappy with the lottery approach, most observers considered it the best model to follow in the event of future drug shortages. Given that many new drugs are likely to be the product of genetic engineering, the next shortage may not lie far in the future.

CHAPTER 8

Paying for Health Care

CLASSIC CASE PRESENTATION

Robert Ingram: Dilemma of the Working Poor

Robert Ingram (as I'll call him) was fifty-two years old and very worried about himself, a result of two months of having episodes of sharp, stabbing pains on the left side of his chest. When the pains came, he felt cold and sweaty, and although he tried to ignore them, he found he had to stop what he was doing and wait until they passed.

He hadn't mentioned the pains to Jeri, his wife, right at first. He half-expected and half-hoped they would simply go away, but they hadn't. Eventually he'd had to tell her, when the stabbing came at home while he was moving a large upholstered chair with a broken frame out to the trash. She'd seen him put the chair down and put his hand on his chest.

When he told her how long he'd been having the pains, she'd made him call up Lane Clinic for an appointment. He hadn't wanted to miss most of a day's work. He operated Bob's Express, which picked up car and truck parts from the smaller supply houses and delivered them to mechanics and garages within a twenty-mile radius. He'd founded the business only a year ago, after working as a mechanic himself for almost thirty years.

He had hoped to be able to expand, but there weren't as many deliveries to make as he'd counted on. The big supply houses had their own distribution system, and he had to scramble to get business from the wrecking yards and the rebuilders.

He was making enough money to pay the operating expenses and the rent, but not much more. All he had to show for his work was one Chevy Silverado pickup and a ten-year-old Ford station wagon. He had one part-time employee, Phil Archer. Jeri took the phone orders from their home office, and he and Phil made the rounds. He was his own boss, and that's what he and Jeri most liked about the business. He worked hard, but he didn't have to answer to anybody.

On Wednesday, the day of his appointment, he asked Phil to work the whole day. He drove the Ford to the clinic, so he'd be able to go directly from there to Ace Distributors and pick up the shirttail full of parts he knew he had to deliver. If anybody called with more orders for Ace, he could get them too.

Dr. Tran was a short, thin, Asian man who looked young enough to be a teenager. But he seemed to know exactly what he was doing. He moved the stethoscope over Robert's chest, listening to his heart. He had him walk across the room, then listened to it again.

Dr. Tran asked about Robert's parents and grandparents. Robert told him both grandfathers had died of heart attacks in their late fifties. One of his grandmothers was still alive, but the other had also died of a heart attack.

Then Dr. Tran asked questions about the chest pain. How long had he had it? What did it feel like? How long did it last? Did anything in particular seem to bring it on? Did he ever get it while sleeping? Did it start when he was carrying grocery bags or simply walking? Did the pain seem to radiate down his left arm? Did his arm feel numb? Did the last two fingers tingle?

Robert did his best to answer all the questions, but he didn't see the point to them. He was almost sorry he'd come. It was easy to believe nothing was seriously wrong with him while he was sitting on the edge of the examining table talking to Dr. Tran. He needed to be making his deliveries. Otherwise, Phil would get hopelessly behind. Late deliveries could lose customers.

Dr. Tran finished his examination and asked Robert to get dressed and have a seat in the chair beside the small built-in desk. Dr. Tran left the room for ten minutes or so, then returned. He took the swivel chair beside the desk.

"I'm worried that you may be on the verge of a heart attack," Dr. Tran told Robert. "You may already have had one or more small attacks."

"Wouldn't I have known it?" Robert could hardly believe what he was hearing.

"Not necessarily," Dr. Tran said. "The blood gets blocked for a moment, some tissue dies. You feel pain, then it's over." He paused. "But what concerns me most is that your coronary arteries may be significantly blocked by plaque, and if that's so, the outcome could be devastating."

"You mean I could die."

"Exactly," Dr. Tran said. "We need to know what shape your heart's in, so I want you to have a coronary angiogram. I'm going to refer you to a cardiologist, and she may want you to have ultrasound as well."

Seeing Robert's blank look, Dr. Tran explained what was involved in the angiogram, then talked about the images sonography could produce.

"Do you really need to take a look at my heart like that?" Robert asked. "Couldn't you just let it go at listening?"

"We need to find out if you've got some blocked coronary arteries," Dr. Tran said. "We also need to get some sense of how your valves are working and what size your heart is. Otherwise, we'd just be guessing and basing a treatment on what we thought was happening. Technology lets us go beyond that."

Dr. Tran leaned forward and touched Robert's knee.

"Don't worry. Angiography is quite safe, really. And the ultrasound amounts to nothing at all."

"But what will they *cost?*"

"I'm not sure exactly," Dr. Tran said. "Probably in the neighborhood of $5000 to $7000. Maybe more if Dr. Goode needs for you to spend the night at the hospital."

"Then it's all out of the question," Robert said. "I don't have the money."

"Your insurance will cover both procedures."

"I don't have insurance, Doctor." Robert shook his head. "I run my own business, and I put all my money into keeping it going. I can't even mortgage my house, because it's rented."

"You're not old enough to qualify for Medicare," Dr. Tran said. "Do you own some property or jewelry? Something you can sell?"

"All I own is a broken-down station wagon and part of a pickup truck. I still owe money on the truck. Maybe I could sell it for enough to pay it off and pay for those tests you want me to have."

"If the tests show what I think they might," Dr. Tran said, "you'll need coronary artery bypass surgery. That will cost in the neighborhood of $30,000. Perhaps as much as $50,000, depending on complications and hospital stays."

"That's just laughable," Robert said. "No way I could raise $30,000. Not even if my life depended on it."

"I suspect it does," Dr. Tran said. "But selling your truck would have the advantage of qualifying you for Medicaid. In this state, if you have assets under $3000, you qualify."

"But if I sold my truck, I'd have to go out of business," Robert said. "I wouldn't have any way to earn a living, and my wife's sickly. She can't work a regular job, because of her headaches."

"Don't you have some family you could borrow from?"

"Maybe I could borrow $1000 from Jeri's mother, but she lives on Social Security. And there's nobody else. The few friends we have haven't got any more money than we do."

"I don't know what to say."

"Can't you just give me some pills?"

"I don't see any alternative," Dr. Tran said. "But I'm uncomfortable doing it, because I don't know exactly what we're up against. Like I told you, you could be on the verge of having a heart attack. We could help you with the right tests and, if necessary, the right sort of surgery. But as it is. . . ."

"I'll just have to take my chances," Robert said. "Until I'm either rich enough or poor enough to get the right treatment."

Briefing Session

Some historians of medicine estimate that it was not until the middle 1930s that the intervention of a physician in the treatment of an illness was likely to affect the outcome in a substantial way. The change was brought about by the discovery and development of antibiotic agents such as penicillin and sulfa drugs. They made it possible, for the first time, both to control infection and to provide specific remedies for a variety of diseases. Additional advances in treatment modalities, procedures, and technology have helped establish contemporary medicine as an effective enterprise.

Before these dramatic changes occurred, there was little reason for anyone to be particularly concerned with the question of the distribution of medical care within society. The situation in the United States has altered significantly, and a number of writers have recently argued that everyone ought to be guaranteed at least some form of medical care. In part this is a reflection of the increased effectiveness of contemporary medicine, but it is also no doubt due to a growing awareness of the serious difficulties faced by disadvantaged groups within society.

The last chapter focused on one aspect of the problem of the distribution of medical resources—that of allocating limited resources among competing individuals in a particular situation. Here we need to call attention to some of the broader social issues. These issues transcend moral decisions about particular people and raise questions about the basic aims and obligations of society.

A great number of observers believe that the United States is currently faced with a health-care crisis. Some of the reasons supporting this belief, as well as some proposed solutions, are outlined in the Social Context parts of this chapter, and we need not repeat them here. But one element of the crisis is often said to be the lack of any program to provide health care for everyone in the society. That people should be forced to do without needed health care for primarily financial reasons has seemed to some a morally intolerable state of affairs.

This point of view has frequently been based on the claim that everyone has a right to health care. Thus, it has been argued, society has a duty to provide that care; if it does not, then it is sanctioning a situation that is inherently wrong. To remedy the situation requires redesigning the health-care system and present practices to see to it that all who need health care have access to it.

The language of "rights" is very slippery. To understand and evaluate arguments that involve claiming (or denying) rights to health care, it is important to understand the nature of the claim. The word "rights" is used in several distinct ways, and a failure to be clear about the use in any given case leads only to unproductive confusion.

The following distinctions may help capture some of the more important sorts of things that people have in mind when they talk about rights.

CLAIM-RIGHTS, LEGAL RIGHTS, AND STATUTORY RIGHTS

Suppose I own a copy of the book *Fan Mail*. If so, then I may be said to have a right to do with the book whatever I choose. Other people may be said to have a duty to recognize my right in appropriate ways. Thus, if I want to read the book, burn it, or sell it, others have a duty not to interfere with me. If I loan the book to someone, then he or she has a duty to return it.

Philosophers of law generally agree that a *claim-right* to something serves as a ground for other people's duties. A claim-right, then, always entails a duty or duties on the part of someone else.

Generally speaking, *legal rights* are claim-rights. Someone has a legal right when someone else has a definable duty, and legal remedies are available when the duty is not performed. Either the person can be forced to perform the duty, or damages of some sort can be collected for failure to perform. If I pay someone to put a new roof on my house by a certain date, she has contracted a duty to perform the work we have agreed to. If the task is not performed, then I can turn to the legal system for enforcement or damages.

Statutory rights are claim-rights that are explicitly recognized in legal statutes or laws. They impose duties on certain classes of people under specified conditions. A hospital contractor, for example, has a duty to meet certain building codes. If he fails to meet them, he is liable to legal penalties. But not all legal rights are necessarily statutory rights. Such considerations as "customary and established practices" may sometimes implicitly involve a legally enforceable claim-right.

MORAL RIGHTS

A *moral right,* generally speaking, is one that is stated in or derived from the principles of a moral theory. More specifically, to say that someone has a moral right to certain goods or manner of treatment is to say that others have a moral duty to see to it that she receives what she has a right to. A moral right is a certain kind of claim-right. Here, though, the source of justification for the right and for the corresponding duty lies in moral principles and not in the laws or practices of a society.

According to Ross, for example, people have a duty to treat other people benevolently. This is a duty that is not recognized by our legal system. We may, if we wish, treat others in a harsh and unsympathetic manner and in doing so violate no law.

Of course, many rights and duties that are based upon the principles of moral theories are also embodied in our laws. Thus, to take Ross again as an example, we have a prima facie duty not to injure or kill anyone. This duty, along with its correlative right to be free from injury or death at the hands of another, is reflected in the body of statutory law and common law that deals with bodily harm done to others and with killing.

The relationship between ethical theories and the laws of a society is complicated and controversial. The fundamental question is always the extent to which laws should reflect or be based upon an ethical theory. In a society such as ours, it does not seem proper that an ethical theory accepted by only a part of the people should determine the laws that govern us all. It is for this reason that some object to laws regulating sexual activity, pornography, and abortion. These are considered best regarded as a part of personal morality.

At the same time, however, it seems that we must rely upon ethical theories as a basis for evaluating laws. Unless we are prepared to say that what is legal is, in itself, what is right, we must recognize the possibility of laws that are bad or unjust. But what makes a law bad? A possible answer is that a law is bad when it violates a right derived from the principles of an ethical theory. Similarly, both laws and social practices may be criticized for failing to recognize a moral right. An ethical theory, then, can serve as a basis for a demand for the reform of laws and practices.

Clearly there is no sharp line separating the moral and the legal. Indeed, virtually all of the moral theories we discussed in Part V have been used by philosophers and other thinkers as the basis for principles applying to society as a whole. Within such frameworks as utilitarianism, natural law theory, and Rawls's theory of a just society, legal and social institutions are assigned roles and functions in accordance with more general moral principles.

POLITICAL RIGHTS

Not everyone attempts to justify claims to rights by referring such claims directly to a moral theory. Efforts are frequently made to provide justification by relying upon principles or commitments that are generally acknowledged as basic to our society. (Of course, to answer how these are justified may force us to invoke moral principles.) Our society, for example, is committed to individual autonomy and equality, among other values. It is by reference to commitments of this sort that we evaluate proposals and criticize practices.

From this point of view, to recognize health care as a right is to acknowledge it as a *political right*. This means showing that it is required by our political commitments or principles. Of course, this may also mean resolving any conflicts that may arise from other rights that also seem to be demanded by our principles. But this is a familiar state of affairs. We are all aware that the constitutional guarantee of freedom of speech, for example, is not absolute and unconditional. It can conflict with other rights or basic commitments, and we look to the courts to provide us with guidelines to resolve the conflicts.

HEALTH CARE AS A RIGHT

With the distinctions that we have discussed in mind, let us return now to the question of a general right to health care. What can those who make such a claim be asserting?

Obviously everyone in our society is free to seek health care and, when the proper arrangements are made, to receive it. That is, health care is a service available in society, and people may avail themselves of it. At the same time, however, no physician or hospital has a duty to provide health care that is sought. The freedom to seek does not imply that others have a duty to provide what we seek.

There is not in our society a legally recognized claim-right to health care. Even if I am sick, no one has a legal duty to see to it that I receive treatment for my illness. (Hospitals receiving federal money have a legal duty to treat people faced with life-threatening emergencies until they are stabilized.) I may request care, or I may attempt to persuade a physician that it is his or her moral duty to provide me with care. But I have no legal right to health care, and, if someone refuses to provide it, I cannot seek a legal remedy.

I may, of course, contract with a physician, clinic, or hospital for care, either in general or for a certain ailment. If I do this, then the other party acquires a legally enforceable duty to provide me the kind of care that we agreed upon.

Contracting for health care, in this respect, is not relevantly different from contracting for a new roof on my house.

Those who assert that health care is a right cannot be regarded as making the obviously false claim that there is a legal right to care. Their claim, rather, must be interpreted as one of a moral or political sort. They might be taken as asserting something like "Everyone in our society ought to be entitled to health care, regardless of his or her financial condition."

Anyone making such a claim must be prepared to justify it by offering reasons and evidence in support of it. The ultimate source of the justification is most likely to be the principles of a moral theory. For example, Kant's principle that every person is of inherent and equal worth might be used to support the claim that every person has an equal right to medical care, simply by virtue of being a person.

Justification might also be offered in terms of principles that express the aims and commitments of the society. A society that endorses justice and equality, one might argue, must be prepared to offer health care to all, if it offers it to anyone.

However justification is offered, to claim that health care is a right is to go beyond merely expressing an attitude. It is to say more than something like "Everyone would like to have health care" or "Everyone needs health care."

The language of "rights" is frequently used in a rhetorical way to encourage us to recognize the wants and needs of people—or even other organisms, such as animals and trees. This is a perfectly legitimate way of talking. But, at bottom, to urge that something be considered a right is to make a claim requiring justification in terms of some set of legal, social, or moral principles.

OBJECTIONS

Why not recognize health care for all as a right? Virtually everyone would admit that in the abstract it would be a good thing. If this is so, then why should anyone wish to oppose it? Briefly stated, arguments against a right to health care are most frequently of two kinds.

First, those who subscribe to a position sometimes called "medical individualism" argue that to recognize a right to health care would have the consequence of violating the rights of physicians and other medical practitioners. Physicians, they claim, would be required to employ their intelligence, knowledge, and skills in a way dictated by society. Thus, physicians would be deprived of their autonomy and, in a very real sense, made slaves of the state.

Second, some critics have pointed out that, while it is possible to admit health care to the status of a right, we must also recognize that health care is only one social good among others. Education, transportation, housing, legal assistance, and so on are other goods that are also sought and needed by members of our society. It is impossible to admit all of these (and perhaps others) to the status of rights, for the society simply cannot afford to pay for them.

The first line of argument, medical individualism, fails to recognize that the health-care situation is perhaps best regarded as one in which there is a conflict of rights (between patients and providers) and not just one in which the rights of physicians are being restricted.

The second line of argument does not necessarily lead to the conclusion that we should not recognize a right to health care. It does serve to warn us that we must be careful to specify exactly what sort of right—if any—we want to support. Do we want to claim, for example, that everyone has a right to a certain minimum of health care? Or do we want to claim that everyone has a right to equal health care (whatever anyone can get, everyone can demand)?

Furthermore, this line of argument warns us that we have to make decisions about what we, as a society, are willing to pay for. Would we, for example, be willing to give up all public support for education in order to use the money for health care? Probably not. But we might be willing to reduce the level of support for education in order to increase that for health care. Whatever we decide, we have to face up to the problem of distributing our limited resources. This is an issue that is obviously closely connected with what sort of right to health care (or, really, the right to what sort of health care) we are prepared to endorse.

The need for health care by those unable to purchase it calls attention to fundamental issues about rights, values, and social goals. If we are to recognize a right to health care, we must be clear about exactly what this involves.

Are we prepared to offer only a "decent minimum"? Does justice require that we make available to all whatever is available to any? Are we prepared to restrict the wants of some people in order to satisfy the basic needs of all people?

Such questions are of more than academic interest, and they concern more than just a handful of patients and physicians. How they are resolved will affect us all, directly and indirectly, through the character of our society. We are the richest nation in the history of the world, yet we have not solved the problem of providing needed medical care to all our citizens.

SOCIAL CONTEXT

Costs of Care

It was one of the most effective political ads of all time.

Harry and Louise, a forty-something couple, are sitting at the kitchen table browsing through the stacks of paper of the 1994 Clinton health plan. "Things are going to change, and not all for the better," says an announcer in a voice-over. "The government may force us to pick from a few health care plans designed by government bureaucrats."

Looking at Harry, Louise says, "Having choices we don't like is no choice at all."

The ad, which was sponsored by the Health Insurance Association of America, tapped into the worries and anxieties felt by millions of Americans as they contemplated the prospect of abandoning the old and familiar fee-for-service medical care system funded mostly by private insurance. If the Clinton plan passed into law, they would then find themselves in a system of managed competition in which they would be required to choose from a variety of medical plans with varying price tags. Although the insurance companies would administer the plans, the plans themselves would need to meet federal requirements and be subject to government oversight.

Due in large part to the Harry and Louise ad, the reforms of the Clinton plan were defeated politically. Ironically, the old fee-for-service system that Harry and Louise appeared to favor, virtually disappeared within a couple of years after the ad had done its work. In 1988 about 71 percent of employees in the U.S. were enrolled in traditional medical insurance plans, but by 1998 more than 85 percent were enrolled in managed-care plans. Since then, the fee-for-service medical system has virtually disappeared.

The plans now available aren't ones designed by a government bureaucracy of the sort feared by Harry and Louise. But so far as "having choices we don't like" is concerned, rather than being able to choose from a large variety of health-care plans, most Americans' choices are limited to the few offered to them by their employer.

Employers, concerned about profits, negotiate with managed-care companies to offer plans that are relatively inexpensive. The companies, focused on their own profits, try to lower the costs of the health care they deliver through the physicians, hospitals, testing laboratories, and clinics with whom they have contracts.

Has the movement to managed care and the radical change in the way that most Americans receive and pay for their health care resolved the crisis that prompted the efforts at reform that so disturbed Harry and Louise? Not really.

Indeed, dissatisfactions with the managed-care system have driven people to demand other alternatives. Also, hospitals and doctor's groups, unwilling to agree to the fees and restrictions imposed by insurers have started to negotiate with insurers to promote their own interests.

These changes have led to higher costs to insurance companies and to newer versions of managed care in which controls over care have been reduced. The result is that the costs of medical treatment is again on the rise. Managed care has not so much failed as we have refused to accept the rationing that it requires to reduce costs.

CRISIS

A crisis exists in a social institution when factors are present that tend to destroy it or render it ineffective in achieving its goals. Two major factors are present in the American health-care system that put it in a state of crisis: the increasing cost to the society of health care and the failure to deliver at least a decent minimum of health care to everyone who needs it.

Despite the widespread expectation that managed care plus a combination of legislative approaches would deal with the crisis, this has not happened. The way in which most Americans now receive health care has been drastically altered, but the crisis continues. We'll examine briefly a few of the key factors producing it, then consider some solutions that have been offered.

CURRENT COSTS

In 1960 health spending in the United States amounted to some $27 billion. In 1970 it rose to $75 billion, and in 1983 it increased to $356 billion. Despite the coming of widespread managed care plans starting around 1994, spending continued to increase. By 1996 U.S. health care costs had climbed to an astounding $1 trillion. This was 4.4 percent more than in 1995; even so, it was the smallest increase in 37 years.

By 2000 spending on health care topped the scale at $1.3 trillion. This was an increase of 6.9 percent over 1993, the year major health-care reform was first proposed. Health-care costs now account for 13.3 percent of the nation's gross domestic product, up .1 percent from 1999 and 1.1 percent from 1998.

The 2000 costs of $1.3 trillion represents spending an average of $4637 on each person. Spending in earlier years reflects the continuing increase: $2966 in 1991; $4001 in 1997; and $4377 in 1999.

Salaries in health care and insurance premiums have mirrored these increases. But the major reason for the increase during the last few years economists believe to be opposition to the strictures of managed care by physicians and patients.

MANAGED CARE AVOIDED

The spread of managed care initially succeeded in bringing costs under control. This was done by instituting policies—some controversial, others objectionable, and nearly all disliked—governing treatments and drugs that would be paid for, access to medical specialists, and length of hospital stays. Although such controls reduced medical costs at first, by 1998 they began to rise again, and the figures for 2000 (the most recent available) show the trend has continued.

When given the choice, consumers in growing numbers prefer a form of managed care that has fewer restrictions than the older plans that required vigilant "gatekeepers" to restrict the tests and treatment options physicians could choose. Traditional health maintenance organizations (HMOs), with their rigid regulations, are now no longer the preferred model for health-care delivery.

The second factor in the weakening of managed care is the product of the new negotiating strengths of health-care providers. Consolidations of hospitals and the organization of physicians into practice groups have given health-care providers more bargaining power when dealing with insurers. They can negotiate higher payments for services and greater autonomy in decisionmaking.

HOSPITAL CARE AND DRUGS

In 2000, national health care spending increased almost $84 billion over the 1999 amount. Hospital care and prescription drugs account for 45 percent of the increase. The cost of hospital care rose by about $10 billion to $412 billion, while the cost of drugs increased by almost $18 billion to some $122 billion.

Drugs have become the focus of much debate about health reform. From 1995–2000, the cost of drugs doubled, and from 1990–2000, the cost tripled. The increase was about 15 percent a year from 1996 to 2000. Drug manufactures cite the costs of research for producing new and effective drugs, while critics point to new "me-too" drugs that are no more than expensive variations on old drugs. The new drugs, they say, are often no more effective than the older and cheaper ones. That people want them is often due to consumer advertising on television. Thus, Xela is perceived as being superior to Zola merely because of heavy promotion. In this respect, health-care costs are being driven up with little or no improvement in anybody's health.

WHY DO COSTS RISE?

Various explanations have been given for the rising costs of health care. Economists point out that in medicine a surplus of services does not drive prices down. Instead, it may drive up demand. The availability of laboratories, high-technology equipment, hospital beds, and a variety of medical services increases the probability that they will be used.

While managed care can exert some control over demand, the control cannot be total. Managed-care plans must compete for contracts, and the plan that offers the most services at the lowest prices has a competitive advantage. Also, with hospitals and physicians' groups now at the negotiating table, insurers and their business clients can no longer make take-it-or-leave-it offers to health-care providers.

Apart from the way the health-care system operates, other factors having to do with a changing population and the state of medicine itself are responsible to some extent for increasing costs. Here are a few of them:

✦ Children born during the baby boom of the 1940s are reaching late middle age, so the median age of the population has increased. An aging population requires more, as well as more expensive, medical care than a younger population.

✦ Advancements in medical technology now make it possible to provide a greater number of services to hospitalized patients. Hence, more people are likely to be hospitalized in order to receive the services. Similarly, while sophisticated medical tests, such as CT scans, sonograms, and endoscopic examinations can now be done on an outpatient basis, that very fact may increase the likelihood of their use.

✦ Also, surgical procedures like knee or cataract operations that once would have been performed in a hospital may now be performed on outpatients. Yet any possible savings are offset by the increase in the number of the procedures performed.

✦ Improvements in medicine and surgery now make it possible to provide therapies for diseases that once would not have been treated. The availability of such treatments means increasing the hospital population, and the success of such treatments means that more people will be alive who can benefit from additional care.

✦ The treatments themselves are likely to be expensive. Surgery, radiation, chemotherapy, and bone marrow transplants may all be used in treating breast cancer. A liver transplant may cost $100,000, and the combination drug therapy now used in the treatment of AIDS can cost from $12,000 to $20,000 a year.

The very success of medicine creates, in a sense, the need for more medicine. Americans have traditionally refused to accept less effective medical treatments when more effective ones are available, even though the best treatments come with a higher price tag.

Similarly, Americans have taken a more interventionist approach toward dealing with disease, and most people, when faced with a serious illness, choose an aggressive approach to treating it. This, too, usually costs more money. Also, Americans have an unwillingness to accept the explicit rationing of resources that would involve, for example, denying heart transplants to people in their eighties or mammograms to women in their forties. No doubt the whole complex of American attitudes about health care is responsible to a large degree for the amount spent on care in our society.

THE NEED FOR HEALTH CARE REFORM

While efforts over the past two decades have improved access to health care for low-income and minority groups, a significant portion of this population is still not receiving needed care.

The number of people without medical insurance has reached 44 million (almost 19 percent of the population), up from 29 million in 1979. Because people leave and enter the insurance rolls, some analysts estimate that as many as 50 to 60 million people are uninsured for at least some of the time during the year. Half those without insurance are children or families with children. Children themselves make up about 25 percent of the uninsured.

The 1994 Clinton health plan was a proposal to provide access to at least basic health care for everyone. In rejecting the plan, Congress showed an unwillingness to pass any kind of comprehensive national health plan that would address the problems of the uninsured. Those with no sort of medical insurance, as well as those with inadequate coverage, did not disappear when the comprehensive health plan was defeated. Indeed, since that time, despite a period of high employment, a strong economy, and new laws intended to extend health benefits, the number of people without health insurance has continued to rise.

The number has increased steadily since 1987 and has now reached the figure of 44 million mentioned above. This is roughly one-sixth of the nation's population. Why do so many people lack medical coverage? The answers are diverse and complex.

Lost Jobs, New Jobs, Smaller Companies

The economy generated about 14 million new jobs from 1993 to 2000, but the economic downturn beginning that year meant that people who had been counting on their employer to provide them with health insurance found themselves out of a job and responsible for paying the full cost of their policies. For many, the cost was more than they could afford, and they allowed their coverage to lapse. (See the discussion of the Kassebaum-Kennedy plan on the next page for details on how that plan was supposed to help.) They joined the ranks of the uninsured.

Even when the economy was booming, most new jobs were in small companies not likely to offer group health insurance. Such employers often say they can't afford to pay even part of the insurance premiums for their employees and still make a profit. Employers are not required by law to offer health insurance, and often they do so only as a fringe benefit to attract the work force they want. With a downturn in business, the need to attract employees lessens, and employers may eliminate health insurance as part of the job package.

Some employers also say employees prefer higher wages to health insurance. Because employees usually have to contribute to paying insurance premiums in a group plan, those in low-wage jobs frequently say they can't afford health insurance, even when an employer pays part of the cost. A worker making $800 a month who has to pay even as little as $75 a month for insurance coverage is left with a substantially reduced income.

Finally, even if an employee is in a group health plan, the plan may not cover the employee's spouse or children. If it doesn't, the family is then faced with paying for private policies that most of them simply can't afford.

Failure of Kassebaum-Kennedy Law

After the political defeat of the Clinton health proposal, various laws were passed with the aim of helping groups of vulnerable people get health care coverage and assisting working people in keeping their health insurance. Generally, the laws have not worked as their framers and advocates intended.

The Kassebaum-Kennedy law of 1996 was supposed to allow people to change jobs without losing their health insurance. Before the law was passed, an insurance company could drop its coverage on an employee who left a group health plan to take another job. If that happened, someone with a preexisting condition, such as asthma or heart disease, might find it impossible to locate an insurance company willing to insure her. For this reason, many people reported they couldn't risk changing jobs, because they would lose their insurance. Those who got fired from their jobs often automatically lost their insurance.

The Kassebaum-Kennedy law guarantees that people leaving a job with group insurance will, regardless of any preexisting condition, be covered by the group insurance of another employer, if the employer offers group insurance.

The General Accounting Office recently reported to Congress, however, that the law is not working as intended. While the law requires insurers to give policies to individuals who leave their jobs, it does not regulate the fees the insurer can charge. One study showed that some insurance companies charged an individual $10,000 to $15,000 or more a year for a policy. One company charged "high risk" people five times the usual rate.

Critics say insurers get rid of the people they don't want—those who may cost them money—by charging them so much they cannot afford to pay. The law's failure thus leaves people who lose or change jobs in the same position as before. Moreover, the law applies only to those who already have group coverage. Those without it may simply be turned down by insurance companies, who have no obligation to accept them as risks.

Failure of Children's Program

The aim of the 1997 Children's Health Insurance Program was to provide health benefits for the country's 10 million (or more) uninsured children. The initial legislation provided $24 billion to be spent over five years in a joint federal-state program.

So far, however, the program has left the problem of uninsured children relatively unsolved. Many who qualify for Medicaid are simply not enrolled. In January

1998 the federal government estimated that the number was 3 million, and in May the estimate was increased to almost 5 million.

One reason the program has not been successful is that parents are not aware they can get health coverage for their children, coverage generally better than that provided by private insurers. Parents who work at low-paying jobs may earn enough to disqualify them from Medicaid coverage, but not their children. Similarly, while welfare laws limit the time an adult may be on welfare and eligible for Medicaid, the same limits do not apply to their children. Parents may mistakenly assume that they must qualify for Medicaid for their children to qualify. State officials don't always check to see whether the children are eligible, even though their parents aren't.

Other factors also may play a role. For example, the application process in many states is both long and confusing, and this discourages parents whose children might qualify from applying. Also, some parents are not able to take time off from work to apply, and Medicaid offices are not open in the evenings. Others may think Medicaid coverage smacks of charity and will have nothing to do with it.

Not Poor Enough

Not all those who are uninsured can qualify for Medicaid coverage, even if they are poor. According to federal statistics, 43.3 percent of people defined as poor in terms of income, were covered by Medicaid at some time during 1997. However, Medicaid is a joint federal-state program, and some states set the level of income required for qualification so low that it is below the federal poverty line.

Childless adults, in particular, find it quite difficult to qualify for Medicaid in several states. Having assets in excess of $3000 to $4000 may be enough to disqualify someone. Hence, to secure medical care, people may be required to divest themselves of virtually all their assets. Many, for the sake of dignity, are unwilling to impoverish themselves to qualify for Medicaid, and so they choose to go without needed care.

Lack of Care and Delayed Care

The lack of medical coverage suggests that many people in need of medical care fail to get it. Some studies show that more than 10 percent of the population receive no care at all and that more than 4 million people seriously in need of care are forced to do without it.

Evidence also indicates that when uninsured people are admitted to hospitals, they are discharged earlier and receive fewer diagnostic and therapeutic procedures than those who have insurance. Some see results of this kind as proof that the United States has already moved to at least a two-tier medical system in which the poor are provided with second-class care, while those able to pay receive the best care available.

Studies also show that the underinsured often delay seeking medical treatment. The frequent result is that a disease that could have been treated effectively and inexpensively at an early stage must subsequently be treated with greater expense and less effectiveness.

Rational Fear

The fear of being in medical need and not being able to get care has become a specter haunting many Americans. People rarely suffer from not being able to buy new cars or better clothes, but when they cannot afford health care, they may pay a permanent and serious price.

Their worry may be quite rational. Anyone out of a job and unable to afford health insurance risks not being able to get needed medical treatment in the event of a serious illness or accident. The American dream can quickly turn into a peculiarly American nightmare—the best of treatments is in sight, but not within reach.

SOCIAL CONTEXT
Solving the Problem?

The failure of our society to guarantee an adequate level of health care (a "decent minimum") to everyone needing it continues to be the major force behind efforts to establish a national health plan that would provide universal coverage. Few people, including legislators, doubt that the United States needs some sort of plan.

While many hoped that managed care would move in the direction of solving the problem, this has not turned out to be the case. Costs are still increasing, and so are the number of people who cannot afford medical care.

Managed care generated a new set of problems. People were (and some still are) unhappy with the extent to which their medical choices were limited, and physicians were displeased with restrictions on their discretion. The need of managed care companies to make a profit can also seriously compromise the quality of medical care and weaken the trust between physicians and their patients.

Dissatisfaction with restrictive health maintenance organizations (HMOs) has undermined the attempt to reduce medical costs by rationing care. We no longer have the old fee-for-service system, but for higher fees people can choose managed care plans that place fewer restrictions on them and their physicians.

The present system, as a result, is still one that offers two kinds of medicine— one for the rich and one for the poor. And it too often happens that the medicine for the poor is none at all.

PROPOSED SOLUTIONS

The intense national debate about health care in 1994 produced a number of proposals for radically reforming the ways in which medical care is financed and delivered. All the proposals addressed the conjoined issues of increasing costs and the need to provide greater access to health care, but the proposals differed significantly in advocating ways in which costs might be controlled and in recommending how and to what extent access might be provided.

Managed Competition

People in a geographical region would be clustered into state-based pools or "health alliances." The pools would include the uninsured, people now paying for their own insurance, and those working for small companies. Companies with many employees would, in effect, constitute their own health alliance.

The health alliances (and large companies) would bargain with the representatives of various health plans (including those operated by private, for-profit insurance companies) to obtain a standard set of basic benefits for reasonable rates.

The plan would offer universal care, and everyone would have access to the same basic insurance. However, group members would be offered the choice of several plans. People without resources would have no option but to choose one of the basic plans. Tax incentives would encourage all members to choose lower-cost plans, but if members could pay extra, they would get extra coverage or privileges (for example, consulting a physician who is not in the health plan).

Physicians, hospitals, and insurers would join together to form provider groups. The provider groups would offer health plans to the health alliances. Most plans would probably be like those now offered by HMOs, in which for a set yearly fee the HMO undertakes to provide all needed medical care. The provider groups would compete with one another to offer plans to attract the most patients. Plans would be judged in terms of price and quality. Hence, the mechanism of competition should keep prices as low as possible, while providing as much quality as possible. The role of government would be to supervise the process, guarantee the quality of care, and make sure that the poor are enrolled in alliances.

The managed-competition plan could be financed in a variety of ways. Under the 1994 Clinton proposal, it would be paid for by a combination of taxes, employee premiums, and an "employer mandate" (that is, an insurance premium paid by employers). Small businesses and the poor (including the working poor) would be subsidized by the government.

Advantages. Managed competition offers universal coverage, portability of insurance (people can move from one health alliance to another without losing insurance), and comprehensiveness (coverage for all medically necessary conditions). In addition, managed competition promises to control costs, while also providing high-quality medical care.

Criticisms. Most people are happy with the care they receive under the present system and managed competition would force them into a new and untried system. The HMO-type plans would require people to choose physicians from an approved list, and people would be forced to deal with a "gatekeeper" to gain access to specialists.

Provider groups, forced to lower prices in response to competition, might reduce the quality of care they give to patients. Even with government oversight, the pressure on investor-owned groups to make a profit is likely to lead to undertreatment, undertesting, and a delay in referring patients to needed specialists.

The awkward structure of a health–alliance/provider–group system would only add to the already high costs of paperwork. The almost 25 percent of health costs now spent on administration could be better spent on improving care. If private investors (insurance companies) were removed from the system, savings would be even greater.

The system is completely untried, and as a result, it is not clear that the savings from implementing it would be as great as they need to be to control health costs. Also, from a practical perspective, how would the system handle rural areas, where there can be no competition because there are few physicians? What could be done about plans that attract a disproportionately large number of older or sicker patients?

These criticisms are not necessarily unanswerable. They are some of the questions raised about the 1994 managed-competition health plan proposal.

Single-Payer Plan

All citizens and legal residents would be automatically enrolled in a program of national health insurance established by the federal government and administered by the states. Everyone would be provided with a basic minimum of medical care and allowed to choose personal physicians. Private insurance premiums could be replaced by a combination of taxes that would include payroll taxes on employers and a tax on employee's income. Private insurers would offer policies for benefits not covered in the basic-services packages.

Advantages. The single-payer plan offers universal coverage, portability of insurance, access to medical care, and comprehensiveness. It offers the possibility of controlling costs, while providing high-quality medical care. It reduces overhead expenses, preserves people's freedom to choose physicians, and breaks the control that the insurance industry has on American medical care. The emphasis on primary care and prevention would not only save money, but also lead to a general improvement in the health of the nation.

The single-payer system is the simplest and most direct way of providing for universal coverage. Further, it has a proven track record in Canada.

Criticisms. The change is too radical to be accepted by Americans, and it involves the government too deeply in health care. There is no reason to believe that the system will control costs adequately, and it is likely to lead to long delays in treatment and even a rationing system. The emphasis on primary care would eventually result in slowing the advance in American medical technology.

Managed Care

Managed care is the name given to medical care that is provided in such a way that costs are controlled by restricting access to the more expensive forms of testing and treatment. Typically, patients are limited to seeing specific physicians and being admitted to particular hospitals. In principle, emphasis is placed on preventive care, and patients receive only the testing and therapies that they genuinely require.

The current American system has become predominantly a managed-care system as businesses have steadily moved away from group health insurance plans that pay fees-for-service.

The earliest and most popular form of managed care is the health maintenance organization. An HMO is a medical plan in which a fixed annual fee is paid to an organized group of physicians and hospitals ("health-care providers"). The group then undertakes to supply the individual with most kinds of needed medical services, at no additional charge.

Enrollment in HMOs soared from 12.5 million in 1983 to 45.2 million in 1993. The HMO became so popular with businesses, because it offers them a chance to reduce the medical costs they must pay by negotiating fees with the provider group.

The provider group agrees to supply medical care in accordance with specific rules. These rules are designed to avoid unnecessary tests and procedures, because the profit of the provider group is determined by the money remaining after the expenses of patients have been paid.

Patients are penalized for going "out of network" to other physicians and hospitals, and physicians must follow strict rules in approving or denying care. Often, there is a personal financial incentive for the physician not to refer a patient to a specialist. In every case, the primary-care physician serves as a "gatekeeper," controlling the patient's access to specialized testing and care.

Advantages. Better patient care is claimed to result from HMOs because they encourage patients to consult a physician at the beginning of an illness, rather than waiting until it grows serious. This is advantageous both to the patient and the HMO, which can avoid spending a larger part of its budget treating the patient's more serious condition.

The managed-care concept can be employed in various forms. Some HMOs have actual physical locations, while others are "HMOs without walls." Preferred provider organizations (PPOs) have the advantage of allowing individuals to choose their physicians from a list of those who have entered into the arrangement. In this way, a major complaint against HMOs—that the individual is required to receive care from a group and has no physician of his own—is avoided. A range of plans, some more expensive than others and allowing more flexibility can be offered. Those willing to pay more can expect better medical service.

Managed care, in the view of some analysts, offers the best approach to providing universal coverage. As an approach to medical care, it is compatible with a number of plans for providing care—including the two previously discussed.

Managed care can reduce health-care costs for particular groups by restricting access to secondary and tertiary health care. Further, by emphasizing preventive care and keeping out-of-pocket expenses low, people are encouraged to consult physicians more often. The outcomes of treatment rules are typically researched, with the result that a rational basis for decisions can be established.

Criticisms. Economists question whether managed care provides overall savings on health care. Contracts negotiated with providers may be so low that they result in physicians and hospitals shifting some of the cost of a managed-care patient to patients with more insurance benefits.

Both managers and physicians have an incentive to encourage physicians to provide less-than-optimal care to maximize profits. Patients may be dissatisfied with the care they receive and yet not be able to do much about it. For example, an HMO may refuse to pay for the long-term use of an expensive drug to treat an enlarged prostate, but be willing to pay for prostate surgery. The choice is not left up to the patient. Acting as gatekeepers, physicians (often, in practice, their staff) are empowered to turn down requests for medical services or consultations.

Disability-rights groups have asserted strongly that the disabled should have access to the best specialists, even if they are not part of the network. Also, anecdotal evidence suggests that many individuals accustomed to taking charge of their own medical care become highly dissatisfied with managed care.

Physicians have often been critical of managed care. Some have felt that the rules imposed on them by the managers of particular plans do not allow them to practice medicine in the best way. Even when they do not disagree with the rules, some say that they find the rules irksome, narrow, and demeaning.

Physicians have also complained of being excluded from membership in managed-care organizations. If the physicians do not follow the rules, they may be dropped from a group without recourse. Or if they are in an area dominated by managed-care groups, they might wish to join one or more of the groups, yet be turned down. This could be financially and professionally disastrous for them.

Some critics point out that the initial success of managed care in reducing medical costs was the result of two factors that have now changed. First, physicians and hospitals were not organized into groups that could bargain effectively with insurers. Thus, the insurers often extracted lower prices, because the health-care providers had no realistic option to agreeing to fees set by insurers.

Second, employees had to accept the insurance plan offered by their employer, even if it was a highly restrictive plan. Bitter criticisms of such plans, illustrated with horror stories of treatment denials, soon made it clear that Americans were not willing to accept a rigid plan. Some made avoiding such a plan a consideration in employment decisions. With increased demand for employees beginning in the 1990s, companies often had to offer medical plans with less restrictive options to attract workers.

INCREMENTAL SOLUTIONS

The debates over health care in 1994 left many people pessimistic about the possibility of a wholesale change in American health care. Neither the political nor the public will to make the change seemed present. Others became convinced that there was no need to make wholesale changes and that the problems of increasing costs and access to care could be solved merely by altering some aspects of the current system.

The American Medical Association, with a membership of 42 percent of licensed physicians in the United States, abandoned its ambitious plan for health-care reform that would include universal coverage and recommended that the nation "search for ways to expand access to care with an incremental reform approach." Then-Executive Vice President James Todd said, "Our goal of universal coverage has not changed, it's just that we need to find ways of getting there in an incremental fashion."

The following are among the numerous proposals being discussed for patching up the present system of health care:

1. **Subsidies.** To deal with the uninsured and the underinsured, provide direct government subsidies to pay for the cost of their insurance. Critics fear that such a program would encourage employers to reduce even further the insurance coverage they provide their workers. Why should a business pay for a high level of benefits, if the government will make up the difference between the cost of care covered by insurance and the cost billed to the patient?

2. **Standard benefits.** Insurers should be required to offer a minimal level of benefits. In this way, those who are underinsured would be covered. Critics see such a step as an unwarranted interference with market forces.

3. **Insurance regulations.** Insurers should be required to cover people with preexisting conditions. They should also be required to make insurance portable without increasing the premium cost, so that people can take their coverage with them when they change jobs or become unemployed.

4. **Community rating.** Insurers currently charge different rates to different segments of the population. The rates are based on the expected frequency of diseases in the various segments. Thus, the old pay higher rates than the young. Community rating would even out premiums to reflect the average cost of insuring the whole community.

Critics claim that this would unfairly penalize young people and lead many of them to drop their insurance. Indeed, something like this happened in 1993 when the state of New York ended rate variation based on age. Rates went down for people in their sixties, while rising for the young and healthy. A half million younger people canceled their insurance. The result was that the premiums of those remaining sharply increased because those left in the pool were, on the average, sicker than before.

5. **State experiments.** Several states have already attempted innovative health-care plans for their citizens. In 2001 a referendum in Maine endorsed (52 percent to 48) a measure to make the state the first to offer universal health coverage for its citizens. (The proposal was opposed by the insurance industry, which funded "Harry-and-Louise"-style attack ads.) Several other states, including Oregon and Maryland, are discussing the possibility. A large number of states have worked out plans for providing care for some people unable to pay.

Critics point out that having a variety of state health-care programs will make it difficult for companies that do business across the country to operate. They will be faced with a patchwork of laws and regulations. Furthermore, state programs may become so entrenched that they stand in the way of eventually achieving a needed national reform.

6. **Extend Medicare.** In 2002 the Bush administration authorized the extension of Medicare coverage to pay for the treatment of Alzheimer's disease. Until that happened, reimbursements for the cost of mental-health care, physical therapy, hospice care, and home-health care for Alzheimer's patients were usually automatically denied. Although the cost is expected to be several billion dollars, a significant part of it is expected to be defrayed by allowing patients to remain at home longer, saving on the costs of institutionalization.

The broadening of Medicare to cover special segments of the population could be a way of incrementally extending health care until everyone in the society has some form of coverage. For example, everyone becomes eligible for Medicare at age 65, but it is often during their fifties that people are likely to become unemployable and unable to afford health insurance. This is also the time when they are more likely to need medical care than in earlier decades. By lowering the Medicare age limit by ten years, millions of the uninsured and underinsured would qualify for needed care.

The main criticism of this proposal is that it would shift to taxpayers an even heavier Medicare burden. Many critics already see the Medicare system as requiring too much money, and in implementing the Balanced Budget Act of 1997, the agency has significantly reduced payments to physicians and hospitals. Indeed, reductions have been so severe that some physicians no longer are willing to accept Medicare patients, claiming that the fees paid to them by Medicare are lower than their costs. Hospitals also say that they lose money on Medicare patients. Extending Medicare, then, would require a significant change of political attitude in our society. Congress would have to be willing to provide the money to fund the system adequately to cover its new responsibilities.

Faced with the failure of complete health reform, yet recognizing the nagging persistence of a host of problems, most analysts and politicians are willing to endorse some small-scale changes. Their attitude is summed up in health economist Uwe Reinhardt's statement about incremental change: "It's like fixing a car, and in some ways this car is going to get worse, but it will still carry you some miles."

The crisis in health care has not abated, yet the system has not collapsed either. Significant reform probably lies in the future, but meanwhile, we must deal with today.

CASE PRESENTATION

The Canadian System as a Model for the United States?

The United States remains the only nation in the industrialized Western world in which parents worry about being able to pay for the medical care needed by their child, workers worry about losing their medical coverage by changing jobs, people without jobs worry about paying for medical insurance, and husbands and wives worry about going bankrupt to pay for the long-term care needed by an ailing spouse.

A SINGLE-PAYER SYSTEM?

During the course of debate in recent years, some critics have pointed to these failings of the present health-care system and recommended that it be replaced by a so-called single-payer system. Under such a system, universal coverage would be provided to all citizens, regardless of their ability to pay, and the single payer would be the federal government.

"Socialized medicine" was the phrase once used to condemn all single-payer systems. The phrase was a label suggesting something like political heresy. How could a capitalist society adopt a plan exempting medical care from the rules of the market economy? Medical care, like house painting, was a service one could purchase from a provider for an agreed upon fee. The physician-provider, like the painter-provider, was an independent economic agent, and to suggest otherwise would be to recommend the practice of socialism.

Of course, those unable to pay a physician's fee would have to do without the service. A charitable organization or a benevolent physician might provide treatment for some truly in need. This wasn't something to be counted on, and in neither case was need a basis for demanding the service. Clearly, just as you couldn't expect a painter to paint your house without pay, so you couldn't expect a physician to provide you with medical care for nothing. Nor did anyone expect the government to pick up the bill. The role of the government in a market economy is not to provide some citizens with free goods, whether it is painting their houses or providing them with medical care.

CHANGING ATTITUDES

For decades this view dominated public discussions about national health programs. Critics of a proposed program hardly had to do more than apply the label "socialized medicine" to it to bring discussion to a close. Then attitudes began to change for a complex of reasons, including the spiraling cost of health care, the increasing power and value of medical intervention, and the growing number of citizens needing care but lacking insurance.

The introduction of the Medicare program in 1965 provided care to millions of people, many of whom would have received no medical assistance at all. Medicare also helped change the thinking of many people. They came to realize that a social insurance plan like Medicare was not "socialized medicine" and that a plan for universal medical care might be offered along the same lines.

Other factors have also encouraged many to look with favor on the introduction of a single-payer plan. The steady increase in the number of citizens lacking health insurance and unable to pay for even basic medical care is the most dramatic. The number of people in this predicament is estimated at 44 million, and the number has been growing at a rate of 1 million per year.

Even people with medical insurance are willing to consider other ways of supporting health care, for they do not feel secure. Most are aware, either from news accounts or personal experience, that their coverage may not be adequate to pay for their medical needs and that they may be forced to do without care or go into debt to pay for it.

People also fear that their policies might be canceled because their medical expenses are too high or their insurer sees them as too much of a risk. Some fail even to get needed medical attention out of fear that their insurer will cancel their policy. The loss of insurance because of a rate increase after a change in jobs or unemployment is also feared. Those who suffer from a "preexisting condition," such as diabetes, may find it impossible to buy insurance or, if they can, to afford the extraordinarily high premiums that are likely.

Factors such as these may have been responsible for prompting 75 percent of Americans surveyed to say they favor a government program to make sure people have some sort of medical insurance. In an earlier survey, 75 percent said they were in favor of abandoning the private fee-for-service medical system in favor of some form of government-backed national health system.

Many proponents of a single-payer system consider the Canadian system a model for what the American health-care system should become. At least at first sight, Canada and the United States seem much alike in relevant respects. They are both democracies with partially regulated, free-market economies. Furthermore, both have a central, federal government, as well as a number of independent provincial or state governments. These similarities suggest that the Canadian experience with its health-care system might provide detailed guidance for reforming the United States system.

THE CANADIAN HEALTH-CARE SYSTEM

Canada established universal health insurance coverage in 1971. It did not nation-alize hospitals or make physicians government employees, as did Great Britain. Rather, it eliminated most forms of private medical insurance and enrolled citizens in a government plan administered by the ten provinces. The plan is paid for by a variety of federal and provincial taxes. The system is not "socialized medicine." It is, rather, a form of tax-based insurance and does not differ in principle from the United States' Social Security or Medicare.

In addition to physician services, diagnostic testing, hospitalization, and surgery, the plan provides for long-term care, prescription drugs for those over 65, and mental-health care. Benefits vary slightly among provinces, and private insurance is used only to bridge the gaps in provincial coverage.

PRINCIPLES OF THE HEALTH ACT

The details of insurance coverage are decided by each province, but every plan adopted must conform to the five principles spelled out in the Canadian Health Act:

1. Universality. Every citizen is covered.

2. Portability. People can move to another province, change jobs, or be unem-ployed and retain their coverage.

3. Accessibility. Everyone has access to physicians, hospitals, and other ele-ments of the health-care system.

4. Comprehensiveness. Medically necessary treatments must be covered.

5. Public administration. The system is publicly operated and publicly accountable.

The first four of these principles are often mentioned as ones that should guide re-form of the United States' system. However, suggestions that the fifth one be adopted have occasioned much controversy.

CANADIAN CITIZENS AS PATIENTS

Every Canadian citizen is guaranteed access to a physician, and she may see any primary-care physician she chooses. If hospitalization, testing, or surgery is neces-sary, then the government insurance plan will pay for it without any direct cost to the patient.

Patients do not receive bills, fill out claim forms, make copayments, or wait for reimbursement. Instead, they need only show their identification card to receive medical services. Their physician bills the insurance plan of the province, and pay-ment is made within two to four weeks. Paperwork is kept at a minimum, and this helps lower administrative costs.

POPULARITY AND EFFECTIVENESS OF THE PROGRAM

The medical system is highly popular with Canadian citizens. In a 1992 survey, 7 out of 10 said they receive good or excellent care, and 9 out of 10 said the health-care system "is one of the things that makes Canada the best country in the world in which to live." Only 3 percent of Canadians in another poll said that they would "prefer a health-care system like that in the United States." Over the last ten years, Canadians have become less pleased with their system (as we will see later), but they are by no means ready to exchange it for an American model.

Various objective measures of health care show that the Canadian system has been successful. The infant mortality rate of 7.1 per 1000 live births is superior to the U.S. rate of 8.9. The Canadian life expectancy is 77.2 years (from 1992), while life expectancy in the United States is 75.2 years. Cost control also has been successful under the plan. In 1991, Canada spent about 9.2 percent of its national income for medical care; the United States spent 12.3 percent. In 1971, the year Canadian Medicare became universal, the proportions were 7.3 percent and 7.4 percent, respectively. This suggests that the Canadians were able to provide both universal coverage and high-quality care, while successfully controlling costs.

CANADIAN PHYSICIANS

Canadian physicians, like U.S. physicians, practice in their own offices and provide care for the patients who choose to consult them. The significant difference is that Canadian physicians must charge for their services according to a fee schedule. The schedule is negotiated by the Ministry of Health and the Provincial Medical Association. Canadian physicians were initially bitterly opposed to the universal health-care system. Many now approve of it, though, for it has turned out to have aspects they like. Although they cannot charge as much as physicians in the United States, they need not contend with the paperwork burden. Nor do they have to argue with insurance representatives who challenge their judgment about a needed medical service.

Physicians' fees in the United States are more than double that of Canadian fees. Canadian physicians have been able to maintain incomes equal to two-thirds that of U.S. physicians. The reason the incomes are not lower is that Canadian physicians see more patients.

Canada has 100 primary-care or family physicians per 100,000 people. The United States has 20. Even when pediatricians, gynecologists, internists, and family and general practitioners are considered, only 30 percent of physicians in the United States offer primary care to their patients. Provincial plans encourage patients to seek a referral to a specialist from a general practitioner. If a specialist sees a patient without a referral, the specialist can bill only for the same amount as a general practitioner would charge. (As sometimes happens, the specialist calls the general practitioner only after the patient has seen her.)

The preponderance of Canadian physicians committed to primary care means that it is possible to emphasize disease prevention. In the long run, this may help prevent the need for costly treatments. Furthermore, primary-care physicians are not as likely to order expensive diagnostic testing as are specialists.

COVERAGE AND COSTS

Canada spends little more than half of the $4637 per capita (all dollars are U.S.) on health care. For that amount of money, it covers, for the entire population of the country, hospitalization, physician visits, rehabilitation therapy, most dental work, prescription drugs for the poor and those over sixty-five, and most laboratory tests.

The United States has no coverage standards for insurance, so many people who are insured have uneven coverage. In addition, the 19 percent of the U.S. population that is uninsured receives little or no health care.

DRAWBACKS OF THE SYSTEM

The Canadian system has aspects that can be viewed as negative. One of the ways in which costs are kept down is to restrict investment in high-cost medical technology. The United States has 1500 cardiac catheterization labs (166 people per unit), while Canada has 31 (816 people per unit). Canada has 12 magnetic resonance imagers (2108 people per unit), while the United States has 1375 (182 people per unit). Similarly, Canada has increased the number of general practitioners and pediatricians, but it has cut back the number of people in medical specialties. Canada has only 11 heart surgery units, while the United States has 793.

RESTRICTED ACCESS

The strength of the Canadian system is its emphasis on basic care and prevention. Its weakness is the restricted access it permits to specialized care, equipment, and procedures. Patients may have to wait from three to six months for heart surgery, a hip replacement, or a bed in a cancer unit. Care is not explicitly rationed, but it is organized so that those with a greater need are given higher priorities. In fairness, the restrictions on care may not be as serious as critics sometimes claim. Government statistics show that the majority of Canadians receive medical care within seven days of requesting it. Hundreds of therapeutic and diagnostic procedures—general surgery, endoscopy, thyroid function tests, X rays, ultrasound, amniocentesis, EKGs, and so on—are performed regularly and with little or no waiting.

Canadian physicians are definitely more sparing in the use of MRIs and other high technology, and patients must wait longer to receive whatever benefits it offers than in the United States. The only other option, defenders of the system say, is to waste resources by unnecessarily duplicating equipment. By not taking this path, Canada has avoided the dizzying cost increases that plague the United States.

Restrictions on care can go too far, and in a 2000 survey of 3000 Canadians, 93 percent said that improving health care should be the government's top priority. Another poll found that 74 percent of the people supported the introduction of user fees that would reduce the demand on the medical system and reduce waiting times.

During the 1990s the federal government also cut revenue sharing with the provinces. This resulted in closing or merging a number of hospitals. Also, places in Canadian medical schools were reduced. In Canada the ratio of medical students to people is 1 per 20,000, while in the U.S. and Britain it is 1 per 13,000.

Despite these cutbacks, demand on the system has continued to grow. Like the U.S., Canada has an aging population, and within thirty years, the number of people over 65 is expected to double to 25 percent. The increasing demand for medical services has meant that Canada has moved in the direction of a two-tier system. Ninety percent of Canadians live within 100 miles of the U.S. border, and those who can afford to, often travel to the U.S. to receive services like hip replacements, MRIs, chemotherapy, and prostate or heart bypass surgery they might have to wait months for in Canada. Ironically, the treatments may even be administered by a Canadian physician who has immigrated to the U.S. for the prospect of making more money.

The emergence of this double-tier system has provoked harsh comments from defenders of the Canadian system. In their view, those who travel to the U.S. for medical treatment are, in effect, buying a place at the head of the line. This violates the sense of social equality the Canadian system aims to reflect.

By contrast, others point to people's need to go to the U.S. for medical services as evidence for revising Canadian health policy. It should allow, they argue, private hospitals to open in Canada to serve Canadian citizens who are willing and able to pay for treatments. But others see this as offering American profit-making hospitals a wedge for undermining the health-care system.

A CANADIAN SYSTEM FOR THE UNITED STATES?

Would the single-payer Canadian system work in the United States? Some observers who know both systems well express doubts. According to economist Victor Fuchs, "There is reason to doubt that the quality of our civil services is up to the quality of the Canadian civil services. There is also reason to question whether the organization and degree of discipline in the [medical] profession is as strong as in Canada. We are very much individualists, and that includes physicians."

Similar doubts have been expressed by David Woods, who sees the different systems of health care as expressions of "national character." "Canada's system is a centralized public enterprise, cautious and based upon ingrained notions (or delusions) of egalitarianism. America's system is decentralized, market-driven, entrepreneurial, and with 37 [now 39] million citizens uninsured by it, certainly unequal in terms of access."

Further, access to specialized care and technology is highly restricted in the Canadian system, something Americans would find particularly galling. Also, Canadians have indicated a greater willingness to pay much higher taxes, both explicit and hidden, to guarantee universal access than have Americans.

Despite these doubts and criticisms, many continue to believe that a single-payer system, with attributes of the Canadian system, would solve a significant number of the problems that plague the present system:

1. The money now spent on private insurance, with its high administrative costs and spotty coverage for individuals, when combined with Medicaid and Medicare

funds, could be used to extend basic coverage to all citizens. The problems of what to do about the uninsured and the underinsured would disappear.

2. People would no longer have to worry about having their policies canceled, exceeding the limits of their coverage, or being uninsurable because of a preexisting medical condition.

3. Universal access would encourage individuals to get medical help early, and rapid intervention would lead to cost savings from prevention and early detection and treatment.

4. The single payer would be able to negotiate with physicians, hospitals, laboratories, and pharmaceutical companies to hold down prices.

The big financial losers in a single-payer system are private health insurance companies. The role they play is reduced to that of offering policies covering treatments not included in the single-payer plan. To a lesser extent, physicians, hospitals, and suppliers also stand to lose more financially in the change to a single-payer system. However, erosions in income due to HMOs and other forms of managed care have already taken place in all sectors of the health economy.

What physicians might expect to gain from a switch to a single-payer system is freedom from some of the more rigid and time-consuming utilization review processes of managed care. In this respect, physicians may be able to regain some of the autonomy that some claim has been declining steadily as third-party payers have taken a more active role in determining what procedures and treatments they are willing to pay for.

What remains unanswered is the basic question of whether the virtues of the Canadian single-payer system could be reproduced in the United States and whether the United States would be satisfied with a system that, for many people, is more restrictive than the one they are accustomed to. The Canadian system has flaws—the long waiting times for testing and treatment, in particular—nevertheless, it is one the United States ought to consider carefully, with an eye to altering its own system, if not forsaking it.

As T. R. Marmor and John Godfrey observe, "Canada is the country closest to ours in wealth, geography, ethnic diversity, and patterns of medical practice. If we cannot learn from Canada, we cannot learn from any country."

Perhaps aspects of the Canadian system combined with aspects of the American system might offer a way to support and deliver medical care so that those unable to pay could receive at least a decent minimum. The United States already has a two-tier (or even multi-tier) system of health care, but what it lacks is a way of providing for the medical needs of those who are uninsured (or underinsured) without forcing them into indigence.

PART **IV**

Terminations

CHAPTER 9

Abortion

CLASSIC CASE PRESENTATION

When Abortion Was Illegal: Mrs. Sherri Finkbine and the Thalidomide Tragedy

Background Note: The following case concerns an event that took place before the U.S. Supreme Court decision in Roe v. Wade *was handed down in 1973. That decision had the effect of legalizing abortion in the United States. Before the decision, most state laws permitted abortion only for the purpose of saving the life of the mother. The case presented here illustrates the kinds of problems faced by many women who sought an abortion for other reasons.*

In 1962 Mrs. Sherri Finkbine was the mother of four normal children and was pregnant. Her health was good, but she was having some trouble sleeping. Rather than talking with her doctor, she simply took some of the tranquilizers that her husband had brought back from a trip to Europe. The tranquilizers were widely used there, and, like aspirin, they could simply be bought over the counter.

Subsequently, Mrs. Finkbine read an article that told of the great increase in the number of deformed children being born in Europe. Some of the children's arms and legs failed to develop or developed only in malformed ways; other children were blind and deaf or had seriously defective internal organs. The birth defects had been traced to the use in pregnancy of a supposedly harmless and widely used tranquilizer. Its active ingredient was thalidomide.

Mrs. Finkbine was worried enough to ask her doctor to find out if the pills she had been taking contained thalidomide. They did. When he learned this, her doctor told her, "The odds are so against you that I am recommending termination of pregnancy." He explained that getting approval for an abortion should not be difficult. She had good medical reasons, and all she had to do was explain them to the three-member medical board of Phoenix. Mrs. Finkbine agreed with her doctor's advice. But then she began to think that maybe it was her duty to inform other women who may have been taking thalidomide about its disastrous consequences. She called a local newspaper and told her story to the editor. He agreed not to use her name, but on a front page, bordered in black, he used the headline "BABY-DEFORMING DRUG MAY COST WOMAN HER CHILD HERE."

The story was picked up by the wire services, and it was not long before Mrs. Finkbine's identity became known. The medical board had already approved her request for an abortion, but because of the great publicity her case received they canceled their approval. The State of Arizona abortion statute legally sanctioned abortion only when it was required to save the life of the mother. The board was afraid that their decision might be challenged in court and that the decision could not stand up to the challenge.

Mrs. Finkbine became the object of a great outpouring of antiabortion feelings. *Il Osservatore Romano,* the official Vatican newspaper, condemned Mrs. Finkbine and her husband as murderers. Although she received some letters of support, others were abusive. One writer said: "I hope someone takes the other four children and strangles them, because it is all the same thing." Another wrote from the perspective of the fetus: "Mommy, please dear Mommy, let me live. Please, please, I want to live. Let me love you, let me see the light of day, let me smell a rose, let me sing a song, let me look into your face, let me say Mommy."

Although Mrs. Finkbine tried to obtain a legal abortion outside her own state, she was unable to do so. Eventually, she went to Sweden. After a rigorous investigation by a medical board, Mrs. Finkbine was given an abortion in a Swedish hospital.

Mrs. Finkbine saw her own problem as solved at last. But she continued to have sympathy with those thousands of potential parents of thalidomide children who lacked the money to follow the course of action she had been forced to take by abortion laws she considered to be restrictive and inhumane.

Briefing Session

Hardly more than three decades ago, most Americans considered abortion a crime so disgusting that it was rarely mentioned in public. Back-alley abortionists with dirty hands and unclean instruments were real enough, but they were also the villains of cautionary tales to warn women against being tempted into the crime. Abortion was the dramatic stuff of novels and movies portraying "girls in trouble" or women pushed to the brink. To choose to have an abortion was to choose to be degraded.

The Supreme Court decision in *Roe v. Wade* changed all that in 1973. The decision had the effect of legalizing abortion, and since then abortion has gained an ambivalent acceptance from a majority of the population. Yet controversy over the legitimacy of abortion continues to flare. Indeed, no other topic in medical ethics has attracted more attention or so polarized public opinion. The reason is understandable. In the abortion question, major moral, legal, and social issues are intertwined to form a problem of great subtlety and complexity.

Before focusing on some of the specific issues raised by abortion, it is useful to have in hand some of the relevant factual information about human developmental biology and the techniques of abortion.

HUMAN DEVELOPMENT AND ABORTION

Fertilization occurs when an ovum is penetrated by a sperm cell and the nuclei of the two unite to form a single cell containing forty-six chromosomes. This normally occurs in the Fallopian tube (or oviduct), a narrow tube leading from the ovary into the uterus (womb). The fertilized ovum—zygote, or conceptus—continues its passage down the Fallopian tube, and during its two- to three-day passage it undergoes a number of cell divisions that increase its size. (Rarely, the zygote does not descend but continues to develop in the Fallopian tube, producing an ectopic pregnancy. Because the tube is so small, the pregnancy has to be terminated surgically.) After reaching the uterus, a pear-shaped organ, the zygote floats free in the intrauterine fluid. Here it develops into a *blastocyst,* a ball of cells surrounding a fluid-filled cavity.

By the end of the second week, the blastocyst becomes embedded in the wall of the uterus. At this point and until the end of the eighth week, it is known as an embryo. During the fourth and fifth weeks, organ systems begin to develop, and the external features take on a definitely human shape. During the eighth week, brain activity usually becomes detectable. At this time, the embryo comes to be known as a fetus.

Birth generally occurs about nine months after fertilization or, to be more accurate, around forty-plus weeks. It is customary to divide this time into three three-month (13 week) periods or trimesters. At present, pregnancy cannot be diagnosed with certainty by ordinary methods until ten to fourteen days after a woman has missed her menstrual period.

More sensitive pregnancy tests make it possible to detect pregnancy as soon as the embryo is implanted in the uterus, seven to ten days after fertilization. Also, improvements in ultrasound imaging allow the gestational sac surrounding the embryo to be detected in its earliest stages. Hence, a woman may be found to be pregnant even before she has missed an expected period.

Abortion is the termination of pregnancy. It can occur because of internal biochemical factors or as a result of physical injury to the woman. Terminations from such causes are usually referred to as "spontaneous abortions," but they are also commonly called miscarriages.

Abortion can also be a deliberate process resulting from human intervention. The methods used in contemporary medicine depend to a great extent on the stage of the pregnancy. The earliest intervention involves the use of drugs (like RU-486 or the hormones in birth control pills) to prevent the embedding of the blastocyst in the uterine wall.

Because the new tests and ultrasound make it possible to detect pregnancy as early as a week or ten days after fertilization, a pregnancy can be terminated at that point. A physician dilates (widens) the cervix (the narrow opening to the uterus), then uses a hand-operated syringe to suction out the contents of the uterus.

Subsequent intervention during the first trimester (up to about twelve weeks) commonly employs the same technique of uterine or vacuum aspiration. After the cervix is dilated, a small tube is inserted into the uterus, and its contents are emptied by suction. The procedure is known as dilation and evacuation. The classical abortion procedure is dilation and curettage. The cervix is dilated and its contents are gently scraped out by the use of a curette, a spoon-shaped surgical instrument. The procedure has been almost wholly replaced by evacuation in developed countries.

After twelve weeks, when the fetus is too large to make the other methods practical, the most common abortion technique involves dilating the cervix and extracting the fetus. (See the Social Context: The "Partial-Birth Abortion" Controversy later in this chapter for discussion.)

These facts about pregnancy and abortion put us in a position to discuss some of the moral problems connected with them. We won't be able to untangle the skein of issues wrapped around the abortion question. We'll only attempt to state a few of the more serious ones and to indicate the lines of argument that have been offered to support positions taken with respect to them; afterward we'll sketch out some possible responses that might be offered on the basis of the ethical theories we discuss in *Part V: Foundations of Bioethics.*

THE STATUS OF THE FETUS

It is crucial for the application of the principles of any moral theory that we have a settled opinion about the objects and subjects of morality. Although principles are generally stated with respect to rational individuals, every theory recognizes that there are people who in fact cannot be considered rational agents. For example, mental and physical incapacities may diminish or destroy rationality. But ethical theories generally recognize that we still have duties to people who are so incapacitated.

The basic problem that this raises is: Who or what is to be considered a person? Are there characteristics that we can point to and say that it is by virtue of possessing these characteristics that an individual must be considered a person and thus accorded moral treatment?

The abortion issue raises this question most particularly with regard to the fetus. (We will use the term "fetus," for the moment, to refer to the developing organism at any stage.) Just what is the status of the fetus in the world? We must find a satisfactory answer to this question, some writers have suggested, before we can resolve the general moral problem of abortion.

Let's consider the possible consequences of answering the question one way or the other. First, if a fetus is a person, it has a serious claim to life. We must assert the claim on its behalf, for, like an unconscious person, the fetus is unable to do so. The claim of the fetus as a person must be given weight and respect in deliberating about any action that would terminate its life. Perhaps only circumstances as extreme as a threat to the life of the mother would justify abortion.

Assuming the fetus is a person, then an abortion would be a case of killing and something not to be undertaken without reasons sufficient to override the fetus's claim to life. In effect, only conditions of the same sort that would justify our killing an adult person (for example, self-defense) would justify our killing a fetus. Thus, the moral burden in every case would be to demonstrate that abortion is not a case of wrongful killing.

By contrast, if a fetus is not a person in a morally relevant sense, the abortion need not be considered a case of killing equivalent to the killing of an adult. In one view, it might be said that an abortion is not essentially different from an appendectomy. According to this way of thinking, a fetus is no more than a complicated clump of organic material, and its removal involves no serious moral difficulty.

In another view, it could be argued that, even though the fetus is not a person, it is a potential person, and thus is a significant and morally relevant property. The fetus's very potentiality makes it unique and distinguishes it from a diseased appendix or a cyst or any other kind of organic material. Thus, because the fetus can become a person, abortion does present a moral problem. A fetus can be destroyed only for serious reasons. Thus, preventing a person from coming into existence must be justified to an extent comparable to the justification required for killing a person. (Some have suggested that the justification does not have to be identical because the fetus is only a potential person. The justification we might present for killing a person would thus serve only as a guide for those that might justify abortion.)

So far we have used the word "fetus," and this usage tends to obscure the fact that human development is a process with many stages. Perhaps it is only in the later stages of development that the entity becomes a person. But exactly when might this happen?

The difference between a fertilized ovum and a fully developed baby just a few minutes before birth are considerable. The ovum and the blastocyst seem just so much tissue. But the embryo and the fetus present more serious claims to being persons. Should abortion be allowed until the fetus becomes visibly human, or until the fetus shows heartbeat and brain waves, or until the fetus can live outside the uterus (becomes viable)?

The process of development is continuous, and so far it has proved impossible to find differences between stages that can be generally accepted as morally relevant. Some writers on abortion have suggested that it is useless to look for such differences, because any place where the line is drawn will be arbitrary. Others have claimed that it is possible to draw the line by relying on criteria that can be rationally defended. A few have even argued that a reasonable set of criteria for determining who shall be considered a person might even deny the status to infants.

PREGNANCY, ABORTION, AND THE RIGHTS OF WOMEN

Pregnancy and fetal development are normal biological processes, and most women who choose to have a child carry it to term without unusual difficulties. However, it is important to keep in mind that even a normal pregnancy involves changes and stresses that are uniquely burdensome. Once the process of fetal growth is initiated, a woman's entire physiology is altered by the new demands placed on it and by the biochemical changes taking place within her body. For example, metabolic rate increases, the thyroid gland grows larger, the heart pumps more blood to meet fetal needs, and a great variety of hormonal changes take place. The growing fetus physically displaces the woman's internal organs and alters the size and shape of her body.

As a result of such changes, the pregnant woman may suffer a variety of ailments. More common ones include severe nausea and vomiting ("morning sickness"), muscle cramps, abdominal pain, anemia, tiredness, and headaches. For many women such complaints are relatively mild or infrequent, while for others they are severe or constant. Nausea and vomiting can lead to dehydration and malnutrition so serious as to be life-threatening. Women who suffer from diseases like diabetes are apt to face special health problems as a result of pregnancy.

Partly because of hormonal changes, women are also more likely to experience psychological difficulties when pregnant, such as emotional lability (mood swings), severe depression, and acute anxiety. Such conditions are often accompanied by quite realistic concerns about the loss of freedom associated with becoming a parent, compromised job status, loss of sexual attractiveness due to the change in body shape, and the pains and risks of childbirth.

The woman who intends to carry a child to term is also likely to have to alter her behavior in many ways. She may have to curtail the time she spends working, take a leave of absence, or even quit her job. Any career plans she has are likely to suffer. She may be unable to participate in social activities to the extent she previously did, and forced to give up some entirely. In addition, if she recognizes an obligation to the developing fetus and is well informed, she may have to alter her diet, stop smoking, and strictly limit the amount of alcohol she consumes.

In summary, the physical and emotional price paid by a woman for a full-term pregnancy is high. Even a normal pregnancy, one that proceeds without any special difficulties, exacts a toll of discomfort, stress, restricted activity, and worry.

Women who wish to have a child are generally willing to undergo the rigors of pregnancy to satisfy this desire. But is it a woman's duty to nurture and carry to term an unwanted child? Pregnancies resulting from rape and incest are the kinds of dramatic cases frequently mentioned to emphasize the seriousness of the burden imposed on women. But the question is also important when the conditions surrounding the pregnancy are more ordinary.

Suppose that a woman becomes pregnant unintentionally and decides that having a child will be harmful to her career or her way of life. Or suppose she simply does not wish to subject herself to the pains of pregnancy. Does a woman have a moral duty to see to it that the developing child comes to be born?

A number of writers have taken the position that women have an exclusive right to control their own reproductive function. In their view, such a right is based upon the generally recognized right to control what is done to our bodies. Since pregnancy is something that involves a woman's body, the woman concerned may legitimately decide whether to continue the pregnancy or terminate it. The decision is hers alone, and social or legal policies that restrict the free exercise of her right are unjustifiable.

Essentially the same point is sometimes phrased by saying that women own their bodies. Because their bodies are their own "property," women alone have the right to decide whether to become pregnant and, if pregnant unintentionally, whether to have an abortion.

Critics have pointed out that this general line of argument, taken alone, does not support the strong conclusion that women should be free from all constraints in making abortion decisions. Even granting that women's bodies are their own property, we nevertheless recognize restrictions on exercising property rights. We have no right to shoot trespassers, and we cannot endanger our neighbors by burning down our house. Similarly, if any legitimate moral claims can be made on behalf of the fetus, then the right of women to decide whether to have an abortion may not be unrestricted.

Some philosophers (Judith Jarvis Thomson, for example) have taken the view that, although women are entitled to control their bodies and make abortion decisions, the decision to have an abortion must be supported by weighty reasons. They have suggested that, even if we grant that a fetus is a person, its claim to life cannot be given unconditional precedence over the woman's claim to control her own life. She is entitled to autonomy and the right to arrange her life in accordance with her own concept of the good. It would be wrong for her to destroy the fetus for a trivial reason, but legitimate and adequate reasons for taking the life of the fetus might be offered.

Others, by contrast, have argued that when a woman becomes pregnant she assumes an obligation for the life of the fetus. It is, after all, completely dependent on her for its continued existence. She has no more right to take its life in order to seek her own best interest than she has to murder someone whose death may bring benefits to her.

THERAPEUTIC ABORTION

Abortion is sometimes required to save the life of the mother or in order to provide her with medical treatment considered essential to her health. Abortion performed for such a purpose is ordinarily regarded as a case of self-defense. For this reason, it is almost universally considered to be morally unobjectionable. (Strictly speaking, the Roman Catholic view condemns abortion in all of its forms. It does approve of providing medical treatment for the mother, even if this results in the death of the fetus, but the death of the fetus must never be intended.)

If the principle of preserving the life and health of the mother justifies abortion, then what conditions fall under that principle? If a woman has cancer of the uterus and her life can be saved only by an operation that will result in the death of the fetus, then this clearly falls under the principle. But what about psychological conditions? Is a woman's mental health relevant to deciding whether an abortion is justified? What if a psychiatrist believes that a woman cannot face the physical rigors of pregnancy or bear the psychological stresses that go with it without developing severe psychiatric symptoms? Would such a judgment justify an abortion? Or is the matter of psychological health irrelevant to the abortion issue?

Consider, too, the welfare of the fetus. Suppose that prenatal tests indicate that the developing child suffers from serious abnormalities. (This was the case of the "thalidomide babies.") Is abortion for the purpose of preventing the birth of such children justifiable?

It might be argued that it is not, that an impaired fetus has as much right to its life as an impaired person. We do not, after all, consider it legitimate to kill people who become seriously injured or suffer from diseases that render them helpless. Rather, we care for them and work to improve their lives—at least we ought to.

Some might argue, however, that abortion in such cases is not only justifiable, but a duty. It is our duty to kill the fetus to spare the person that it will become a life of unhappiness and suffering. We might even be said to be acknowledging the dignity of the fetus by doing what it might do for itself if it could—what any rational creature would do. Destroying such a fetus would spare future pain to the individual and his or her family and save society from an enormous expense. Thus, we have not only a justification to kill such a fetus, but also the positive obligation to do so.

In this chapter, we will not deal explicitly with the issues that are raised by attempting to decide whether it is justifiable to terminate the life of an impaired fetus. Because such issues are directly connected with prenatal genetic diagnosis and treatment, we discuss them more fully in Chapter 6. Nonetheless, in considering the general question of the legitimacy of abortion, it is important to keep such special considerations in mind.

ABORTION AND THE LAW

Abortion in our society has been a legal issue as well as a moral issue. Until the Supreme Court decision in *Roe v. Wade,* nontherapeutic abortion was illegal in virtually all states. The *Webster* decision (see the Social Context: Crucial Legal and Policy Decisions) is a recent indication that the Court is willing to accept more state restrictions than previously, but even so abortions are far from being illegal. However, even though groups still lobby for a constitutional amendment to protect a fetus's "right to life" and prohibit elective abortion, the position has little popular support.

The rightness or wrongness of abortion is a moral matter, one whose issues can be resolved only by appealing to a moral theory. Different theories may yield incompatible answers, and even individuals who accept the same theory may arrive at different conclusions.

Such a state of affairs raises the question of whether the moral convictions or conclusions of some people should be embodied in laws that govern the lives of all people in the society. The question can be put succinctly: Should the moral beliefs of some people serve as the basis for laws that will impose those beliefs on everyone?

This question cannot be answered in a straightforward way. To some extent, which moral beliefs are at issue is a relevant consideration. So too are the political principles that we are willing to accept as basic to our society. Every ethical theory recognizes that there is a scope of action that must be left to individuals as moral agents acting freely on the basis of their own understanding and perceptions. Laws requiring the expression of benevolence or gratitude, for example, seem peculiarly inappropriate.

Yet, one of the major aims of a government is to protect the rights of its citizens. Consequently, a society must have just laws that recognize and enforce those rights. In a very real way, then, the moral theory we hold and the conclusions arrived at on the basis of it will determine whether we believe that certain types of laws are justified. They are justified when they protect the rights recognized in our moral theories—when political rights reflect moral rights. (See the Briefing Session in Chapter 7 for a fuller discussion of moral rights and their relation to political rights.)

An ethical theory that accords the status of a person to a fetus is likely to claim also that the laws of the society should recognize the rights of the fetus. A theory that does not grant the fetus this position is not likely to regard laws forbidding abortion as justifiable.

ETHICAL THEORIES AND ABORTION

Theories like those of Mill, Kant, Ross, and Rawls attribute to individuals autonomy or self-direction. An individual is entitled to control his or her own life, and it seems reasonable to extend this principle to apply to one's own body. If so, then a woman should have the right to determine whether or not she wishes to have a child. If she is pregnant with an unwanted child, then, no matter how she came to be pregnant, she might legitimately decide on an abortion. Utilitarianism also suggests this answer on consequential grounds. In the absence of other considerations, if it seems likely that having a child will produce more unhappiness than an abortion would, then an abortion would be justifiable.

If the fetus is considered to be a person, however, the situation is different for some theories. The natural law view holds that the fetus is an innocent person and that direct abortion is never justifiable. Even if the pregnancy is due to rape, the fetus cannot be held at fault and made to suffer through its death. Even though she may not wish to have the child, the mother has a duty to preserve the life of the fetus.

For deontological theories like those of Kant and Ross, the situation becomes more complicated. If the fetus is a person, it has an inherent dignity and worth. It is an innocent life which cannot be destroyed except for the weightiest moral reasons. Those reasons may include the interests and wishes of the woman, but deontological theories provide no clear answer as to how those are to be weighed.

For utilitarianism, by contrast, even if the fetus is considered a person, the principle of utility may still justify an abortion. Killing a person is not, for utilitarianism, inherently wrong. (Yet it is compatible with rule utilitarianism to argue that permitting elective abortion as a matter of policy would produce more unhappiness than forbidding abortion altogether. Thus, utilitarianism does not offer a definite answer to the abortion issue.)

As we have already seen, both utilitarianism and deontological theories can be used to justify therapeutic abortion. When the mother's life or health is at stake, the situation may be construed as one of self-defense. Both Kant and Ross recognize that we each have a right to protect ourselves, even if it means taking the life of another person. For utilitarianism, preserving one's life is justifiable, for being alive is a necessary condition for all forms of happiness.

We have also indicated that abortion "for the sake of the fetus" can be justified by both utilitarianism and deontological theories. If by killing the fetus we can spare it a life of suffering, minimize the sufferings of its family, and preserve the resources of the society, then abortion is legitimate on utilitarian grounds. In the terms of Kant and Ross, destroying the fetus might be a way of recognizing its dignity. If we assume that it is a person, then by sparing it a life of indignity and pain we are treating it in the way that a rational being would want to be treated.

The legitimacy of laws forbidding abortion is an issue that utilitarianism would resolve by considering their effects. If such laws promote the general happiness of the society, then they are justifiable. Otherwise, they are not. In general, Kant, Ross, Rawls, and natural law theory recognize intrinsic human worth and regard as legitimate laws protecting that worth, even if those holding this view are only a minority of the society. Thus, laws discriminating against blacks and women, for example, would be considered unjust on the basis of these theories. Laws enforcing equality, by contrast, would be considered just.

But what about fetuses? The Roman Catholic interpretation of natural law would regard the case as exactly the same. As full human persons, they are entitled to have their rights protected by law. Those who fail to recognize this are guilty of moral failure, and laws permitting abortion are the moral equivalent of laws permitting murder.

For Kant and other deontologists, the matter is less clear. As long as there is substantial doubt about the status of the fetus, it is not certain that it is legitimate to demand that the rights of fetuses be recognized and protected by law. It is clear that the issue of whether or not the fetus is considered a person is most often taken as the crucial one in the abortion controversy.

The battle over abortion is certain to continue in the courts, streets, media, and classrooms. The issues are of great social importance, yet highly personal and explosively emotional. The best hope for a resolution continues to rest with the condemnation of violence and an emphasis on the traditional strategies of verbal persuasion, rational argument, and the appeal to basic moral principles.

The following Social Context pieces and the Case Presentations illustrate not only the conflict of opposing views, but the willingness of most people to attempt to find a nuanced response to the many issues presented by abortion.

SOCIAL CONTEXT
How Americans View Abortion: Tolerant Ambivalence

January 2002 marked the thirtieth anniversary of the Supreme Court decision legalizing abortion in the United States. Yet even after three decades, abortion has not become a standard, uncontroversial medical procedure.

Although more than a million abortions are performed every year, Americans remain ambivalent and divided on its moral acceptability. In some respects, abortion has become even less accepted than it was a decade or more ago.

POLL RESULTS SHOW MIXED FEELINGS

The country's mixed feelings about abortion are revealed in a January 2000 poll by the Gallup Organization. When people were asked, "With respect to the abortion issue, would you consider yourself to be pro-choice or pro-life?" those answering pro-life rose to 44 percent from the previous 33 percent of 1995. Those describing themselves as pro-choice declined from 56 to 48 percent.

Percent describing themselves as

	1995	2000
Pro-life	33	44
Pro-choice	56	48

Source: Gallup Organization; January 2000

This shift was not accompanied by a significant increase in the number wanting to see abortion outlawed. Only 17–19 percent endorsed this view, while 51 percent said abortion should be legal under some circumstances. Another 28 percent said it should be legal in any circumstance.

These new results are similar to those of a *New York Times/CBS News* poll taken on the twenty-fifth anniversary of the *Roe v. Wade* decision. (See the Social Context: Crucial Legal and Policy Decisions for a discussion of this and other court rulings.) The poll provides us with the most detailed picture available of American attitudes about abortion.

Half the population considers abortion "the same thing as murder," but even so, 32 percent of those in this group think abortion is "sometimes the best course of action in a bad situation." While 60 percent of the respondents said they thought the Supreme Court ruling establishing a woman's constitutional right to an abortion was good on the whole, almost 80 percent supported a mandatory waiting period and, in the case of minors, parental consent. People were split almost evenly on the question of whether the abortion dispute is about a woman's ability to control her body or about the life of the fetus. While 45 percent said it is about the life of the fetus, 44 percent said it is about a woman's controlling her body.

Despite favoring regulations, nearly 60 percent of those polled thought the government should stay out of abortion decisions. While the idea of a constitutional amendment banning abortion was seen as a political possibility by abortion opponents in the 1980s, more than 75 percent of those polled reject the notion. The clearest message sent by these results seems to be that people believe a decision about having an abortion ought to be thought of as a private moral matter and not a public legal one.

ABORTION FOR ANY REASON?

While abortion rights advocates have long held that women should be free to have an abortion for any reason they believe adequate, the poll results suggest the view is no longer as widely shared as it once was. Almost half (49 percent) of those who had a view on why women have abortions considered the reasons "not serious

---

Abortion Should . . .

not be permitted	22%
be generally available	32%
be available with strict limits	45%

Source: New York Times/CBS News Poll 1998

---

enough." This was up from the 41 percent of a 1989 poll. In 1989 also, 50 percent of the people surveyed said they didn't think a woman's not wanting to marry the man by whom she became pregnant was a good enough reason to have an abortion. By 1998, the figure had increased to 62 percent.

TIME OF FETAL DEVELOPMENT

The time of fetal development has become an important consideration in weighing the legitimacy of abortion for most people. In 1989 half the respondents in a poll thought abortions during the first trimester (first three months) of pregnancy should be permitted, and by 1998 the percentage had risen to 61. However, only 15 percent thought abortion should be allowed in the second trimester, and that figure fell to 7 percent for the last three months.

Time also seems to be a relevant factor for most people in determining the acceptability of drug-induced abortion. In fact, 65 percent of those asked said they would consider a drug that prevents a fertilized egg from becoming implanted in the uterus a form of birth control and not abortion at all. Only 20 percent said they would regard such intervention as abortion. Similarly, while 50 percent of those asked favored "chemical abortion" using a drug like RU-486 (employed in the first seven weeks of pregnancy) as an alternative to surgical abortion, 36 percent opposed it.

WOMEN AND MEN

The views of women and men, as represented by the poll results, are virtually the same with respect to the availability of abortion and to the extent that access to abortion should be restricted or forbidden. Thirty-two percent of women and 31 percent of men believe it should be generally available. While 44 percent of women and 45 percent of men favor strict limits, only 21 percent of women and 23 percent of men think abortion should not be permitted.

AGE AND RELIGION

Nor does age seem to matter much. While 21 percent of those 18–29 years old say they believe abortion should not be permitted, the figure rises to 23 percent for those 30–44, drops to 20 percent for those 45–64, then increases to only 25 percent for those 65 or older.

While Roman Catholics are usually perceived as wholly opposed to abortion for everyone, 74 percent said they thought it should be available either generally or under strict limits. The corresponding figures for Protestants was 76 percent. A relatively low 26 percent of Catholics and 24 percent of Protestants believed abortion should not be permitted at all.

However, those who said religion was "extremely important" or "very important" in their daily lives were also most likely to think (43 percent and 23 percent respectively) that abortion shouldn't be allowed. This view was endorsed by only 9 percent of those who said religion was not so important in their daily lives.

EDUCATION

The survey found that the more educated the respondents, the less likely they were to be completely opposed to abortion. Of those without a high school diploma,

---

Abortion Rates

Age (1994)

Under 15	1%
15–19	19%
20–24	37%
25–29	20%
30–34	14%
35–39	7%
40–	2%

Race and Ethnicity (1995)

White/Hispanic	60%
African-American	38%
Other	2%

Previous Children (1995)

None	44%
1	27%
2	18%
3	8%
4+	3%

As result of rape or incest

1%

Number of Abortions (1994)

First	52%
Second	29%
Third	11%
Fourth +	8%

Source: Centers for Disease Control and Prevention

28 percent said abortion should not be permitted, but the figure fell to 24 percent for high school graduates. For those with some college it fell to 19 percent, then to 18 percent for those with college degrees.

REASONS

Over the years since the *Roe v. Wade* decision, public attitude toward abortion has remained relatively consistent on several possible reasons for having one. About 80 percent of those surveyed believe a woman should be able to obtain an abortion if her health is significantly endangered by the pregnancy. About 75 percent believe she should also be able to get an abortion if there is "a strong chance of a serious defect in the baby."

Only 43 percent believe the family having a low income and not being able to afford another child is a good enough reason for an abortion, and the figure drops to 39 percent if the woman is married and simply doesn't want any more children.

NEW MEDICAL TECHNOLOGY

To a considerable extent, the ambivalence about abortion and the public clash of opinions about its moral legitimacy are due to the development of new reproductive and life-sustaining technology, as well as to an increase in awareness of the character of the fetus.

When a genetic disease like Tay–Sachs is present in a family, in vitro fertilization and the selection of an embryo free of the disease for implantation can avoid a problem that might lead to abortion. While for some, discarding unused embryos created by in vitro fertilization is equivalent to abortion, most people are more comfortable with the idea of destroying embryos than of aborting a fetus.

Reproductive technology has also made more familiar the concept of "selectively reducing" one or more developing fetuses in a multiple pregnancy resulting from the use of fertility drugs. For some, selective reduction is simply abortion by another name, but for others it is a procedure necessary to give the remaining fetuses a better chance to develop normally.

Also, as the statistics mentioned earlier show, the majority of people aren't troubled by preventing pregnancy by treatment with a "morning after" drug or by using a drug like RU-486 to stop pregnancy from occurring. This may be because most people do not think of a fertilized egg as a fetus until development in the uterus is well underway. Thus, they do not equate it with a baby.

The other relevant development in technology is the ability to keep alive babies that are so premature that in important aspects they are still developing fetuses. A baby is considered full-term if it is born forty weeks after conception, but a state-of-the-art neonatal unit staffed with trained and experienced people can save the lives of infants who have had only twenty-three or twenty-four weeks of development.

These babies often do not do well and suffer serious lifelong problems. Even so, the fact that such small babies can survive outside the uterus has led many people to become more restrained in their endorsement of abortion or to favor restrictions on when it can be performed. After all, the second trimester ends at around twenty-five weeks. (See the discussion of the *Webster* decision later in this chapter.)

NUMBER OF ABORTIONS

In 1990 the number of women who had an abortion was 1.6 million. By 1995 the figure was down to 1,210,833, and by 1997 it had fallen to 1.328 million. Thus, from 1990 to 1997 (the last year with complete figures), abortion declined 17.4 percent.

The reasons for the decline are unclear, but some believe it is connected with the aging of the population, the wider availability of contraception, and fewer unwanted pregnancies. Others think the decline reflects a change of attitude toward abortion, as well as changes in society (antiabortion protests, shrinking number of abortion providers, stiffer regulation) that make it more difficult for a woman to secure an abortion.

While the number of abortions is likely to vary slightly from year to year, experts think it is unlikely any increase will reach the 1990 high point. Some suggest that a less-accepting attitude toward abortion will keep the number lower than might be expected otherwise.

THE MIDDLE POSITION

The abstract and absolute positions represented by statements like "A woman has a right to choose to have an abortion for any reason at all" and "A fertilized egg is as much a person as a born child and has just as much right to life" have become less representative of the beliefs of most people over the last three decades. The majority of people tend toward the view that the most reasonable position on abortion lies somewhere between these extremes.

To sum up in a phrase, Americans appear to think abortion should be "safe, legal, and rare." But of course agreement to such a general proposition doesn't translate into agreements about what restrictions are appropriate. While abstract positions may have blurred for most people, debates over particular policies remain as divisive and acrimonious as they ever were.

SOCIAL CONTEXT

The "Partial-Birth Abortion" Controversy

In 1995 debate began to rage around abortion performed after twenty weeks of gestation, often focusing on a specific surgical procedure used to terminate a pregnancy. Technically known as intact dilation and extraction, the procedure was named "partial birth abortion" by those opposed to abortion.

The debate, now abating, is characterized to an unusual extent by a lack of information and a reliance on misinformation by participants on both sides. Instead of laying out the issues as the opponents present them, it is more useful to begin by considering some of the facts relevant to evaluating the various positions taken.

LATE-TERM ABORTION

While abortion opponents often portray "abortion doctors" as employing brutal procedures to destroy viable fetuses in order to satisfy the whims of pregnant women, those favoring abortion rights present women as opting for such measures in only rare and extreme cases. The best estimates available suggest that neither picture is accurate.

More than half (52.2 percent) of all abortions are performed less than nine weeks after conception, and about a quarter (24.7 percent) are performed in weeks nine and ten. Indeed, 98.9 percent of all abortions are performed within twenty weeks of conception. Thus, later-term abortion, defined as abortion after twenty weeks, is relatively rare, accounting for only 1.1 percent of all abortions.

No statistics are available on the reasons women have late-term (instead of early) abortions. The best information comes from the congressional testimony of physicians who perform abortions. They suggest that one group of women have abortions because their own health is threatened by pregnancy. For example, the pregnancy may have triggered an autoimmune disease or the woman may have developed cancer and needs treatment with chemotherapy and radiation.

A second group of women have late-term abortions because the fetus has developed a severe defect. For example, ultrasound may reveal that the growing child's cerebral hemispheres have failed to develop. If the pregnancy continues, the child that is born will not only lack all cognitive capacity, but will die within a few days or weeks.

The third and largest group are those who have failed to get an early abortion for a variety of mostly social reasons. The group includes teenagers in psychological denial about being pregnant until they (or a parent) had to face the undeniable fact. Also included are indigent women, who may be homeless, mentally retarded, or socially unskilled. Drug users, who engage in their own form of denial, are included in this third group, as are women with menstrual periods so irregular they don't suspect they are pregnant until several months have passed.

Proponents of abortion rights tend to overlook this third group and focus, instead, on the other two. Being able to cite the pressing need of a pregnant woman to save her life or the cruelty of forcing a pregnant woman to carry to term a fetus with a serious developmental defect makes it easier for them to defend their case.

Opponents of abortion, by contrast, tend to discuss late-term abortion as if it were the general rule, rather than very much the statistical exception. When 98.9 percent of all abortions are performed before twenty weeks, it is misleading to condemn all abortion by focusing on the 1.1 percent as representative. They also tend to ignore powerful reasons for having a late-term abortion, preferring to use cases producing the strongest negative emotional response.

FETAL VIABILITY

Abortion opponents have focused on fetal viability as the crucial grounds for outlawing late-term abortion. In making their case, they have suggested that late abortions involve killing babies that otherwise would live and thrive. This has made the debate over late-term abortion particularly contentious, for determinations of viability cannot be made in definite and reliable ways.

Perinatologists (specialists in newborns) say that too many factors are involved in determining viability to allow anyone to make reliable generalizations about which fetuses will live and which will die at any given stage of development. In addition to characteristics such as a fetus's weight and the developmental stage of the

Timing of Abortions

Weeks	Number	Percentage
–9	798,850	52.2
9–10	377,570	24.7
11–12	181,960	11.9
13–15	94,060	6.2
16–20	60,040	3.9
21–22	10,340	
23–24	4,940	
25–26	850	1.1
26+	32	
	1,528,930	

Source: Estimates by Alan Gutmacher Institute based on survey, Centers for Disease Control, and National Center for Health Statistics Data, 1997.

organs, factors like the health of the mother, her socioeconomic status, and her access to health care also play a role. So do the race and gender of the fetus. In development, a white fetus lags a week behind a black one of the same age, and a male fetus lags the same amount behind a female.

The viability of a fetus is also connected with the state of medical technology and management. At the time of the *Roe v. Wade* decision in 1973, fetal viability was around 26 weeks, but now it is closer to 24, with 22 weeks being possible. A *micropremie* weighs 500 to 600 grams (a bit over a pound) and is hardly larger than the palm of a man's hand. Babies of this age and size, even if they survive, are likely to have irreversible physical and mental deficits.

The American College of Obstetrics and Gynecology estimates that fewer than 4 percent of babies are born during weeks 23 to 25 of the normal 40 week gestation period, but their survival is conditional on the factors mentioned. Even with aggressive intervention and intensive care, some experts doubt that more than about 1 percent of even 25-week-old fetuses would survive. Some hospitals and state laws make 23 or 24 weeks the cutoff point for elective abortions, while others follow a more restrictive policy and make 20 weeks the limit. After the cutoff, a factor like the health and safety of the mother or a fetal abnormality must be present to justify an abortion.

How viable a fetus is and how likely one is to survive without serious and permanent mental and physical deficits is a clinical judgment that can only be made case by case. A claim to the effect that thousands or even hundreds of viable fetuses are destroyed by abortion is not supported by the evidence.

METHODS

Opponents of abortion have focused attention on a method to perform late-term abortion known as intact dilation and extraction. The procedure involves using a drug to dilate (widen) the pregnant woman's cervix, then manipulating the fetus by hand until it can be pulled though the birth canal. Usually, to ease the passage and make the procedure easier on the woman, the fetal brain is extracted by suction so the skull can be collapsed (fenestrated). It is this procedure abortion opponents have called *"partial-birth abortion,"* a name coined for rhetorical purposes and not one used in medicine.

Intact dilation and extraction may also be performed by injecting digoxin into the uterus to stop the fetal heart. After the death of the fetus, the woman is induced into labor with a hormone injection, and the fetus is delivered vaginally. Some obstetricians consider this form of the procedure too psychologically stressful for the woman. Others believe it is sufficiently well tolerated to make it the preferred method.

The third or classic method of dilation and extraction does not involve removing an intact fetus. After a woman's cervix is dilated, instruments are used to dismember the fetus and extract the parts through the birth canal. The fetus is either killed by a prior injection or by the process itself. Ultrasound may be used to guide the instruments, and the procedure may take twenty minutes or longer.

Surgeons who prefer intact dilation and extraction point to the time and risks associated with the classic procedure. The woman's uterus may be damaged by an instrument or punctured by a sharp bone fragment. It is safer for the woman, if the intact fetus is pulled out by hand.

About 86 percent of abortions performed after twenty weeks are done by one of these three procedures. "Any procedure done at this stage is pretty gruesome," said one high-risk pregnancy specialist.

LEGISLATION

In 1996 Congress passed legislation banning late-term abortion, along with intact dilation and extraction, but it was vetoed by President Clinton on the ground that the bill made no provision for protecting the health of the pregnant woman.

A second attempt at passing legislation began a year later. The House passed a bill by a margin large enough (295 to 136) to override a presidential veto. The Senate passed (64 to 36) a similar ban, yet it was short of the votes needed to survive a veto. President Clinton announced he would veto any bill that did not allow an abortion to protect the health of a pregnant woman, but both the House and Senate bills would protect only the life of the pregnant woman. Abortion opponents claimed that allowing an exception for health would virtually be equivalent to no regulation at all, given the nebulous nature of claims about health, particularly mental health.

The final version of the Senate bill was revised to reflect the proposal framed and endorsed by the American Medical Association. In the first endorsement of any position on abortion, the AMA proposal made it clear that dilation and *evacuation,* the procedure most often used in early abortions, was not banned. Also, the proposal protected physicians from criminal penalties, if they had to perform a dilation and extraction because of unforeseen circumstances during a delivery. Finally, the proposal allowed physicians accused of violating the ban to appear before a state medical board, instead of a trial court.

In contrast with the AMA, the American College of Obstetricians and Gynecologists and the American Academy of Pediatrics both opposed any ban on dilation and extraction. Some saw a danger in the AMA's position, suggesting that it invited politicians to make decisions about what medical procedures are appropriate.

STATE LAWS

Impatient with the slowness of Congress in passing a law banning "partial-birth abortion," by 1997 about 22 states had passed their own laws. By 1998, however, at least half of those laws had been ruled unconstitutional by the courts. The most common flaw was that the language of the laws was so broad it would also apply to abortions performed before the fetus could possibly be viable. Also, like the original bill passed by Congress, the laws made no exception to protect the pregnant woman's health.

In 1995 the Ohio legislature passed a law banning all abortion past the point of fetal viability. Viability was presumed to occur 24 weeks after conception. The only exception to the ban was for abortions a physician decided needed to be performed to "prevent the death of the pregnant woman or a serious risk of the substantial and irreversible impairment of a major bodily function of the pregnant woman."

The law also included a provision making it a crime for a physician to end a pregnancy "by purposely inserting a suction device into the skull of a fetus to remove its brain."

In *Voinovich v. Women's Medical Professional Corporation,* a case brought to challenge the law, the U.S. Sixth Circuit Court of Appeals in Cincinnati ruled that the law unconstitutionally restricted a woman's right to abortion by defining the prohibited procedure so broadly that it had the consequence of banning the most common method of performing a surgical abortion during the second trimester.

The ruling was appealed to the Supreme Court. In a 1998 decision (6 to 3), the Court refused to hear the case, letting the Appeals Court decision stand. In the dissenting opinion, Justice Thomas made clear that the dissenters' concern was not with late-term abortion, but with whether the prohibition of later-term abortion except to protect the life and health of the mother can limit the health protected to physical health and exclude mental. In the 1973 decision *Roe v. Bolton,* the Court had held that "emotional" and "psychological" factors may be considered by physicians in deciding whether an abortion after fetal viability is necessary to preserve the health of the pregnant woman.

A 2000 ruling by the United States Supreme Court on a Nebraska law resulted in nullifying more than thirty state laws prohibiting late-term abortion. The 1997 Nebraska law banned "an abortion procedure in which the person performing the abortion partially delivers vaginally a living unborn child before killing the unborn child and completing the delivery." The phrase "partial delivery" was defined as "deliberately and intentionally delivering into the vagina a living unborn child or a substantial proportion thereof."

The Supreme Court held in a 5-to-4 vote that the government cannot prohibit physicians from employing an abortion procedure that may be the most medically appropriate way of terminating some pregnancies. The Nebraska law, the Court decided, did not contain provisions for protecting the health and safety of the mother. Justice Steven wrote in the majority opinion that it was "impossible for me to understand how a state has any legitimate interest in requiring a doctor to follow any procedure other than the one he or she reasonably believes will best protect the woman" in exercising her constitutional right to abortion.

The Supreme Court decision effectively declared that all legislation, state or federal, aimed at regulating abortion by specifying what procedures are illegitimate is unconstitutional. Whether this will put an end to efforts to prohibit late-term abortion is uncertain.

Many observers believe there was never a need for laws banning late-term abortion. In keeping with the *Roe v. Wade* decision granting states the power to regulate abortion to protect the interest of the fetus after the first trimester and in keeping with the *Webster* decision (see Social Context: Crucial Legal and Policy Decisions), more than forty states have laws banning abortion after fetal viability has occurred. The problem of determining viability is vexing and perhaps unsolvable, but an additional law banning late-term abortion, even if constitutional, would not help resolve the problem.

Advocates for abortion rights and even some opponents of abortion have expressed the view that the controversy over late-term abortion is primarily a way to keep abortion issues at the forefront of political discussion and to pressure politicians to modify their endorsement of elective abortion. Some have also seen the controversy as a way to raise money for all anti-abortion activities.

While these analyses may be inaccurate, or even cynical, it seems fair to say that the debate over late-term abortion introduced no new ethical issues into the discussion. The old problems remain as complex and perhaps intractable as before.

SOCIAL CONTEXT
Crucial Legal and Policy Decisions

ROE V. WADE

Norma McCorvey of Dallas was unmarried, poor, and pregnant. She wished to have an abortion, but under Texas law, abortion was a criminal offense, except when required to save the woman's life. California law was less restrictive, and McCorvey believed she could get an abortion there, but she lacked money for travel and expenses. Unwillingly, she bowed to legal and economic necessity and carried the fetus to term. She then gave up the newborn child for adoption.

When McCorvey was later approached by a public interest attorney and asked if she would agree to be the plaintiff in a class-action suit against Henry Wade, the district attorney of Dallas County, challenging the constitutionality of the Texas abortion law, she readily consented. Federal courts ruled that the Texas statute was void, but Wade appealed to the Supreme Court.

Because McCorvey wished her identity to be protected by a pseudonym, the 1973 Supreme Court decision in the case was titled *Roe v. Wade*. In a 7-to-2 decision, written by Justice Harry A. Blackmun, the court found the Texas law unconstitutional. In doing so, the court effectively decriminalized abortion, for abortion laws in most other states differed little from the Texas statute.

The *Roe* decision did not require that abortion be unregulated, but it placed limits on the restrictions states could impose. According to the ruling, during the first twelve weeks (the first trimester) of pregnancy, states cannot restrict a woman's decision about abortion. During the second trimester, states may restrict abortion to protect the health of the woman. In the final trimester, because the fetus may be considered viable, states may limit abortions to those necessary to preserve the health of the woman.

After the *Roe* decision, abortions became easily obtainable by most women who wanted them. Yet the decision also triggered a firestorm of controversy between proponents of relatively unregulated choice ("prochoice" advocates) and opponents of so-called abortion on demand ("prolife" or "right-to-life" advocates) that shows no sign of dying down. While those who favor making abortion a matter of individual decision were pleased by the *Roe* decision, those morally opposed to abortion were not.

Many, if not most, who believe abortion is morally wrong also think it should be illegal, except in very special cases. Within the limits of regulation imposed by the *Roe* decision, opponents of abortion have taken various legal measures to attempt to slow or halt its practice. They have become politically active and have often succeeded in getting laws passed that impose requirements on abortion that make it difficult to get one. As this has happened, advocates of personal choice have often charged that the laws are unconstitutional and have filed suits that have frequently ended up before the Supreme Court.

SUPREME COURT DECISIONS AFTER *ROE V. WADE*

The conflict over abortion has been expressed, in part, in a continuing series of legal skirmishes that have produced a number of Supreme Court decisions seeking to define abortion rights and limits. To get some sense of the way in which laws, regulations, and practices have changed since the *Roe* decision in 1973, it is instructive to review a few Court decisions briefly and consider in more detail the ones that have most influenced the direction of public policy on abortion.

ROE V. BOLTON (1973). The Court rejected the requirement that abortions had to be performed in hospitals, thus opening the way for abortion clinics. The Court also found that emotional and psychological factors connected with the health of the pregnant woman could be considered by physicians in deciding whether an abortion after the first trimester was justifiable.

PLANNED PARENTHOOD V. DANFORTH (1976). The Missouri law requiring a husband's consent for an abortion was struck down. Also, parents of minor, unmarried girls were found not to have an absolute veto over their daughter's decision to have an abortion.

MAHER V. ROE (1977). The Court decided states do not have a constitutional obligation to pay for abortions for the poor. Hence, the Court left it up to states to decide whether they wished to include funding for abortion as part of their contribution to the Medicaid program.

HARRIS V. McRAE (1980).   The Court upheld the Hyde Amendment, the federal law banning the use of federal Medicaid funds to pay for abortions. Hence, those wanting an abortion and unable to pay for it would have to depend on money from other sources. (States, however, have no constitutional obligation to provide money for abortions.)

CITY OF AKRON V. AKRON CENTER FOR REPRODUCTIVE HEALTH (1983).   The Court struck down a law requiring that women wanting an abortion receive counseling that includes the statement that "the unborn child is a human life from the moment of conception," then wait at least twenty-four hours before reaffirming their decision.

WEBSTER V. REPRODUCTIVE HEALTH SERVICES (1989).   The Missouri law in the *Webster* case is similar to laws the Court had previously held to be void. However, the law was carefully crafted by prolife advocates to avoid the specific difficulties that had led the Court to reject them. While the preamble of the law asserts that "life begins at conception," at issue were three provisions restricting abortion.

1. Public employees, including physicians and nurses, are forbidden to perform an abortion, except when necessary to save a woman's life.
2. Public hospitals, clinics, or other tax-supported facilities cannot be used to perform abortions not necessary to save a woman's life, even if no public funds are involved.
3. Physicians are required to perform tests to determine the viability of a fetus, if they have reason to believe the woman has been pregnant for at least twenty weeks.

On July 3, 1989, the Supreme Court in a 5-to-4 decision upheld the constitutionality of the law. Chief Justice William Rehnquist, writing the majority opinion, held that the Court did not have to rule against the claim that life begins at conception, for such language is only an expression of a permissible value judgment. Furthermore, "Nothing in the Constitution requires States to enter or remain in the business of performing abortions. Nor . . . do private physicians and their patients have some kind of constitutional right of access to public facilities for the performance of abortions."

So far as viability is concerned, Rehnquist saw a problem, not with the Missouri law, but with *Roe v. Wade*'s "rigid trimester analysis of the course of a pregnancy." That is, he found the law more sensitive to the issue of viability than the trimester rule, which holds that the state can regulate abortion in the second trimester to protect a woman's health and regulate it more stringently, down to prohibiting it, in the last trimester. Furthermore, "the key elements" of *Roe v. Wade* are "not found in the text of the Constitution or in any place else one would expect to find a constitutional principle."

Justice Harry A. Blackmun, the author of the majority opinion in *Roe v. Wade*, wrote the dissenting opinion in Webster. He made clear that he regarded the Court's decision as an outright attack on *Roe*. Rehnquist, he argued, failed to consider the case for viability on appropriate grounds—namely, the right to privacy or autonomy, on which *Roe* was decided. Instead, he misread the Missouri law in a way that seemed to conflict with the trimester structure established in *Roe* to balance the state's interest in maternal health and potential life against the right to privacy.

The hope of abortion opponents was that the Court would use the *Webster* case to overturn *Roe v. Wade*. The Court stopped short of doing that, but the *Webster* decision made it clear that the Court was willing to approve restrictions on abortion of a sort that it had held unconstitutional until then. Various new state and local regulations were formulated and passed into law.

PLANNED PARENTHOOD V. CASEY (1992).   The Pennsylvania Abortion Control Act was one of those pieces of legislation framed with the intention of making abortions more difficult to secure. It included the following restrictions:

1. A physician must inform a woman seeking an abortion about the procedure and its risks, the stage of the pregnancy, and the alternative of carrying the fetus to term.

2. The woman must wait at least twenty-four hours after receiving this information before having an abortion.

3. A girl under the age of eighteen must secure the informed consent of at least one parent before having an abortion, and a parent must accompany the girl to counseling. Alternatively, consent may be sought from a court.

4. A married woman must (except under certain circumstances) sign a statement that she has notified her husband of her intention to have an abortion.

The 5-to-4 Court ruling upheld most sections of the Pennsylvania law, but it rejected the provision requiring a married woman to notify her husband of her intention to have an abortion.

However, in the view of some observers, the most important outcome of the *Casey* decision was that it reaffirmed what it called the "essence" of the constitutional right to an abortion, while also introducing a new legal standard for testing the constitutional legitimacy of regulations governing abortions. The Court considered the provisions of the Pennsylvania law in terms of whether they had the purpose or result of imposing an "undue burden" on a woman seeking an abortion. In the Court's definition, a burden is "undue" if it places a "substantial obstacle in the path of a woman seeking an abortion before the fetus attains viability." Only the spousal notification requirement, in the Court's view, imposed such a burden.

The undue-burden standard makes it clear that, in the opinion of the Court, laws that attempt to prohibit abortions outright or those that attempt to reduce the frequency of abortions by making them extraordinarily difficult to obtain are unconstitutional.

In its decision, the Court explicitly endorsed *Roe v. Wade* as having established "a rule of law and a component of liberty that we cannot renounce." The majority held that *Roe* has acquired a "rare precedential force" and could be repudiated only "at the cost of both profound and unnecessary damage to the Court's legitimacy and to the nation's commitment to the rule of law."

Until the *Webster* decision, abortion was considered a fundamental right that could not be restricted, except to serve a compelling state interest. This meant that during the first two trimesters of pregnancy, almost all restrictions were considered unconstitutional. After *Webster,* it seemed to many that the way was open for more and heavier regulation of abortion. However, although the "undue-burden" standard introduced in *Casey* permits considerable regulation during this period, it does not allow opponents of abortion to regulate the practice so heavily as to make it virtually unavailable.

MADSEN V. WOMEN'S HEALTH CENTER (1994).   In 1993 a Florida circuit court issued an injunction to protect access to the clinic operated by the Aware Woman Center for Choice in Melbourne, Florida. Demonstrators from Operation Rescue and related organizations were made subject to the injunction. The order imposed a 300-foot protected zone around the clinic, forbade the display of signs that could be seen from inside the clinic, and barred demonstrators from making excessive noise.

The case was appealed, and in a 6-to-3 ruling the Supreme Court upheld the basic provisions of the injunction. It approved an approximately thirty-six-foot buffer zone to keep protesters away from the clinic's entrance and parking lot and off a public right-of-way. The buffer zone "burdens no more speech than necessary to accomplish the government's interest," Justice Rehnquist wrote.

SCHENCK V. PRO-CHOICE NETWORK (1997).   In a New York State case in which a group opposed to abortion appealed an injunction ordering them to cease blockading the entrances to a clinic and stop harassing and intimidating the women seeking an abortion, the Supreme Court in a 6-to-3 decision upheld the lower court's decision to keep the protesters from blocking doorways and driveways.

The Court struck down (8 to 3) a section of the New York law that established a "floating" fifteen-foot buffer zone between protesters and people entering or leaving a clinic, because the indefinite character of the zone raised the prospect of suppressing more speech than necessary to protect the state's interest in public safety. Yet the Court upheld (6 to 3) a section of the injunction allowing only two protesters at a time to come within a fixed fifteen-foot buffer zone to talk to women in a non-threatening way and to "cease and desist" and to withdraw outside the zone if asked to do so.

The Court's tacit endorsement of a fixed buffer zone around abortion clinics is significant, because about 300 of the 900 abortion clinics in the country are protected by buffer zones spelled out in court injunctions. Both the Florida and New York rulings are considered important indicators of the Court's view of the Freedom of Access to Clinic Entrances Act. It is designed to provide federal remedies, including criminal penalties, to restrict violent protests at abortion clinics.

HILL V. COLORADO (2000).   The Court held in a 6-to-3 ruling that a Colorado law aimed at protecting abortion clinic physicians, patients, and visitors from harassment by protestors did not violate the protestors' First Amendment rights to free expression. The law holds that within one hundred feet of any health-care facility no one can approach anyone closer than eight feet to talk or pass out leaflets, unless the person approached permits it.

FEDERAL POLICIES

President George W. Bush, on his first full day in office, issued an executive order that would cut off federal funds to international family planning programs that provide abortions or even abortion counseling. Thus, Bush reinstated the ban first imposed during the Reagan administration and lifted only by President Clinton.

Some critics consider the need for the order debatable. Legislation passed in 1999 restoring U.S. financing of the United Nations already contained a clause prohibiting the United States Agency for International Development from using money to promote or provide abortions. Nevertheless, the ban made clear the position the Bush administration planned to take on abortion. With world population now standing at 6 billion and increasing by 60 to 80 million a year, even some opposed to abortion worry that withholding funds from family-planning organizations will make it difficult to achieve the goal of stabilizing the population and thus relieving the pressure on natural resources.

Such stability would require a fertility rate of 2.1 children per woman, but most undeveloped countries have a much higher rate. In sub-Saharan Africa, for example, women frequently have six or more children. Also, an estimated 45 percent of pregnancies worldwide are either unwanted or unintended.

The Bush administration's policy on abortion has also come into conflict with the demands of scientists and disease-advocacy groups that embryonic stem cells be made available for research. Because embryonic stem cells can be acquired only by destroying a human embryo, many opponents of abortion object to their use. Others, however, distinguish between an embryo and a fetus and see no incompatibility between opposing abortion and favoring the use of stem cells.

The potential of stem cells to treat injuries and diseases for which now we have no effective therapies (e.g., spinal-cord damage and Parkinson's disease) has both split traditional abortion allies and broadened the debate. (See Chapter 6.)

SOCIAL CONTEXT

RU-486—"The Abortion Pill"

Sandra Crane, as we'll call her, decided she had missed her period. She was thirty-one years old, and ordinarily her menstrual cycle was as regular as the calendar. Since she was now a week overdue, she felt sure she was pregnant.

The feeling was familiar. She had two children already, six-year-old Jennifer and two-year-old Thomas. She and her husband had decided they weren't going to have any more. They had discussed the matter, and she resolved that if she became pregnant, she would seek medical help to end her pregnancy.

The next morning Sandra Crane consulted her gynecologist, and a day later she received a phone call informing her that she was pregnant. She explained that she wanted the pregnancy ended as soon as possible, and was told to return to the clinic, where she was given two tablets to swallow—a 600-milligram dosage of the drug RU-486.

Two days later, as directed, Sandra returned to the clinic and took a 400-milligram dosage of misoprostol (a prostaglandin), a drug to make her uterus contract. Later, she began to experience cramping and bleeding, but soon the uterine lining was expelled. She felt some discomfort, but the process differed little from an unusually heavy menstrual period.

After a day of rest, she felt almost her usual self again. Two weeks later, she returned to the clinic for an examination to make sure the abortion was complete.

RU-486, or mifepristone, was developed by the French endocrinologist Etienne-Émile Baulieu. The drug works by blocking the action of progesterone, the hormone that prepares the uterine wall for the implantation of the fertilized egg. The dose of prostaglandins then induces uterine contractions that expel the sloughed-off lining, including the zygote. To be most effective, the drug must be taken during the first five to seven weeks of pregnancy. Physicians urge that the drug be taken as early as possible, but some researchers suggest that its use might be extended even to the tenth week of pregnancy.

If RU-486 is taken early in pregnancy, it blocks the action of progesterone, and as a result, a fertilized egg will not be able to follow its usual course of implanting itself in the uterine wall. Hence, the drug also has the possibility of serving as a "morning-after pill" for preventing pregnancy, even after fertilization. But the drug's major use lies in its power to induce an abortion chemically.

In initial testing, 100 women volunteers less than a month pregnant were given RU-486. Of these, 85 percent aborted within four days, without reporting the pain or psychological difficulties that can accompany surgical abortion. The later use of prostaglandin injections in conjunction with the drug increased the speed of the process. An oral dose of prostaglandins later replaced the injection. Women tolerated this better, and the price was significantly lower.

Additional clinical trials in France and the use of the drug by more than 200,000 women showed it to be safe and 95.5 percent effective. With the use of the oral prostaglandins, the effectiveness rises to 96.9 percent. Some women taking the drug bleed excessively and a proportion do not abort as expected (about 3 percent, according to a French study) and require surgical intervention. For these reasons, the drug is intended for use only under close medical supervision. All in all, however, the evidence shows that the use of the drug is safer and cheaper than surgical abortion. It is now used by more than 70 percent of French women seeking an abortion and no more than seven weeks pregnant.

Recent studies of RU-486 indicate that it may be of value in preventing endometriosis (a major cause of infertility) and fibroid tumors, which often require a hysterectomy. Thus, the drug may have a role in aiding women in getting pregnant, as well as in preventing or ending pregnancies. Other studies suggest that the drug may help prevent breast cancer and Cushing's syndrome (a metabolic disorder).

THE CONFLICT

The drug was developed in 1980 by the pharmaceutical company Roussel-Uclaf and approved for use in France in September 1988. A month later, in response to a boycott of the company's products by abortion opponents, Roussel took the drug off the market. This provoked public protests, and Health Minister Claude Evin notified the company that if it did not release the drug the government, which owned 36.25 percent of the company, would permanently transfer the patent to another company. "From the moment the governmental approval of the drug was granted, RU-486 became the moral property of women, not just the property of the drug company," Evin said. Two days later the company resumed marketing the drug.

THE UNITED STATES

Roussel licensed the drug for use in China, Sweden, and Britain. Initial plans to market the drug in the United States were abandoned because of opposition from right-to-life groups. Opponents of abortion generally consider RU-486 as no more than a biochemical means for producing an abortion and so oppose its use. According to the president of the National Right-to-Life Coalition, RU-486 represents "chemical warfare against an entire class of innocent humans."

The National Right-to-Life Coalition (NRL) and other groups opposed to abortion informed drug companies that they would boycott all of a company's products if it tried to market an abortion-inducing drug. "Our basic position is that death drugs designed to kill unborn babies have no place in America," the NRL education director said.

Baulieu, the drug's developer, claims that fears of such reprisals have kept RU-486 from being distributed worldwide. Indeed, the fear of boycotts of Roussel and Hoechst, the German pharmaceutical company that is its majority stockholder, led the company to decide against trying to get approval to sell the drug in the United States. Fear of the response of the prolife movement also kept U.S. drug companies from applying to the Food and Drug Administration (FDA) for approval.

Baulieu also charges that Roussel should not have put approval of the drug for international use in the hands of the World Health Organization (WHO). The WHO, he claims, has delayed its approval because it is so financially dependent on the United States that a reprisal in the form of a withdrawal of U.S. funds would severely cripple its operations.

"I believe the key to the future of RU-486 lies in the United States," Baulieu said at a news conference. He said that because of the drug's simplicity, it could dramatically reduce the number of illegal abortions and related maternal deaths throughout the world. "How can we ignore that 500 women a day die as a result of badly executed abortions?" he asked. "At present, things are so bad in the Third World that anything that improves the situation is welcome. I think it is our moral duty to act."

Louise B. Tyrer of Planned Parenthood similarly characterized the lack of availability of the drug, calling it "discriminatory to women" and "a threat to their safety and health." In her view and in the opinion of prochoice advocates, "Women should have a choice between medical and surgical abortion."

In April 1993, the situation changed when Roussel-Uclaf agreed to license the drug and the technology used to make it to the Population Council, a nonprofit research organization. The council agreed to find a manufacturer, establish a clinical trial, and then apply to the FDA to license the drug for use in the United States.

In 1996 the Council presented data from the French studies to the FDA. The agency gave its preliminary approval of the drug, pronouncing it safe and effective and making it legal to manufacture, sell, and prescribe it in the United States. Still, no company could be found willing to make the drug.

In 1998 the Council published data produced by its own tests of the drug. The results were similar to those of the French. The study was conducted from September 1994 to September 1995 and involved 2121 woman from ages 18 to 35 who were given the drug at seventeen clinics. The drug was most effective in the 849 women who were no more than 49 days pregnant. For 92 percent of them, drugs alone terminated the pregnancy. Only 1 percent were still pregnant after taking the drugs, and the remainder had surgical abortions, because of heavy bleeding.

The Population Council, working with a group of private investors, made arrangements with Danco Laboratories, a small pharmaceutical company, to produce RU-486 under the trade name Mifeprex. All that was required was final FDA approval.

APPROVAL

On September 28, 2000, the FDA at last recognized RU-486, or Mifeprex, as safe and effective, and made it a legitimate prescription drug. Danco promised to have supplies of the drug available to physicians by the end of October. Although the FDA had considered placing unusually severe restrictions on the use of the drug, in the end it decided any physician qualified to determine the length of a pregnancy and practicing within one hour of facilities able to offer a surgical abortion could administer the drug in the office.

Reactions to the approval were predictably mixed. George W. Bush denounced the FDA as "wrong," and abortion opponents, calling the drug a "baby poison," vowed to lobby for legislation to prohibit its use. Pro-choice advocates celebrate the approval, saying it would allow women to keep their abortion decisions private. Also, women living in rural areas without easy access to surgical abortion would now have a safe option. A survey by the Kaiser Family Foundation found that 44 percent of physicians involved in women's health care would be at least "somewhat likely" to prescribe Mifeprex.

IN PRACTICE

Most of the hopes that pro-choice advocates pinned on getting mifepristone (RU-486) approved have not materialized. Many physicians still prefer the speed and reliability of surgical abortions. A procedure takes only a few minutes, then the patient is on the way to recovery. RU-486 is limited to use during the first seven weeks of pregnancy, and, once given the drug, the woman must return to the office two more times. The process takes about three weeks.

Many physicians, furthermore, who thought they were likely to prescribe the drug to patients wanting a medical abortion have come to realize that abortion is typically regulated by a bewildering complexity of state laws. Some states require that a physcian performing abortions must have an ultrasound machine, life-support equipment, and an operating suite available. Other laws stipulate the standard the facility must satisfy—the hall width, temperature of the running water, and amount of ventilation.

Thirteen states require counseling before an abortion is performed and dictate a waiting period. Some states require that the fetal tissue be inspected, while others demand it be disposed of by cremation or burial. While the laws of some states regulate abortion in general, those in other states specifically mention drug-induced abortion.

It is not surprising, given the circumstances, that the availability of a drug to produce abortion has had little impact so far on the practice of abortion. Most abortions are still performed in clinics by the same people who provided them before, and most of those people still prefer the surgical method. To what extent the situation would be different without state laws passed over the last three decades to discourage abortion is a matter of speculation.

SOCIAL CONTEXT
The "Morning-After Pill"

About 3.5 million unwanted pregnancies occur each year. Although some 1 million of them are terminated by abortion, a great number of women end up having children they don't want. Many of these unwanted pregnancies could be prevented by contraceptive drugs that are taken *after* intercourse.

Emergency contraception is a way to prevent pregnancy by delaying or inhibiting ovulation, inhibiting fertilization, or preventing a fertilized egg from implanting itself in the uterine wall. The drugs that can function in this way are already available as birth control pills.

Although the Federal Drug Administration has reviewed these drugs and found them safe and effective in preventing pregnancy and invited manufacturers to submit proposals for relabeling the drugs for use as emergency contraception, so far drug companies have not made any submissions. Even so, because the drugs already have FDA approval, they can be legitimately prescribed by a physician for emergency use. (RU-486 can also prevent pregnancy if used early enough. See the previous Social Context.)

Eight brands of birth control pills can be used for emergency contraception. Seven contain a combination of the hormones estrogen and progestin. If one of these pills is taken within seventy-two hours of having sex and a second pill is taken twelve hours afterward, the chance of preventing pregnancy is 75 percent. Statistically, 8 of 100 women engaging in unprotected sex during the second or third week of their menstrual cycle will become pregnant. If they take the birth control pills as described, only two will.

The second type of birth control pill contains levonorgestrel (a progestin). One dose taken forty-eight hours after sex and a second dose twelve hours later will also reduce by 75 percent the chance of pregnancy.

Emergency contraception can also be achieved mechanically by the insertion of the copper-T IUD (intrauterine device) by a physician. The IUD effectively blocks the migration of the fertilized egg into the uterus. It is more than 99 percent effective in preventing pregnancy.

The major side effects of the double dose of birth control pills is nausea and vomiting. One- to two-thirds of women taking the pills experience nausea for about two days, and some 12 to 22 percent have episodes of vomiting. An antinausea drug taken at the same time as the contraceptives can reduce the side effects.

Because there is no way to tell when an egg becomes fertilized after intercourse, emergency contraception blurs the line between contraception and abortion. A majority of Americans have no objections either to contraception or to early abortion, so to them emergency contraception is a favored way to prevent an unwanted pregnancy.

Even the National Right to Life Committee, a group opposed to abortion, does not condemn emergency contraception outright. "Some chemical compounds may work to either prevent fertilization or kill the developing human being which has begun to grow," the group said in an official comment. The statement went on to recommend that a woman consult her physician to see whether in the physician's "best medical judgment" taking the pill would prevent fertilization or cause an abortion.

Washington, Alaska, California, and Oregon are among those states now operating pilot programs providing "morning-after" pills without a prescription. Washington's laws allow a pharmacist to acquire from a physician the right to dispense certain prescription drugs when, in the pharmacist's judgment, they are needed. More than 30,000 women have now received the pills, known as Plan B, under the law.

In France a similar drug can be dispensed by a nurse. Norway was the first country to make a drug like Plan B available over the counter, but it has since been followed by Great Britain.

CASE PRESENTATION
A Problem Not of Her Own Making

For months doctors told eleven-year-old Visna (as we will call her) and her parents that her abdominal pains were nothing but indigestion. Then in July 1998 the truth finally emerged—Visna was twenty-seven weeks pregnant.

Visna's family had emigrated from India to the Detroit suburb of Sterling Heights, Michigan, only the previous summer. Her parents found factory jobs and rented a two-bedroom apartment, and Visna shared one of the rooms with Hari, her sixteen-year-old brother. Sometime during the winter after their arrival in the U.S., Visna told her parents, Hari raped her, but this emerged only after Visna, who had turned twelve, was found to be pregnant.

As soon as Visna's parents discovered her condition, they made plans to take her to Kansas for an abortion. Visna would have to have a late-term abortion, and because Michigan law bans almost all abortions after twenty-four weeks, her family would have to take her out of state. But their plans were frustrated when they were leaked to a family court judge. Charges of parental negligence were filed by prosecutors against her parents, and the court immediately removed Visna from her family and made her a ward of the state.

At a court hearing, Visna's doctor argued that if her pregnancy were allowed to continue, it could cause her both physical and psychological damage. A psychologist testified that, because Visna was a Hindu, if she were forced to have an illegitimate child, it would make her unfit for marriage by another Hindu. Her parents also expressed their worry that if Visna had a child, the child might suffer from genetic abnormalities and, in particular, might be mentally retarded, because her brother would be the father.

Abortion opponents made public statements about Visna's case. They begged her not to have an abortion, and offered her money to let the pregnancy proceed. They promised they would find someone to adopt the baby. They said they considered it irrelevant that the child was conceived as the result of rape and incest.

At the end of the court hearing, the prosecution announced that it was convinced pregnancy might endanger Visna's life and dropped the negligence charge against her parents. Visna was reunited with her family, and her parents pursued their original plan of taking her to Kansas.

In Wichita, Dr. George Tiller, who had been shot in 1993 by a prolife activist, performed the abortion. He stopped the fetus's heart and used drugs to induce labor. Visna was in her twenty-ninth week of pregnancy, and this made the procedure a late-term abortion. Visna resumed life with her family, but her brother was charged with rape.

CHAPTER 10

Euthanasia and Physician-Assisted Suicide

CLASSIC CASE PRESENTATION
Karen Quinlan: The Debate Begins

At two in the morning on Tuesday, April 14, 1975, Mrs. Julie Quinlan was awakened by a telephone call. When she hung up she was crying. "Karen is very sick," Mrs. Quinlan said to her husband, Joseph. "She's unconscious, and we have to go to Newton Hospital right away."

The Quinlans thought their twenty-one-year-old adopted daughter might have been in an automobile accident. But the doctor in the intensive care unit told them that wasn't so. Karen was in a critical comatose state of unknown cause and was being given oxygen through a mask taped over her nose and mouth. She had been brought to the hospital by two friends who had been with her at a birthday party. After a few drinks, she had started to pass out, and her friends decided she must be drunk and put her to bed. Then someone checked on her later in the evening and found that Karen wasn't breathing. Her friends gave her mouth-to-mouth resuscitation and rushed her to the nearest hospital.

Blood and urine tests showed that Karen had not consumed a dangerous amount of alcohol. They also showed the presence of .6 milligram of aspirin and the tranquilizer Valium. Two milligrams would have been toxic, and five lethal. Why Karen stopped breathing was mysterious. But it was during that time that part of her brain died from oxygen depletion.

After Karen had been unconscious for about a week, she was moved to St. Clare's Hospital in nearby Denville, where testing and life-support facilities were better. Dr. Robert J. Morse, a neurologist, and Dr. Arshad Javed, a pulmonary internist, became her physicians. Additional tests were made. Extensive brain damage was confirmed, and several possible causes of the coma were ruled out.

NO LONGER THE SAME

During the early days, the Quinlans were hopeful. Karen's eyes opened and closed, and her mother and her nineteen-year-old sister, Mary Ellen, thought that they detected signs Karen recognized them. But Karen's condition began to deteriorate. Her weight gradually dropped from 120 pounds to 70 pounds. Her body began to contract into a rigid fetal position, until her five-foot-two-inch frame was bent into a shape hardly longer than three feet. She was now breathing mechanically, by means of an MA-1 respirator that pumped air through a tube in her throat. By early July, Karen's physicians and her mother, sister, and brother had come to believe it was hopeless to expect her ever to regain consciousness.

Only her father continued to believe it might be possible. But when he told Dr. Morse about some encouraging sign he had noticed, Dr. Morse said to him "Even if God did perform a miracle so that Karen would live, her damage is so extensive she would spend the rest of her life in an institution." Mr. Quinlan then realized that Karen would never again be as he remembered her. He now agreed with Karen's sister: "Karen would never want to be kept alive on machines like this. She would hate this."

NEED TO GO TO COURT

The Quinlans' parish priest, Father Thomas Trapasso, had also assured them that the moral doctrines of the Roman Catholic Church did not require the continuation of extraordinary measures to support a hopeless life. Before making his decision, Mr. Quinlan asked the priest, "Am I playing God?" Father Thomas said "God has made the decision that Karen is going to die. You're just agreeing with God's decision, that's all."

On July 31, after Karen had been unconscious for three and a half months, the Quinlans gave Drs. Morse and Jared their permission to take Karen off the respirator. The Quinlans signed a letter authorizing the discontinuance of extraordinary procedures and absolving the hospital from all legal liability. "I think you have come to the right decision," Dr. Morse said to Mr. Quinlan.

But the next morning Dr. Morse called Mr. Quinlan. "I have a moral problem about what we agreed on last night," he said. "I feel I have to consult somebody else and see how he feels about it." The next day, Dr. Morse called again. "I find I will not do it," he said. "And I've informed the administrator at the hospital that I will not do it."

The Quinlans were upset and bewildered by the change in Dr. Morse. Later they talked with the hospital attorney and were told by him that, because Karen was over twenty-one, they were no longer her legal guardians. The Quinlans would have to go to court and be appointed to guardianship. After that, the hospital might or might not remove Karen from the respirator.

Mr. Quinlan consulted attorney Paul Armstrong. Because Karen was an adult without income, Mr. Quinlan explained, Medicare was paying the $450 a day it cost to keep her alive. The Quinlans thus had no financial motive in asking that the respirator be taken away. Mr. Quinlan said that his belief that Karen should be allowed to die rested on his conviction that it was God's will, and it was for this reason that he wanted to be appointed Karen's guardian.

LEGAL ARGUMENTS

Mr. Armstrong filed a plea with Judge Robert Muir of the New Jersey Superior Court on September 12, 1975. He explicitly requested that Mr. Quinlan be appointed Karen's guardian so that he would have "the express power of authorizing the discontinuance of all extraordinary means of sustaining her life."

Later, on October 20, Mr. Armstrong argued the case on three constitutional grounds. First, he claimed that there is an implicit right to privacy guaranteed by the Constitution and that this right permits individuals or others acting for them to terminate the use of extraordinary medical measures, even when death may result. This right holds, Armstrong said, unless there are compelling state interests that set it aside.

Second, Armstrong argued that the First Amendment guarantee of religious freedom extended to the Quinlan case. If the court did not allow them to act in accordance with the doctrines of their church, their religious liberty would be infringed. Finally, Armstrong appealed to the "cruel and unusual punishment" clause of the Eighth Amendment. He claimed that "for the state to require that Karen Quinlan be kept alive, against her will and the will of her family, after the dignity, beauty, promise, and meaning of earthly life have vanished, is cruel and unusual punishment."

Karen's mother, sister, and a friend testified that Karen had often talked about not wanting to be kept alive by machines. An expert witness, a neurologist, testified that Karen was in a "chronic vegetative state" and that it was unlikely that she would ever regain consciousness. Doctors testifying for St. Clare's Hospital and Karen's physicians agreed with this. But, they argued, her brain still showed patterns of electrical activity, and she still had a discernible pulse. Thus, she could not be considered dead by legal or medical criteria.

On November 10, Judge Muir ruled against Joseph Quinlan. He praised Mr. Quinlan's character and concern, but he decided that Mr. Quinlan's anguish over his daughter might cloud his judgment about her welfare so he should not be made her guardian. Furthermore, Judge Muir said, because Karen is still medically and legally alive, "the Court should not authorize termination of the respirator. To do so would be homicide and an act of euthanasia."

APPEAL

Mr. Armstrong appealed the decision to the New Jersey Supreme Court. On January 26, 1976, the court convened to hear arguments, and Mr. Armstrong argued substantially as before. But this time the court's ruling was favorable. The court agreed that Mr. Quinlan could assert a right of privacy on Karen's behalf and that whatever he decided for her should be accepted by society. It also set aside any criminal liability for removing the respirator, claiming that if death resulted it would not be homicide and that, even if it were homicide, it would not be unlawful. Finally, the court stated that, if Karen's physicians believed that she would never emerge from her coma, they should consult an ethics committee to be established by St. Clare's Hospital. If the committee accepted their prognosis, then the respirator could be removed. If Karen's present physicians were then unwilling to take her off the respirator, Mr. Quinlan was free to find a physician who would.

Six weeks after the court decision, the respirator still had not been turned off. In fact, another machine, one for controlling body temperature, had been added. Mr. Quinlan met with Morse and Jared and demanded that they remove the respirator. They agreed to "wean" Karen from the machine, and soon she was breathing without mechanical assistance. Dr. Morse and St. Clare's Hospital were determined that Karen would not die while under their care. Although she was moved to a private room, it was next door to the intensive-care unit. They intended to put her back on the respirator at the first sign of breathing difficulty.

Because Karen was still alive, the Quinlans began a long search for a chronic-care hospital. Twenty or more institutions turned them away, and physicians expressed great reluctance to become involved in the case. Finally, Dr. Joseph Fennelly volunteered to treat Karen, and on June 9 she was moved from St. Clare's to the Morris View Nursing Home.

THE END—AFTER TEN YEARS

Karen Quinlan continued to breathe. She received high-nutrient feedings and regular doses of antibiotics to ward off infections. During some periods she was more active than at others, making reflexive responses to touch and sound.

On June 11, 1985, at 7:01 in the evening, ten years after she lapsed into a coma, Karen Quinlan finally died. She was thirty-one years old.

Her father died of cancer on December 10, 1996 at the Karen Quinlan Center of Hope, a hospice Joseph and Julia Quinlan had founded in 1980 with money they received from the film and book rights to their daughter's story. Joseph Quinlan continued to support the right of patients and their families to discontinue the use of life-sustaining technologies, but he opposed all forms of physician-assisted suicide.

Briefing Session

Death comes to us all. We hope that when it comes it will be swift and allow us to depart without prolonged suffering, our dignity intact. We also hope that it will not force burdens on our family and friends, making them pay both financially and emotionally by our lingering and hopeless condition.

Such considerations give euthanasia a strong appeal. Should we not be able to snip the thread of life when the weight of suffering and hopelessness grows too heavy to bear? The answer to this question is not as easy as it may seem, for hidden within it are a number of complicated moral issues.

Just what is euthanasia? The word comes from the Greek for "good death," and in English it has come to have the meaning "easy death." But this does little to help us understand the concept. For consider this: If we give ourselves an easy death, are we committing suicide? If we assist someone else to an easy death (with or without that person's permission), are we committing murder? Anyone who opposed killing (either of oneself or of others) on moral grounds might also consider it necessary to object to euthanasia.

It may be, however, that the answer to both of these questions is no. But if it is, then it is necessary to specify the conditions that distinguish euthanasia from both suicide and murder. Only then would it be possible to argue, without contradiction, that euthanasia is morally acceptable but the other two forms of killing are not.

Someone believing that suicide is morally legitimate would not object to euthanasia carried out by the person herself, but he would still have to deal with
the problem posed by the euthanasia/murder issue.

ACTIVE AND PASSIVE EUTHANASIA

We have talked of euthanasia as though it involved directly taking the life of a
person, either one's own life or the life of another. However, some philosophers
distinguish between "active euthanasia" and "passive euthanasia," which in turn
rests on a distinction between killing and letting die.

To kill someone (including oneself) is to take a definite action to end his or
her life (administering a lethal injection, for example). To allow someone to die,
by contrast, is to take no steps to prolong a person's life when those steps seem
called for—failing to give a needed injection of antibiotics, for example. Active
euthanasia, then, is direct killing and is an act of commission. Passive euthanasia
is an act of omission.

This distinction is used in most contemporary codes of medical ethics (for example, the American Medical Association's Code of Ethics) and is also recognized in the Anglo-American tradition of law. Except in special circumstances, it
is illegal to deliberately cause the death of another person. It is not, however, illegal (except in special circumstances) to allow a person to die. Clearly, one might
consider active euthanasia morally wrong, while recognizing passive euthanasia
as morally legitimate.

Some philosophers, however, have argued that the active–passive distinction is
morally irrelevant with respect to euthanasia. Both are cases of causing death,
and it is the circumstances in which death is caused, not the manner of causing
it, that is of moral importance.

Furthermore, the active–passive distinction is not always clear-cut. If a person
dies after special life-sustaining equipment has been withdrawn, is this a case of
active or passive euthanasia? Or is it a case of euthanasia at all?

VOLUNTARY, INVOLUNTARY, AND
NONVOLUNTARY EUTHANASIA

Writers on euthanasia have often thought it important to distinguish between
voluntary, involuntary, and nonvoluntary euthanasia. *Voluntary euthanasia* includes cases in which a person takes his or her own life, either directly or by refusing treatment. But it also includes cases in which a person deputizes another
to act in accordance with his wishes.

Thus, someone might instruct her family not to permit the use of artificial
support systems should she become unconscious, suffer from brain damage, and
be unable to speak for herself. Or someone might request that he be given a lethal
injection, after suffering third-degree burns over most of his body, suffering uncontrollable pain, and being told he has little hope of recovery.

Finally, assisted suicide, in which the individual requests the direct help of someone else in ending his life, falls into this category. (Some may think that one or more of the earlier examples are also cases of assisted suicide. What counts as assisted suicide is both conceptually and legally unclear.) That the individual explicitly consents to death is a necessary feature of voluntary euthanasia.

Involuntary euthanasia consists in ending the life of someone contrary to that person's wish. The person killed not only fails to give consent, but expresses the desire not to be killed. No one arguing in favor of nonvoluntary euthanasia holds that involuntary euthanasia is justifiable. Those who oppose both voluntary and nonvoluntary euthanasia often argue that to permit either runs the risk of opening the way for involuntary euthanasia.

Nonvoluntary euthanasia includes those cases in which the decision about death is not made by the person who is to die. Here the person gives no specific consent or instructions, and the decision is made by family, friends, or physicians. The distinction between voluntary and nonvoluntary euthanasia is not always a clear one. Physicians sometimes assume that people are "asking" to die, even when no explicit request has been made. Also, the wishes and attitudes that people express when they are not in extreme life-threatening medical situations may be too vague for us to be certain that they would choose death when they are in such a situation. Is "I never want to be hooked up to one of those machines" an adequate indication that the person who says this does not want to be put on a respirator should she meet with an accident and fall into a comatose state?

If the distinctions made here are accepted as legitimate and relevant, we can distinguish eight cases in which euthanasia becomes a moral decision:

1. Self-administered euthanasia
   a. active
   b. passive
2. Other-administered euthanasia
   a. active and voluntary
   b. active and involuntary
   c. active and nonvoluntary
   d. passive and voluntary
   e. passive and involuntary
   f. passive and nonvoluntary

Even these possibilities don't exhaust the cases euthanasia presents us with. For example, notice that the voluntary–nonvoluntary distinction doesn't appear in connection with self-administered euthanasia in our scheme. Yet it might be argued that it should, for a person's decision to end his life (actively or passively) may well not be a wholly voluntary or free decision. People who are severely depressed by their illness and decide to end their lives, for example, might be thought of as not having made a voluntary choice.

Hence, one might approve of self-administered voluntary euthanasia, yet think that the nonvoluntary form should not be permitted. It should not be allowed not because it is necessarily morally wrong, but because it would not be a genuine decision by the person. The person might be thought to be suffering from a psychiatric disability. Indeed, the current debate about physician-assisted suicide turns, in part, on just this issue.

DEFINING "DEATH"

The advent of new medical technologies, pharmaceutical agents, and modes of treatment raises the question of when we should consider someone dead. Suppose someone's heartbeat, blood pressure, respiration, and liver and kidney functions can be maintained within the normal range of values by medical intervention. Should we still include this individual among living persons, even though she is in an irreversible coma or a chronic vegetative state?

If we consider the individual to be a living person, we need to decide how she ought to be treated. Should she be allowed to die or be maintained by medical means? This is the kind of question faced by families, physicians, and the courts in the Quinlan and Cruzan cases (see the Case Presentations), and it is one faced every day in dozens of unpublicized, though no less agonizing, cases.

But what if an unconscious individual lacking higher cortical functioning is no longer a living person? Could a physician who disconnected a respirator or failed to give an antibiotic be said to have killed a person? If nutrition and hydration are withheld from a "brain dead" individual or even if the individual is given a lethal injection, is it reasonable to say that this is a case of killing? Perhaps the person died when her brain stopped functioning at a certain level. Or perhaps she died when she lapsed into coma.

A practical question that advances in medicine have made even more pressing is when or whether a comatose individual may be regarded as a source of transplant organs. If the individual remains a living person, it may be morally wrong (at least prima facie) to kill him to obtain organs for transplant. But what if the comatose individual is not really alive? What if he is dead already and no longer a person? Then there seem to be no reasonable grounds for objecting to removing his organs and using them to save the lives of those who need them. (See Chapter 7 for a discussion of organ donation.)

Questions like the ones raised here have prompted various attempts to define the notion of death. In the view of many commentators, the traditional notion of death is no longer adequate to serve as a guide to resolving issues about the treatment of individuals who, through disease or accident, have fallen into states in which many of their basic physiological functions can be maintained by medical means, although they remain comatose or lacking in higher-brain function.

Until recently, the traditional notion of death has been enshrined in laws defining crimes such as homicide and manslaughter. Given the change in medical technology, actions like removing a respirator, which might once have been regarded as criminal for causing the death of a person, perhaps should now be viewed in a different way. Perhaps a person may be dead already, even though major physiological systems are still functioning.

Four major notions or concepts of death have emerged during the last two decades. We'll list each of them, but it's important to keep in mind that there is a difference between specifying the concept of death (or, as it is sometimes put, defining "death") and the criteria for determining that the concept fits in particular cases. This is analogous to defining "the best team" as the one winning the most games, then providing criteria for determining what counts as winning a game.

The concepts are merely sketched and the criteria for applying them only hinted at.

1. *Traditional.* A person is dead when he is no longer breathing and his heart is not beating. Hence, death may be defined as the permanent cessation of breathing and blood flow. This notion is sometimes known as the "cardiopulmonary" or "heart-lung criterion" for death.

2. *Whole-brain.* Death is regarded as the irreversible cessation of all brain functions. Essentially, this means that there is no electrical activity in the brain, and even the brain stem is not functioning. Application of the concept depends on the use of electroencephalographic or imaging data.

3. *Higher-brain.* Death is considered to involve the permanent loss of consciousness. Hence, someone in an irreversible coma would be considered dead, even though the brain stem continued to regulate breathing and heartbeat. Clinical, electroencephalographic, and imaging data are relevant to applying the concept. So, too, are statistics concerning the likelihood of the individual's regaining consciousness.

4. *Personhood.* Death occurs when an individual ceases to be a person. This may mean the loss of features that are essential to personal identity or (in some statements) the loss of what is essential to being a person. Criteria for personal identity or for being a person are typically taken to include a complex of such activities as reasoning, remembering, feeling emotion, possessing a sense of the future, interacting with others, and so on. The criteria for applying this concept have more to do with the way an individual functions than with data about his brain.

Technology makes it necessary to take a fresh look at the traditional notion of death, but technology also provides data that have allowed for the development of new notions. It would be pointless, for example, to talk about brain death without having some means to determine when the concept might be satisfied.

The whole-brain concept of death was proposed by the 1981 *Report of the President's Commission for the Study of Ethical Problems in Medicine* and included in the Uniform Death Act. As a consequence, state laws employing the traditional concept of death generally have been modified in keeping with the whole-brain concept.

The whole-brain concept has the advantage of being relatively clear-cut in application. However, applying the concept is not without difficulty and controversy. In the view of some, the concept is too restrictive and so fails to resolve some of the difficulties that prompted the need for a new concept. For example, both Karen

Quinlan and Nancy Cruzan would have been considered alive by the whole-brain criteria. However, those who favor concepts of death based on the loss of higher-brain function or the loss of personhood might argue that both cases were ones in which the affected individuals were, in the respective technical senses, dead.

Furthermore, critics charge, the whole-brain concept is not really as straight-forward in its application as it might seem. Even when there appears to be complete lack of cognitive functioning and even when basic brain-stem functions appear to have disappeared, a brain may remain electrically active to some degree. Isolated cells or groups of cells continue to be alive, and monitoring of the brain yields data that are open to conflicting interpretations.

The higher-brain and personhood concepts face even greater difficulties. Each must formulate criteria that are accepted as nonarbitrary and as sufficient grounds for deciding that an individual is dead. No one has yet solved either of these problems for either of these concepts. The fact that there can be controversy over whole-brain death indicates how much harder it is to get agreement about when higher-brain functions are lost. Also, securing agreement on criteria for determining when an entity either becomes or ceases to be a person is a conceptual difficulty far from being resolved to the satisfaction of most philosophers. (See the discussion of persons in connection with abortion in Chapter 9, "Status of the Fetus" for more on this topic.)

ADVANCE DIRECTIVES

Like so many issues in bioethics, euthanasia has traditionally been discussed only in the back rooms of medicine. Often decisions about whether to allow a patient to die are made by physicians acting on their own authority. Such decisions do not represent so much an arrogant claim to godlike wisdom as an acknowledgment of the physician's obligation to do what is best for the patient.

Most physicians admit that allowing or helping a patient to die is sometimes the best assistance that can be given. Decisions made in this fashion depend on the beliefs and judgment of particular physicians. Because these may differ from those of the patient concerned, it is quite possible that the physician's decision may not reflect the wishes of the patient.

But covert decisions made by a physician acting alone are becoming practices of the past as euthanasia is discussed more widely and openly. Court cases, such as *Quinlan* and *Cruzan,* have both widened the scope of legally permissible actions and reinforced the notion that an individual has a right to refuse or discontinue life-sustaining medical treatment. Such cases have also made it clear that there are limits to the benefits that can be derived from medicine—that, under some conditions, individuals may be better off if everything that technologically can be done is not done. Increasingly, people want to be sure that they have some say in what happens to them should they fall victim to hopeless injury or illness.

One indication of this interest is that the number of states permitting individuals to sign "living wills" or advanced directives has now increased to include all states. The first living-will legislation was the "Natural Death Act," passed by the

California legislature on August 30, 1977. The act is generally representative of all such legislation. It permits a competent adult to sign a directive that will authorize physicians to withhold or discontinue "mechanical" or "artificial" life-support equipment if the person is judged to be "terminal" and if "death is imminent."

The strength of advance directives is that they allow a person to express in an explicit manner how he or she wishes to be treated before treatment is needed. In this way, the autonomy of the individual is recognized. Even though unconscious or comatose, a person can continue to exert control over his or her life. This, in turn, means that physicians need not and should not be the decisive voice in determining the continuation or use of special medical equipment.

Critics of advance-directive legislation have claimed that it does not go far enough in protecting autonomy and making death easier (where this is what is wanted). They point out that the directive specified in the California bill and most others would have made no difference in the case of Karen Quinlan. She had not been diagnosed as having a "terminal condition" at least two weeks prior to being put on a respirator, yet this is one of the requirements of the act. Consequently, the directive would have been irrelevant to her condition.

Nor, for that matter, would those people be allowed to die who wish to, if their disease or injury does not involve treatment by "artificial" or "mechanical" means. Thus, a person suffering from throat cancer would simply have to bear the pain and wait for a "natural" death. Finally, at the moment, some states explicitly exclude nutrition and hydration as medical treatments that can be discontinued. The Supreme Court in the *Cruzan* case accepted the notion that the nutrition received by Nancy Cruzan through a feeding tube implanted in her stomach was a form of medical treatment that could be withdrawn. However, the Court did not rule on the Missouri law that forbids withdrawal. Until this law or some other like it is successfully challenged in court, an advance directive does not necessarily guarantee that such treatment will be discontinued, even when requested.

Limitations of such kinds on living wills have led some writers to recommend that individuals sign a legal instrument known as a durable power of attorney. In such a document, an individual can name someone to act on his behalf should he become legally incompetent to act. Hence, unlike the advance directive, a durable power of attorney allows a surrogate to exercise control over novel and unanticipated situations. For example, the surrogate may order the discontinuation of artificial feeding, something that an advance directive might not permit.

The widespread wish to have some control over the end of one's life is reflected in a federal law that took effect in 1991. The Patient Self-Determination Act is sometimes referred to as a "medical Miranda warning."

It requires that hospitals, nursing homes, and other health-care facilities receiving federal funding provide patients at the time of admission with written information about relevant state laws and the rights of citizens under those laws to refuse or discontinue treatment. Patients must also be told about the practices and policies at that particular institution so they can choose a facility willing to abide by their decisions. The institutions must also record whether a patient has provided a written "advance directive" (e.g., a living will or power of attorney for health care) that will take effect should the patient become incapacitated.

Another sign of change is the recent concern with the medical circumstances in which people die. The medical ideal of a "hospital death," one in which the patient's temperature, pulse rate, and respiration are brought within normal limits by medication and machinery, is being severely challenged. This is reflected in the policy of the AMA that holds that it may be morally appropriate to withhold "all means of life prolonging medical treatment," including artificial feeding, from patients in irreversible comas.

A new ideal of natural death also seems to be emerging. In this view, the kind of support a dying patient needs is psychological counseling and contact with family and friends, rather than heroic medical efforts. An acceptance of death as a normal end of life and the development of new means of caring for the dying may ease the problem of euthanasia. If those who face imminent death are offered an alternative to either euthanasia or an all-out medical effort to preserve their lives, they may choose that alternative. "Death with dignity" need not always mean choosing a lethal injection.

ETHICAL THEORIES AND EUTHANASIA

Roman Catholicism explicitly rejects all forms of euthanasia as being against the natural law duty to preserve life. It considers euthanasia as morally identical with either suicide or murder. This position is not so rigid as it may seem, how-

---

Public Views on Euthanasia

	Agree	Disagree	Neither
1. If a person has a fatal illness, that person should have the right to have all life-sustaining devices removed, including feeding tubes.	79%	12%	9%
2. If a person is in a coma that cannot be reversed, relatives should be allowed to tell doctors to remove all life-sustaining devices, including feeding tubes.	81%	11%	8%
3. In case of fatal illness, doctors should be allowed to help that person end his or her life.	49%	35%	16%
4. If a person has been diagnosed as having a fatal illness, he or she should be allowed to take his or her own life.	39%	45%	16%

Source: *Parade Magazine* (9 February 1992) mail survey of 3750 people aged twenty-one or older; 2203 respondents. Reprinted with permission from *Parade*, copyright © 1992.

ever. The principle of double effect (see Part V: Foundations of Bioethics) makes it morally acceptable to give medication for the relief of pain—even if the indirect result of the medication will be to shorten the life of the recipient. The intended result is not the death of the person but the relief of suffering. The difference in intention is thus considered to be a morally significant one. Those not accepting the principle of double effect would be likely to classify the administration of a substance that would relieve pain but would also cause death as a case of euthanasia.

Furthermore, on the Catholic view there is no moral obligation to continue treatment when a person is medically hopeless. It is legitimate to allow people to die as a result of their illness or injury, even though their lives might be lengthened by the use of extraordinary means. Additionally, we may legitimately make the same decisions about ourselves that we make about others who are in no condition to decide. Thus, without intending to kill ourselves, we may choose measures for the relief of pain that may secondarily hasten our end. Or we may refuse extraordinary treatment and let "nature" take its course, let "God's will" determine the outcome. (See Foundations of Bioethics for a fuller discussion of the Roman Catholic position on euthanasia and extraordinary means of sustaining life.)

At first sight, utilitarianism would seem to endorse euthanasia in all of its forms. Whenever suffering is great and the condition of the person is one without legitimate medical hope, then the principle of utility might be invoked to approve putting the person to death. After all, in such a case we seem to be acting to end suffering and to bring about a state of affairs in which happiness exceeds unhappiness. Thus, whether the person concerned is ourself or another, euthanasia would seem to be a morally right action.

A utilitarian might argue in this way, but this is not the only way in which the principle of utility could be applied. It could be argued, for example, that since life is a necessary condition for happiness, it is wrong to destroy that condition because by doing so the possibility of all future happiness is lost. Furthermore, a rule utilitarian might well argue that a rule like "The taking of a human life is permissible when suffering is intense and the condition of the person permits no legitimate hope" would be open to abuse. Consequently, in the long run the rule would actually work to increase the amount of unhappiness in the world. Obviously, it is not possible to say there is such a thing as "the utilitarian view of euthanasia." The principle of utility supplies a guide for an answer, but it is not itself an answer.

Euthanasia presents a considerable difficulty for Kant's ethics. For Kant, an autonomous rational being has a duty to preserve his or her life. Thus, one cannot rightly refuse needed medical care or commit suicide. Yet our status as autonomous rational beings also endows us with an inherent dignity. If that status is destroyed or severely compromised, as it is when people become comatose and unknowing because of illness or injury, then it is not certain that we have a duty to maintain our lives under such conditions. It may be more in keeping with our freedom and dignity for us to instruct others either to put us to death or to take no steps to keep us alive should we ever be in such a state. Voluntary euthanasia may be compatible with (if not required by) Kant's ethics.

By a similar line of reasoning, it may be that nonvoluntary euthanasia might be seen as a duty that we have to others. We might argue that by putting to death a comatose and hopeless person we are recognizing the dignity that person possessed in his or her previous state. It might also be argued that a human being in a vegetative state is not a person in the relevant moral sense. Thus, our ordinary duty to preserve life does not hold.

According to Ross, we have a strong prima facie obligation not to kill a person except in justifiable self-defense—unless we have an even stronger prima facie moral obligation to do something that cannot be done without killing. Since active euthanasia typically requires taking the life of an innocent person, there is a moral presumption against it. However, another of Ross's prima facie obligations is that we keep promises made to others. Accordingly, if someone who is now in an irreversible coma with no hope of recovery has left instructions that in case of such an event she wishes her life to be ended, then we are under a prima facie obligation to follow her instructions. Thus, in such a case we may be justified in overriding the presumption against taking an innocent life.

What if there are no such instructions? It could be argued that our prima facie obligation of acting beneficently toward others requires us to attempt to determine what someone's wishes would be from what we know about him as a person. We would then treat him the way that we believe that he would want us to. In the absence of any relevant information, we might make the decision on the basis of how a rational person would want to be treated in similar circumstances. Of course, if anyone has left instructions that his life is to be maintained, if possible, under any circumstances, then we have a prima facie obligation to respect this preference also.

SOCIAL CONTEXT
The Physician-Assisted Suicide Law in Oregon

On March 24, 1998, an anonymous woman in her mid-eighties became the first known person to choose physician-assisted suicide under an Oregon law authorizing physicians to prescribe doses of drugs that terminally ill patients can use to end their lives.

The woman, who lived in Portland, died shortly after swallowing a lethal dose of barbiturates, which she washed down with a glass of brandy. She was suffering from terminal breast cancer and had been given less than two months to live. In an audiotape she made two days before her death, she said she "looked forward" to her coming suicide. "I will be relieved of all the stress I have." She said she had grown tired of fighting cancer and had trouble breathing and walking. "I can't see myself living a few more months like this," she said. She died about half an hour after taking the prescribed drugs.

The woman may not have been the first person to commit suicide under the provisions of the law. It allows strict privacy, and the woman's death was made public with her consent by an advocacy group that supports the law.

THE LAW

Oregon's 1994 "Written Request for Medication to End One's Life in a Humane and Dignified Manner" or Death with Dignity Act is the first physician-suicide measure passed by any state. The measure does not permit a physician to play an active role in ending a patient's life. The major provision of the measure is that it allows physicians to prescribe lethal drugs for terminally ill patients without risking criminal prosecution.

The law spells out a set of conditions that must be met by patients and physicians:

1. A primary-care physician and a consulting physician must both agree that the patient has six months or less to live.
2. The patient must make two oral requests (at least forty-eight hours apart) for drugs to use to terminate his or her life.
3. The patient must wait at least fifteen days after the initial oral request, then make a written request to the physician.
4. If either physician thinks the patient has a mental disorder or is suffering from impaired judgment from depression, they must recommend the patient for counseling.
5. The patient can terminate the request at any time during the process.

Under the law, a physician is not permitted to assist a patient to die by any means more active than prescribing a medication that can cause death and indicating the manner in which it can be used. Hence, such practices as lethal injections remain as illegal as before.

A LONG TIME COMING

In 1994 the Oregon law was approved by the slight margin of 52 percent to 48 percent of the vote. Immediately after it was clear that the law had passed, it was challenged in court. The legal wrangles took three years, and in 1997 opponents of the law mounted an effort through a voter initiative to have it repealed. The effort failed, and the law was approved by 60 percent of the voters.

Despite voter approval, physicians were still uncertain about what might happen to them if they acted in accordance with the law and assisted a patient in killing himself. Thomas Constantine, the head of the Drug Enforcement Administration, responding to pressure by two politically conservative members of Congress, announced that the agency would impose severe sanctions on any physicians who prescribed lethal doses of drugs. Constantine claimed that prescribing drugs for use in suicide wasn't a legitimate medical use under the federal drug laws. Although the DEA cannot cancel a physician's license to practice, it has the power to withdraw the license to prescribe drugs. The threat to physicians was thus very real.

It was not until June 1998 that Attorney General Janet Reno removed the final legal obstacle to implementing the Oregon law. The DEA is a branch of the Justice Department, and Reno said the policy statement threatening to take action against physicians who acted in accordance with the Oregon law had been issued without

---

Survey of Oncologists

Support physician-assisted suicide:	22.5%
Taken part in at least one:	10.8%
Taken part in five or more:	18%
Performed euthanasia at least once:	3.7%
Of the previous group, five or more times:	12%
n = 3299	

Source: Survey by Ezekiel Emanuel of Society of Clinical Oncology, *Annals of Internal Medicine*, October, 2000.

---

her knowledge or consent. Overruling Constantine, Reno said the drug laws were intended to block illicit drug dealing and that there was no evidence that Congress ever meant for the DEA to have a role in resolving the moral problems presented by the Oregon law.

The law explicitly protects only physicians from prosecution. Hence, it leaves in doubt the legal status of nurses. Many terminally ill patients are paralyzed or too weak to take prescribed medications without assistance. Nurses typically help patients take prescribed medications, but what if they help the patient take a lethal dose of drugs? Does this make them liable for legal prosecution?

Also, from a moral point of view, if a nurse is opposed to euthanasia or suicide, does the general responsibility he has to assist a patient require him to help the patient take lethal drugs? Nurses in Oregon are facing these questions, although apparently very few (if any) have had to deal with them in a practical way.

Some pharmacists in Oregon also have trouble with the physician-assisted suicide law. Because they must fill the prescriptions written by physicians, the law makes them, to an extent, participants in the suicide. Some have argued that drugs prescribed for potential use in a suicide should be labeled as such on the prescription. That way pharmacists who object to assisted suicide can avoid becoming involved in one. The prescription could be filled by some other pharmacist.

Physicians object to this proposal, though. They point out that if prescriptions were labelled as potential suicide agents, then the patient's confidentiality would be violated. Particularly in small towns, if word got out, the families of those who chose assisted suicide might become the targets of public criticism or worse.

In March 1998, Oregon state officials decided to make physician-assisted suicide available to residents who cannot pay for it under the state's Medicaid program. The state will have to bear the full cost, because by law federal funds cannot be used to pay for physician-assisted suicide.

Critics claim that the use of state funds is a tacit endorsement of suicide, while supporters claim it is only an extension of the "comfort care" already covered by Medicaid. Those who believe mental health services are underfunded think that supporting physician-assisted suicide is a serious mistake. It suggests to patients that death is the only help available to them. Some observers believe the Oregon legislature will remove physician-assisted suicide as a procedure covered by the state's Medicaid plan.

IS THE LAW NEEDED?

Proponents of the Oregon law would like to see other states pass similar legislation. They point out that terminally-ill people who decide to end their lives are often frustrated in carrying out their wishes, even though the society has endorsed in principle a "right to die."

The federal Patient Self-Determination Act requires hospitals to inform patients that they have the right to refuse or discontinue treatment and that by living wills and powers of attorney for health care, they can put their decisions into practice. The Supreme Court in the *Cruzan* decision implicitly acknowledges a "right to die," in that it permits the withdrawal of life-sustaining treatment when clear and compelling evidence shows that this reflects the wishes of an individual. Yet despite the legal possibility of exercising control over medical care during the last stages of one's life, various barriers stand in the way of actual control:

◆ Surveys of physicians and health-care workers show that many are not aware of the legal options open to patients or are not willing to respect them. Many in health care are not aware of laws that allow them to withhold or discontinue such care as mechanical ventilation, kidney dialysis, or even feeding tubes. Many believe that once a treatment has been started, it is illegal to discontinue it. Courts have repeatedly upheld the right of individuals to decide that, at a certain point in their treatment, they do not want to be provided with food or water, yet 42 percent of health-care workers rejected this as an option patients could choose.

◆ Many physicians and hospitals simply ignore the oral instructions patients give them about discontinuing their care. In one study of over 4000 seriously ill patients, researchers found that while a third of the patients asked not to be revived by cardiopulmonary resuscitation, 50 percent of the time, "Do not resuscitate" was never written in their charts.

◆ The living wills or powers of attorney made out by patients may not be followed in practice. In a 1997 study of 4804 terminally ill patients, only 688 had written directives, and only 22 of these contained instructions explicit enough to guide the care they received. Even these instuctions were ignored about half the time, and physicians knew about the patient's instructions only about a quarter of the time.

Also, advance directives are sometimes not included among the documents constituting a patient's medical chart. In another study, when seventy-one patients were moved to a nursing home, twenty-five of them had living wills that were not sent with them.

As a result, despite the efforts patients may make to control what happens to them at the end of their lives, they may be forced to accept decisions about their care made by physicians or nurses in accordance with their own values or institutional policies.

◆ Families may override the wishes expressed by patients in their living wills. Even though the views of the patient take legal precedence over those of a relative, in practice a physician or hospital may do as the relative wishes. Families never sue because of the overtreatment of a patient, but they do because of withholding or discontinuing treatment.

Laws like the one in Oregon are viewed by many as the only way patients can be sure that in the final days of their lives they can exercise control. Many fear that if they enter a hospital, they cannot trust nurses and physicians to know their wishes and to respect them.

The extent of the desire people have to exercise control over how their lives end is shown by the popularity of Derek Humphry's best-selling *Final Exit*. The book is a guide to effective methods for committing suicide or, as the subtitle puts it, the book is about "The Practicalities of Self-Deliverance and Assisted Suicide for the Dying."

Journalist Betty Rollins's foreword to the book describes the hundreds of letters she received from people who read her book, *Last Wish*, on her mother's suicide because of a terminal illness. The saddest of the letters, she said, were from those who had tried to die, failed in their attempt, and suffered even more as a result. "Until there is a law which would allow physicians to help these people who want a final exit, there is Derek Humphry's book, fittingly named, to guide them."

Various polls suggest that nearly a majority of the American people favor a policy of voluntary physician-assisted suicide, and in cases less well known than the Kevorkian case, in which physicians have been charged with aiding the death of their patients, they have typically been found not guilty or been given suspended sentences.

HOW MANY CASES?

The Oregon law is written so that only Oregon residents can ask physicians to assist them in suicide under the stipulated conditions. Thus, sick people have not migrated to the state with the idea of getting a physician's help in killing themselves.

Although the way seems clear for any terminally ill Oregon resident to seek help in dying, so far few people seem to have done so. In February 1999 state officials reported that in the first year under the new law, fifteen people in the state ended their lives with drugs legally prescribed for that purpose. (There were 29,000 deaths in Oregon in 1998.) The average age of the eight men and seven women was 69. Thirteen had cancer, one congestive heart failure, and the other chronic lung disease. Fourteen had lived in the state at least six months, and one had come to be with family members.

Eight other people in 1998 were certified as terminally ill and had received authorization to receive lethal doses of drugs, but six died of their diseases without taking the medications. The other two were still alive at the end of the year. For the fifteen who acted under the law, the cause of death was listed as "Drug overdose, legally prescribed."

In 2000, forty-four people obtained drugs under the Death with Dignity legislation, but only twenty-one used them. This was down from twenty-seven people the previous year, the same figure as for 1998. So far only about 125 people have ended their lives with assistance.

According to a state report, those choosing physician-assisted suicide were "not disproportionately poor, uneducated, uninsured, fearful of the financial consequences of their illnesses" or "lacking end-of-life care." The primary factor mentioned by individuals was "the importance of autonomy and personal control."

Neither financial worries nor the pain of a long illness was mentioned by them as a decisive factor.

The average time to unconsciousness after taking the prescribed drugs was 5 minutes (with a range of 3 to 20), and the average time to death was 26 minutes (with a range of 15 minutes to 11.5 hours).

That relatively few have taken advantage of the Oregon law may support the idea of those favoring it that most people simply want to know that if they are terminally ill and in pain, a way out is available to them. To this extent, then, the Oregon experience may support the movement in other states to allow physician-assisted suicide.

NEW FEDERAL ACTIONS

In November 2001, Attorney General Ashcroft sent a letter to the Drug Enforcement Agency authorizing agents to take legal action against physicians prescribing drugs for the purpose of ending the lives of terminally ill patients.

Ashcroft wrote that "prescribing, dispensing or administering federally controlled substances to assist suicide" is "not a legitimate medical purpose" and so would violate the 1970 federal Controlled Substances Act. He thus reinstalled the roadblock to the Oregon law that Janet Reno had lifted in 1997.

Critics of Ashcroft claimed he had wrongly interpreted the Act. It is supposed to prevent the illegal trafficking in drugs, not interfere with a state's right to regulate the practice of medicine.

The State of Oregon filed suit against the Justice Department in the Federal District Court in Portland. Justice Robert E. Jones issued a restraining order keeping Ashcroft's directive from being followed. The outcome of the trial will determine the immediate status of the Oregon law. Ultimately, however, it may take a Supreme Court ruling to settle the issue.

CASE PRESENTATION

The Cruzan *Case: The Supreme Court Upholds the Right to Die in a Landmark Decision*

In the early morning of January 11, 1983, twenty-five-year-old Nancy Cruzan was driving on a deserted county road in Missouri. The road was icy and the car skidded, then flipped over and crashed. Nancy was thrown from the driver's seat and landed face down in a ditch by the side of the road.

An ambulance arrived quickly, but not quickly enough to save her from suffering irreversible brain damage. Nancy never regained consciousness, and her physicians eventually concluded that she had entered into what is known medically as a persistent vegetative state, awake but unaware. The higher brain functions responsible for recognition, memory, comprehension, anticipation, and other cognitive functions had all been lost.

Her arms and legs were drawn into a fetal position, her knees against her chest, and her body stiff and contracted. Only loud sounds and painful stimuli evoked responses, but even those were no more than neurological reflexes.

"We've literally cried over Nancy's body, and we've never seen anything," her father, Joe Cruzan, said. "She has no awareness of herself."

Nancy was incapable of eating, but her body was sustained by a feeding tube surgically implanted in her stomach. She was a patient at the Missouri Rehabilitation Center, but no one expected her to be rehabilitated. She could only be kept alive.

"If only the ambulance had arrived five minutes earlier—or five minutes later," her father lamented.

The cost of Nancy Cruzan's care was $130,000 a year. The bill was paid by the state. Because she was a legal adult when her accident occurred, her family was not responsible for her medical care. Had she been under twenty-one, the Cruzans would have been responsible for her medical bills, as long as they had any financial resources to pay them.

EIGHT YEARS LATER

In 1991, eight years after her accident, Nancy was almost thirty-three years old, and her physicians estimated she might live another thirty years. She was like some 10,000 other Americans who are lost in the dark, dimensionless limbo lying between living and dying. Those who love them can think of them only with sadness and despair. Given a choice between lingering in this twilight world and dying, most people find it difficult to imagine anyone would choose not to die.

Hope eventually faded even for Nancy Cruzan's parents. They faced the fact she would never recover her awareness, and the time came when they wanted their daughter to die, rather than be kept alive in her hopeless condition. They asked that the feeding tube used to keep her alive be withdrawn. Officials at the Missouri Rehabilitation Center refused, and Joe and Louise Cruzan were forced to go to court.

LOWER COURT DECISIONS

During the court hearings, the family testified that Nancy would not have wanted to be kept alive in her present condition. Her sister Christy said Nancy had told her that she never wanted to be kept alive "just as a vegetable." A friend testified that Nancy had said that if she were injured or sick she wouldn't want to continue her life, unless she could live "half-way normally." Family and friends spoke in general terms of Nancy's vigor and her sense of independence.

In July 1988, Judge Charles E. Teel of the Jasper County Circuit Court ruled that artificially prolonging the life of Nancy Cruzan violated her constitutional right. As he wrote, "There is a fundamental right expressed in our Constitution as 'the right to liberty,' which permits an individual to refuse or direct the withholding or withdrawal of artificial death-prolonging procedures when the person has no cognitive brain function."

Missouri Attorney General William Webster said Judge Teel's interpretation of the Missouri living-will law was much broader than the legislature intended and appealed the ruling. In November 1988, the Missouri Supreme Court in a 4-to-3 decision overruled the decision of the lower court—Nancy Cruzan's parents would not be allowed to disconnect the feeding tube.

The court focused on the state's living-will statute. The law permits the withdrawing of artificial life-support systems in cases in which individuals are hopelessly ill or injured and there is "clear and convincing evidence" this is what they would want done. The act specifically forbids the withholding of food and water. Judge Teel's reasoning in the lower court decision was that the surgically implanted tube was an invasive medical treatment that the Missouri law permitted her parents, as guardians, to order it withdrawn.

The Missouri Supreme Court held that the evidence as to what Nancy Cruzan would have wanted did not meet the "clear and convincing" standard required by the law. Also, the evidence did not show that the implanted feeding tube was "heroically invasive" or "burdensome." In the circumstance, then, the state's interest in preserving life should override other considerations.

The court found "no principled legal basis" to permit the Cruzans "to choose the death of their ward." Thus, "in the face of the state's strongly stated policy in favor of life, we choose to err on the side of life, respecting the right of incompetent persons who may wish to live despite a severely diminished quality of life." William Colby, the Cruzans' attorney, appealed the ruling to the United States Supreme Court, and for the first time the Court agreed to hear a case involving "right to die" issues.

SUPREME COURT DECISION

On June 25, 1990, the Supreme Court issued a landmark ruling. In a 5-to-4 decision, it rejected Colby's argument that the Court should overturn as unconstitutional the State of Missouri's stringent standard requiring "clear and convincing evidence" as to a comatose patient's wishes. The decision came as a cruel disappointment to Nancy Cruzan's parents, because it meant they had lost their case.

Yet for the first time in U.S. judicial history, the Court recognized a strong constitutional basis for living wills and for the designation of another person to act as a surrogate in making medical decisions on behalf of another. Unlike the decisions in *Roe v. Wade* and *Quinlan*, which found a right of privacy in the Constitution, the Court decision in *Cruzan* appealed to a Fourteenth Amendment "liberty interest." The interest involves being free to reject unwanted medical treatment. The Court found grounds for this interest in the common-law tradition, according to which, if one person even touches another without consent or legal justification, then battery is committed.

The Court regarded this as the basis for requiring that a patient give informed consent to medical treatment. The "logical corollary" of informed consent, the Court held, is that the patient also possesses the right to withhold consent. A difficulty arises, though, when a patient is in no condition to give consent. The problem becomes one of knowing what the patient's wishes would be.

Justice Rehnquist, in the majority opinion, held that the Constitution permits states to decide on the standard that must be met in determining the wishes of a comatose patient. Hence, Missouri's rigorous standard that requires "clear and convincing proof" of the wishes of the patient was allowed to stand. The Court held that it was legitimate for the state to err on the side of caution, "because an erroneous decision not to terminate treatment results in the maintenance of the status quo," while an erroneous decision to end treatment "is not susceptible of correction."

Justice William Brennan dissented strongly from this line of reasoning. He pointed out that making a mistake about a comatose patient's wishes and continuing treatment also has a serious consequence. Maintaining the status quo "robs a patient of the very qualities protected by the right to avoid unwanted medical treatment."

Justice Stevens, in another dissent, argued that the Court's focus on how much weight to give previous statements by the patient missed the point. The Court should have focused on the issue of the best interest of the patient. Otherwise, the only people eligible to exercise their constitutional right to be free of unwanted medical treatment are those "who had the foresight to make an unambiguous statement of their wishes while competent."

One of the more significant aspects of the decision was that the Court made no distinction between providing nutrition and hydration and other forms of medical treatment. One argument on behalf of the state was that providing food and water was not medical treatment. However, briefs filed by medical associations made it clear that determining the formula required by a person in Nancy Cruzan's condition and regulating her feeding are medically complex procedures. The situation is more comparable to determining the contents of an intravenous drip than to giving someone food and water.

The Missouri living-will statute explicitly forbids the withdrawal of food and water. However, the law was not directly at issue in the *Cruzan* case, because Nancy Cruzan's accident occurred before the law was passed. The Court's treatment of nutrition and hydration as just another form of medical treatment has since served as a basis for challenging the constitutionality of the Missouri law, as well as laws in other states containing a similar provision.

The Supreme Court decision placed much emphasis on the wishes of the individual in accepting or rejecting medical treatment. In doing so, it underscored the importance of the living will as a way of indicating our wishes, if something should happen to render us incapable of making them known directly. In some states, though, living wills have a legal force only when the individual has a terminal illness (Nancy Cruzan did not) or when the individual has been quite specific about what treatments are unwanted. Because of such limitations, some legal observers recommend that individuals sign a durable power of attorney designating someone to make medical decisions for them if they become legally incompetent.

The Court decision left undecided the question of the constitutionality of assisted suicide. Some state courts have held that, although individuals have a right to die, they do not have a right to the assistance of others in killing themselves. While more than twenty states have passed laws against assisted suicide, only Oregon has made it legal for physicians to prescribe drugs to help patients end their lives.

A FINAL COURT RULING

What of Nancy Cruzan? The State of Missouri withdrew from the case, and both the family's attorney and the state-appointed guardian filed separate briefs with the Jasper County Circuit Court asking that the implanted feeding tube be removed. A hearing was held to consider both her medical condition and evidence from family and friends about what Nancy Cruzan would wish to be done. On December 14, 1990, Judge Charles Teel ruled that there was evidence to show that her intent, "if mentally able, would be to terminate her nutrition and hydration," and he authorized the request to remove the feeding tube.

Even after the tube was removed, controversy did not end. About twenty-five protesters tried to force their way into Nancy Cruzan's hospital room to reconnect the feeding tube. "The best we can do is not cooperate with anyone trying to starve an innocent person to death," one of the protest leaders said.

Twelve days after the tube was removed, on December 26, 1990, Nancy Cruzan died. Her parents, sisters, and grandparents were at her bedside. Almost eight years had passed since the accident that destroyed her brain and made the remainder of her life a matter of debate.

"We all feel good that Nancy is free at last," her father said at her graveside.

The *Cruzan decision,* by acknowledging a "right to die" and by finding a basis for it in the Constitution, provides states with new opportunities to resolve the issues surrounding the thousands of cases as tragic as Nancy Cruzan's.

CASE PRESENTATION

Dr. Jack Kevorkian: Physician-Assisted Suicide Activist

On August 5, 1993, Thomas W. Hyde, Jr., a thirty-year-old Michigan construction worker with a wife and a two-year-old daughter, was taken inside a battered white 1968 Volkswagen bus parked behind the apartment building in the Detroit suburb of Royal Oak where sixty-five-year-old retired pathologist Dr. Jack Kevorkian lived.

Dr. Kevorkian fitted a respiratory mask over Hyde's face and connected the plastic tubing leading from the mask to a short cylinder of carbon monoxide gas. Dr. Kevorkian placed a string in Hyde's hand. At the opposite end of the string was a paper clip crimping the plastic tubing and shutting off the flow of gas. Hyde jerked on the string, pulled loose the paper clip, then breathed in the carbon monoxide flowing into the mask. Twenty minutes later, he was dead.

Mr. Hyde suffered from amyotrophic lateral sclerosis (Lou Gehrig's disease), a degenerative and progressive neurological disorder. He was paralyzed, unable even to swallow, and, without suctioning, he would have choked to death on his own saliva. He reported that he was in great pain, and like hundreds before him, he approached Dr. Kevorkian to help him end his life.

In a videotape made on July 1, 1993, Mr. Hyde said to Dr. Kevorkian, "I want to end this. I want to die." Dr. Kevorkian agreed to help, and Mr. Hyde became the twentieth person since 1990 whom Dr. Kevorkian had assisted in committing suicide.

TRIAL

After the death of Thomas Hyde, Dr. Kevorkian was arrested and charged with violating the 1992 Michigan law that had been enacted specifically to stop his activities. The law applies to anyone who knows another person intends to commit suicide and either "provides the physical means" or "participates in a physical act" by which the suicide is carried out. However, the law explicitly excludes those administering medications or procedures that may cause death, "if the intent is to relieve pain or discomfort."

On May 2, 1994, a jury found Dr. Kevorkian was innocent of the charge of assisting suicide. As one juror said, "He convinced us he was not a murderer, that he was really trying to help people out." According to another, Dr. Kevorkian had acted to relieve Mr. Hyde's pain, and that is allowed by the law.

Several jurors expressed skepticism and resentment at the attempt to legislate behavior falling within such a private sphere. "I don't feel it's our obligation to choose for someone else how much pain and suffering they can go through," one said. "That's between them and their God."

After the decision, Dr. Kevorkian reiterated his position that people have a right to decide when to end their lives. He acted, he said, to protect that right. "I want that option as I get older, and I want it unencumbered, unintimidated, free with my medical colleagues," he said. "So I did it for myself, too, just as any competent adult would want to do."

Kevorkian always insisted he practiced physician-assisted suicide only in accordance with stringent safeguards. "You act only after it is absolutely justifiable," he said. "The patient must be mentally competent, the disease incurable." He maintained that other physicians should determine that a candidate for assisted suicide was incurable and that a psychiatrist assess the patient's mental state and determine that he or she was competent. In practice, Kevorkian did not proceed in this fashion, because other physicians refused to cooperate with him.

CRITICS

Critics charged that without the safeguard of a psychiatric evaluation, patients who sought out Kevorkian to help them kill themselves were likely to be suffering from depression. Hence, they couldn't be regarded as having made an informed, rational decision to end their lives.

Other critics worried that, if physicians are allowed to play a role in terminating the lives of patients, that role could expand. Physicians might begin by assisting those who ask their help, but then move on to making their own decisions about who should live. Or they might even be recruited to carry out a government policy identifying those who should be "assisted" in dying. The potential for abuse is so serious physicians should not be associated in any way with procedures intended to end the lives of patients.

Finally, some critics, though disagreeing with Kevorkian, believed he had successfully pointed out a major flaw in the health-care system—the medical profession is so committed to preserving life it has not developed ways of dealing with death in cases in which it is inevitable. Rather than help people kill themselves, critics said, physicians ought to surrender the idea of treatment and concentrate on making those with terminal illnesses pain free so they could spend their remaining time enjoying the comfort of their families and friends.

It was in keeping with such an aim that hospitals and other institutions set up hospices to provide nursing care and support for the dying. Even after decades, however, hospices remain at the margins of the medical establishment, and physicians associated with them are given little respect by their colleagues.

A CHARGE OF MURDER

In 1998 the Michigan Department of Consumer and Industry Services, the state agency responsible for licensing physicians, charged that Jack Kevorkian was practicing medicine without a license by assisting forty-two people in committing suicide. (Kevorkian said he assisted about 120 people.)

Although the agency had issued a cease-and-desist order, Kevorkian continued to help terminally ill people die. The Michigan legislature, that same year, passed a law making assisting in suicide a crime, but Kevorkian announced he would continue his activities, despite the law.

In September 1998, Dr. Kevorkian administered a lethal injection to Thomas Youk, a fifty-two-year-old man in an advanced stage of the motor neuron disease ALS (amyotrophic lateral sclerosis). For the first time, Kevorkian by his own direct action caused the death of a person, thus moving from physician-assisted suicide to active euthanasia.

Kevorkian videotaped the event and offered the tape to the CBS program *Sixty Minutes,* which broadcast excerpts from the tape on national television on November 22. About 15.6 million households watched the program.

Kevorkian said he had given the tape to CBS in the hope that it would lead to his arrest and become a test case for assisted suicide and active euthanasia.

"I want a showdown," Kevorkian told a reporter. "I want to be prosecuted for euthanasia. I am going to prove that this is not a crime, ever, regardless of what words are written on paper."

On November 25, the prosecutor of Oakland County, Michigan, filed first-degree murder charges against Jack Kevorkian. David G. Gorcyca, the prosecutor, said that Dr. Kevorkian's actions clearly fit the definition of premeditated murder and that the consent of the man killed was no legal defense.

On April 13, 1999, Jack Kevorkian was found guilty of second-degree murder and sentenced to a prison term of ten to twenty-five years. "This trial was not an opportunity for a referendum," Judge Jessica Cooper said at the sentencing.

Those sympathetic to Jack Kevorkian believe he did more than anyone else to force society to face an issue it has chosen to ignore. His critics believe he made a circus of what should be a serious and deliberative discussion.

CASE PRESENTATION

A Canadian Tragedy

Robert Latimer admitted that he killed his twelve-year-old daughter Tracy by putting her in the cab of his pickup truck, then rolling up the windows and letting the engine run until the cab filled up with deadly carbon monoxide gas.

But he said he did it because he loved her.

Tracy was born with cerebral palsy, a birth-disorder involving physical and sometimes mental impairments of varying degrees of severity. A year before she died, Tracy's father said she had been "a happy little girl," living with her parents and three siblings on a 1280-acre wheat and canola farm in Saskatchewan, Canada. Then she had surgery that was supposed to improve her condition. Instead, it turned her into a child who was in constant agony and who could not walk, talk, or feed herself. She lost so much weight that at the time of her death she weighed only forty pounds.

Yet Tracy's doctors wanted her to have additional surgery. They wanted to do extensive surgery on her hip to stabilize the metal rods they had inserted into her back to help her stay upright. They also wanted to insert a feeding tube into her stomach, because the antiseizure medication she had to take interfered with her appetite and her digestion. That was when Bob Latimer decided Tracy would be better off dead.

Latimer was charged with second-degree murder, and found guilty by a jury in 1994. The conviction was overturned on a technicality, and although he was convicted a second time, the jury made it clear they had done so reluctantly and only because they were required to consider only the facts presented in court. They took the unusual step of asking the judge to sentence Latimer to only one year in prison.

The general public was as sympathetic toward Latimer as the jury. "Bob Latimer is not a murderer, and he's no threat to society," said one of his neighbors. "It's a shame to take him away from his family and lock him up."

But advocates for the disabled did not share the jury's and public's forgiving attitude toward Latimer. In their view, he deserved to be given a stiff prison term to make it clear that the lives of severely disabled people are worth just as much as the lives of others.

"If you can make your own choice, that's a different thing," said Ron Bort, the president of the local chapter of Voice of People with Disabilities. "For someone else to decide your life is not worth living—that's the scary part."

The point was echoed by the vice president of another advocacy group, the Canadian Association for Community Living. "Tracy Latimer did not choose to die," Diane Richler said. "She was murdered, and justice should be served."

Latimer told a reporter he had felt he had no choice. "People are saying this is a handicap issue, but they're wrong," he said. "This was a torture issue. It was about mutilation and torture for Tracy. She had bedsores, she was in pain all the time, and she wasn't eating well. With the combination of a feeding tube, rods in her back, her leg cut and flopping around, and bedsores, how can people say she was a happy little girl?"

Latimer said he and his wife were never concerned with any legal problems he might have by causing Tracy's death. "We were just concerned with Tracy," he said.

The Canadian Senate debated in 1995 the question of whether a special category should be introduced into the criminal code to cover cases of "mercy killing" like that carried out by Robert Latimer. While a recommendation for such a change was drafted, the law was never changed.

Consequently, despite the jury's wishes, Robert Latimer's conviction of second-degree murder carried with it a mandatory sentence of twenty-five years in prison, with no possibility of parole until after ten years.

CASE PRESENTATION

The Lingering Death of Baby Owens

On a chilly December evening in 1976, Dr. Joan Owens pushed through the plate glass doors of Midwestern Medical Center and walked over to the admitting desk. Dr. Owens was a physician in private practice and regularly visited Midwestern to attend to her patients.

But this night was different. Dr. Owens was coming to the hospital to be admitted as a patient. She was pregnant, and shortly after 9:00 she began having periodic uterine contractions. Dr. Owens recognized them as the beginnings of labor pains. She was sure of this not only because of her medical knowledge, but because the pains followed the same pattern they had before her three other children were born.

While her husband, Phillip, parked the car, Dr. Owens went through the formalities of admission. She was not particularly worried, for the birth of her other children had been quite normal and uneventful. But the pains were coming more frequently now, and she was relieved when she completed the admission process and was taken to her room. Phillip came with her, bringing her small blue suitcase of personal belongings.

At 11:30 that evening, Dr. Owens gave birth to a 4.5-pound baby girl. The plastic bracelet fastened around her wrist identified her as Baby Owens.

BAD NEWS

Dr. Owens was groggy from exhaustion and from the medication she had received. But when the baby was shown to her, she saw at once that it was not normal. The baby's head was misshapen and the skin around her eyes strangely formed.

Dr. Owens recognized that her daughter had Down syndrome.

"Clarence," she called to her obstetrician. "Is the baby mongoloid?"

"We'll talk about it after your recovery," Dr. Clarence Ziner said.

"Tell me now," said Dr. Owens. "Examine it!"

Dr. Ziner made a hasty examination of the child. He had already seen that Dr. Owens was right and was doing no more than making doubly certain. A more careful examination would have to be done later.

When Dr. Ziner confirmed Joan Owens's suspicion, she did not hesitate to say what she was thinking. "Get rid of it," she told Dr. Ziner. "I don't want a mongoloid child."

Dr. Ziner tried to be soothing. "Just sleep for a while now," he told her. "We'll talk about it later."

Four hours later, a little before 5:00 in the morning and before it was fully light, Joan Owens woke up. Phillip was with her, and he had more bad news to tell. A more detailed examination had shown that the child's small intestine had failed to develop properly and was closed off in one place—the condition known as *duodenal atresia*. It could be corrected by a relatively simple surgical procedure, but until the surgery was performed the child could not be fed. Phillip had refused to consent to the operation until he had talked to his wife. Joan Owens had not changed her mind: She did not want the child.

"It wouldn't be fair to the other children to raise them with a mongoloid," she told Phillip. "It would take all of our time, and we wouldn't be able to give David, Sean, and Melinda the love and attention they need."

"I'm willing to do whatever you think best," Phillip said. "But what can we do?"

"Let the child die," Joan said. "If we don't consent to the surgery, the baby will die soon. And that's what we have to let happen."

Phillip put in a call for Dr. Ziner, and, when he arrived in Joan's room, they told him of their decision. He was not pleased with it.

"The surgery has very low risk," he said. "The baby's life can almost certainly be saved. We can't tell how retarded she'll be, but most DS children get along quite well with help from their families. The whole family will grow to love her."

"I know," Joan said. "And I don't want that to happen. I don't want us to center our lives around a defective child. Phillip and I and our other children will be forced to lose out on many of life's pleasures and possibilities."

"We've made up our minds," Phillip said. "We don't want the surgery."

"I'm not sure the matter is as simple as that," Dr. Ziner said. "I'm not sure we can legally just let the baby die. I'll have to talk to the Director and the hospital attorney."

APPLYING FOR A COURT ORDER

At 6:00 in the morning, Dr. Ziner called Dr. Felix Entraglo, the director of Midwestern Medical Center, and Isaac Putnam, the head of the center's legal staff. They agreed to meet at 9:00 to talk over the problem presented to them by the Owenses.

They met for two hours. It was Putnam's opinion that the hospital would not be legally liable if Baby Owens were allowed to die because her parents refused to give consent for necessary surgery.

"What about getting a court order requiring surgery?" Dr. Entraglo asked. "That's the sort of thing we do when an infant requires a blood transfusion or immunization and his parents' religious beliefs make them refuse consent."

"This case is not exactly parallel," said Mr. Putnam. "Here we're talking about getting a court to force parents to allow surgery to save the life of a defective infant. The infant will still be defective after the surgery, and I think a court would be reluctant to make a family undergo significant emotional and financial hardships when the parents have seriously deliberated about the matter and decided against surgery."

"But doesn't the child have some claim in this situation?" Dr. Ziner asked.

"That's not clear," said Mr. Putnam. "In general we assume that parents will act for the sake of their child's welfare, and when they are reluctant to do so we look to the courts to act for the child's welfare. But in a situation like this . . . who can say? Is the Owens baby really a person in any legal or moral sense?"

"I think I can understand why a court would hesitate to order surgery," said Dr. Entraglo. "What sort of life would it be for a family when they had been pressured into accepting a child they didn't want? It would turn a family into a cauldron of guilt and resentment mixed in with love and concern. In this case, the lives of five normal people would be profoundly altered for the worse."

"So we just stand by and let the baby die?" asked Dr. Ziner.

"I'm afraid so," Dr. Entraglo said.

THE FINAL DAYS

It took twelve days for Baby Owens to die. Her lips and throat were moistened with water to lessen her suffering, and in a small disused room set apart from the rooms of patients, she was allowed to starve to death.

Many nurses and physicians thought it was wrong that Baby Owens was forced to die such a lingering death. Some thought it was wrong for her to have to die at all, but such a protracted death seemed needlessly cruel. Yet they were cautioned by Dr. Entraglo that anything done to shorten the baby's life would probably constitute a criminal action. Thus, fear of being charged with a crime kept the staff from administering any medication to Baby Owens.

The burden of caring for the dying baby fell on the nurses in the obstetrics ward. The physicians avoided the child entirely, and it was the nurses who had to see to it that she received her water and was turned in her bed. This was the source of much resentment among the nursing staff, and a few nurses refused to have anything to do with the dying child. Most kept their ministrations to an absolute minimum.

But one nurse, Sara Ann Moberley, was determined to make Baby Owens's last days as comfortable as possible. She held the baby, rocked her, and talked soothingly to her when she cried. Doing all for the baby that she could do soothed Sara Ann as well.

But even Sara Ann was glad when Baby Owens died. "It was a relief to me," she said. "I almost couldn't bear the frustration of sitting there day after day and doing nothing that could really help her."

The baby's parents took responsibility for disposing of her body.

SOCIAL CONTEXT
Physician-Assisted Suicide: The Dutch Experience

In 2000 the Dutch Parliament passed a law establishing specific rules to allow physicians to assist in the suicide of a terminally ill patient or to kill the patient at the patient's explicit request without risking criminal prosecution. The new law gives a new legal status to a practice that has been followed in the Netherlands for almost fifteen years.

Under a 1993 act, ending a patient's life or assisting in suicide remained illegal, although the law provided physicians with protection from prosecution, if they followed the provisions of the law. The Dutch criminal code previously provided as much as twelve years in prison for anyone who "takes the life of another at his or her explicit and serious request."

In a 1972 case involving a physician who put her mother to death at the mother's request, however, a court refused to impose a penalty. Since then and with the reenforcement of a major court decision in 1984, the extralegal practice of voluntary, active, physician-administered euthanasia became established in the Netherlands. The new legislation made the Netherlands the first nation to legalize assisted suicide.

CONDITIONS

The 2000 law, following the provisions of the 1993 legislation, requires that a physician follow an extensive checklist to avoid prosecution. The safeguards built into the law include the following:

1. Patient-initiated request. The physician must be convinced that the patient's request for euthanasia is "voluntary and well-considered." The request must be made entirely of the patient's own free will and not under pressure from others, including family, friends, or physicians. The patient must make the request personally, and relatives cannot make a request on behalf of a patient.

2. Patient competence. At the time of the decision, the patient must be in a rational state of mind and able to make informed decisions. Those who suffer from dementia or are in a coma are not candidates for euthanasia.

3. Patient understanding. The patient must have a correct and clear understanding of his or her situation and prognosis.

4. Informed as to alternatives. The patient must be informed about alternatives to assisted-suicide or euthanasia. The patient should then be encouraged to discuss them with physicians, family, and advisors.

5. Enduring decision. Requests to physicians made on impulse or ones that may be the result of depression cannot be regarded as legitimate.

6. Unbearable suffering. "The patient must experience his or her suffering as perpetual, unbearable, and hopeless." The physician must be able to make the reasonable judgment that the suffering the patient is experiencing is unendurable. The patient's condition does not have to be terminal.

7. Professional consultation. The physician must consult with at least one other physician who has had experience in dealing with patients requesting euthanasia or help in dying.

8. Medically appropriate. The physician must end the patient's life in a medically appropriate manner.

9. Government report. The physician must submit a report to the government in which the patient's medical history is presented and the physician declares that all the conditions required for assisting in suicide or performing euthanasia have been observed.

The patient must also sign a witnessed explicit authorization for the act to be carried out. Typically, the physician then injects a barbiturate to induce sleep, combined with curare to produce death.

MINORS EXCLUDED

Part of the initial bill would make it possible, in exceptional cases, for minors between the ages of twelve and sixteen to request euthanasia against the wishes of their parents. This provision of the bill was strongly criticized and was eventually withdrawn.

STATISTICS

A study conducted by the Dutch government reported that in 1990 there were 2300 deaths by voluntary euthanasia and about 400 cases of assisted suicide. These represented some 2 percent of the total number of deaths in the Netherlands that year. The report also indicated that physicians had reported a total of 9000 requests for euthanasia. Apparently, a majority of requests were turned down.

Between 1990 and 1995, cases of euthanasia rose from 1.8 percent of total deaths to 2.4 percent, but the proportion of cases involving physician-assisted suicide remained about the same.

A preliminary report indicates that 2216 patients were assisted in ending their lives by physicians in 1999, but the actual number is thought to be closer to 5000. (Evidence indicates that, as a rule, only half the cases of physician-assisted suicide are reported.) Almost nine out of ten of the reported cases involved people in the final stages of cancer.

Despite the new law and the fact that physician-assisted suicide has been de facto legal since 1993, physicians are reluctant to practice it. Surveys show that about two-thirds of the people who ask physicians to end their lives are turned down.

An opinion poll conducted in 1993 in the Netherlands showed that 78 percent of those questioned supported the right of the terminally ill to ask for euthanasia. (A previous poll showed that about 50 percent of Roman Catholics also favor this.) Ten percent were opposed, and 71 percent said that physicians who act in accordance with the rules should not have to justify themselves in a court of law. A 2000 poll revealed that about 10 percent of the Dutch people and 10 percent of their physicians are vigorously opposed to the new law.

NO RIGHT

While the new law decriminalizes euthanasia, it does not recognize a right to euthanasia. Physicians have a right to refuse to cooperate if asked to assist in a suicide, even if the conditions required by the law are satisfied.

One difficulty with the new law, even its proponents admit, is that it is unclear about how to deal with cases in which someone has made a request for assisted suicide while of sound mind, then comes to suffer dementia. Should the request be honored? The Dutch Ministry of Health has explicitly stated that dementia itself cannot be grounds for assisted suicide. The patient would have to be suffering from intolerable pain and a very early stage of dementia for a request to be acted on.

MODEL FOR THE UNITED STATES?

Dutch practice and laws are often mentioned in the United States as an example of what a reasonable euthanasia policy might include. In particular, the practice is offered as a model for providing an option to continuing treatment of individuals suffering from a lingering terminal illness. People with AIDS and those suffering from the intractable pain of terminal cancer, for example, have often expressed a wish for a social and legal policy that would permit active, voluntary euthanasia or assisted suicide. These are just the sort of people the Dutch practice has evolved to deal with.

However, the medical care situation in the United States is different in what may be considered a relevant and important way. Dutch citizens are almost universally participants in health plans that cover their medical costs. Hence, individuals are not under economic pressures to make decisions about ending their lives. They need not worry that they are running out of insurance coverage or may be bankrupting their families by remaining alive.

Furthermore, the Dutch practice does not deal with the type of cases that have caused much concern and controversy in this country. Until recently, the proper treatment of individuals in irreversible comas, as in the *Quinlan* and *Cruzan* cases, has been at the focus of dispute. Since the practice in Holland requires that individuals be conscious and intellectually competent, it embodies no principles that could be appealed to for resolving the troublesome issues involved in dealing with those in persistent vegetative states.

Nevertheless, the Dutch experience may still be valuable in showing whether it is possible to have a social policy permitting assisted suicide and voluntary euthanasia without the abuses or corruption of medical power feared by critics.

PART V

Foundations of Bioethics

Ethical Theories, Moral Principles, and Medical Decisions

"He's stopped breathing, Doctor," the nurse said. She sounded calm and not at all hysterical. By the time Dr. Sarah Cunningham had reached Mr. Sabatini's bedside, the nurse was already providing mouth-to-mouth resuscitation. But Mr. Sabatini still had the purplish blue color of cyanosis, caused by a lack of oxygen in his blood.

Dr. Cunningham knew that, if he was to survive, Mr. Sabatini would have to be given oxygen fast and placed on a respirator. But should she order this done?

Mr. Sabatini was an old man, almost ninety. So far as anyone knew, he was alone in the world and would hardly be missed when he died. His health was poor. He had congestive heart disease and was dying slowly and painfully from intestinal cancer.

Wouldn't it be a kindness to Mr. Sabatini to allow him this quick and painless death? Why condemn him to lingering on for a few extra hours or weeks?

The decision that Sarah Cunningham faces is a moral one. She has to decide whether she should take the steps that might prolong Mr. Sabatini's life or not take them and accept the consequence that he will almost surely die within minutes. She knows the medical procedures that can be employed, but she has to decide whether she should employ them.

This kind of case rivets our attention because of its immediacy and drama. But there are many other situations that arise in the context of medical practice and research that present problems that require moral decisions. Some are equal in drama to the problem facing Dr. Cunningham, while others are not so dramatic but are of at least equal seriousness. There are far too many to catalog, but consider this sample: Is it right for a woman to have an abortion for any reason? Should children with serious birth defects be put to death? Do people have a right to die? Does everyone have a right to medical care? Should physicians ever lie to their patients? Should people suffering from a genetic disease be allowed to have children? Can parents agree to allow their children to be used as experimental subjects?

Most of us have little tolerance for questions like these. They seem so cold and abstract. Our attitude changes, however, when we find ourselves in a position in which we are the decision makers. It changes, too, when we are in a position in which *we* must advise those who make the decisions. Or when we are on the receiving end of the decisions.

But whether we view the problems abstractly or concretely, we are inclined to ask the same question: Are there any rules, standards, or principles that we can use as guides when we are faced with moral decisions? If there are, then Dr. Cunningham need not be wholly unprepared to decide whether she should order steps taken to save Mr. Sabatini. Nor need we be unprepared to decide issues like those in the questions above.

The branch of philosophy concerned with principles that allow us to make decisions about what is right and wrong is called *ethics* or *moral philosophy*. *Medical ethics* is specifically concerned with moral principles and decisions in the context of medical practice, policy, and research. Moral difficulties connected with medicine are so complex and important that they require special attention. Medical ethics gives them this attention, but it remains a part of the discipline of ethics. Thus, if we are to answer our question as to whether there are any rules or principles to use when making moral decisions in the medical context, we must turn to general ethical theories and to a consideration of moral principles that have been proposed to hold in all contexts of human action.

In the first section, we will discuss five major ethical theories that have been put forward by philosophers. Each of these theories represents an attempt to supply basic principles we can rely on in making moral decisions. We'll consider these theories and examine how they might be applied to moral issues in the medical context. We will discuss the reasons that have been offered to persuade us to accept each theory, but we will also point out some of the difficulties each theory presents.

In the second section, we will examine and illustrate several moral principles that are of special relevance to medical research and practice. These principles are frequently appealed to in discussions of practical ethical problems and are sufficiently uncontroversial as to be endorsed in a general way by any of the ethical theories mentioned in the first section. (Those who defend theories without principles do not of course endorse them as principles.)

In the third and last section, we will consider the basic concepts of three ethical theories that are usually offered as theories free of principles—virtue ethics, care ethics, and feminist ethics. We will consider how the theories might be used in making moral decisions, but we will also call attention to some of the criticisms urged against each of them.

The three sections are not dependent on one another, and it is possible to profit from one without reading the others. (The price for this independence is a small amount of repetition.) Nevertheless, reading all three sections is recommended. The Case Presentations and Social Contexts presented in the majority of this book can most easily be followed by someone who has at least some familiarity with basic moral theories.

Also, some points in discussions turn upon questions about the applicability of certain familiar moral principles or whether it is possible to operate without any principles. Being acquainted with those principles makes it easier to understand and evaluate such discussions.

Basic Ethical Theories

Ethical theories attempt to articulate and justify principles that can be employed as guides for making moral decisions and as standards for the evaluation of actions and policies. In effect, such theories define what it means to act morally, and in doing so they stipulate in a general fashion the duties or obligations that fall upon us.

Ethical theories also offer a means to explain and justify actions. If our actions are guided by a particular theory, then we can explain them by demonstrating that the principles of the theory required us to act as we did. In such cases, the explanation also constitutes a justification. We justify our actions by showing that, according to the theory, we had an obligation to do what we did. (In some cases, we may justify our actions by showing that the theory *permitted* our actions— that is, didn't require them, but didn't rule them out as wrong.)

Advocates of a particular ethical theory present what they consider to be good reasons and relevant evidence in its support. Their general aim is to show that the theory is one that any reasonable individual would find persuasive or would endorse as correct. Accordingly, appeals to religion, faith, or nonnatural factors are not considered to be either necessary or legitimate to justify the theory. Rational persuasion alone is regarded as the basis of justification.

In this section, we will briefly consider four general ethical theories and one theory of justice that has an essential ethical component. In each case, we will begin by examining the basic principles of the theory and the grounds offered for its acceptance. We will then explore some of the possibilities of applying the theory to problems that arise within the medical context. Finally, we will mention some of the practical consequences and conceptual difficulties that raise questions about the theory's adequacy or correctness.

UTILITARIANISM

The ethical theory known as utilitarianism was given its most influential formulation in the nineteenth century by the British philosophers Jeremy Bentham (1748–1832) and John Stuart Mill (1806–1873). Bentham and Mill did not produce identical theories, but both their versions have come to be spoken of as "classical utilitarianism." Subsequent elaborations and qualifications of utilitarianism are inevitably based on the formulations of Bentham and Mill, so their theories are worth careful examination.

THE PRINCIPLE OF UTILITY

The foundation of utilitarianism is a single apparently simple principle. Mill calls it the "principle of utility" and states it this way: *"Actions are right in proportion as they tend to promote happiness, wrong as they tend to produce the reverse of happiness."*

The principle focuses attention on the *consequences* of actions, rather than upon some feature of the actions themselves. The "utility" or "usefulness" of an action is determined by the extent to which it produces happiness. Thus, no action is *in itself* right or wrong. Nor is an action right or wrong by virtue of the actor's hopes, intentions, or past actions. Consequences alone are important. Breaking a promise, lying, causing pain, or even killing a person may, under certain circumstances, be the right action to take. Under other circumstances, the action might be wrong.

We need not think of the principle as applying to just one action that we are considering. It supplies the basis for a kind of cost–benefit analysis to employ in a situation in which several lines of action are possible. Using the principle, we are supposed to consider the possible results of each action. Then we are to choose the one that produces the most benefit (happiness) at the least cost (unhappiness). The action we take may produce some unhappiness, but it is a balance of happiness over unhappiness that the principle tells us to seek.

Suppose, for example, that a woman in a large hospital is near death: she is in a coma, an EEG shows only minimal brain function, and a respirator is required to keep her breathing. Another patient has just been brought to the hospital from the scene of an automobile accident. His kidneys have been severely damaged, and he is in need of an immediate transplant. There is a good tissue match with the woman's kidneys. Is it right to hasten her death by removing a kidney?

The principle of utility would probably consider the removal justified. The woman is virtually dead, while the man has a good chance of surviving. It is true that the woman's life is threatened even more by the surgery. It may in fact kill her. But, on balance, the kidney transplant seems likely to produce more happiness than unhappiness. In fact, it seems better than the alternative of doing nothing. For in that case, both patients are likely to die.

The principle of utility is also called the "greatest happiness principle" by Bentham and Mill. The reason for this name is clear when the principle is stated in this way: *Those actions are right that produce the greatest happiness for the greatest number of people.* This alternative formulation makes it obvious that in deciding how to act it is not just my happiness or the happiness of a particular person or group that must be considered. According to utilitarianism, every person is to count just as much as any other person. That is, when we are considering how we should act, everyone's interest must be considered. The right action, then, will be the one that produces the most happiness for the largest number of people.

Mill is particularly anxious that utilitarianism not be construed as no more than a sophisticated justification for crude self-interest. He stresses that in making a moral decision we must look at the situation in an objective way. We must, he says, be a "benevolent spectator" and then act in a way that will bring about the best results for all concerned. This view is summarized in a famous passage:

> The happiness which forms the utilitarian standard of what is right in conduct, is not the agent's own happiness, but that of all concerned. As between his own happiness and that of others, utilitarianism requires him to be as strictly impartial as a disinterested and benevolent spectator. In the golden rule of Jesus of Nazareth, we read the complete spirit of the ethics of utility. To do as you would be done by, and to love your neighbor as yourself, constitute the ideal perfection of utilitarian morality.

The key concept in both formulations of the principle of utility is "happiness." Bentham simply identifies happiness with pleasure—pleasure of any kind. The aim of ethics, then, is to increase the amount of pleasure in the world to the greatest possible extent. To facilitate this, Bentham recommends the use of a "calculus of pleasure and pain," in which characteristics of pleasure such as intensity, duration, and number of people affected are measured and assigned numerical values. To determine which of several possible actions is the right one, we need only determine which one receives the highest numerical score. Unfortunately, Bentham does not tell us what units to use nor how to make the measurements.

Mill also identifies happiness with pleasure, but he differs from Bentham in a major respect. Unlike Bentham, he insists that some pleasures are "higher" than others. Thus, pleasures of the intellect are superior to, say, purely sensual pleasures. This difference in the concept of pleasure can become significant in a medical context. For example, in the choice of using limited resources to save the life of a lathe operator or of an art historian, Mill's view might assign more value to the life of the art historian. That person, Mill might say, is capable of "higher pleasures" than the lathe operator. (Of course, other factors would be relevant here for Mill.)

Both Mill and Bentham regard happiness as an intrinsic good. That is, it is something good in itself or for its own sake. Actions, by contrast, are good only to the extent to which they tend to promote happiness. Therefore, they are only instrumentally good. Since utilitarianism determines the rightness of actions in terms of their tendency to promote the greatest happiness for the greatest number, it is considered to be a *teleological* ethical theory. (*Teleological* comes from the Greek word *telos,* which means "end" or "goal.") A teleological ethical theory judges the rightness of an action in terms of an external goal or purpose— "general happiness" or utility for utilitarianism. However, utilitarianism is also a *consequentialist* theory, for the outcomes or consequences of actions are the only considerations relevant to determining their moral rightness. Not all teleological theories are consequentialist.

Some more recent formulations of utilitarianism have rejected the notion that happiness, no matter how defined, is the sole intrinsic good that actions or policies must promote. Critics of the classical view have argued that the list of things we recognize as valuable in themselves should be increased to include ones such as knowledge, beauty, love, friendship, liberty, and health. According to this *pluralistic* view, in applying the principle of utility we must consider the entire range of intrinsic goods that an action is likely to promote. Thus, the right action is the one that can be expected to produce the greatest sum of intrinsic goods. In most of the following discussion, we will speak of the greatest happiness or benefit, but it is easy enough to see how the same points can be made from a pluralistic perspective.

ACT AND RULE UTILITARIANISM

All utilitarians accept the principle of utility as the standard for determining the rightness of actions. But they divide into two groups over the matter of the application of the principle.

Act utilitarianism holds that the principle should be applied to particular acts in particular circumstances. *Rule utilitarianism* maintains that the principle should be used to test rules, which can in turn be used to decide the rightness of particular acts. Let's consider each of these views and see how it works in practice.

Act utilitarianism holds that an act is right if, and only if, no other act could have been performed that would produce a higher utility. Suppose a child is born with severe impairments. The child has an open spine, severe brain damage, and dysfunctional kidneys. What should be done? (We will leave open the question of who should decide.)

The act utilitarian holds that we must attempt to determine the consequences of the various actions that are open to us. We should consider, for example, these possibilities: (1) Give the child only the ordinary treatment that would be given to a normal child; (2) give the child special treatment for its problems; (3) give the child no treatment—allow it to die; (4) put the child to death in a painless way.

According to act utilitarianism, we must explore the potential results of each possibility. We must realize, for example, that when such a child is given only ordinary treatment it will be worse off, if it survives, than if it had been given special treatment. Also, a child left alone and allowed to die is likely to suffer more pain than one killed by a lethal injection. Furthermore, a child treated aggressively will have to undergo numerous surgical procedures of limited effectiveness. We must also consider the family of the child and judge the emotional and financial effects that each of the possible actions will have on them. Then, too, we must take into account such matters as the "quality of life" of a child with severe brain damage and multiple defects, the effect on physicians and nurses in killing the child or allowing it to die, and the financial costs to society in providing long-term care.

After these considerations, we should then choose the action that has the greatest utility. We should act in the way that will produce the most benefit for all concerned. Which of the possibilities we select will depend on the precise features of the situation: how impaired the child is, how good its chances are for living an acceptable life, the character and financial status of the family, and so on. The great strength of act utilitarianism is that it invites us to deal with each case as unique. When the circumstances of another case are different, we might, without being inconsistent, choose another of the possible actions.

Act utilitarianism shows a sensitivity to specific cases, but it is not free from difficulties. Some philosophers have pointed out that there is no way that we can be sure that we have made the right choice of actions. We are sure to be ignorant of much relevant information. Besides, we can't know with much certainty what the results of our actions will really be. There is no way to be sure, for example, that even a severely impaired infant will not recover enough to live a better life than we predict.

The act utilitarian can reply that acting morally doesn't mean being omniscient. We need to make a reasonable effort to get relevant information, and we can usually predict the probable consequences of our actions. Acting morally doesn't require any more than this.

Another objection to act utilitarianism is more serious. According to the doctrine, we are obligated to keep a promise only if keeping it will produce more utility than some other action. If some other action will produce the same utility, then keeping the promise is permissible but not obligatory. Suppose a surgeon promises a patient that only he will perform an operation, then allows a well-qualified resident to perform part of it. Suppose all goes well and the patient never discovers that the promise was not kept. The outcome for the patient is exactly the same as if the surgeon had kept the promise. From the point of view of act utilitarianism, there is nothing wrong with the surgeon's failure to keep it. Yet critics charge that there is something wrong, that in making the promise the surgeon took on an obligation. Act utilitarianism is unable to account for obligations engendered by such actions as promising and pledging, critics say, for such actions involve something other than consequences.

A third objection to act utilitarianism arises in situations in which virtually everyone must follow the same rules in order to achieve a high level of utility, but even greater utility can be achieved if a few people do not follow the rules. Consider the relationship between physicians and the Medicaid program. The program pays physicians for services provided to those poor enough to qualify for the program. The program would collapse if nearly all physicians were not honest in billing Medicaid for their services. Not only would many poor people suffer, but physicians themselves would lose a source of income.

Suppose a particular physician believes that the requirements to qualify for Medicaid are too restrictive and that many who urgently need medical care cannot afford it. As an act utilitarian, she reasons that it is right for her to get money to open a free clinic under the program. She intends to bill for services she does not provide, then use that money to treat those not covered by Medicaid. Her claims will be small compared to the entire Medicaid budget, so it is unlikely that anyone who qualifies for Medicaid will go without treatment. Since she will tell no one what she is doing, others are not likely to be influenced by her example and make false claims for similar or less worthy purposes. The money she is paid will bring substantial benefit to those in need of health care. Thus, she concludes, by violating the rules of the program, her actions will produce greater utility than would be produced by following the rules.

The physician's action would be morally right, according to act utilitarians. Yet, critics say, we expect an action that is morally right to be one that is right for everyone in similar circumstances. If every physician in the Medicaid program acted in this way, however, the program would be destroyed and thus produce no utility at all. Furthermore, according to critics, the physician's action produces unfairness. Although it is true that the patients she treats at her free clinic gain a benefit they would not otherwise have, similar patients must go without treatment. The Medicaid policy, whatever its flaws, is at least prima facie fair in providing benefits to all who meet its requirements. Once again, then, according to critics, more seems to be involved in judging the moral worth of an action than can be accounted for by act utilitarianism.

In connection with such objections, some critics have gone so far as to claim that it is impossible to see how a society in which everyone was an act utilitarian could function. We could not count on promises being kept nor take for granted that people were telling us the truth. Social policies would be no more than general guides to action, and we could never be sure that people would regard themselves as obligated to adhere to their provisions. Decisions made by individuals about each individual action would not obviously lead to the promotion of the highest degree of utility. Indeed, some critics say, such a society might collapse, for communication among individuals would be difficult, if not impossible, social cohesion would be weakened, and general policies and regulations would have very uncertain effects.

The critics are not necessarily right, of course, and defenders of act utilitarianism have made substantial efforts to answer the criticisms we have presented. Some have denied that the theory has those implications and argued that some of our generally accepted moral perceptions should be changed. In connection with this last point, Carl Wellman provides an insight into the sort of conflict between moral feelings and rational judgment that the acceptance of act utilitarianism can produce. Concerning euthanasia, Wellman writes:

> Try as I may, I honestly cannot discover great hidden disutilities in the act of killing an elderly person suffering greatly from an incurable illness, provided that certain safeguards like a written medical opinion by at least two doctors and a request by the patient are preserved. In this case I cannot find any way to reconcile my theory with my moral judgment. What I do in this case is to hold fast to act-utilitarianism and distrust my moral sense. I claim that my condemnation of such acts is an irrational disapproval, a condemnation that will change upon further reasoning about the act. . . . That I feel wrongness is clear, but I cannot state to myself any rational justification for my feeling. Hence, I discount this particular judgment as irrational.

Rule utilitarianism maintains that an action is right if it conforms to a rule of conduct that has been validated by the principle of utility as one that will produce at least as much utility as any other rule applicable to the situation. A rule like "Provide only ordinary care for severely braindamaged newborns with multiple impairments," if it were established, would allow us to decide about the course of action to follow in situations like that of our earlier example.

The rule utilitarian is not concerned with assessing the utility of individual actions but of particular rules. In practice, then, we do not have to go through the calculations involved in determining in each case whether a specific action will increase utility. All that we have to establish is that following a certain rule will in general result in a situation in which utility is maximized. Once rules are established, they can be relied on to determine whether a particular action is right.

The basic idea behind rule utilitarianism is that having a set of rules that are always observed produces the greatest social utility. Having everyone follow the same rule in each case of the same kind yields more utility for everybody in the long run. An act utilitarian can agree that having rules may produce more social utility than not having them. But the act utilitarian insists that the rules be regarded as no more than general guides to action, as "rules of thumb." Thus, for act utilitarianism it is perfectly legitimate to violate a rule if doing so will maximize utility in that instance. By contrast, the rule utilitarian holds that rules must generally be followed, even though following them may produce less net utility (more unhappiness than happiness) in a particular case.

Rule utilitarianism can endorse rules like "Keep your promises." Thus, unlike act utilitarianism, it can account for the general sense that in making promises we are placing ourselves under an obligation that cannot be set aside for the sake of increasing utility. If "Keep your promises" is accepted as a rule, then the surgeon who fails to perform all of an operation himself, when he has promised his patient he would do so, has not done the right thing, even if the patient never learns the truth.

Rule utilitarians recognize that circumstances can arise in which it would be disastrous to follow a general rule, even when it is true that *in general* greater happiness would result from following the rule all the time. Clearly, we should not keep a promise to meet someone for lunch when we have to choose between keeping the promise and rushing a heart-attack victim to the hospital. It is consistent with the theory to formulate rules that include appropriate escape clauses. For example, "Keep your promises, unless breaking them is required to save a life" and "Keep your promises, unless keeping them would lead to a disastrous result unforeseen at the time the promise was made" are rules that a rule utilitarian might regard as more likely to lead to greater utility than "Always keep your promises no matter what the consequences may be." What a rule utilitarian cannot endorse is a rule like "Keep your promises, except when breaking a promise would produce more utility." This would in effect transform the rule utilitarian into an act utilitarian.

Of course, rule utilitarians are not committed to endorsing general rules only. It is compatible with the view to offer quite specific rules, and in fact there is no constraint on just how specific a rule may be. A rule utilitarian might, for example, establish a rule like "If an infant is born with an open spine, severe brain damage, and dysfunctional kidneys, then the infant should receive no life-sustaining treatment."

The possibility of formulating a large number of rules and establishing them separately opens this basic version of rule utilitarianism to two objections. First, some rules are likely to conflict when they are applicable to the same case, and basic rule utilitarianism offers no way to resolve such conflicts. What should a physician do when faced both with a rule like that above and with another that directs him to "Provide life-sustaining care to all who require it"? Rules which, when considered individually, pass the test of promoting utility, may when taken together express contradictory demands. A further objection to basic rule utilitarianism is that establishing rules to cover many different circumstances and situations results in such an abundance of rules that employing the rules to make moral decisions becomes virtually impossible in practice.

Partly because of such difficulties, rule utilitarians have taken the approach of establishing the utility of a set of rules or an entire moral code. The set can include rules for resolving possible conflicts, and an effort can be made to keep the rules few and simple to minimize the practical difficulty of employing them. Once again, as with individual actions or rules, the principle of utility is employed to determine which set of rules, out of the various sets considered, ought to be accepted.

In this more sophisticated form, rule utilitarianism can be characterized as the theory that an action is right when it conforms to a set of rules that has been determined to produce at least as much overall utility as any other set. It is possible to accept the present forms of social and economic institutions, such as private property and a market economy, as constraints, then argue for the set of rules that will yield the most utility under those conditions. However, it is also possible to be more radical and argue for a particular set of rules that would lead to the greatest possible utility, quite apart from present social forms. Indeed, such a set of rules might be proposed and defended in an effort to bring about changes in present society that are needed to increase the overall level of utility. Utilitarianism, whether act or rule, is not restricted to being a theory about individual moral obligation. It is also a social and political theory.

We have already seen that rule utilitarianism, unlike act utilitarianism, makes possible the sort of obligation we associate with making a promise. But how might rule utilitarianism deal with the case of the physician who files false Medicaid claims to raise money to operate a free clinic? An obvious answer, although certainly not the only one possible, is that any set of rules likely to be adopted by a rule utilitarian will contain at least one rule making fraud morally wrong. Without a rule forbidding fraud, no social program that requires the cooperation of its participants is likely to achieve its aim. Such a rule protects the program from miscalculations of utility that individuals may make for self-serving reasons, keeps the program focused on its goal, and prevents it from becoming fragmented. Even if some few individuals commit fraud, the rule against it is crucial in discouraging as many as possible. Otherwise, as we pointed out earlier, such a program would collapse. By requiring that the program operate as it was designed, rule utilitarian also preserves prima facie fairness, because only those who qualify receive benefits.

The most telling objection to rule utilitarianism, according to some philosophers, is that it is inconsistent. The justification of a set of moral rules is that the rules maximize utility. If rules are to maximize utility, then it seems obvious that they may require that an act produce more utility than any other possible act in a particular situation. Otherwise, the maximum amount of utility would not result. But if the rules satisfy this demand, then they will justify exactly the same actions as act utilitarianism. Thus, the rules will consider it right to break promises, make fraudulent claims, and so on. When rule utilitarianism moves to block these possibilities by requiring that rules produce only the most utility overall, it becomes inconsistent: the set of rules is said to maximize utility, but the rules will require actions that do not maximize utility. Thus, rule utilitarianism seems both to accept and reject the principle of utility as the ultimate moral standard.

PREFERENCE UTILITARIANISM

Some philosophers have called into question the idea of using happiness or any other intrinsic value (knowledge or health, for example) as a criterion of the rightness of an action. The notion of an intrinsic value, they have argued, is too imprecise to be used as a practical guide. Furthermore, it is not at all clear that people share the same values, and even if they do, they are not committed to them to the same degree. Someone may value knowledge more than health, whereas someone else may value physical pleasure over knowledge or health. As a result, there can be no clear-cut procedure for determining what action is likely to produce the best outcome for an individual or group.

The attempt to develop explicit techniques (such as those of decision theory) to help resolve questions about choosing the best action or policy has led some thinkers to replace considerations of intrinsic value with considerations of actual preferences. What someone wants, desires, or prefers can be determined, in principle, in an objective way by consulting the person directly. In addition, people are often able to do more than merely express a preference. Sometimes they can rank their preferences from that which is "most desired" to that which is "least desired."

Such a ranking is of special importance in situations involving risk, for people can be asked to decide how much risk they are willing to take to attempt to realize a given preference. A young woman with a hip injury who is otherwise in good health may be willing to accept the risk of surgery to increase her chances of being restored to many years of active life. By contrast, an elderly woman in frail health may prefer to avoid surgery and accept the limitations that the injury imposes on her physical activities. For the elderly woman, not only are the risks of surgery greater because of her poor health, but even if the surgery is successful, she also will have fewer years to benefit from it.

By contrast, the older woman may place such a premium on physical activity that she is willing to take the risk of surgery to improve her chances of securing even a few more years of it. Only she can say what is important to her and how willing she is to take the risk required to secure it.

These considerations about personal preferences can also be raised about social preferences. Statistical information about what people desire and what they are willing to forgo to see their desires satisfied becomes relevant to institutional and legislative deliberations about what policies to adopt. For example, a crucial question facing our own society is whether we are willing to provide everyone with at least a basic minimum of health care, even if this requires increasing taxes or reducing our support for other social goods, such as education and defense.

Employing the satisfaction of preferences as the criterion of the rightness of an action or policy makes it possible to measure some of the relevant factors in some situations. The life expectancy of infants with particular impairments at birth can be estimated by statistics; a given surgical procedure has a certain success rate and a certain mortality rate. Similarly, a particular social policy has a certain financial cost, and if implemented, the policy is likely to mean the loss of other possible benefits and opportunities.

Ideally, information of this kind should allow a rational decision maker to calculate the best course of action for an individual or group. The best action will be the one that best combines the satisfaction of preferences with other conditions (financial costs and risks, for example) that are at least minimally acceptable. To use the jargon of the theorists, the best action is the one that maximizes the utilities of the person or group.

A utilitarianism that employs preferences has the advantage of suggesting more explicit methods of analysis and rules for decision making than the classical formulation. It also has the potential for being more sensitive to the expressed desires of individuals. However, preference utilitarianism is not free from specific difficulties.

Most prominent is the problem posed by preferences that we would generally regard as unacceptable. What are we to say about those who prefer mass murder, child abuse, or torturing animals? Obviously, subjective preferences cannot be treated equally, and we must have a way to distinguish acceptable from unacceptable ones. Whether this can be done by relying on the principle of utility alone is doubtful. In the view of some commentators, some other moral principle (or principles) is needed. (See the discussion of justice immediately following.)

DIFFICULTIES WITH UTILITARIANISM

Classical utilitarianism is open to a variety of objections. We will concentrate on only one, however, for it seems to reveal a fatal flaw in the structure of the entire theory. This most serious of all objections is that the principle of utility appears to justify the imposition of great suffering on a few people for the benefit of many people.

Certain kinds of human experimentation forcefully illustrate this possibility. Suppose an investigator is concerned with acquiring a better understanding of brain functions. She could learn a great deal by systematically destroying the brain of one person and carefully noting the results. Such a study would offer many more opportunities for increasing our knowledge of the brain than those studies that use as subjects people who have damage to their brains in accidental ways. We may suppose that the experimenter chooses as her subject a person without education or training, without family or friends, who cannot be regarded as making much of a contribution to society. The subject will die from the experiment, but it is not unreasonable to suppose that the knowledge of the human brain gained from the experiment will improve the lives of countless numbers of people.

The principle of utility seems to make such experiments legitimate because the outcome is a greater amount of good than harm. One or a few have suffered immensely, but the many have profited to an extent that far outweighs that suffering.

Clearly what is missing from utilitarianism is the concept of *justice*. It cannot be right to increase the general happiness at the expense of one person or group. There must be some way of distributing happiness and unhappiness and avoiding exploitation.

Mill was aware that utilitarianism needs a principle of justice, but most contemporary philosophers do not believe that such a principle can be derived from the principle of utility. In their opinion, utilitarianism as an ethical theory suffers severely from this defect. Yet some philosophers, while acknowledging the defect, have still held that utilitarianism is the best substantive moral theory available.

KANT'S ETHICS

For utilitarianism, the rightness of an action depends upon its consequences. In stark contrast to this view is the ethical theory formulated by the German philosopher Immanuel Kant (1724–1804) in his book *Fundamental Principles of the Metaphysics of Morals*. For Kant, the consequences of an action are morally irrelevant. Rather, an action is right when it is in accordance with a rule that satisfies a principle he calls the "categorical imperative." Since this is the basic principle of Kant's ethics, we can begin our discussion with it.

THE CATEGORICAL IMPERATIVE

If you decide to have an abortion and go through with it, it is possible to view your action as involving a rule. You can be thought of as endorsing a rule to the effect "Whenever I am in circumstances like these, then I will have an abortion." Kant calls such a rule a "maxim." In his view, all reasoned and considered actions can be regarded as involving maxims.

The maxims in such cases are personal or subjective, but they can be thought of as being candidates for moral rules. If they pass the test imposed by the categorical imperative, then we can say that such actions are right. Furthermore, in passing the test, the maxims cease to be merely personal and subjective. They gain the status of objective rules of morality that hold for everyone.

Kant formulates the categorical imperative in this way: Act only on that maxim which you can will to be a universal law. Kant calls the principle "categorical" to distinguish it from "hypothetical" imperatives. These tell us what to do if we want to bring about certain consequences—such as happiness. A categorical imperative prescribes what we ought to do without reference to any consequences. The principle is an "imperative" because it is a command.

The test imposed on maxims by the categorical imperative is one of generalization or "universalizability." The central idea of the test is that a moral maxim is one that can be generalized to apply to all cases of the same kind. That is, you must be willing to see your rule adopted as a maxim by everyone who is in a situation similar to yours. You must be willing to see your maxim universalized, even though it may turn out on some other occasion to work to your disadvantage.

For a maxim to satisfy the categorical imperative, it is not necessary that we be agreeable in some psychological sense to see it made into a universal law. Rather, the test is one that requires us to avoid inconsistency or conflict in what we will as a universal rule.

Suppose, for example, that I am a physician and I tell a patient that he has a serious illness, although I know that he doesn't. This may be to my immediate advantage, for the treatment and the supposed cure will increase my income and reputation. The maxim of my action might be phrased as, "Whenever I have a healthy patient, I will lie to him and say that he has an illness."

Now suppose that I try to generalize my maxim. In doing so, I will discover that I am willing the existence of a practice that has contradictory properties. If "Whenever any physician has a healthy patient, she will lie to him and say he has an illness" is made a universal law, then every patient will be told that he has an illness. Trust in the diagnostic pronouncements of physicians will be destroyed, while my scheme depends on my patients' trusting me and accepting the truth of my lying diagnosis.

It is as if I were saying, "Let there be a rule of truth telling such that people can assume that others are telling them the truth, but let there also be a rule that physicians may lie to their patients when it is in the interest of the physician to do so." In willing both rules, I am willing something contradictory. Thus, I can will my action in a particular case, but I can't will that my action be universal without generating a logical conflict.

Kant claims that such considerations show that it is always wrong to lie. Lying produces a contradiction in what we will. On one hand, we will that people believe what we say—that they accept our assurances and promises. On the other hand, we will that people be free to give false assurances and make false promises. Lying thus produces a self-defeating situation, for, when the maxim involved is generalized, the very framework required for lying collapses.

Similarly, consider the egoist who seeks only his self-interest and so makes "Never show love or compassion for others" the maxim of his actions. When universalized, this maxim results in the same kind of self-defeating situation that lying does. Since the egoist will sometimes find himself in need of love and compassion, if he wills the maxim of his action to be a universal law, then he will be depriving himself of something that is in his self-interest. Thus, in willing the abolition of love and compassion out of self-interest, he creates a logical contradiction in what he wills.

ANOTHER FORMULATION

According to Kant, there is only one categorical imperative, but it can be stated in three different ways. Each is intended to reveal a different aspect of the principle. The second formulation, the only other we will consider, can be stated in this way: Always act so as to treat humanity, either yourself or others, always as an end and never as only a means.

This version illustrates Kant's notion that every rational creature has a worth in itself. This worth is not conferred by being born into a society with a certain political structure, nor even by belonging to a certain biological species. The worth is inherent in the sheer possession of rationality. Rational creatures possess what Kant calls an "autonomous, self-legislating will." That is, they are able to consider the consequences of their actions, make rules for themselves, and direct their actions by those self-imposed rules. Thus, rationality confers upon everyone an intrinsic worth and dignity.

This formulation of the categorical imperative perhaps rules out some of the standards that are sometimes used to determine who is selected to receive certain medical resources (such as kidney machines) when the demand is greater than the supply. Standards that make a person's education, accomplishments, or social position relevant seem contrary to this version of the categorical imperative. They violate the basic notion that each person has an inherent worth equal to that of any other person. Unlike dogs or horses, people cannot be judged on "show points."

For Kant, all of morality has its ultimate source in rationality. The categorical imperative, in any formulation, is an expression of rationality, and it is the principle that would be followed in practice by any purely rational being. Moral rules are not mere arbitrary conventions or subjective standards. They are objective truths that have their source in the rational nature of human beings.

DUTY

Utilitarianism identifies the good with happiness or pleasure and makes the production of happiness the supreme principle of morality. But, for Kant, happiness is at best a conditional or qualified good. In his view, there is only one thing that can be said to be good in itself: a good will.

Will is what directs our actions and guides our conduct. But what makes a will a "good will"? Kant's answer is that a will becomes good when it acts purely for the sake of duty.

We act for the sake of duty (or from duty) when we act on maxims that satisfy the categorical imperative. This means, then, that it is the motive force behind our actions—the character of our will—that determines their moral character. Morality does not rest on results—such as the production of happiness—but neither does it rest on our feelings, impulses, or inclinations. An action is right, for Kant, only when it is done for the sake of duty.

Suppose that I decide to donate one of my kidneys for transplanting. If my hope is to gain approval or praise or even if I am moved by pity and a genuine wish to reduce suffering, and this is the only consideration behind my action, then, although I have done the morally right thing, my action has no inner moral worth. By contrast, I may have acted *in accordance with duty* (done the same thing as duty would have required), but I did not act *from duty.*

This view of duty and its connection with morality captures attitudes we frequently express. Consider a nurse who gives special care to a severely ill patient. Suppose you learned that the nurse was providing such extraordinary care only because he hoped that the patient or her family would reward him with a special bonus. Knowing this, you would be unlikely to say that the nurse was acting in a morally outstanding way. We might even think the nurse was being greedy or cynical, and we would say that he was doing the right thing for the wrong reasons.

Kant distinguishes between two types of duties: perfect and imperfect. (The distinction corresponds to the two ways in which maxims can be self-defeating when tested by the categorical imperative.) A *perfect duty* is one we must always observe, but an *imperfect duty* is one that we must observe only on some occasions. I have a perfect duty not to injure another person, but I have only an imperfect duty to show love and compassion. I must sometimes show it, but when I show it and which people I select to receive it are entirely up to me.

My duties determine what others can legitimately claim from me as a right. Some rights can be claimed as perfect rights, while others cannot. Everyone can demand of me that I do him or her no injury. But no one can tell me that I must make him or her the recipient of my love and compassion. In deciding how to discharge my imperfect duties, I am free to follow my emotions and inclinations.

For utilitarianism, an action is right when it produces something that is intrinsically valuable (happiness). Because actions are judged by their contributions to achieving a goal, utilitarianism is a teleological theory. By contrast, Kant's ethics holds that an action has features in itself that make it right or in accordance with duty. These features are distinct from the action's consequences. Such a theory is called *deontological,* a term derived from the Greek word for "duty" or "obligation."

KANT'S ETHICS IN THE MEDICAL CONTEXT

Four features of Kant's ethics are of particular importance in dealing with issues in medical treatment and research:

1. No matter what the consequences may be, it is always wrong to lie.
2. We must always treat people (including ourselves) as ends and not as means only.
3. An action is right when it satisfies the categorical imperative.

4. Perfect and imperfect duties give a basis for claims that certain rights should be recognized.

We can present only two brief examples of how these features can be instrumental in resolving ethical issues, but these are suggestive of other possibilities.

Our first application of Kant's ethics bears on medical research. The task of medical investigators would be easier if they did not have to tell patients that they were going to be made part of a research program. Patients would then become subjects without even knowing it, and more often than not their risk would be negligible. Even though no overt lying would be involved, on Kantian principles this procedure would be wrong. It would require treating people as a means only and not as an end.

Likewise, it would never be right for an experimenter to deceive a potential experimental subject. If an experimenter told a patient, "We would like to use this new drug on you because it might help you" and this were not really so, the experimenter would be performing a wrong action. Lying is always wrong.

Nor could the experimenter justify this deception by telling herself that the research is of such importance that it is legitimate to lie to the patient. On Kant's principles, good results never make an action morally right. Thus, a patient must give voluntary and informed consent to become a subject of medical experimentation. Otherwise, he or she is being deprived of autonomy and treated as a means only.

We may volunteer because we expect the research to bring direct benefits to us. But we may also volunteer even though no direct personal benefits can be expected. We may see participation in the research as an occasion for fulfilling an imperfect duty to improve human welfare.

But, just as Kant's principles place restrictions on the researcher, they place limits on us as potential subjects. We have a duty to treat ourselves as ends and act so as to preserve our dignity and worth as humans. Therefore, it would not be right for us to volunteer for an experiment that threatened our lives or threatened to destroy our ability to function as autonomous rational beings without first satisfying ourselves that the experiment was legitimate and necessary.

Our second application of Kant's ethics in a medical context bears on the relationship between people as patients and those who accept responsibility for caring for them. A physician, for example, has only an imperfect duty to accept me as a patient. He has a duty to make use of his skills and talents to treat the sick, but I cannot legitimately insist on being the beneficiary. How he discharges his duty is his decision.

If, however, I am accepted as a patient, then I can make some legitimate claims. I can demand that nothing be done to cause me pointless harm, because it is never right to injure a person. Furthermore, I can demand that I never be lied to or deceived. Suppose, for example, I am given a placebo (a harmless but inactive substance) and told that it is a powerful and effective medication. Or suppose that a biopsy shows that I have an inoperable form of cancer, but my physician tells me, "There's nothing seriously wrong with you." In both cases, the physician may suppose that he is deceiving me "for my own good": the placebo may be psychologically effective and make me feel better, and the lie about cancer may save me from useless worry. Yet, by being deceived, I am being denied the dignity inherent in my status as a rational being. Lying is wrong in general, and in such cases as these it also deprives me of my autonomy, of my power to make decisions and form my own opinions. As a result, such deception dehumanizes me.

As an autonomous rational being, a person is entitled to control over his or her own body. This means that medical procedures can be performed on me only with my permission. It would be wrong even if the medication were needed for my "own good." I may voluntarily put myself under the care of a physician and submit to all that I am asked to, but the decision belongs to me alone.

In exercising control over my body, however, I also have a duty to myself. Suppose, for example, that I refuse to allow surgery to be performed on me, although I have been told it is necessary to preserve my life. Since I have a duty to preserve my life, as does every person, my refusal is morally unjustifiable. Even here, however, it is not legitimate for others to force me to "do my duty." In fact, in Kantian ethics it is impossible to force another to do his or her duty because it is not the action but the maxim involved that determines whether or not one's duty has been done.

It is obvious even from our sketchy examples that Kantian ethics is a fruitful source of principles and ideas for working out some of the specific moral difficulties of medical experimentation and practice. The absolute requirements imposed by the categorical imperative can be a source of strength and even of comfort. By contrast, utilitarianism requires us to weigh alternative courses of actions by anticipating their consequences and deciding whether what we are considering doing can be justified by those results. Kant's ethics saves us from this kind of doubt and indecision—we know we must never lie, no matter what good may come of it. Furthermore, the lack of a principle of justice that is the most severe defect of utilitarianism is met by Kant's categorical imperative. When every person is to be treated as an end and never as only a means, the possibility of legitimately exploiting some for the benefit of others is wholly eliminated.

DIFFICULTIES WITH KANTIAN ETHICS

Kant's ethical theory is complex and controversial. It has problems of a theoretical sort that manifest themselves in practice and lead us to doubt whether the absolute rules determined by the categorical imperative can always provide a straightforward solution to our moral difficulties. We will limit ourselves to discussing just three problems.

First, Kant's principles may produce resolutions to cases in which there is a conflict of duties that seems intuitively wrong. I have a duty to keep my promises, and I also have a duty to help those in need. Suppose, then, that I am a physician and I have promised a colleague to attend a staff conference. Right before the conference starts, I am talking with a patient who lapses into an insulin coma. If I get involved in treating the patient, I'll have to break my promise to attend the conference. What should I do?

The answer is obvious: I should treat the patient. Our moral intuition tells us this. But for Kant, keeping promises is a perfect duty, while helping others is an imperfect one. This suggests, then, that according to Kantian principles I should abandon my patient and rush off to keep my appointment. Something is apparently wrong with a view that holds that a promise should never be broken—even when the promise concerns a relatively trivial matter and the consequences of keeping it are disastrous.

Another difficulty with the categorical imperative arises because we are free to choose how we formulate a maxim for testing. In all likelihood none of us would approve a maxim such as "Lie when it is convenient for you." But what about one like "Lie when telling the truth is likely to cause harm to another"? We would be more inclined to make this a universal law. Now consider the maxim "Whenever a physician has good reason to believe that a patient's life will be seriously threatened if she is told the truth about her condition, then the physician should lie." Virtually everyone would be willing to see this made into a universal law.

Yet these three maxims could apply to the same situation. Since Kant does not tell us how to formulate our maxims, it is clear that we can act virtually any way we choose if we are willing to describe the situation in detail. We might be willing to have everyone act just as we are inclined to act whenever they find themselves in exactly this kind of situation. The categorical imperative, then, does not seem to solve our moral problems quite so neatly as it first appears to.

A final problem arises from Kant's notion that we have duties to rational beings or persons. Ordinarily, we have little difficulty with this commitment to persons, yet there are circumstances, particularly in the medical context, in which serious problems arise. Consider, for example, a fetus developing in its mother's womb. Is the fetus to be considered a person? The way this question is answered makes all the difference in deciding about the rightness or wrongness of abortion.

A similar difficulty is present when we consider how we are to deal with an infant with serious birth defects. Is it our duty to care for this infant and do all we can to see that it lives? If the infant is not a person, then perhaps we do not owe him the sort of treatment it would be our duty to provide a similarly afflicted adult. It's clear from these two cases that the notion of a person as an autonomous rational being is both too restrictive and arbitrary. It begs important moral questions.

Another difficulty connected with Kant's concept of a rational person is the notion of an "autonomous self-regulating will." Under what conditions can we assume that an individual possesses such a will? Does a child, a mentally retarded person, or someone in prison? Without such a will, in Kant's view, such an individual cannot legitimately consent to be the subject of an experiment or even give permission for necessary medical treatment. This notion is very much in need of development before Kant's principles can be relied on to resolve ethical questions in medicine.

The difficulties that we have discussed require serious consideration. This does not mean, of course, that they cannot be resolved or that because of them Kant's theory is worthless. As with utilitarianism, there are some philosophers who believe the theory is the best available, despite its shortcomings. That it captures many of our intuitive beliefs about what is right (not to lie, to treat people with dignity, to act benevolently) and supplies us with a test for determining our duties (the categorical imperative) recommends it strongly as an ethical theory.

ROSS'S ETHICS

The English philosopher W. D. Ross (b. 1877) presented an ethical theory in his book *The Right and the Good* that can be seen as an attempt to incorporate aspects of utilitarianism and aspects of Kantianism. Ross rejected the utilitarian notion that an action is made right by its consequences alone, but he was also troubled by Kant's absolute rules. He saw not only that such rules fail to show sensitivity to the complexities of actual situations, but also that they sometimes conflict with one another. Like Kant, Ross is a deontologist, but with an important difference. Ross believes it is necessary to consider consequences in making a moral choice, even though he believes that it is not the results of an action taken alone that make it right.

MORAL PROPERTIES AND RULES

For Ross there is an unbridgeable distinction between moral and nonmoral properties. There are only two moral properties—rightness and goodness—and these cannot be replaced by, or explained in terms of, other properties. Thus, to say that an action is "right" is not at all the same as saying that it "causes pleasure" or "increases happiness," as utilitarianism claims.

At the same time, however, Ross does not deny that there is a connection between moral properties and nonmoral ones. What he denies is the possibility of establishing an identity between them. Thus, it may be right to relieve the suffering of someone, but right is not identical with relieving suffering. (More exactly put, the rightness of the action is not identical with the action's being a case of relieving suffering.)

Ross also makes clear that we must often know many nonmoral facts about a situation before we can legitimately make a moral judgment. If I see a physician injecting someone, I cannot say whether she is acting rightly without determining what she is injecting, why she is doing it, and so on. Thus, rightness is a property that depends partly on the nonmoral properties that characterize a situation. I cannot determine whether the physician is doing the right thing or the wrong thing until I determine what the nonmoral properties are.

Ross believes that there are cases in which we have no genuine doubt about whether the property of rightness or goodness is present. The world abounds with examples of cruelty, lying, and selfishness, and in these cases we are immediately aware of the absence of rightness or goodness. But the world also abounds with examples of compassion, reliability, and generosity in which rightness and goodness are clearly present. Ross claims that our experience with such cases puts us in a position to come to know rightness and goodness with the same degree of certainty as when we grasp the mathematical truth that a triangle has three angles.

Furthermore, according to Ross, our experience of many individual cases puts us in a position to recognize the validity of a general statement like "It is wrong to cause needless pain." We come to see such rules in much the same way that we come to recognize the letter A after having seen it written or printed in a variety of handwritings or typefaces.

Thus, our moral intuitions can supply us with moral rules of a general kind. But Ross refuses to acknowledge these rules as absolute. For him they can serve only as guides to assist us in deciding what we should do. Ultimately, in any particular case we must rely not only on the rules but also on reason and our understanding of the situation.

Thus, even with rules, we may not recognize what the right thing to do is in a given situation. We recognize, he suggests, that there is always some right thing to do, but what it is may be far from obvious. In fact, doubt about what is the right way of acting may arise just because we have rules to guide us. We become aware of the fact that there are several possible courses of action, and all of them seem to be right.

Consider the problem of whether to lie to a terminally ill patient about his condition. Let us suppose that, if we lie to him, we can avoid causing him at least some useless anguish. But then aren't we violating his trust in us to act morally and to speak the truth?

In such cases, we seem to have a conflict in our duties. It is because of such familiar kinds of conflicts that Ross rejects the possibility of discovering absolute, invariant moral rules like "Always tell the truth" and "Always eliminate needless suffering." In cases like the one above, we cannot hold that both rules are absolute without contradicting ourselves. Ross says that we have to recognize that every rule has exceptions and must in some situations be overridden.

ACTUAL DUTIES AND PRIMA FACIE DUTIES

If rules like "Always tell the truth" cannot be absolute, then what status can they have? When our rules come into conflict in particular situations, how are we to decide which rule applies? Ross answers this question by making use of a distinction between what is actually right and what is prima facie right. Since we have a duty to do what is right, this distinction can be expressed as one between *actual duty* and *prima facie duty.*

An actual duty is simply what my real duty is in a situation. It is the action that, out of the various possibilities, I ought to perform. More often than not, however, I may not know what my actual duty is. In fact, for Ross, the whole problem of ethics might be said to be the problem of knowing what my actual duty is in any given situation.

Prima facie literally means "at first sight," but Ross uses the phrase to mean something like "other things being equal." Accordingly, a prima facie duty is one that dictates what I should do when other relevant factors in a situation are not considered. If I promised to meet you for lunch, then I have a prima facie duty to meet you. But suppose I am a physician and, just as I am about to leave for an appointment, the patient I am with suffers cardiac arrest. In such circumstances, according to Ross's view, I should break my promise and render aid to the patient. My prima facie duty to keep my promise doesn't make that fact obligatory. It constitutes a moral reason for meeting you, but there is also a moral reason for not meeting you. I also have a prima facie duty to aid my patient, and this is a reason that outweighs the first one. Thus, aiding the patient is both a prima facie duty and, in this situation, my actual duty.

The notion of a prima facie duty permits Ross to offer a set of moral rules stated in such a way that they are both universal and free from exceptions. For Ross, for example, lying is always wrong, but it is wrong prima facie. It may be that in a particular situation my actual duty requires that I lie. Even though what I have done is prima facie wrong, it is the morally right thing to do if some other prima facie duty that requires lying in the case is more stringent than the prima facie duty to tell the truth. (Perhaps only by lying am I able to prevent a terrorist from blowing up an airplane.) I must be able to explain and justify my failure to tell the truth, and it is of course possible that I may not be able to do so. It may be that I was confused and misunderstood the situation or failed to consider other alternatives. I may have been wrong to believe that my actual duty required me to lie. However, even if I was correct in my belief, that I lied is still prima facie wrong. It is this fact (and for Ross it is a fact) that requires me to explain and justify my action.

We have considered only a few simple examples of prima facie duties, but Ross is more thorough and systematic than our examples might suggest. He offers a list of duties that he considers binding on all moral agents. Here they are in summary form:

1. *Duties of fidelity:* telling the truth, keeping actual and implicit promises, and not representing fiction as history

2. *Duties of reparation:* righting the wrongs we have done to others

3. *Duties of gratitude:* recognizing the services others have done for us

4. *Duties of justice:* preventing a distribution of pleasure or happiness that is not in keeping with the merit of the people involved

5. *Duties of beneficence:* helping to better the condition of other beings with respect to virtue, intelligence, or pleasure

6. *Duties of self-improvement:* bettering ourselves with respect to virtue or intelligence

7. *Duties of nonmaleficence:* avoiding or preventing an injury to others

Ross doesn't claim that this is a complete list of the prima facie duties that we recognize. However, he does believe that the duties on the list are all ones that we acknowledge and are willing to accept as legitimate and binding without argument. He believes that if we simply reflect on these prima facie duties we will see that they may be truly asserted. As he puts the matter:

> I . . . am claiming that we know them to be true. To me it seems as self-evident as anything could be, that to make a promise, for instance, is to create a moral claim on us in someone else. Many readers will perhaps say that they do not know this to be true. If so I certainly cannot prove it to them. I can only ask them to reflect again, in the hope that they will ultimately agree that they also know it to be true.

Notice that Ross explicitly rejects the possibility of providing us with reasons or arguments to convince us to accept his list of prima facie duties. We are merely invited to reflect on certain kinds of cases, like keeping promises, and Ross is convinced that this reflection will bring us to accept his claim that these are true duties. Ross, like other intuitionists, tries to get us to agree with his moral perceptions in much the same way as we might try to get people to agree with us about our color perceptions. We might, for example, show a paint sample to a friend and say, "Don't you think that looks blue? It does to me. Think about it for a minute."

We introduced the distinction between actual and prima facie duties to deal with those situations in which duties seem to conflict. The problem, as we can now state it, is this: What are we to do in a situation in which we recognize more than one prima facie duty and it is not possible for us to act in a way that will fulfill them? We know, of course, that we should act in a way that satisfies our actual duty. But that is just our problem. What, after all, is our actual duty when our prima facie duties are in conflict?

Ross offers us two principles to deal with cases of conflicting duty. The first principle is designed to handle situations in which just two prima facie duties are in conflict: *That act is one's duty which is in accord with the more stringent prima facie obligation.* The second principle is intended to deal with cases in which several prima facie duties are in conflict: *That act is one's duty which has the greatest balance of prima facie rightness over prima facie wrongness.*

Unfortunately, both these principles present problems in application. Ross does not tell us how we are to determine when an obligation is "more stringent" than another. Nor does he give us a rule for determining the "balance" of prima facie rightness over wrongness. Ultimately, according to Ross, we must simply rely upon our perceptions of the situation. There is no automatic or mechanical procedure that can be followed. If we learn the facts in the case, consider the consequences of our possible actions, and reflect on our prima facie duties, we should be able to arrive at a conclusion as to the best course of action—in Ross's view something that we as moral agents must and can do.

To return to specific cases, perhaps there is no direct way to answer the abstract question, Is the duty not to lie to a patient "more stringent" than the duty not to cause needless suffering? So much depends on the character and condition of the individual patient that an abstract determination of our duty based on "balance" or "stringency" is useless. However, knowing the patient, we should be able to perceive what the right course of action is.

Ross further believes that there are situations in which there are no particular difficulties about resolving the conflict between prima facie duties. For example, most of us would agree that, if we can save someone from serious injury by lying, then we have more of an obligation to save someone from injury than we do to tell the truth.

ROSS'S ETHICS IN THE MEDICAL CONTEXT

Ross's moral rules are not absolute in the sense that Kant's are; consequently, as with utilitarianism, it is not possible to say what someone's duty would be in an actual concrete situation. We can discuss in general, however, the advantages that Ross's theory brings to medical–moral issues. We will mention only two for illustration.

First and most important is Ross's list of prima facie duties. The list of duties can serve an important function in the moral education of physicians, researchers, and other medical personnel. The list encourages each person responsible for patient care to reflect on the prima facie obligations that he or she has toward those people and to set aside one of those obligations only when morally certain that another obligation takes precedence.

The specific duties imposed in a prima facie way are numerous and can be expressed in terms relevant to the medical context: Do not injure patients; do not distribute scarce resources in a way that fails to recognize individual worth; do not lie to patients; show patients kindness and understanding; educate patients in ways useful to them; do not hold out false hopes to patients; and so on.

Second, like utilitarianism, Ross's ethics encourages us to show sensitivity to the unique features of situations before acting. Like Kant's ethics, however, Ross's also insists that we look at the world from a particular moral perspective. In arriving at decisions about what is right, we must learn the facts of the case and explore the possible consequences of our actions. Ultimately, however, we must guide our actions by what is right, rather than by what is useful, or by what will produce happiness, or anything of the kind.

Since for Ross actions are not always justified in terms of their results, we cannot say unequivocally, "It's right to trick this person into becoming a research subject because the experiment may benefit thousands." Yet, we cannot say that it is always wrong for a researcher to trick a person into volunteering. An action is right or wrong regardless of what we think about it, but in a particular case circumstances might justify an experimenter in allowing some other duty to take precedence over the duty of fidelity.

Fundamentally, then, Ross's ethics offers us the possibility of gaining the advantages of utilitarianism without ignoring the fact that there seem to be duties with an undeniable moral force behind them that cannot be accounted for by utilitarianism. Ross's ethics accommodates not only our intuition that certain actions should be performed just because they are right but also our inclination to pay attention to the results of actions and not just the motives behind them.

DIFFICULTIES WITH ROSS'S MORAL RULES

The advantages Ross's ethics offers over both utilitarianism and Kantianism are offset by some serious difficulties. To begin with, it seems false that we all grasp the same principles. We are well aware that people's beliefs about what is right and about what their duties are result from the kind of education and experience that they have had. The ability to perceive what is good or right does not appear to be universally shared. Ross does say that the principles are the convictions of "the moral consciousness of the best people." In any ordinary sense of "best," there is reason to say that such people don't always agree on moral principles. If "best" means "morally best," then Ross is close to being circular: the best people are those who acknowledge the same prima facie obligations, and those who recognize the same prima facie obligations are the best people.

Some have objected that Ross's list of prima facie duties seems incomplete. For example, Ross does not explicitly say that we have a prima facie obligation not to steal, but most people would hold that if we have any prima facie duties at all, the duty not to steal must surely be counted among them. Of course, it is possible to say that stealing is covered by some other obligation—the duty of fidelity, perhaps, since stealing may violate a trust. Nevertheless, from a theory based on intuition, the omission of such duties leaves Ross's list peculiarly incomplete.

Further, some critics have claimed that it is not clear that there is always even a prima facie obligation to do some of the things Ross lists. Suppose that I promise to lie about a friend's physical condition so that she can continue to collect insurance payments. Some would say that I have no obligation at all to keep such an unwise promise. In such a case, there would be no conflict of duties, because I don't have even a prima facie duty to keep such a promise.

Finally, Ross's theory, some have charged, seems to be false to the facts of moral disagreements. When we disagree with someone about an ethical matter, we consider reasons for and against some position. Sometimes the discussion results in agreement. But, according to Ross's view, this should not be possible. Although we may discuss circumstances and consequences and agree about the prima facie duties involved, ultimately I arrive at my judgment about the duty that is most stringent or has the greatest degree of prima facie rightness, and you arrive at yours. At this point, it seems, there can be no further discussion, even though the two judgments are incompatible. Thus, a choice between the two judgments about what act should be performed becomes arbitrary.

Few contemporary philosophers would be willing to endorse Ross's ethical theory without serious qualifications. The need for a special kind of moral perception (or "intuition") marks the theory as unacceptable for most philosophers. Yet many would acknowledge that the theory has great value in illuminating such aspects of our moral experience as reaching decisions when we feel the pull of conflicting obligations. Furthermore, at least some would acknowledge Ross's prima facie duties as constituting an adequate set of moral principles.

RAWLS'S THEORY OF JUSTICE

In 1971 the Harvard philosopher John Rawls published a book called *A Theory of Justice*. The work continues to attract a considerable amount of attention and has been described by some as the most important book in moral and social philosophy of the twentieth century.

One commentator, R. P. Wolfe, points out that Rawls attempts to develop a theory that combines the strengths of utilitarianism with those of the deontological position of Kant and Ross, while avoiding the weaknesses of each view. Utilitarianism claims outright that happiness is fundamental and suggests a direct procedure for answering ethical–social questions. But it is flawed by its lack of a principle of justice. Kant and Ross make rightness a fundamental moral notion and stress the ultimate dignity of human beings. Yet neither provides a workable method for solving problems of social morality. Clearly, Rawls's theory promises much if it can succeed in uniting the two ethical traditions we have discussed.

THE ORIGINAL POSITION AND THE PRINCIPLES OF JUSTICE

For Rawls, the central task of government is to preserve and promote the liberty and welfare of individuals. Thus, principles of justice are needed to serve as standards for designing and evaluating social institutions and practices. They provide a way of resolving conflicts among the competing claims that individuals make and a means of protecting the legitimate interests of individuals. In a sense, the principles of justice constitute a blueprint for the development of a just society.

But how are we to formulate principles of justice? Rawls makes use of a hypothetical device he calls "the original position." Imagine a group of people like those who make up our society. These people display the ordinary range of intelligence, talents, ambitions, convictions, and social and economic advantages. They include both sexes and members of various racial and ethnic groups.

Furthermore, suppose that this group is placed behind what Rawls calls "a veil of ignorance." Assume that each person is made ignorant of his or her sex, race, natural endowments, social position, economic condition, and so on. Furthermore, assume that these people are capable of cooperating with one another, that they follow the principles of rational decision making, and that they are capable of a sense of justice and will adhere to principles they agree to adopt. Finally, assume that they all desire what Rawls calls "primary goods": the rights, opportunities, powers, wealth, and such that are both worth possessing in themselves and are necessary to securing the more specific goods an individual may want.

Rawls argues that the principles of justice chosen by such a group will be just if the conditions under which they are selected and the procedures for agreeing on them are fair. The original position, with its veil of ignorance, characterizes a state in which alternative notions of justice can be discussed freely by all. Since the ignorance of the participants means that individuals cannot gain advantage for themselves by choosing principles that favor their own circumstances, the eventual choices of the participants will be fair. Since the participants are assumed to be rational, they will be persuaded by the same reasons and arguments. These features of the original position lead Rawls to characterize his view as "justice as fairness."

We might imagine at first that some people in the original position would gamble and argue for principles that would introduce gross inequalities in their society. For example, some might argue for slavery. If these people should turn out to be masters after the veil of ignorance is stripped away, they would gain immensely. But if they turn out to be slaves, then they would lose immensely. However, since the veil of ignorance keeps them from knowing their actual positions in society, it would not be rational for them to endorse a principle that might condemn them to the bottom of the social order.

Given the uncertainties of the original situation, there is a better strategy that these rational people would choose. In the economic discipline known as game theory, this strategy is called "maximin," or maximizing the minimum. When we choose in uncertain situations, this strategy directs us to select from the alternatives the one whose worst possible outcome is better than the worst possible outcome of the other alternatives. (If you don't know whether you're going to be a slave, you shouldn't approve a set of principles that permits slavery when you have other options.)

Acting in accordance with this strategy, Rawls argues that people in the original position would agree on the following two principles of justice:

1. Each person is to have an equal right to the most extensive total system of equal basic liberties compatible with a similar system of liberty for all.

2. Social and economic inequalities are to be arranged so that they are both: (a) to the greatest benefit of the least advantaged . . . , and (b) attached to offices and positions open to all under conditions of fair equality of opportunity.

For Rawls, these two principles are taken to govern the distribution of all social goods: liberty, property, wealth, and social privilege. The first principle has priority. It guarantees a system of equal liberty for all. Furthermore, because of its priority, it explicitly prohibits the bartering away of liberty for social or economic benefits. (For example, a society cannot withhold the right to vote from its members on the grounds that voting rights damage the economy.)

The second principle governs the distribution of social goods other than liberty. Although society could organize itself in a way that would eliminate differences in wealth and abolish the advantages that attach to different social positions, Rawls argues that those in the original position would not choose this form of egalitarianism. Instead, they would opt for the second principle of justice. This means that in a just society differences in wealth and social position can be tolerated only when they can be shown to benefit everyone and to benefit, in particular, those who have the fewest advantages. A just society is not one in which everyone is equal, but one in which inequalities must be demonstrated to be legitimate. Furthermore, there must be a genuine opportunity for acquiring membership in a group that enjoys special benefits. Those not qualified to enter medical schools because of past discrimination in education, for example, can claim a right for special preparation to qualify them. (Of course, in a Rawlsian society, there would be no discrimination to be compensated for.)

Rawls argues that these two principles are required to establish a just society. Furthermore, in distributing liberty and social goods, the principles guarantee the worth and self-respect of the individual. People are free to pursue their own conception of the good and fashion their own lives. Ultimately, the only constraints placed on them as members of society are those expressed in the principles of justice.

Yet Rawls also acknowledges that those in the original position would recognize that we have duties both to ourselves and to others. They would, for example, want to take measures to see that their interests are protected if they should meet with disabling accidents, become seriously mentally disturbed, and so on. Thus, Rawls approves a form of paternalism: others should act for us when we are unable to act for ourselves. When our preferences are known to them, those acting for us should attempt to follow what we would wish. Otherwise, they should act for us as they would act for themselves if they were viewing our situation from the standpoint of the original position. Paternalism is thus a duty to ourselves that would be recognized by those in the original position.

Rawls is also aware of the need for principles that bind and guide individuals as moral decision makers. He claims that those in the original position would reach agreement on principles for such notions as fairness in our dealings with others, fidelity, respect for persons, and beneficence. From these principles we gain some of our obligations to one another.

But, Rawls claims, there are also "natural duties" that would be recognized by those in the original position. Among those Rawls mentions are (1) the duty of justice—supporting and complying with just institutions; (2) the duty of helping others in need or jeopardy; (3) the duty not to harm or injure another; (4) the duty to keep our promises.

For the most part, these are duties that hold between or among people. They are only some of the duties that would be offered by those in the original position as unconditional duties.

Thus, Rawls in effect endorses virtually the same duties as those that Ross presents as prima facie duties. Rawls realizes that the problem of conflicts of duty was left unsolved by Ross and so perceives the need for assigning priorities to duties—ranking them as higher and lower. Rawls believes that a full system of principles worked out from the original position would include rules for ranking duties. Rawls's primary concern, however, is with justice in social institutions, and he does not attempt to establish any rules for ranking.

RAWLS'S THEORY OF JUSTICE IN THE MEDICAL CONTEXT

Rawls's "natural duties" are virtually the same as Ross's prima facie duties. Consequently, most of what we said earlier about prima facie duties and moral decision making applies to Rawls.

Rawls endorses the legitimacy of paternalism, although he does not attempt to specify detailed principles to justify individual cases. He does tell us that we should consider the preferences of others when they are known to us and when we are in a situation in which we must act for them because they are unable to act for themselves. For example, suppose we know that a person approves of electroconvulsive therapy (shock treatments, or ECT) for the treatment of severe depression. If that person should become so depressed as to be unable to reach a decision about his own treatment, then we would be justified in seeing to it that he received ECT.

To take a similar case, suppose you are a surgeon and have a patient who has expressed to you her wish to avoid numerous operations that may prolong her life six months or so but will be unable to restore her to health. If in operating you learned that she has a form of uterine cancer that had spread through her lower extremities and if in your best judgment nothing could be done to restore her to health, then it would be your duty to her to allow her to die as she chooses. Repeated operations would be contrary to her concept of her own good.

The most important question in exploring Rawls's theory is how the two principles of justice might apply to the social institutions and practices of medical care and research. Most obviously, Rawls's principles repair utilitarianism's flaw with respect to human experimentation. It would never be right, in Rawls's view, to exploit one group of people or even one person for the benefit of others. Thus, experiments in which people are forced to be subjects or are tricked into participating are ruled out. They involve a violation of basic liberties of individuals and of the absolute respect for persons that the principles of justice require.

A person has a right to decide what risks she is willing to take with her own life and health. Thus, voluntary consent is required before someone can legitimately become a research subject. However, society might decide to reward research volunteers with money, honors, or social privileges to encourage participation in research. Provided that the overall structure of society already conforms to the two principles of justice, this is a perfectly legitimate practice so long as it brings benefits (ideally) to everyone and the possibility of gaining the rewards of participation is open to all.

Regarding the allocation of social resources in the training of medical personnel (physicians, nurses, therapists, and so on), one may conclude that such investments are justified only if the withdrawal of the support would work to the disadvantage of those already most disadvantaged. Public money may be spent in the form of scholarships and institutional grants to educate personnel, who may then derive great social and economic benefits from their education. But, for Rawls, the inequality that is produced is not necessarily unjust. Society can invest its resources in this way if it brings benefits to those most in need of them.

The implication of this position seems to be that everyone is entitled to health care. First, it could be argued that health is among the "primary goods" that Rawls's principles are designed to protect and promote. After all, without health an individual is hardly in a position to pursue other more specific goods, and those in the original position might be imagined to be aware of this and to endorse only those principles of justice that would require providing at least basic health care to those in the society. Furthermore, it could be argued that the inequalities of the health care system can be justified only if those in most need can benefit from them. Since this is not obviously the case with the present system, Rawls's principles seem to call for a reform that would provide health care to those who are unable to pay.

However, it is important to point out that it is not at all obvious that a demand to reform our health-care system follows from Rawls's position. For one thing, it is not clear that Rawls's principles are intended to be directly applied to our society as it is. Our society includes among its members people with serious disabilities and ones with both acute and chronic diseases. If Rawls's principles are intended to apply only to people with normal physical and psychological abilities and needs, as he sometimes suggests, then it is not clear that those who are ill can be regarded as appropriate candidates. If they are considered appropriate, then the results may be unacceptable. The principles of justice may require that we devote vast amounts of social resources to making only marginal improvements in the lives of those who are ill.

Furthermore, Rawls does not explicitly mention the promotion of health as one of the primary goods. It may seem reasonable to include it among them, given the significance of health as a condition for additional pursuits, but this is a point that requires support. (Norman Daniels is one who has argued for considering health a primary good.) This seems the most promising position to take if Rawls's principles are to be used as a basis for evaluating our current health policies and practices.

It seems reasonable to hold that Rawls's principles, particularly the second, can be used to restrict access to certain kinds of health care. In general, individuals may spend their money in any way they wish to seek their notions of what is good. Thus, if someone wants cosmetic surgery to change the shape of his chin and has the money to pay a surgeon, then he may have it done. But if medical facilities or personnel should become overburdened and unable to provide needed care for the most seriously afflicted, then the society would be obligated to forbid cosmetic surgery. By doing this it would then increase the net access to needed health care by all members of society. The rich who desired cosmetic surgery would not be permitted to exploit the poor who needed basic health care.

These are just a few of the possible implications that Rawls's theory has for medical research and practice. It seems likely that more and more applications of the theory will be worked out in detail in the future.

DIFFICULTIES WITH RAWLS'S THEORY

Rawls's theory is currently the subject of much discussion in philosophy. The debate is often highly technical, and a great number of objections have been raised. At present, however, there are no objections that would be acknowledged as legitimate by all critics. Rather than attempt to summarize the debate, we will simply point to two aspects of Rawls's theory that have been acknowledged as difficulties.

One criticism concerns the original position and its veil of ignorance. Rawls does not permit those in the original position to know anything of their own purposes, plans, or interests—of their conception of the good. They do not know whether they prefer tennis to Tennyson, pleasures of mind over pleasures of the body. They are allowed to consider only those goods—self-respect, wealth, social position—that Rawls puts before them. Thus, critics have said, Rawls has excluded morally relevant knowledge. It is impossible to see how people could agree on principles to regulate their lives when they are so ignorant of their desires and purposes. Rawls seems to have biased the original position in his favor, and this calls into question his claim that the original position is a fair and reasonable way of arriving at principles of justice.

A second criticism focuses on whether Rawls's theory is really as different from utilitarianism as it appears to be. Rawls's theory may well permit inequalities of treatment under certain conditions in the same way that the principle of utility permits them. The principles of justice that were stated earlier apply, Rawls says, only when liberty can be effectively established and maintained. Rawls is very unclear about when a situation may be regarded as one of this kind. When it is not, his principles of justice are ones of a "general conception." Under this conception, liberties of individuals can be restricted, provided that the restrictions are for the benefit of all. It is possible to imagine, then, circumstances in which we might force individuals to become experimental subjects both for their own benefit and for that of others. We might, for example, require that all cigarette smokers participate in experiments intended to acquire knowledge about lung and heart damage. Since everyone would benefit, directly or indirectly, from such knowledge, forcing their participation would be legitimate. Thus, under the general conception of justice, the difference between Rawls's principles and the principle of utility may in practice become vanishingly small.

NATURAL LAW ETHICS
AND MORAL THEOLOGY

The general view that the rightness of actions is something determined by nature itself, rather than by the laws and customs of societies or the preferences of individuals, is called *natural law theory*. Moral principles are thus regarded as objective truths that can be discovered in the nature of things by reason and reflection. The basic idea of the theory was expressed succinctly by the Roman philosopher Cicero (103–43 B.C.). "Law is the highest reason, implanted in Nature, which commands what ought to be done and forbids the opposite. This reason, when firmly fixed and fully developed in the human mind, is Law." The natural law theory originated in classical Greek and Roman philosophy and has immensely influenced the development of moral and political theories. Indeed, all the ethical theories we have discussed are indebted to the natural law tradition. The reliance upon reason as a means of settling upon or establishing ethical principles and the emphasis on the need to reckon with the natural abilities and inclinations of human nature are just two of the threads that are woven into the theories that we have discussed.

PURPOSES, REASON, AND THE MORAL LAW
AS INTERPRETED BY ROMAN CATHOLICISM

The natural law theory of Roman Catholicism was given its most influential formulation in the thirteenth century by St. Thomas Aquinas (1225–1274). Contemporary versions of the theory are mostly elaborations and interpretations of Aquinas's basic statement. Thus, an understanding of Aquinas's views is important for grasping the philosophical principles that underlie the Roman Catholic position on such issues as abortion.

Aquinas was writing at a time in which a great number of the texts of Aristotle (384–322 B.C.) were becoming available in the West, and Aquinas's philosophical theories incorporated many of Aristotle's principles. A fundamental notion borrowed by Aquinas is the view that the universe is organized in a teleological way. That is, the universe is structured in such a way that each thing in it has a goal or purpose. Thus, when conditions are right, a tadpole will develop into a frog. In its growth and change, the tadpole is following "the law of its nature." It is achieving its goal.

Humans have a material nature, just as a tadpole does, and in their own growth and development they too follow a law of their material nature. But Aquinas also stresses that humans possess a trait that no other creature does—reason. Thus, the full development of human potentialities—the fulfillment of human purpose—requires that we follow the direction of the law of reason, as well as being subjected to the laws of material human nature.

The development of reason is one of our ends as human beings, but we also rely upon reason to determine what our ends are and how we can achieve them. It is this function of reason that leads Aquinas to identify reason as the source of the moral law. Reason is practical in its operation, for it directs our actions so that we can bring about certain results. In giving us directions, reason imposes an obligation on us, the obligation to bring about the results that it specifies. But Aquinas says that reason cannot arbitrarily set goals for us. Reason directs us toward our good as the goal of our action, and what that good is, is discoverable within our nature. Thus, reason recognizes the basic principle "Good is to be done and evil avoided."

But this principle is purely formal, or empty of content. To make it a practical principle we must consider what the human good is. According to Aquinas, the human good is that which is suitable or proper to human nature. It is what is "built into" human nature in the way that, in a sense, a frog is already "built into" a tadpole. Thus, the good is that to which we are directed by our natural inclinations as both physical and rational creatures.

Like other creatures, we have a natural inclination to preserve our lives; consequently, reason imposes on us an obligation to care for our health, not to kill ourselves, and not to put ourselves in positions in which we might be killed. We realize through reason that others have a rational nature like ours, and we see that we are bound to treat them with the same dignity and respect that we accord ourselves. Furthermore, when we see that humans require a society to make their full development possible, we realize that we have an obligation to support laws and practices that make society possible.

Thus, for example, as we have a natural inclination to propagate our species (viewed as a "natural" good), reason places on us an obligation not to thwart or pervert this inclination. As a consequence, to fulfill this obligation within society, reason supports the institution of marriage.

Reason also finds in our nature grounds for procedural principles. For example, because everyone has an inclination to preserve his life and well-being, no one should be forced to testify against himself. Similarly, because all individuals are self-interested, no one should be permitted to be a judge in his own case.

Physical inclinations, under the direction of reason, point us toward our natural good. But, according to Aquinas, reason itself can also be a source of inclinations. For example, Aquinas says that reason is the source of our natural inclination to seek the truth, particularly the truth about the existence and nature of God.

Just from the few examples we have considered, it should be clear how Aquinas believed it was possible to discover in human nature natural goods. Relying upon these as goals or purposes to be achieved, reason would then work out the practical way of achieving them. Thus, through the subtle application of reason, it should be possible to establish a body of moral principles and rules. These are the doctrines of natural law.

Because natural law is founded on human nature, which is regarded as unchangeable, Aquinas regards natural law itself as unchangeable. Moreover, it is seen as the same for all people, at all times, and in all societies. Even those without knowledge of God can, through the operation of reason, recognize their natural obligations.

For Aquinas and for Roman Catholicism, this view of natural law is just one aspect of a broader theological framework. The teleological organization of the universe is attributed to the planning of a creator—goals or purposes are ordained by God. Furthermore, although natural law is discoverable in the universe, its ultimate source is divine wisdom and God's eternal law. Everyone who is rational is capable of grasping natural law. But because passions and irrational inclinations may corrupt human nature and because some people lack the abilities or time to work out the demands of natural law, God also chose to reveal our duties to us in explicit ways. The major source of revelation, of course, is taken to be the biblical scriptures.

Natural law, scriptural revelation, the interpretation of the Scriptures by the Church, Church tradition, and the teachings of the Church are regarded in Roman Catholicism as the sources of moral ideals and principles. By guiding one's life by them, one can develop the rational and moral part of one's nature and move toward the goal of achieving the sort of perfection that is suitable for humans.

This general moral–theological point of view is the source for particular Roman Catholic doctrines that have special relevance to medicine. We will consider just two of the most important principles.

THE PRINCIPLE OF DOUBLE EFFECT.   A particular kind of moral conflict arises when the performance of an action will produce both good and bad effects. On the basis of the good effect, it seems it is our duty to perform the action; but on the basis of the bad effect, it seems our duty not to perform it.

Let's assume that the death of a fetus is in itself a bad effect and consider a case like the following: A woman who is three months pregnant is found to have a cancerous uterus. If the woman's life is to be saved, the uterus must be removed at once. But if the uterus is removed, then the life of the unborn child will be lost. Should the operation be performed?

The principle of double effect is intended to help in the resolution of these kinds of conflicts. The principle holds that such an action should be performed only if the intention is to bring about the good effect and the bad effect will be an unintended or indirect consequence. More specifically, four conditions must be satisfied:

1. The action itself must be morally indifferent or morally good.
2. The bad effect must not be the means by which the good effect is achieved.
3. The motive must be the achievement of the good effect only.
4. The good effect must be at least equivalent in importance to the bad effect.

Are these conditions satisfied in the case that we mentioned? The operation itself, if this is considered to be the action, is at least morally indifferent. That is, in itself it is neither good nor bad. That takes care of the first condition. If the mother's life is to be saved, it will not be *by means of* killing the fetus. It will be by means of removing the cancerous uterus. Thus, the second condition is met. The motive of the surgeon, we may suppose, is not the death of the fetus but saving the life of the woman. If so, then the third condition is satisfied. Finally, since two lives are at stake, the good effect (saving the life of the woman) is at least equal to the bad effect (the death of the fetus). The fourth condition is thus met. Under ordinary conditions, then, these conditions would be considered satisfied, and such an operation would be morally justified.

The principle of double effect is most often mentioned in a medical context in cases of abortion. But, in fact, it has a much wider range of application in medical ethics. It bears on cases of contraception, sterilization, organ transplants, and the use of extraordinary measures to maintain life.

THE PRINCIPLE OF TOTALITY.   The principle of totality can be expressed in this way: An individual has a right to dispose of his or her organs or to destroy their capacity to function only to the extent that the general well-being of the whole body demands it. Thus, it is clear that we have a natural obligation to preserve our lives, but, by the Roman Catholic view, we also have a duty to preserve the integrity of our bodies. This duty is based on the belief that each of our organs was designed by God to play a role in maintaining the functional integrity of our bodies, that each has a place in the divine plan. As we are the custodians of our bodies, not their owners, it is our duty to care for them as a trust.

The principle of totality has implications for a great number of medical procedures. Strictly speaking, even cosmetic surgery is morally right only when it is required to maintain or ensure the normal functioning of the rest of the body. More important, procedures that are typically employed for contraceptive purposes—vasectomies and tubal ligations—are ruled out. After all, such procedures involve "mutilation" and the destruction of the capacity of the organs of reproduction to function properly. The principle of totality thus also forbids the sterilization of the mentally retarded.

As an ethical theory, natural law theory is sometimes described as teleological. In endorsing the principle "Good is to be done and evil avoided," the theory identifies a goal with respect to which the rightness of an action is to be judged. As the principle of double effect illustrates, the intention of the individual who acts is crucial to determining whether the goal is sought. In a sense, the intention of the action, what the individual wills, defines the action. Thus, "performing an abortion" and "saving a woman's life" are not necessarily the same action, even in those instances in which their external features are the same. Unlike utilitarianism, which is also a teleological theory, natural law theory is not consequentialist: The outcome of an action is not the sole feature to consider in determining the moral character of the action.

APPLICATIONS OF ROMAN CATHOLIC
MORAL-THEOLOGICAL VIEWPOINTS
IN THE MEDICAL CONTEXT

Roman Catholic ethicists and moral theologians have written and developed a body of widely accepted doctrine. We will consider only four topics.

First, the application of the principle of double effect and the principle of totality have definite consequences in the area of medical experimentation. Since we hold our bodies in trust, we are responsible for assessing the degree of risk present in an experiment in which we are asked to be a subject. Thus, we need to be fully informed of the nature of the experiment and the risks that it holds for us. If after obtaining this knowledge we decide to give our consent, it must be given freely and not as the result of deception or coercion.

Because human experimentation carries with it the possibility of injury and death, the principle of double effect and its four strictures apply. If scientific evidence indicates that a sick person may benefit from participating in an experiment, then the experiment is morally justifiable. If, however, the evidence indicates that the chances of helping that person are slight and he or she may die or be gravely injured, then the experiment is not justified. In general, the likelihood of a person's benefiting from the experiment must exceed the danger of that person's suffering greater losses.

A person who is incurably ill may volunteer to be an experimental subject, even though she or he cannot reasonably expect personal gain in the form of improved health. The good that is hoped for is good for others, in the form of increased medical knowledge. Even here, however, there are constraints imposed by the principle of double effect. There must be no likelihood that the experiment will seriously injure, and the probable value of the knowledge expected to result must balance the risk run by the patient. Not even the incurably ill can be made subjects of trivial experiments.

The good sought by healthy volunteers is also the good of others. The same restrictions mentioned in connection with the incurably ill apply to experimenting on healthy people. Additionally, the principle of totality places constraints on what a person may volunteer to do with his or her body. No healthy person may submit to an experiment that involves the probability of serious injury, impaired health, mutilation, or death.

A second medical topic addressed by Roman Catholic theologians is whether "ordinary" or "extraordinary" measures are to be taken in the preservation of human life. While it is believed that natural law and divine law impose on us a moral obligation to preserve our lives, Catholic moralists have interpreted this obligation as requiring that we rely upon only ordinary means. In the medical profession, the phrase "ordinary means" is used to refer to medical procedures that are standard or orthodox, in contrast with those that are untried or experimental. But from the viewpoint of Catholic ethics, "ordinary" used in the medical context applies to "all medicines, treatments, and operations which offer a reasonable hope of benefit for the patient and which can be obtained and used without excessive expense, pain, or other inconvenience." Thus, by contrast, extraordinary means are those that offer the patient no reasonable hope or whose use causes serious hardship for the patient or others.

Medical measures that would save the life of a patient but subject her to years of pain or would produce in her severe physical or mental incapacities are considered extraordinary. A patient or her family are under no obligation to choose them, and physicians are under a positive obligation not to encourage their choice.

The third medical topic for consideration is euthanasia. In the Roman Catholic ethical view, euthanasia in any form is considered immoral. It is presumed to be a direct violation of God's dominion over creation and the human obligation to preserve life. The Ethical Directives for Catholic Hospitals is explicit on the matter of taking a life:

> The direct killing of any innocent person, even at his own request, is always morally wrong. Any procedure whose sole immediate effect is the death of a human being is a direct killing. . . . Euthanasia ("mercy killing") in all its forms is forbidden. . . . The failure to supply the ordinary means of preserving life is equivalent to euthanasia.

According to this view, it is wrong to allow babies suffering from serious birth defects to die. If they can be saved by ordinary means, there is an obligation to do so. It is also wrong to act to terminate the lives of those hopelessly ill, either by taking steps to bring about their deaths or by failing to take steps to maintain their lives by ordinary means.

It is never permissible to hasten the death of a person as a direct intention. It is, however, permissible to administer drugs that alleviate pain. The principle of double effect suggests that giving such drugs is a morally justifiable action even though the drugs may indirectly hasten the death of a person.

Last, we may inquire how Roman Catholicism views abortion. According to the Roman Catholic view, from the moment of conception the conceptus (later, the fetus) is considered to be a person with all the rights of a person. For this reason, direct abortion at any stage of pregnancy is regarded as morally wrong. Abortion is "direct" when it results from a procedure "whose sole immediate effect is the termination of pregnancy." This means that what is generally referred to as therapeutic abortion, in which an abortion is performed to safeguard the life or health of the woman, is considered wrong. For example, a woman with serious heart disease who becomes pregnant cannot morally justify an abortion on the grounds that the pregnancy is a serious threat to her life. Even when the ultimate aim is to save the life of the woman, direct abortion is wrong.

We have already seen, however, that the principle of double effect permits the performance of an action that may result in the death of an unborn child if the action satisfies the four criteria for applying the principle. Thus, *indirect* abortion is considered to be morally permissible. That is, the abortion must be the outcome of some action (for example, removal of a cancerous uterus) that is performed for the direct and total purpose of treating a pathological condition affecting the woman. The end sought in direct abortion is the destruction of life, but the end sought in indirect abortion is the preservation of life.

DIFFICULTIES WITH NATURAL LAW ETHICS AND MORAL THEOLOGY

Our discussion has centered on the natural law theory of ethics as it has been interpreted in Roman Catholic theology. Thus, there are two possible types of difficulties: those associated with natural law ethics in its own right and those associated with its incorporation into theology. The theological difficulties go beyond the scope of our aims and interests. We will restrict ourselves to considering the basic difficulty that faces natural law theory as formulated by Aquinas. Since it is this formulation that has been used in Roman Catholic moral theology, we shall be raising a problem for it in an indirect way.

The fundamental difficulty with Aquinas's argument for natural law is caused by the assumption, borrowed from Aristotle, that the universe is organized in a teleological fashion. (This is the assumption that every kind of thing has a goal or purpose.) This assumption is essential to Aquinas's ethical theory, for he identifies the good of a thing with its natural mode of operation. Without the assumption, we are faced with the great diversity and moral indifference of nature. Inclinations, even when shared by all humans, are no more than inclinations. There are no grounds for considering them "goods," and they have no moral status. The universe is bereft of natural values.

Yet, there are many reasons to consider this assumption false. Physics surrendered the notion of a teleological organization in the world as long ago as the seventeenth century—the rejection of Aristotle's physics also entailed the rejection of Aristotle's teleological view of the world. This left biology as the major source of arguments in favor of teleology. But contemporary evolutionary theory shows that the apparent purposive character of evolutionary change can be accounted for by the operation of natural selection on random mutations. Also, the development and growth of organisms can be explained by the presence of genetic information that controls the processes. The tadpole develops into a frog because evolution has produced a genetic program that directs the sequence of complicated chemical changes. Thus, no adequate grounds seem to exist for asserting that the teleological organization of nature is anything more than apparent.

Science and "reason alone" do not support teleology. It can be endorsed only if one is willing to assume that any apparent teleological organization is the product of a divine plan. Yet, because all apparent teleology can be explained in nonteleological ways, this assumption seems neither necessary nor legitimate.

Without its foundation of teleology, Aquinas's theory of natural law ethics seems to collapse. This is not to say, of course, that some other natural law theory, one not requiring the assumption of teleology, might not be persuasively defended.

Major Moral Principles

Making moral decisions is always a difficult and stressful task. Abstract discussions of issues never quite capture the feelings of uncertainty and self-doubt we characteristically experience when called upon to decide what ought to be done or to judge whether someone did the right thing. There are no mechanical processes or algorithms we can apply in a situation of moral doubt. There are no computer programs to supply us with the proper decision when given the relevant data.

In a very real sense, we are on our own when it comes to making ethical decisions. This does not mean that we are without resources and must decide blindly or even naively. When we have the luxury of time, when the need to make a decision is not pressing, then we may attempt to work out an answer to a moral question by relying upon a general ethical theory like those discussed earlier. However, in ordinary life we rarely have the opportunity or time to engage in an elaborate process of reasoning and analysis.

A more practical approach is to employ moral principles that have been derived from and justified by a moral theory. A principle such as "Avoid causing needless harm" can serve as a more direct guide to action and decision making than, say, Kant's categorical imperative. With such a principle in mind, we realize that, if we are acting as a physician, then we have a duty to use our knowledge and skills to protect our patients from injury. For example, we should not expose a patient to the needless risk of a diagnostic test that does not promise to yield useful information.

In this section, we will present and illustrate five moral principles. All are ones of special relevance to dealing with the ethical issues presented by decisions concerning medical care. The principles have their limitations. For one thing, they are in no sense complete. Moral issues arise, even in the context of medicine, for which they can supply no direct guidance. In other situations, the principles themselves may come into conflict and point toward incompatible solutions. (How can we both avoid causing harm and allow a terminally ill patient to die?) The principles themselves indicate no way such conflicts can be resolved, for, even taken together, they do not constitute a coherent moral theory. To resolve conflicts, it may be necessary to employ the more basic principles of such a theory.

It is fair to say that each of the five basic moral theories we have discussed endorses the legitimacy of these principles. Not all would formulate them in the same way, and not all would give them the same moral weight. Nevertheless, each theory would accept them as expressing appropriate guidelines for moral decision making.

Indeed, the best way to think about the principles is as guidelines. They are in no way rules that can be applied automatically. Rather, they express standards to be consulted in attempting to arrive at a justified decision. As such, they provide a basis for evaluating actions or policies as well as for making individual moral decisions.

They help guarantee that our decisions are made in accordance with our principles and not according to our whims or prejudices. By following them we are more likely to reach decisions that are reasoned, consistent, and applicable to similar cases.

THE PRINCIPLE OF NONMALEFICENCE

"Above all, do no harm" is perhaps the most famous and most quoted of all moral maxims in medicine. It captures in a succinct way what is universally considered to be an overriding duty of anyone who undertakes the care of a patient. We believe that in treating a patient a physician should not by carelessness, malice, inadvertence, or avoidable ignorance do anything that will cause injury to the patient.

The maxim is one expression of what is sometimes called in ethics the principle of nonmaleficence. The principle can be formulated in various ways, but here is one relatively noncontroversial way of stating it: *We ought to act in ways that do not cause needless harm or injury to others.* Stated in a positive fashion, the principle tells us that we have a duty to avoid maleficence, that is to avoid harming or injuring other people.

In the most obvious case, we violate the principle of nonmaleficence when we intentionally do something we know will cause someone harm. For example, suppose a surgeon during the course of an operation deliberately severs a muscle, knowing that by doing so he will cripple the patient. The surgeon is guilty of maleficence and is morally (as well as legally) blameworthy for her action.

The principle may also be violated when no malice or intention to do harm is involved. A nurse who carelessly gives a patient the wrong medication and causes the patient to suffer irreversible brain damage may have had no intention of causing the patient any injury. However, the nurse was negligent in his actions and failed to exercise due care in discharging his responsibilities. His actions resulted in an avoidable injury to his patient. Hence, he failed to meet his obligation of nonmaleficence.

The duty imposed by the principle of nonmaleficence is not a demand to accomplish the impossible. We realize that we cannot reasonably expect perfection in the practice of medicine. We know that the results of treatments are often uncertain and may cause more harm than good. We know that the knowledge we have of diseases is only partial and that decisions about diagnosis and therapy typically involve the exercise of judgment, with no guarantee of correctness. We know that an uncertainty is built into the very nature of things and that our power to control the outcome of natural processes is limited. Consequently, we realize that we cannot hold physicians and other health professionals accountable for every instance of death and injury involving patients under their care.

Nevertheless, we can demand that physicians and others live up to reasonable standards of performance. In the conduct of their professions, we can expect them to be cautious and diligent, patient and thoughtful. We can expect them to pay attention to what they are doing and to deliberate about whether a particular procedure should be done. In addition, we can expect them to possess the knowledge and skills relevant to the proper discharge of their duties.

These features and others like them make up the standards of performance that define what we have a right to expect from physicians and other health professionals. In the language of the law, these are the standards of "due care," and it is by reference to them that we evaluate the medical care given to patients. Failure to meet the standards opens practitioners (physicians, nurses, dentists, therapists) to the charge of moral or legal maleficence.

In our society, we have attempted to guarantee that at least some of the due-care standards are met by relying upon such measures as degree programs, licensing laws, certifying boards, and hospital credentials committees. Such an approach offers a way of ensuring that physicians and others have acquired at least a minimum level of knowledge, skill, and experience before undertaking the responsibilities attached to their roles. The approach also encourages such values as diligence, prudence, and caution, but there is of course no way of guaranteeing that in a particular case a physician will exhibit those virtues. Haste, carelessness, and inattention are always possible, and the potential that a patient will suffer an injury from them is always present.

The standards of due care are connected in some respects with such factual matters as the current state of medical knowledge and training and the immediate circumstances in which a physician provides care. For example, in the 1920s and 1930s, it was not at all unusual for a general practitioner to perform relatively complicated surgery. This was particularly true of someone practicing in a rural area. In performing surgery, he would be acting in a reasonable and expected fashion and could not be legitimately charged with violating the principle of nonmaleficence.

However, the change in medicine from that earlier time to the present has also altered our beliefs about what is reasonable and expected. Today, a general practitioner who has had no special training and is not board certified and yet performs surgery on her patients may be legitimately criticized for maleficence. The standards of due care in surgery are now higher and more exacting than they once were, and the general practitioner who undertakes to perform most forms of surgery causes her patients to undergo an unusual and unnecessary risk literally at her hands. Their interest would be better served if their surgery were performed by a trained and qualified surgeon.

Such a case also illustrates that no actual harm or injury must occur for someone to be acting in violation of the principle of nonmaleficence. The general practitioner performing surgery may not cause any injury to his patients, but he puts them in a position in which the possibility of harm to them is greater than it needs to be. It is in this respect that he is not exercising due care in his treatment and so can be charged with maleficence. He has subjected his patients to *unnecessary risk*, risk greater than they would be subject to in the hands of a trained surgeon.

It is important to stress that the principle of nonmaleficence does not require that a physician subject a patient to no risks at all. Virtually every form of diagnostic testing and medical treatment involves some degree of risk to the patient, and to provide medical care at all, a physician must often act in ways that involve a possible injury to the patient. For example, a physician who takes a thorough medical history and performs a physical examination, then treats a patient with an antibiotic for bacterial infection cannot be held morally responsible if the patient suffers a severe drug reaction. That such a thing might happen is a possibility that cannot be foreseen in an individual case.

Similarly, a serious medical problem may justify subjecting the patient to a serious risk. (Gaining the consent of the patient is an obvious consideration, however.) A life-threatening condition, such as an occluded right coronary artery, may warrant coronary-bypass surgery with all its attendant dangers.

In effect, the principle of nonmaleficence tells us to avoid needless risk and, when risk is an inevitable aspect of an appropriate diagnostic test or treatment, to minimize the risk as much as is reasonably possible. A physician who orders a lumbar puncture for a patient who complains of occasional headaches is acting inappropriately, given the nature of the complaint, and is subjecting his patient to needless risk. By contrast, a physician who orders such a test after examining a patient who has severe and recurring headaches, a fever, pain and stiffness in his neck, and additional key clinical signs is acting appropriately. The risk to the patient from the lumbar puncture is the same in both cases, but the risk is warranted in the second case and not in the first. A failure to act with due care violates the principle of nonmaleficence, even if no harm results, whereas acting with due care does not violate the principle, even if harm does result.

THE PRINCIPLE OF BENEFICENCE

"As to diseases, make a habit of two things—to help or at least to do no harm." This directive from the Hippocratic writings stresses that the physician has two duties. The second of them ("at least to do no harm") we discussed in connection with the principle of nonmaleficence. The first of them ("to help") we will consider here in connection with the principle of beneficence.

Like the previous principle, the principle of beneficence can be stated in various and different ways. Here is one formulation: *We should act in ways that promote the welfare of other people.* That is, we should help other people when we are able to do so.

Some philosophers have expressed doubt that we have an actual duty to help others. We certainly have a duty not to harm other people, but it has seemed to some that there are no grounds for saying that we have a duty to promote their welfare. We would deserve praise if we did, but we would not deserve blame if we did not. From this point of view, being beneficent is beyond the scope of duty.

We need not consider whether this view is correct in general. For our purposes, it is enough to realize that the nature of the relationship between a physician and a patient does impose the duty of acting in the patient's welfare. That is, the duty of beneficence is inherent in the role of physician. A physician who was not acting for the sake of the patient's good would, in a very real sense, not be acting as a physician.

That we recognize this as a duty appropriate to the physician's role is seen most clearly in cases in which the physician is also a researcher and her patient is also an experimental subject. In such instances, there is a possibility of a role conflict, for the researcher's aim of acquiring knowledge is not always compatible with the physician's aim of helping the patient. (See Chapter 1 for a discussion of this problem.)

The duty required by the principle of beneficence is inherent in the role not only of physicians but also of all health professionals. Nurses, therapists, clinical psychologists, social workers, and others accept the duty of promoting the welfare of their patients or clients as an appropriate part of their responsibilities. We expect nurses and others to do good for us, and it is this expectation that leads us to designate them as belonging to what are often called "the helping professions."

The extent to which beneficence is required as a duty for physicians and others is not a matter easily resolved. In practice, we recognize that limits exist to what can be expected from even those who have chosen to make a career of helping others. We do not expect physicians to sacrifice completely their self-interest and welfare on behalf of their patients. We do not think their duty demands that they be totally selfless. If some do, we may praise them as secular saints or moral heroes, but that is because they go beyond the demands of duty. At the same time, we would have little good to say of a physician who always put his interest above that of his patients, who never made a personal sacrifice to service their interests.

Just as there are standards of due care that explicitly and implicitly define what we consider to be right conduct in protecting patients from harm, so there seem to be implicit standards of beneficence. We obviously expect physicians to help patients by providing them with appropriate treatment. More than this, we expect physicians to be prepared to make *reasonable* sacrifices for the sake of their patients. Even in the age of "health-care teams," a single physician assumes responsibility for a particular patient when the patient is hospitalized or treated for a serious illness. It is this physician who is expected to make the crucial medical decisions, and we expect her to realize that discharging that responsibility may involve an interruption of private plans and activities. A surgeon who is informed that her postoperative patient has started to bleed can be expected to cancel her plan to attend a concert. Doing so is a reasonable duty imposed by the principle of beneficence. If she failed to discharge the duty, in the absence of mitigating circumstances, she would become the object of disapproval by her patient and by her medical colleagues.

It would be very difficult to spell out exactly what duties are required by the principle of beneficence. Even if we limited ourselves to the medical context, there are so many ways of promoting someone's welfare and so many different circumstances to consider that it would be virtually impossible to provide anything like a catalog of appropriate actions. However, such a catalog is hardly necessary. Most people most often have a sense of what is reasonable and what is not, and it is this sense that we rely on in making judgments about whether physicians and others are fulfilling the duty of beneficence in their actions.

The principles of nonmaleficence and beneficence impose social duties also. In the most general terms, we look to society to take measures to promote the health and safety of its citizens. The great advances made in public health during the nineteenth century were made because the society recognized a responsibility to attempt to prevent the spread of disease. Water treatment plants, immunization programs, and quarantine restrictions were all in recognition of society's duty of nonmaleficence.

These and similar programs have been continued and augmented, and our society has also recognized a duty of beneficence in connection with health care. The Medicaid program for the poor and Medicare for the elderly are major efforts to see to at least some of the health needs of a large segment of the population. Prenatal programs for expectant mothers and public clinics are among the other social responses we have made to promote the health of citizens.

Less obvious than programs that provide direct medical care are ones that support medical research and basic science. Directly or indirectly, such programs contribute to meeting the health needs of our society. Much basic research is relevant to acquiring an understanding of the processes involved in both health and disease, and much medical research is specifically aimed at the development of effective diagnostic and therapeutic measures.

In principle, social beneficence has no limits, but in practice it must. Social resources like tax revenues are in restricted supply, and the society must decide how they are to be spent. Housing and food for the poor, education, defense, the arts, and the humanities are just some of the areas demanding support in the name of social beneficence. Medical care is just one among many claimants, and we must decide as a society what proportion of our social resources we want to commit to it. Are we prepared to guarantee to all whatever medical care they need? Are we willing to endorse only a basic level of care? Do we want to say that what is available to some (the rich or well-insured) must be available to all (the poor and uninsured)? Just how beneficent we wish to be—and can afford to be—is a matter still under discussion (see Chapter 8).

THE PRINCIPLE OF UTILITY

The principle of utility can be formulated in this way: *We should act in such a way as to bring about the greatest benefit and the least harm.* As we discussed earlier, the principle is the very foundation of the moral theory of utilitarianism. However, the principle need not be regarded as unique to utilitarianism. It can be thought of as one moral principle among others that present us with a prima facie duty, and as such it need not be regarded as always taking precedence over others. In particular, we would never think it was justified to deprive someone of a right, even if by doing so we could bring benefit to many others.

We need not repeat the discussion of the principle of utility presented earlier, but it may be useful to consider here how the principle relates to the principles of nonmaleficence and beneficence. When we consider the problem of distributing social resources, it becomes clear that acting in accordance with the principles of nonmaleficence and beneficence usually involves trade-offs. To use our earlier example, as a society we are concerned with providing for the healthcare needs of our citizens. To accomplish this end, we support various programs—Medicare, Medicaid, hospital-building programs, medical research, and so on.

However, there are limits to what we can do. Medical care is not the only concern of our society. We are interested in protecting people from harm and in pro moting their interests, but there are many forms of harm and many kinds of interest to be promoted. With finite resources at our disposal, the more money we spend on health care, the less we can spend on education, the arts, the humanities, and so on.

Even if we decided to spend more money on health care than we are currently spending, there would come a point at which we would receive only a marginal return for our money. General health would eventually reach such a level that it would be difficult to raise it still higher. To save even one additional life, we would have to spend a vast sum of money. By contrast, at the start of a health-care program, relatively little money can make a relatively big difference. Furthermore, money spent for marginal improvements would be directed away from other needs that had become even more crucial because of underfunding. Thus, we could not spend all our resources on health care without ignoring other social needs.

The aim of social planning is to balance the competing needs of the society. Taken alone, the principles of nonmaleficence and beneficence are of no help in resolving the conflicts among social needs. The principle of utility must come into play to establish and rank needs and to serve as a guide for determining to what extent it is possible to satisfy one social need in comparison with others. In effect, the principle imposes a social duty on us all to use our resources to do as much good as possible. That is, we must do the most good *overall,* even when this means we are not able to meet all needs in a particular area.

The application of the principle of utility is not limited to large-scale social issues, such as how to divide our resources among medical care, defense, education, and so on. We may also rely on the principle when we are deliberating about the choice of alternative means of accomplishing an aim. For example, we might decide to institute a mandatory screening program to detect infants with PKU but decide against a program to detect those with Tay–Sachs. PKU can often be treated successfully if discovered early enough, whereas early detection of Tay–Sachs makes little or no difference in the outcome of the disease. Furthermore, PKU is distributed in the general population, whereas Tay–Sachs occurs mostly in a special segment of the population. In general, then, the additional money spent on screening for Tay–Sachs would not be justified by the results. The money could do more good, produce more benefits, were it spent some other way.

The principle of utility is also relevant to making decisions about the diagnosis and treatment of individuals. For example, as we mentioned earlier, no diagnostic test can be justified if it causes the patient more risk than the information likely to be gained is worth. Invasive procedures are associated with a certain rate of injury and death (morbidity and mortality). It would make no sense to subject a patient to a kidney biopsy if the findings were not likely to affect the course of treatment or if the risk from the biopsy were greater than the risk of the suspected disease itself. Attempts are well under way in medicine to employ the formal theories of decision analysis to assist physicians in determining whether a particular mode of diagnosis, therapy, or surgery can be justified in individual cases. Underlying the details of formal analysis is the principle of utility, which directs us to act in a way that will bring about the greatest benefit and the least harm.

PRINCIPLES OF DISTRIBUTIVE JUSTICE

We expect (and can demand) to be treated justly in our dealings with other people and with institutions. If our insurance policy covers up to thirty days of hospitalization, then we expect a claim against the policy for that amount of time to be honored. If we arrive in an emergency room with a broken arm before the arrival of someone else with a broken arm, we expect to be attended to before that person.

We do not always expect that being treated justly will work to our direct advantage. Although we would prefer to keep all the money we earn, we realize that we must pay our share of taxes. If a profusely bleeding person arrives in the emergency room after we do, we recognize that he is in need of immediate treatment and should be attended to before we are.

Justice has at least two major aspects. Seeing to it that people receive that to which they are entitled, that their rights are recognized and protected, falls under the general heading of *noncomparative justice.* By contrast, *comparative justice* is concerned with the application of laws and rules and with the distribution of burdens and benefits.

The concern of comparative justice that is most significant to the medical context is *distributive justice.* As the name suggests, distributive justice concerns the distribution of such social benefits and burdens as medical services, welfare payments, public offices, taxes, and military service. In general, the distribution of income has been the focus of recent discussions of distributive justice. In medical ethics, the focus has been the distribution of health care. Is everyone in the society entitled to receive health-care benefits, whether or not she or he can pay for them? If so, then is everyone entitled to the same amount of health care? (See Chapter 8 for a discussion of this issue.)

Philosophical theories of justice attempt to resolve questions of distributive justice by providing a detailed account of the features of individuals and society that will justify our making distinctions in the ways we distribute benefits and burdens. If some people are to be rich and others poor, if some are to rule and others serve, then there must be some rational and moral basis for such distinctions. We look to theories of justice to provide us with such a basis. (See the earlier discussion of John Rawls's theory for an outstanding recent example.)

Theories of justice differ significantly, but at the core of all theories is the basic principle that "Similar cases ought to be treated in similar ways." The principle expresses the notion that justice involves fairness of treatment. For example, it is manifestly unfair to award two different grades to two people who score the same on a multiple-choice exam. If two cases are the same, then it is arbitrary or irrational to treat them differently. To justify different treatment, we would have to show that in some relevant respect the cases are also dissimilar.

This fairness principle is known as the *formal* principle of justice. It is called "formal" because, like a sentence with blanks, it must be filled in with information. Specifically, we must be told what factors or features are to be considered *relevant* in deciding whether two cases are similar. If two cases differ in relevant respects, we may be justified in treating them differently. We may do so without being either irrational or arbitrary.

Theories of distributive justice present us with *substantive* (or *material*) principles of justice. The theories present us with arguments to show why certain features or factors should be considered relevant in deciding whether cases are similar. The substantive principles can then be referred to in determining whether particular laws, practices, or public policies can be considered just. Further, the substantive principles can be employed as guidelines for framing laws and policies and for developing a just society.

Arguments in favor of particular theories of justice are too lengthy to present here. However, it is useful to consider briefly four substantive principles that have been offered by various theorists as ones worthy of acceptance. To a considerable extent, differences among these principles help explain present disagreements in our society about the ways in which such social "goods" as income, education, and health care should be distributed. Although the principles themselves direct the distribution of burdens (taxation, public service, and so on) as well as benefits, we will focus on benefits. The basic question answered by each principle is "Who is entitled to what proportion of society's goods?".

THE PRINCIPLE OF EQUALITY

According to the principle of equality all benefits and burdens are to be distributed equally. Everyone is entitled to the same size slice of the pie, and everyone must bear an equal part of the social load. The principle, strictly interpreted, requires a radical egalitarianism—everyone is to be treated the same in all respects.

The principle is most plausible for a society above the margin of production. When there is enough to go around but not much more, then it is manifestly unfair for some to have more than they need and for others to have less than they need. When a society is more affluent, the principle may lose some of its persuasiveness. When greater efforts by a few produce more goods than the efforts of the ordinary person, it may be unfair not to recognize the accomplishments of a few by greater rewards. Rawls's theory remains an egalitarian one, while providing a way to resolve this apparent conflict. According to Rawls, any departure from equality is arbitrary, unless it can be shown that the inequality will work out to *everyone's* advantage.

THE PRINCIPLE OF NEED

The principle of need is an extension of the egalitarian principle of equal distribution. If goods are parceled out according to individual need, those who have greater needs will receive a greater share. However, the outcome will be one of equality. Since the basic needs of everyone will be met, everyone will end up at the same level. The treatment of individuals will be equal, in this respect, even though the proportion of goods they receive will not be.

What is to count as a need is a significant question that cannot be answered by a principle of distribution alone. Obviously, basic biological needs (food, clothing, shelter) must be included, but what about psychological or intellectual needs? The difficulty of resolving the question of needs is seen in the fact that—even in our affluent society, the richest in the history of the world—we are still debating the question of whether health care should be available to all.

THE PRINCIPLE OF CONTRIBUTION

According to the principle of contribution, everyone should get back that proportion of social goods that is the result of his or her productive labor. If two people work to grow potatoes and the first works twice as long or twice as hard as the second, then the first should be entitled to twice as large a share of the harvest.

The difficulty with this principle in an industrialized, capitalistic society is that contributions to production can take forms other than time and labor. Some people risk their money in investments needed to make production possible, and others contribute crucial ideas or inventions. How are comparisons to be made? Furthermore, in highly industrialized societies it is the functioning of the entire system, rather than the work of any particular individual, that creates the goods to be distributed. A single individual's claim on the outcome of the whole system may be very small.

Nonetheless, it is individuals who make the system work, so it does seem just that individuals should benefit from their contributions. If it is true that it is the system of social organization itself that is most responsible for creating the goods, then this is an argument for supporting the system through taxation and other means. If individual contributions count for relatively little (although for something), there may be no real grounds for attempting to distinguish among them in distributing social benefits.

THE PRINCIPLE OF EFFORT

According to the principle of effort, the degree of effort made by the individual should determine the proportion of goods received by the individual. Thus, the file clerk who works just as hard as the president of a company should receive the same proportion of social goods as the president. Those who are lazy and refuse to exert themselves will receive proportionally less than those who work hard.

The advantage of the principle is that it captures our sense of what is fair— that those who do their best should be similarly rewarded, while those who do less than their best should be less well rewarded. The principle assumes that people have equal opportunities to do their best and that if they do not it is their own fault. One difficulty with this assumption is that, even if the society presents equal opportunities, nature does not. Some people are born with disabilities or meet with accidents, and their misfortunes may make it difficult for them to want to do their best, even when they are given the opportunity.

Each principle has its shortcomings, but this does not mean that adjustments cannot be made to correct their weaknesses. A complete theory of justice need not be limited in the number of principles that it accepts, and it is doubtful that any theory can be shown to be both fair and plausible if it restricts itself to only one principle. Although all theories require adjustment, theories fall into types in accordance with the principles they emphasize. For example, Marxist theories select need as basic, whereas libertarian theories stress personal contribution as the grounds for distribution. Utilitarian theories employ that combination of principles that promises to maximize both private and public interests.

Joel Feinberg, to whom the preceding discussion is indebted, may be mentioned as an example of a careful theorist who recommends the adoption of a combination of principles. Feinberg sees the principle of equality based on needs as the basic determination of distributive justice. After basic needs have been satisfied, the principles of contribution and effort should be given the most weight.

According to Feinberg, when there is an economic abundance, then the claim to "minimally decent conditions" can reasonably be made for every person in the society. To have one's basic needs satisfied under such conditions amounts to a fundamental right. However, when everyone's basic needs are taken care of and society produces a surplus of goods, then considerations of contribution and effort become relevant. Those who contribute most to the increase of goods or those who work the hardest to produce it (or some combination) can legitimately lay claim to a greater share.

The principles of justice we have discussed may seem at first to be intolerably abstract and so irrelevant to the practical business of society. However, it is important to keep in mind that it is by referring to such principles that we criticize our society and its laws and practices. The claim that society is failing to meet some basic need of all of its citizens and that this is unfair or unjust is a powerful charge. It can be a call to action in the service of justice. If the claim can be demonstrated, it has more than rhetorical power. It imposes upon us all an obligation to eliminate the source of the injustice.

Similarly, in framing laws and formulating policies, we expect those who occupy the offices of power and influence to make their decisions in accordance with principles. Prominent among these must be principles of justice. It may be impossible in the conduct of daily business to apply any principle directly or exclusively, for we can hardly remake our society overnight. Yet if we are committed to a just society, then the principles of justice can at least serve as guidelines when policy decisions are made. They remind us that it is not always fair for the race to go to the swift.

THE PRINCIPLE OF AUTONOMY

The principle of autonomy can be stated this way: *Rational individuals should be permitted to be self-determining.* According to this formulation, we act autonomously when our actions are the result of our own choices and decisions. Thus, autonomy and self-determination are equivalent.

Autonomy is associated with the status we ascribe to rational beings as persons in the morally relevant sense. We are committed to the notion that persons are by their very nature uniquely qualified to decide what is in their own best interest. This is because, to use Kant's terms, they are ends in themselves, not means to some other ends. As such, they have an inherent worth, and it is the duty of others to respect that worth and avoid treating them as though they were just ordinary parts of the world to be manipulated according to the will of someone else. A recognition of autonomy is a recognition of that inherent worth, and a violation of autonomy is a violation of our concept of what it is to be a person. To deny someone autonomy is to treat her or him as something less than a person.

This view of the nature of autonomy and its connection with our recognition of what is involved in being a person is shared by several significant moral theories. At the core of each theory is the concept of the rational individual as a moral agent who, along with other moral agents, possesses an unconditional worth. Moral responsibility itself is based on the assumption that such agents are free to determine their own actions and pursue their own aims.

Autonomy is significant not only because it is a condition for moral responsibility, but because it is through the exercise of autonomy that individuals shape their lives. We might not approve of what people do with their lives. It is sad to see talent wasted and opportunities for personal development rejected. Nevertheless, as we sometimes say, "It's his life." We recognize that people are entitled to attempt to make their lives what they want them to be and that it would be wrong for us to take control of their lives and dictate their actions, even if we could. We recognize that a person must walk to heaven or hell by her own freely chosen path.

Simply put, to act autonomously is to decide for oneself what to do. Of course, decisions are never made outside of a context, and the world and the people in it exert influence, impose constraints, and restrict opportunities. It is useful to call attention to three interrelated aspects of autonomy in order to get a better understanding of the ways in which autonomy can be exercised, denied, and restricted. We will look at autonomy in the contexts of actions, options, and decision making.

AUTONOMY AND ACTIONS

Consider the following situations: A police officer shoves a demonstrator off the sidewalk during an abortion protest. An attendant in a psychiatric ward warns a patient to stay in bed or be strapped down. A corrections officer warns a prison inmate that if he does not donate blood he will not be allowed out of his cell to eat dinner. A state law requires that anyone admitted to a hospital be screened for the HIV antibody.

In each of these situations, either actual force, the threat of force, or potential penalties are employed to direct the actions of an individual toward some end. All involve some form of coercion, and the coercion is used to restrict the freedom of individuals to act as they might choose. Under such circumstances, the individual ceases to be the agent who initiates the action as a result of his or her choice. The individual's initiative is set aside, wholly or partially, in favor of someone else's.

Autonomy is violated in such cases even if the individual intends to act in the way that is imposed or demanded. Perhaps the prison inmate would have donated blood anyway, and surely some people would have wanted to be screened for HIV. However, the use of coercion makes the wishes or intentions of the individual partly or totally irrelevant to whether the act is performed.

Autonomy as the initiation of action through one's own intervention and choice can clearly be restricted to a greater or lesser degree. Someone who is physically forced to become a subject in a medical experiment, as in a Nazi concentration camp, is totally deprived of autonomy. The same is true of someone tricked into becoming a subject without knowing it. In the infamous Tuskegee syphilis studies, some participants were led to believe they were receiving appropriate medical treatment, when in fact they were part of a control group in the experiment. The situation is somewhat different for someone who agrees to become a subject in order to receive needed medical care. Such a person is acting under strong coercion, but the loss of autonomy is not complete. It is at least possible to refuse to participate, even if the cost of doing so may be extremely high.

In situations more typical than those above, autonomy may be compromised, rather than denied. For example, someone who is by nature nonassertive or someone who is poor and uneducated may find it very difficult to preserve his power of self-determination when he becomes a patient in a hospital. Medical authority, represented by physicians and the hospital staff, may be so intimidating to such a person that she does not feel free to exercise her autonomy. In such a case, although no one may be deliberately attempting to infringe on the patient's autonomy, social and psychological factors may constitute a force so coercive that the patient feels she has no choice but to do what she is told.

AUTONOMY AND OPTIONS

Autonomy involves more than freedom from duress in making decisions. There must be genuine possibilities to decide among. A forced option is no option at all, and anyone who is in the position of having to take what he can get can hardly be regarded as self-determining or as exercising free choice.

In our society, economic and social conditions frequently limit the options available in medical care. As a rule, the poor simply do not have the same choices available to them as the rich. Someone properly insured or financially well off who might be helped by a heart transplant can decide whether or not to undergo the risk of having one. That is an option not generally available to someone who is uninsured and poor.

Similarly, a woman who depends on Medicaid and lives in a state in which Medicaid funds cannot be used to pay for abortions may not have the option of having an abortion. Her choice is not a genuine one, for she lacks the means to implement it. The situation is quite different for a middle-class woman faced with the same question. She may decide against having an abortion, but whatever she decides, the choice is real. She is autonomous in a way that the poor woman is not.

Those who believe that one of the goals of our society is to promote and protect the autonomy of individuals have frequently argued that we must do more to offer all individuals the same range of health-care options. If we do not, they have suggested, then our society cannot be one in which everyone has an equal degree of autonomy. In a very real sense, those who are rich will have greater freedom of action than those who are poor.

AUTONOMY AND DECISION MAKING

More is involved in decision making than merely saying yes or no. In particular, relevant information is an essential condition for genuine decision making. We are exercising our autonomy in the fullest sense only when we are making *informed* decisions.

It is pointless to have options if we are not aware of them; we can hardly be said to be directing the course of our lives if our decisions must be made in ignorance of information that is available and relevant to our choices. These are the reasons that lying and other forms of deception are so destructive of autonomy. If someone with a progressive and ordinarily fatal disease is not told about it by her physician, then she is in no position to decide how to shape what remains of her life. The lack of a crucial piece of information—that she is dying—is likely to lead her to make decisions different from the ones she would make were she in possession of the information.

Information is the key to protecting and preserving autonomy in most medical situations. A patient who is not informed of alternative forms of treatment and their associated risks is denied the opportunity to make his own wishes and values count for something in his own life. For example, someone with coronary artery disease who is not told of the relative merits of medical treatment with drugs but is told only that he is a candidate for coronary artery-bypass surgery, is in no position to decide what risks he wishes to take and what ordeals he is prepared to undergo. A physician who does not supply the patient with the information the patient needs is restricting the patient's autonomy. The principle of autonomy requires *informed* consent, for consent alone does not involve genuine self-determination.

Making decisions for "the good" of others (paternalism), without consulting their wishes, deprives them of their status as autonomous agents. For example, some people at the final stages of a terminal illness might prefer to be allowed to die without heroic intervention, while others might prefer to prolong their lives as long as medical skills and technological powers make possible. If a physician or family undertakes to make a decision in this matter on behalf of the patient, then no matter what their motive, they are denying to the patient the power of self-determination.

Because autonomy is so bound up with informed consent and decision making, special problems arise in the case of those unable to give consent and make decisions. Patients who are comatose, severely brain damaged, psychotic, or seriously mentally impaired are not capable of making decisions on their own behalf. The nature of their condition has already deprived them of their autonomy. Of course, this does not mean that they have no status as moral persons or that they have no interests. It falls to others to see that their interests are served.

The situation is similar for those, such as infants and young children, who are incapable of understanding. Any consent that is given must be given by others. But what are the limits of consent that can be legitimately given for some other person? Consenting to needed medical care seems legitimate, but what about rejecting needed medical care? What about consenting to becoming a subject in a research program? These questions are as crucial as they are difficult to resolve.

RESTRICTIONS ON AUTONOMY

Autonomy is not an absolute or unconditional value. We would regard it as absurd for someone to claim that she was justified in committing a murder because she was only exercising her power of self-determination. Such a defense would be morally ludicrous.

However, we do value autonomy and recognize a general duty to respect it and even to promote its exercise. We demand compelling reasons to justify restricting the power of individuals to make their own choices and direct their own lives.

We will briefly examine four principles that are frequently appealed to in justifying restrictions on autonomy. The principles have been discussed most in the context of social and legal theory, for it is through laws and penalties that a society most directly regulates the conduct of its citizens. However, the principles can also be appealed to in justifying policies and practices of institutions (such as hospitals) and the actions of individuals that affect other people.

Appealing to a principle can provide, at best, only a prima facie justification. Even if a principle can be shown to apply to a particular case in which freedom of action is restricted, we may value the lost freedom more than what is gained by restricting it. Reasons suggested by the principle may not be adequately persuasive. Furthermore, the principles themselves are frequently the subjects of controversy, and, with the exception of the harm principle, it is doubtful that any of the principles would be universally endorsed by philosophers and legal theorists.

THE HARM PRINCIPLE.   According to the harm principle, we may restrict the freedom of people to act if the restriction is necessary to prevent harm to others. In the most obvious case, we may take action to prevent violence like rape, robbery, killing, or assault. We may act to protect someone who is in apparent risk of harm from the action of someone else. The risk of harm need not be the result of the intention to harm. Thus, we might take steps to see that a surgeon whose skills and judgment have been impaired through drug use is not permitted to operate.

The risk that he poses to his patients warrants the effort to keep him from acting as he wishes. The harm principle may also be used to justify laws that exert coercive force and so restrict freedom of action. Laws against homicide and assault are clear examples, but the principle extends also to the regulation of institutions and practices. People may be robbed at the point of a pen, as well as at the point of a knife, and the harm produced by fraud may be as great as that produced by outright theft. Careless or deceptive medical practitioners may cause direct harm to their patients, and laws that regulate the standards of medical practice restrict the freedom of practitioners for the protection of patients.

THE PRINCIPLE OF PATERNALISM.   In its weak version, the principle of paternalism is no more than the harm principle applied to the individual himself. According to the principle, we are justified in restricting someone's freedom to act if doing so is necessary to prevent him from harming himself. Thus, we might force an alcoholic into a treatment program and justify our action by claiming that we did so to prevent him from continuing to harm himself by his drinking.

In its strong version, the principle of paternalism justifies restricting someone's autonomy if by doing so we can benefit her. In such a case, our concern is not only with preventing the person from harming herself, but also with promoting her good in a positive way. The principle might be appealed to even in cases in which our actions go against the other's known wishes. For example, a physician might decide to treat a patient with a placebo (an inactive drug), even if she has asked to be told the truth about her medical condition and her therapy. He might attempt to justify his action by claiming that if the patient knew she was receiving a placebo, then the placebo would be less likely to be effective. Since taking the placebo while believing that it is an active drug makes her feel better, the physician may claim that by deceiving her he is doing something to help her.

Paternalism may be expressed in laws and public policies, as well as in private actions. Some have suggested the drug laws as a prime example of governmental paternalism. By making certain drugs illegal and inaccessible and by placing other drugs under the control of physicians, the laws aim to protect people from themselves. Self-medication is virtually eliminated, and the so-called recreational use of drugs is prohibited. The price for such laws is a restriction on individual autonomy. Some have argued that the price is too high and that the most the government should do is warn and educate the individual about the consequences of using certain drugs.

THE PRINCIPLE OF LEGAL MORALISM. The principle of legal moralism holds that a legitimate function of the law is to enforce morality by turning the immoral into the illegal. Hence, the restrictions placed on actions by the law are justified by the presumed fact that the actions are immoral and so ought not to be performed.

To a considerable extent, laws express the values of a society and the society's judgments about what is morally right. In our society, homicide and theft are recognized as crimes, and those who commit them are guilty of legal, as well as moral, wrongdoing. Society attempts to prevent such crimes and to punish offenders.

The degree to which the law should embody moral judgments is a hard question. It is particularly difficult to answer in a pluralistic society like ours, in which there may be sharp differences of opinion about the moral legitimacy of some actions. Until quite recently, for example, materials considered obscene could not be freely purchased, birth-control literature could not be freely distributed nor contraceptives legally prescribed in some states, and the conditions of divorce were generally stringent and punitive. Even now many states outlaw homosexual solicitation and acts, and prostitution is generally illegal. The foundation for such laws is the belief by many that the practices proscribed are morally wrong.

The current heated debate over abortion reflects, in some of its aspects, the conflict between those who favor strong legal moralism and those who oppose it. Many who consider abortion morally wrong would also like to see it made illegal once more. Others, even though they may oppose abortion, believe that it is a private moral matter and that the attempt to regulate it by law is an unwarranted intrusion of state power.

THE WELFARE PRINCIPLE. The welfare principle holds that it is justifiable to restrict individual autonomy if doing so will result in providing benefits to others. Those who endorse this principle are not inclined to think that it demands a serious self-sacrifice for the welfare of others. Rather, in their view, an ideal application of the principle would be the case in which we give up just a little autonomy to bring about a great deal of benefit to others.

For example, transplant organs are in short supply at the moment because their availability depends mostly on their being freely donated. The situation could be dramatically changed by a law requiring that organs from the recently dead be salvaged and made available for use as transplants.

Such a law would end the present system of voluntary donation, and by doing so it would restrict our freedom to decide what is to be done with our bodies after death. However, it would be easy to argue that the tremendous value that others might gain from such a law easily outweighs the slight restriction on autonomy that it would involve.

These four principles are not the only ones that offer grounds for abridging the autonomy of individuals, but they are the most relevant to decision making and policy planning in medicine. It is important to keep in mind that merely appealing to a principle is not enough to warrant a limit on autonomy. A principle points in the direction of an argument, but it is no substitute for one. The high value we place on autonomy gives its preservation a high priority, and compelling considerations are required to justify compromising it. In the view of some philosophers, who endorse the position taken by Mill, only the harm principle can serve as grounds for legitimately restricting autonomy. Other theorists find persuasive reasons to do so in other principles.

Theories without Principles

Most of traditional Western ethics is based on the assumption that ethical beliefs are best represented by a set of rules or abstract principles. Thus, Kant's categorical imperative, Mill's principle of utility, and Ross's list of prima facie duties attempt to supply guides for moral action and decision making that apply in all circumstances.

Moral decisions thus typically involve bringing a case under a rule, in much the same way that law courts apply statutory laws to cases brought before them. Much ethical dispute, like much legal dispute, is over whether an abstract rule does or does not apply in a concrete case.

In recent decades, some ethical theorists have turned away from the principle-governed, legalistic approach to ethics in favor of another approach from the Western tradition. Some of the new theorists have emphasized the importance of character as the source of moral action, whereas others have stressed the central role of shared concerns and the crucial importance of social practices and institutions in shaping our moral lives.

We will present brief sketches of ethical theories that (according to their proponents) cannot be reduced to sets of abstract principles. Although moral theorists debate such questions as whether the virtue of being a truthful person (a character trait) isn't ultimately derived from the duty to tell the truth (a principle), we will steer clear of these issues. Rather, as with theories based on principles, we will restrict ourselves to a general statement of each theory, indicate how it might be applied in a medical context, and then discuss some of the difficulties it faces as a moral theory.

The three theories discussed here have been presented by their proponents in a variety of versions, some of them quite elaborate and philosophically sophisticated. Keep in mind that we are presenting only sketches.

VIRTUE ETHICS

J. D. Salinger's character Holden Caulfield dislikes "phonies" and dreams of standing in a field and keeping little kids from running off the edge of the cliff beyond. He wants to be a "catcher in the rye."

Millions of us who have read *The Catcher in the Rye* have admired Holden and wanted to be like him in some ways. We too would like to avoid phoniness, particularly in ourselves, and we would like to do something to make the world a better place, particularly for children. Holden isn't a perfect person, but even so, he's a moral hero, a sort of icon or example of what we wish we could be in some respects.

Every culture is populated by real and fictional characters representing the sort of people we should try to become. Some characters are seen as perfect, while others are people who, despite their flaws, show what they were capable of in confronting life's problems and struggles. To name only a few historically important people, consider Socrates, Jesus, Gautama Buddha, Moses, Florence Nightingale, Confucius, Martin Luther King, Susan B. Anthony, Anne Frank, Gandhi, and Mother Teresa. It would be easy to make an even longer list of fictional characters who evoke our admiration and make us feel we would be better people if we could be more like them.

Virtue ethics is ethics based on character. Its fundamental idea is that a person who has acquired the proper set of dispositions will do what is right when faced with a situation involving a moral choice. Thus, virtue ethics doesn't involve invoking principles or rules to guide actions.

The virtuous person is both the basic concept and the goal of virtue ethics. The virtuous person is one who acts right, because she or he is just that sort of person. Right actions flow out of character, and the virtuous person has a disposition to do the right thing. Rules need not be consulted, calculations need not be performed, abstract duties need not be considered.

People become virtuous in the way they become good swimmers. Upbringing, education, the example of others, reflection, personal effort, and experience all play a role. As with swimming, some people may be more naturally inclined to become virtuous than others. Those who are naturally patient, reflective, and slow to anger may find it easier than those who are impatient, impulsive, and possessed of a fiery temper.

Families and social institutions—like schools, clubs, and athletic teams, as well as religious institutions—play a role in shaping our moral character. They tell us how we should behave when we lose a school election or win a softball game. They teach us what we should do when we have a chance to take money without anyone's finding out, when we witness a case of discrimination, when we ourselves are treated unfairly.

Quite apart from explicit teachings or doctrines, the lives of historical figures like Jesus, Mohammed, and Buddha have served as examples of what it is possible for a person to become. Perhaps no one believes she or he can achieve the level of moral perfection that such people represent, but they offer us models for fashioning ourselves. In the way a swimmer may study the backstroke, we can study the way moral heroes have dealt with the moral questions that face us.

When a Christian asks, "What would Jesus do?" it is not typically an attempt to call on divine guidance. Rather, it is an occasion for reflection, of attempting to imagine what someone trying to live a life like Jesus' would do. We try to improve our character by becoming more like those who are admirable. Hence, in addition to education and social influences, we must engage in self-criticism and make deliberate efforts to improve.

THE VIRTUES

The virtuous person is disposed to demonstrate virtues through behavior. *Virtue* is a translation of the Greek word *arete,* which also has much the same meaning as *excellence.* (Virtue ethics is also called *aretaic ethics.*) The excellent tennis player demonstrates in playing tennis that he possesses characteristics needed to play the game well. Similarly, the virtuous person demonstrates through living that she possesses the appropriate range of excellences.

Virtues have traditionally been divided into moral and practical, or nonmoral, virtues:

Moral virtues: benevolence, compassion, honesty, charity, sincerity, sympathy, respect, consideration, kindness, thoughtfulness, loyalty, fairness, and so on

Nonmoral virtues: rationality (or intelligence), tenacity, capability, patience, prudence, skillfulness, staunchness, shrewdness, proficiency, and so on

The distinction between moral and non-moral virtues is far from clear, but the rough idea is that those in one set are associated with living a good (moral) life, while those in the other are associated with the practical aspects of living. A thief can be patient (a nonmoral virtue), but not honest (a moral one). By contrast, an honest (moral virtue) person may lack patience. (How to classify *courage* has always been a problem. A courageous thief may be more successful than a cowardly one, but a benevolent person lacking the courage to put his views into practice will be ineffective.)

VIRTUE ETHICS IN THE MEDICAL CONTEXT

Consider Dr. Charles Holmes, an emergency room trauma surgeon who chose his specialty because the money is good and the hours reasonable. He treats the patients, then he goes home. Holmes is technically expert, but he lacks compassion for his patients and is not interested in their worries or fears. He shows no tact in dealing with patients and barely acknowledges they are people.

Dr. Holmes is far removed from our notion of what a physician as a compassionate healer should be. In treating his patients as broken machines, he may help them in important ways, but his skills as a physician are deficient. Holmes, we might say, lacks the dispositions necessary to be a good physician.

From at least the time of the ancient Greeks, the Western tradition has expected physicians to be virtuous, and more recently, we have broadened that expectation to include nurses, medical technicians, and all who care for patients. The tradition is resplendent with stories of those who behaved in ways that make them moral examples for all who commit themselves to providing patient care. Scores of European physicians at the time of the Black Death (the bubonic plague) in the fourteenth century tended to their patients, even though they knew they risked infection themselves. The eighteenth-century American physician Benjamin Rush did his best to help cholera sufferers, although he knew he was likely to get the disease. Florence Nightingale, braving harsh conditions and the risk of sickness, helped care for British troops during the Crimean War and fought to establish nursing as a profession.

Virtue ethics calls attention to the strength of medicine at its moral (and practical) best. Courage, loyalty, integrity, compassion, and benevolence, along with determination and intelligence, are virtues associated with physicians and others who provide what we consider the right sort of care for their patients. We expect everyone involved in patient care to display in their behavior a similar constellation of virtues. Virtue ethics, with its emphasis on character and behavioral dispositions, comes closer to capturing our concept of the ideal health professional than does a rule-based view of moral decision making like Kant's ethics or utilitarianism.

DIFFICULTIES WITH VIRTUE ETHICS

A fundamental difficulty with virtue ethics is that it provides us with no explicit guidance in deciding how to act in particular circumstances. Suppose someone is terminally ill, in great pain, and asks assistance in dying. Should we agree to help? We may ask, "What would Jesus do?" and the answer may be, "I don't know." If we have been brought up to be virtuous, perhaps we should have no need to ask such questions. But how are we to know who among us has been properly brought up, and for those of us who aren't sure, what should we do?

Medicine is repeatedly faced with the problem of deciding about what actions ought to be taken, but virtue ethics is about character and dispositions. However, even a benevolent person (one disposed to act benevolently) may not know how to distribute organs that are in scarce supply. Further, virtue ethics does not supply any clear way to resolve moral conflicts. What if Assiz thinks it would be wrong to abort a fetus twenty-four weeks after conception, but Puzo does not. How can they go about resolving their dispute? The answer is not clear.

Also, virtues, like duties, can be incompatible when they are translated into action. If I am a transplant coordinator and try to express my gratitude to my physics teacher by allowing her to jump to the head of the waiting list for a new liver, this will conflict with my commitment to fairness. But if virtues are not ranked, how do I decide what to do in such a case? Surely we don't think it would be right for me to put my teacher at the head of the list, but on what grounds can virtue ethics say that it would be wrong?

CARE ETHICS

Care ethics is an outgrowth of feminist ethics or, perhaps more accurately, is a particular strand of feminist ethics. Care ethics is not a unified doctrine that can be captured in a set of abstract statements. Indeed, care ethics, like feminist ethics in general, rejects abstract principles as the basis for ethics. It is perhaps best characterized as a family of beliefs about the way values should be manifested in character and in behavior. It is unified by a set of shared concerns and commitments, as well as by the rejection of the traditional philosophical view that ethics can be adequately represented by rules and principles.

Much of the philosophical work in care ethics has been developed on the basis of psychologist Carol Gilligan's research on moral development. Lawrence Kohlberg's earlier studies suggest that women are "less developed" in their moral reasoning skills than men because they are not as adept at applying moral principles to particular cases. Gilligan does not conclude that Kohlberg is wrong but, rather, that women have a *style* of moral reasoning that is entirely different from the style employed by men. The title Gilligan gave to her book, *In a Different Voice,* is an allusion to the impression she formed in listening to women discuss how they would resolve moral difficulties that she was hearing a voice different from the strident and judgmental male voice of traditional ethical theory.

Gilligan claims that when women are presented with cases of moral conflict, they focus on the details of the people involved in the situation and their personal relationships. They then try to find a way to resolve the conflict that will avoid causing harm to anyone and satisfy, to the extent possible, the interests of everyone concerned. To accomplish such a resolution, women are prepared to look for compromises and points of agreement, to be flexible in their demands, and to take novel approaches to find resolutions that all parties to the dispute will accept.

Unlike the approach taken by women, Gilligan claims, when men are presented with a case of moral conflict, they focus on analyzing the situation with the aim of deciding what abstract rule it would be appropriate to follow to resolve the case. They take little interest in the people as individuals who have their own concerns and needs. Once men have identified a rule they believe fits the case at hand, they act (and try to make others act) in a way that most closely conforms to it. Men are prepared to follow rules in the interest of justice, even if securing justice involves sacrificing the interests of some of the people involved in the conflict.

Gilligan characterizes the way women respond to situations of moral conflict as expressing an *ethic of care* and the way in which men respond as expressing an *ethic of justice*. She emphasizes, however, that there isn't a perfect correlation between these types of response and gender. Ideally, according to Gilligan, moral agents should employ both approaches in moral decision making. Not only is there room for both, but there is also a need for both.

Some philosophers have refined Gilligan's original distinction and divided "feminist ethics" from "care ethics." *Feminist ethics,* they emphasize, involves acknowledging the validity of women's experience in dealing with people and society, expressing a commitment to social equality, and exploring ways to empower women (see the discussion of feminist ethics later in this chapter). *Care ethics* need not have such explicit feminist concerns, although it shares the same general aims and point of view.

Even so, most feminists see the question of whether care ethics should be distinguished from feminist ethics as less important than the need to make sure women's perspectives and concerns are represented within ethics. According to them, the tradition of philosophical ethics has concentrated on the development of comprehensive abstract theories that fail to acknowledge the importance of values prized by women and thus assign those values no role in moral decision making or the moral life. Care ethics is a means of bringing women's concerns with the lives of individual women, children, families, and the society into ethics.

VALUES, NOT PRINCIPLES

Ethical theories as diverse as utilitarianism and Kantian ethics have in common a reliance upon abstract principles both as an expression of the theory and as a means of resolving moral conflicts. Thus, to decide whether an action is morally legitimate, we can appeal to the principle of utility or to the categorical imperative. Moral theories can be viewed as providing a decision procedure for arriving at morally justified conclusions in particular cases—to justify an action, bring it under a rule.

Care ethics holds that it is not even appropriate to think in terms of rules or principles where certain kinds of relationships are concerned. Do we need to perform a utilitarian calculation before giving a friend a ride to the hospital? Should parents consult the categorical imperative before deciding whether to immunize their children against polio? Of course not. These relationships require that we give of ourselves and provide assistance and care of an appropriate sort. Such a requirement is bound up with the nature of being a friend or a parent. Other relationships—being a nurse, physician, teacher, manager, therapist, trainer—have similar requirements bound up with them. In general, rules and principles seem both inappropriate and unnecessary where certain human relationships are concerned.

Care ethics rejects outright the idea that abstract principles can capture everything relevant to making moral decisions. Hence, feminist/care ethics explicitly denies there can be a decision procedure consisting only in bringing a case "under a rule" or showing it to be an "instance" of a general principle. What is crucial for care ethics, rather, is an understanding of the complexities of the particular situation in which a moral problem has occurred. It requires a deep and detailed understanding of the people and their interests and feelings. Only then is it possible to resolve the problem in a way that is sensitive to the needs of everyone.

In understanding a complex situation, we must use intelligence to grasp relationships and details about the people, the circumstances, and the problem. But equally important, we must use *empathy* to understand the concerns and feelings of the people involved. We must identify with those in need or conflict, see what is at stake from their point of view, and ascertain their worries and concerns. We must also bring to the situation of moral conflict or doubt such traditional "women's values" as caring, consideration, kindness, concern for others, compassion, understanding, generosity, sympathy, helpfulness, and a willingness to assume responsibility.

These are the very values we must rely on to resolve moral conflicts and see to the needs of the people involved. The point is not to show who is in the wrong or being treated unfairly. Rather, the point is to find a way out of the conflict that takes into account the concerns and feelings of those involved.

According to care ethics, the traditional ethical model of a disinterested, detached, and dispassionate judge reviewing the objective facts in a case and then issuing an impartial decision about the moral acceptability of an action is inappropriate and mistaken. It excludes the very values that are most relevant to moral situations and most important to the people who are involved. Moral decisions should not be impartial, in an abstract and bloodless way, rather, they should show partiality to *everyone* involved.

Like virtue ethics, care ethics emphasizes the development of an appropriate character. As a society we should make an effort, by teaching and example, to develop individuals, male and female, who respond appropriately to moral situations. They should be people who recognize the importance of personal relationships, respect individuals, and accept responsibility. In their dealings with others, if they have acquired the proper character, they will bring to bear the values (see above) we associate with caring for and about people.

CARE ETHICS IN THE MEDICAL CONTEXT

Suppose the parents of a severely impaired newborn boy are told by the child's physicians that his treatment ought to be discontinued and he should be given only "comfort care" and allowed to die. The parents' initial response is to reject the recommendation and insist that everything possible be done to continue the life of their child. How might such a conflict be resolved by the approach advocated by care ethics?

The parties in the conflict must discuss freely and openly each of their positions. (We need not assume only two positions are involved.) The physicians must explain in detail the baby's medical condition, discuss the therapy they may be able to offer, and be forthcoming about its limitations. If they believe the baby will die in a few hours or days, no matter what they do, they must be frank about their expectation. They might point out that the only therapy possible involves extensive and painful surgery, that it is almost certain to be unsuccessful, that it will be expensive, and that it will demand the resources of the hospital, the society, and the parents themselves.

For their part, the parents might talk about their hopes for the child and their willingness to love and nurture even a child with severe physical and mental problems. They might discuss the guilt they would feel about giving up the struggle and allowing the child to die. They might discuss their experiences with other children or talk about the difficulties they had conceiving the one who is now not expected to live.

No particular outcome can be predicted from such a discussion. We might imagine education taking place and compromises developing among all the participants. We might imagine the physicians coming to a greater appreciation of what the child means to the parents and why they are so reluctant to allow the child to die. The parents, for their part, might come to understand that the physicians are concerned with their child and are also frustrated and saddened by their inability to help the child get better.

The outcome might involve adjustments on the part of all participants. The parents might come to realize that their child is almost sure to die no matter what is done. The physicians might realize that they might make the child's death easier for the parents to bear by allowing the parents to hold the child and spend time with him.

Other moral conflicts or questions might be approached in a similar fashion. Should Ladzewell's request that he be assisted in dying be followed? Should Terema's request for an abortion in the second trimester of pregnancy be honored? Dozens of similar questions arise in the area of health care, and care ethics suggests that the proper approach is not to invoke principles, but instead to deal with the people involved as individuals and behave in accordance with the values of care.

Medicine, nursing, and allied areas have traditionally been associated with the values of caring. We have expected practitioners to manifest in their character and conduct concern, compassion, sympathy, kindness, and willingness to take responsibility and to help patients in their charge. In this respect, care ethics is asking us to recognize a traditional approach to patients. However, care ethics also reassures us that this approach is legitimate, even though no abstract principles are involved. More than this, though, it tells us to rely on those same values and dispositions when we are faced with moral conflicts in medicine. Again, care ethics reassures us that we can put our trust in the values of care and need not reach for principles to resolve the conflict.

DIFFICULTIES WITH CARE ETHICS

A frequent criticism of care ethics is that Gilligan's empirical claims about the differences between the moral reasoning of women and men do not stand up to the challenge of more recent data. Without taking a stand on this question, it is enough to observe that Gilligan's empirical claims are not crucial to care ethics. It is enough for the care ethics theorist to demonstrate the importance of the values that belong to the ethic of care by showing how they can play a role in the moral life of individuals and society and how they can be employed as guides in resolving cases of moral doubt and conflict.

Also, not all care advocates have accepted a radical division between two "ethics." Some critics have pointed out, for example, that the principle of beneficence ("Act so as to promote the good of others") can be construed as implying the need for caring. Hence, according to this line of criticism, care ethics can be seen as a part of the traditional enterprise of philosophical ethics. Care ethics usefully emphasizes values and approaches relatively ignored or unappreciated in traditional ethical theory, but it does not stand as an alternative to a moral theory like utilitarianism or even Ross's intuitionism.

A more important criticism may be that, like virtue ethics, which also rejects principles as necessary to ethics, care ethics provides us with no obvious way to resolve moral conflicts. We may bring to a conflict the ethics of care, but we may still not know how to make a decision. When a number of people are in need of the same kidney for transplant, how should we decide who gets the kidney? Should we, in the manner suggested by care ethics, have a discussion with them all, assess their needs and feelings, then make a decision? It seems unlikely such a group could reach a consensus, particularly in the short time allowed under such circumstances. If we make the decision affecting them, then most would probably claim they had been treated unfairly. Such cases suggest that the abstract principle of justice may yield more satisfactory results than the values of care ethics alone.

Finally, values, like virtues and duties, can be incompatible when they have to be translated into action. While I may be moved by sympathy and want the mother with two young children to receive the bone marrow that may save her life, I may also be moved by my compassion for the sufferings of a six-year-old boy who might have a long life ahead of him and want him to receive it. If I am forced to choose who gets the bone marrow, even if I learn much more about the people involved, my choice ultimately seems arbitrary.

These objections might be answered satisfactorily by a care ethics theorist. Even so, they are prima facie shortcomings that require serious responses.

FEMINIST ETHICS

Feminist ethics in general, like care ethics in particular, rejects the traditional notion that ethics can be represented by a set of abstract rules or principles and that the morality of actions and policies can be assessed by reference to them.

From the feminist perspective, the "principlism" of traditional ethics is compromised by the facts of the social world. The unequal distribution of political and social power and the inequalities attached to the accidents of birth, race, and gender mean that even such an apparently basic principle as the autonomy (self-directedness) of the individual is restricted in its application. In some states, for example, a woman who cannot pay for an abortion is not free to get one. Thus, her autonomy as an abstract right is meaningless in practical terms. The focus of ethics, according to feminist philosophers, must be on social arrangements, practices, and institutions, not abstract principles. Further, the overall aim of ethics must be to eliminate (or at least reduce) the oppression of women, races, and other subordinate groups in societies throughout the world.

Although care ethics originated in feminism, some feminists regard associating it with feminism as a threat to feminism. They fear that caring will be seen as a uniquely female trait and that feminist ethics will be undercut. First, it may be dismissed as based on an inferior form of reasoning (Gilligan's "ethic of care") more appropriate to the largely female "helping" professions of nursing and social work than to the predominantly male profession of medicine. Second, the view that caring is a woman's way of thinking may reinforce the stereotypes that confine women to the lower ranks of the health-care hierarchy. Caring has a legitimate place in feminist ethics, but it must be seen as a disposition desirable for all people to have across all divisions of gender, race, and class.

For many feminist philosophers, *equality* lies at the core of ethics. Their primary concern is with gender equality, and their aim is to critique the institutions and practices of society to expose the ways they keep women subjected to men. More broadly, though, most feminists support an effort to expose and eradicate the domination of any one group by another. They recognize that women may suffer compound injustices because they belong to races and classes that have been subordinated. A woman who is Asian, sick, and old needs to have all the ways she is subordinated addressed by ethics and redressed by society.

For feminists, ethics is part of the ongoing effort to uncover and eliminate the sources of social inequality. As Susan Sherwin puts the point, feminist ethics cannot be satisfied just by calculating increases in happiness and invoking moral principles. Rather, it must also ask *whose* happiness is increased and how the principles affect the oppressed as well as the oppressor. In the final analysis, she writes, "Positive moral value attaches to actions or principles that help relieve oppression, and negative value attaches to those that fail to reduce oppression or actually help to strengthen it."

Traditional ethics is among the practices scrutinized by feminist philosophers. As discussed earlier, the concept of individuals as self-directing, or autonomous, is compromised by social realities. Equality is necessary for the exercise of autonomy, and under present conditions, most people are not autonomous. Thus, appealing to the principle of autonomy is more a way of saying that those who are socially privileged and economically and politically powerful may do as they wish than a way of putting power into the hands of people who are oppressed. People limited by social disadvantages, dependence on others, or responsibility for the care of others are not equal to those free of such burdens, and thus lack their autonomy.

Because of the importance feminists attach to social equality, they are concerned with the ways medicine as a social institution tends to subordinate women to men. They point to the fact that most nurses are still female, while most physicians are male. Also, some feminists tend to see the "medicalization" of women's reproductive lives—through assisted-reproduction procedures like in vitro fertilization, hospitalized deliveries by obstetricians, or hormone-replacement therapy at menopause—as ways for men to exercise control over women. Further, some feminists view the techniques of assisted reproduction as a means for powerful males to produce genetically connected offspring at the expense of subordinated females.

Various feminists also question some of society's fundamental assumptions about the value of medicine. For example, some have argued that providing expensive health care for the very sick is not the best way to pursue health. It could be more effectively pursued by the equal distribution of resources like food, shelter, security, and education that help keep people healthy. We could get (as it were) more health by distributing our resources than we could by treating sick people with expensive drugs, equipment, and expertise.

FEMINIST ETHICS IN THE MEDICAL CONTEXT

Because feminist ethics can't be represented by a set of principles and isn't a unified set of beliefs, it's not likely that particular examples of how feminist doctrines might be put into practice would be accepted as accurate by most feminists. Nevertheless, we can at least suggest in a general way how a few cases might be approached from the perspective of feminist ethics.

Feminist ethics, because of its views about how reproduction and child rearing have been employed to keep women subordinate to men, supports the idea that women must have unfettered access to abortion. Without such access, women cannot control their own lives and are forced to submit to regulation by others. They are therefore in a state of subjection. On the question of when abortions are permissible—whether late-term abortions are acceptable or whether abortions are permitted when contraception has not been used, when it has been used, or only when a rape has occurred—feminist theorists differ. Even on the topic of abortion, not all feminists agree; some argue that the ready availability of abortion deprives women of the strongest support for saying no to male sexual aggression.

Assisted reproduction is another area in which feminists disagree among themselves. Some hold that the new technologies that allow women who would otherwise be infertile (even postmenopausal women) to have a child empower women. Others hold, however, that reproductive technology is dangerous to women and an instrument of male dominance, a way of forcing women to have children. Women who seem to seek out such technology on their own may simply have been misled by our male-dominated society to believe that their choice is free.

A feminist ethics approach to a particular case might involve asking questions about the power relations among those involved. For example, suppose a seventy-two-year-old woman with leukemia is considering whether she should refuse a second course of chemotherapy and wait for death with only home care and no further medical intervention. Feminist ethics would want us to ask: (1) whether the attitude of the mostly male hospital staff that an old woman has no useful life is influencing her decision; (2) whether her experience of caring for others is making her reluctant to impose a burden on her daughter or daughter-in-law, whereas an old man might simply feel entitled to care; (3) whether society's view that an old woman has no function might not result in her thinking of herself in the same way—thus ignoring herself as a repository of wisdom and a link with the past or (assuming she regains her health) as someone able to exercise her skills in whatever way she sees fit. In sum, from the perspective of feminist ethics, instead of regarding the decision to discontinue treatment as a straightforward matter of exercising autonomy, we are enjoined to look at the hidden factors that may be influencing the woman's decision and making it less than free.

DIFFICULTIES WITH FEMINIST ETHICS

Proponents of traditional ethical theories question whether feminist ethics can be of much use in actual cases in which decisions must be made. What does it mean to promote gender equality when deciding whether life support should be terminated or late-term abortion allowed? How do we go about practical decision making? Even asking a feminist doesn't seem to be of much use, because they differ among themselves on how such questions should be answered.

The multiplicity of feminist views has led some critics to charge that feminist ethics is not a unified and coherent ethical theory in the way that, say, utilitarianism is. Feminists respond that they reject the notion of moral knowledge as essentially theoretical and deny that the role of ethics is to tell us what to do. (Those in power may believe or wish this were so, but that is only because traditional ethics allows them to employ principles to subjugate women.) Rather, ethics is about people, and it has the aim of facilitating their mutual understanding and adjusting the differences among them. Working together, they resolve conflicts and find a solution to their problems.

One problem with this view of ethics is that, like care and virtue ethics, it appears to provide us with no way to resolve moral conflicts. Suppose someone who is HIV positive claims he has no responsibility to warn sexual partners of his HIV status or to practice safe sex. "It's their lookout," he says. What, from the point of view of feminist ethics, might he be told to persuade him he has an obligation not to put others at risk of a deadly disease by his behavior? Or what grounds could be offered to support his position? The answer is not clear. And if the approach assumed in these questions (asking for "grounds") is wrong, what is the right approach to resolve the problem of someone's acting in ways that will endanger others needlessly?

A second difficulty of this view of ethics is that it seems to open feminist ethics to the charge of relativism. If ethics is (in Margaret Urban Walker's phrase) "socially embodied" and can only facilitate agreement among those who accept the values of a particular culture, how can feminist ethics criticize the culture? More to the point, even if the culture is one that subjugates women, feminist ethics seems to be committed to going along with its practices and values.

In fact, some cultural practices, such as so-called female circumcision (genital mutilation) in some countries, have divided feminists. Many want to condemn it, but the feminist view of ethics doesn't seem to provide a means for doing so. As with virtue ethics and care ethics, the commitment to doing without principles or rules doesn't seem to offer a way of assessing actions, policies, and practices from the outside.

Retrospect

The two major tasks of this chapter have been to provide information about several important ethical theories and to formulate and illustrate several generally accepted moral principles. One aim in performing these tasks was to make it easier to follow the arguments and discussions in this book.

Another and ultimately more serious aim has been to call attention to ethical theories and principles you may wish to consider adopting. From this standpoint, the problems and issues raised in the Case Presentations and Social Contexts can be considered tests for the theories and principles. You may find that some of the theories that we have discussed are inadequate to deal with certain moral issues in the medical context, although they may seem satisfactory in more common or simpler cases. Or you may discover that certain commonly accepted moral principles lead to contradictory results or to conclusions that you find difficult to accept. Other theories or principles may appear to give definite and persuasive answers to medical–moral problems, but you may find that they rest on assumptions that it does not appear reasonable to accept. Such a dialectical process of claims and criticism is slow and frustrating. Yet it offers the best hope of settling on theories and principles that we can accept with confidence and employ without misgivings.

During the last quarter century, a great amount of effort has been expended addressing the moral problems of medical practice and research. Without question, progress has been made in developing a better understanding of a number of issues and securing agreement about how they are to be dealt with. Nevertheless, a large number of moral issues in medicine remain unsettled or even unexplored. Even in the absence of moral consensus on these issues, the demands of practical decision making generate a force that presses us for immediate solutions.

In such a situation, we cannot afford to try to settle all doubts about moral principles in an abstract way and only then apply them to problems in medicine. The dialectical process must be made practical. Formulating and testing theories and principles must go on at the same time as we are actually making moral decisions. We must do our best to discover the principles of aerodynamics while staying aloft.

To a considerable extent, that is what this book is about. Biomedical ethics is still an area in which there are more legitimate questions than there are satisfactory answers, but the answers that we do have are better supported and better reasoned than those available even twenty years ago.

Notes and References

Chapter 1: Research Ethics and Informed Consent

The Jesse Gelsinger Case Presentation draws heavily from Paul Gelsinger's statement to the National Human Research Protections Advisory Committee Meeting at Bethesda, MD on 29 January 2002. Additional information is from Sheryl Gay Stolberg, "The Biotech Death of Jesse Gelsinger," New York Times Magazine (28 November 1999).

Materials on clinical trials, HIV, and Pregnancy were drawn from the New York Times articles: S. G. Stolberg, "Research on AIDS in Poor Nations Raises an Outcry" (17 September 1997) and "Defense for Third-World HIV Experiments" (1 October 1997); Howard W. French, "AIDS Research in Africa: Juggling Risks and Hopes" (8 October 1997); on the journal resignations, see Lawrence K. Altman, "AIDS Experts Leave Journal After Studies Are Criticized" (15 October 1997); Saba and Ammann state their views in "A Cultural Divide on AIDS Research" (20 September 1997); on discontinuing placebos, see Sheryl Gay Stolberg, "Placebo Use Is Suspended in Overseas AIDS Trials" (19 February 1998); for more recent results, see Lawrence K. Altman, "Report Dims Hope for AIDS Therapy to Protect Babies" (7 July 2000) and "AIDS Studies on Infants Appear to Conflict" (13 July 2000).

The Social Context on radiation research is based on the following New York Times articles: Keith Schneider, "Nuclear Scientists Irradiated People in Secret Research" (17 December 1993); "1950 Memo Shows Worry over Radiation Tests" (28 December 1993); "Signatures in Experiment Called Forgery" (12 April 1994); and John H. Cushman, Jr., "Study Sought on All Testing on Humans" (10 January 1994). More recent developments are reported in the New York Times: Philip J. Hilts, "Secret Radioactive Experiments to Bring Compensation by the U.S." (20 November 1996) and Matthew L. Wald, "Rule Adopted to Prohibit Secret Tests on Humans" (29 March 1997). See also the Associated Press story "Settlement is Reached in Suit Over Radioactive Oatmeal" (31 December 1997.)

Details of the experiments in the Willowbrook case are taken from Saul Krugman and Joan P. Giles, "Viral Hepatitis: New Light on an Old Disease," JAMA, 212 (1970): 1019–1021. "Echoes of Willowbrook or Tuskegee?" is based on Philip J. Hilts, "Ethics Officials to Investigate Drug Experiments on Children," New York Times (15 April 1998).

The Baby Fae Case Presentation is based on the following New York Times stories: L. K. Altman, "Learning from Baby Fae," (18 November 1984); Philip M. Boffey, "Medicine Under Scrutiny" (20 November 1984); Sandra Blakeslee, "Baboon Implant in Baby Fae Assailed" (20 December 1985). For a detailed discussion, see Ronald Munson, Raising the Dead: Organ Transplants, Ethics, and Society (New York: Oxford University Press, 2002), Chapter 7.

The account of Nazi experiments is from the indictment in United States v. Karl Brandt, excerpted in Hastings Center Report, "Special Supplement: Biomedical Ethics and the Shadow of Nazism" (6 August 1976): 5. On drug testing, see Ross J. Baldessarini, Chemotherapy in Psychiatry (Cambridge, Mass.: Harvard University Press, 1977), pp. 4–11.

The paternalistic view of consent is expressed in Eugene G. Laforet, "The Fiction of Informed Consent," JAMA 235 (12 April 1976): 1579–1585. Placebos are discussed in Sissela Bok, "The Ethics of Giving Placebos," Scientific American 231 (November 1974): 17–23. The discussion of research and children is indebted to Joan D. Lockhart, "Pediatric Drug Testing," Hastings Center Report 7 (June 1977): 8–10. Prisoners and research is discussed in Jessica Mitford, Kind and Usual Punishment (New York: Knopf, 1973). The historical cases of research on the poor are from M. H. Pappworth, Human Guinea Pigs (Boston: Beacon Press, 1961), pp. 61–62. The Tuskegee case details are from the "Final Report of the Tuskegee Syphilis Study Ad Hoc Advisory Panel," U.S. Public Health Service (Washington, D.C., 1973), excerpted in S. J. Reiser et al., Ethics in Medicine (Cambridge, Mass.: MIT Press, 1977), pp. 316–321. On fetal experimentation, I am indebted to "Individual Risks vs. Societal Benefits: The Fetus," in Experiments and Research with Humans: Values in Conflict (Washington, D.C.: National Academy of Sciences, 1975), pp. 59–90. HHS regulations on children as research subjects were published in the *Federal Register* (8 March 1983). They are summarized in "Finally, Final Rules on Children Who Become Research Subjects," *Hastings Center Report* 13 (August 1983): 2–3. See also Robert Pear, "Proposal to Test Drugs in Children Meets Resistance," *New York Times* (30 November 1997).

On the tamoxifen trial, see, "Scientists Cancel Tamoxifen Test," Associated Press (7 April 1998). On foreign drug testing, see Elisabeth Rosenthal, "For More Drugs, First Test Is Abroad," *New York Times* (7 August 1990) and Warren E. Leary, "U.S. Ethics Are Questioned by Critics of Vaccine Test in Italy and Sweden," *New York Times* (13 March 1994).

The account of the controversy over the use of the Pernkopf anatomy is based on Nicholas Wade, "Doctors Question Use of Nazi's Medical Atlas," *New York Times* (26 November 1996).

Chapter 2: Physicians, Patients, and Others

The Case Presentation is based on the documentary film *Dax's Case*, by Unicorn Medical (Dallas, Texas) for the Council for Dying (New York, New York); produced by Donald Pasquella and Keith Burton; directed by Donald Pasquella. On development of licensing procedures for physicians, see John Duffy, *The Healers: The Rise of the Medical Establishment* (New York: McGraw-Hill, 1977). An influential account of the doctor–patient relationship as a social role is Talcott Parsons, "Illness and the Role of the Physician: A Sociological Perspective," in Clyde Kluckhohn and H. A. Murray, eds. *Personality in Nature, Society, and Culture* (New York: Knopf, 1961). The multiple sclerosis study is reported in *Hastings Center Report* 13 (June 1983): 2–3.

On the medical I.D. question, see Sheryl Gay Stolberg in the *New York Times:* "Health Identifier for All Americans Runs into Hurdles" (19 July 1998) and "Medical I.D.'s and Privacy" (26 July 1998). The Social Context on pregnancy and prosecution is based on: Martha Field, "Controlling the Woman to Protect the Fetus," *Law Medicine and Health Care* 2 (1989): 114–129 for the Monson and similar cases; *New York Times* (15 January 1986; 30 August 1988) for effects of alcohol and other drugs; (4 May 1989; 9 May 1989) for the Illinois cases; (2 February 1990) for a Wyoming case; (30 May 1990) for the New York court ruling; (18 August 1992) for the Connecticut Supreme Court ruling; (19 July 1990) for racial bias; (28 October 1992) for the Gillespie case; (24

July 1992) for the Florida Supreme Court decision; *Time* (19 September 1988) for statistics about crack babies and hospital experiences in California and South Carolina. See also the following *New York Times* articles: Tamar Lewin, "Detention of Pregnant Woman for Drug Use is Struck Down" (28 April 1997), "Florida Court Says Hurting One's Fetus Isn't Crime" (31 October 1997), "Abuse Laws Cover Fetus a High Court Rules" (30 October 1997); Rick Bragg, "Defender of God, South and Unborn Addict" (13 January 1998). See also Associated Press, "Woman Who Used Crack Is Guilty in Death of Fetus" (3 December 1997) and "More Women Report Alcohol Use in Pregnancy" (25 April 1997). The Supreme Court decision is reported in Linda Greenhouse, "Drug Tests Curbed During Pregnancy," *New York Times* (21 March 2001).

The Twitchell Case Presentation draws substantially from David Margolic, "Death and Faith, Law and Christian Science," *New York Times* (6 August 1990). Other sources were *New York Times* (3, 6 July 1990) and "Convicted of Relying on Prayer," *Time* (16 July 1990). The overturn of the conviction was reported on CNN in November 1994.

Chapter 3: HIV/AIDS

The Thompson case is based on accounts by a number of people with AIDS. On AIDS and suicide, see Seth Mydans, "AIDS Patients' Silent Companion Is Often Suicide," *New York Times* (25 February 1990). On combination therapy, see Michael Waldhoz, "AIDS Drug Cocktails in Use Since 1996 Cause Steep Drop in Deaths Study Finds," *Wall Street Journal* (26 March 1998); AP, "AIDS Related Deaths Fall by 26 percent in 1996" (10 January 1998); L. K. Altman, "AIDS Deaths Drop 48% in New York," *New York Times* (2 February 1998); AP, "HIV Infection Rate Steady, But Rate of AIDS Has Slowed" (24 April 1998); S. G. Stolbert, "Despite New AIDS Drugs, Many Still Lose the Battle" (21 August 1997); Sheryl Gay Stolberg, "In AIDS War, New Weapons and New Victims," *New York Times* (2 June 2001); on drug resistance, see Lawrence K. Altman, "Study Reports Drug Resistant Strains Have Increased to 14 Percent Among New HIV Cases," *New York Times* (7 February 2001). On HIV drug advertising, see Stuart Elliott, "A Campaign for AIDS Drug Adds Warning," *New York Times* (10 May 2001). On the history of the disease see, L. K. Altman, "Study of HIV Family Tree Places Origins a Decade Earlier," *New York*

Times (3 February 1998); on infection estimates see the following *New York Times* articles, Robert Pear, "New Estimate Doubles Rate of HIV Spread" (25 December 1997), Elizabeth Olson, "AIDS Infections Rise Globally," 25 November 2000), Ian Fisher, "Stigma Lingers as AIDS Spreads Across Ukraine" (26 January 2002); on prevention see, S. G. Stolbert, "President Decides Against Financing Needle Programs," *New York Times* (20 April 1998). On the Bergalis case, see Lawrence K. Altman's articles in *New York Times:* "AIDS Mystery That Won't Go Away" (5 July 1994) and "AIDS and a Dentist's Secrets" (6 June 1993). Also, see Gina Kolata, "The Face That Haunts," *New York Times* (10 July 1994).

On vaccine, see *New York Times* articles: L. K. Altman, "Vaccine Protects Two Chimps from AIDS" (30 April 1997) and "U.S. to Begin Study of Vaccine's Ability to Suppress HIV Levels" (11 May 2000); Nicholas Wade, "DNA Innovation Lets Team Undermine the AIDS Virus" (21 July 2000), Gina Kolata "New Kind of Vaccine, Made of DNA, Controls Virus in Early Tests on Monkeys" (2 October 2000); also see Geoffrey Cowley, "Can He Find A Cure?" *Newsweek* (11 June 2001) and J. S. Fischer, "Searching For That Ounce of Prevention," *U.S. News and World Report* (17 July 2000).

On AIDS in Africa, see *New York Times:* Rachel L. Swarns, "AIDS Is Chief Cause of Death in South Africa, Study Says" (16 October 2001) and "Newest Statistics Show AIDS Still Spreading in Africa" (1 March 2001); David A. Sanger, "South African Links AIDS to Broader Issue of Poverty" (27 June 2001); on financing see: Editorial, "Toward a Global AIDS Fund" (2 May 2001); Barbara Crossette, "Annan in Washington to Seek AIDS Funds" (10 May 2001); David E. Sanger, "Bush Says U.S. Will Give $200 Million to World AIDS Fund" (11 May 2001); Jane Perlez, "U.N. Chief Calls on U.S. Companies to Donate to AIDS Fund" (1 June 2001). On drugs and treatments see from the same source Rachel L. Swarns, "AIDS Drug Battle Deepens in Africa" (8 March 2001) and "Despite Legal Victory, South Africa Hesitates on AIDS Drugs" (21 April 2001); Sheryl Gay Stolberg, "Africa's AIDS War: Pressure for Affordable Medicine" (9 March 2001); Rachel L. Swarns, "Drug Makers Drop South African Suit Over AIDS Medicine" (20 April 2001); Barbara Crossette, "A Wider War on AIDS in Africa and Asia: Experts Say That Cheaper Drug Treatments Alone Are Not Enough" (27 April 2001); Stephanie Flanders, "In the Shadow of AIDS, a World of Other Problems"

(24 June 2001) [on infectious diseases]; Jennifer Steinhauer, "U.N. United in AIDS Fight But Split Over What to Do" (27 June 2001). Sections of the U.N.'s Declaration are reprinted in *New York Times,* "From the U.N. Statement on AIDS" (29 June 2001).

Chapter 4: Race, Gender, and Medicine

The Tuskegee Case Presentation is based on the classic study of the case, James H. Jones, *Bad Blood: The Tuskegee Syphilis Experiment,* New and Expanded Edition (New York: Free Press, 1993) and Alison Mitchell, "Survivors of Tuskegee Study Get Apology From Clinton," *New York Times* (17 May 1997).

The section on African–American health issues draws from the *New York Times* articles: W. E. Leary, "Discrimination May Impair Black's Health" (24 October 1996) and "Even When Covered by Insurance Black and Poor People Receive Less Health Care" (12 September 1996); Lynda Richardson, "An Old Experiment's Legacy: Distrust of AIDS Treatment" (21 April 1997); C. K. Yoon, "Families Emerge as Silent Victims of Tuskegee Syphilis Experiments" (10 March 1997); P. T. Kilborn, "Black Americans Trailing Whites in Health, Studies Say" (26 January 1998); S. G. Stolberg, "Cultural Issues Pose Obstacles in Cancer Fight" (14 March 1998); Richard Rothstein, "Linking Infant Mortality to Schooling and Stress" (6 January 2002). See also Christine Gorman, "Why Do Blacks Die Young?" *Time* (16 September 1991; "Collaboration Urged to Ease Prostate Cancer Burden, Especially Among African Americans," *Nation's Health* (February, 1998); Office of Minority Health Affairs, "Progress Report for: Black Americans," n.d. (issued in 1998) and "Trends in the Health of African American Children," n.d. (issued in 1998); D. S. Pinkney, "Barriers to Health Care Remain, Especially for Blacks," *American Medical News* (28 November 1994), p. 20ff. For an analysis of the roots of long-standing distrust of medicine by blacks, see V. N. Gamble, "Under the Shadow of Tuskegee," *American Journal of Public Health* (November, 1997), pp. 1773–1779. See also H. E. Flack and E. D. Pellegrino, ed., *African–American Perspectives on Biomedical Ethics* (Washington, D.C.: Georgetown University Press, 1992). For the recent study on blacks and cardiac catheterization, see Sheryl Gay Stolbert, "Blacks Found on Short End of Heart Attack Procedure," *New York Times* (10 May 2001). The CDC review of "health indicators" as reported by Associated Press

(24 January 2002). For an outstanding historical perspective, see Linda A. Clayton and W. Michael Byrd, *An American Health Dilemma: A Medical History of African Americans and the Problems of Race: Beginnings to 1900* (New York: Routledge, 2000).

The discussion of the health problems of American Indians and Alaska Natives is based on Office of Minority Health Affairs, "Progress Report for American Indians and Alaska Natives," n.d. (issued in 1998); Jo Ann Kauffman and Yvette K. Joseph-Fox, "American Indian and Alaska Native Women, in Marcia Bayne-Smith, ed. *Race, Gender, and Health* (Thousand Oaks, CA: Sage Publications, 1996), pp. 121–171. On the problems of Asian Americans and Pacific Islanders, see R. H. True and Tessi Guillerno, "Asian/Pacific Islander American Women," in Bayne-Smith, pp. 94–120 and Department of Health and Human Services, "Progress Review: Asian Americans and Pacific Islanders" (13 September 1997). On the problems of Hispanics/Latinos, see A. L. Gichaello, "Latino Women in Bayne-Smith, pp. 21–171, and Department of Health and Human Services, "Progress Review: Hispanic Americans," 29 April 1997. Comparative figures for disease incidence and mortality for all ethnic groups are from Department of Health and Human Services, *Health United States 1996–1997 and Injury Chartbook* (Hyattsville, MD: 1997).

The discussion of the lack of women as research participants is based on Office of Minority Health, "Including Women and Minorities in Clinical Trials, *Closing the Gap* (December/January, 1998), p. 11; Michael Wines, "In Research, the Sincerest Form of Concern Is Money," *New York Times* (22 June 1997); the American Medical Association Council on Ethical and Judicial Affairs' report and the Public Health Service's report of the Task Force on Women's Health Issues are quoted in John M. Smith, *Women and Doctors* (New York: Delta Books, 1992); on treatment, see references in Lawrence K. Altman, "Mastectomy Alternative Often Ignored, Study Says," *New York Times* (19 May 1998). The GAO report charging recent failures of researchers to enroll a sufficient number of women in studies is reported in Robert Pear, "Studies Find Research on Women Lacking," *New York Times* (29 April 2000).

For the Hmong Case Presentation, see "Girl Flees After Clash of Cultures on Illness," *New York Times* (12 November 1994); for background and an additional case, see Anne Fadiman, *The Spirit Catches You and You Fall Down: A Hmong Child, Her American Doctors, and the Collision of Two Cultures* (New York: Farrar, Straus, and Giroux, 1997); see Richard Bernstein's review "Doctors vs. Demons," *New York Times* (24 September 1997); for the more recent news about Lor Lee, see *Fresno Bee* (2 November 1996) and (2 February 1995).

The Social Context on the mammography debate draws from *New York Times* articles: Gina Kolata, "Mammograms for Women in 40s Debated by Experts" (22 January 1997), "Mammogram Talks Prove Indefinite" (25 January 1997), "Stand on Mammograms Greeted by Outrage" (25 January 1997); "Women Benefit from Breast Screening in 40s" [Letters], (28 January 1997); Kathy Conway, "Luckily, I Had a Mammogram" (24 February 1997); "Let Mammography Be Guided by Facts" [Letters], (4 February 1997); Marjorie Connelly, "On Breast Cancer, the Vote Favors Aggressive Screening," (22 June 1997); other material was drawn from Sharon Begley, "The Mammogram War," *Newsweek* (24 February 1997) and Jeffry Kluger, "Mammogram Two-Step," *Time* (7 April 1997), and Associated Press, "Risk of False Alarm from Mammogram is 50% Over Decade" (15 April 1998). For continuation of the debate, see these *New York Times* articles by Gina Kolata: "Expert Panel Cites Doubts on Mammogram's Worth" (23 January 2002); "Dispute Builds over Value of Mammography (1 February 2002).

The Susan Arcadan case is based on an interview with a breast cancer patient at Johns Hopkins Hospital conducted in March of 1998; the name and details have been changed.

The prostate cancer section is based on Leon Jaroff, "The Man's Cancer," *Time* (1 April 1996); Patrick Walsh and Janet Worthington, *The Prostate: A Guide for Men and the Women Who Love Them* (Baltimore: Johns Hopkins University Press, 1996); Robert Lipsyte, "Hot Gland," *American Health* (March, 1994); W. E. Leary, "Men Are Told to Reconsider How to Treat Prostate Gland," *New York Times* (9 February 1994); "Collaboration Urged to Ease Prostate Cancer Burden, Especially Among African Americans," *Nation's Health* (February, 1998). See also the following *New York Times* articles: A. E. Pollack, "Routine Screening for Prostate Cancer Is Said to Cut Deaths," (19 May 1998); David Kirby, "More Options for Men with Prostate Cancer" (3 October 2000); Kenneth Chang, "Findings Fuel Debate on

Prostate Test" (2 May 2000) and Susan Brink, "Prostate Dilemmas," *U.S. News & World Report* (22 May 2000).

Chapter 5: Genetic Control

The Huntington's Disease Classic Case Presentation relies heavily on Gina Kolata, "Closing In on a Killer Gene, *Discover* (March 1984): 83–87. See also Lawrence K. Altman, "Researchers Report Genetic Test Detects Huntington's Disease," *New York Times* (9 November 1983) and Albert Rosenfeld, "At Risk for Huntington's Disease," *Hastings Center Report* 14 (June 1984): 5–8. Nancy Wexler's views on genetic testing are quoted from Mary Murray, "Nancy Wexler," *New York Times Magazine* (13 February 1993): 28–31. For a profile of Wexler see *Time* (10 February 1992). On more recent developments, see the following *New York Times* articles: Sandra Blakeslee, "Unusual Clues Help in Long Fight to Solve Huntington's Disease" (27 October 1992) and Natalie Angier, "Action of Gene in Huntington's Is Proving a Tough Puzzle" (2 November 1993).

The account of PKU screening is drawn from National Academy of Sciences, *Genetic Screening: Programs, Principles, and Research* (Washington, D.C.: National Academy of Sciences, 1975). For an account of alpha-fetoprotein screening, see Barbara Gastel et al., eds., *Maternal Serum Alpha Fetoprotein: Issues in the Prenatal Screening and Diagnosis of Neural Tube Defects* (U.S. Department of Health and Human Services Publication HE 20.2: M41, 1981). For social problems caused by PKU laws and sickle–cell screening, see Philip Reilly, "There's Another Side to Genetic Screening," *Prism* (January 1976): 55–57.

Genetic screening and the problems it poses for rights is considered by Susan West, "Genetic Testing on the Job," *Science* 82 (September 1982): 16. See also Morton Hunt, "The Total Gene Screen," *New York Times Magazine* (19 January 1986). Specific uses of genetic engineering are reported in: *New York Times* (25 June 1995) on flu vaccine; (30 May 1997) on mouse–human hybrids; (1 May 1997) on increasing muscle growth; (30 October 1997) on sickle–cell model.

The Human Genome Project account draws from the following *New York Times* articles by Nicholas Wade: "Genetic Code of Human Life is Cracked by Scientists" (27 June 2000), "Big Stride for Researchers in Human Gene Mapping," *New York Times* (15 March 1997), "Genome's Riddle" (13 February 2001), "Now the Hard Part: Putting the Genome to Work" (27 June 2000). For a patient-centered discussion, see Lois Wingerson, *Mapping Our Genes: The Genome Project and the Future of Medicine* (New York: Dutton, 1990); for the genome from the point of view of the chromosomes, see Matt Ridley, *Genome: The Autobiography of a Species in 23 Chapters* (New York: Harper-Collins, 1999); for the story of the scientific "race," see Kevin Davies: *Cracking the Genome: Inside the Race to Unlock Human DNA* (New York: Free Press, 2001).

On genetic testing, see Sandra Blakeslee, "Cause of Brain Cells' Death in 7 Diseases Is Discovered," *New York Times* (8 August 1997); Nicholas Wade, "Two Gene Discoveries Help Explain Misfires of Epilepsy in the Brain," *New York Times* (30 December 1997), "Newly Discovered Gene Offers Clues on Deafness," (14 November 1997), "Gene Mutation Tied to Colon Cancers in Askenazi Jews (26 August 1997), "Gene from a Mideast Ancestor May Link 4 Disparate Peoples," (22 August 1997) on familia Mediterranean fever disease and "Genetic Cause Found for Some Cases of Human Obesity" (27 June 1997; Denise Grady, "Gene Link to Incurable Eye Disease Is Found," *New York Times* (19 September 1997); Associated Press, "Blood Test Uncovers Inherited Diseases in Fetuses, (4 November 1996) and "Two Genes Found to Be Causing Some Diabetes" (5 December 1996); Natalie Angiers, "Scientists Zero in on Gene Tied to Prostate Cancer" *New York Times* (22 November 1996). For an account of how getting good news about Huntington's disease can be stressful and disorienting, see Patrick Cooke, "A Genetic Test for Huntington's Let Colin MacAllister See His Future, And That's When His Free Fall Began," *Health* (July–August, 1993), 81–86. On recent breast cancer conclusions, see Jeffry Kluger, *Time* (26 May 1997). Poll results are from a 1994 *Time*/CNN survey cited in *Time* (17 January 1994), p. 50.

On genetic disorders that worsen over generations, see Anastasia Toufexis, "The Generational Saga of the Vicious Gene," *Time* (17 February 1992): 72; and Gina Kolata, "Discovery Upsets Geneticists' Ideas on Inherited Ills," *New York Times* (6 February 1992). As background on genes affecting breast cancer, see Rachel Nowa, "Breast Cancer Gene Offers Surprises," *Science* (23 September 1994): 1796–1799; Gregory Cowley, "Family Matters: Hunt for a Breast Cancer Gene," *Newsweek* (6 December 1993): 46–52; and Kenneth Offit, "Hostage to Our Genes?" *New York Times* (22 September 1994).

On cystic fibrosis, see Andrew Purvis, "Laying Siege to a Deadly Gene," *Time* (24 February 1992) and Natalie Angier, "Researchers Trace Primary Cause of Cystic Fibrosis to the Stone Age," *New York Times* (1 June 1994). The account of the discovery of the cystic fibrosis gene is based on Sandra Blakeslee, "Discovery May Help Cystic Fibrosis Victims," *New York Times* (24 August 1989). See the Associated Press stories "Gene Defect for a Type of Dwarfism Is Found" (31 July 1994, on Canavan disease); "Researchers Find Key to Rare Brain Disorder" (4 October 1993); "Gene Linked for First Time to High Blood Pressure" (7 October 1992); "Gene Linked to Diabetes Found" (12 January 1993); and "Genetic Defect Linked to Alzheimer's" (23 October 1992). See E. Pennisi, "Free-Radical Scavenger Gene Tied to ALS," Science News (6 March 1993). See the following *New York Times* stories: Tim Hilchey, "Researchers Find Genetic Defect that Causes Rare Immune Disease" [namely, severe-combined-immunodeficiency disease] (9 April 1993) and Natalie Angier, "Gene Is Found that Causes Rare Type of Hypertension" (16 January 1992). For a discussion of issues of genetic discrimination, see *Science News* (21 January 1989): 40–42; Gina Kolata, "Nightmare or the Dream of a New Era in Genetics," *New York Times* (7 December 1993); Sharon Begley, "When DNA Isn't Destiny," *Newsweek* (6 December 1993): 53–55; and George J. Annas, "Who's Afraid of the Human Genome?" *Hastings Center Report* (July/August 1989), 19–21. Guidelines on sickle-cell testing are in Warren E. Leary, "Sickle-Cell Screen Urged for All Newborns," *New York Times* (28 April 1993); on treatments, see Leary's "Intractable Pain of Sickle Cell Begins to Yield," *New York Times* (7 June 1994). The discussion of ethical issues about testing and children is based on Gina Kolata's, "Should Children Be Told If Genes Predict Illness?" *New York Times* (26 September 1994). For general review and references, see Philip Kitcher, *The Lives to Come: The Genetic Revolution and Human Possibilities* (New York: Simon and Schuster, 1996).

The Gene Therapy Case Presentation draws information from Eve K. Nicholas, *Human Gene Therapy* (Cambridge, Mass.: Harvard University Press, 1988). The plan to initiate ADA gene therapy is described in Natalie Angier, "Gene Implant Therapy," *New York Times* (8 March 1990), and her account of the first case is in "Girl, 4, Becomes First Human to Receive Engineered Genes," (15 September 1990). Biographical details of Ashanthi Desilva and additional treatments are reported in Larry Thompson, "The First Kids with New Genes," *Time* (7 June 1993): 50–53. The first case, as well as plans for future ones, is discussed in W. French Anderson, "Human Gene Therapy," *Science* (8 May 1992): 808–813. An excellent review of the ethical issues is Leroy Walters and Julie Gage Palmer, *Ethics of Human Gene Therapy* (New York: Oxford University Press, 1996).

Chapter 6: Reproductive Control

The Case Presentation discussion of obtaining stem cells is indebted to National Institutes of Health, "Stem Cells: A Primer" (May 2000), www.nih.gov/news/stemcell/primer/htm. For a discussion of the therapeutic possibilities of stem cells and extensive references, see Ronald Munson, *Raising the Dead: Organ, Transplants, Ethics, and Society* (New York: Oxford University Press, 2002), Chapter 11, "Grow Your Own Organs: Stem-Cell Engineering and Regenerative Medicine." The official Roman Catholic view of stem cells is found in Pontifical Academy of Life, "Declaration on the Production and the Scientific and Therapeutic Use of Human Embryonic Stem Cells," issued at Vatican City: 25 August 2000. For accounts of the recent research and criticisms, I am indebted to the magisterial series of articles by Nicholas Wade in the *New York Times:* "Embryo Cell Research: A Clash of Values," (2 July 1999); "Stem Cells Yield Promising Results" (31 March 2001); "Findings Deepen Debate on Using Embryonic Stem Cells" (3 April 2001); "Experiment Offers Hope for Tissue Repair" (22 January 1999).

Statistics on fertility treatments are cited in S. G. Stolberg, "U.S. Publishes First Guide to Infertility," *New York Times* (18 December 1997). For report on personal experiences, see Stolberg, "For the Infertile, A High-Tech Treadmill," *New York Times* (14 December 1997). For information about techniques, see Lawrence J. Kaplan and Rosemarie Tong, *Controlling Our Reproductive Destiny* (Cambridge: MIT Press, 1996). On fertility clinics see *New York Times:* Gina Kolata, "Reproductive Revolution Is Jostling Old Views," (11 January 1993) and Glenn Kramon, "Infertility Chain: The Good and Bad in Medicine" (19 June 1992). The account of the debate about the selling of ova is based on Gina Kolata, "Young Women Offer to Sell Their Eggs to Infertile Couples," *New York Times* (10 November 1991). On transplanting ovaries from aborted fetuses, see Gina Kolata, *New York Times,* "Fetal Ovary

Transplant Is Envisioned" (6 January 1994). For problems over embryos, see Gina Kolata, "Frozen Embryos: Few Rules in a Rapidly Growing Field," *New York Times* (5 June 1992). The historical background on artificial insemination is presented in R. Snowden and G. D. Mitchell, *The Artificial Family* (London: Allen and Unwin, 1981).

The influential New York law regulating surrogacy is summarized in Lisa Belkin, "Childless Couples Hang on to Last Hope, Despite Laws," *New York Times* (28 July 1992). The Kim Cotton case is reported in the AP story "Surrogate Mother's Child in English Court Custody" (9 January 1985).

The cloning Case Presentation is indebted to: Michael Specter with Gina Kolata, "After Decades and Many Missteps, Cloning Success," *New York Times* (3 March 1997); Gina Kolata, "Panel Recommends a Ban on Human Cloning Efforts," *New York Times* (8 June 1997); "Clinton Seeks to Ban Human Cloning," Associated Press (9 June 1997); Sharon Begley, "Little Lamb Who Made Thee," *Newsweek* (10 March 1997), 53–59; Wray Herbert et al., "The World After Cloning," *U.S. News & World Report* (10 March 1997), 59–63; Madeline Nash, "The Age of Cloning," (10 March 1997), 64–65; Gina Kolata, "For Some Fertility Experts, Human Cloning Is a Dream," *New York Times* (7 June 1997). For recent developments, see Gina Kolata, "In Big Advance in Cloning, Biologists Create 50 Mice," *New York Times* (27 July 1998). The Hall and Stillman "twinning" experiments are discussed in Geoffrey Cowley, "Clone Hype," *Newsweek* (8 November 1993): 60–64 and David Gelman, "How Will the Clone Feel," same issue, (65–66). The cloning story is told in Gina Kolata, *Clone* (New York: William Morrow, 1998) and in Ian Wilmut, Keith Campbell, and Colin Tudge, *The Second Creation: Dolly and the Age of Biological Control* (Cambridge, MA: Harvard University Press, 2000).

The Louise Brown Case Presentation is based on *Newsweek* (7 August 1978); *Time* (7 August 1978); and *U.S. News and World Report* (7 August 1978). On Louise Brown see "Where Are They Now," *Time* (15 August 1996). "Motherhood after Menopause" draws on "World's Oldest Mother Just Wanted Baby," AP (27 April 1997); Gina Kolata, "A Record and Big Questions as a Woman Gives Birth at 63," *New York Times* (24 April 1997); Claudia Kalb, "How Old Is Too Old?" *Newsweek* (5 May 1997); Margaret Carlson, "Old Enough to Be Your Mother," *Time* (10 January 1994): 41; AP "California Woman,

53, Gives Birth to Twins" (11 November 1992); and the Gina Kolata, "When Grandmother Is the Mother, Until Birth" *New York Times* (5 August 1991). Also see Gina Kolata, "Clinics Enter a New World of Embryo 'Adoption,'" *New York Times* (23 November 1997) and "Scientists Face New Ethical Quandaries in Baby-Making," (19 August 1997); M. D. Lemonick, "Sorry Your Time Is Up," *Time* (12 August 1996).

The septuplets Case Presentation is based on Pam Belluck, "Iowan Makes U.S. History, Giving Birth to 7 Live Babies," *New York Times* (20 November 1997) and "Heartache Frequently Visits Parents with Multiple Births," *New York Times* (3 January 1997); Gina Kolata, "Many Specialists Are Left in No Mood for Celebration," *New York Times* (21 November 1997). For personal details of the family also see M. D. Lemonick, "'It's a Miracle,'" *Time* (1 December 1997), 35–39; on technology see Lemonick's "The New Revolution in Making Babies," 41–46.

Information about the Baby M case is drawn from *New York Times* articles (4, 5, 6, 10, 26, 27 January 1987; 2, 3, 9, 10, 11, 17 February 1987; 5, 9, 10, 31 March 1987; 2 April 1987). Additional information about the Rios case is from James Lieber, "The Case of the Frozen Embryos," *Saturday Evening Post* (October, 1989): pp. 50–53. The Calvert case is based on Carol Lawson, "Couple's Own Embryos Used in Birth Surrogacy," *New York Times* (12 August 1990); Seth Mydans, "Surrogate Loses Custody Bid in Case Defining Motherhood," *New York Times* (22 October 1990); and *Time* (22 August 1990).

Chapter 7: Scarce Medical Resources

The Brattle County, Texas, Case Presentation is fictional, but it represents the problem faced by dialysis centers when programs were starting. For the classic account of a committee (at Swedish Hospital, Seattle, Washington, in 1961), see Shana Alexander, "They Decide Who Lives, Who Dies" *Life* (1962).

For a discussion (with extensive references) of major issues in organ transplants, see Ronald Munson, *Raising the Dead: Organ Transplants, Ethics, and Society* (New York: Oxford University Press, 2002). For current survival rates, see the United Network for Organ Sharing website. On special topics see R. W. Evans et al., "The Potential Supply of Organ Donors," *JAMA*, 259 (1992), 1546–1547; "P. A. Singer et al., "Ethics of Liver Transplantation with Living Donors," *New England Journal of Medicine* (1989) 321, 620–622;

S. J. Younger and R. M. Arnold, "Ethical, Psychosocial, and Public Policy Implications of Procuring Organs from Non-Heart-Beating Cadaver Donors," *JAMA*, 269 (1993), 2769–2774. On selling organs, see the following *New York Times* articles: Peter S. Young, "Moving to Compensate Families in Human Organ Market" (8 July 1994); Sanjoy Hazarka, "India Debates Ethics of Buying Transplant Kidneys" (17 August 1992); Chris Hedges, "Egypt's Doctors Impose Kidney Transplant Curbs" (23 January 1992) and "Egypt's Desperate Trade" (22 September 1991). See also, "Trading Flesh Around the Globe," *Time* (17 June 1991): 61. The classic sociological study on dialysis and transplants is Renee C. Fox, "A Sociological Perspective on Organ Transplantation and Hemodialysis," *Annals of the New York Academy of Sciences* 169 (1970): 406–428.

The facts and opinions in the Ayala case are presented in Lance Morrow, "When One Body Can Save Another," *Time* (7 June 1991) 54–58; the Associated Press story, "Mom, 43, Having Baby to Save Daughter's Life" (17 February 1990); Irene Chang, "Bone Marrow Baby Is Born to the Ayalas," *Los Angeles Times* (6 April 1990); the marriage of Anissa is reported in Rebecca Norris, "Made in Heaven," *American Health* (October 1994): 100.

The account of the public debate on fetal-cell transplants is based on J. Eric Ahlskog, "Cerebral Transplantation for Parkinson's Disease: Current Progress and Future Prospects," *Mayo Clinic Proceedings* 68 (1993): 578–591; Associated Press, "Fetal Tissue Study Approved, the First Since the Ban Was Lifted" (4 January 1994); "Fetal Tissue Grafts Reverse Parkinson's," *Science News* (28 November 1992): 372; and the following *New York Times* articles: Warren Leary, "Call to Regulate Transplant Tissue" (15 August 1993), Gwen Ifill, "House Approves Fetal Tissues in Federally Funded Research" (26 June 1991), and Gina Kolata, "Fetal Tissue Implant Said to Be Aiding a Parkinson Patient" (2 February 1990).

On the shortage of Betaseron, see Associated Press, "Computer Lottery Will Distribute a New M.S. Drug," (2 September 1993); Tamar Lewis, "Prize in Unusual Lottery: A Scarce Experimental Drug," *New York Times* (7 January 1994); and Laura Johanes, "New Drug Aims to Win Over Sufferers," *Wall Street Journal* (20 April 1996).

For the Sepulveda case, see Bruce Lambert, "Jesse Sepulveda Is Dead at Seven," *New York Times* (18 July 1993). For the Bosze case, see Isabel Wilkerson, "Search for Marrow Donor Questions Nature of Altruism and Child Rights,"

New York Times (30 July 1990) and "Setback for Boy Needing Marrow," Associated Press (28 September 1990). For the Benton case, see Terry Trucco, "Sales of Kidneys Prompt New Laws and Debate," *New York Times* (1 August 1990).

Chapter 8: Paying for Health Care

The Case Presentation is a composite, one representing the situation of the 44 million Americans lacking health insurance. These are most often people with jobs or small businesses.

The discussion of rights in the Briefing Session is indebted to Joel Feinberg, "The Nature and Value of Rights," *Journal of Value Inquiry* 4 (1970): 243–257. See also Charles J. Dougherty, *American Health Care: Realities, Rights, and Reforms* (New York: Oxford University Press, 1988).

The materials on health-care costs and controversies are drawn from the following *New York Times* articles: Robert Pear, "In a First, Medicare Coverage is Authorized for Alzheimer's" (30 March 2002), "Propelled by Drugs and Hospital Costs, Health Spending Surged in 2000" (7 January 2002); Sam Howe Verhovek, "Frustration Grows with Cost of Health Insurance" (16 September 2000); Robin Toner, "Harry and Louise Were Right, Sort Of" (24 November 1996); Peter Kilborn, "Looking Back at Jackson Hole" (22 March 1998). On HMOs and proposals for change, see David Sibley, "Nasty, Costly Battle Shapes Up Over Changing Managed Care" (3 June 1998), "What the Texas Experiment Shows About HMO Liability," (7 August 1998); Lasette Alvarez, "A Conservative Battles Corporate Health Care," 12 February 1998); Milt Freudenheim, "Health Insurers Seek Big Increases in Their Premiums" (24 April 1998); on attempts to extend care to particular groups, see Robert Pear, "Policy Changes Fail to Fill Gaps in Health Coverage" (8 August 1998), "Senators Reject Bill to Regulate Care by HMOs" (9 October 1998)," Health Care Bills Don't Meet Goals, Budget Aids Say" (2 July 1997), "Clinton Ordering Effort to Sign Up Medicaid Children" (28 December 1997), "Clinton to Expand Medicaid for Some of the Working Poor" (3 August 1998), "New Health Plans Due for Elderly" (9 June 1998); Peter T. Kilborn, "States to Provide Health Insurance to More Children" (21 September 1997); Adam Clymer, "With Health Overhaul Dead, a Search for Minor Repairs" (28 August 1994). On costs and consumer complaints, see Ian Fisher, "HMO Premiums Rising Sharply, Stoking Debate on Managed Care" (11 January 1998); Peter T. Kilborn,

"Complaints About HMOs Rise as Awareness Grows" (10 October 1998). For more on costs, see Milt Freudenheim, "Health Care Costs Edging Up and a Bigger Surge Is Feared" (2 January 1997); Peter T. Kilborn, "HMO Fiscal Incentives Linked to Doctor's Discontent" (19 November 1998), "Doctor's Pay Regains Ground Despite the Effects of HMOs" (22 April 1998). On the uninsured or underinsured, see Peter T. Kilborn, "Illness is Turning into Financial Catastrophe for More of the Uninsured" (1 August 1997), "The Uninsured Find Fewer Doctors in the House" (30 August 1998).

Statistics in the Canadian Case Presentation are mostly drawn from Karen Dnelan, et. al. "All Payer, Single Payer, Managed Care, No Payer: Patients' Perspectives in Three Nations [U.S., Canada, Germany]," *Health Affairs*, 15 (1996), 256–265. The case is also based on the following *New York Times* articles: James Brooke, "Full Hospitals Make Canadians Wait and Look South" (16 January 2000); Anthony De Palma, "Doctor, What's the Prognosis for Canada" (15 December 1996); also used were Anthony Schmitz, "Health Assurance," in *Health* (January/February 1991): 39–47 and *Consumer Reports* (September 1992): 579–592. For a detailed comparison of the U.S. system with those in Canada and Germany, see Donald Drake, Susan Fitzgerald, and Mark Jaffe, *Hard Choices: Health Care At What Cost?* (Kansas City: Andrews and McMeel, 1993).

Chapter 9: Abortion

The Finkbine Case Presentation is based on Allen F. Guttmacher, *The Case for Legalized Abortion* (Berkeley, CA: Diablo Press, 1977), pp. 15–17.

On birth defects, see the following *New York Times* articles: Kurt Eichenwald, "Push for Royalties Threatens the Use of Down Syndrome Test" (25 May 1997); Denise Grady, "Research Finds Risk in Early Test of Fetus," (27 January 1998), and the Associated Press, "Small Amount of Folic Acid Bars Defects" (4 December 1997). For specific developmental or genetic anomalies, see Clayman, Charles B., ed. *American Medical Association Encyclopedia of Medicine* (New York: Random House, 1989.)

The Social Context Gallup statistics are cited in Robin Toner, "The Abortion Debate, Stuck in Time," *New York Times* (21 January 2000). The statistics from the *New York Times*/CBS poll cited in the Social Context appear in the newspaper for 16 January 1998; I have also drawn from Carey Goldberg and Janet Elder, "Public Still Backs Abortion But Wants Limits, Poll Says" on the same date and the following *New York Times* articles: Tamar Lewis, "Debate Distant for Many Having Abortions" (17 June 1998); Carey Goldberg, "Shifting Certainties in the Abortion War" (11 January 1998).

On the "partial-birth" abortion debate, see *New York Times:* Linda Greenhouse, "Overturning of Late-Term Abortion Ban Is Let Stand" (24 March 1998); Deborah Sontage, "'Partial Birth' Just One Way, Physicians Say" (21 March 1997); Neil A. Lewis, "Ban on Method of Late Abortion Passes House Despite Veto Threat," (9 October 1997); Katharine Q. Seelye, "Senate Votes Ban on Late Abortion: Bill Faces a Veto," (21 May 1997), "Medical Group Supports Ban on a Type of Late Abortion" (19 May 1997, "As Federal Bans Face a Veto, States Outlaw Late Abortions" (3 May 1997), "Group Defends Late-Term Abortion Procedure" (27 February 1997); Frank Burni, "The Partial Truth Abortion Fight" (9 March 1997); Sheryl Gay Stolberg, "Definitions of Fetal Viability Is Focus of Debate in Senate" (15 May 1997); Linda Greenhouse, "Justices to Rule on Law That Bans Abortion Method" (14 January 2000), and on the Nebraska and Colorado decisions, "Court Rules That Government Can't Outlaw Type of Abortion" (28 June 2000).

On legal and policy decisions, information about the Pennsylvania case (Casey) and the U.S. Supreme Court decision from *New York Times* (22 January 1992; 23 April 1992; 30 June 1992; 13 May 1993; 30 January 1994). Information about the Webster case is from *Newsweek* (1 May 1989; 17 July 1989) and *Time* (1 May 1989). Response to the Webster decision is based on Linda Greenhouse, "Supreme Court Upholds Sharp State Limits on Abortion," *New York Times* (4 July 1990) and E. Dionne, "On Both Sides, Advocates Predict a 50-State Battle" in the same issue.

Difficulty in getting access to abortion is covered in *New York Times* (5 January 1992, 15 March 1992). The Court ruling on access to clinics and its background is reported in *New York Times* (25 January 1994, 1 July 1994). See too Linda Greenhouse, "High Court Upholds Buffer Zone of 15 Feet at Abortion Clinics," *New York Times* (20 February 1997) and, on the Colorado law, "Court Rules That Governments Can't Outlaw Types of Abortion" (28 June 2000); Peter T. Kilborn, "Definition of Abortion Is Found to Vary Abroad" (23 November 1999); Frank Bruni and Marc Lacey, "Bush Acts to Deny Money Overseas Tied to Abortion" (22 January 2001); Daniel E.

Pellegrom, "A Deadly Global Gag Rule" (27 January 2001).

The Social Context on RU-486 is based on *New York Times* stories: (28 October 1994; 28 March 1994; 18 February 1994; 2, 20 April 1993; 27 July 1990; 22 June 1990; 18 November 1993; 23 February 1992; 13 October 1993; 23 September 1989; 26, 27, 29, 30 October 1988; 22 February 1988). It also draws from *Newsweek* (22 November 1993); *Time* (14 July 1993; 4 June 1994; 4 October 1992; 7 November 1988); and Steven Greenhouse, "A Fierce Battle," *New York Times Magazine* (12 February 1989). For an account of the seizure of RU-486 by U.S. customs, see *New York Times* (2, 17 July 1992). More recent material on RU-486 is drawn from Gina Kolata, "Abortion Pill Tests Well in the United States, Drug's Sponsor Says" (30 April 1998) and "Doctors Looking at Abortion Pill Are Often Unaware of Obstacles" (30 September 2000), as well as Nancy Gibbs, "The Pill Arrives," *Time* (8 October 2000). On emergency contraception involving "preconceptive" drugs, see the *New York Times* articles: Tamar Lewin, "A New Procedure Makes Abortions Possible Earlier" (21 December 1997) and Jane Brody, "Personal Health" (2 September 1997), and Gina Kolata, "Morning After Pill Becomes Available Without a Doctor" (8 October 2000).

The Visna Case is based on Suzanne Siegel and Bill Roy, "Youth, Incest, and Abortion," *Newsweek* (10 August 1998).

Chapter 10: Euthanasia and Physician-Assisted Suicide

The Quinlan Case Presentation is based on Phyllis Battelle, "The Story of Karen Quinlan," *Ladies' Home Journal* 93 (September 1976): 69–76, 172–180. Direct quotations are from Battelle. I have also drawn from B. D. Colen, *Karen Ann Quinlan: Dying in the Age of Eternal Life* (New York: Nash, 1976) and *In the Matter of Karen Quinlan: The Complete Legal Briefs, Court Proceedings, and Decisions* (Arlington, VA.: University Publications of America, 1975). On the death of Joseph Quinlan, see Robert Hanley's obituary in *New York Times* (11 December 1996).

On the Oregon measure, see Associated Press, "Voters in Oregon Allow Doctors to Help the Terminally Ill" (10 November 1994) and "Suicide Plan Would Permit Prescription for Lethal Drugs" (15 October 1994). For more background, see the following *New York Times* stories: Timothy Egan, "Suicide Law Placing Oregon on Several Uncharted Paths" (20 November 1994); for criticisms, Robert A. Burt, "Death Made Too Easy" (16 November 1994); the first statistics are from, Sam W. Verhovek, "Legal Suicide Has Killed 8, Oregon Says" (18 August 1998); on Ashcroft's letter and more recent statistics, see Sam W. Verhovek, "U.S. Acts to Stop Assisted Suicides" (7 November 2001); for the suit see, "Stay Extended Against U.S. on Oregon's Suicide Law" (20 November 2001); "As Suicide Approvals Rise in Oregon, Half Go Unused" (7 February 2002).

The Social Context on the Cruzan case draws from: *Time* (11 December 1989; 19 March 1990; 9 July 1990); *Newsweek*, Marcia Angell, "The Right to Die in Dignity" (23 July 1990); *New York Times* (17 November 1988; 29 July 1988; 25 July 1989; 19 January 1990; 26, 27 June 1990; 23 July 1990).

The discussion of Kevorkian and assisted suicide draws material from *Time* (31 May 1993; *New York Times*, David Margolick, "Jurors Acquit Dr. Kevorkian in Suicide Case" (3 May 1994); "Michigan Panel Narrowly Backs Suicide" (5 March 1994); Lawrence K. Altman, "A How-to Book on Suicide Surges to the Top of the Best-Seller List" (August 1991); and Jane Gross, "Voters Turn Down Legal Euthanasia" (7 November 1991).

The discussion on euthanasia in the Netherlands is based on articles from the *New York Times*: Tom Kuntz, "Helping a Man Kill Himself as Shown on Dutch TV" (includes partial transcript of dialogue during the process) (14 November 1994); Marliese Simons, "Dutch Move to Enact Law Making Euthanasia Easier" and "Dutch Parliament Approves Law Permitting Euthanasia" (9, 10 February 1993); and F. X. Klines, "Dutch Quietly in Lead in Euthanasia Requests" (31 October 1986). See also Maurice A. M. de Wachter, "Euthanasia in the Netherlands," *Hastings Center Report* (April 1992): 23–33; and Robert I. Misbin, ed. *Euthanasia*, "Part II: Euthanasia in the Netherlands," (Fredrick, Md.: University Publishing Group, 1992), pp. 55–107. Information about and the criticisms of the California Natural Death Act are from Karen Lebacqz, "On Natural Death,'" *Hastings Center Report* 7 (1977): 14. The Timothy Quill Scenario is based on "State Won't Press Case on Doctor in Suicide," *New York Times* (17 August 1991).

Foundations of Bioethics

My discussion of ethical theories is indebted to Richard B. Brandt, *Ethical Theory* (Englewood

Cliffs, N.J.: Prentice Hall, 1959) and William K. Frankena, *Ethics*, 2nd ed. (Englewood Cliffs, N.J.: Prentice-Hall 1973). My treatment of utilitarianism owes much to the essay by Paul Taylor in his *Problems of Moral Philosophy* (Belmont, CA: Dickenson, 1971), pp. 137–151. Mill's statement of the principle of utility is from *Utilitarianism* (Indianapolis: Bobbs-Merrill, 1971), p. 18; the second quotation is from p. 24. In the discussion of act and rule utilitarianism and their difficulties, I am indebted to Michael D. Bayles and Kenneth Henley's introduction in their *Right Conduct* (New York: Random House, 1983), pp. 86–94, and to Carl Wellman, *Morals and Ethics* (New York: Scott, Foresman, 1975), pp. 39–42, 47–50. The quotation is from p. 49.

The statements of Kant's categorical imperative are more paraphrases than literal translations. They are from his *Groundwork of the Metaphysics of Morals*, translated by H. J. Paton (New York: Harper & Row, 1964). Some of the criticisms of Kant are based on those of Brandt (*Ethical Theory*, pp. 27–35) and Frankena (*Ethics*, pp. 30–33).

The quotation from Ross is from his *The Right and the Good* (New York: Oxford University Press, 1930), p. 24. The prima facie duties are found on pp. 21–22 and the "rules" for resolving conflict on pp. 41–42. My exposition is indebted to G. J. Warnock, *Contemporary Moral Philosophy* (New York: St. Martin's Press, 1967) and to Fred Feldman, *Introductory Ethics* (Englewood Cliffs, N.J.: Prentice-Hall, 1978), pp. 149–160.

Rawls's theory is presented in *A Theory of Justice* (Cambridge, Mass.: Harvard University Press, 1971). The principles are quoted from p. 203; "natural duties" are discussed on pp. 340–350. My statement of the theory is indebted to Norman Daniels's introduction to *Reading Rawls* (New York: Basic Books, 1976). The first criticism is one made by Thomas Nagel, "Rawls on Justice" (Daniels, pp. 1–16) and Ronald Dworkin, "The Original Position" (Daniels, pp. 16–53). The second criticism is urged by R. M. Hare, "Rawls's Theory of Justice" (Daniels, pp. 81–108) and David Lyons, "Nature and Soundness of the Contract and Coherence Arguments" (Daniels, pp. 141–169).

For Aquinas's view on "man," see his *Summa Theologica*, Part II (First Part), vol. 6, translated by Fathers of the English Dominican Province (London: Burns Oates and Washbourne, 1914). For his views on natural law and law in general, see vol. 8, "Treatise on Law." For an interpretation of Aquinas, see Frederick Copleston, *A His-*tory of Philosophy*, vol. 2, part 2 (New York: Doubleday, 1962), pp. 126–131, to which my account is indebted. For the presentation of the current Catholic natural law view I am indebted to Charles J. McFadden, *Medical Ethics*, 6th ed. (Philadelphia: F. A. Davis, 1967). The doctrine of double effect is treated on pp. 121–155; euthanasia, extraordinary means, and medical experimentation, pp. 239–270. The quotations from the Directives are from the appendix in McFadden: abortion, p. 441, euthanasia, p. 442.

My discussion of moral principles is indebted to Tom L. Beauchamp and James F. Childress, *Principles of Biomedical Ethics* (New York: Oxford University Press, 1979), pp. 56–201, and to Beauchamp's and LeRoy Walters's introduction in *Contemporary Issues in Bioethics*, 2nd ed. (Belmont, CA: Wadsworth, 1982), pp. 26–32. The discussion of liberty-limiting principles is based on Joel Feinberg, *Social Philosophy* (Englewood Cliffs, N.J.: Prentice-Hall, 1973), pp. 20–33, as is the discussion of principles of justice, pp. 98–119.

The account of virtue ethics is indebted to Louis P. Pojman, *Ethics: Discovering Right and Wrong*, 2nd ed. (Belmont, California: Wadsworth Publishing Company, 1995), 166–181. See also Alasdair McIntyre, *After Virtue* (University of Notre Dame Press, 1981), the book that revived current discussions of virtue ethics, and Philippa Foot, *Virtues and Vices* (Oxford: Blackwell, 1978), a collection of essays by a virtue ethicist who addresses problems in medical ethics. For the beginnings of feminist-care ethics, see Carol Gilligan, *In a Different Voice* (Cambridge, MA: Harvard University Press, 1982; for its philosophical development, see Annette Bair, *Postures of the Mind* (Minneapolis: University of Minnesota Press, 1985). Care ethics and feminist ethics are points of view still developing, and my sketch of them represents the ideas of no one theorist. Nell Noddings in *Caring: A Feminine Approach to Ethics and Moral Education* (Berkeley: University of California Press, 1988) argues that everyone ought to follow the ethic of caring and abandon abstract principles. Some feminist writers do not want the emphasis on care to overwhelm feminism and its concerns. See Susan Sherwin, *No Longer Patient: Feminist Ethics and Health Care* (Philadelphia: Temple University Press, 1992) and Helen B. Holmes and Laura M. Purdy, ed. *Feminist Perspectives in Medical Ethics* (Bloomington: Indiana University Press, 1992). See the *Resources by Chapter and Topic*, found at the book's Web site, for more references.

General Resources in Bioethics

The number of books and articles dealing with bioethics is staggering, and it is growing larger at a rapid rate. Merely extending the list of additional sources in the section following this one would be of marginal utility. Likely to be more useful, I think, is a brief guide to some of the more important bibliographical sources, databases, and online sites.

This approach will permit those who want to follow the course of debate in certain areas to gain access to the most recent publications and information. Similarly, those interested in the history of a debate can find references allowing them to trace it to its origins. A book cannot provide up-to-the-minute references, nor can it supply complete bibliographies in specialized areas.

Better, then, to provide a few tools to allow readers to mine what they need from the vast deposits of books, articles, and online data. Even so, please keep in mind that the materials listed here are no more than a sample of those currently available. Keep in mind too that Web addresses change often, and the sites themselves tend to be ephemeral—they spring up, only to be cut down.

InfoTrac COLLEGE EDITION

Accompanying this book is access to InfoTrac College Edition, a fully searchable, online database of full-text articles and accompanying images from more than 900 periodicals. Materials are updated daily and maintained in the database for four years. This source is particularly good for following the course of popular debates on such biomedical topics as stem cells, abortion, physician-assisted suicide, cloning, health care costs, and so on.

GUIDES TO ONLINE RESOURCES

Gibbs, Scott, Micaela Sullivan-Fowler, and Nigel W. Rowe. *Mosby's Medical Surfari: A Guide to Exploring the Internet and Discovering the Top Health Care Resources.* St. Louis: Mosby, 1998. Advice on searching online health sites as well as a categorized listing of health sites.

Goldstein, Douglas E. *The On-Line Guide to Health Care Management and Medicine.* Chicago: Irving Professional, 1997. A guide to online sites of health-care resources and services, including medical management of specific disorders, pharmacology, support groups, medical centers, and so on. Not particularly useful for bioethics sites.

Sharp, Vicki F. and Richard M. Sharp. *Web-Doctor: Finding the Best Health Care Online.* Quality Medical Home Health Library. New York: St. Martin's Griffin, 1998. Catalogues selected health sites and organizes them by major topics.

ONLINE SITES AND DATA BASES

AIDSLINE

ADDRESS: Accessed free through the National Library of Medicine, the Centers for Disease Control, and other Web sites.

Indexes over 3000 journals in the clinical, research, epidemiology, and social policy literature of the disease.

Biomedical Ethics Unit McGill University

ADDRESS: http://www.mcgill.ca/bioethics

Links to other sites, plus news and information relevant to biomedical ethics.

Bioethicsline

ADDRESS: Accessed free through the National Library of Medicine and many university Web sites.

Includes ethics-related publications in medicine, law, religion, philosophy, the social sciences, and popular media. Produced by the Information Retrieval Project at the Kennedy Institute of Ethics, Georgetown University. Updated bi-monthly. To order free bibliographical computer searches, call the National Reference Center for Bioethics Literature, Kennedy Institute of Ethics, Georgetown University, at 800-633-3849.

Center for Bioethics University of Pennsylvania

ADDRESS: http://www.med.upenn.edu/-bioethics/

Offers a variety of relevant resources, including Genetics and Ethics Resource Project, lists of journals and books, and access to *American Journal of Ethics in Medicine*, an online journal written by medical students. Has a link to Episteme, a philosophy site with links to others.

Centers for Disease Control

ADDRESS: http://www.cdc.gov

Health information, data, and statistics; links to other sites such as National AIDS Clearinghouse, Library of Congress, National Library of Medicine, World Health Organization, and Agency for Health Care Policy and Research. CDC Wonder provides access to CDC reports, guidelines, and public health data.

Hastings Center

ADDRESS: http://www.thehastingscenter.org

Limited to information about the center, but plans include the introduction of an interactive network permitting information sharing and access to library resources.

Health and Humanities Links
Michigan State University

ADDRESS: http://www.medlib.ipui.edu/ethics

Links to other health and humanities sites provided by the Interdisciplinary Program in Health and Humanities.

LexisNexis

A commercial database providing access to the full text an enormous variety of publications, including national and foreign newspapers, popular magazines, and technical journals in medicine and law. Access to MEDLINE, Bioethicsline, and other data bases. Available through some university libraries. More often available is a pared-down version known as *Academic Universe*. Mead Data Central, Box 933, Dayton, OH 94501.

MacLean Center
for Clinical Medical Ethics
University of Chicago

ADDRESS: http://ccme-mac4.bsd.uchicago.edu/CCMEHomePage.html

Comprehensive list of links, well organized and easy to use.

MCW Bioethics Database
Medical College of Wisconsin

ADDRESS: http://www.mcw.edu/bioethics/

Scholarly and comprehensive, with links to other bioethics Web sites.

MEDLINE

ADDRESS: Accessed free through the National Library of Medicine and other web sites.

Contains abstracts of articles in clinical and research medicine and related areas. Includes articles on ethics, economics, and society as related to medicine; over 250,000 records are added each year.

MEDLINE-PLUS

ADDRESS: Accessed free through National Library of Medicine

Provides links to community health organizations, associations, clearinghouses, self-help groups, and clinical trials. Also links to CANCERLIT, National Cancer Institute, CancerNet, HIV/AIDS resources.)

Medical Matrix, University of Kansas

ADDRESS: http://kuhttp.cc.ukans.edu/cwis/units/medcntr/Lee/HOMEPAGE.HTML

Useful for links to other medically related sites.

National Bioethics Advisory Commission

ADDRESS: http://www.bioethics.gov

The committee appointed by the executive branch to address bioethical issues.

National Health Care Expenditures

ADDRESS: http://www.hcfa.gov/stats

Database of health care expenditures that can be searched; links to other agencies of the Health Care Finance Administration.

National Institutes of Health (NIH)

ADDRESS: http://www.nih.gov

Resources include CancerNet, AIDS information, Women's Health Institute; online library catalogues and journals; access to NIH search engine. Also, access to NIH Clinical Center, BioEthics Program site.

National Library of Medicine

ADDRESS: http://www.nlm.nih.gov

Search the library, order fact sheets, newsletters, publications, software, and images. Links to a variety of databases. Free access to MEDLINE and MEDLINE-PLUS.

Office of Minority Health
Care Resource Center

ADDRESS: http://www.omhcrc.gove/frames.htm

News, publications, policy statements, and databases on minority health care. Links to other relevant sites.

Transweb

ADDRESS:　http://www.transweb.org

News and information about solid organ transplantation, personal accounts of the transplant experience; press releases, media reports, and legislation about transplants. Contains a subject index and links to other major transplant sites.

United Network for Organ Sharing (UNOS)

ADDRESS:　http://www.unos.org

News, policy statements, and extensive database about organ transplants; searching is possible. Links to transplant centers, organ procurement organizations, patient and donor organizations, and transplant physicians.

Yahoo

ADDRESS:　http://www.yahoo.com/health

Searchable database on health related topics.

Online medical information is plentiful, and any search engine will produce a number of sites for almost any disease. Large national organizations like the American Heart Association have their own sites (www.amhrt.org) with links to others, and medical centers like the Mayo Clinic (www.mayohealth.org) often supply considerable medical information.

JOURNALS IN BIOETHICS

Bioethics
Cambridge Quarterly of Healthcare Ethics
Hastings Center Report
Journal of Clinical Ethics
Journal of Law, Medicine & Ethics
Journal of Medical Ethics (British)
Journal of Medical Humanities
Kennedy Institute of Ethics Journal

JOURNALS THAT INCLUDE ARTICLES ON BIOETHICS

American Journal of Law and Medicine
American Journal of Public Health
Annals of Internal Medicine
Health Affairs
Health Matrix
Lancet (British)
JAMA (Journal of the American Medical Association)
Journal of Health Politics, Policy, and Law
Milbank Quarterly
New England Journal of Medicine
Pediatrics
Perspectives in Biology and Medicine
Philosophy and Public Affairs
Public Affairs Quarterly
Social Theory and Practice
Theoretical Medicine
Transplantation Proceedings

Law journals in general (e.g., Yale Law Journal, George Washington University Law Review) often contain articles directly relevant to biomedical issues. This is also true of nursing journals (e.g., American Journal of Nursing) and journals of health care and hospital management.

BIBLIOGRAPHIES

Arizona State University Center for the Study of Law, Science and Technology. "The Human Genome Project: Bibliography of Ethical, Social, Legal, and Scientific Aspects." Jurimetrics Journal 32 (1992): 223–311.

Basic Resources in Bioethics (1991); Teaching Ethics in the Health Care Setting, Part I: Survey of the Literature (1991); Teaching Ethics in the Health Care Setting, Part II: Sample Syllabus (1991). Bibliographies available from the National Reference Center for Bioethics Literature, Kennedy Institute of Ethics, Georgetown University, Washington, D.C. 20057. Published in the Kennedy Institute of Ethics Journal, beginning in 1991.

Leatt, Peggy et. al. Perspectives on Physician Involvement in Resource Allocation and Utilization Management: An Annotated Bibliography. Toronto: University of Toronto, 1991.

Lineback, Richard H., ed. Philosopher's Index. Bowling Green, Ohio: Philosophy Documentation Center, Bowling Green State University. Provides abstracts from journals and books in philosophy and related fields. The journals are indexed from 1940, and the file contains more than 200,000 items and is updated regularly.

Musgrove, Michèle, comp. Artificial Insemination Bibliography. Ottawa: Royal Commission on New Reproductive Technologies, 1992.

Walter, LeRoy and Tamar Joy Kahn, eds. Bibliography of Bioethics, Washington, D.C.: Kennedy Institute of Ethics. A regularly updated bibliography.

About the Author

Ronald Munson is Professor of Philosophy of Science and Medicine at the University of Missouri–St. Louis. He received his Ph.D. from Columbia University and was a Postdoctoral Fellow in Biology at Harvard University. He has been a Visiting Professor at the University of California, San Diego, the Johns Hopkins University School of Medicine, and Harvard Medical School.

He has served as bioethicist for a National Institutes of Health multicenter study, the National Cancer Institute, the Monsanto Recombinant DNA Advisory Committee, and the Washington University School of Medicine Human Subjects Committee.

His articles have appeared in *Philosophy of Science, British Journal for the Philosophy of Science, History and Philosophy of Science, Journal of Medicine and Philosophy, Kennedy Institute of Ethics Journal, Politics and the Life Sciences,* and *New England Journal of Medicine.*

His books include *Reasoning in Medicine* (with Daniel Albert and Michael Resnik); *Way of Words; Man and Nature: Philosophical Issues in Biology; Elements of Reasoning;* and *Basics of Reasoning* (both with David Conway). His *Intervention and Reflection: Basic Issues in Medical Ethics, 6th edition* is the nation's most widely used bioethics text. His most recent book is *Raising the Dead: Organ Transplants, Ethics, and Society* (N.Y.: Oxford University Press, 2002).

Ronald Munson is also author of the novels *Nothing Human, Fan Mail,* and *Night Vision.*